MW01410400

Ancient History: Adam to Messiah

A Multi Level,

Bible Focused Unit Study

Utilizing

the Charlotte Mason Approach,

the 4Mat System,

and the Internet!

By Robin Sampson

Contributing Authors: Nanette Cole and Dennis Ward

Heart of Wisdom Publishing
http://HeartofWisdom.com

Heart of Wisdom Store
http://Homeschool-Books.com

Day by Day Lesson Plans
Heartofwisdom.com/homeschool

About the Author

Robin Sampson is a home schooling mother of eleven, grandmother of eleven, and author of several acclaimed books including *What Your Child Needs to Know When*, *A Family Guide to the Biblical Holidays*, and *The Heart of Wisdom Teaching Approach*.

Robin has been writing and speaking, covering a broad spectrum of home school topics, from education philosophies to Biblical studies for over fifteen years. Robin has authored articles for magazines such as *Homeschool Today*, *Teaching Home*, *Home School Digest*, *The Old Schoolhouse*, and *Restore Magazine*.

Robin actively lives her subject as she continues to home-educate her youngest children. Several of Robin's children are grown, married, and homeschooling their own children. Robin's husband, Ronnie, is a retired deputy director for Homeland Security in Washington, D.C. They reside in TN

Visit Robin's blog at Heartofwisdom.com/blog

Revised edition published August 2003
Reprint March 2008, August 2011

Heart of Wisdom Publishing
Shelbyville, TN 37160

First Copyright May 2001

Web Site: http://HeartofWisdom.com
E-mail: Support@Heartofwisdom.com

ISBN: 0-9701816-3-9

Printed in the United States of America

Dedication

To My Loving Husband Ronnie

You are the wind beneath my wings!
Without you this book would not be possible.
Thank you for your constant, tireless support.
Your commitment, dedication, and unselfish giving is a
beautiful picture of the love described in Ephesians 5:25:
*Husbands, love your wives, even as Christ also loved the church,
and gave himself for it.*

To My Children

Tammy, Belinda, Rebecca, Victoria, Daniel, Connie, Regina,
Anthony, Michael, David, and Christopher.

and To My Grandchildren

Jennifer, Abigail, Stephen, AnnMarie, Timothy, Tiffany,
Kaitlyn, Brandon, John, Joseph, Jordan, Sierra,
and those yet to be born.

and To All Future Blessings

Statement of Faith

We believe the scriptures to be the verbally inspired Word of God, without error in the original writings, the complete revelation of His will for the salvation of men, and the only absolute authority for genuine faith and practice.

We believe in one God, Creator of all things, infinitely perfect and eternally rules His universe and is bringing all things to their proper end according to His omniscient plan.

We believe that Jesus Christ is the Messiah, is true God and true man, having been conceived by the Holy Spirit and born of the virgin Mary. He died on the cross as a perfect sacrifice for our sins and He rose bodily from the dead, later ascending triumphantly into heaven where he intercedes for us in God's presence.

We believe that the primary ministry of the Spirit is to glorify the Lord Christ our Messiah. To accomplish this, He convicts men, regenerates those He intends to save, indwells, guides, instructs and empowers believers for godly living and service.

We believe that man, originally created perfect in God's image, fell into sin in Adam, and consequently we are all by nature under God's wrath and subject to both sin and death if left to our own dispositions and designs.

We believe that unless man accepts the Jesus the Messiah as his Savior, he is condemned to eternal damnation. We believe that salvation is by grace through faith. No man can do anything to earn salvation.

We believe we should uphold the commandments of God if we love Christ with all our heart (John 14:15, Romans 3:31, 7:22, Galatians 3:21-22, I John 5:1-3) and teach others to do so (Matthew 5:17-19, Revelation 22:13-14).

We believe that Christ will return with power and glory to bring earthly history to its close according to His wise plan. We believe that all men will be resurrected bodily, the believers to everlasting blessedness in the presence of God and the unbelievers to judgment and everlasting conscious torment in the lake of fire, along with Satan and his angels.

Disclaimer

Heart of Wisdom is nondenominational functioning entirely apart from any denominational agenda. The main objective and focus of our unit studies are on students and parents learning God's Word and establishing a relationship with Him. The resources and links are provided as a service. Opinions and materials contained therein are those of the ministries and/or authors and may or may not reflect this author's position on particular issues. Many scholars with varying doctrinal opinions are able to contribute to specific areas of research. This book includes research or recommended resources by Christians of several different denominations, Jews, Messianics, fundamentalists, etc. when it was evident that their area of expertise was correct in investigating the truth concerning history. This does not mean the author or publisher is in doctrinal agreement with authors of contributed scholarly text or recommended resources.

Table of Contents

How to Use this Book

Introduction

Introduction 1
Interacting With Our Web Site 3

The Teaching Approach

HOW Teaching Approach 4
Bible First Philosophy 5
Delight-Directed Studies 7
Charlotte Mason Philosophy 9
The 4Mat Lessons 10
Writing to Learn 14
Correcting Written Work 15

Getting Started

Scheduling 16
Creating a Portfolio 18
Creating a Time Line Book 19
Creating a Vocabulary Notebook . .22
Creating a Spelling Notebook 23
Graphic Organizers 26

Resources

About the Resources 27
Required Resources 29
Choosing Resources? 30
Key Resource List 31
Key Resources in Several Units . . .32
Alternative Resources 37

Timeline

Adam to Messiah Time Line 39

Adam to Abraham Unit

Adam to Abraham Overview 42
Adam to Abraham Objectives 43
Adam to Abraham Time Line 44
Adam to Abraham Vocabulary 45
Adam to Abraham Resources 46

Adam to Abraham Lessons

Introduction 48
Creation 50
Garden of Eden 54
Adam and Eve 56
The Fall 60
Cain and Abel 64
Seth to Noah 67
Corruption of Man 69
The Flood .73
After the Flood 77
The Tower of Babel 79
Beginning of Nations 81
The Nation's Religions 85
The Calling of Abram 88
Abram Enters Canaan 92
Genesis Reveals the Messiah 96

Table of Contents continued...

Mesopotamia Unit

Mesopotamia Overview 102
Mesopotamia Objectives 103
Mesopotamia Vocabulary 104
Mesopotamia Time Line 105
Mesopotamia Resources 106

Lessons

Cradle of Civilization 111
Ancient Civilizations and the Bible .116
Sumer and Akkad (3500–2000) 129
Cuneiform 134
Assyria (1200–612) 137
Babylonia (625–536) 143
Hanging Gardens of Babylon 150
Hammurabi Code 153
Persia (612–330) 156
Art in Mesopotamia 161
Daily Life in Mesopotamia 164
Religion in Mesopotamia 168
Science and Technology 170

Ancient Egypt Unit

Ancient Egypt Overview 174
Ancient Egypt Objectives 176
Ancient Egypt Time Line 177
Ancient Egypt Vocabulary 178
Ancient Egypt Resources 179

History of Ancient Egypt

Introduction 185
History of Ancient Egypt 187
Geography of Ancient Egypt 191
Egypt's Neighbors 193

Pyramids in Ancient Egypt 195
Ancient Egypt in the Bible 198
Joseph in Ancient Egypt (c. 1659) . .202
Moses in Ancient Egypt (c. 1533) .206
The Plaques (c. 1454) 209
Passover (c. 1454) 214
The Exodus (c. 1454) 218
Pharaohs of Ancient Egypt 221
King Tutankhamen (1003-994) 224
Alliance with Israel 227

Life in Ancient Egypt

Agriculture in Ancient Egypt 229
Architecture in Ancient Egypt . . .231
Archaeology 234
Art in Ancient Egypt 236
Pottery in Ancient Egypt: 240
Cities in Ancient Egypt 242
Clothing in Ancient Egypt 244
Economy and Trade in Egypt 246
Daily Life in Ancient Egypt 248
Education in Ancient Egypt 252
Food in Ancient Egypt 254
Government in Ancient Egypt . . .256
Hieroglyphics 260
Language in Ancient Egypt 262
Literature in Ancient Egypt 265
Medicine in Ancient Egypt 267
Mummies in Ancient Egypt 270
The Nile River 273
Men in Ancient Egypt 277
Women in Ancient Egypt 279
Religion in Ancient Egypt 283
Science and Technology in Egypt .286
Slavery in Ancient Egypt 288
Egypt Today 291

Table of Contents continued...

Ancient Israel Unit

Ancient Israel Overview 296
Ancient Israel Objectives 297
Ancient Israel Time Line 299
Ancient Israel Vocabulary 300
Ancient Israel Resources 302

History of Ancient Israel

Father Abraham 313
God's Covenant with Israel 316
The Patriarchs (2000-1700 B.C.) 322
Egyptian Bondage (1700-1275 B.C.) . .325
The Exodus and Passover 328
Wilderness Wanderings (1275-1235 B.C.)332
The Law 335
The Tabernacle 340
The Priesthood 343
The Twelve Spies 346
Occupation of Canaan (1250 B.C.) . .348
The Twelve Tribes 353
Ancient Israel Geography 355
Period of the Judges (1235-1050 B.C.) 358
United Kingdom (1050-922 B.C.) 362
King Saul (1020-1000 B.C.) 364
King David (1000-960 B.C.) 367
Jerusalem 370
King Solomon (960-920 B.C.) 374
Solomon's Temple 378
Assyrian Captivity (721 B.C.) 382
Divided Kingdom 385
The Babylonian Exile (587-539 B.C.) .388
The Diaspora 393
Restoration/Second Temple 396
The Persian Period (539-332 B.C.) . .398
Queen Esther 401
The Hellenistic Period (19 B.C.) . . .404
The Maccabean Period 406

The Roman Period 411
Herod's Temple 415
Israel History Review 418

Life in Ancient Israel

Agriculture in Ancient Israel 419
Archaeology in Ancient Israel . . .423
Clothing: the Tallit 428
Clothing: General 431
Education in Ancient Israel 434
Family Life in Ancient Israel 438
Food in Ancient Israel 441
Israel's Holidays 446
Prayer in Ancient Israel 450
The Sabbath 455
Women in Ancient Israel 458

Ancient Greece Unit

Ancient Greece Overview 464
Ancient Greece Objectives 466
Ancient Greece Time Line 467
Ancient Greece Vocabulary 468
Ancient Greece Resources 469

History of Ancient Greece

Geography of Ancient Greece 474
Trojan War (1200 B.C.) 477
Government of Ancient Greece . . .480
Greek Mythology (c. 1200-800 B.C.) . .482
The Olympics (first 776 B.C.) 485
Ancient Greek Astronomy (585 B.C.)488
Greek Philosophers (c. 550-250 B.C.) .491
Pythagoras (569-475 B.C.) 496
Persian Wars (497-490 B.C.) 499
Peloponnesian War (431-404 B.C.) . .502
Alexander the Great (356-323 B.C.) .504

Table of Contents continued...

Hebrews in Greece (332-363 B.C.) 508
Archimedes (287-212 B.C.) 511
Archimedes' Principle 514
Hanukkah (165 B.C.) 517

Life in Ancient Greece

Ancient Greek Architecture 520
Art in Ancient Greece 524
Cities: Athens 526
Cities: Sparta 529
Funerals in Ancient Greece 531
Weddings in Ancient Greece 533
Drama in Ancient Greece 535
Education in Ancient Greece . . .537
Daily Life in Ancient Greece 542
Food in Ancient Greece 545
Men in Ancient Greece 547
Women in Ancient Greece 549
Literature: Fables 552
Medicine in Ancient Greece 554
Religion in Ancient Greece 557
Science in Ancient Greece 560

Ancient Rome Unit

Ancient Rome Overview 564
Ancient Rome Objectives 566
Ancient Rome Vocabulary 568
Ancient Rome Time Line 569
Ancient Rome Resources 570

History of Ancient Rome

Geography 579
Founding of Rome (753 B.C.) 583
The Etruscan Dynasty (800-B.C.) . . .586
The Roman Republic (508-27 B.C). . .589
The Punic Wars (264-146 B.C.) 593

Julius Caesar (100-44 B.C.) 597
Julius Caesar: The Play 602
Antony & Octavian (44-30 B.C.) 605
The Roman Empire (27 B.C.-A.D.-410) 609
The Jewish Revolts (A.D. 132-135) . .614
Barbarian Invasions (A.D. 235) 618
Constantine A.D. (361-395) 622
Birth of Christianity (A.D. 379) 627
The Fall of the Roman Empire . .633
Science in Ancient Rome 637

Life in Ancient Rome

Agriculture in Ancient Rome 639
Architecture in Ancient Rome . . .641
Art in Ancient Rome 644
Calendars in Ancient Rome 648
Citizenship in Ancient Rome 650
Clothing in Ancient Rome 652
Customs in Ancient Rome 655
Daily Life in Ancient Rome 657
Men in Ancient Rome 660
Women in Ancient Rome 662
Economy in Ancient Rome 666
Education in Ancient Rome 668
Famous Romans 670
Food in Ancient Rome 673
Gladiators and the Colosseum . . .675
Language in Ancient Rome 678
Laws in Ancient Rome 681
Literature in Ancient Rome 683
Medicine in Ancient Rome 687
Military in Ancient Rome 690
Money in Ancient Rome 694
Philosophy in Ancient Rome 696
Religion in Ancient Rome 698

Table of Contents *continued...*

The Messiah Unit

Messiah Overview 702
Messiah Objectives 704
Messiah Time Line 705
Messiah Resources 706

Introduction: Mind of Christ 710

Messiah in the Old Testament

Messianic Prophecies 713
Christ, Our Passover Lamb 715
Type of Christ: Joseph 717
Type of Christ: Moses 721
Type of Christ: Boaz 723

Messiah in the Gospels

Geography at the Time of Christ .724
Culture at the Time of Christ 726
The Gospels 729
Genealogy of the Messiah 732
Birth of Christ 734
Christ's Disciples 737
The Bible Jesus Read 739
The Kingdom of God 742
Attitude Toward Lepers 744
Teachings on Law 746
Teachings Through Parables 750
Miracles Performed by Christ 754
Attitude Toward Adulteress 757
Christ, Our Shepherd 759
Attitude Toward Women 761
Attitude Toward Children 763
Christ, Our Bridegroom 765
Attitude Toward the Poor 767
Teachings on Love 769
Teachings on Forgiveness 772
Crucifixion/Resurrection 774

Reproducible Pages

Scrapbooking to Learn 781
Paper People Patterns 783

Resource Suppliers

List of Suppliers 787

See Heart of Wisdom Day by Day Lesson Plans at Heartofwisdom.com/homeschool

Key to Symbols

Resource Symbols

 Book or Magazine

 Internet Site

 Audio Resource

 Suitable for all ages (read aloud).

 Key Resource (see pages 32-36)

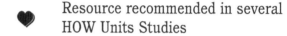 Resource recommended in several HOW Units Studies

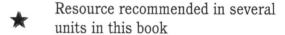 Resource recommended in several units in this book

 Resource recommended in several lessons in a unit.

Activity Symbols

 Writing assignment

 Vocabulary or list

 Copy passages; outline; fill in a worksheet

 Examine

 Map work

 Answer questions

 Add to Time Line Book, make a chart, or graphic organizer

 Expand research

 Think and Discuss

 Write a letter

 Prepare a meal or recipe

 Get a picture or illustration

See Heart of Wisdom Day by Day Lesson Plans at Heartofwisdom.com/homeschool

How to Use This Book

Introduction

Introduction .1
Interacting With Our Web Site 3

The Teaching Approach

HOW Teaching Approach 4
Bible First Philosophy 5
Delight-Directed Studies 7
Charlotte Mason Philosophy 9
The 4Mat Lessons 10
Writing to Learn 14
Correcting Written Work 15

Getting Started

Scheduling 16
Creating a Portfolio 18
Creating a Time Line Book 19
Creating a Vocabulary Notebook . .22
Creating a Spelling Notebook 23
Graphic Organizers 26

Resources

About the Resources 27
Required Resources 29
Choosing Resources? 30
Key Resource List 31
Key Resources in Several Units . . .32
Alternative Resources 37
Timeline .39

Student Portfolio Pages

See more scrapbook pages and Scrap-Lap Books at Heartofwisdom.com/scrapbook

Introduction

The first goal of this book is to inspire students to become "hearers and doers" of God's Word and to encourage them to search the Scriptures and apply them to everyday situations. The second goal is to teach students a love of learning that will last a lifetime.

This book covers a time frame from Creation through the time of Christ in two unique ways:

1. This book's focus is on Bible history, as opposed to most ancient-history studies (even many Christian-based texts), which concentrate on the pagans in ancient times, ignoring God's people. For example, in this book's Ancient Egypt Unit the focus is on Joseph, Moses, the Exodus, and God's people (rather than on the pyramids and gods of Egypt). Our Ancient Greece and Rome units focus on the Israelites fighting against idolatry under Greek and Roman rule (rather than on Greek mythology and Roman gods). We also include an in-depth unit study of Ancient Israel.

2. This book is much more than a basic history study: It is a thematic unit study. You will lead your student(s) chronologically on a fascinating journey through the Bible as they learn to study, write, research, and reason through many subjects including: Bible History, Geography, Literature, Government, Composition, Agriculture, Religion, Science, Economics, and more. As your students study, they will have a number of valuable experiences. They will write essays, summaries, and editorials. They will have the opportunity to publish their work online. They will dramatize and teach others. These activities will develop their ability to think, which is an asset that will benefit them throughout their lives.

Bible Focus

It is crucial that students understand the ancient times if they are to have a good grasp of the Bible. God teaches us through stories about His people. This book is your introduction to the Mesopotamian world of the patriarchs, the Egyptian world of the Exodus, the Babylonian world of Daniel, the Persian world of Esther, and other Bible stories that show us not only the faithfulness of our God, and the greatness of our privileges, but also the marvelous wisdom of the plan of salvation.

Seventy-eight percent of the entire Bible writings (not counting the OT references in the NT), focus on Israel! In this book, you will examine the interaction between the Israelites and the Canaanite, Mesopotamian, Egyptian, Greek, and Roman cultures, which will open your eyes to new-found truths.

A Christian's roots are deep in Judaism through Christ, all the way back to Abraham! *And if ye be Christ's, then are ye Abraham's seed, and heirs according to the promise* (Gal. 3:29). Throughout the Word of God, Abraham is held before us as an example of faith and grace. The Lord God called Abraham, "My friend" (Isa. 41:8). The letter to the Galatians, who were Gentiles by birth and by nature, declares that all who believe on the Lord Jesus Christ are "the children of Abraham" (v. 7), and that we are "blessed with faithful Abraham" (v. 9). God's focus was on Abraham and his family; shouldn't our study of world history have the same focus?

To fully comprehend our Christian faith, we should have a complete understanding of our Hebrew heritage. As Christians, we study a Hebrew book written by Hebrews; we serve a Hebrew Lord who had Hebrew disciples; we desire to follow the first-century church, which was first predominately Hebrew; and through Christ, we are grafted into a Hebrew family! It therefore makes sense to study the Hebrew culture and its effect on world history. This is a refreshing, new, and exciting way to view the Bible! Much of the Bible is a mystery to most Americans. The perplexing phrases, the puzzling actions, the sometimes difficult-to-understand words of Jesus, the unconventional holidays, and the parables can only be understood with an awareness of the Hebrew culture.

Studying Scripture from our Western/American/Greek view is like looking for gold in a dark mine with a dim pen light—you can see enough to stumble around, but you need more light to see clearly. A good grasp of the ancient Hebraic customs and terminology provides a powerful floodlight, exposing intricate details and treasures as you re-examine Scripture.

We believe that *Ancient History: Adam to Messiah* will be a fascinating study for parents as well as for their students. May God bless you and your family as you seek Him and make Him your focus through your studies.

Interacting With Our Web Site

This book is available in a hyper-linked electronic form (Ebook). Ebook users are assigned a special download area at http://Homeschool-Books.com where you can access and download seven individual Ebooks (one for each unit). Each Ebook includes hundreds of Internet links to help your student(s) study the lessons. With Ebooks you have the ability search through the unit for keywords or to print out pages (by unit or lesson or in its entirety) for each member of your family. Ebooks include access to downloading any revisions or updates of this book for two years.

Every time you see this symbol or underlined text in this book, it indicates that there is an active link in the Ebook which will take you to one of the following: another page on our site (containing a worksheet or detailed instructions), an external site with relevant information, or a site from which you can purchase resources.

The links include: interactive sites; illustrated sites; video clips; audio clips; lessons from schools and colleges; dozens of encyclopedias; information on where to buy each resource; etc. Giving your student the opportunity to do research in a variety of ways increases his interest! Our site is continually updated, so we offer new resources and alternatives for books that go out-of-print.

The Internet is a large part of our future. Students will be using the Internet in almost any profession they choose to enter. The Internet is an open door to an enormous, exciting library. The wealth of information on the Internet can be overwhelming because a search for a single topic can lead to thousands of links; but Heart of Wisdom guides you to the best and most appropriate Web sites for each lesson. Throughout the lessons in this book, students not only utilize the Internet, they also learn to navigate it successfully, use search engines and directories, and evaluate Web sites. Because URLs (Internet addresses) change frequently, we do not include them in this book. Instead, we direct you to our site, where you can click through to the appropriate sites for that lesson.

Utilizing the Internet can create engaged, involved, and active learners. But remember, sitting in front of a computer reading through Web pages is only part of learning. Studies show that seventy-five percent of students need more than reading to retain information. Heart of Wisdom incorporates the Internet into the Four-Step Process in each lesson. This process motivates students to learn, and guides them to activities that help them organize the information that they have learned and use it for developing communication skills through writing assignments.

Don't Have Internet Access? There is more than enough information and book resources in this book to study ancient history without access to the Internet.

UPDATE: See the Link Library for updated links at Heartofwisdom.com/homeschool/?cat=224

The Heart of Wisdom Teaching Approach

The homeschool movement has brought about (or restored) many superior, efficient, and exciting teaching approaches. These methods verify that we need to renew our thinking concerning education. The chart below gives nutshell descriptions of each approach.

Bible First Philosophy	The Bible is the center of education, and all subordinate studies should be brought into the circle of light radiating from the Bible. Academics play an important part, but they are secondary. Students spend half the school day studying God's Word, and the other half studying God's world.
A Return to Biblical Hebraic Education	The Bible outlines how we should teach our children. The ancient Hebraic aim of education was ethical and religious. Study is a form of worship. The method of instruction in the home was oral, and learning was accomplished by practice. The ancient Hebrew taught no distinction between sacred and secular areas of life. Every detail of life, therefore, must be set aside and consecrated to the glory of God.
Charlotte Mason's Philosophy	Students should develop a love of learning by reading real books—classic literature—as opposed to twaddle, or "dumbed-down" literature. This method also incorporates narration: the assimilating of information, retelling (sorting, sequencing, selecting, connecting, rejecting, and classifying), creating a Time Line Book, and developing a "Nature Diary."
The 4Mat System	These four steps are a cycle of instruction based on the Four Learning Styles developed by Dr. Bernice McCarthy (see "The 4Mat Lessons"). This system is an organized method of using all of the approaches listed on this page.
Integrated Unit Study	The "unit" or "theme" part of the name refers to the idea of studying a topic as a whole instead of as several "subjects." A unit study takes a topic and "lives" with it for a period of time, integrating science, social studies, language arts, and fine arts as they apply.
Lifestyle of Learning	An approach outlined in *Wisdom's Way of Learning* by Marilyn Howshall. The emphasis is on parents relying on the Holy Spirit's guidance to provide the needed resources so that children can develop expertise in their fields of interest. Howshall explains how using these simple and natural tools (with the emphasis on the process of learning rather than the product of learning) will allow your children to begin to develop their own lifestyle of learning.
Delight-Directed Learning	Students acquire basic concepts of learning (reading, reasoning, writing, researching, etc.) during the process of examining the topic they are interested in. Education ought to be about building learners' abilities to do useful things.
Writing to Learn	Students think on paper—think to discover connections, describe processes, express emerging understandings, raise questions, and find answers; encouraging higher-level thinking skills. This method forces the student to internalize; learning in such a way that he/she understands better and retains longer.

The Heart of Wisdom teaching approach is a beautiful, exciting blend of several of these teaching methods. The remainder of this chapter gives highlights of our approach. To find out more, see our Web site at http://HomeSchoolUnitStudies.com, or the book, *The Heart of Wisdom Teaching Approach*.

UPDATE: See this approach explained at HeartofWisdom.com/Homeschoollinks

Bible First Philosophy

The primary focus of each Heart of Wisdom Unit Study is the Bible. Academics play an important part, but they are secondary. Students spend about half the school day studying God's Word (direct studies) and half studying God's world (derived studies).

The first goal of the Heart of Wisdom Teaching Approach is for each family to read though the Bible (chronologically) once a year. In the first year, your family will read most of the Bible chronologically, intertwined with academic studies, by completing this book, *Ancient History: Adam to Messiah.* The first unit, "Adam to Abraham" takes your family through Genesis 1-12. The "Ancient Israel Unit" takes you from Abraham through the Old Testament into the time of Christ. The "Messiah Unit" focuses on the four Gospels. The other units provide the historical background of Bible times and include a significant amount of Bible reading.

After completing *Ancient History: Adam to Messiah*, we suggest you reread the entire Bible each year using *The Narrated Bible.* (See why we recommend *The Narrated Bible* on page 29). Although it only takes fifteen to twenty minutes per day to accomplish this goal, you should set aside one to two hours (depending on your children's ages) to thoroughly study what you have read. *The Heart of Wisdom Teaching Approach* gives you several ideas to continue this approach.

The Heart of Wisdom Approach will teach you to:

- Develop a habit of daily Bible reading
- Read through the Bible with your family once a year
- Create a portfolio
- Create a Time Line Book
- Learn to use Bible study tools (concordances, lexicons, and dictionaries)
- Learn Biblical history and geography
- Learn to integrate writing and grammar skills with Bible studies
- Learn the way to righteousness
- Learn Biblical languages (at least some rudimentary Greek and Hebrew)
- And more.

The ultimate desire for Christian parents should be for their children to have a heart of wisdom—true wisdom from God. To teach true wisdom, a curriculum should spend a significant amount of time studying God's Word. *For the word of God is quick, and powerful, and sharper than any two edged sword, piercing even to the dividing asunder of soul and spirit, and of the joints and marrow, and is a discerner of the thoughts and intents of the heart* (Heb. 4:12).

Although academic school requirements are included in this curriculum, the main objective of this book is for students and parents to learn God's Word and establish a relationship with God. Author David Mulligan explains the importance of Scripture-centered curriculum in *Far Above Rubies: Wisdom in the Christian Community*. He also reveals the surprising hesitancy Christians feel about this approach to curriculum. He states:

> The idea of spending a lot of school time on the study of Scripture may at first be disturbing. We are so used to dividing "religious" activities from the rest of our time [that] it seems as if Bible study just does not fit, except in a minor way, in our regular school day. We think of Bible study as suitable for family devotions, church services, Sunday school classes, and if the study gets "deep," in the seminary. How much Bible can children get without detracting from other studies?
>
> In asking this question we uncover in ourselves something of the tension that exists in the Western world between learning and religion. We know somehow the question is not right; we should be first giving place to Scripture, but can not quite let go of the other side of things. And rightly so! The other side, God's creation, is vastly important, but still Scripture should come first, and all other studies find their place in relation to it. We should turn the question around: "How many secular studies can a student pursue without detracting from his knowledge of God's Word?!" Christian education must be built upon a pattern that maintains Scripture at its center and bring all subordinate studies into the circle of light radiating from thence.

Marilyn Howshall explains in *Lifestyle of Learning*, that we must consider the problems confronting us as Christian homeschoolers:

> We come from a generation that was not taught how to learn. Few Christians know how to access the Word of God for themselves and fewer still know how to access the Lord for themselves in an intimate way. Many parents were, themselves, not given a love of learning as children and are now lacking in purpose, and training their own children in the same way. With only the raw material of our fragmented lives to work with, we attempt to implement our new godly desires and goals into our existing lifestyles and systems. In so doing, we create an additional problem—burn-out! We use the world's methods and means to produce something they were not designed to produce. When we finally accept the truth that the old way will not produce the results we want, we are ready to receive the suggestion of a new way. Now we are ready to learn.

1. For more about Bible First Philosophy see: Far Above Rubies: Wisdom in the Christian Community by David Mulligan. Available from Messenger Publishing PO Box 251, Marshfield, VT 05658, 802-426-4018

Delight-Directed Studies

Delight-directed learning places students in charge of their own learning, helping them to find something which they want to accomplish. The delight-directed method uses natural curiosity to motivate the student. The student acquires basic concepts of learning (reading, reasoning, writing, researching, etc.) during the process of examining the topic of interest. Less control can lead to more learning.

Each lesson in this book provides enough resources and activities to lead your student into a great deal of in-depth study on a topic. We encourage you to touch on each lesson in each unit, but also to allow students to study in-depth the lessons they find of interest. When your student takes the initiative to do this, set aside any restricted schedules (don't focus on getting through the book), and allow your student to enjoy the process of learning!

Students learn when there is delight not through rigid formal structured studies and schedules. Instead of looking at state standards seek God and ask Him what He would have you teach your children. Listen to the Holy Spirit. God promises us wisdom if we ask for it. When following God's guidance not only lead you what to teach your unique individual child but you will learn to walk a surrendered life, by faith.

All children love to learn—at least all children love to learn before they go to school. Forced learning can destroy the natural love for learning that our children are born with. Children locked into studying something they find boring are no different than adults locked into boring, irrelevant meetings. If adults cannot see the relevance of the material covered in a meeting, they will "tune out" or "drop out." If children do not understand how the subject will help to address the concerns of their lives, they will tune out. Would you, for example, read this page if it were titled "Basic Plumbing Concepts"? You might if you had a kitchen-sink leak or a basement full of water. In the same way, students need to have an interest in the topic they are learning.

If we allow students a free choice, they can concentrate on learning what they might need in their lives. Freedom to choose what not to study implies freedom to learn more about what one cares about, and freedom to explore new interests.

Roger Schank of The Institute for the Learning Sciences explains, in Engines for Education, the importance of individualized education. "Depending on an individual's situation and goals, there are many things that might be worth learning. In order to give a very detailed prescription for what knowledge a student should acquire, we must take into account that not every child will need or want to do the same things. A curriculum must therefore be individualized. It must be built around an understanding of what situations a particular learner might want to be in, or might have to be in later in life, and what abilities he will require in those situations. The methods and the curriculum are molded by the questions that appear on the standardized achievement tests administered to every child from the fourth grade on. Success no longer means being able to do. Success comes to mean "academic success," a matter of learning to function within the system, of learning the "correct" answer, and of doing well at multiple-choice exams. Success also means, sadly, learning not to ask difficult questions. When we ask how our children are doing in school, we usually mean, "are they measuring up to the prevailing standards?" rather than, "are they having a good time and feeling excited about learning?" We should purpose to be flexible in the way we try to tap into our children's innate interests. When we are interacting with the student we can evaluate whether learning has taken place.

A teacher's or parent's first job is to spark the desire in children to read something, to motivate them to care, so that the natural order of learning can kick into action. The educator's job is to provide the one item which today's educational system leaves out: motivation. (Schank, 1994). When students are given good instructional materials, they can and will teach themselves, and they will eventually learn to locate their own resources (books, Web sites, people, materials, classes, etc.).

The Delight-Directed Method is Biblical

The Bible instructs parents to recognize that each child is a unique individual, with a "way" already established that needs to be recognized, acknowledged, and reckoned with by means of the truth of Scripture.

Proverbs 22:6 says *Train up a child in the way he should go, Even when he is old he will not depart from it.* This verse shows us that a parent's training must be based on knowing his or her child. The Hebrew text is written with the personal pronoun attached to the noun "way." It reads, "his way" and not simply "in the way he should go." "Way" is the Hebrew *derek*, "way, road, journey, manner." Parents need to recognize the way each of their children is bent by the way God has designed each of them. If parents fail to recognize this, they may also fail to help launch their children into God's plan for their lives.

Marlyn Howshall's Lifestyle of Learning approach[1] is based on leaning on the Holy Spirit and delight directed learning. She explains, "If the goal of your instruction is love from a pure heart (which will only come with an emptying of self) then you will provide a strong foundation of character in your children that will enable them with your help to acquire a strong and unique, God-designed education which will include creative vocational purpose. If you want godly fruit, you have to know God and do things His way. You won't learn what His way is until you decide you want to know what it is and surrender your will to become completely teachable of the Holy Spirit."

---

1. For more about Marylin Howshall's Life Style of Learning approach see: The Lifestyle of Learning Approach, Wisdom's Way of Learning. Available from Lifestyle of Learning, P.O. Box 145, Bedford, VA 24523. Email LOLearning@aol.com.

Charlotte Mason Philosophy

Charlotte Mason was an educator in England during the previous century, and her methods are currently experiencing a rebirth among American home schools. Mason believed children should be educated through a wide curriculum using a variety of real, living books. "Twaddle" and "living books" are terms coined by Mason. "Twaddle" refers to dumbed-down literature; absence of meaning. "Living books" refers to books that are well written and engaging—they absorb the reader—the narrative and characters "come alive"; living books are the opposite of cold, dry textbooks. Charlotte Mason's concern was for students to develop a lifetime love of learning. She based her philosophy on the Latin word for education, "educare," which means "to feed and nourish." This method focuses on the formation of good habits, reading a variety of books, narration, copying work, dictation, keeping a nature diary, keeping a spelling notebook, and preparing a time line book). In each lessons in this book, we've organized each of Mason's unique methods into a four-step process. (See illustration on page 11).

Narration
Narration is literally "telling back" what has been learned. Students are instructed to read a passage from the Bible, text from a suggested resource, or content from a Web site and "tell" what they have learned, either orally or in writing. This is a perfect activity for the third and fourth steps of the 4Mat System. This process involves sorting, sequencing, selecting, connecting, rejecting, and classifying. Narration increases the student's ability to remember, making review work unnecessary.

Copy Work and Dictation
Copy work and dictation are underrated. Both provide on-going practice for handwriting, spelling, grammar, etc. Both are good exercises for teaching accuracy and attention to detail, and students discover things about the text they are copying that they would be unlikely to notice otherwise. In dictation, the parent reads as the child writes. Students learn correct spelling, capitalization, punctuation, and other language mechanics when they compare their work to the original and correct mistakes.

Time Line Book
Charlotte Mason's students created a Time Line Book (originally called a Museum Sketch Book; sometimes called a Book of the Centuries) to help students pull together seemingly unrelated information. As students learn historical facts, they make notes and sketches in their book on the appropriate page about famous people, important events, inventions, wars, etc. (See directions and samples on pages 19-20).

1. For more on this subject see: A Charlotte Mason Education and More Charlotte Mason Education by Catherine Levison; Charlotte Mason's Original Homeschooling Series; A Charlotte Mason Companion by Karen Andreola; For the Children's Sake by Susan S. MacAulay and The Charlotte Mason Study Guide by Penny Gardner.

The 4Mat Lessons

Each lesson in this book contains four basic steps. These four steps are a cycle of instruction based on the four learning styles identified in *The 4Mat System* developed by Dr. Bernice McCarthy. Each of the four steps teaches to one of these four learning styles. This cycle of learning is based on the fact that different individuals perceive and process experiences in different, preferred ways; these preferences comprise our unique learning styles. Students become comfortable with their own best ways of learning, and grow through experience with alternative modes. The chart below gives an overview of the four learning styles.

Type 1	Type 2	Type 3	Type 4
A Type One learner is one who perceives concretely and processes by thinking through an idea.	A Type Two learner is one who perceives abstractly and processes actively working with an idea.	A Type Three learner is one who perceives abstractly and processes by thinking through an idea.	A Type Four learner is one who perceives concretely and processes actively working with an idea.
Type Ones are "people" people. They learn by listening and sharing ideas and by personalizing information. They need to be personally involved and seek commitment. They tackle problems by reflecting alone and then brainstorming with others. They demonstrate concern for people. They excel in viewing concrete situations from many perspectives and model themselves on those they respect.	Schools are made for these types of learners. They are eager learners who think through ideas. They are thorough and industrious, and excel in traditional learning environments. They are excellent at discerning details and at sequential thinking. They tackle problems rationally and logically. They are less interested in people than concepts.	Ninety-five percent of the engineers tested are Type 3. They excel at down-to-earth problem solving. They are common-sense people. They have a limited tolerance for fuzzy ideas. They experiment and tinker with things. They tackle problems by acting (often without consulting others). They need to explore, manipulate, and experience things to understand how things work.	These types of learners seek to influence others. They learn by trial and error. They are self-discovery learners. They thrive on challenge. They adapt to change and relish it. They tend to take risks and are at ease with people. They perceive things with emotions and process by doing. They need to be able to use what they have learned.

The most important thing to realize about learning styles is that one style is not better than another. We all have different intellectual strengths. No one fits into a box; we are all unique individuals created by God. Each of us is a combination of the four types, more or less, in one or two categories. Studies show that seventy percent of children do NOT learn well through the way the schools teach—lecture/textbook/test—most students need more. The Bible teaches that we are all different parts of the body of Christ and that one part is no better than another part (1 Corinthians 12:12-25).

The 4MAT® model consists of four instructional goals:

1. Motivating students
2. Teaching ideas and facts
3. Experimenting with Concepts & Skills
4. Integrating new learning into real life.

It addresses four styles of learners:

1. Those who learn by listening and sharing ideas
2. Those who learn by conceptualizing — integrating their observations into what is known,
3. Those who learn by experimenting—testing theories in practice
4. Those who learn by creating—acting and then testing their new experience

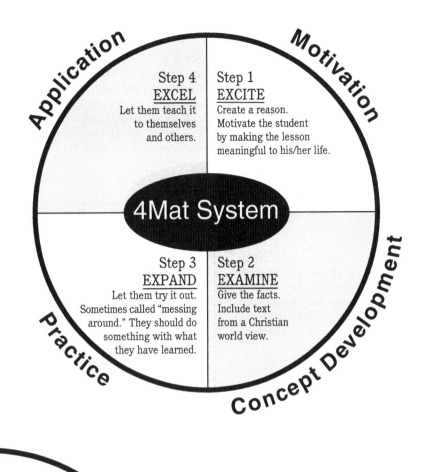

Application Motivation

Step 4
EXCEL
Let them teach it
to themselves
and others.

Step 1
EXCITE
Create a reason.
Motivate the student
by making the lesson
meaningful to his/her life.

4Mat System

Step 3
EXPAND
Let them try it out.
Sometimes called "messing
around." They should do
something with what
they have learned.

Step 2
EXAMINE
Give the facts.
Include text
from a Christian
world view.

Practice Concept Development

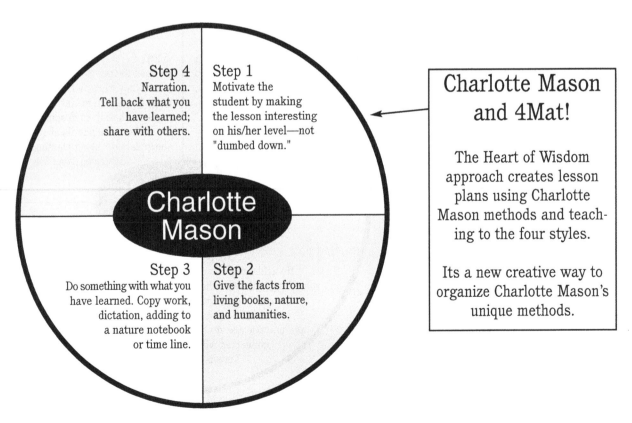

Step 4
Narration.
Tell back what you
have learned;
share with others.

Step 1
Motivate the
student by making
the lesson interesting
on his/her level—not
"dumbed down."

Charlotte Mason

Step 3
Do something with what you
have learned. Copy work,
dictation, adding to
a nature notebook
or time line.

Step 2
Give the facts from
living books, nature,
and humanities.

Charlotte Mason and 4Mat!

The Heart of Wisdom approach creates lesson plans using Charlotte Mason methods and teaching to the four styles.

Its a new creative way to organize Charlotte Mason's unique methods.

Step 4
Israel was to instruct all nations in divine holiness and redemption as Yahweh's instrument of light to the nations.

Step 1
Motivation—Israel's mandate was to diligently teach their children to love God, and to know and obey his statutes and ordinances (Deut 6:1-9).

Education in Bible Times

Step 3
Oral and written recitation. Repetition in observation, experiential learning (doing), listening, reciting, and imitating.

Step 2
The aim of education was ethical and religious, centering on the Torah and recognizing and remembering events of divine providence in history.

Modern-day science may have come up with the 4Mat System, but is it really a new way to teach or have we had this pattern all along?

Ultimately, biblical education is instruction in a lifestyle. For this reason, the apostle Paul reminded his pupil Timothy, *you ... know all about my teaching, my way of life ... continue in what you learned ...* (2 Tim 3:10,14). Not only is biblical education a lifestyle —it is a lifetime!

The 4Mat lessons are designed so that all learning styles are addressed, in order that more than one type of student may be permitted to both "shine" and "stretch." Each lesson contains "something for everybody," so each student not only finds the mode of greatest comfort for him/her, but is challenged to adapt to other, less comfortable but equally valuable modes.

Step 4
He asked them to go and tell others. "Go ye therefore, and teach all nations..."

Step 1
He took the people where they were and made the lesson meaningful to their lives in some way. He spoke to shepherds about sheep, farmers about planting, fishermen about fish, etc.

How Jesus Taught

Step 3
He asked them to do something with what they learned—to actively respond—doing and practice are vitally connected with knowing.

Step 2
He brought in the facts—Scripture, "It is written,..."

Studies show that this four-step method motivates students to comprehend the material better and retain the information longer. Dozens of studies have been done comparing the 4Mat System to traditional textbooks. These studies show again and again that students learning under the 4Mat System achieved significantly greater gains than students in the textbook group.[1]

Since the development of this teaching approach, Dr. McCarthy has achieved national recognition as a leader in the instructional field. The 4MAT System is being used by hundreds of thousands of teachers throughout the country to design and develop unit plans for every age group; kindergarten, college, law, medical schools, etc. In documented field studies of the 4Mat System the following outcomes have been found to recur consistently:

Improved Retention ....From the earliest stages of implementation, students show significantly better recall of information when taught with the 4MAT System.

Higher Achievement ....On objective achievement tests measuring knowledge, comprehension, application, and analysis, 4MAT students score significantly higher than their traditionally taught counterparts.

Increased Motivation ....Qualitative studies show that teachers and students display more-positive attitudes toward learning with 4MAT than with traditional methods. Teachers report more frequent collaboration, greater commitment to assessment, and a deeper appreciation of the teacher's role as a motivator.

Improved Thinking Skills ..In studies measuring analytical and creative thinking, 4MAT students show a substantially better command of basic thinking skills than control groups. Improvements tend to be most dramatic in verbal and figural creative thought.

Lower Remediation ....4MAT substantially improves success rates with at-risk and special-education students. The need for re-teaching also declines.

1. For more on this subject see: The 4MAT System, Teaching to Learning Styles with Right and Brain Processing Techniques by Bernice McCarthy; *4Mat in Action* by Susan Morris and Bernice McCarthy; *The 4Mat System Workbook; 4Mation Developer Software* by Excel, Inc; *4Mation Lesson Bank* by Excel, Inc.

Writing to Learn

One of the best ways for a student to understand a topic is to write about it. Students must comprehend the material, restructure the new information, and then share their new understanding. "Writing to Learn"[1] is much more than an accumulation of report writing; it helps students think and learn carefully and completely. Writing assignments are about creating both ideas and learning. During writing assignments, students learn how to assess information and determine its appropriateness, to evaluate and compare, analyze and discern, add their own feelings, organize information, and communicate conclusions. Through these processes, students learn to manage and use information to solve problems, interrelate knowledge, and effectively communicate learning outcomes. Students develop excellence in achievement by producing the required quality assignments; they develop diligence by continually practicing clarity, accuracy, relevance, prioritizing, consistency, depth, and breadth through writing activities.

Charlotte Mason's narration methods for younger children involve "telling back" favorite stories read by parents. In later years, students progress to reading passages and "telling back" in verbal or written form what they have learned. Talking it out, whether aloud or on paper, helps students think.

Often teachers use writing as a way of testing. They use it to find out what students already know, rather than as a way of encouraging them to learn. But the active processes of seeking information, compiling notes, and evaluating, analyzing, and organizing content, as well as the processes of personal reflection, choosing and constructing words, and expressing ideas in writing, are valuable learning tools which students will use the rest of their lives.

Catherine Copley explains in *The Writer's Complex:*

> Writing provides food for thought—it enables you to knead small, half-baked words and sentences into great big loaves of satisfying thought that then lead to more thoughts. Developing ideas involves getting some ideas—in whatever form—onto paper or screen so you can see them, return to them, explore them, question them, share them, clarify them, change them, and grow them. It really is almost like growing plants or kneading bread and waiting for the results: plant the seed, start the process, and then let your mind, including your unconscious, take over. Go to sleep and let your dreaming continue to develop your ideas. Humans were born to think; it's almost impossible to stop us. Writing helps us to bring all that activity into consciousness, helps to clarify and direct our thinking, and generate more thinking. Writing, thinking, and learning are part of the same process.[2]

1. For more on this subject see the "Writing to Learn" chapter in Writers INC or Writing to Learn by William Zinsser, HarperCollins; ISBN: 0062720406.
2. Copley, Catherine. (1995) *The Writer's Complex*, Empire State College <http://www.esc.edu/htmlpages/writer/copley/hmpg.htm>

Correcting Written Work

You and your student will need a writing handbook to use with this book. We recommend *Writers Inc: A Student Handbook for Writing and Learning* (see description on page 29); you or your student will be referring to this book in almost every lesson.

You will correct spelling, capitalization, punctuation, grammar, sentence structure, subject/verb agreement, consistent verb tense, and word usage in all writing by marking each error with a number that corresponds with a rule from *Writers INC*. The student refers to the rule in the book, corrects his paper, and turns it back in.

Read through "The Writing Process" in *Writers INC* with your student. It is important for your student to understand the stages in the writing process: Prewriting, Drafting, Revising, Editing, and Publishing. Explain to your student that you will accept his or her writing in different stages. Requiring all work to be "published" can discourage writing. Throughout the lessons your student will be asked to write summaries, paraphrases, letters, essays, etc. Much of the time you can accept rough drafts, but occasionally (especially in adding work to the Portfolio) your student needs to go through the entire process.

Through the writing assignments, students will learn:

- Writing Skills: Context, form, mechanics, editing, and revision.
- Spelling Skills: Create a personal Spelling Dictionary.
- Vocabulary Skills: Create a personal Vocabulary Notebook.
- Handwriting Skills: Practice writing Bible verses.
- Critical Thinking Skills: Manage and use information to solve problems, interrelate knowledge, and effectively communicate learning outcomes.
- Character Development through assignment completion: Attentiveness, commitment, confidence, decisiveness, efficiency, faithfulness, perseverance, promptness, responsibility, and self-control.

Online Writing Tutors

If you don't feel qualified to teach or proofread your students' work we can connect you to a professional online writing tutor available monthly or annually. If you purchase the program your student works with a mentor to improve upon various writing skills. If your child needs help with any Heart of Wisdom writing assignment --research papers, book reviews, journal writing, grammar, poetry-- he or she will be assigned a mentor who can coach them. All contact is via e-mail and the turn around is within 24 hours, so feedback, input, and new lessons arrive promptly and result in an incredibly high level of student interest and enthusiasm. You can use a tutor until you feel comfortable teaching your student or use the tutor long term. For more information e-mail support@heartofwisdom.com.

Getting Started

The whole foundation of the Heart of Wisdom philosophy is to give up man's standards and lean on God for what He would have us teach our children. Matthew 6:33 is our focus, "*Seek ye first the kingdom of God, and his righteousness; and all these things shall be added unto you.*" If we focus on teaching our children God's Word he will take care of any other needs. Have faith! Pray and seek God's leading. There is no better way to plan —let Him take you through His book at His pace! God's yoke is easy, and His burden is light—let the Spirit direct your schooling. When we lean on Him, He will transform every area of our lives! (Mat 11:28–30.)

There are several ways that you can use this book. The schedule listed is only a guideline to complete this book in a one year (36 week) period. There are enough resources and activities listed to spend one year studying a single unit or even several months on some of the lessons. Use the schedule below as a very loose guide. Remember the goals:

1. To learn and obey God's Word.
2. To develop a love of learning, and a lifestyle of learning.

Unit		Lessons	One Year Schedule	Schedule for Your Family
1	Adam to Abraham	16	4 Weeks	
2	Mesopotamia	13	3 Weeks	
3	Ancient Egypt	38	6 Weeks	
4	Ancient Israel	43	7 Weeks	
5	Ancient Greece	31	5 Weeks	
6	Ancient Rome	38	7 Weeks	
7	Messiah	27	4 Weeks	

Follow your student's delight and allow them study topics of interest in depth. Adjust this schedule to fit the needs of your family as the Lord leads. A typical school year is 180 days or 36 weeks. There are 206 lessons in this book. Using the one year schedule, students should complete 5 to 6 lessons a week. Some homeschoolers are finding two years in this book gives a good foundation of Bible times.

You decide the pace. Understand you can certainly complete more than one lesson a day. For example the Ancient Greece Lessons about funerals, weddings, drama and education can be completed in few hours in one day. More important lessons like understanding God's covenant with Abraham might take two days study time. *Be anxious for nothing, but in everything by prayer and supplication, with thanksgiving, let your requests be made known to God;and the peace of God, which surpasses all understanding, will guard your hearts and minds through Christ Jesus.* Php 4:6-8 If God, in His loving mercy, promises the sun to rise and set each day, will He not promise that our purpose will come to pass as well?

Think of the story of the Twelve Spies. Don't be like the ten spies who shrank in fear. Have the faith of Joshua and Caleb. God has brought you out of Egypt and to the threshold of the promise land. Will you fear the giants or go in an enjoy the milk and honey? (Number 13-14).

Before You Begin this Book:
  1. Set up the Portfolio (see page 18).
  2. Set up a Time Line Book (see pages 19-21).
  3. Set up a Vocabulary Notebook (see page 22).
  4. Set up a Spelling Notebook (see page 23).

Before You Begin a Unit
Plan the lessons you'll complete each week,and organize your resources. Keeping your resources organized it very helpful.

  1. *Pray* and decide the number of weeks you'll be spending on the unit.
  2. Browse through the unit. Choose and list:
    a) The lessons you will complete each week.
    b) The activities you would like to complete in each lesson.
    c) The Resources you have on hand.
    d) The Resources you'll get from the library or another source.

● Multi-Level Teaching

This book was designed for homeschool families who use a multi-age approach. Most home-schooler are teaching more than one child covering a span of ages. The approach lends itself to individual and family learning. You will work through the lessons teaching your 4th grader, 7th grader, and 11th grader at the same time, and they will each be learning and absorbing at their own level (just like the one room schoolhouse).

Each lesson includes a list of resources for different levels and suggestions to read aloud as a family. Lessons include a range of activities; many are easy enough for elementary students, while others are challenging enough for high school students. Older students will have more difficult assignments and be expected to learn at higher levels. Younger students will pick up what they are ready to learn and their assignments can be adjusted accordingly. Parents can easily adapt older-student resources to suit younger children by reading the text (from a Web site or book) and summarizing it for the student. (Charlotte Mason's narration method in reverse.) If you're using this book with younger students, you may wish to repeat the book in a few years. See our Web site for high school credit information.

Creating a Portfolio

A Portfolio is simply a three-ring notebook that is used to store the student's work for each unit, including writing assignments, artwork, small collections, letters, photos, brochures, maps, etc. To set up your Portfolio you will need: a three-ring notebook with a clear-plastic pocket cover, a variety of paper, cardstock, top-loading sheet protectors (for photos, brochures, maps, etc.), and a three-hole punch.

Scrapbooking to Learn

Combine scrapbooking techniques with Charlotte Mason's copy methods for a great display or addition to your unit study portfolio. Some students thrive on creativity; for them, we suggest scrapbook supplies (memory albums, stickers, die cuts, paper, cardstock, scissors, pens, punches, templates, rulers, idea books, etc.). Students can decorate papers with illustrations, stickers, frames, etc. There are thousands of scrapbook ideas on the Internet; you can find them by simply typing "scrapbook" into any Search Engine. Scrapbooking is incredibly rewarding, Students show enthusiasm about almost any subject if there are able to scrapbook. See the last page of this book for more on "scrapbooking to learn" and patterns for paper people. See our web site for students samples.

Cover

Students can create a cover by drawing on paper with markers or crayons, making a collage, using pictures from the Internet, or enlarging a color photo at a local copy center. Students can then slide the finished product into the pocket covering their notebook. If your student experiences a block in creating a cover design, leave the cover blank until he or she feels inspired.

Division

Students can use index dividers or colored paper dividers, and make a title page for each unit: Adam to Abraham; Ancient Mesopotamia; Ancient Egypt; Ancient Israel; Ancient Greece; Ancient Rome; and The Messiah. If you prefer, you can make an entire notebook for each time period.

Contents

Your students will include essays, reports, stories, poems, songs, Bible verses, journal entries, book reviews, dictation lessons, photographs of projects, computer-produced graphics, memorabilia, recipes, maps, Internet printouts, illustrations, etc. Your students should demonstrate correct grammar, punctuation, spelling, and vocabulary usage in all writing, and complete all corrections, rewrites, and improvements. They can store oversized artwork easily by folding poster board in half, stapling the sides perpendicular to the fold (which has now become the bottom), and slipping artwork in the top.

Creating a Time Line Book

In her writings, Charlotte Mason recommended preparing a handmade Time Line Book (originally called a Museum Sketch Book; sometimes called a Book of the Centuries). This activity is based upon one of the major keys to motivation: the active involvement of students in their own learning. Students learn by doing, making, writing, designing, creating, and solving. Creating this Time Line Book is a marvelous way for students to not only be actively involved but to "pull it all together" and grasp the flow of biblical and historical events.

In a short period of time, students can complete an illustrated time line page that tells a story, resulting in immediate feedback that is satisfying and rewarding. Then, as your students learn historical facts, they will make notes and sketches in their book, on the appropriate dated page, about famous people, important events, inventions, wars, etc. (Work that includes undated information about a time period, such as daily life, education, etc., fits better into the Portfolio, but you can combine the two books if you wish.)

To get started, you can purchase a blank <u>Book of the Centuries</u> published by Small Ventures Press, or make your own with the instructions below.

To Set Up Your Time Line Book

You will need: a three-ring notebook with a clear-plastic pocket cover, blank 8.5" x 11" pages, smaller lined pages (8.5" x 11" cut down to 8.5" x 9"), and a three-hole punch. An option is to choose a color for the pages of each unit (peach for Mesopotamia, pink for Rome, blue for Israel, etc.).

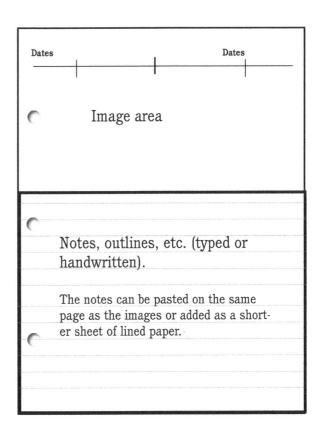

Decide upon the units of time you will use (decades, centuries, etc.) to divide your time line into segments. A time line documenting the period from Adam to the Messiah will begin with Creation (before 2000 B.C.) and end with the resurrection of Christ (c. A.D. 30). (The nice thing about the notebook style timeline is that it's cumulative; every year's study can be added in. You can continue this time line as you study later periods by adding pages.) As you study each period, there will be times when you will document decades on one page, and other times when you will document several centuries on one page. Place the appropriate section of the time line across the top of each 8.5" x 11" page to represent increments. The shorter lined pages will go in between these pages to hold notes. If there is not room on your time line to include all of your chronology, cull some of the dates or add pages with larger segments that leave more room. Use the time lines in this book as a guide.

Time Line Illustrations

There are many ways to illustrate the pages.
    1. Students can draw, trace, or sketch illustrations.
    2. Print out clip art from the Internet. Thousands of illustrations, maps, Christian clip art, etc., are available on the Internet. A few examples are shown on the sample pages.
    3. Photo copy illustrations from book. Below are samples from <u>Reproducible Maps, Charts, Time Lines and Illustrations (What the Bible Is All About Resources)</u>.

MOSES

A Note About Bible Dates

Don't be surprised to find several hundred years difference in B.C. time lines (such as those on the Internet, in <u>Holman Bible Atlas</u>, or in <u>Reproducible Maps, Charts, Time Lines and Illustrations</u>). Scholars disagree about Bible dates, especially before Abraham (c. 2100 B.C.). The time lines in this book are based on conventional chronologies. The most important thing is that students see the chronological progression. Explain to your student(s) that the "c." stands for circa which means "approximately": it is used before a date to indicate that it is approximate or estimated. Use the dates which you feel are most accurate.

Moses, Passover, the Exodus   Wanderings Begin

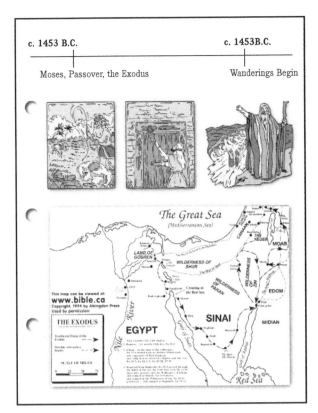

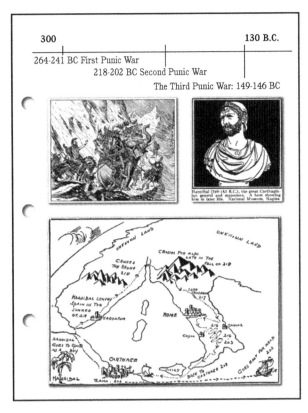

1743 Hatshepsut Crowned

1455 Hatshepsut dethroned

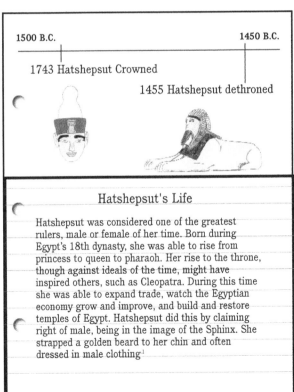

Hatshepsut's Life

Hatshepsut was considered one of the greatest
rulers, male or female of her time. Born during
Egypt's 18th dynasty, she was able to rise from
princess to queen to pharaoh. Her rise to the throne,
though against ideals of the time, might have
inspired others, such as Cleopatra. During this time
she was able to expand trade, watch the Egyptian
economy grow and improve, and build and restore
temples of Egypt. Hatshepsut did this by claiming
right of male, being in the image of the Sphinx. She
strapped a golden beard to her chin and often
dressed in male clothing[1]

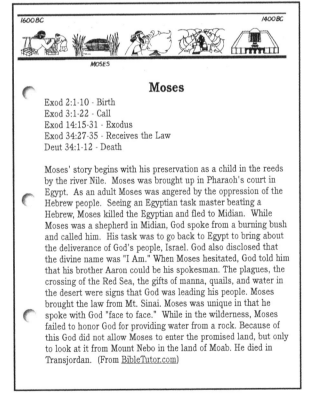

Moses

Exod 2:1-10 - Birth
Exod 3:1-22 - Call
Exod 14:15-31 - Exodus
Exod 34:27-35 - Receives the Law
Deut 34:1-12 - Death

Moses' story begins with his preservation as a child in the reeds
by the river Nile. Moses was brought up in Pharaoh's court in
Egypt. As an adult Moses was angered by the oppression of the
Hebrew people. Seeing an Egyptian task master beating a
Hebrew, Moses killed the Egyptian and fled to Midian. While
Moses was a shepherd in Midian, God spoke from a burning bush
and called him. His task was to go back to Egypt to bring about
the deliverance of God's people, Israel. God also disclosed that
the divine name was "I Am." When Moses hesitated, God told him
that his brother Aaron could be his spokesman. The plagues, the
crossing of the Red Sea, the gifts of manna, quails, and water in
the desert were signs that God was leading his people. Moses
brought the law from Mt. Sinai. Moses was unique in that he
spoke with God "face to face." While in the wilderness, Moses
failed to honor God for providing water from a rock. Because of
this God did not allow Moses to enter the promised land, but only
to look at it from Mount Nebo in the land of Moab. He died in
Transjordan. (From BibleTutor.com)

See more timelines, scrapbook pages and Scrap-Lap Books at HeartofWisdom.com/scrapbook.

Creating a Vocabulary Notebook

To set up your student's Vocabulary Notebook, divide a spiral notebook into 26 sections (one for each letter of the alphabet), allowing two or three pages per letter. Read "Improving Vocabulary Skills" in *Writers INC*.

It's best to keep vocabulary separate from the Unit Portfolios, because many of the new words your student will learn along the way will not be specific to the thematic unit. Vocabulary Notebook pages can be helpful for students not only to observe their progress, but also to establish an increasing awareness in reading. Research has shown that it is much easier to remember words in context than in simple lists. Computer option: students can also keep their vocabulary words in a file on the computer.

Each day, students should make a vocabulary list of unknown words found while reading. At the end of the reading, students will be expected to make vocabulary entries into their notebooks. If the student does not come across any new words, choose new words from the "Vocabulary" section of the current unit study. The student should arrange the entries as follows:

1. Write the date of the entry next to the word.
2. Include the sentence where you first found the word.
3. Write the definition of the word from context.
4. Write the antonym of the word as derived from context.
5. Write one complete sentence using the word.

Example

intact – (7/9/00) "The deck was torn and scattered, but the precious engine was intact." "The Lawgiver" p. 239.
Definition: unharmed, untouched.
Antonym: destroyed, torn apart.
Sentence: I was pleased to find my house intact after the tornado warnings had passed.

Root Words

Students should study word roots. Many English words have Latin roots. When a student learns one root, he/she can often learn many new words. For example, the Latin root "tele" means "to distance," and this root is found in many English words, such as the following: telephone, telescope, etc.

Review

Once a week, verbally go over a random list of words. Ask the student to use each word in a sentence. Check off the words that the student masters. Review all words at the end of the semester.

Creating a Spelling Notebook

To set up your student's Spelling Notebook, divide a spiral notebook into 26 sections (one for each letter of the alphabet). Add any words that the student has trouble spelling. Read "Steps to Become a Better Speller," "Spelling Rules," and "Commonly Misspelled Word List" in *Writers INC*.

Each time you notice a misspelled word in a student's written work, write the word on a list for the student. (Remember to add misspelled words that the spell-checker finds in work written using a word processor.) If the word is again misspelled in written work, the student must add it to his/her Spelling Notebook.

Overcoming Continually Misspelled Words

If students turn in work over and over with the same words misspelled, you may need to become more firm. Businesses and corporations are faced with employees who cannot spell, and use different methods for correcting these problems. One effective example, although it's a bit extreme, is used by the Orlando Police Department. Police officers in training are required to write lengthy reports (back and front of a page in ink) that are turned in to their sergeants for review. The sergeant reviews the report with a red pen, circling any misspelled words. One error results in the officer rewriting the entire report (back and front). The trainee officers quickly learn to carry a pocket dictionary and carefully proofread reports. We're not suggesting that you use this approach; you don't want to discourage writing. But you can modify this approach by allowing students to use erasable ink. Hand back papers with spelling mistakes and ask for corrections. Encourage students to proofread aloud, always with pencil or pen in hand, and to proofread backwards.

Hebrew and Greek Notebook

Several of the lessons in this book include references to Hebrew or Greek words. Encourage students to look up the Hebrew or Greek word in a Lexicon. (See our web site for active links to Crosswalk's New Testament Greek lexicon based on *Thayer's and Smith's Bible Dictionary* and Crosswalk's Old Testament Hebrew lexicon based on *Brown, Driver, Briggs, Gesenius Lexicon*.) Your student should have an assigned place to keep these words and the definitions in a notebook, or in a section of his/her Portfolio.

Graphic Organizers

Throughout the lessons you will see several organization activities. These are convenient ways of organizing notes and thoughts about a topic. Graphic Organizers can be powerful teaching tools; students remember text better if it is turned into a graphic. The next few pages show examples of different types of Graphic Organizers.

Mind Mapping

A Mind Map (or Concept Map) is a convenient way of organizing notes and thoughts about a topic. Your students can use it in brainstorming and planning, to help them grasp and expand learned concepts. Mind mapping is a nonlinear activity which generates ideas, images and feelings around a stimulus word. As students "cluster," their thoughts tumble out, enlarging their word bank for writing and often enabling them to uncover patterns in their ideas.

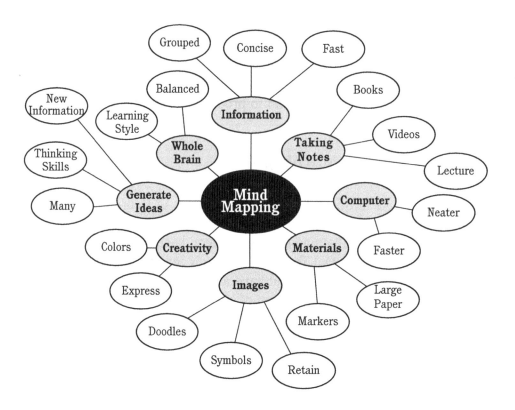

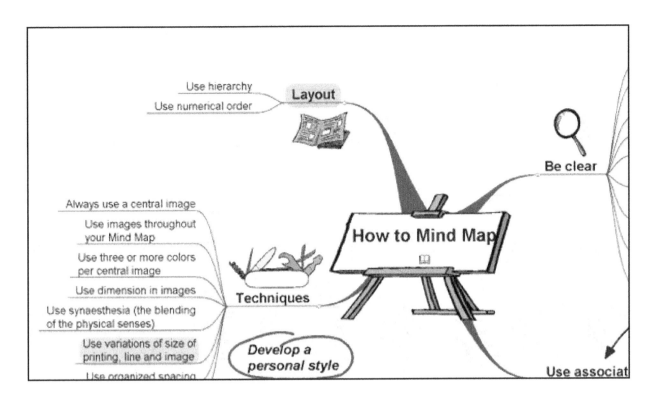

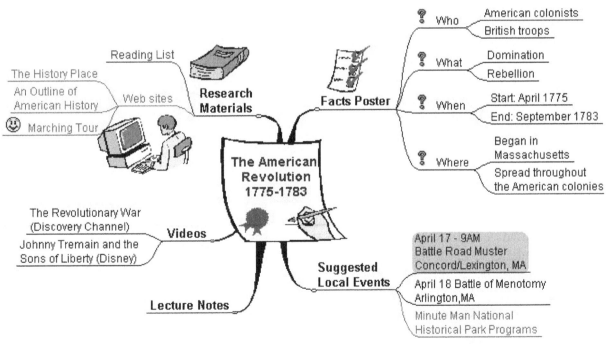

Mind maps on this page are by eMindMaps: Trial free mind-mapping software. See http://www.mindjet.com.

Contrast-and-Compare Graphics

	Item 1	Item 2
Attribute 1		
Attribute 2		
Attribute 3		

A comparison is a systematic strategy for analyzing and evaluating the similarities of two or more things. (A contrast is simply a comparison that emphasizes differences rather than similarities.) An effective comparison attempts to demonstrate one of three general purposes: Two things thought to be different are actually similar; two things thought to be similar are really quite different; two things, although comparable, are not equal—one is better than the other.

Venn Diagram

The Venn Diagram is made up of two or more overlapping circles. It is often used in mathematics to show relationships between sets. In language arts instruction, the Venn Diagram is useful for examining similarities and differences between characters, stories, poems, etc. It is frequently used as a prewriting activity to enable students to organize thoughts or textual quotations prior to writing a compare/contrast essay. This activity enables students to organize similarities and differences visually.

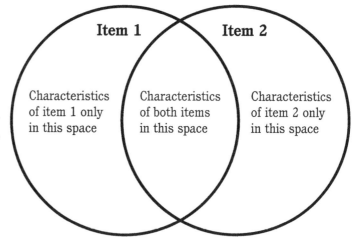

Storyboards

A storyboard (or flowchart) is a graphic, sequential depiction of a narrative. A time line is a form of storyboarding. It helps students to think visually about the sequence of scenes. It develops defining and analyzing processes while building a step-by-step picture of the process for analysis, discussion, or communication purposes. A storyboard can be a simple cartoon strip with illustrations, or boxes with text that tell a story.

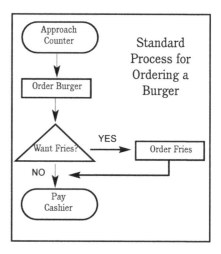

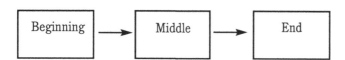

Underlined text refers to Internet link.

About the Recommended Resources

Four Types of Resources Recommended

1. Bible Study Tools
2. Reference Books: Students read specific portions of the reference books for each lesson.
3. Literature and Classics (novels and stories): to be read during the course of the unit.
4. Internet Sources

Bible Study Tools

You should have several Bible study tools on hand: a KJV Bible; *The Narrated Bible* (explained in the Required Resources Section), a Bible Atlas (we recommend *The Holman Bible Atlas*), a Bible dictionary; a Bible handbook (Customs and Manners); a concordance, a Greek and Hebrew Lexicon, etc. (many of these are available on the Internet). For a full list of recommended Bible study tools, a plan for reading through the Bible in a year, and a plan for creating a Bible portfolio, see our Web site or the book *The Heart of Wisdom Teaching Approach*.

Required Resources	none	See page 31
Key Resources recommended in several units	⚷— ♥ or ⚷— ★	Pages 34-36
Alternative Resources recommended in several units	♥ or ★	Page 37-40
Resources recommended in several lessons in a unit	◆	In the unit
Alternative Resources recommended in a specific unit		In the unit
Resources recommended in a lesson	none	In the lesson

Reference Books

Thematic units should offer your children choices of both nonfiction reference and fiction books as sources of information. Frequently, we recommend heavily illustrated reference books because they provide the best source of factual information (in an interesting and user-friendly manner), nurture students' excitement, promote an interest in learning, and spark curiosity. Some reference books, such as *The Usborne Book of the Ancient World* or *The Holman Bible Atlas* contain information pertinent to every unit and are referred to in several lessons. Some reference books, such as *Eyewitness to Ancient Rome*, only pertain to a single unit. These types of books make good read-alouds. They can stimulate interest in any topic you may be introducing. They also build background knowledge for students, expand vocabu-

---

Resources recommended in ◆several lessons, ★ several units, ▯other HOW Units. ⚷—Key Resource (see beginning of unit or page 32).

lary, and encourage students to share interests. Read to your students with enthusiasm. Share photos and illustrations. Encourage students to browse through the book and read the sections they are interested in.

Literature and Classics

 Look for this symbol in each unit for novels that are to be read over a period of time. Students are more interested in and fascinated with what they are learning when they learn from stories. Literature paints for us a picture of a time and place, of customs and society and manners. It makes historical figures come alive, giving them depth and character, and helping us share in their thoughts and feelings, their struggles and joys. We recommend that you choose at least one such book for each unit. Elizabeth Wilson explains in her book, *Books Children Love*:

> Books contain the throb of human life; the magic entrances, fascinates, sets the right imagination, opens doors of interest and curiosity, informs and triggers questioning. Restless bodies become still and concentrated-thinking is encouraged. Reading aloud fosters warm ties in human relationships. The experience is shared, and then interesting and meaningful conversation ensues. Developing the ability and desire to pursue reading is education.

We try to include several story type books or biographies in each unit. Books from a Christian perspective about ancient times are scarce but we found a few for each unit. Set aside a special time each day to read the recommended literature aloud as a family or offer your older student choice from a few of these books for silent substained reading (SSR - students silently read a book of their choice for a few minutes each day).

Don't forget the best stories of all times are in the Bible. The Bible is unique in its composition. It has a wealth of manuscript authority unsurpassed by any other classic. Educated men and peasants, kings and farmers had a hand in its composition. Some of the pages were written in the desert and some by the sea; some in the king's palace and some in a shepherd's hut; many of its pages were slipped out a prison window in the cramped handwriting of an old man. Part of it was written full of action; some of it full of poetry and song. Read aloud Bible stories from the Narrated Bible or Bible story books or listen to the Bible dramatized Audio Bible on CD. God's Word never returns void!

Internet Sources

There is a wealth of information on the Internet: you and your student can access video clips, interactive sites, audio clips, illustrated sites, lessons from schools and colleges, dozens of encyclopedias, etc. Giving your student the opportunity to do research in a variety of ways increases his interest! You're not expected to use all the Internet sources. We usually recommend several Internet sources in each lesson because sites move or go off-line daily. If we list several, you have a better chance of finding the information.

Underlined text refers to Internet link.

Required Resources

The only required resources are a Bible and a writing handbook. (Think of the Bible as your main textbook and this book as your guide.) All other resources are *optional*. We recommend *The Narrated Bible* and *Writers Inc: A Student Handbook for Writing and Learning*.

The Narrated Bible

The Narrated Bible is arranged chronologically, so the readings corre- spond with the lessons in this book. (The Bible references are also given in the lesson if you choose to use another Bible.) Throughout the lessons you will see a Bible icon with numbers. The numbers correspond to page numbers in *The Narrated Bible*. We recommend *The Narrated Bible* for several reasons:

74-96

The Narrated Bible

1. The chronological arrangement helps students see how various Scriptures fit with each other and with their historical settings.
2. The modern English used is familiar and easy to understand. It is amazingly easy to read through several books of the Bible in one sitting with this story format.
3. Because it is written in everyday English, the text can be used for dictation and copy- ing lessons, (teaching handwriting, grammar, capitalization, and punctuation).
4. The layout of the book is ideal for teaching students how to outline. Each section includes excellent titles and subtitles, which give a concise overview of the theme.
5. Helpful background information (narrative commentary) is written to integrate with most Scriptures in such a way that it is part of an unfolding story (in a separate and distinct typeface and color).
6. Throughout the presentation of scripture, chapter and verse designations are placed in the margin for easy reference.
7. Proverbs, Ecclesiastes, and the Song of Solomon are divided thematically. Topic examples: Discipline, Temper, Patience, Greed, Flattery, Controlled Speech, etc. We have created a Cause and Effect Worksheet to use with these readings.

Writers Inc: A Student Handbook for Writing and Learning

Your student will be referring to this book in almost every lesson. Read how to use this book to correct your student's written work on page 15. We do not refer to page numbers in this book because it is frequently revised. Writing, reading, and additional study skills are com- bined in this comprehensive writing manual. The fundamental principles of writing are explained throughout for quick reference. The process of organizing, researching, and writing a paper is laid out in easy-to-understand language. The book outlines strategies for writing with computers, including instruction in writing multimedia reports and publishing online. Also included is information on thinking and learning skills, such as viewing, notetaking, and test-taking skills and more. Paperback (August 1995) Write Source; ISBN: 0669388130. Grade level: 9-12 but can be used for grades 4-12 with parent's guidance.

Resources recommended in ◆several lessons, ★ several units, ⬙ other HOW Units. ☞ Key Resource (see beginning of unit or page 32).

Heart of Wisdom Publishing   29

Choosing Resources (Purchase or Library?)

A large part of the appeal of unit studies is flexibility. When choosing resources, this means that each family will need to consider their homeschool budget, time available, the number of children that will be using this program, and their personal interests.

Many of the lessons in this book contain enough resource material in themselves that any further research is not required. However, there are several recommendations included for those who desire to branch out and learn more. We provide you with hundreds of resources (and a select number of Key Resources) to choose from. Don't think of this choice as overwhelming. Think of it as an opportunity to find out where your students' interests (their delight) lie.

You are going to make two investments in your homeschool: time and money. Investing in good resources will save time. Utilizing the library and inter-library loan will save money. Some families enjoy a weekly library trip. But for other families that live far from the library or that have infants and/or toddlers, library trips can be very inconvenient. Building a home library saves a tremendous amount of time and effort. A well-equipped home library to a homeschooler is like a well-equipped kitchen to a cook. How much time and effort is saved by having the right ingredients and not having to substitute! (Explain this to your husband by comparing it to having the right tool for a job in the toolbox.)

Bear with me as I use another food analogy. Let's compare the options of making dessert available to making resources available. Your choice depends on the time and money available. (The second option will work for most homeschool families.)

	Three Ways to Provide Dessert	Three Ways to Provide Resources
1	If you have the time, you can save money by preparing a cake from scratch.	If you have the time, you can save money by getting all your resources from the library (or inter-library loan).
2	If you lack the time, you can invest more money by purchasing a cake mix.	If you lack the time, you can invest more money by purchasing the Key Resources used in several units (books marked with a ◐━ ♥ or ◐━ ★) and go to the library once before each unit for other resources.
3	If you're really pressed for time and have the funds, you can purchase a cake at a bakery.	If you're really pressed for time and have the funds, you can purchase all the Key Resources.

Underlined text refers to Internet link.

Key Resources

The Key Resources are our favorite books and are suggested many times throughout the lessons. These books are *optional* but a great addition to a homeschool library. We recommend you purchase the Key Resources used in several units (books marked with a ●━ ♥ or ●━ ★) and go to the library for other resources before beginning each unit. *Nelson's Illustrated Encyclopedia of the Bible* would be extremely useful as a companion to this book.

Key Resources for Grades 4-12 Click on blue title for Purchasing information	Adam to Abraham	Mesopotamia	Ancient Egypt	Ancient Israel	Ancient Greece	Ancient Rome	The Messiah
Bible	▓	▓	▓	▓	▓	▓	▓
Writing Handbook (students level)	▓	▓	▓	▓	▓	▓	▓
Victor Journey Through the Bible ●━ ♥ 4-8 9-12	▓			*			
Kingfisher Illustrated History of The World ●━ ♥ 4-8 9-12	▓						
Usborne Book of the Ancient World ●━ ♥ 4-8 9-12	▓						
Genesis: Finding Our Roots ●━ ♦ 4-8 9-12	▓						
Adam and His Kin ●━ ♦ 4-8 9-12	▓						
Kingdoms and Empires: The Rise, Fall, and Rescue of the Jewish Nation ●━ ♥ 4-8 9-12		*		*			
Ancient Egypt (Eyewitness) ●━ ♦ 4-8 9-12			▓				
Nelson's Illustrated Encyclopedia of the Bible ●━ ♥ 4-8 9-12	▓			*			
Ancient Greece(Eyewitness) ●━ ♦ 4-8 9-12					▓		
Ancient Rome (Eyewitness) ●━ ♦ 4-8 9-12						▓	
Daily Life at the Time of Jesus ●━ ♥ 4-8 9-12							▓

Optional Key Resources to add for Grades 9-12 or Parents							
Writers INC ●━ ♥ 9-12	▓	▓	▓	▓	▓	▓	▓
Our Father Abraham ●━ ♥ 9-12	▓			*			
Holman Bible Atlas ●━ ♥ 9-12	▓	▓	▓	▓			
Ancient Egypt and the Old Testament ●━ ★ 4-8 9-12			▓				
The Greco-Roman World of the New Testament Era ●━ ★ 9-12					▓	▓	
Yeshua: A Guide to the Real Jesus and the Original Church ●━ ♥ 9-12							▓

*Many of these resources are suggested in several units the astrick (*) indicates the resource focus.

Resources recommended in ♦several lessons, ★ several units, ▷ other HOW Units. ●━Key Resource (see beginning of unit or page 32).

Resources Recommended in Several Units

The resources listed here are entirely optional and provided merely for your convenience. The ⚷ resources suggested are considered the "best of the best"—home-school favorites—therefore, we have included them in the lessons with reading suggestions (indicating page numbers) to enhance and increase your instruction. A very important part of teaching your child to love to learn is making available interesting resources. It is also enormously valuable to demonstrate essential study skills such as pulling together information from several different resources (particularly when researching Bible topics).

Books with a ◐ symbol are appropriate for grades 4-12 or family read aloud. All other books are appropriate for high school or adults.

Daily Life at the Time of Jesus by Miriam Feinberg Vamosh ⚷ ♥ 4-8 9-12
Vivid original illustrations of life in New Testament times, maps, photographs of the Holy Land and the most significant archaeological finds of the past half-century combine to bring alive the times of Jesus in a novel and fascinating way. From the inspiring historical background of the unique period which has affected the lives of so many of the succinct, in-depth explanations that accompany each illustration, this is a perfect book for all ages. Paperback - 104 pages (February 2001). Palphot Ltd. Israel. ISBN: 0570052920.

Encyclopedia of the Bible (Nelson's Illustrated) ⚷ ♥ 4-8 9-12
This is an excellent overview of culture and geography of Hebrews and their neighbors. The section on People and Empires is great for the Mesopotamia unit. Includes lavish illustrations, and hundreds of color photographs, maps, and charts. Drawing on the latest scholarship in archaeology and theology, you get close-up views of the ancient civilizations where people lived under the perceived protection or punishment of their gods, and where the mundane and miraculous overlap. An all-in-one, easy-to-understand, heavily illustrated, must have book to understand Bible times. A complete library of Bible historical references in one convenient volume! Accessible and up-to-date, this outstanding resource features a detailed study of Jesus' life; outlines of Bible books; a comprehensive survey of social customs, religious beliefs, and significant events; and more. Colorful illustrations, photographs, maps, and timelines make this resource perfect for sermon preparation. 320 pages, softcover. Thomas Nelson (2001) ISBN: 0785246142.

The Greco-Roman World of the New Testament Era ⚷ ♥ 9-12
Many Bible background books are available for scholars but this one a delight to read and easy to-understand. Any student of the New Testament eager to understand its Greco-Roman setting will profit greatly from this excellent book!

Underlined text refers to Internet link.

An eye-opening book that advances our understanding of the New Testament and early Christianity. Paperback, 352 pages. (October 1999) Intervarsity Pr; ISBN: 0830815899.

The Holman Bible Atlas: A Complete Guide to the Expansive Geography of Biblical History by Thomas C. Brisco ⊶❤ 9-12
The Atlas is laid out in chronological order. It begins taking a general look at the geography of the ancient Near East. It ends with the expansion of Christianity up to 300 AD. Maps, charts and color photographs guide readers through each Biblical era, illustrating the land, sites, and archaeology of the ancient world of the Bible. Features 140 full-color photographs, 140 maps, and an Index of important Biblical places. January 1999) Broadman & Holman Publishers; ISBN: 1558197095. Suitable for family read aloud.

The Kingfisher History Encyclopedia ⊶❤ 4-8 9-12
A homeschooler's delight! Homeschoolers rave about this book they pull off the shelves over and over to complement history, science and Bible studies. This lavishly illustrated global overview of historical events from 40,000 B.C. to 1993 is suitable for collections from middle school on up. Short essays, time charts, biographies, boxed articles, and comparative tables create a picture of what was occurring simultaneously in various cultures at any given time. Each time division includes thematic essays on such topics as arts and crafts, communication and transportation, food and farming, religion, science and technology, trade and money, and war and weapons. World maps summarize the international situation at the beginning of each section. There are numerous color drawings and photographs on every page. (Booklist review) (September 1999) Larousse Kingfisher Chambers; ISBN: 0753451948.

The Kingfisher Illustrated History of the World ⊶❤ 4-8 9-12
This book is now out of print; it has been replaced by the book above. However, many homeschoolers and libraries still have this book; therefore we are including readings from both *The Kingfisher Illustrated History of the World* and *The Kingfisher History Encyclopedia* throughout the history units. Hardcover - 761 pages (October 1993) Kingfisher Books; ISBN: 1856978621. Reading level: Ages 9-12. Sometimes available through Bibliofind.com.

Our Father Abraham: Jewish Roots of the Christian Faith by Marvin R. Wilson ⊶❤ 9-12
Recommended in all seven units in this book. Wilson explains "Other ancient civilizations produced histories intended primarily to glorify a ruler among his subjects or to exalt that nation in the eyes of the world. Hebrew history, however, was written to glorify the Lord of the universe. It was written to inspire faith and trust in the living God." Christian Century magazine listed *Our Father Abraham* as an

Resources recommended in ◆several lessons, ★ several units, ▷ other HOW Units. ⊶Key Resource (see beginning of unit or page 32).

Heart of Wisdom Publishing   33

"all-time best seller" in its field. Many Christians are regrettably uninformed about the rich Hebrew heritage of the church. Must reading for every Christian wanting to delve deeply into the very foundations of the Christian faith. (April 1989) W.B. Eerdman's Pub. Co.; 374 pages. ISBN: 0802804233.

The Narrated Bible by F. Lagard Smith ♥
See description on page 29.

Usborne Book of the Ancient World by J. Chisolm ☞★
This is a Combined Volume of Usborne's Illustrated World History books. It includes the three volumes: *Early Civilization*, *The Greeks*, and *The Romans*. Introduces the highlights of ancient history throughout the world, from the earliest farmers of the Middle East to the end of the Roman empire, and discusses religion, society, and everyday life. This colorfully illustrated compendium of the ancient cultures of the world presents a breadth, but not depth, of information. The reader can learn about events and advances in various civilizations from the beginning of time to A.D. 500. All illustrations are captioned and placed contiguous to the appropriate text. This is a secular book. Paperback 288 pages (February 1992) E D C Publications; ISBN: 0746012330.

Writers INC ♥
See description on page 29.

The Victor Journey Through the Bible ☞ ♥
If you only purchase one resource this should be the one! This easy-to-read, visual exploration of the Bible allows you to follow the action from Genesis to Revelation. The stories of Scripture will come alive as you travel story-by-story through Bible lands and times. You will discover how ancient people really lived-the foods they ate, the homes they lived in, the clothes they wore, the work they performed.Every library-home, church, and school-will want this complete reference work on its shelves. It will enrich Sunday School lesson preparation, Bible storytelling, family devotions, and Bible study. The Victor Journey through the Bible is unparalleled as a user-friendly resource! Includes: over 400 colorful pages of photographs, drawings, maps, and charts, more than 100 drawings from objects or monuments of Bible times, over 200 photographs of Bible lands today, photographs of more than 50 archaeological discoveries, scores of reconstructions and diagrams, and dozens of colorful maps. Hardcover: 416 pages, Chariot Victor Books; Reprint edition (1996)ISBN: 156476480X.

Yeshua: A Guide to the Real Jesus and Original Church by Ron Mosley ☞ ♥
This is a well-researched and fascinating study of the Jewishness of the historical Jesus. The author explores the structure and mission of the original church in the Jewish culture of the first century. The book combines scholarship with an

understandable writing style resulting in a book that can be easily read but challenging to the reader. This book is a must for every serious student of the Bible in enlightening us as to our Jewish heritage. With forwards by Brad Young, Ph.D., Dr. Marvin Wilson, and Dwight Prior. We recommend readings in the "Ancient Israel Unit," "Messiah Unit," and the "Early Church Unit" (in another HOW book). Paperback - 213 pages (July 1998) Jewish New Testament Publishers; ISBN: 1880226685. Reading level: Grades 9 and up.

Alternative Resources

These are book recommended in several units. Books recommended in specific units are in the beginning of that unit. The ★ symbol indicates resources recommended in several units in this book. The ♥ symbol indicates resources recommended in several Heart of Wisdom Unit Studies.

Ancient Civilizations (Exploring History) by Philip Brooks ★ 4-8 9-12 Beginning with the dawn of civilization, this book tackles all aspects of civilized life, from settlement, agriculture and trade to crafts, language, and transportation. Sections on Sumer, Babylonia, the Hittites, Assyria, the Persian Empire, the Parthians and Sassanians, the Islamic Empire, on through to the civilizations of the Andes, the Olmec, and the Maya, create a real sense of history for young readers. Hardcover - 64 pages 1 Ed. edition (October 1, 1999) Lorenz Books; ISBN: 0754802116. Reading level: Ages 9-12.

The Bible Comes Alive by Dr. Clifford Wilson (Vol. 1, Vol. 2, Vol. 3) ★ 9-12 Dr. Wilson, an eminent biblical archaeologist, presents a pictorial summary of his extensive archaeological work in support of his conviction that the Bible is true—historically, scientifically, and theologically.
In Volume One, The Bible Comes Alive Creation to Abraham, Dr. Wilson presents the archaeological and historical evidence supporting the authenticity of the book of Genesis, and brings to life the age of the patriarchs. (February 1997) New Leaf Pr; ISBN: 0892213493.
In Volume Two, The Bible Comes Alive Moses to David, Dr. Wilson presents the archaeological evidence that brings to life the period of Egyptian exile in Israel's national history, and covers the Egyptians, the Canaanites, Jericho, and the settling of Israel, through the reign of David, her greatest king. (August 1998) New Leaf Pr; ISBN: 0892214198.
In Volume Three, The Bible Comes Alive Solomon in All his Glory, Dr. Wilson brings forth the evidence of the golden age of Israel and its influence over other nations, and introduces us to the societies and histories of Assyria and Babylon, while illuminating the biblical record. (January 2000) New Leaf Pr; ISBN: 0892214864.

Resources recommended in ♦several lessons, ★ several units, ⬕♥other HOW Units. ☞—Key Resource (see beginning of unit or page 32).

Heart of Wisdom Publishing   35

Bible History: Old Testament by Alfred Edersheim ★ 9-12
Grasping "the big picture" of God's story in the Old Testament helps readers understand the finer points of theology. And it is this "grasp of the big picture" that Alfred Edersheim offers in an unparalleled way. Since its original appearance in 1890, this work has encountered many rivals but no successors, and its relevance for the Christian faith has only been reinforced during the intervening decades. Henderickson Publishers' unique, newly typeset edition of the complete and unabridged work will be a milestone contribution to the libraries of believers. Hardcover Updated edition (September 1995) Henderickson Publishers, Inc.; ISBN: 156563165X. All seven volumes of this book are available online.

Bible Lands by Jonathan Tubb, Alan Hills ★ 4-8
Through intriguing text and striking photographs of archaeological finds, this compelling title gives historical perspective on the ancient peoples of the Holy Land, from the Israelites to the Greeks. Agriculture, clothing, jewelry, weaponry, art, and trade practices are brought to life in this survey of an area that has been in turmoil since ancient times. Hardcover. Reading level: Ages 9-12.

Creation to Canaan ★ 4-8
The biblical lines of the godly and ungodly are clearly defined in this rich volume. A chronological book about the extremely important beginning of time. Chapters include: Creation to the Flood, Spread of Humanity, Beginning of the Jewish Nation, Growth and Development of Israel. Heavily illustrated and packed with charts, maps, diagrams, and family trees, making this period come alive for all ages. Paperback. Rod and Staff Publishers. Reading level: Seventh grade.

A Family Guide to the Biblical Holidays ★ K-3 4-8 9-12
Description: Robin Sampson (author of this book) presents an extensive look at the nine annual holidays: Passover, Unleavened Bread, Firstfruits, Pentecost, Trumpets, Day of Atonement, Tabernacles, Hanukkah, Purim and the weekly holiday—the Sabbath! This books explains the historical, agricultural, spiritual, and prophetic purposes of each holiday, showing how each points to Christ, and includes creative ways to teach them to your children! Includes projects, crafts, recipes, games, and songs for celebrating each holiday. When you have this book at your fingertips it will be like having a library on the Bible holidays. This book includes information that will fill ten books: one on each of the seven holidays in Leviticus, the Sabbath, plus Hanukkah and Purim, and tons of information about the importance of our Hebrew Roots."In 34 years of publishing Messianic Catalogs we have never seen such a creative contribution to the body of Messiah ..." -- review from Manny Brotman, founder of *The Messianic Jewish Movement International*. Several excerpts are available on the Internet.

Underlined text refers to Internet link.

Far Above Rubies: Wisdom in the Christian Community by David Mulligan ★ 9-12 This book answers the following questions: What is the real purpose of education? What makes "Christian education" Christian? Why do Christian schools insist on using Greek and Roman standards for education? Does the Bible give a pattern of learning? What is wisdom; what is the Christian community? In response to the moral deficiency, academic weakness, and spiritual hostility of the atmosphere of the modern educational system, thousands of Christians have removed their children from public schools, and with the great sacrifice of time and money have pursued their children's education under the banner of Christ. Specific readings are recommended though out several lessons in the Israel, Greece and Rome lessons (especially those on education). 284 pages (1994) Messenger Publishing. 802-426-4018.

From Mesopotamia to Modernity: Ten Introductions to Jewish History and Literature by Burton L. Visotzky (Editor), David E. Fishman (Editor)♥ 9-12 a one volume introduction to both Jewish history and literature from its earliest times up to the present. Specific readings are recommended in the Israel, Greece Rome and Messiah lessons. Paperback (July 1999) Westview Press; ISBN: 0813367174.

A Historical Survey of the Old Testament by Eugene H. Merrill ★ 9-12 A comprehensive but concise study of the first 39 books of the Bible. Merrill approaches it as God's revelation to the world, through Israel, His chosen people. Includes: Insights from the Middle East, geographic backgrounds, archeological perspectives, as well a cultural, religious and social points of view. A short review of intertestamental history is also included. 332 pages 2nd edition (December 1992) Baker Book House; ISBN: 0801062837.

Introducing the Old Testament by John Drane 9-12 *Introducing the Old Testament* provides an excellent and informative introduction to a collection of writings that lie at the heart of the Judeo-Christian tradition, and is illustrated throughout with maps, charts, and photographs. Drane also wrote *Nelsons Illustrated Encyclopedia of the Bible*. Hardcover: 368 pages Revised edition (January 2003) ISBN: 0800634322.

Manners and Customs in the Bible by Victor Harold Matthews ★ 9-12 Insight into the Bible's culture, its people and how they lived. What people wore, what they ate, what they built, how they exercised justice, how they mourned, and how they viewed family and legal customs all are manners and customs, and all vary from period to period throughout Israel's history. Paperback - 283 pages Rev edition (September 1993) Henderickson Publishers, Inc.; ISBN: 0943575818.

Resources recommended in ♦several lessons, ★ several units, ▯♦other HOW Units. ●━Key Resource (see beginning of unit or page 32).

Heart of Wisdom Publishing   37

Reproducible Maps, Charts, Time Lines and Illustrations: What the Bible Is All about Resources ♥ 4-8 9-12
The books of the Bible, timelines, history, maps of Bible times, etc. that can be copied make this a reference book you will use again and again. Paperback, 287 Pages, Gospel Light Publications, January 1998 ISBN: 0830719385

The Student Bible Atlas by Tim Dowley, Richard Scott ★ 4-8
This richly illustrated and informative guidebook gives students an introduction to the books of the Bible and shows what it was like to live during biblical times. (1996) Augsburg Fortress Publishers; ISBN: 0806620382.

Streams of Civilization Volume 1 ★ 9-12
A comprehensive overview of history from a Christian perspective. Extensive vocabulary questions and suggested projects are listed throughout the text. Contains beautiful illustrations and numerous high-quality, two-color maps. Vol. One covers history from Creation to the 1620s. Answer Key and Test Packets can be purchased separately. The Time Line provides students with an excellent overview of the key personalities who have shaped history from ancient times to the present. Christian Liberty; ISBN: 0890510172. Grade level: 9-10.

Usborne Book of Discovery: Inventors/Scientists/Explorers ♥ 4-8 9-12
Three books in one combined volume. Marvel at the ideas of brilliant scientists from Aristotle to Einstein. Looks at the lives and careers of the men and women whose achievements in invention, science and exploration have changed the world. Charts, diagrams and archival photographs provide detailed historical facts and looks at men and women whose discoveries and achievements have changed the world. Paperback (June 1994) E D C Publications; ISBN: 074601872X. Reading level: Ages 9-12.

Audio

What in the World is Going On Here? A Judeo Christian Primer of World History by Diana Waring 4-8 9-12
Description: Learn history like you never have before! Diana Waring takes you on a whirlwind tour of world history with enthusiasm and humor. You will explore the Old Testament as the ultimate "textbook" for ancient World history. You'll learn about archaeology, ancient historians, Old Testament prophecies and contemporary research in a style that will help you put world events into a simplified, usable time frame Excellent for the entire family. P.O. Box 7697, Newark, DE 19714-7697, Phone: (302) 369-9176.

Underlined text refers to Internet link.

Bible Timeline

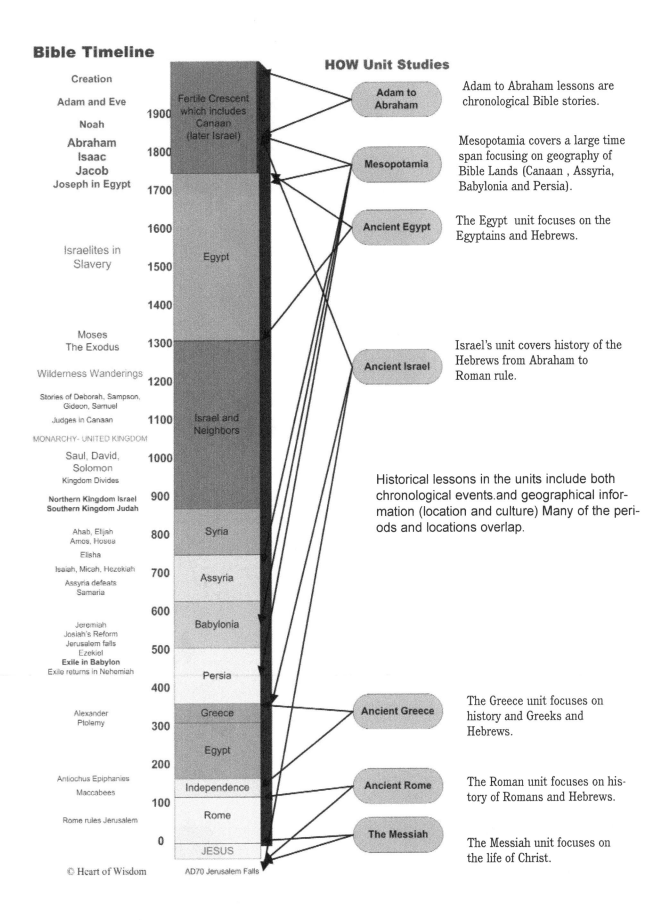

HOW Unit Studies

Creation

Adam and Eve

Noah

1900

**Abraham
Isaac
Jacob**

Joseph in Egypt

1800

1700

1600

Israelites in
Slavery

1500

1400

Moses
The Exodus

1300

Wilderness Wanderings

1200

Stories of Deborah, Sampson,
Gideon, Samuel

Judges in Canaan

1100

MONARCHY- UNITED KINGDOM

Saul, David,
Solomon

1000

Kingdom Divides

**Northern Kingdom Israel
Southern Kingdom Judah**

900

Ahab, Elijah
Amos, Hosea

800

Elisha

Isaiah, Micah, Hezekiah

700

Assyria defeats
Samaria

600

Jeremiah
Josiah's Reform
Jerusalem falls
Ezekiel
Exile in Babylon
Exile returns in Nehemiah

500

400

Alexander
Ptolemy

300

200

Antiochus Epiphanies

Maccabees

100

Rome rules Jerusalem

0

© Heart of Wisdom

AD70 Jerusalem Falls

Fertile Crescent
which includes
Canaan
(later Israel)

Egypt

Israel and
Neighbors

Syria

Assyria

Babylonia

Persia

Greece

Egypt

Independence

Rome

JESUS

**Adam to
Abraham**

Adam to Abraham lessons are
chronological Bible stories.

Mesopotamia

Mesopotamia covers a large time
span focusing on geography of
Bible Lands (Canaan , Assyria,
Babylonia and Persia).

Ancient Egypt

The Egypt unit focuses on the
Egyptains and Hebrews.

Ancient Israel

Israel's unit covers history of the
Hebrews from Abraham to
Roman rule.

Historical lessons in the units include both
chronological events.and geographical information (location and culture) Many of the periods and locations overlap.

Ancient Greece

The Greece unit focuses on
history and Greeks and
Hebrews.

Ancient Rome

The Roman unit focuses on history of Romans and Hebrews.

The Messiah

The Messiah unit focuses on
the life of Christ.

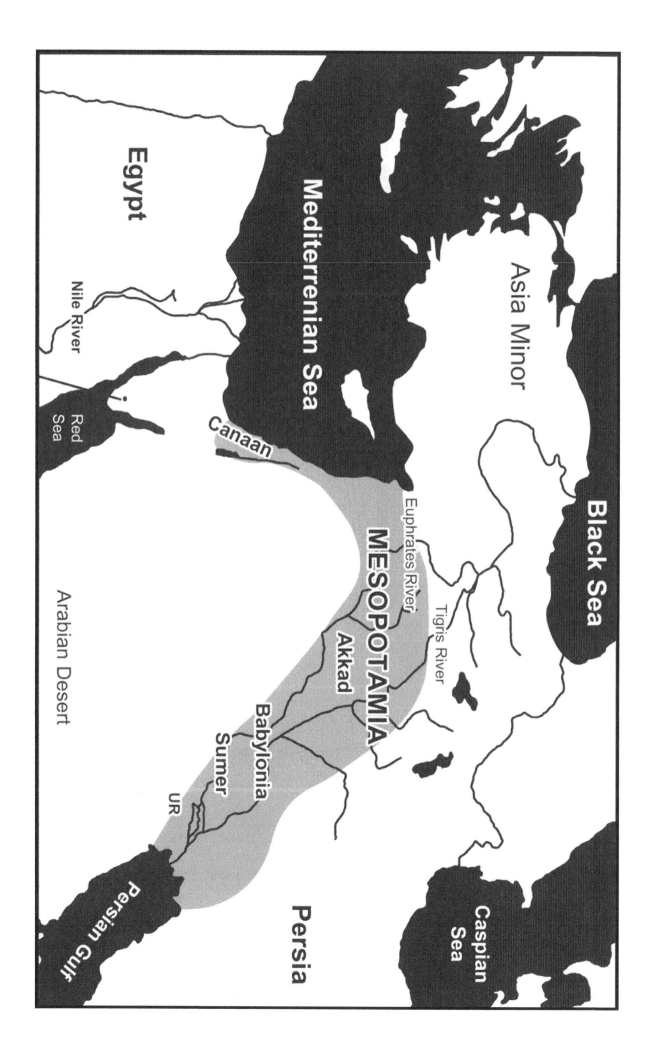

Adam to Abraham Unit

Unit Overview

Adam to Abraham Overview 42

Adam to Abraham Objectives 43

Adam to Abraham TimeLine 44

Adam to Abraham Vocabulary 45

Adam to Abraham Resources 46

Lessons

Introduction 48

Creation 50

Garden of Eden 54

Adam and Eve 56

The Fall .60

Cain and Abel 64

Seth to Noah 67

Corruption of Man 69

The Flood 73

After the Flood 77

The Tower of Babel 79

Beginning of Nations 81

The Nation's Religions 85

The Calling of Abram 88

Abram Enters Canaan 92

Genesis Reveals the Messiah 96

This unit takes a historical look at creation. Heart of Wisdom's book *Creation: An Internet Linked Unit Study* examines creation and evolution theories in depth.

Adam to Abraham Overview

The Old Testament stories and prophecies lay the foundation for understanding the life of Jesus Christ in the New Testament. We cannot fully know about Christ and His purpose for coming into our world without studying the Old Testament. It gives us a picture of Christ's sacrifice for sin.

The Book of Genesis is the book of origins. The word genesis (Hebrew b'resheet) comes from a Greek word that means "origin," "source," or "beginning." The first eleven chapters of Genesis begin with Creation and the first man and woman and move to the seventy nations of the world considered "The Table of Nations" in Genesis chapter 10. Genesis chapters 12–50 comprise the ancestral story. The focus of this unit study is on Genesis 1–12, with a brief introduction to the call of Abram (God later changed Abram's name to Abraham) and the promised Land. (The culture of the Mesopotamian world of Abraham is covered in the Mesopotamia Unit Study, and the Hebrews' ancestral story is told in detail in the Ancient Israel Unit Study.)

Genesis 1–12 stories include the divine act that brings humanity and history into existence and enables humanity to exist, multiply, diversify, and disperse upon the earth. It is the story of how God creates a world that is good but becomes corrupted by sin, which enters the world through human disobedience. Adam and Eve ate fruit which was forbidden to them, and Cain murdered his brother Abel. God later commanded Noah to build an ark in which pairs of all living things were preserved from the great Flood which God sent to purge the earth. God set the rainbow as a remembrance of His covenant with Noah. Afterward, people began building a tower that would reach to heaven in order to make a name for themselves, but God confused their speech and scattered them. Then God again appointed a man—Abraham—with whom to establish His covenant.

The messages taught in Genesis is taught through the rest of the Bible:

1. God is sovereign. (above or superior to all, greatest, supreme)
2. God has a plan which He is carrying out.
3. God is able to take the bad and the evil and cause it to serve His eternal purposes, thus bringing great good out of it all.

The entire Bible finds its meaning and explanation in the redemption provided by Jesus Christ. Each lesson in this book reveals shadows and types of the great doctrine of salvation by grace through faith in the death and resurrection of Christ. As you teach your children about the Creator of universe—the story of the Fall, of corruption, the Flood, the call of Abram—remind them that God takes control of every situation in our lives. He is the One who commands the wind and the waves , and He is the One who knows us by name. He is the One we can call on at any time.

See Heart of Wisdom Day by Day Lesson Plans at Heartofwisdom.com/homeschool

---

Underlined text refers to Internet link at http://Homeschool-Books.com

Adam to Abraham Objectives

Upon completion of this unit, your student should:

- Gain a closer relationship with God through study of His Word.
- Understand that Creation took place in a series of six days, which were the same as the days of 24 hours we now experience.
- Appreciate how creation reveals God.
- See the sovereignty of God in His actions in respect to four outstanding events: Creation, the Fall, the Flood, and the Babel dispersion.
- Understand the growth of the human race and its developing culture.
- Understand the key events, people, and places in Genesis 1-12.
- Be able to place the key events and people from Genesis 1-12 in chronological order.
- Have a grasp of the historical background of the world's beginning from a Christian world view.
- Learn to think in a distinctively biblical way (Rom. 12 1; Cor. 2:16).
- Be able to speculate what the Garden of Eden must have been like.
- Understand the effect that sin had and has on mankind.
- Be familiar with the generations from Seth to Noah.
- Realize that Noah's flood was world-wide and extinguished all human and animal life except for the lives of those in the ark.
- Be familiar with the generations from Noah to Abram.
- Understand the racial, linguistic, and political divisions of the genealogy of nations.
- Appreciate the Flood and its effect on the earth.
- Be able to trace Abraham's travels from Ur to Canaan.
- Grasp the story of the Tower of Babel and explain its effect on today's world.
- Understand the land and people of Canaan.
- Be able to share findings and encourage others to study the Word of God.
- Learn to gather and use information for research purposes.
- Learn to use a variety of resource materials to gather information for research topics.
- Be able to analyze how specific historical events would be interpreted differently based on newly uncovered records and/or information.
- Be able to write compositions that are focused on different audiences and that fulfill different purposes.
- Be able to write fictional, biographical, autobiographical, and observational narrative compositions.
- Be able to write in response to literature.

Adam to Abraham Time Line

Approx. Time	Person	Years Lived
Creation c. 5500 B.C.	Adam (Gen. 1 & 2; 5:5)	930
	Seth (Gen. 5:3; 5:8)	912
	Enos (Gen. 5:6; 5:11)	905
	Cainan (Gen. 5:9; 5:14)	910
	Mahalaleel (Gen. 5:12; 5:17)	895
	Jared (Gen. 5:15; 5:20)	962
	Enoch (Gen. 5:18; 5:23)	365
	Methuselah (Gen. 5:21; 5:27)	969
	Lamech (Gen. 5:25; 5:31)	777
The Flood c. 3113 B.C.	Noah (Gen. 5:28; 9:29)	950?
	Shem (Gen. 5:32; 11:11)	600?
	Arphaxad (Gen. 11:10; 11:13)	438
	Salah (Gen. 11:12; 11:15)	433
	Eber (Gen. 11:14; 11:17)	464
	Peleg (Gen. 11:16; 11:19)	239
	Reu (Gen. 11:18; 11:21)	239
	Serug (Gen. 11:20; 11:23)	230
	Nahor (Gen. 11:22; 11:25)	148
	Terah (Gen. 11:24; 11:32)	205
c. 1775 B.C.	Abraham's Migration	175

Adam to Abraham Vocabulary

See Vocabulary Instructions on page 22.

A.D.	descendant	primeval story
ancestor	Divine Council	primogeniture
animal husbandry	Eden	Promised Land
antediluvian	ethnic	Pseudepigrapha
antiquity	Eve	rebellion
babble	Fall	repentance
Babel	Fertile Crescent	Sabbath
banish	Flood	Table of Nations
B.C.	forefathers	Torah
Canaan	genealogy	Tower of Babel
catastrophic	lineage	utopia
C.E.	metallurgy	vagabond
cosmology	myth	ziggurat
covenant	nation	God (names)
		Adonai
Creation	Noah	Elohim
		El Shaddai
cubit	origins	YHVH
		Hakadosh Baruch Hu
		Ribono shel Olam
deluge	Pentateuch	Harachaman
		Avinu Shebashamayim

Adam to Abraham Resources

The resources are completely optional. This unit study includes so many links to information on the Internet you could actually use this unit without purchasing any resources. However, students need to read (and feel and smell) real books! We include several sources popular with homeschoolers so you can utilize what you have on hand. You are going to make two investments in your homeschool: time and money. Investing in good resources will save time. Utilizing the library and inter-library loan will save money. Each family will need to consider the resources they need based on their homeschool budget, time available, the number of children that will be using this program, and their personal interests.

The ◑ symbol indicates a resource appropriate for grades 4-12 or family read aloud. All other books are appropriate for young adults or adults.

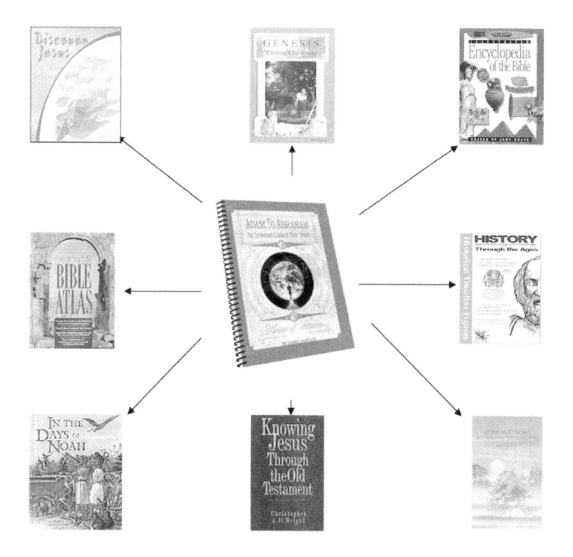

Key Resources for this Unit

Discover Jesus in Genesis by Larry Edison and Deborah Obeid ⊶ ♦
Description:Deborah Obeid and Larry Edison have collaborated together to come up with this book designed to help readers of all ages understand the manner in which Jesus is both the theme and the Promise of Genesis. You'll find many major events from Genesis portrayed in picture form, each displaying the biblical event along with the manner in which God took pains to gradually yet clearly teach His people about the promise and coming of the Messiah. In His actions, God painted a picture so that His people might see Jesus in Genesis. Each chapter consists of one painting on high gloss paper along with full page explanation of the Biblical text. Winepress Publishing (2002). ISBN 1579213898.

Adam and His Kin: The Lost History of Their Lives and Times by Ruth Beechick ⊶ ♦
Drawing on linguistics, archaeology, astronomy, the Bible, and other history, Dr. Ruth Beechick writes an enlightening and entertaining history of Adam and his offspring. An engaging, enjoyable, informative, easy-to-read account of Genesis from creation to Abraham. Includes information from science, and ancient traditions. Paperback (January 1991) Arrow Pr; ISBN: 0940319071. Interest level: Ages 11-Adult.

Genesis: Finding Our Roots by Ruth Beechick ⊶ ♦
This book provides a unique look at Genesis 1-11, integrating history with art, literature, and other disciplines. Startling insights into how ancient art, literature, world history, language, and even ancient myths prove that the Bible is a true historical record. Includes maps, charts, a time line, and beautiful full-color reproductions of ancient art. Hardcover - 112 pages (February 1998) Educational Services Corp.; ISBN: 094031911X. Intended for family study.

Encyclopedia of the Bible (Nelson's Illustrated) ⊶ ♦
See description in the "Key Resources" section beginning on page 32.

The Holman Bible Atlas ⊶ ♥
See description in the "Key Resources" section beginning on page 32.

Our Father Abraham ⊶ ♥
See description in the "Key Resources" section beginning on page 32.

The Victor Journey Through the Bible ♥
See description in the "Key Resources" section beginning on page 32.

Who's Who in the Bible by Stephen Motyer ⊶ ♥
See description in the "Key Resources" section beginning on page 32.

Resources recommended in ♦several lessons, ★ several units, ♥other HOW Units. ⊶Key Resource (see beginning of unit or page 32).

Introduction

Step 1 Excite

Create a time line using index cards (or sticky notes) without looking at any references. Put each major event and each key person from Genesis on a separate index card. Shuffle the cards and try to line them up in chronological order.

Abel	Enoch	Methuselah
Abraham	The Fall	Noah
Adam	The Flood	Seth
Cain	Ham	Shem
Creation	Japheth	Tower of Babel

Step 2 Examine

Research the time period between Adam and Abraham. Use any resource (an encyclopedia, a nonfiction book, or the Internet). We recommend the following:

Books

The Holman Bible Atlas ☞ ♥
Read: "Introduction" (2).

Who's Who in the Bible ☞ ♥
Read: "First People of Genesis" (6-7), "Abraham and His People" (8-9).

What in the World is Going On Here? A Judeo Christian Primer of World History by Diana Waring
Description: See description on page 38. These tapes will give you an excellent chronological foundation of God's unfolding plan through history that you can build upon throughout the units. Listen to and discuss the tapes "Creation to the Destruction of Assyria."

The Bible Comes Alive: Volume One, Creation to Abraham ★
Read: Section I "Early Genesis Is Factual History."

An Historical Survey of the Old Testament ★
Read: "In the Beginning" (45-72).

Video

The Bible: In the Beginning
Description: The Bible is brought to the screen with astounding scope in this internationally acclaimed film that depicts the first 22 chapters of Genesis. ASIN: 6304386168.

Step 3 Expand

Activity 1: Create an Outline
Create an outline of Genesis 1-12. Refer to the Outline Example.

Activity 2: Write Summaries
Write a summary paragraph for each of the key events in Gen. 1-12. Younger children can narrate or dictate.
1. The creation of the world and man (1-2)
2. The corruption of man, the fall (3-5)
3. The destruction of man, the flood (6-9)
4. The dispersion of man, the nations (10-11)
5. The Calling of Abram (12:1-9)
6. First entry into Canaan (12:5-7)

Activity 3: Create a Mind Map
Use sheets of unlined paper and colored markers or pencils. Put an image or circle in the center along with the phrase "Adam to Abram." As you study this unit, draw lines out from the center as you determine the major categories of information (creation, corruption, Babel, Noah, The Flood, dispersion, Abram, Canaan, etc.). Branch lines from these will hold subtopics. Use different colors for each cluster of information. Ask yourself, "Who?" "What?" "Where?" "When?" and "How?" Color and patterns will organize your ideas into meaningful groups that will make connections and relationships more clear. Also use symbols, numbers, arrows, or other "doodles" on your Mind Map (trees, ark, tower, etc.). Continue adding to this Mind Map in each lesson.

Step 4 Excel

Now that you have studied Genesis you should be able to line up the index cards in chronological order. Place the appropriate Bible reference on each card and share your time line with others.

Resources recommended in ♦several lessons, ★ several units, ♥other HOW Units. ●—Key Resource (see beginning of unit or page 32).

Heart of Wisdom Publishing   49

Creation

Note: This lesson is an overview of creation. The "Creation Unit Study" examines creation and evolution theories in depth.

Step 1 Excite

Romans chapter 1 tells us that God has planted evidence of Himself throughout His creation so that we are without excuse. The psalmist, in beautiful poetic language, made reference to God's creative work. Here are a few choice allusions: *When I look at thy heavens, the work of thy fingers, the moon and the stars which thou hast established* (Ps. 8:3); *The heavens are telling the glory of God; and the firmament proclaims his handiwork* (Ps. 19:1); *By the word of the Lord the heavens were made, and all their host by the breath of his mouth. He gathered the waters of the sea as in a bottle; he put the deeps in storehouses* (Ps. 33:6,7).

Psalm 136 draws attention to the character of God as displayed in the Creation as well as in other mighty works. The worshiper should give thanks to God, *for he is good: his mercy endures forever* (v. 1). In verses 5–8 the psalmist gives details of God's creation, reflecting the Genesis chapter 1 account. The writer of Psalm 148 bid every part of God's creation—the sun, the moon, the shining stars—to praise the name of the Lord, *for he commanded and they were created .(Ps 148:5)* In this way, the psalmist leads us to see the worthiness of God to receive praise and glory for His creation. God tells us about Himself through creation. Our responsibility is to hear His voice and respond to Him.

Dr. Albert Green, founder of Alta Vista College, stated in his book *Thinking Christianly*[1],

> A Biblical way of looking at creation will have consequences on your life. As the Holy Spirit grips your heart with the realization that creation reveals God and can be offered back to him in our ordinary daily activities, praise will well up in your heart as never before. Further, you will find your life come together with new integrity. No more sacred/secular dualism! Christ really is Lord of all! What a glorious message the gospel is!

Watch a video. You might be able to rent these videos from your local Christian bookstore or homeschool support group.

God of Creation
Description: This video unveils the power and majesty of the world God created—from the smallest organisms to the largest stars in the universe. Order from Moody Video 1-800-842-1223.

The Wonders of God's Creation
Description: In three spectacular hours, this award-winning series takes you on one of the most exceptional journeys imaginable—from high above planet

Earth to the very heart of the human body. Join us and see bow the Master Creator reveals Himself through the glorious miracle of creation. Order from Moody Video 1-800-842-1223.

Step 2 Examine

In the ancient world, Near Eastern creation myths began with either mythological gods or objects (like the sun or moon) treated as "gods" in conflict with one another in the heavens. In one story the creator Baal struggles with an adversary, Mot; in another Baal battles the Sea. In the Babylonian creation myth, the god Marduk kills Tiamat (chaos) after a violent battle, which results in creation. The ancient Egyptian myths say that creation began from a chaos of churning, bubbling water, called Nu or Nun, from which Atum (later called Re, Ra, and/or Khepri) created the world. Today's modern evolution myths mirror the ancient myths that somehow our orderly world was created, by accident, out of chaos.

In the Genesis Creation story, God is shown as a personal God in complete control, calling the entire universe into creation by His spoken Word. Human beings, male and female, are created "in the image and likeness of God." Genesis emphasizes the awesome power of our Creator, while illustrating that human beings are the clear focus of God's loving concern.

What a difference between the pagan stories and the Genesis story. All the myths are cold, dead, lifeless, uncaring, while the Creation story is warm, vital, loving, alive. Christians know that our heavenly Father created the world and each person for a reason. By faith we understand that the universe was formed at God's command (Heb. 11:3). Knowing this gives us value, a special sense of comfort and joy, and hope for our lives and our future. Those who believe that life gradually evolved from single cells into complex forms find no real meaning in life, believing that they and everything around them resulted from a freak accident.

Jesus was there with God in the beginning of time: He is before all things, and in Him all things hold together (Col. 1:17). When replying to a question from theologians, Jesus said unto them, *"Verily, verily, I say unto you, Before Abraham was, I am."* (John 8:58). In a prayer Jesus said, *"Father, I will that they also, whom thou hast given me, be with me where I am; that they may behold my glory, which thou hast given me: for thou lovedst me before the foundation of the world"* (John 17:24).

Read John 1:1–18, Eph. 1:3–14, Col. 1:15–20, and Heb. 1:1–4 for further insight on God's eternal nature. Now, read aloud the Creation story in Genesis chapters 1–2 with your family. You've probably heard these words before. Take time to reflect on how the Creation story reflects the person of God. Observe the distinct sequences, order, consistency, and priorities. Most English versions of the Bible translate Elohim as "GOD" (all caps) and Yahweh as "LORD" (all caps). Yahweh is used when the Bible stresses God's personal relationship with his people. Elohim refers to God as the Creator of the whole universe and the source of all

---

Resources recommended in ◆several lessons, ★ several units, ◆other HOW Units. ◉━Key Resource (see beginning of unit or page 32).

life. For this reading, replace the titles for GOD or LORD with Elohim and Yahweh. Read about Creation from one of the resources. Use an encyclopedia, books in the library, or the Internet. We recommend the following:

Books

The Victor Journey through the Bible ♥
Read: Creation (10-11).

Discover Jesus in Genesis ⚷– ♦
Read: "Creation: the Beginning" (4-5).

Adam and His Kin ⚷– ♦
Read: Chapter 1 "The Beginning of Time" and Chapter 2 "In the Garden."

Genesis: Finding Our Roots ⚷– ♦
Read: "Creation: The Beginning" (4-5).

The Bible Comes Alive: Volume One, Creation to Abraham ★
Read: Section II "In the Beginning."

Bible History: Old Testament ★
Read: Chapter 1 of Volume 1. It discusses the importance of Jesus Christ in Creation.

Internet Sources

The 6 Days of Creation
Description: An excellent study, the first part of "Old Testament Bible Study of the Creation to Abraham Genesis 1 to Genesis 12." Includes the basic views concerning the origin of the universe.

The Literal Week of Creation
Description: Article by Henry Morris from the Institute for Creation Research.

Creation - Man in the Garden of Eden - The Fall
Description: Discusses the importance of Jesus Christ in Creation from chapter 1 of Volume 1 in Bible History: Old Testament by Alfred Edersheim.

God's Creation
Description: Part 1 of "God's Story: From Creation to Eternity" from ChristianAnswers.net. (Follow the "next" buttons on the bottom of each page.)

Step 3 Expand

Choose and complete one of the following activities:

Activity 1: Write a Poem
Write a poem about creation. Refer to "Writing Poetry" in *Writers INC.*

Activity 2: Learn Hebrew Words
Look up each of these words in a Hebrew lexicon. Add the word, phoneic spelling and meaning to your Hebrew Notebook. See The Old Testament Hebrew Lexicon.

The Hebrew word for created is *bara*; Hebrew actually has several words for "creating" "making," "building," or "forming," "created"—*bara* is used only in referring to God in the Hebrew Bible. It occurs in Gen. 1:1, also in v.21, 27. Usually *bara* is understood to be creation *ex nihilo*, "out of nothing." Only God can call things into existence that do not exist. The Hebrew word *rosh* means "head." It is used in the word *Rosh HaShanah* (New Year or "head of the year"), rosh avot ("head of the family"), *rosh pinah* ("cornerstone of head of the stone"), *Rosh Chodesh* ("head of the month" or "new moon").

Activity 3: Study Art
Find and study, at a library or museum, a copy of the painting *The Creation of Adam* by Michelangelo, from Rome's Sistine Chapel. Make a copy of the painting to include in your portfolio. Write a description of the painting.

Activity 4: Copy Passages
Copy (by hand or typing) two or more paragraphs from your research. Or have someone dictate the passage to you. Younger students can copy one or two sentences or narrate (tell back) what has been learned.

Activity 5: Share with a Child
Tell the story of Creation and complete the The Creative Days Worksheet with an elementary-aged child.

Step 4 Excel

Share what you have learned with a friend or family member. Correct written work to demonstrate correct punctuation and spelling, and effective use of grammar. Add corrected written work or any illustrations to your portfolio.

Footnote
1. Green, Albert. (1990) *Thinking Christianly*, Seattle, WA: Alta Vista College Press.

Resources recommended in ♦several lessons, ★ several units, ♥other HOW Units. ●━Key Resource (see beginning of unit or page 32).

Garden of Eden

Step 1 Excite

The Narrated Bible

The Bible says that when God created a thing, "He saw that it was good." The Lord God created a perfect environment for Adam. The Garden was certainly a most wonderful place. Adam sinned and this perfect environment became corrupted. Not much is written about the Garden, so we have to picture it using our imagination and a glimpse of what God will do in the future. God, in His timing, will once again make a perfect world. In this future place we know that the wolf will dwell with the lamb, the Leopard will lie down with the kid, and the child will play at the den of the viper and not worry (Isaiah 11).

The site of the Garden is somewhere along the course of the great streams of the Tigris and the Euphrates of Western Asia, in "the land of Shinar" or Babylonia. Find this area on a Bible map.

Step 2 Examine

In Isaiah 65, God describes the new earth that He will create one day. He says, *For, behold, I create new heavens and a new earth: and the former shall not be remembered, nor come into mind. But be ye glad and rejoice for ever in that which I create: for, behold, I create Jerusalem a rejoicing, and her people a joy. And I will rejoice in Jerusalem, and joy in my people: and the voice of weeping shall be no more heard in her, nor the voice of crying.*

Again in Isaiah 65 it says, *And they shall build houses, and inhabit them; and they shall plant vineyards, and eat the fruit of them. They shall not build, and another inhabit; they shall not plant, and another eat: for as the days of a tree are the days of my people, and mine elect shall long enjoy the work of their hands. They shall not labour in vain, nor bring forth for trouble; for they are the seed of the blessed of the LORD, and their offspring with them. And it shall come to pass, that before they call, I will answer; and while they are yet speaking, I will hear. The wolf and the lamb shall feed together, and the lion shall eat straw like the bullock: and dust shall be the serpent's meat. They shall not hurt nor destroy in all my holy mountain, saith the LORD.*

Do research about this topic. Use any resource (an encyclopedia, a non-fiction book, a historical novel, or the Internet). We recommend the following:

Books

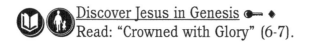
Discover Jesus in Genesis ☉━ ◆
Read: "Crowned with Glory" (6-7).

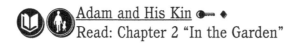
Adam and His Kin ☉━ ◆
Read: Chapter 2 "In the Garden"

Genesis: Finding Our Roots ●━ ◆
Read: Unit 2 "Book of Adam."

The Holman Bible Atlas ●━ ♥
Read: "The Garden of Eden" (33).

Bible History: Old Testament ★
Read: Chapter 1 "Creation - Man in the Garden of Eden."

Internet Sources

Creation - Man in the Garden of Eden
Description: Chapter 1 from Bible History: Old Testament by Alfred Edersheim.

The Garden of Eden
Read: Article from the *Condensed Biblical Cyclopedia*.

Where Was The Garden of Eden?
Description: Bible study from Daily Bible Study.

Step 3 Expand

Choose and complete one of the following activities:

Activity 1: Write an Essay
Write an essay on what you perceive the Garden to have been like. The essay should be at least 100 words, but not more than 500 words. Refer to "Structure of the Traditional Essay" and "Sample of a Traditional Essay" in *Writers INC*, or "How to Write an Essay."

Activity 2: Copy Passages
Copy (by hand or typing) two or more Bible references about the Garden of Eden: Genesis 2:8-17; 3:23,24; 4:16; Isaiah 51:3; Ezekiel 28:13; 31:9,16,18; 36:35; and Joel 2:3.

Step 4 Excel

Share what you have learned about the Garden of Eden with a friend or family member. Correct all written work to demonstrate correct punctuation and spelling, and effective use of grammar. Add corrected written work or any illustrations to your portfolio.

Resources recommended in ◆several lessons, ★ several units, ♥other HOW Units. ●━Key Resource (see beginning of unit or page 32).

Adam and Eve

Step 1 Excite

The Narrated Bible

O n the sixth day of Creation God created all the living creatures and, "in his own image," man both "male and female." The Hebrew word *adam* means "mankind," "men and women," "people." The first act of Adam was his giving names to the beasts of the field and the fowls of the air. After that, God caused a deep sleep to fall upon him, and while he was unconscious, God took one of his ribs, and made a woman. God presented her to Adam. Adam received her as his wife, and said, "This is now bone of my bones, and flesh of my flesh: she shall be called Woman, because she was taken out of Man." He called her Eve, because she was the mother of all living beings. God then blessed the couple, told them to be "fruitful and multiply," and gave them dominion over all other living things.

If God had formed Eve from the ground Adam might have felt differently toward her. But Eve shared both Adam's flesh and spirit. Man and women are formed of one flesh. The woman was taken from his side to remain at his side to be a helpmeet.

Read God's story of creation in Genesis 1:1-31 and Genesis 2:4-7. What was God's attitude about His creation and particularly Adam?

Step 2 Examine

When Jesus was crucified on the cross, He was crucified as the Last Adam. As the Last Adam, Jesus wiped out the old race; and brings in the new race.

> The first Adam was lord over a limited domain, the last Adam is Lord of all (Acts 10:36). The first Adam was tempted and failed the test, and in him, we all continue to sin and die. The Last Adam was tempted, as was the first, but remained sinless and lived a perfect life of righteousness. The first Adam disobeyed God. The last Adam was 'obedient unto death, even the death of the cross.' (Philippians 2:8) The first Adam began with everything provided for him in the Garden of Eden and he lost everything. The Last Adam began with nothing in a stable and ended with everything. The first Adam gave life to all his descendants. The last Adam, Jesus Christ, communicates 'life' and 'light' to all men, and gives eternal life to those who receive Him and believe on His name (John 1:1–14).

Do research about Adam and Eve. Use any resource (an encyclopedia, a non-fiction book, a historical novel, or the Internet). We recommend the following:

Books

🕮👪 <u>Discover Jesus in Genesis</u> ☞ ◆
Read: "The Promised Battle" (8-9).

🕮👪 <u>Adam and His Kin</u> ☞ ◆
Read: Chapter 1 "The Beginning of Time."

🕮👪 <u>Genesis: Finding Our Roots</u> ☞ ◆
Read: Unit 2 "Book of Adam."

🕮👪 <u>Who's Who in the Bible</u> ☞ ♥
Read: "The First People of Genesis" (6-7).

🕮👪 <u>The Bible Comes Alive Volume One, Creation to Abraham</u> ◆
Read: "Adam Was an Actual Man... Contrasted with Jesus" (133-136).

🕮 <u>An Historical Survey of the Old Testament</u> ★
Read: "The Genealogy of Adam and Eve" (45-48).

Internet Sources

ⓘ👪 <u>What Was Adam Like?</u>
Description: Article from Answers Online, Answers in Genesis Ministries.

ⓘ👪 <u>Adam</u>
Description: Brief biography of Adam from <u>BibleTutor.com.</u>

ⓘ👪 <u>Eve</u>
Description: Brief biography of Eve from <u>BibleTutor.com.</u>

ⓘ👪 <u>Adam & Eve: Excuses, Excuses, Excuses</u>
Description: Modern-day parable between father and son relating to Adam and Eve's excuses for sin.

ⓘ <u>The Creation of Man</u>
Description: An excellent study, part of "Old Testament Bible Study of the Creation to Abraham Genesis 1 to Genesis 12."

ⓘ <u>Regenerating Ribs</u>
Description: Interesting article, from Answers in Genesis Ministries, explaining thoracic (chest) surgeons routinely remove ribs, and these often grow back, in whole or in part.

Resources recommended in ◆several lessons, ★several units, ♥other HOW Units. ☞Key Resource (see beginning of unit or page 32).

Step 3 Expand

Choose and complete one of the following activities:

Activity 1: Write a Story
Write the story of the creation of Adam and Eve in your own words (minimum 150 words). Refer to "Writing about an Event" in *Writers INC*. (Younger students can dictate the story.)

Activity 2: Contrast and Compare
Make a contrast-and-compare graphic (see page 26) of the first Adam and the Last Adam, Jesus. Corinthians 15:45,47 gives two names or titles for Jesus. He is spoken of as "the Last Adam" and "the Second Man". As the Last Adam, Christ is the sum total of humanity; as the Second Man He is the Head of a new race. So we have here two unions, the one relating to His death and the other to His resurrection.

When Jesus was crucified on the cross, He was crucified as the Last Adam. As the Last Adam Jesus wiped out the old race; as the second Man He brings in the new race. All who accept Christ as Lord are included in both illustrations. *For if we have become united with him by the likeness of his death, we shall be also by the likeness of his resurrection* (Romans 6:5). All who accept Christ as Lord, died in Him as the last Adam and live in Him as the second Man. The first Adam was tempted and failed the test, and in him, we all continue to sin and die. The Last Adam was tempted, as was the first, but remained sinless, and lived a perfect life of righteousness. The first Adam began with everything provided for him in the Garden of Eden and he lost everything. The Last Adam began with nothing in a stable and ended with everything.

The Hebrew word for side is *tsela* and in Greek is *pleura*. The same Greek word occurs in the crucifixion account, when Adam's rib was removed from his side and when the soldiers pierced Jesus' side (John 19:34-36). Include the piercing sides on your chart. Can you think of more similarities? What was Adam's relationship to his bride and Christ's relationship to his bride, the church? Read Gen. 2-21-23. List as many similarities as you can and then read the article listed below.

Adam, the Second
Description: Article from *Baker's Evangelical Dictionary of Biblical Theology*.

Activity 3: Answer Questions

1. Who named Eve? (Genesis 2:23; 3:20)

2. Who was first fooled by Satan? (Genesis 3; 2 Corinthians 11:3; 1 Timothy 2:14)

3. How does the serpent display craftiness tempting the woman? Compare Genesis verses 4 and 5 to 3:22. Did the serpent lie?

4. What is the woman's punishment given in 3:16?

3. Who were the children of Adam and Eve? (Genesis 4:1,2,25; 5:3,4)

4. How old was Adam when he died? (Genesis 5:5)

Activity 4: Learn Hebrew Words
Look up each of these words in a Hebrew lexicon. Add the word, phonetic spelling and meaning to your Hebrew Notebook. See The Old Testament Hebrew Lexicon. The Hebrew word adam is ~da (phonetic- aw-dam'). It means "mankind," or "people." The Hebrew word for Eve is *hwwx* (phonetic - khav-vaw'). It means "life" or "living." The Hebrew word for side is *tsela* (phonetic- tsay-law'). It means "side," "rib," or "beam."

Activity 5: Discuss
"Have you ever faced a strong temptation? What did you do? Did you walk away or succumb?" Satan focused Eve's attention upon a specific thing. He got her to focus on what she didn't have when all around her was paradise. He determines the time of the temptation. He waits for the vulnerable moments. His ultimate strategy is to destroy us. He can't do that, but he can destroy our joy, peace, contentment, and assurance if we allow him to do it. Discuss different temptations in your life. Are there any that occur over and over? In order for us to walk godly in Christ, our thoughts must be in submission to the Holy Spirit. (2 Corinthians 10:3-5) Read Ephesians 6:10-14. Discuss what you can do next time you are tempted.

Activity 6: Share with a Child
Tell the story of Adam and Eve and complete the The Serpent's Lie Worksheet with an elementary-aged child.

Activity 7: Illustrate a Comic
Draw a comic-book page complete with conversations in bubbles showing the story of Adam and Eve.

Step 4 Excel

Share what you have learned about Adam and Eve with a friend or family member. Correct all written work to demonstrate correct punctuation and spelling, and effective use of grammar. Add corrected written work or any illustrations to your portfolio.

Resources recommended in ◆several lessons, ★ several units, ● other HOW Units. ●— Key Resource (see beginning of unit or page 32).

The Fall

The Narrated Bible

Step 1 Excite

Even though God created the perfect environment, sin entered into the world. God had to deal with man's sin. God had a plan and it would not be stopped.

God created everything else, and then He created Adam. Adam was God's masterpiece, created in God's own image. From Adam, all mankind came about. Adam had the first "personal" relationship with God: he walked with God, talked with God, and he tended God's creation. Yet, it was in this perfect relationship that Adam sinned. However, even after Adam sinned, God loved Adam and made the first sacrifice for him.

Read Genesis 3:6,11,12; and Romans 5:12,15,19.

Step 2 Examine

> The history of the Fall is recorded in Genesis 2 and 3. That history is to be literally interpreted. It records facts which underlie the whole system of revealed truth. It is referred to by our Lord and his apostles not only as being true, but as furnishing the ground of all God's subsequent dispensations and dealings with the children of men. The record of Adam's temptation and fall must be taken as a true historical account, if we are to understand the Bible at all as a revelation of God's purpose of mercy. [1]

Satan is a subtle liar from the beginning (John 8:44), all his lies have a common theme: one can sin and get away with it. But death is the penalty for sin (Gen. 2:17). The beautiful harmony of God's Creation was shattered by this entry of human sin.

When a man obeys God, he demonstrates his complete faith in the wisdom of God. Beginning with Adam, God has consistently demonstrated His will in the context of instruction or commands. Breaking the commands is disobedience and causes separation from God. God's commands are never unfair or too strict but man being a sinner by nature falls short in obeying God.

Lured by the temptation of instant pleasure Eve succumbed and persuaded her husband also to eat. Their opened eyes saw only their naked bodies, and they attempted to hide from each other and from God. Sin unchecked produces more evil. When the heart of a person no longer looks toward God, every thought and every action becomes based on sin. It is this condition in which Man found himself, and it is this condition that God was sorry to see. Since Adam, sin has kept Man separated from God.

Sin unchecked produces more evil. When the heart of a person no longer looks toward God, every thought and every action becomes based on sin. It is this condition in which man found himself, and it is this condition that God was sorry to see. Since Adam, sin has kept man separated from God.

Mark 10:18 *And Jesus said unto him, Why callest thou me good? There is none good but one, that is, God.*

Rom. 3:10 *As it is written, There is none righteous, no, not one.* (Also 1 John 1:8,10; Rom. 3:12, 5:12; Gal. 3:22.)

Research the Fall of Man. Use any resource (an encyclopedia, nonfiction book, historical novel, or the Internet). We recommend the following:

Books

The Victor Journey through the Bible ●▬ ♥
Read: The Fall (12-13).

Discover Jesus in Genesis ●▬ ♦
Read: "Out of the Garden Banashed" (10-11).

Adam and His Kin ●▬ ♦
Read: Chapter 3 "The Punishment."

Genesis: Finding Our Roots ●▬ ♦
Read: Unit 2 "Book of Adam."

An Historical Survey of the Old Testament ★
Read: "The Fall of Man" (56-58).

Internet Sources

The Fall of Humankind
Description: Part of "God's Story: From Creation to Eternity" from ChristianAnswers.net. (Follow the "next" buttons on the bottom of each page.)

The Fall of Man
Description: An excellent study, part of "Old Testament Bible Study of the Creation to Abraham Genesis 1 to Genesis 12."

Resources recommended in ♦several lessons, ★ several units, ♥ other HOW Units. ●▬ Key Resource (see beginning of unit or page 32).

Step 3 Expand

Choose and complete one of the following activities:

Activity 1: Create a Storyboard
A storyboard is a graphic, sequential depiction of a narrative. Gather the materials you would need to tell the story of the Fall. You can either draw this story or cut out pictures to tell this story to your family and friends. Refer to Storyboard directions (page 26).

Activity 2: Copy Verses
Copy (by hand or typing) two or more verses about the Fall of Man: Genesis 3:1-19; 2:16,17; Job 31:33; Ecclesiastes 7:29; Isaiah 43:27; Hosea 6:7; Romans 5:12,14,18,19,21; 1 Corinthians 15:21,22; 2 Corinthians 11:3; and 1 Timothy 2:14.

Activity 3: Create a Chart
Create a chart showing the three forms of temptation and subsequent sin: "lust of the eye," "lust of the flesh," and "the pride of life." See the chart below. Re-read Adam's and Eve's temptations, and notice how each of these forms is

Sin	Lust of the Eye	Lust of the Flesh	The Pride of Life	Penalty	God's Answer
1. Stealing	X	X	X	Death and Separation from God	Paid in full by Jesus

present in the first sin. God's response to these sins shows both judgment and mercy. It shows judgment because Adam and Eve were separated from the close relationship they had enjoyed with God. It shows mercy because God did not let Adam and Eve live forever in this separated state, but gave a way of redemption. (Read Genesis 3:21). God made a way for all men to return to a relationship with Him. God's first sacrifice was from among His animals, which provided the skins He gave to Adam and Eve to "cover" their "shame," i.e., to cover their sin. God finally gave His Son as the last sacrifice. Read John 3:13-17. Notice that there are three types of application for the tree of the knowledge of good and evil:

A tree that was good for food (natural food for the physical body).
A tree that was pleasant to the eyes (carnal food for the mind).
A tree desirable to make one wise (spiritual food).

Discuss with a family member what "Paid in Full" means. Discuss what this means to you.

Activity 4: Rewrite a Passage
Henry Thiessen wrote: "The thought is something like this. At first God and man stood face to face with each other in perfect harmony. In sinning, Adam turned his back upon God. . . . Christ's death has satisfied the demands of God and now God has again turned his face toward man. It remains for man to turn around and face God. Since God has been reconciled by the death of his Son, man is now entreated to be reconciled to God." Rewrite this passage in your own words.

Activity 5: Share with a Child
Tell the story of Adam and Eve and complete the The Serpent's Lie Worksheet with an elementary-aged child.

Step 4 Excel

Share what you have learned about the Fall of Man with a friend or family member. Correct written work to demonstrate correct punctuation and spelling, and effective use of grammar. Add corrected written work or any illustrations to your portfolio.

Footnotes:
1. Easton, Matthew George. "Entry for Fall", *Easton's Bible Dictionary*: Crosswalk.com, Inc.

Resources recommended in ◆several lessons, ★ several units, ● other HOW Units. ●—Key Resource (see beginning of unit or page 32).

Heart of Wisdom Publishing   63

Cain and Abel

Step 1 Excite

6-8

The Narrated Bible

The story of Cain and Abel is in Genesis Chapter 4. Read Genesis 4:1-16; Hebrews 11:4; 1 John 3:12; and Jude 1:11. Here were two children brought up in the same home, under absolutely identical circumstances, with the same background, the same teaching concerning the true God etc., and yet their lives turned out so differently.

Two sacrifices were made. Abel made a sacrifice of the firstborn of his flock, while Cain made a sacrifice of the fruit of the ground. Why do you think one sacrifice was acceptable to God and the other was not? What part did faith play in Cain's and Abel's sacrifices?

Step 2 Examine

Cain was the first-born son of Adam and Eve (Genesis 4). He became a tiller of the ground, as his brother Abel followed the pursuits of pastoral life. He was "a sullen, self-willed, haughty, vindictive man; wanting the religious element in his character, and defiant even in his attitude towards God." It came to pass "in process of time" (marg. "at the end of days"), i.e., probably on the Sabbath, that the two brothers presented their offerings to the Lord. Abel's offering was of the "firstlings of his flock and of the fat," while Cain's was "of the fruit of the ground." Abel's sacrifice was "more excellent" (Hebrews 11:4) than Cain's, and was accepted by God. On this account Cain was "very wroth," and cherished feelings of murderous hatred against his brother, and was at length guilty of the desperate outrage of putting him to death (1 John 3:12). For this crime he was expelled from Eden, and henceforth led the life of an exile, bearing upon him some mark which God had set upon him in answer to his own cry for mercy, so that thereby he might be protected from the wrath of his fellow-men; or it may be that God only gave him some sign to assure him that he would not be slain (Genesis 4:15). Doomed to be a wanderer and a fugitive in the earth, he went forth into the "land of Nod," i.e., the land of "exile", which is said to have been in the "east of Eden," and there he built a city, the first we read of, and called it after his son's name, Enoch. His descendants are enumerated to the sixth generation. They gradually degenerated in their moral and spiritual condition until they became wholly corrupt before God. This corruption prevailed, and at length the Deluge was sent by God to prevent the final triumph of evil. [1]

Cain's character continued in his descendants. Four generations later, Lamech was a polygamist (Genesis 4:17-19 (compare 2:24)) Lamech was also a murderer and wrongly expected God's grace (Genesis 4:23-24).

Research Cain and Abel. Use any resource (an encyclopedia, nonfiction book, historical novel, or the Internet). We recommend the following:

Books

📖👨 Discover Jesus in Genesis ⊶ ◆
Read: "Murder Near Paradise" (12-13).

📖👨 Adam and His Kin ⊶ ◆
Read: Chapter 5 "Cain."

📖👨 Genesis: Finding Our Roots ⊶ ◆
Read: Unit II "The Book of Adam."

📖👨 Who's Who in the Bible ⊶ ❤
Read: "First People of Genesis" (6-7).

📖 An Historical Survey of the Old Testament ★
Read: "The Genealogy of Adam and Eve" (58-60).

📖 Bible History: Old Testament ★
Read: Chapter 2 "Cain and Abel: The Two Ways and the Two Races."

Internet Sources

ⓘ The Birth of Cain and Abel
Description: An excellent study, part of "Old Testament Bible Study of the Creation to Abraham Genesis 1 to Genesis 12."

ⓘ Cain and Abel: The Two Ways and the Two Races
Description: Chapter 2 from Bible History: Old Testament by Alfred Edersheim.

ⓘ👨 The Broken Family of Cain and Abel
Description: Part 10 of "God's Story: From Creation to Eternity" from ChristianAnswers.net.

Step 3 Expand

Choose and complete one of the following activities:

✍👨 Activity 1: Write a Description
Faith plays a vital role in God's people. The covenants that God has kept are founded in His faithfulness. It is God's faithfulness that should be the guide for our faithfulness. Read Romans 3:25-30. Use a Bible Concordance, Topical Bible, or other Bible reference, and describe in one or two paragraphs some of the aspects of God's faithfulness. (Younger students can dictate the description.)

Resources recommended in ◆several lessons, ★ several units, ❤ other HOW Units. ⊶ Key Resource (see beginning of unit or page 32).

Heart of Wisdom Publishing   65

Activity 2: Contrast and Compare
Just as the "best fruit" of Cain would not please God, neither will the sinner's "best" works get him into heaven. God only accepted one offering—the blood lamb of Abel. Make a contrast and compare graphic (see page 26) comparing Abel's offering with Jesus, the Lamb of God.

Activity 3: Add to Your Time Line Book
Add Cain and Abel to your Time Line Book. Refer to Reproducible Maps, Charts, Timelines & Illustrations (13)

Activity 4: Create a Storyboard
Gather the materials you would need to tell the story of Cain and Abel. A storyboard is a graphic, sequential depiction of a narrative. You can either draw this story or cut out pictures to tell this story to your family and friends. Refer to Storyboard directions (see page 26).

Activity 5: Write a Summary
Both Cain and Abel brought offerings to God, but their heart attitudes were different. Write and share a paragraph explaining the term "Man looks on the outward appearance, but God looks at the heart." Younger students can dictate or narrate (tell back) what they learned.

Activity 6: Think about and Discuss
When Cain murdered Abel, what emotion preceded the act? (Genesis 4:3-7). Anger is perhaps the strongest, and potentially the most destructive of our emotions. Unbridled anger is the source for many outward acts of violence and inward roots of bitterness. Anger is not sin (Luke 4:28-30; 2 Corinthians 12:10; Galatians 5:20). Ephesians 4:26 tells us to be angry but not to sin. When does anger turn into sin? Talk to your parents about ways to deal with anger. What are biblical steps to release it to God and experience His peace?

Activity 7: Share with a Child
Tell the story of Cain and Abel and complete the The Cain and Abel Crossword Puzzle with an elementary aged child.

Step 4 Excel

Share what you have learned about Cain and Abel with a friend or family member. Correct all written work to demonstrate correct punctuation and spelling, and effective use of grammar. Add corrected written work or illustrations to your portfolio.

Footnotes:

1. Easton, Matthew George. "Entry for Cain", *Easton's Bible Dictionary*: Crosswalk.com, Inc.

Seth to Noah

8-10

The Narrated Bible

Step 1 Excite

Alfred Edersheim said in *Bible History: Old Testament*, "The place of Abel could not remain unfilled if God's purpose of mercy were to be carried out." Seth was the third son of Adam and Eve mentioned in the Bible. Seth's recorded descendants down to Noah are Enos, Cainan, Mahalaleel, Jared, Enoch, Methuselah, Lamech, and Noah.

There is an exciting message in the names of the descendants of Adam through his son Seth down to Noah! Ray C. Stedman analyzes these names in his book *Understanding Man*,

> "...a way of escape [for man] is indicated again in a most fascinating way in this chapter by the meaning of the names listed. There is some difference among authorities as to the meaning of these names, depending upon the root from which they are judged to be taken. But one authority gives a most interesting sequence of meanings. The list begins with Seth, which means "Appointed."

> Enosh, his son, means "Mortal;" and his son, Kenan, means "Sorrow." His son Mahalalel, means "The Blessed God." He named his boy Jared which means "Came Down," and his boy, Enoch, means "Teaching." Methuselah, as we saw, means "His death shall bring," Lamech means "Strength," and Noah, "Comfort." Now put that all together:

> *God has Appointed that Mortal man shall Sorrow;*
> *but The Blessed God, Came Down, Teaching,*
> *that His Death Shall Bring,*
> *Strength and Comfort.*

Step 2 Examine

Seth means "substituted." Gen. 4:25 says, *And Adam knew his wife again; and she bare a son, and called his name Seth: For God, said she, hath appointed me another seed instead of Abel, whom Cain slew.* While Adam and Eve had more children, it is through Seth that God's promised salvation would come. Read Luke 3:38.

Resources recommended in ◆several lessons, ★ several units, ● other HOW Units. ●━Key Resource (see beginning of unit or page 32).

Not much is written about the genealogy from Seth to Abram. We do know certain things about some of these men. For example, we know the ages to which these men lived, and we know their ages when they fathered the next in the genealogy. We know that Enoch walked with God, and we know that God took him so that Enoch did not see death.

Research the genealogy between Seth and Noah. Use any resource (an encyclopedia, nonfiction book, historical novel, or the Internet). We recommend the following:

Books

> Who's Who in the Bible ⌐ ♥
> Read: "First People of Genesis" (6-7),

> Bible History: Old Testament ★
> Read: Chapter 3 "Seth and his Descendants - The Race of Cain."

Internet Sources

> The Genealogy of the Rotal Line from Adam to Noah
> Description: An excellent study, part of "Old Testament Bible Study of the Creation to Abraham Genesis 1 to Genesis 12."

> The Stone Age to the Flood to before 2000 BC
> Description: MustardSeed Media annotated time line.

> Seth and his Descendants - The Race of Cain
> Description: Chapter 3 from Bible History: Old Testament by Alfred Edersheim.

Step 3 Expand

> Activity 1: Add to Your Time Line Book
> Using the ages mentioned in Genesis, make a time line chart of the lives of each of the men in the genealogy chain from Adam to Noah.

Step 4 Excel

Share what you have learned about the genealogy between Seth and Noah with a friend or family member. Correct all written work to demonstrate correct punctuation and spelling, and effective use of grammar. Add corrected written work or any illustrations to your portfolio.

Corruption of Man (Pre flood - Antediluvian)

11

The Narrated Bible

Step 1 Excite

Adam and Eve are good but immature, fine but breakable, like glass dishes. They are without flaw, yet capable of marring themselves. Satan uses a serpent to tempt Eve and Adam, first to question God, then to rebel against him. First, Satan introduces doubts about God's authority and goodness. Did God really say, *"You must not eat from any tree in the garden"*? (Gen. 3:1). He invites Eve to consider how the fruit of the tree of knowledge is good for food and for knowledge. We see the tendency of sin to begin with a subtle appeal to something attractive and good in itself, to an act that is somehow plausible and directed toward some good end; the first sins disclose the essence of later sins. Sin involves the refusal of humankind to accept its God-given position between the Creator and lower creation. It flows from decisions to reject God's way, and to steal, curse, and lie simply because that seems more attractive or reasonable. [1]

Antediluvian man became very corrupt, so corrupt that God "repented" that He had made man. Sometimes a superficial look is taken at the corruption of man; however, the corruption of creation caused by sin is far deeper than we can sometimes imagine. All sickness and all disease came from this corruption. The very building blocks of man himself (the DNA) became corrupt.

Genesis 4 gives a brief glimpse into the society and culture of mankind before the Flood. It describes cities, polygamy, Nomadic herdsmen, musical instruments, bronze, and iron. Read Genesis 4.

Step 2 Examine

Two days before the crucifixion of Christ, His disciples asked Him, *"What shall be the sign of thy coming, and of the end of the age?"* (Matthew 24:3). His reply pointed to a number of "signs," all of which together would occur in that generation which would see the signs, and which would be the sign they had requested. These signs were climaxed with the prophetic warning, *But as the days of Noe were, so shall the coming of the Son of Man be, For as in the days that were before the Flood, they were eating and drinking, marrying and giving in marriage, until the day that Noe entered into the Ark, and knew not until the Flood came and took them all away; so shall also the coming of the Son of Man be.* (Matthew 24:37-39). Thus did Jesus not only verify the historicity of antediluvian culture and the great Flood, and remind us of the relationship between wickedness and judgment, but He also encouraged us to study closely the characteristics of the days before the Flood, because these would also characterize the days just before His return. [2]

Resources recommended in ◆several lessons, ★ several units, ◆other HOW Units. ◉━Key Resource (see beginning of unit or page 32).

To corrupt means "to make morally depraved." It means to pervert what is good and upright. It means to make unclean what was once clean. It means to spoil what was once good and unspoiled. The word corrupt always implies a former state that was unspoiled, clean, good, or upright. It is never used to speak of the original created nature of man. It speaks of what man has become because of spoiling or perverting the nature with which he was created. [3]

Research the corruption of man. Use any resource (an encyclopedia, nonfiction book, historical novel, or the Internet). We recommend the following:

Books

Adam and His Kin
Read: Chapter 8 "Noah" and Chapter 9 "The Year 1656."

Genesis: Finding Our Roots
Read: Unit 3 "Book of Noah."

Bible History: Old Testament ★
Read: Chapter 5 "The Universal Corruption of Man - Preparation for the Flood."

Internet Sources

The Population of the Pre-Flood World
Description: Chapter 5 from Bible History: Old Testament by Alfred Edersheim.

Sin, Repentance and Forgiveness
Description: An article from "Israel Teaching Letter" discussing Christianity's theology of "original sin," and Judaism's theology that man has the "proclivity to sin" by Clarence H. Wagner, Jr.

The Fall of Man. Genesis 3:1-24
Description: An excellent study, part of "Old Testament Bible Study of the Creation to Abraham Genesis 1 to Genesis 12."

Step 3 Expand

Choose and complete one of the following activities:

Activity 1: Make a List
When the Bible says, "it repented God," what do you think this meant? Consider the genealogy you have studied. How many people are listed in such a way that they could be considered "people after God's heart"? Make a list of these people.

Activity 2: Write a Description
Write a description of society and culture of mankind before the Flood from the verses in Genesis 4. Younger students can dictate the description.

Activity 3: Write an Article
Look at today's newspaper, or listen to a news broadcast. What do you think is God's reaction to the stories in that paper or on that broadcast? Pick out one story and try to see what God sees. Write an article explaining what you think God feels, and what you think our response should be to God's reaction.

Activity 4: Expand Research
Find out about the four major theological theories on original sin. These theories did not exist until about the third century A.D., and there was no generally accepted doctrine until the fifth century A.D.[5]

1. The Wesleyanism (also called Mediate Imputation or Theory of Condemnation for Depravity) view states that we inherit corruption (sin nature) from Adam, but not actual sin.
2. Augustinianism is a view from Augustine (also called the Theory of Adam's Natural Headship and the Realistic Theory). He believed that we were actually present in Adam when he sinned, which is how we can be held guilty for what he did.
3. The Federal Theory (also called Immediate Imputation) says God holds us guilty of the same sin Adam committed, from the moment we are born.
4. The Pelagianism belief is there is no original sin; we are responsible for our own sin only. This is the theological doctrine propounded by Pelagius, a British monk, who believed humans can merit heaven by leading righteous lives.

Whether you believe in theology of "original sin," or that man has the "proclivity to sin," the bottom line is the same: man can, and does, sin against God and man. Humans are not animals, and because we have understanding and moral

---

Resources recommended in ◆several lessons, ★ several units, ◆other HOW Units. ☞Key Resource (see beginning of unit or page 32).

consciousness, we are responsible for our actions, which have consequences. We know from the Bible, that the *wages of sin is death* (Rom. 6:23), which effectively separates us from God, now and in eternity. Deuteronomy 24:16 makes it clear that *each [person] is to die for his own sin*. This death has both spiritual and physical dimensions, and no one can escape paying the price.[4]

To find out more on this topic see:

> Are Men Born Sinners? The Myth of Original Sin
> Description: An online book written by A. T. Overstreet. Overstreet explains that original sin is several differing theories that have evolved from heathen philosophy, and that it was made a dogma of the Roman Catholic Church in the 5th century A.D.

Step 4 Excel

Share what you have learned about the corruption of man with a friend or family member. Correct all written work to demonstrate correct punctuation and spelling, and effective use of grammar. Add corrected written work or any illustrations to your portfolio.

Footnotes
1.   Elwell, Walter A. (1997). "Entry for 'Sin'", *Evangelical Dictionary of Theology*.
2.   Unruh, J. Timothy. (1995). "The Days of Noah and the Sons of God," Lambert Dolphin's Research Library. <http://www.ldolphin.org/unruh/giants.html> (Accessed August 2000).
3.   Overstreet, A. T. "Are Men Born Sinners?". <http://www.gospeltruth.net/menbornsinners/mbs04.htm> (Accessed August 2000).
4.   Wagner, Clarence H., Jr. "Sin, Repentance And Forgiveness," "Israel Teacher Letter." Bridges For Peace. <http://bridgesforpeace.com> (Accessed December 2000).
5.   The focus of the activity is not to determine the theory of original sin. It is to show students that many doctrines accepted as biblical fact, actually came into existence years after the Bible.

The Flood

12-14

The Narrated Bible

Step 1 Excite

Noah found favor in the eyes of the Lord. Noah was a righteous man, blameless among the people of his time, and he walked with God. Can you imagine being Noah when God told him He was going to put an end to all mortals on earth? Can you imagine being the only righteous person living in a spiritual and moral wasteland? How do think Noah found favor in the eyes of the Lord? Can you imagine being asked to build a boat 4 1/2 stories high and as long as a football field and a half, 500 miles or more away from the closest body of water? Can you imagine the public ridicule? As you study this lesson, think about your life. Are you willing to do things God's way rather than your own? Are you willing to trust God's ability rather than your agenda?

Read Genesis 6, 7, 8, and Matthew 24:37-39.

Step 2 Examine

The Genesis account of the Flood of Noah is quite explicit. It describes the Flood as more than a local flood, more even than a regional catastrophe. Suffice it to say that the Hebrew word used in the original text (kataklusmos) means "cataclysm" and is applied only to the Genesis Flood. It is clear that this yearlong flood was not only worldwide, but also one that produced dramatic desolation. Indeed, it must have been a world-restructuring event. So great was its force that in all likelihood even Noah would not have been able to recognize his former homeland. It is very unlikely that any vestiges of the pre-flood civilizations survived, at least in any recognizable form. Noah's Ark, therefore, constitutes the one remaining archaeological link to the world before the Flood. No other major antediluvian artifact is likely ever to be found. [1] The Flood covered the entire earth to the tops of the mountains. As awesome as it sounds, the waters of the Flood covered the deepest valley to the highest mountain.

In Matthew 24:37-39 Jesus uses the account of the universal Flood and its destruction to point to His second coming and judgment, which is also a universal event. As in the days of Noah, when all who were outside the ark were destroyed, so it will be at the coming of the Son of Man when all those outside the ark of safety, Jesus Christ (those who have not accepted Him as Saviour), shall be judged and condemned.

Read more about the Flood. Use any resource (an encyclopedia, nonfiction book, historical novel, or the Internet).We recommend the following:

Resources recommended in ◆several lessons, ★ several units, ●other HOW Units. ●—Key Resource (see beginning of unit or page 32).

Books

The Victor Journey through the Bible ☞ ♥
Read: Noah Builds the Ark (14-15).

Discover Jesus in Genesis ☞ ♦
Read: "The Flood" (14-15).

Adam and His Kin ☞ ♦
Read: Chapter 10 "The Great Flood."

Genesis: Finding Our Roots ☞ ♦
Read: Unit 3 "Book of Noah."

Grand Canyon: Monument to Catastrophe by Steven A. Austin
Description: True science will not disagree with God. This means that we must always test the so-called "sciences" in the light of truth. For example, evolution would tell you that species evolved into higher forms of life. However, science also tells you that the universe is in a state of decline. Both cannot be true, and since the later position is provable by consistent laboratory example, the first must be false. (September 1995) Institute for Creation Research; ISBN: 0932766331.

An Historical Survey of the Old Testament ★
Read: "The Flood" (60-71).

Bible History: Old Testament ★
Read: Chapter 6 "The Flood."

The Genesis Flood by Henry M. Morris and John C. Whitcomb
Description: This is the book which many recognize as having started the modern revival of creationism and catastrophism. Although it has gone through over 32 printings, it is still the most definitive treatment of the biblical and scientific evidence of the global flood in the days of Noah. ISBN: 0-87552-338-2.

Internet Sources

The Flood
Description: Chapter 6 from Bible History: Old Testament by Alfred Edersheim.

The Great Flood Begins
Description: An excellent study, part of "Old Testament Bible Study of the Creation to Abraham Genesis 1 to Genesis 12."

(i) (👪) Noah and the Great Flood
Description: Part of God's Story: From Creation to Eternity from ChristiansAnswers.net. (Follow the "next" buttons on the bottom of each page.)

(i) From Where Came the Extra Water for the Great Flood?
Description: Explanation of the earth's water sources before and during the Flood from God's Point of View.

Videos

(📼) (👪) The Quest for Noah's Ark
Description: "High atop a Mountain in Eastern Turkey is a 5,000 Year Old Wooden Ship. Is it Noah's Ark? Did the biblical story of Noah and the flood actually happen? Has the Ark really been located? New expeditions and scientific investigations using satellites, computers, and aerial spy cameras have provided amazing answers to these questions. Winner of the Dove Family Approved Seal Award." (Publisher's description).

(📼) The Search for Noah's Ark
Description: An incredible docu-lecture. Dr. John Morris, veteran of numerous Ararat expeditions, presents awesome footage and informative slides to produce a faith-affirming video on this ongoing search. Interest level: Junior High-Adult. To Order, Call 1-800-422-4253.

(📼) The World that Perished: Evidence of the Global Flood of Genesis
Description: Combines special effects animation with other outstanding visuals. Brings to light the scientific and historic evidence that God's judgment - Noah's Flood - was real and global. Reveals the fascinating facts and planet-changing nature of the Flood. Biblically accurate. Answers the doubts of skeptics and strongly strengthens faith in the Bible. This much-translated film illustrates that God does judge sin, and concludes with an excellent soul-winning message. Produced by Films for Christ. Available from Paradise Gardens 1-800-332-2261.

Step 3 Expand

Choose and complete one of the following activities:

(⚖️) (👪) Activity 1: Contrast and Compare
Make a contrast and compare graphic (see page 26). Compare man's wickedness in the days of Noah with today. Watch television and notice how many times God's commandments are broken or ridiculed in a typical comedy or drama.

Resources recommended in ◆several lessons, ★ several units, ● other HOW Units. ●━Key Resource (see beginning of unit or page 32).

Activity 2: Add to Your Time Line Book
Add the story of the Flood to your Time Line Book. Refer to
<u>Reproducible Maps, Charts, Timelines & Illustrations</u> (11-13).

Activity 3: Write an Article
Imagine you are writing for a newspaper. Using the results of your
research, write an article about flooding. Compare the different types of floods and
the damage they can cause. As you will see from your research, even localized
floods cause millions and possibly billions of dollars of damage a year. Be aware
that the total sum of all floods in the world can be considered minor when compared to the Flood.

Activity 4: Write a Description
Use Scripture references to write a description of the ark. Include size
and materials. Hint: The dimensions of the ark are given in cubits. A cubit was the
distance from a man's elbow to the tip of his fingers; generally about 18 inches.

Activity 5: Answer Questions

1. How was the Flood foretold? (Genesis 6:13,17)
2. Was does the NT say about the Flood? (Matthew 24:38; Luke 17:26,27;
   Hebrews 11:7; 1 Peter 3:20; 2 Peter 2:5)
3. What promise did God make? (Genesis 8:20,21; Isaiah 54:9)
4. How was Noah in the spiritual wilderness like Jesus in the wilderness?

Activity 6: Expand Your Research
Study the effects of local floods and major catastrophic flooding. Use the
encyclopedia, news articles, or other sources. Floods are one of the most deadly
and damaging natural disasters known to mankind. The amount of power in even
a relatively small flood is staggering. In 1931 the Huang He River in China flood-
ed, causing 80 million people to become homeless, and killing over one million
people.

Activity 7: Write a Paper
From your research, write a paper titled "Arguments for a Universal Flood."
Hints: the depth (7:19-20), the duration, New Testament references (II Peter 3:6-
7), and size of the ark.

Step 4 Excel

Share what you have learned about the Flood with a friend or family member. Correct written
work to demonstrate correct punctuation and spelling, and effective use of grammar. Add
corrected written work or any illustrations to your portfolio.

After the Flood

14-16

The Narrated Bible

Step 1 Excite

After the Flood, nothing was the same; nothing was left unchanged. The earth had been "cleansed." Aside from Noah and his sons and their wives, not only was man gone, everything else was too. Even after the terrible flood waters changed the earth forever, God showed mercy.

As mankind spread around the globe, many people began herding and farming. People had the option of increasing food production through work. Africa, America, and Australia have a few large mammals that can be domesticated for farming. Read Genesis 8:6-12.

Step 2 Examine

The book, *Knowing God through Genesis*[1], explains how we can see God through the Flood: "In God's grief over man's wickedness, we see the disappointment of a loving God who desires our best. In His destruction of the human race, we see the wrath of God poured out on disobedience. In the singling out of Noah for rescue, we see a sovereign God who cares for individuals. In the shimmering rainbow, we see an unending reminder that God keeps His word." The book also explains that we can see ourselves through the Flood: "In the unrestrained evil of the race, we see our own pattern of sin before God's grace transformed us. In the refusal of Noah's neighbors to heed his preaching, we see our own resistance to God's spokesmen for justice and truth. In the faith and obedience of Noah, we are given a model for our own relationship with the Lord. In the new beginning for mankind after leaving the ark, we see reflected our own opportunities to start afresh with God."

Research the period after the Flood. Use any resource (an encyclopedia, nonfiction book, historical novel, or the Internet). We recommend the following:

Books

Discover Jesus in Genesis ●— ◆
Read: "The Promise of Protection: The Rainbow" (16-17).

Adam and His Kin ●— ◆
Read: Chapter 11 "The Calendar Puzzle" and Chapter 12 "Starting up the New World."

Genesis: Finding Our Roots ●— ◆
Read: Unit 4 "Book of the Sons of Noah."

Resources recommended in ◆several lessons, ★several units, ●other HOW Units. ●—Key Resource (see beginning of unit or page 32).

Bible History: Old Testament ★
Read: Chapter 7, "The Universal Corruption of Man - Preparation for the Flood."

Internet Sources

The Flood Waters Subside
Description: An excellent study, part of "Old Testament Bible Study of the Creation to Abraham Genesis 1 to Genesis 12."

The Universal Corruption of Man - Preparation for the Flood
Description: Chapter 7 from Bible History: Old Testament by Alfred Edersheim.

Step 3 Expand

Activity 1: Write a Diary Entry
Write a diary entry as if you were one of the people watching as Noah built the ark. Why did you think he was foolish? Younger students can dictate or narrate (tell back) what a person may have been thinking.

Activity 2: Write a Diary Entry
Write another entry as if you were one of Noah's children. Explain what you see, hear, and feel before boarding the ark and after the ark has landed. Do you feel opportunities to start afresh? Younger students can dictate or narrate (tell back) what Noah's child may have been thinking.

Activity 3: Share with a Child
Tell the story of the rainbow and complete the The Rainbow Covenant Worksheet with an elementary aged child.

Step 4 Excel

The dove and the olive branch are important symbols. In Genesis 8:6-12, it was the dove that brought back the olive branch. Read Matthew 3:14-17 and Romans 11:24. The dove and the branch are reflections of salvation that recur throughout the Bible. Draw an illustration of a dove and an olive branch. Share your drawing with someone.

Footnote
1. Egne, David (1991). *Knowing God Through Genesis*, (The Discovery Series), RBC Ministries, Grand Rapids, MI 49555. Available on the Internet <http://www.gospelcom.net/rbc/ds/sb111/sb111.html>

The Tower of Babel

17

The Narrated Bible

Step 1 Excite

After the Flood most of the people ignored God's command to fill the earth. There they settled together on the plain of Shinar (the future site of Babylon) and started building a tower to their own glory. God confused their language so they could not understand each other. They stopped building the tower of Babel and scattered over the face of the earth.

Step 2 Examine

Read the story of the Tower of Babel in Genesis 11:1-9.

Research The Tower of Babel. Use any resource (Bible, an encyclopedia, a non-fiction book, or the Internet). We recommend the following:

Books

The Victor Journey through the Bible ♦── ♥
Read: Tower of Babel (18-19).

Discover Jesus in Genesis ♦── ♦
Read: "The Tower of Confusion" (18-19).

Adam and His Kin ♦── ♦
Read: Chapter 15 "The Tower of Bel" and Chapter 16 "Aftermath."

Genesis: Finding Our Roots ♦── ♦
Read: Unit 5 "The Book of Shem."

The Bible Comes Alive Volume One, Creation to Abraham ♦
Read: "Babylon: Where the Tower of Babel Was Located" (46-47).

Bible History: Old Testament ★
Read: Chapter 8 "Genealogy of Nations - Babel - Confusion of Tongues."

Internet Sources

The Tower of Babel and Ancestry of Abraham
Description: An excellent study, part of "Old Testament Bible Study of the Creation to Abraham Genesis 1 to Genesis 12."

Resources recommended in ♦several lessons, ★ several units, ♥other HOW Units. ♦──Key Resource (see beginning of unit or page 32).

Is There Archaeological Evidence of the Tower of Babel?
Description: Discussion of the reasons, methods, and culture surrounding the building of the Tower of Babel.

MSN Encarta - Tower of Babel
Description: Presents a brief retelling of the Old Testament story. Read about the Babylonians' attempt to construct a tower to heaven, and the outcome.

Tower of Babel and the Confusion of Languages
Description: Offers a commentary illuminating the symbolic and religious meaning of the Tower of Babel.

Step 3 Expand

Choose and complete one of the following activities:

Activity 1: Write a Poem
Write a poem about Babel. Refer to "Writing Poetry" in *Writers INC.*

Activity 2: Share with a Child
Tell the story of the Tower of Babel and complete the Tower of Babel Crossword Puzzle with an elementary aged child.

Activity 1: Contrast-and-Compare
Genesis recounts that the two cities Shinar and Babel formed the original kingdom of Nimrod. The image of the city of Babel stood in sharp contrast to the nomadic life of Israel's patriarchs. Moreover, the episode at Babel foreshadowed the dangers that Israel faced as it settled among the Canaanite cities with their rich temples and false gods. The main reason God punished His people with the exile in Assyria and Babylon was their persistent desire to accommodate themselves in the idolatry and lifestyles in the nations around them. Make a contrast-and-compare graphic (see page 26) showing how their actions compare with Christians' today. Do we have difficulty living in a corrupt world? Why does God command separation?

Step 4 Excel

Share what you have learned with a friend or family member. Correct written work to demonstrate correct punctuation and spelling, and effective use of grammar. Add corrected written work or any illustrations to your portfolio.

Beginning of Nations

18-22

The Narrated Bible

Step 1 Excite

Genealogy is a fascinating study and a wonderful vehicle for learning. Interview your parents, grandparents, and other family members about your family's ethnic background. What country did your family come from? How did they get to this country? What are some family traditions? Make a chart of three generations of your family. Free downloadable forms are available from the Internet at http://www.familytreemagazine.com/forms/download.html

Have you ever thought about all the different nations on earth? Do you remember the names of Noah's sons? Do you realise that all the people in the world come from these three men? The Bible explains how they were part of the origin of all the nations of the earth.

Step 2 Examine

After the waters of the Flood have receded, Noah and his sons are told to replenish the earth (Gen. 9:1). All nations, all cultures, all tribes, and all peoples are descended from Noah through Shem, Ham, or Japheth. Anthropologists divide all the world's peoples into three races: Caucasian (white), Mongoloid (yellow), and Negroid (black). Within each of Noah's sons was the potential to produce all the variations that are evident within the three races of man. Gen 5:32: And Noah was five hundred years old: and Noah begat Shem, Ham, and Japheth.

Shem: The line of Shem's seed was the covenant line from whom Abraham came, then the patriarchs, then David, and eventually Christ. Semitic, a word which refers to the Jewish race and peoples, comes from the name Shem.

Ham: The peoples of Ham's line populated parts of Asia Minor, the Arabian Peninsula, and eventually the entire continent of Africa - once known as the "Land of Ham."

Japheth: The Japhethite line goes to the non-Jewish (Gentile) nations. The Greek, Roman, and Egyptian peoples can trace their roots to the family of Japheth.

Some have interpreted Genesis chapter 9 to be the Scriptural basis for race discrimination. However, when God commanded Israel to be a "separated people," it was always based on the principle of separation from sin. It is never based on what we determine as race; such as color of hair, skin, or eyes, or physical characteristics.

Resources recommended in ♦several lessons, ★ several units, ♦other HOW Units. ●━Key Resource (see beginning of unit or page 32).

Heart of Wisdom Publishing   81

Which Came First?

The order of the son's of Noah is not clear. Most commentaries believe Japheth was the first born. (Gen 10:21; 9:24) others disagree.

> *The Jewish Encyclopedia* says, "Japheth and his two brothers, Shem and Ham, were born...clearly indicated which of the three brothers was the eldest. Japheth usually comes third in order."

> *Harper's Bible Commentary* says, "The characteristic structure of the unit, in which Noah's sons are dealt with in reverse order of their significance, is also taken from Genesis 10 and becomes characteristic of Chronicles."

> *Smith's Bible Dictionary* lists Shem as the oldest.

> *Commentary Critical and Explanatory on the Whole Bible*: ...the account begins with the descendants of Japheth, and the line of Ham is given before that of Shem though he is expressly said to be the youngest or younger son of Noah; and Shem was the elder brother of Japheth (Ge 10:21),

> *Easton's Bible Dictionary*: Lists Japheth as one of the sons of Noah, mentioned last in order (Gen. 5:32; 6:10; 7:13), perhaps first by birth (10:21; comp. 9:24).

Seventy Nations

> This remarkable text sets Israel within the context of the world known to the OT writers. It lists seventy nations (probably a symbolic round number; cf. the seventy sons of Jacob who went down to Egypt, 46:27), which represent all the peoples of the world, and is not an exhaustive list of all groups known in ancient Israel. It reads a bit like a family tree, but it may be that not all the relationships described are genealogical. In the ancient world, treaties and covenants led to people calling themselves brothers or sons of their treaty-partner. What the Table of Nations describes is the relationship between the different peoples, however they may have originated historically.[1]

Research the genealogy of nations. Use any resource (an encyclopedia or the Internet). We recommend the following:

Books

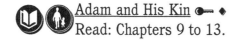
Read: Chapters 9 to 13.

Genesis: Finding Our Roots ❍— ◆
Read: Unit V "The Book of Shem." Focus on the "Table of Nations" beginning on page 80.

The Holman Bible Atlas ❍— ♥
Read: "The Table of Nations" (36).

An Historical Survey of the Old Testament ★
Read: "The Dispersion of Nations" (68-71).

Bible History: Old Testament ★
Read: Chapter 5 "The Population of the Pre-Flood World" and Chapter 8 "Genealogy of Nations - Babel - Confusion of Tongues."

Internet Sources

The Families of Man
Description: Bible study on Genesis 9:18-28 by Ray C. Stedman.

The Table of Nations Genesis 10 and 11
Description: Bible study on Genesis 10 and 11 and genealogical table of the descendants of Noah.

Table of Nations and Genealogy of Mankind
Description: An article on the descendants of Noah.

The Population of the Pre-Flood World
Description: Chapter 5 from Bible History: Old Testament by Alfred Edersheim.

Genealogy of Nations - Babel - Confusion of Tongues
Description: Chapter 8 from Bible History: Old Testament by Alfred Edersheim.

Shem
Description: This is a dictionary entry from the *Illustrated Bible Dictionary*.

Japheth
Description: This is a dictionary entry from the *Illustrated Bible Dictionary*.

Ham
Description: This is a dictionary entry from the *Illustrated Bible Dictionary*.

Resources recommended in ◆several lessons, ★ several units, ♥other HOW Units. ❍—Key Resource (see beginning of unit or page 32).

Heart of Wisdom Publishing   83

Step 3 Expand

Choose and complete one of the following activities:

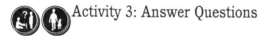Activity 1: Review Maps
Today, the word "nation" is usually taken to mean a geographic boundary containing a large group of people under one government. This large group may or may not be related ethnically or tribally. In the Old Testament however, "nation" usually had more to do with family, tribe, or lineage than geographical boundaries. While these tribes lived in localized areas, they attached themselves to each other more by family than by area. Read Genesis Chapter 10. Make a list of the different nations that came from Shem, Ham, and Japheth. Review the maps of the Old Testament, and locate where these "nations" lived.

Activity 2: Make a Family Tree
Make a family tree of Noah's sons. List their descendants according to Genesis 10 and 11.

Activity 3: Answer Questions

1. Who were the three sons of Noah?
2. How many sons did Japheth have?
3. How many sons did Ham have?
4. Which of Ham's sons has the name of a country?
5. Who was the father of Nimrod?

Activity 4: Learn Hebrew Words
Add the word, phonetic spelling, and meaning to your Hebrew Notebook. See The Old Testament Hebrew Lexicon. The Hebrew word for nation is *ywg* (phonetic -go'-ee) The final words of Jesus' ministry, the Great Commission of Matthew 28:16-20, indicate how His ministry had expanded to "make disciples of all nations." Use a Bible dictionary to look up and define the word "nations."

Step 4 Excel

Share what you have learned about the genealogy of nations with a friend or family member. Correct all written work to demonstrate correct punctuation and spelling, and effective use of grammar. Add corrected written work or illustrations to your portfolio.

Footnotes
1. The Jewish Encyclopedia (NY: Funk and Wagnall, 1905), XII:588-9; The Universal Jewish Encyclopedia (NY:Universal Jewish Encyclopedia Co., 1942), 6:41.

The Nations Religions

18-22

The Narrated Bible

Step 1 Excite

After God confused the language, men began to wander. So did their religions. From the beginning foundation of a belief in God, the various people began to change their religions to suit themselves. Similarities in the various stories about the Flood, Creation, and other things point to the truth of creation and man's history. A primary difference between the truth of God and the tales that man began telling is obvious. Man's stories diminish or leave out God and give glory and credit to man himself. Thus, man began to worship the created rather than the Creator.

At the time Abraham came to Canaan, there were a number of nations in the area. Each seemed to have its own god and religious practices. From Baal to Nebo to Egyptian Mythology, religions abounded. One thing remains. All religions, then and now, attempt to answer these questions: Who is God? Who is Adam (man)? What is sin? What is salvation? The difference between the true God of the Scriptures and these other religions is clear. All other religions try to reach God by works and by man's own strength. The Scriptures tell us differently.

Step 2 Examine

After God confused the languages, men began to wander. So did their religions. As the people moved away from each other they began loosing sight of God and His ways and began practicing pagan religions, starting mythical stories of various gods. Similarities in the various worldwide stories about the Flood, Creation, and other things point to the truth of Creation and Man's history. A primary difference between the truth of God and the tales that Man began telling is obvious: Man's stories diminish or leave out God and give glory and credit to Man himself. Thus, Man began to worship the created rather than the Creator.

One of the most amazing inaccurate claims made today by unbelievers, is that the book of Genesis grew out of the pagan mythologies of nations like Babylon. Unbelievers have a theory that the stories in the Bible were taken from early civilizations(such as the epic of Gilamesh), rather than the other way around. The truth is when God dispersed Men, they took His teachings and perverted them into their own religions.

Each nation was dispersed from Babel, so they carried with them their memories of the stories of Adam, Eve, the serpent, the Fall, and the Flood. As time passed, ancestor worship became worse until the polytheistic systems as the Babylonian, Assyrian and Egyptian. Many of the pagan religions began as distorted stories . As the people started telling stories about many gods they intertwined their stories with distorted versions of facts recorded in

Resources recommended in ◆several lessons, ★ several units, ●other HOW Units. ●━Key Resource (see beginning of unit or page 32).

Heart of Wisdom Publishing   85

Genesis. The biblical account of the Flood is an example of this. People and tribes that have been separated for thousands of years still have a common belief that a deluge destroyed the world.

At the time when Abraham came to Canaan, there were a number of nations in the area. Each seemed to ave its own god and religious practices. From Baal to Nebo to gods of Egyptian mythology, religions abounded. One thing remains the same; all religions, then and now, attempt to answer these questions: Who is God? Who is Adam (Man)? What is sin? What is salvation? The difference between the true God of the Scriptures and these other religions is clear. All other religions try to reach God by works and by Man's own strength. The Scriptures tell us differently.

Do research to find out who or what early civilizations worshiped. Use any resource (an encyclopedia, nonfiction book, historical novel, or the Internet). We recommend the following:

Books

Adam and His Kin ⊶ ◆
Read: Chapter 17 "Gods and Goddesses."

Genesis: Finding Our Roots ⊶ ◆
Read: "The Religion of Sumer" (84) from Unit V "Book of Shem."

Our Father Abraham ⊶ ♥
Read: "The World of the Bible" (9-12).

Bible History: Old Testament ★
Read: Chapter 9 "The Nations and their Religion."

Bible Lands by Jonathan Tubb, Alan Hills (Photographer)
Description: Photographs and text document life in biblical times, surveying the clothing, food, and civilizations of a wide variety of cultures, including the Israelites, Babylonians, Persians, and Romans. A. A. Knopf; ISBN: 0679814574. Reading level: Ages 9-12.

Internet Sources

The Nations and their Religions
Description: Chapter 9 from Bible History: Old Testament by Alfred Edersheim.

Sumer: The Religion
Description: Brief overview of Sumerians worshipping many gods from Mesopotamia: The Sumerians.

Step 3 Expand

Activity 1: Contrast and Compare
God has said that He is the only God and there is no god besides Him. Using an encyclopedia, library, or other sources, make a <u>contrast and compare graphic</u> (see page 26) to compare four of the most common religions of the area during this period. In the essay, describe how these religions look at God, Adam (mankind), Sin, and Salvation. Also describe how they look at the life to come. Compare this with what you believe about the God of the Bible.

Activity 2: Make a List
Make a list of how America is like the Sumerian society.

Activity 3: Contrast and Compare
Make a contrast and compare chart with modern day Judaism, Christianity, and Islam. Include: the history of how religion started, including key people and dates, major beliefs, religious rituals and Customs, books, what happens after death, the meaning of life. Refer to the http://school.discovery.com/lessonplans/programs/islam/ and http://Homeschool-Books.com /Ancienthistory/contrast.htm

Activity 4: Write an Essay
Write a paper titled "The Birth of Paganism." Refer to "Essay Writing" at http://Homeschool-Books.com /writing.htm#essays

Step 4 Excel

Share what you have learned about the nation's religions after Babel with a friend or family member. Correct all written work to demonstrate correct punctuation and spelling, and effective use of grammar. Add corrected written work or any illustrations to your portfolio.

Resources recommended in ♦several lessons, ★ several units, ♥other HOW Units. ☞Key Resource (see beginning of unit or page 32).

The Calling of Abram

23-24

The Narrated Bible

This lesson will introduce you to Abram. We will look at Abraham's life and family more in the "Ancient Israel Unit." (When Abraham's son, Ishmael, was thirteen years old, God changed Abram's name to Abraham.)

Step 1 Excite

Faith plays a very important part in the life of anyone wanting to please God. Read Hebrews 11:6. An important part of faith is obedience. Able was obedient, Enoch was obedient, and Noah was obedient. What part does faith play in your life?

Abram's call begins a new chapter in God's plan to redeem mankind. From Abram's family would come a people who would know how to teach and keep the ways of the Lord. God required obedience and personal commitment from Abram in order for the blessing to be bestowed.

Read about the call of Abram in Genesis 12. Also read Romans 4:1.

Step 2 Examine

Easton's Bible Dictionary states:

> Abraham was father of a multitude, son of Terah, named (Genesis 11:27) before his older brothers Nahor and Haran, because he was the heir of the promises. Till the age of seventy, Abram sojourned among his kindred in his native country of Chaldea. He then, with his father and his family and household, quitted the city of Ur, in which he had hitherto dwelt, and went some 300 miles north to Haran, where he abode fifteen years. The cause of his migration was a call from God (Acts 7:2-4). There is no mention of this first call in the Old Testament; it is implied, however, in Genesis 12. While they tarried at Haran, Terah died at the age of 205 years. Abram now received a second and more definite call, accompanied by a promise from God (Genesis 12:1,2); whereupon he took his departure, taking his nephew Lot with him, "not knowing whither he went" (Hebrews 11:8). He trusted implicitly to the guidance of Him who had called him. ...The history of Abraham made a wide and deep impression on the ancient world, and references to it are interwoven in the religious traditions of almost all Eastern nations. He is called "the friend of God" (James 2:23), "faithful Abraham" (Galatians 3:9), "the father of us all" (Romans 4:16). [1]

Underlined text refers to Internet link at http://Homeschool-Books.com   Heart of Wisdom Publishing

Find out more about Abraham. Use any resource (Bible dictionary, Bible encyclopedia, a non-fiction book, or the Internet). We recommend the following:

Books

The Victor Journey through the Bible ☞ ♥
Read: Abraham's Journeys (18-19).

Discover Jesus in Genesis ☞ ♦
Read: "God's Promise to Abraham" (20-21).

Adam and His Kin ☞ ♦
Read: Chapter 19 "Abram."

Genesis: Finding Our Roots ☞ ♦
Read: Unit VI "Book of Terah."

Who's Who in the Bible ☞ ♥
Read: "Abraham and His People" (8-9).

The Holman Bible Atlas ☞ ♥
Read: "The World of the Patriarchs" (41-48).

An Historical Survey of the Old Testament ★
Read: "The Founding Fathers" (73-84).

Bible History: Old Testament ★
Read: Chapter 10 "The Chronology of the Early History of the Bible - Commencement of the History of God's Dealings with Abraham and his Seed," and Chapter 11 "The Calling of Abram - His Arrival in Canaan and Temporary Removal to Egypt."

Internet Sources

The Call of Abraham
A Slide Show from Lake View Church.

People of The Bible Abraham
Description: Bible study from Intouch Ministries explaining that Abraham willingly obeyed God, not out of obligation but out of love.

The Chosen People
Description: Brief overview of Abraham's relation to the Jews, from "Daily Bible Study."

Resources recommended in ♦several lessons, ★ several units, ♥other HOW Units. ☞Key Resource (see beginning of unit or page 32).

Abraham's Faith Tested
Description: A Bible study with questions to answer.

The Birth of a Nation (Abraham to Joseph)
Description: Part 10 of "God's Story: From Creation to Eternity" from ChristianAnswers.net. (Follow the "next" buttons on the bottom of each page.)

The Call of Abraham. Genesis 12:1-20 ⚷ ★
Description: An excellent study, part of "Old Testament Bible Study of the Creation to Abraham Genesis 1 to Genesis 12."

Those Who Have Faith Are the Sons of Abraham
Description: Excellent article describes how Jew or Gentile, rich or poor, male or female, white or black or brown, quick-witted or slow, old or young-anyone can be a child of Abraham. By John Piper, Pastor of Bethlehem Baptist Church.

God Keeps His Promises
Description: An article from Discovery Publishing, a ministry of Peninsula Bible Church.

Video

Abraham
Description: (from the back cover) "Emmy winner Joseph Sargent brings us the first in a series of magnificent Biblical epics from Turner Home Entertainment. *Abraham* is a powerful film, based on the most dramatic and moving tale from the Old Testament in which an ordinary shepherd is called upon by God to show his abiding faith in extraordinary ways." ASIN: 6303257828.

Step 3 Expand

Choose and complete one of the following activities:

Activity 1: Fill out a Worksheet
Compile information from your research to fill out a Person Worksheet about Abram.

Activity 2: Fill out a Worksheet
Choose an event in Abram's life to focus on. Fill out an Event Worksheet.

Activity 3: Write a Précis
Write a précis about Abram (minimum 100 words). Refer to "Writing a Précis" (182) in *Writers INC*. Share the précis with your family.

Activity 4: Trace a Map

Genesis 11:27-32; 15:7; and Nehemiah 9:7 describe Ur as the starting point of the migration westward to Palestine of the family of Abraham around 1900 B.C. Ur was one of the first village settlements founded by the so-called Ubaidian inhabitants of Sumer. A map of Abraham's migration can be found in the Holman Bible Atlas (page 46).

Activity 5: Examine & Memorize Scripture

Abraham's call involved separating himself from his country, his kinsmen, and his father's house. God was establishing an important principle: that His people were to separate themselves from all that hinders His purpose for their lives. The Bible says, "Wherefore come out from among them and be ye separate, saith the Lord, and touch not the unclean thing; and I will receive you." (I Cor. 6:17-18) Separation is a continual requirement for God's people, from the corrupt world (Ex. 23:24; John 17:5; 16:2; 1 Tim. 3:1-5; James 1:27; 4:4); and from those in the church in sin, who don't repent (Matt. 18:15-17; 1 Cor. 5:9-11; 2 Thes. 3:6-15).

Pray and examine where you are in your life. Discuss these questions with your parents: Are you "separate" and out from among the world? Do you have friends who are unbelievers? Do you have friends in unrepentant sin? The Bible firmly states that bad company corrupts good morals. What can seem to be innocent can result in great sin. What are the consequences of not separating? Read 2 Corinthians 6:16 and Romans 8:15-16. We must obey God's commands. Study and discuss each verse listed above. Memorize the two that speak to you most.

Activity 6: Write a Summary

Abraham possessed the faith that expressed itself in obedience. Write a summary of how Abraham's faith and obedience is a portrait of the saving faith we receive through God's son. Younger students can dictate the description of Abraham's faith.

Activity 7: Share with a Child

Tell the story of the call of Abram and complete the The Call of Abram Worksheet with an elementary aged child.

Step 4 Excel

Share what you have learned about the call of Abram with a friend or family member. Correct written work to demonstrate correct punctuation and spelling, and effective use of grammar. Add corrected written work or any illustrations to your portfolio.

Footnotes
1.   Easton, Matthew George. "Entry for Abraham." *Easton's Bible Dictionary*.

Resources recommended in ♦several lessons, ★ several units, ♥other HOW Units. ●—Key Resource (see beginning of unit or page 32).

Heart of Wisdom Publishing   91

Abram Enters Canaan

Step 1 Excite

God unconditionally promised to Abraham and his descendants "all the land of Canaan" (Gen. 22:15-18). The land of Canaan (Israel, the Promised Land, and the Holy Land) is the most important place on earth. You need to know where it is and what countries surround it.

This land is the birthplace of the Judeo-Christian heritage. More blood has been shed for this land than for any other spot on earth. God Himself refers to Jerusalem, and to no other place on earth, as "My City" (Isa. 45:13) or more often, "My Holy Mountain" (Isa. 11:9; 56:7; 57:13; Eze. 20:40; Joel 2:1; 3:17). It is the place where God has His temple built and where He dwelt (Ps. 87:1-2). The Bible is a book about Israel. The Bible commands us to "pray for the peace of Jerusalem." It is the place where Jesus Christ will come and establish Jerusalem as the capital of the whole world and rule over the whole earth (Isa. 11:9). If we understand God's purpose for the ancient nation of Israel, we can fully appreciate and understand God's redemptive plan for the world.

Few people today recognize how important the modern state of Israel is in God's plan. The Bible says that the sons and daughters of Israel would return to their land, the land of Israel, just before He would send them their Messiah. In 1948, Israel was re-established as a nation after almost 2000 years of not having a national homeland. The Six Day War fought by Israel in 1967, returned Jerusalem into Jewish control for the first time in 1897 years. Not a day that goes by that Israel is not in our evening news. It is amazing that this little country in the Middle East, 70 miles wide and 300 miles long, has had so much attention.

Isaiah 27:6 says, *Israel shall blossom and bud, and fill the face of the world with fruit.* This prophecy is being fulfilled now. When Jews began resettling their historic homeland in the late 19th century the land was desolate, consisting of desert and swamps. The Hebrews worked on turning barren lands into fertile fields. Israel today is a leading exporter of flowers!

In this lesson we ask you to make a map of Israel out of felt. You can use this map over and over for any Bible study for years to come. You should think of this map as a treasure map! Because it is going to help you see real treasure— by opening your eyes to understanding the stories of the Bible. Maps give your brain a visual path through a story, helping you to understand the order of the events and visualize them. Once you get an understanding of where the events of the Bible took place the stories will become more real to you. Use the map on our site at http://heartofwisdom.com/israelmap.htm or find and trace a map of Israel (or from your Bible, Bible Atlas, or the Internet).

Step 2 Examine

Canaan was a collection of city-states which extended from Sidon to Gaza on the East Mediterranean coast and inland to the Jordan River Valley. At the time of Abraham, Canaan contained about 260,000 inhabitants including many skilled craftsmen in metals, textiles, ceramics, and woodwork; Canaan was destroyed by the Akkadians in around 1600 BC. When you read through Genesis you will see where several decendants of Abraham urged the Hebrews sons not to marry women from the Canaanite peoples.

Do you remember the lesson about Noah's sons? In a strange way, the descendants of Noah are reunited when Abraham came to Canaan. If you recall, Noah placed a curse on his son Canaan (Genesis 9:18-29) and a blessing upon his sons Shem and Ham. Abraham, a descendant of Shem comes to live in the land of Canaan inhabited by the Canaanites.

Some call this Land Palestine, but God calls it Israel. The name Palestine was a regional name that was imposed on the area by the Roman Emperor, Hadrian,

The Land of Milk and Honey refers to the fact that the land could support animals that provide milk and cheese, e.g. sheep, goats, camels, and eventually cattle, as well as flowering fruit trees that provided nectar for bees and fruit for jam. Animals and trees also meant there would be water. The promise of a Land of Milk and Honey confirmed God's blessing for the Israelites, considering the entire region is mostly arid desert. [2]

who suppressed the Second Jewish Revolt in A.D. 135. He was so angry with the Jews that he wanted to humiliate them and emphasize that the Jewish nation had lost its right to a homeland under Roman rule. The name Palaestina was originally an adjective derived from Philistia, the name of the arch-enemies of the Israelites 1000 years earlier.[1] Throughout the Word of God, this Land is always called Israel, never Palestine.

We often think of Bible lands as desert images. But the land is described several times in the Torah as a good land and "a land flowing with milk and honey" (Ex. 3:8).

Research the land or Israel (first called Canaan) and the Canaanites. Use any resource (an encyclopedia, nonfiction book, historical novel, or the Internet). We recommend the following:

Books

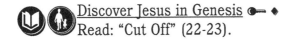
Discover Jesus in Genesis ●— ◆
Read: "Cut Off" (22-23).

Resources recommended in ◆several lessons, ★ several units, ● other HOW Units. ●— Key Resource (see beginning of unit or page 32).

Heart of Wisdom Publishing   93

Encyclopedia of the Bible (Nelson's Illustrated) ♥
"The Canaanites" (56-57).

The Holman Bible Atlas ⚷ ♥
See: "Abraham in Canaan" (47).

First Civilizations (Cultural Atlas for Young People) ⚷ ♦
Read: "Israel and Judah" (66-67). See the description in the Key
Resource section for the Mesopotamian Unit.

An Historical Survey of the Old Testament ★
Read: "Abraham: Genesis 11:26-25:8" (77-84).

Bible History: Old Testament ★
Read: Volume I: "The World Before the Flood, and The History of the
Patriarchs."

Our Father Abraham: Jewish Roots of the Christian Faith ⚷ ♥
Read: Chapter 13 "Jews, Christians, and the Land."

The Promised Land by Linda Robinson Whited
Description: A combination Bible story and activities book. The Bible story
traces God's promise to give the people the land, beginning with the first promise
to Abraham and ending when the Israelites enter Canaan ender the leadership of
Joshua. The story will help children ages nine through twelve make the connections among the various people in the Old Testament stories of the Hebrew people
as they seek the Promised Land. Paperback, 48 pages, Abingdon Press (1999).
ISBN: 0687081912.

365 Fascinating Facts About the Holy Land by Clarence M. Wagner
Description: 365 Fascinating Facts about the Holy Land brings the region to
life, especially for those who have never been there. From general information
about climate, culture, and customs, to concise information about Middle East politics, wars, and efforts for peace. Paperback. 224 pages. New Leaf Press (2000)
ISBN: 0892214899.

The Land of Many Names by Steve Maltz
Description: This is a lively, entertaining and provocative introduction to the
subject for ordinary Christians. The author takes you on a historical journey of the
Land of Many Names, from the Canaan of Abraham to the Promised Land, by way
of the Land of Milk and Honey, Israel and Judah, Judea and Samaria, Palestine,
The Holy Land, Zion, Israel and 'The Zionist Entity.' Authentic Lifestyle (2003),
175 pages. ISBN: 1860242871.

God's Plan for Israel: A Study of Romans 9-11 by Steven A. Kreloff 3
Description: This book will take you from the time God promised the land to Abraham through Israel's history and into the future. This is a small, easy-to-read, much-needed book about a greatly misunderstood topic. "God's Plan for Israel" is an excellent, balanced book explaining God's mercy, grace, and faithfulness to the Jews and Gentiles. Kreloff, a saved Jew, shows how clearly the Scriptures distinguish between the church and Israel. Paperback: 112 pages Loizeaux Brothers; (1995) ISBN: 0872134687.

Internet Sources

Ancient Canaan Unit
Description: An excellent site describing the culture, daily life, geography, government, social life, and industry of ancient Canaan from The William Penn Charter School.

Canaan: The Promised Land
Description: Article from BibleTutor.com.

Into the Land of Canaan
Description: Article from Antiquities Online. Includes an explanation of Canaan before the arrival of the Hebrews.

Canaan
Description: Encyclopedia article from Britannica.com.

Step 3 Expand

Activity 1: Add to Your Time Line Book
Add Abraham entry into Canaan to your Time Line Book.

Activity 2: Copy Passages
Copy (by hand or typing) two or more paragraphs from your research. Or have someone dictate the passage to you. Younger students can copy one or two sentences or narrate (tell back) what has been learned.

Activity 3: Make a Felt Map
You will need:
1. One large piece of dark colored felt (at least 8.5x11).
2. Velcro dots
3. Three or four of felt squares in red, yellow, and white (felt squares are usually sold by pieces 9 X 12 inches).
4. Scissors.
5. Hole punch (optional).

Resources recommended in ◆several lessons, ★ several units, ● other HOW Units. ☛ Key Resource (see beginning of unit or page 32).

Heart of Wisdom Publishing   95

Use the map at http://heartofwisdom.com/israelmap.htm as a pattern or trace a map from an atlas. If possible take it to a copy center and blown up two to four times the size. Cut out the pattern of a dark colored large piece of felt. Use a Bible atlas or links from our site to find Bible maps of this area.

As you complete lessons in the Ancient History units or during Bible study, make "markers" out of the smaller pieces of felt. Mark rivers and bodies of water (the Jordan River, the Sea of Galilee, the Dead Sea, the Mediterranean Sea)with a fine point felt pin. Mark th enames of cities on small pieces of felt. Use velcro dots to hold the felt pieces on to the felt (the felt will "stick on" but the velcro is much sturdier). As you learn about Israel, your "markers" can change to be the name of cities, events, or people. Keep your felt map and "markers" rolled up in a storage container close to your study area. Consider purchasing or making a flannel board to display your map. Flannal boards are avialble at various stores and at http://www.thefeltsource.com.

Activity 4: Contrast and Compare
Make a contrast and compare graphic (see page 26) to compare the first entry into Canaan by Abraham with the Hebrews entering Canaan under Joshua.

Activity 5: Write an Essay
Write a traditional essay about the Canaanites, and include what they looked like, who and how they worshiped, marriage customs, approximate population, government, basic laws, what they used for money, entertainment, clothing, food, what their homes were like, their educational system and written language, the roles of men and women, their weapons and scientific achievements, transportation, agriculture, etc. Refer to "Structure of the Traditional Essay" and "Sample of a Traditional Essay" in *Writers INC*, or "How to Write an Essay."

Step 4 Excel

Share what you have learned with your family. Discuss how the Canaanite's religion affected the other areas of their society. For example, how did their beliefs affect laws, government, and other aspects of their daily lives? Discuss how you think Christianity affects or has affected your society. Take notes on your discussion. When the discussion is finished, review your notes. Put your notes in your portfolio.

Footnotes
1. Wagner, Clarence H. Jr. 12 Keys To Understanding Israel In The Bible.
    <http://www.bridgesforpeace.com/publications/teaching/Article-44.html>
2. Easton, Entry for "Canaan" online. Cited 2000.. Available from World Wide Web:
    <http://bible.crosswalk.com/Dictionaries/EastonsBibleDictionary/ebd.cgi?number=T703>
3. Southern Nazarene University, online. Cited 2000.. Available from World Wide Web: <http://home.snu.edu/~hculbert.fs>

Genesis Reveals the Messiah

Step 1 Excite

The Bible is composed of 66 books by many authors, over a period of many centuries, yet it is one book, in its content, message, and theme. That theme is salvation through Jesus Christ. In the first book of the Bible, Genesis, God speaks creation into existence. The heaven, earth, oceans, plants, birds and fish, animals and humans are created by the spoken Word of God. Soon, corruption came into the world and enslaved man into sin.

The book of John parallels the first chapter of Genesis by opening with a portrayal of God speaking salvation into existence. *In the beginning was the Word, and the Word was with God, and the Word was God. The same was in the beginning with God. All things were made by him; and without him was not any thing made that was made.* (John 1:1-3). God's Word becomes human in the person of Jesus Christ the Messiah. Jesus is the last Adam (1 Cor. 15:45), and He came to earth to save the "generations of Adam." He provides forgiveness and judgment for the broken and fallen. Jesus breaks the power of canceled sin and sets the prisoner free.

During this unit you have seen how the stories in Genesis chapters 1-11 (Adam, Abel, the Flood, Tower of Babel, call of Abram) point to Christ. In this lesson you will review the law of Bible interpretation that is best summed up in the following words by an unknown poet:

> The New is in the Old contained; the Old is in the New explained.
> The New is in the Old concealed, the Old is in the New revealed;
> The New is in the Old enfolded; the Old is in the New unfolded!"

Step 2 Examine

In Jewish society genealogies were very important. A person's ancestry was his identity and status. Bible prophecy foretold that the Messiah would have to meet several requirements; one being the Messiah would be a descendant of Abraham. Matthew, a Jewish believer, begins his story of Christ with the genealogy of Christ. The genealogy in Matthew proves that Jesus comes from the covenant line. There are 16 references to the Old Testament in the first two chapters of Matthew. Matthew wanted to show the prophecies that the Jesus he described was indeed the Messiah Israel had been expecting. Jesus emerges from Israel and fulfills the promise of a Messianic King.

There are hundreds of prophecies about Jesus in the Old Testament. Every detail of Jesus' life is spelled out in advance- from His birth in Bethlehem to His death on the cross. Review how Jesus is revealed in the first 12 chapters of Genesis by reading the text in the following chart.

Research this topic. Use any resource (an encyclopedia, nonfiction book, or the Internet). We recommend the following:

●─Key Resource (see beginning of unit or page 32). Resources recommended elsewhere in this ◆unit, ★book, ●HOW Unit Studies.

Genesis Story	How the Story Reveals Christ
Creation	Genesis begins with the Creation story revealing Jesus *with God All things were made through Him* (John 1:1-3; 1 Cor. 8:6). God rested on the Sabbath—Jesus is Lord of the Sabbath (Luke 6:5)
Adam	Adam was given dominion over all. *All authority has been given to things on earth* (Gen. 1:26,28) *Me* [Jesus] *in heaven and on earth.* (Matt. 28:18). *Far above all principality and might and dominion* (Eph. 1:21).
The Serpent	Adam and Eve were tempted by the Serpent, Satan. Satan is our first enemy in the history of our salvation, he tempted Christ when he was praying and fasting and doing penance in the desert. Jesus came into the world to conquer Satan and to free us from Sin.
The Fall	Adam and Eve's sin corrupted mankind. God Himself makes garments of animal skins to cover the sin and nakedness of His children (Gen 3:21). For the first time spilling innocent blood is needed for the consequence of sin. Jesus is the last Adam (1 Cor. 15:21-22, 45). God sent Christ to be atonement for all sin. *For as by one man's disobedience many were made sinners, so by the obedience of one shall many be made righteous. Moreover the law entered, that the offence might abound. But where sin abounded, grace did much more abound: That as sin hath reigned unto death, even so might grace reign through righteousness unto eternal life by Jesus Christ our Lord.* (Romans 5:19-6:1). Sin and death are destroyed by Christ (Rom. 6:6-9, 1 Cor. 15:26).
Cain and Abel	Abel the shepherd brings a blood offering (Possibly a lamb) that was accepted by God. Jesus Christ is the *lamb of God which taketh away the sin of the world.*(John 1:29; Isa. 53:7; Matt. 26:53, 54; Luke 23:9). In contrast Cain offered fruit of his own work (Hebrews 11:4). God illustrates the awesome power of the sacrificed Lamb. One lamb saves a man, then a household, then a nation, and finally is available through the Lamb of God for the whole world.
Noah and the Flood	The story of the Flood is a picture of salvation by grace. Noah's work brings blessing to all creation is seen from the fact that the animals and birds were also preserved in the ark. *And God remembered Noah, and every living thing, and all the cattle that was with him in the ark* (Genesis 8:1) So, too, the work of Christ shall yet bring blessing to the beasts of the field. At His return to the earth *the creation itself also shall be delivered from the bondage of corruption into the glorious liberty of the children of God* (Rom. 8:21).
Tower of Babel	Man's pride and arrogance were revealed in the story of the Tower of Babel. God confused their languages, they were not able to understand each other, then he and dispersed them around the world. During Pentecost, all understood each other, with the language of love, through Christ.
Call of Abram	Abram believed God. He left everything and went out of his country without knowing where, "*God will provide*" (Ro.4:16, Ge.22:8). God promised Abraham, *Of your descendants, the Messiah will be born, that's why all the nations will be blessed through you...* promise that will be repeated 3 times to him... and it was fulfilled in Mat.1:1.

Underlined text refers to Internet link at http://Homeschool-Books.com

Books

Messianic Christology ★
See description in the Messiah Resources Section.

Knowing Jesus Through the Old Testament ★
See description in the Messiah Resources Section.

The Miracle of the Scarlet Thread by Richard Booker
This is one of the most profound books of the blood of the Messiah ever written! Booker explains how the First and Second Testaments are woven together by the *scarlet thread of the blood covenant* to tell one complete story through the entire Bible. Subjects explained are the blood covenant ritual, the covenant with Abraham, in the tabernacle, in the sacrifices, in the High Priest and Passover. (December 1988) Destiny Image; ISBN: 0914903268.

Internet Sources

Jesus Christ in Genesis
Description: Article from Knowing God Through Genesis.

Fulfilled Messianic Prophecies from Genesis
Description: Several tables with prophecy, fulfillment, and commentary.

Does the New Testament Support Genesis 1-11?
Description: The early chapters of Genesis were frequently referred to by every New Testament writer and Jesus Christ Himself. This site lists sixty-eight direct references in the New Testament that refer back to these foundational chapters of Genesis. (Based in part on the original work of Dr. Henry M. Morris as contained in his book *The Remarkable Birth of Planet Earth*.

Step 3: Expand

Complete one or more of the following activities:

Activity 1: Make a Chart
Create a visual chart. Make either a "Types of Christ from Genesis" chart or a "Prophecies of Christ in Genesis" chart. Include columns showing the similarities and Bible references.

Activity 2 Match the Story
Match the Bible stories in Genesis with the appropriate text on the next page. Look up the Bible verses for hints.

Bible Story	Genesis
1. Creation: God's spoke Creation into existence.	1:1
2. Adam: First man, given dominion over Creation	1:28
3. Eve: First woman, first in the transgression.	3:15
4. Satan: An angel from heaven fell from pride.	
5. The Fall: Corrupted man and placed all mankind into the bondage of sin.	3:1-21
6. Cain and Abel: God accepts the blood sacrifice as temporary atonement for sin.	4:8-10
7. Flood and Rainbow: Salvation from judgement and given a promise.	9:13-15
8. Tower of Babel: Man without God equals confusion.	11:9
9. Promises to Abraham: All the nations will be blessed through him.	22:15-19

How Christ Fulfilled	Verses
a. Jesus came to offer salvation from judgement.	John 3:16
b. Through Christ there is unity.	Acts 2:11
c. When we believe in Christ we are adopted into his family and become heirs with Christ.	Gal 3,
d. Christ came to redeem and set the prisoner free.	GAl 3:13
d. Jesus Christ blood takes away the sin of the world.	Luke 22:20; Heb 9:22; 12:24,
e. Christ is ruler over heaven and on earth.	Romans 5:14; 1Co 15:45
f. Christ was present and active with this was spoken into existence. Christ is the Word in human form.	John 1:1
g. God grace is magnified as the promise of salvation is from the seed of this one.	Luke 3
h. Jesus came into he world to conquer him.	1John 3:8

Step 4 Excel

Share how Genesis reveals Jesus with a friend or family member. Add the chart to your portfolio.

Footnotes
1. Keathley, J. Hampton III. (1998). "Concise Old Testament Survey," Biblical Studies Foundation, <http://www.bible.org/docs/ot/survey/toc.htm> (Accessed April 2000)
2. Egner, David. (1991). "Knowing God Through Genesis," RBC Ministries, <http://www.gospelcom.net/rbc/ds/sb111/>

Mesopotamia Unit

Unit Overview

Mesopotamia Overview 102

Mesopotamia Objectives 103

Mesopotamia Vocabulary 104

Mesopotamia Time Line 105

Mesopotamia Resources 106

Mesopotamia Lessons

Cradle of Civilization 111

Ancient Civilizations and the Bible .116

Sumer and Akkad (3500–2000) 129

Cuneiform 134

Assyria (1200–612) 137

Babylonia (625–536) 143

Hanging Gardens of Babylon 150

Hammurabi Code 153

Persia (612–330) 156

Art in Mesopotamia 161

Daily Life in Mesopotamia 164

Religion in Mesopotamia 168

Science and Technology 170

Mesopotamia Overview

This book is an examination of the effects that Mesopotamia had on the geography and history of the Old Testament World and the influence that the Old Testament world had on Mesopotamia. During this unit you will study the rise of different early civilizations as they formed in the heart of the ancient world in and around the Holy Land (Israel, originally Canaan) in the area known as the Fertile Crescent. The history of the Bible lands and people was greatly influenced by the geographical environment (climate, topography, and geopolitical relationships with neighboring areas). In order to properly understand the biblical periods, we must examine the beginnings of culture in the ancient Near East.

The foundation of the early civilizations was laid in the two lands of the great rivers, Mesopotamia and Egypt. Tracing the influence of Mesopotamia to and from its neighbors is complex. The span of time is enormous, the occasions and opportunities quite varied. The available research differs depending on the author's world view. Bible scholars focus on the Hebrews and search for influence upon the Assyrian and Babylonian occupation of the Promised Land in the eighth through sixth centuries B.C., while classical scholars pick out the orientalizing period of the eighth through seventh centuries B.C. The goal of this unit is to learn about the geography and lifestyles of the Hebrews and their neighbors in the Old Testament world.

One of the major problems in understanding the Scriptures is that of pinning the biblical events down in time and space. Bible geography and history are so deeply interwoven that neither can be fully understood without the help of the other. There is a good deal more to geography than just finding a specific place on a map or globe. Geography involves understanding what the location is like, how it differs from other places, and how the people who reside there interact with their environment.

The last unit flowed chronologically from Adam to Abraham. This unit's first focus is geographical history occurring in the Fertile Crescent geographical area (see the time line on the next page) spanning the time from Abraham all the way to Esther and the Sumerian, Babylonian, Assyrian, and Persian civilizations of Mesopotamia. Later units will go back to more of a detailed chronological study about the systems developed in Egypt and Israel.

As you move through this unit, continue to read your Bible chronologically during your family Bible time as God leads. The background you learn here will help you immensely with future Bible studies. Spend time each day in prayer before you begin your studies.

Page Numbers

The Narrated Bible

NOTE: The Bible symbols in the lessons in this unit might show dozens and even hundreds of pages. This does not mean you have to read them. The page numbers are listed to show you the events that occurred during the period discussed in the lesson.

Underlined text refers to Internet link at http://Homeschool-Books.com

Bible Timeline

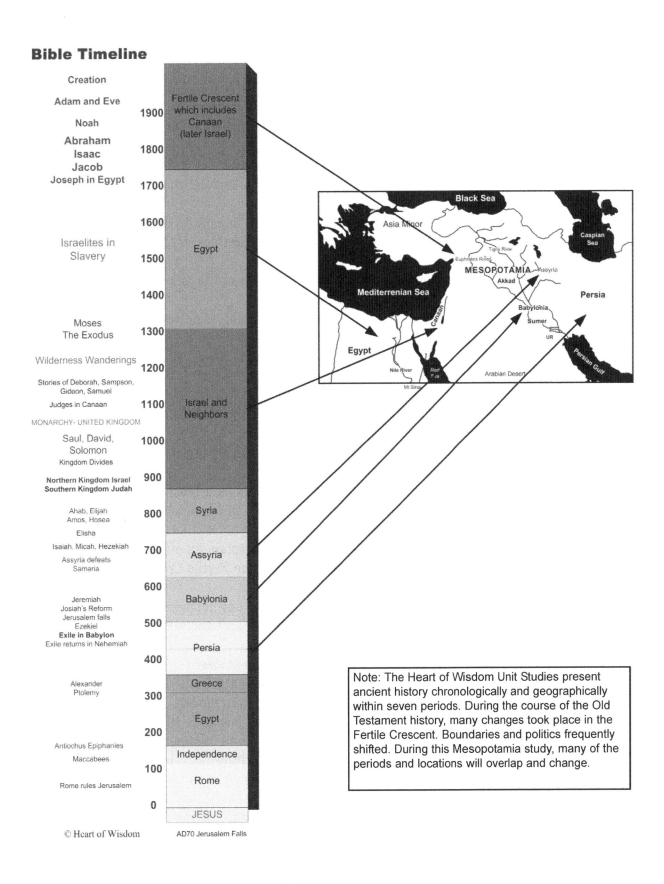

Creation

Adam and Eve

Noah

Abraham
Isaac
Jacob
Joseph in Egypt

Israelites in Slavery

Moses
The Exodus

Wilderness Wanderings

Stories of Deborah, Sampson, Gideon, Samuel

Judges in Canaan

MONARCHY- UNITED KINGDOM

Saul, David, Solomon

Kingdom Divides

Northern Kingdom Israel
Southern Kingdom Judah

Ahab, Elijah
Amos, Hosea

Elisha

Isaiah, Micah, Hezekiah

Assyria defeats Samaria

Jeremiah
Josiah's Reform
Jerusalem falls
Ezekiel
Exile in Babylon
Exile returns in Nehemiah

Alexander
Ptolemy

Antiochus Epiphanies

Maccabees

Rome rules Jerusalem

1900 Fertile Crescent which includes Canaan (later Israel)

1800

1700

1600

1500 Egypt

1400

1300

1200

1100 Israel and Neighbors

1000

900

800 Syria

700 Assyria

600 Babylonia

500

400 Persia

300 Greece

200 Egypt

100 Independence

Rome

0

JESUS

© Heart of Wisdom   AD70 Jerusalem Falls

Black Sea

Asia Minor

Caspian Sea

Tigris River

Euphrates River

MESOPOTAMIA   Assyria

Akkad

Mediterrenian Sea

Persia

Babylonia

Sumer

Canaan

UR

Egypt

Nile River   Red Sea   Arabian Desert

Persian Gulf

Mt Sinai

Note: The Heart of Wisdom Unit Studies present ancient history chronologically and geographically within seven periods. During the course of the Old Testament history, many changes took place in the Fertile Crescent. Boundaries and politics frequently shifted. During this Mesopotamia study, many of the periods and locations will overlap and change.

Resources recommended in ◆several lessons, ★ several units, ▯➡other HOW Units. ●—Key Resource (see beginning of unit or page 32).

Mesopotamia Objectives

Upon completion of this unit your student should:

- Understand that Mesopotamia was an integral part of the BIble landscape in many periods
- Understand that Mesopotamia was Abraham's homeland
- Understand that the Mesopotamian kings from Assyria and Babylon appear frequently in the Bible
- Understand that the Jewish captives spent many years in exile in Babylon
- Understand that Mesopotamia gave birth to many civilizations, including the Sumerian, Akkadian, Babylonian, and Assyrian
- Be able to cite the inventions and general contributions of the Mesopotamians to Western civilization and world culture in general
- Be able to describe the benefits and difficulties of locating societies and establishing them in the Tigris-Euphrates Valley
- Appreciate the importance of agriculture to early civilizations
- Be able to relate the historic origin of various crops
- Be able to explain the evolution of Sumerian writing
- Be able to describe the state of agriculture before the age of metals
- Understand the effects of widespread agriculture in early history
- Be able to explain the process by which the first civilization was created
- Be able to describe life in the early Sumerian city-states
- Be able to discuss the economy, society, and polity of ancient Mesopotamia
- Be able to evaluate the technological and intellectual achievements of the Sumerians
- Understand the importance of laws
- Be able to relate the story of the Tower of Babel and explain its effect on today's world
- Know the location and understand the importance of the Fertile Crescent
- Understand the importance of writing
- Recognize the influence of environment upon religious development
- Recognize the influence of environment upon religious architecture
- Be familiar with ancient views of the after-life
- Have knowledge of the origins and development of city-states
- Have knowledge of the evolution of executive government
- Understand the development of an empire on the Assyrian model
- Understand the creation of the world's first recognized law code (Hammurabi)
- Recognize the river system of the Tigris-Euphrates and its influence upon survival
- Be familiar with the evolution and use of cuneiform writing
- Know the origins of Western literature through various sources (Book of Job, Flood story)
- Recognize the advances made in the technology of warfare by the Assyrians

Underlined text refers to Internet link at http://Homeschool-Books.com

Mesopotamia Vocabulary

See Vocabulary Instructions on page 22.

cereal zones	Gilgamesh	pastoralism	
			Sumerians
city-state	hunter-gatherer	plateau	
			surplus
civilization	hydraulic society	priest-king	
			swidden
Code of Hammurabi	irrigate	raised-field farming	
			technology
Cradle of Civilization	Ishtar	Sargon I	
			terrace agriculture
conquer	merchant	Sargoni	
			tributary
drought	Mesoamerica	scribe	
			Tigris and Euphrates
edubba	Mesopotamia	Semitic	
			urban
emperor	monarchy	silt	
			ziggurat
empire	monotheism	social class	
Fertile Crescent	Neolithic Revolution	Stela of the Vultures	
fisherfolk	nomad		
		stylus	

Resources recommended in ◆several lessons, ★ several units, ▯◆other HOW Units. ◉━Key Resource (see beginning of unit or page 32).

Heart of Wisdom Publishing   105

Mesopotamia Time Line

	Sumerians settle on banks of Euphrates.	Seth
	Democratic assemblies develop into hereditary monarchies.	Noah
	Kish - leading Sumerian city.	Shem, Ham, and Japheth
	Gilgamesh, hero of Sumerian legends, reigns as king of Erech.	
	Lugalannemudu of Abab unites city-states.	Methuselah dies at age 969.
	Ur-Nammu founds Ur's 3rd dynasty.	
1900	Amorites from Syrian desert conquer Sumer.	Abram and Sarai
1800	Hammurabi ascends Babylonian throne.	Joseph in Egypt
1700	Hammurabi brings most of Mesopotamia under his control.	
1600	Hittite invasion from Turkey ends Hammurabi's dynasty.	
1500	Assyria conquered by Hurrians from Anatolia.	
1400	Kurigalzu assumes Babylonian throne.	
1200	Nebuchadnezzar I expels Elamites.	Moses, the Exodus, Joshua
1100	King Tiglath-Pileser I leads Assyria to new era of power.	
1000	Assyrian empire shattered by Aramaean and Zagros tribes.	Saul, David, Solomon
960		Solomon builds the Temple.
800	Tiglath-Pileser II creates great empire.	
700	Assurbanipal extends empire from Nile to Caucasus Mountains. Chaldeans and Iranian Medes overrun Assyria - Neo-Babylonian empire.	Hezekiah develops water supply at Siloam.
600		Nebuchadnezzar captures and destroys Jerusalem, exiles Jews to Babylon.
500	Cyrus the Great, Persian statesman, conquers Babylon.	
400		Nehemiah rebuilds Jerusalem and its walls.
		Persians capture Jerusalem.

All Dates are Approximate

Mesopotamia Resources

The ❶ symbol indicates a resource appropriate for grades 4-12 or family read-aloud. All other books are appropriate for young adults or adults.

Main Resources Suggested in this Unit

Encyclopedia of the Bible (Nelson's Illustrated)☞ ♥
The section on People and Empires is excellent for this Mesopotamia unit. Includes lavish illustrations, and hundreds of color photographs, maps, and charts. See description in the "Key Resources" section beginning on page 32.

Exploring Ancient Cities of the Bible by Michael Carroll ☞ ♥
Investigate stories and mysteries that you've always wondered about through *Exploring Ancient Cities of the Bible*. The mysteries and well-researched answers, the graphic photos and penetrating paintings, the fun facts and sidebars all inform and captivate readers, pressing them toward a better understanding of the history that changed the world. This book will make the Bible come alive and will reveal God's awesome creative power. Hardcover - 48 pages (2001) Cook Communications; ISBN: 0781436958.

First Civilizations (Cultural Atlas for Young People) by Erica C.D. Hunter, Ph.D. and Gillian Evans (Editor) ♦
This volume focuses on the earliest civilizations of Mesopotamia and the ancient Near East, beginning with the region's earliest nomads, following the growth of warring city-states and empires, and culminating with Drain's mighty Persian Empire and its destruction by Alexander the Great in 331 B.C. 220 full-color illustrations and maps. 96 Pages (1994) ISBN: 0816029768.

The Holman Bible Atlas ♥
See description in the "Key Resources" section beginning on page 32.

Mesopotamia and the Fertile Crescent (Looking Back) by Mavis Pilbeam ♦
Focusing on particular periods in four areas of the world, these titles provide broad introductions to each region. Addresses many aspects of the lives of each region's diverse inhabitants, including government, laws, food, science and technology, arts and crafts, religion, and the impact of war on everyday life. Includes maps and attractive color photos. Library Binding - 64 pages (1999) Raintree/Steck Vaughn; ISBN: 081725434X. Reading level: Young adult.

The Student Bible Atlas ♥
See description in the "Key Resources" section beginning on page 32.

Resources recommended in ♦several lessons, ★ several units, ❐♥ other HOW Units. ☞━Key Resource (see beginning of unit or page 32).

Usborne Book of the Ancient World ❤
See description in the "Key Resources" section beginning on page 32.

The Victor Journey through the Bible ●—❤
See description in the "Key Resources" section beginning on page 32.

Alternative Resources

Ancient Civilizations (Exploring History) by Philip Brooks ★
See description in the "Alternative Resources Recommended in Several Units" section beginning on page 37.

Ancient Mesopotamia (Let's See Library Ancient Civilizations) by Robert B. Noyed, Cynthia Fitterer Klingel
Easy-to-understand text and colorful photos explore this ancient civilization. Includes a table of contents, glossary, and index. School & Library Binding - 24 pages (September 2002) Compass Point Books; ISBN: 0756502942. Reading level: Ages 4-8 (grades 1-3).

The Babylonians by Elaine Landau
From the Cradles of Civilization series. Topics covered include daily life and customs of different classes; social roles; notable rulers and their accomplishments; advances made in law, the arts, agriculture, and sciences; and factors leading to the decline of the empire. Large type, open pages, and frequent use of maps, full-color and black-and-white photographs and illustrations of artifacts and architecture enhance the readability. (September 1997) Millbrook Pr; ISBN: 0761302166. Reading level: Ages 9-12.

Daily Life in Ancient Mesopotamia by Karen Rhea Nemet-Nejat ◆
"Readers will discover fascinating details about the lives of these people from the society where writing began—taken from the ancients' own quotations and descriptions. A wealth of information is provided on such varied topics as: education; literature; mathematics and science; city vs. country life; family life; and religion. Similarities between daily life in ancient Mesopotamia and modern-day Iraq are also discussed. Beautifully illustrated, this easy-to-use reference contains a timeline and an historical overview to aid student research." —review by *The Historian*. Hardcover (September 1998) Greenwood Publishing Group; ISBN: 0313294976.

God King: A Story in the Days of King Hezekiah by Joanne Williamson
This novel is inspired by research on the historical King Taharka and his period. By the author of the best-selling *Hittite Warrior*, carries the reader back to Ancient Egypt and to the biblical Jerusalem. Around 701 B.C. Egypt is being ruled by the Kushite dynasty. Young Prince Taharka, a very minor royal son, succeeds

unexpectedly to the throne of Kush and Egypt -- a "divine" rulership. He begins to find his way. . .until a treacherous plot pushes him into sudden exile and into the hands of Amos, an emissary of King Hezekiah seeking help for Judea from the Egyptians against the Assyrians. Far from home, near Jerusalem, and found out in his disguise as a medical assistant, Taharka encounters two kings in conflict. One is the mighty Assyrian, Sennacherib, promising alliance; the other is Hezekiah, the Jew who trusts in Yahweh. Taharka must choose with whom to live or die. Bethlehem Books (2002) Reading level: Young Adult. ISBN: 1883937736. See more on books in this series in the Ancient Israel unit.

Mesopotamia (Cultures of the Past, Group 4) by Pamela F. Service ◆ The "Cultures of the Past" series is hallmarked by excellent writing, colorful graphics, well-chosen pictures, and exceptional design work, showing what can be done within the confines of the series format. In these two volumes, the authors not only provide a survey of the ancient cultures but also put them within a historical context. These tightly focused books provide historical overviews of each ancient society and discuss their religious beliefs and cultural achievements. Excerpts from sacred books, charts comparing the childhood experiences for boys and girls living in these eras, and plentiful color reproductions enhance reader interest. Each volume concludes with a chapter exploring the enduring legacies of the cultures. Library Binding - 80 pages (October 1998) Marshall Cavendish Corp.; ISBN: 0761403019. Reading level: Ages 9-12.

Mesopotamia: The Mighty Kings (The Lost Civilizations Collections) by Time Life
Explores the great empires that flourished during the first and second centuries B.C. in Mesopotamia. Includes the rise of Babylonia in the south, Assyria in the north, and the renaissance of Babylon before it fell to the Persians in 539 B.C. Time Life; (1999) ISBN: 0809490412.

Science in Ancient Mesopotamia (Science of the Past) by Carol Moss
Describes the enormous accomplishments of the Sumerians and Babylonians of ancient Mesopotamia in every scientific area, a heritage which affects our own everyday lives. Many of the clay tablets the ancient Mesopotamians used to record their observations still exist today. By deciphering the text, we know that they were the first group of people to study the human body, use a system of weights and measures, and classify plants and animals. They could also perform complex mathematical calculations, and used a variety of herbal remedies. School & Library Binding - 64 pages Revised edition (September 1998) Franklin Watts, Incorporated; ISBN: 0531203646. Appropriate for the middle grades, but the reading level is about 9th to 12th grade.

Resources recommended in ◆several lessons, ★ several units, ▣▸other HOW Units. ●━Key Resource (see beginning of unit or page 32).

Heart of Wisdom Publishing   109

Usborne First Civilizations

A brilliant, colorful overview of world history from prehistoric times to the early 20th century. Prepared with the help of experts in each period, each book has many illustrations which provide an attractive and stimulating starting point for each subject. Assumes evolution. (June 1978) E D C Publications; ISBN: 0860201384. Reading Level: Ages 8-12. Interest level: Ages 8-16.

Videos

The Dig

Seventh-grade teacher Richard Edwardson manufactures artifacts and archaeological sites and teaches his students excavation techniques. *Archaeology Magazine* called this video an "impressive testimony to an impressive teacher." National Film Board of Canada (1989) VHS and 16mm, 22 min., color. Available to rent from Indiana University, Audio Visual Center; Franklin Hall; Bloomington, Indiana 47405-5901. Call 1 (800) 552-8260.

Lost Civilizations Collection: Mesopotamia: Return to Eden

Join archaeologist unearthing physical clues to the truth behind the biblical stories of Noah and his Ark, the Great Flood, the Tower of Babel, and more. Embark on an extraordinary, thought-provoking "Return to Eden," as you descend through time, layer by layer, from the Jewish Exodus into Babylon to the barbaric reign of the fearsome Assyrians, to the dawn of civilization itself amid the first cities of ancient Sumer. Witness the invention of writing, the wheel, and the concept of law. Time Life Lost Civilizations Collection. Buyindies 1-877-889-7477.

Magazines

Calliope: World History Magazine for Young People (Mesopotamia Issue)

This excellent issue contains information and activities, all written to the level of the student, dealing with a variety of Mesopotamian topics. Especially useful for studying farming; the cities of Ur and Babylon; and the empires of Sargon the Great, the Assyrians, and the Babylonians. Vol. 4, no. 1. Peterborough, New Hampshire: Cobblestone Publishing, Inc., September/October 1993.

Calliope: World History Magazine for Young People (Epic Heroes Issue)

The Mesopotamian hero Gilgamesh is featured in this excellent issue, which also includes information and activities on heroes from other ancient cultures. Vol. 1, no. 3. Peterborough, New Hampshire: Cobblestone Publishing, Inc., January/February 1991.

The Cradle of Civilization HI0201

Step 1 Excite

<History is His Story>

What state do you live in? Have you ever talked to someone from another state or city and compared differences? What about someone from another country? Do you know where New York City and Washington, D.C. are located? Do you know the major Interstate nearest your home?

Set a timer for ten minutes and role play. Someone in your family should pretend they are from another country (they happen to speak English but they have never been to America). Act as if you are describing the area you in which you live to that person. Limit your description to a ten-square-mile area from your home. Do not mention your state or the United States. When your time is up, switch roles and change sides.

How well could you explain so that the other person understood America based on your description? What about the governmental system? the religions? the customs? the geography? To truly understand a person, you need to look at the big picture.

You are about to study the very first civilizations of the world. The regions of Mesopotamia, Egypt (the Nile Valley), and the Indus Valley are the three main areas for studying how people of the world first came together to create civilizations and empires. The history curricula of American public schools focuses on how the civilizations began and the important contributions made by the Mesopotamians. This unit will include the beginnings of civilizations and contributions, but with a focus on Bible location and events.

Pay close attention to the maps and time line in this unit. These visual graphs will help you understand the chronology of Bible events and the geographical locations within the rise of the ancient civilizations. You'll get a grasp of the ancient Near East cultures, learning what they tell us of the days in which Bible stories were written and of the events and conditions which they relate or reflect. By the time you finish this unit , you will have completed several maps, and you should be able to draw a map of the Fertile Crescent area, as well as understand the major events in this time period without any references.

Step 2 Examine

Mesopotamia is called the Cradle of Civilization. "Mesopotamia," "the country between the two rivers," is the name given by the ancient Greeks and Romans to the region between the Euphrates and the Tigris rivers (Genesis 24:10).

Resources recommended in ◆several lessons, ★ several units, ▷ other HOW Units. ●— Key Resource (see beginning of unit or page 32).

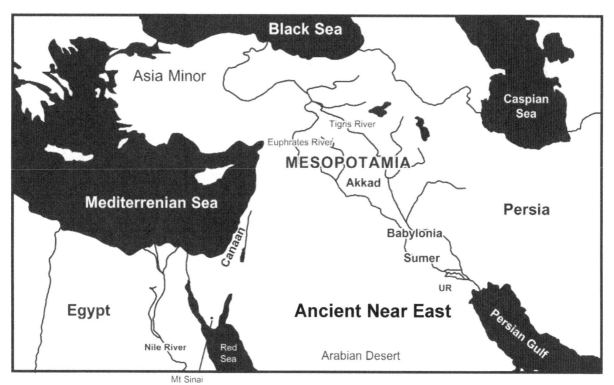

Mesopotamia is a large part of the Fertile Crescent, a crescent-shaped area stretching from the Mediterranean Sea to the Persian Gulf, through the Tigris and Euphrates valley. It includes all of Mesopotamia, present-day Iraq, Israel, Lebanon, Syria, and western Iran. It is called the "Fertile Crescent" because it is shaped like a crescent moon and because of the rich, fertile soil found in the region.

The Fertile Crescent gave birth to, and sustained, many great civilizations, including those of the Assyrian, Sumerians, Canaanites, Philistines, Phoenicians/Carthaginians, Hyksos, Akkadians, Hittites, Hurrians, Mitanni, Kassites, Aramaeans, Amorites, Seleucids, Nabateans, Lakhmids, Ghassanids, Ummayyads, and Abbasids. Lagash, Ur, Eredu, and Uruk were the main cities of Sumer. Kish and Babylon were the major cities of Babylonia. The city of Ur was the capital of the Mesopotamian civilization.

The fertile Mesopotamian river valleys and plains were desirable for settlement, but this was the very thing that made Mesopotamia susceptible to attack. The richness of this area attracted neighboring peoples who were ready and willing to become the occupants of this area. But first they had to take it from those already living there. The early Mesopotamian states needed self-defense as well as irrigation; this led them to build walled settlements for protection and canals for irrigation.

Mesopotamia was the birthplace of the varied civilizations that developed writing, schools, libraries, and written law codes. The Sumerians, Akkadians, Chaldeans, Hittites, Babylonians, Israelites, Phoenicians, Lydians, Assyrian, and Persians established the founda-

Underlined text refers to Internet link at http://Homeschool-Books.com

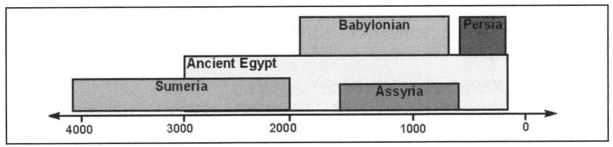

tions for future civilizations. Their contributions included brick cities, the wheel, glass, the sail, coinage, calendars, bronze, iron, monotheism, epic poetry, mathematics, farming, and irrigation.

Each Mesopotamian city-state was like a separate country. The ancient names of its cities continue in the world today: Ur of the Chaldees, Babylon, and Nineveh. The Sumerians first lived in southern Mesopotamia and Uruk (biblical Erech). The Babylonians came after them, and for a time Babylon was the center of the world. For the Assyrians, Ashur was their most ancient capital, Nineveh their royal residence, and Harran their final seat of royalty.

These civilizations that developed between the Tigris and Euphrates rivers are now Iraq and Kuwait. The names of countries and cities change with the empires that move in and out, but the names of the rivers stay the same. In the middle of Iraq lie the ruins of Nebuchadnezzar's Hanging Gardens of Babylon (one of the seven wonders of the ancient world).

Mesopotamia had four dominant forces at different times throughout its history: the Sumerians, the Babylonians, the Assyrians, and the Persians. Each influenced the Greek and Roman civilizations that followed them.

Browse through library books and Web sites to find maps of this time period in the ancient Near East. As you go through the books and sites, take notes of things you would like to learn about. Use any resource from the "Mesopotamia Resources" section, or an encyclopedia, non-fiction book, historical novel, or the Internet.

Books

The Victor Journey through the Bible ⊙—♥
Read: Skim stories and view maps on pages 18-54.

Encyclopedia of the Bible (Nelson's Illustrated) ⊙— ♥
Skim Part 2 "People and Empires" (50-67).

Exploring Ancient Cities of the Bible ♥
Read: "Mesopotamia: Home of the Empires" (18-20).

Resources recommended in ♦several lessons, ★ several units, ◻♦other HOW Units. ⊙—Key Resource (see beginning of unit or page 32).

Heart of Wisdom Publishing   113

First Civilizations (Cultural Atlas for Young People) ◆
Read: "Introduction" (4-5); "Table of Dates" (6-7). Browse through "Part 2: Kingdoms and Empires" (52-91).

Mesopotamia and the Fertile Crescent ◆
Read: "Introduction" (6-8); "From Hunters to Farmers" (9-15) (ignore dates); "From Villages to Empires" (15-25).

Internet Sources

Ancient Mesopotamia
Description: A seventh-grade World History/World Geography unit designed to be used by both students and teachers.

The Fertile Crescent - Cradle of Nine Civilizations
Description: An overview of the Fertile Crescent by high-school teacher Larry Larsen. Includes quizzes and information on the following topics: geography, Sumerians, Akkadians, Babylonians, Hittites, Phoenicians, Hebrews, Assyrian, Chaldeans, and Persians.

Introduction to Mesopotamia
Description: Published for the British History National Curriculum, this site was published to be a resource for primary-school educators who are teaching a unit on ancient Mesopotamia. Includes time line, maps, facts, and more.

Learning Family Studies - Ancient Mesopotamia
Description: The Learning Family founders, the Reisers, share their field trip adventures in Mesopotamia.

Odyssey Online: The Near East
Description: From Emory University, this award-winning educational Web site aimed at middle-school students explores ancient Near Eastern, Egyptian, Greek, and Roman cultures. Includes puzzles, games, and worksheets.

Step 3 Expand

Activity: Make a Map (Do not skip this activity.)
Make a map of the ancient Near East. Trace the one in this unit or print one from our Web site: http://Heartofwisdom.com/maps.htm. You will need several copies of this map for the remaining lessons, as you'll be adding labels and coloring sections to indicate various civilizations.

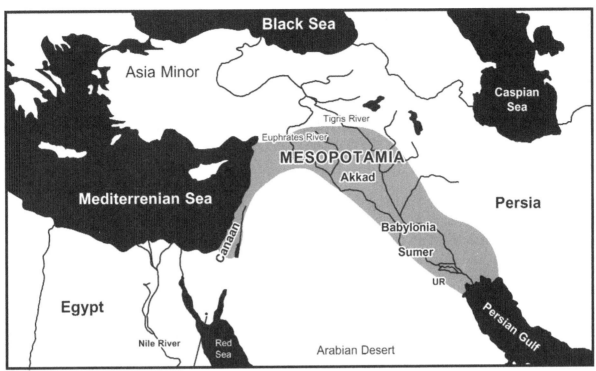

The Fertile Crescent

Memorize the bodies of water and color them blue (use colored pencils so you can view the text through the shading): Tigris River, Euphrates River, Mediterranean Sea, Sea of Galilee, Jordan River, Dead Sea, Nile River, Red Sea, and the Persian Gulf. Memorize and mark each area of land: Mesopotamia, Canaan, Persia, Egypt, Babylon, Assyria, and the city of Ur.

For this lesson you will review the last unit, Adam to Abraham. Place symbols showing the the *approximate* locations (some of the exact locations are not known) of: the Garden of Eden (Gen. 2:10-14), the Tower of Babel (Gen. 2:11-14), where the ark landed (Gen. 8:4), and Abraham's journeys from Ur to Canaan and into Egypt, then back to Canaan.

As you work through the Civilization lessons you will need a map for each lesson. You will color or shade the empires that ruled Canaan and the surrounding areas.

Step 4 Excel

Share your map with a friend or family member. Point out the locations of the major events you learned about in the last unit. Name all the bodies of water on your map. Correct written work to demonstrate correct punctuation and spelling, and effective use of grammar. Add corrected written work or any illustrations to your portfolio.

Resources recommended in ◆several lessons, ★ several units, ▯►other HOW Units. ●—Key Resource (see beginning of unit or page 32).

Ancient Civilizations and the Bible

Step 1 Excite

The Narrated Bible
*See note on page 102

In the last unit you studied the time from Adam to Abraham chronologically. In this unit you'll take a quick look at the big picture of the time period and geography from Abraham to the end of the Old Testament.

Create a time line using index cards (or sticky notes) without looking at any references. Put each major event and each key person listed below on a separate index card. Shuffle the cards and try to line them up in chronological order as best you can.

Aaron	Israel	Passover
Abraham	Israelites' Slavery in Egypt	Rachel
Daniel	Jacob	Rebekah
David	Jericho	Ruth
Elijah	Jonah	Samuel
Elisha	Joseph	Saul
Esau	Joshua	Solomon
Esther	Judah	Tabernacle
Exodus	Judges	Temple
Ezra	Kingdom Divided	Ten Commandments
Gideon	Kingdom United	Twelve Spies
Isaac	Miriam	Wilderness Wanderings
Isaiah	Moses	
Ishmael	Nehemiah	

Step 2 Examine

The history of geography records the gradual development which men made and the results of that progress in enlarged views of life and increased civilization. Understanding the geographical distributions, routes taken, culture, and history is of primary importance to understanding God's Word.

Underlined text refers to Internet link at http://Homeschool-Books.com

The land of the Bible is the stage on which the men and women of the Bible act out their roles. God constructed the set. To really grasp the greatest story of all time, we need to "see" this stage. The Bible is a living book about real people living in real places. Once you understand the locations' relationships to each other, and they become identifiable places in real time periods, you will have a much better understanding. When we understand Bible times and places, we can think about the ways in which people related to each other in Bible days. Where they lived in many ways determined who were their friends and who were their enemies.

Civilization developed in Mesopotamia simultaneously with that in Egypt. The patriarchs, Abraham, Isaac, and Jacob migrated through the Fertile Crescent (Babylonia, Mesopotamia, Syria, Canaan, Egypt). The Fertile Crescent is also the part of the world from which Nimrod sprung, as well as King Hezekiah, King Josiah, the prophet Isaiah, and more. The northern portion of this fertile plateau was the original home of the ancestors of the Hebrews (Gen. 11; Acts 7:2). From this region Isaac obtained his wife Rebekah (Gen. 24:10,15), and here also Jacob sojourned, dreamed of the ladder, (Gen. 28:2-7) and obtained his wives, and here most of his sons were born (Gen. 35:26; 46:15). Abraham led the Hebrews from Mesopotamia to Canaan. Moses led the people from Egypt to Canaan.

In the middle of Babylonia lie the ruins of Nebuchadnezzar's Hanging Gardens of Babylon (Babel), near to the place where Shadrach, Meshach, and Abednego walked in the midst of the fiery furnace. Here Daniel read for Nebuchadnezzar the mysterious handwriting *mene tekel peres* ("counted, weighed, divided") which was written on the wall in the Aramaic or Chaldean language. This is also where, under the later rule of Darius, Daniel sat unharmed in the lions' den.

The Bible events that occurred in this area are numerous and discussed in detail in other units. Here we will take a quick look at some major events to get an understanding of the locations.

This lesson can be a one-hour review lesson or a one-month study. You can stop and expand on each topic with the Bible or *The Victor Journey through the Bible* (see page numbers in Step 2) or focus on the geography of each event. Your decision should be based on your knowledge and your students' knowledge of historical events and geographical locations. The goal is not to get through a certain material in a certain amount of time. The goal is to learn what God wants you to learn. This lesson should at least give you a good overview of the chronological events and geographical areas. Pray and let the Lord lead!

As you read or listen to these events, place your index cards in the proper chronological order. All of the events occurred in or near Canaan (later called Israel). Find each location and person listed in bold and mark the event on your ancient Near East map from the previous lesson.

Resources recommended in ◆several lessons, ★ several units, ◻▸other HOW Units. ●▬Key Resource (see beginning of unit or page 32).

Overview

Abraham and Sarah

In the last unit, you learned that Abram left **Ur** to go to live in **Canaan** (later called Israel). God promised Abraham a son. Sarah, his wife, felt she was too old to have children, so she gave Abraham her handmaiden, Hagar, to have a child for Abraham. Hagar gave birth to Ishmael. A few years later Sarah did become pregnant and gave birth to Isaac. At that time, Abraham was 100 and Sarah was ninety years old.

Isaac

Isaac was born in Canaan. When Isaac became a man, Abraham insisted he marry a girl from Haran (in Mesopotamia) from his father's family, instead of from Canaan (because the Canaanites practiced idolatry). Isaac married Rebekah, his cousin, who gave birth to twins, Jacob and Esau. You will learn more about Isaac in the *Ancient Israel Unit Study.*

Jacob (Israel)

Jacob tricks his father and steals his brother's birthright and blessing. Jacob flees to **Haran** and then serves his uncle for twenty years in order to marry Leah and Rachel. He returns to to Canaan. After wrestling with a spirit, Jacob's name is changed to Israel. Jacob's twelve sons become the Twelve Tribes of Israel. You'll learn more about Jacob in the *Ancient Israel Unit Study.*

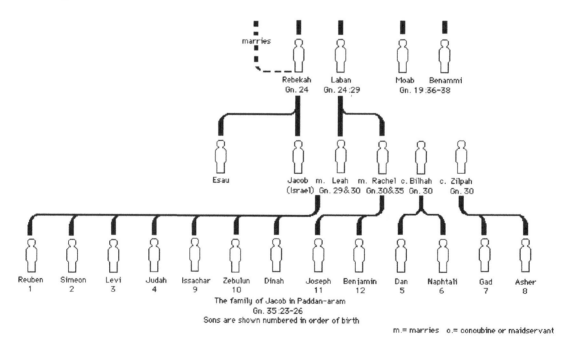

The family of Jacob in Paddan-aram
Gn. 35:23-26
Sons are shown numbered in order of birth

m.= marries c.= concubine or maidservant

Joseph

Jacob has twelve sons, who become the Twelve Tribes of Israel. Joseph, first son of Jacob and Rachel, is Jacob's favorite. His jealous brothers sell him into slavery to some Egyptians. While in **Egypt**, Joseph becomes a servant of the potiphar. Joseph is falsely accused of a

---

Underlined text refers to Internet link at http://Homeschool-Books.com

crime and sent to prison, where he shows his relationship to God by interpreting dreams. The pharaoh hears of the interpretations and consults Joseph about his dreams. Joseph gives him the meaning and the pharaoh releases Joseph from prison. Seven years of famine cause Jacob and his family to leave Canaan and come to Egypt. The family is reunited with Joseph and settles in **Goshen**. After Joseph and his brother die, the new pharaoh is concerned with the Hebrew people's population, so the Hebrews become slaves in Egypt for the next four hundred years. You'll learn more about Joseph in the *Ancient Egypt Unit Study*.

Moses

Over 300 years after the Hebrews became slaves in Egypt, Moses is born to a Hebrew woman. The pharaoh in charge during this time orders all the Hebrew male children to be killed. Moses' mother saves Moses by placing him in a floating basket in the river, where the pharaoh's daughter finds the baby and takes him to raise as her own. Moses grows up in the pharaoh's palace, and Moses' sister, Miriam, brings her mother to the princess as a nurse-maid for Moses. As an adult Moses kills an Egyptian for beating a Hebrew slave. Moses flees to Median for forty years. You'll learn more about Moses in the *Ancient Egypt* and *Ancient Israel Unit Study*.

Exodus

In the **Sinai** area, Moses becomes familiar with the land that he will later lead the Hebrews through. On a mountain top in a fiery bush, God tells Moses to lead the people from Egypt. At eighty years of age, Moses returns to Egypt to face the pharaoh's with his brother Aaron. (Aaron later becomes the founder of the priesthood and the first high priest). Aaron helps Moses lead the Israelites out of Egyptian bondage. You'll learn more about Moses, the Passover, and the Exodus in the *Ancient Egypt* and *Ancient Israel Unit Study*.

Wilderness Wanderings

God gives the people mana, which sustains them in the wilderness. Moses receives the Ten Commandments on top of **Mt. Sinai**. When the Hebrews arrive at Kadesh Barnea, gateway to the promised land, they send twelve spies to check out the land and people. The spies return with both good and bad news. The good news is that the land is wonderful, but the bad news is that the Canaanites are hostile giants. Two of the spies, Caleb and Joshua, have faith to overcome the Canaanites, but the other ten spies are afraid and convince the Israelites not to go and take Canaan as God had wanted. As a consequence of rebellion, they remain in the wilderness for forty years. Moses, Aaron, and Miriam die during this period. Since, of the twelve spies sent by Moses to enter Canaan, Joseph and Caleb alone gave a favorable description, they are the only ones allowed to enter the Promised Land. Joseph becomes leader of the Israelites after Moses' death. You'll learn more about the Wilderness Wanderings in the *Ancient Israel Unit Study*.

Crossing the Jordan

At the end of the Wilderness Wanderings, Joshua leads the Hebrews across the **Jordan River** and into the Promised Land. When Israel crosses the Jordan, it is the time of harvest and the river is at flood stage, but God makes it possible for them to cross. The priests go before the

---

Resources recommended in ◆several lessons, ★ several units, ● other HOW Units. ●━Key Resource (see beginning of unit or page 32).

people and bear the ark containing the law of God, and as their feet are dipped in the brim of Jordan, the waters are cut off from above and the priests pass on, bearing the ark. When the priests are halfway over Jordan, they are commanded to stand in the bed of the river until all the host of Israel has passed over.

Conquest of Canaan

The first great Canaanite battle to take the land is the battle of Jericho (Joshua 6). By following God's instructions, the Israelites go around the city once a day for six days. On the seventh day, they go around the city seven times, then the priests blow the trumpets and the people shout. The walls fall down and the army of Israel enters the city. You'll learn more about the conquest of Canaan in the *Ancient Israel Unit Study*.

Period of the Judges

The Israelites do not drive all the Canaanites out of the land, rather, they decide to live among them. God sends judges to help lead and guide the people. Four major judges rule over Israel, each of them for forty years. They are Othniel, Deborah, Barak, and Gideon. Gideon becomes known for his victory over the Midianites with only 300 men. The period of the judges lasts roughly from 1200 B.C. to 1020 B.C.

Samson also lives during this period. He becomes known for his great strength in defeating the Philistines. In his final moments, he pulls down the two pillars of the Philistine temple and kills thousands of Philistines.

The story of Ruth also takes place during this time. Ruth and Naomi go from **Moab** to Israel. Boaz has compassion on Ruth and takes care of her, redeems and marries her.

Also during this period, Samuel's mother Hannah prays earnestly for a child and promises to give her child to God for service. Samuel is born and later given to the care of the High Priest Eli, to grow up and work for God. He serves as a prophet, priest and judge of Israel.

Period of Kings

Later, the people demand a King. God chooses Samuel to anoint the first two kings, Saul and David. David's son Solomon becomes the king after David. You'll learn more about these three kings in the *Ancient Israel Unit Study*.

Kingdom Divides

When the kingdom is divided, the ten northern tribes become **Israel** and the two southern tribes become **Judah**. For the first sixty years, the kings of Judah aim at re-establishing their authority over the kingdom of the other ten tribes, so that there is a state of perpetual war between them. For the next eighty years, there is no open war between them. For about another century and a half, Judah has a somewhat checkered existence after the termination of the kingdom of Israel until its final overthrow in the destruction of the temple. The kingdom maintains a separate existence for three hundred and eighty-nine years. You'll learn more about the divided kingdom period in the *Ancient Israel Unit Study.*

Israel, the Northern Kingdom (931–722 B.C.)
Jeroboam rules the Northern Kingdom, of which **Samaria** is the capitol. Every king that rules this area is unrighteous. From 800 to 875 B.C., two great prophets, Elijah and Elisha, are used by God to save Israel. God raises up **Assyria** to conquer the Northern kingdom, which is scattered across the world and never restored. This is known as the exile of the Ten Northern Tribes.

Judah, the Southern Kingdom (931–586 B.C.)
Judah is first ruled by Solomon's son, Rehoboem. **Jerusalem** becomes the capital of Judah. Rehoboem and nineteen other kings of Judah are unrighteous. In between them, eight righteous Kings reign over Judah. King **Hezekiah** repairs the damage caused to the Temple by his father; inspires his people to seek and serve the Lord; celebrates the Passover, something that hadn't been done in generations; and brings peace (for a time) to his people.

The Exile
Exile is a term used to refer to the period in the sixth century B.C. when part of the Judean population is exiled to Babylonia. Isaiah is a prophet and adviser to Hezekiah during this time. During Hezekiah's reign Assyria is active in Israel, capturing Samaria and Philistine cities. Sennacherib, king of Assyria, invades the country and captures every walled city *except* Jerusalem. This is considered a miraculous, divine intervention in the Bible. Judah is caught between the great powers of Egypt and Babylonia. The prophet Jeremiah tells Jehoiachin, the last king of Judah, to submit to Babylonia, but he rebels. Jeremiah foretells that Babylon will rule Judah for seventy years. Nebuchadnezzar, the Chaldean king, destroys Jerusalem, killing Jehoiachin and sending some 10,000 Jews into Babylonian captivity. Daniel is taken captive at that time. You'll learn more about the period of the Exile in the *Ancient Israel Unit Study.*

The Return
Judah has been in captivity for seventy years. Then in 539 B.C., Cyrus, a leader of Persians and Medes, conquers Babylon and brings an end to the Babylonian empire. God prompts Cyrus to allow the people to return to Israel and begin the rebuilding of the Temple in Jerusalem. Nearly 50,000 people make this journey. Esther, a Jewess, becomes Xerxes' wife and Queen of Persia. Haman plots against the Jews to have them all killed. With the help and advice of Mordecai, Esther saves the Jews from the massacre. The Feast of Purim commemorates this event. Esther had paved the way for the work of Ezra and Nehemiah in rebuilding Jerusalem.

When the people begin to rebuild the Temple, they become discouraged by opposition. After encouragement from Haggai and Zechariah, they return to the task and complete the Temple. Ezra, the high priest, teaches the people about the law of God as they rebuild physically and spiritually. Nehemiah leads the building of the walls under the king of Persia.

Resources recommended in ◆several lessons, ★ several units, ◖▶other HOW Units. ◑▬Key Resource (see beginning of unit or page 32).

Between the Testaments

At the close of the Old Testament, Jerusalem is ruled by Persia. Alexander the Great had ruled the world, and after his death, his four generals continue his reign. One of them, Antiochus Epiphanies, re-conquers Israel. He devastates Jerusalem, desecrates the Temple by sacrificing a pig on the sacred altar, and kills the Jews that will not bow down to Greek idols or give up the Sabbath. This provokes a revolt to take back Jerusalem, led by Mattathias, a priest, and his five sons. The Temple is purified and re-dedicated. By 164 B.C. the Hebrews have gained control of the Temple and rededicated it to God.

You can expand on any of the previous listed Bible events using any resource (the Bible, Bible study tools, or the Internet). We recommend the following:

Books

Exploring Ancient Cities of the Bible ♥
Read: Skim text and view maps (8-29).

The Victor Journey through the Bible ♥
Read: Skim or read stories and view maps (18-54).

The Holman Bible Atlas ♥
Read: Skim or read stories and view maps (40-188).

The Student Bible Atlas ♥
Read: View maps #3-17.

30 Days to Understanding What Christians Believe in 15 Minutes a Day by Max Anders

Description: Proven effective by over 200,000 readers, *30 Days to Understanding What Christians Believe* helps you learn to position key Bible characters, places, and events in chronological order so that you can "think your way through" the entire Word of God. Through interesting, memory-enhancing exercises, *30 Days to Understanding What Christians Believe* acquaints readers with the core teachings of Scripture in just fifteen minutes a day! Homeschoolers will appreciate the new teaching plan with activities and directions for a twelve-week group study, complete with overhead transparency masters for class or home group use. ISBN: 0785209999.

Internet Sources

Ancient Mesopotamia
Description: "Overview of the Region" shows the area between the Tigris and Euphrates rivers, which is approximately modern Iran.

(i) <u>Biblical Archaeologist</u>
Description: Perspectives on the Ancient World from Mesopotamia to the Mediterranean

(i) <u>The Hebrews</u>
Description: Explains that the Hebrews were originally a group of nomadic tribes that roamed Mesopotamia, Palestine, and northern Egypt.

(i) <u>Mesopotamia</u>
Description: A free clickable Bible map from DailyBible.com. Includes links to applicable Bible history information.

(i) <u>Mesopotamia</u>
Description: Map with some geographical and climatological background about the ancient Near East, including an introduction to the people (Sumerian, Akkadians, and neighbors), the divine world, and economy.

Step 3 Expand

Choose and complete one of the following activities:

Activity 1: Trace a Map
Use a copy of your map of the ancient Near East to shade the area of the Fertile Crescent. Add this map to your portfolio.

Activity 2: Make a Cookie Map
Make a "cookie map" of Mesopotamia. You'll need: an atlas; a cookie recipe; a can of frosting; a variety of chocolate chips, mini fun chips, or candy dots; and several tubes of cake-decorating gels in a variety of colors. Make a large cookie, then frost it (this becomes the "glue"), and use the candy chips to locate selected cites or towns from the atlas. Use the decorating gels to draw rivers, lakes, parks, or centers of mineral resources on the "map" using the symbols and the map key in the atlas.

Activity 3: Create a Map Worksheet
Develop a map worksheet for younger students. Draw a blank map out-line of the ancient East. Make a list of the geographical features of Fertile Crescent. Make blanks on the map for the students to fill in with names from this list. Share this worksheet with some younger students.

Activity 4: Make a Salt-Dough Map
Make a salt-dough map of Mesopotamia. You will need: 2 level cups plain flour, 1 level cup cooking salt, 3/4 cup water, 2 tsp. cooking oil, food coloring or poster paints (optional), and poster board or other smooth cardboard. Mix the dry

Resources recommended in ◆several lessons, ★ several units, ◗• other HOW Units. ●▬Key Resource (see beginning of unit or page 32).

Heart of Wisdom Publishing   123

ingredients together, then add the water and oil. Turn out onto a work surface and knead for 10 minutes, or until a small amount of the dough can be rolled into a ball without cracking. Divide the dough into parts and add food coloring (blue for water, green for land, etc.) or paint it with poster paints when dry. Draw an outline of ancient Greece on the poster board or cardboard. Spread the salt dough onto the outline, making mountains and other geographical features. Allow the map to dry thoroughly.

Activity 5: Make a Brochure
Prepare a travel brochure for one of the ancient cities you studied in this lesson. Use pictures you have found or drawn. Decide upon four places or topics to feature in your brochure. Be sure to include basic facts about the country as well as interesting and exciting places to visit there.

Activity 6: Answer Questions
Answer the following:
1. What was life like in the city-states?
2. What building was located in the center of each city-state?
3. What materials were used in the construction of this building?
4. If you were to visit one of the cities, what would you most like to see or do there?

Activity 7: Write an Essay
Write about the modern inhabitants of this region from your research above. What has happened to their agriculture? Iraq is draining the marshlands of the lower river valleys; how is this affecting the land and the people of the area? Oil is abundant in this area and is a primary source of wealth; how is this affecting the Fertile Crescent?

Step 4 Excel

Share your work from Step 3 with someone. Share a map of the Fertile Crescent with your pastor or church leader. Explain what you have learned about Abraham, Isaac, and Jacob being in this area. Correct all written work to demonstrate correct punctuation and spelling, and effective use of grammar. Add corrected written work or any illustrations to your portfolio.

Note: The amount of information that follows may seem to be a lot to cover but you can easily read through these stories in less time than it would take to watch a long movie or TV mini-series.

Underlined text refers to Internet link at http://Homeschool-Books.com

Archaeology

Step 1 Excite

What if the entire contents of your home or bedroom—clothes, papers, furniture, etc.—were thrown into a large hole, and then the hole was filled in with dirt and left to stand up against the elements for a few centuries? What would be left? How accurate do you think those remains would be in telling people about your life?[1] Would someone be able to discern the practices or religious customs that you follow? What techniques do you think archaeologist use to interpret evidence? Do you think archaeological research has proved or disproved the Bible?

Step 2 Examine

Much of archaeology is devoted to studying the "lifestyles of the dead and buried," that is, trying to assess what people looked like, how healthy they were, what they ate, and what they died of. The word *archaeology* comes from two Greek words meaning "a study of ancient things."

Archaeology is the field that recovers and investigates the physical evidence of earlier human life and culture. archaeologist have contributed to our understanding of ancient cultures and the history of man. Archaeological research comprises three aspects: discovery and surface survey of the site; the technique of excavation; and the technique of interpretation.[1] The passage of time and the modern-day explosion of knowledge have made archaeology quite complex.

> Archaeology and the Bible are closely related; they inform each other. The process of correlating archaeological evidence and the biblical record is traditionally called biblical archaeology. From the perspective of the biblical scholar this process is a biblical discipline because it is applied for the benefit of biblical studies. Near Eastern archaeologist whose discoveries impinge upon the Bible prefer a geographical or regional designation such as Syro-Palestinian archaeology or the archaeology of the Fertile Crescent as a more accurate description of their discipline. Whatever the nomenclature, archaeological research and biblical studies are best understood as independent but certainly interrelated disciplines.[2]

Resources recommended in ◆several lessons, ★ several units, ◖◉ other HOW Units. ◉— Key Resource (see beginning of unit or page 32).

Archaeology is a complex science, using the other sciences, such as chemistry, anthropology, and zoology. Many talented professionals—including engineers, historians, chemists, paleontologists, photographers, artists, and surveyors—are involved in the discovery and publication of archaeological knowledge. The objects an archaeologist discovers—whether a piece of bone, pottery, metal, stone, or wood—are studied in detail. The archaeologist's work often requires translating ancient writings and studying an ancient city's art and architecture. These detailed studies are carried out in museums and laboratories, but the archaeologist must first recover the material by carefully excavating an ancient city.[3]

What does archaeology tell us about the Bible? Scientific archaeology has delivered an enormous amount of "hard evidence" from the ancient world that correlates with information in the Old and New Testaments. The very "stones cry out" the reliability of the biblical record. Dr. Robert Dick Wilson, former professor of Semitic philology at Princeton Theological Seminary, said,

> "After forty-five years of scholarly research in biblical textual studies and in language study, I have come now to the conviction that no man knows enough to assail the truthfulness of the Old Testament. Where there is sufficient documentary evidence to make an investigation, the statements of the Bible, in the original text, have stood the test."

Dr. J. O. Kinnaman said:

> "Of the hundreds of thousands of artifacts found by the archaeologist, not one has ever been discovered that contradicts or denies one word, phrase, clause, or sentence of the Bible, but always confirms and verifies the facts of the Biblical record."

Research archaeology. Find out about the scientific discipline, methods, and tools of archaeology. Use any resource (an encyclopedia, nonfiction book, historical novel, or the Internet). We recommend the following:

Books

Exploring Ancient Cities of the Bible ◆
Read: "The World of Biblical Archeology" (4-7); "Old Testament Discoveries" (8-13).

The Bible Comes Alive Volume One, Creation to Abraham ◆
Read: "Section I: Early Genesis is Factual History" (13-50).

First Civilizations (Cultural Atlas for Young People) ◆
Read: "Physical Background"; "Archaeology in the Near East" (8-13);
and "Archaeology, War and Looting" (90-91).

Kingfisher History Encyclopedia ♥
Read: "What is History?"

Kingfisher Illustrated History of the World ♥
Read: Use the index to look up "Archaeology."

Streams of Civilizations: Earliest Times to Discovery ★
Read: "Introducing History."

Internet Sources

Ancient Texts Relating to the Bible
Description: Explains how archaeological discoveries shed light on the world
of the Bible.

Archaeology and the Bible
Description: Associates for Biblical Research explain how the discoveries of
archaeology verify the reliability of the Bible as a historical document.

Archaeology & the Patriarchs
Description: Article explaining how archaeology has added a tremendous
amount to our knowledge and understanding of the Bible.

Archaeology Resources
Description: List of links about ancient Mesopotamia, Egypt, Nubia, and
Israel from the WWW Virtual Library on the Middle East.

Finding and Interpreting the Evidence
Description: Learn about important concepts in archaeology, such as interpreting evidence and dating artifacts.

Step 3 Expand

Choose and complete one of the following activities:

Activity 1: Make a Brochure
Make a brochure depicting the tools archaeologist use. Illustrate, identify, and tell what each tool is used for.

Resources recommended in ◆several lessons, ★ several units, ◖▸other HOW Units. ●▬Key Resource (see beginning of unit or page 32).

Heart of Wisdom Publishing   127

Activity 2: Contrast and Compare

Make a underline contrast and compare graphic (see page 26). Label one column "Materials Preserved," and the other, "Materials Not Preserved." Place these items in the proper column: animal skins, bone, burnt wood, cloth, feathers, fired clay, metal, paper, plants, and stone.

Activity 3: Experiment

Do this activity with a homeschool group (best to do outside). Visit a flea market, garage sale, or salvage store to find cheap ceramic wares. Purchase inexpensive ceramic items such as plates, cups, mugs, and bowls of varying shapes, sizes, and colors. Break the vessels. Remove several pieces from each vessel. Mix up the remaining pieces and place them on a table. Pretend you are archaeologist. Analyze the items to learn about the culture that left behind the artifacts. Can you tell how many different vessels were found at the site? Can you determine the function of the items? How many different ways did this culture decorate their pottery? Make a chart to classify the pieces into groups according to their characteristics (item number, shape, material, color, etc).

Activity 4: Write a Summary

Write a summary of your research findings about scientific disciplines, methods, and tools of archaeology. (Minimum 200 words).

Activity 5: Write a Document

Create a fictional primary source from ancient Mesopotamia. A primary source is an original written document from the period being studied (newspapers, deeds, tax and census records, photographs, diaries, and maps). Show your source to someone and ask what he or she can tell from it. What questions should be asked?

Step 4 Excel

Share what you have learned about archaeology with a friend or family member. Correct all written work to demonstrate correct punctuation and spelling, and effective use of grammar. Add corrected written work or any illustrations to your portfolio. Add any new words you learned in this lesson to your Vocabulary Notebook (see page 22).

Footnotes
1. Negev, A. 1996, c1990. *The Archaeological Encyclopedia of the Holy Land* (3rd ed.). Prentice Hall Press: New York
2. Achtemeier, P. J. 1985. *Harper's Bible Dictionary*. Includes index. (1st ed.) (Page 44). Harper & Row: San Francisco
3. (1998). "Finding and Interpreting the Evidence," The Annenberg/CPB Project. <http://www.learner.org/exhibits/collapse/mesopotamia_sub.html> (Accessed May 2000).
4. Youngblood, R. F. 1997, c1995. *Nelson's New Illustrated Bible Dictionary*. Thomas Nelson: Nashville

Sumer and Akkad 3500–2000 B. C.

Step 1 Excite

23-96

The Narrated Bible
*See note on page 102

Spend at least ten minutes discussing irrigation and writing. What is irrigation? Why is it important? How would people have to live without irrigation? Why would it make such a difference in early people's lives? Do you think they needed to organize the building and upkeep of the canals?

Discuss writing. Why is it important? How would writing make a difference in people's lives? What type of documents do you think people first recorded? Have you ever played the game "gossip"? This is how it's played: First, sit in a circle with several people and whisper a few sentences to the person seated next to you. Next, each person repeats the sentence to the person on their right. The more people involved, the more the sentence usually changes by the time it reaches the end of the circle. Try playing gossip with your family.

Step 2 Examine

Sumer was the name of the southern area of Mesopotamia near where the Tigris and Euphrates emptied into the Persian Gulf. When the Sumerians settled here sometime after the Flood, they found two groups of people, referred to by archaeologist as Ubaidians and an unidentified Semitic people. By 3800 the Sumerians were the dominant group in the area. At least a dozen city-states developed, including Ur, Uruk, Kish, and Lagash. The Sumerian civilization was at its height between 2800 and 2370 B.C.

The Sumerians created a system of irrigation that allowed them to grow crops and to prosper. The Sumerian civilization is considered by historians to be the first true civilization. People gathered into cities and developed the first writing system (cuneiform).

The Sumerians built canals, established an irrigation system, and were skilled in the use of metals (silver, gold, and copper) to make pottery, jewelry, and weapons. They organized city-states. The farmers produced the food, while city dwellers did other kinds of work. Some were brick makers, canal builders, butchers, potters, and so forth. These workers exchanged their goods and services for food.

The most important Sumerian contribution was the invention of cuneiform writing, a wedge-shaped script formed by pressing a reed stylus into wet clay tablets which were later dried, baked, and stored in libraries. Cuneiform developed about the same time that hieroglyphic writing began in Egypt. Sumerian inscriptions are the oldest literature in history. Most of the cuneiform included administrative, economic, and legal documents, including inventories, promissory notes, receipts, deeds of sale, marriage contracts, wills, and court decisions.

Resources recommended in ♦several lessons, ★ several units, ▷ other HOW Units. ●—Key Resource (see beginning of unit or page 32).

Heart of Wisdom Publishing   129

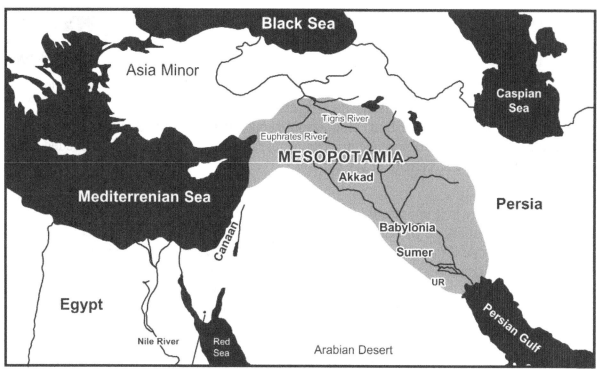

Akkadian Dynasty (c. 2340–2180 B.C.)

The Akkadians, Semitic people from the west, conquered Sumer around 2350 B.C., and the two cultures merged. Nimrod, the son of Ham (Gen. 10:6), built four cities in the land of Shinar somewhere in southern Mesopotamia, extending almost to the Persian Gulf (where the tower of Babel was built). One of the four cities was Akkad (Accad). The Akkadian king Sargon I (not to be confused with Sargon of Assyria) developed a new technique of war with the bow and arrow and soon defeated Sumer in northern Mesopotamia. He knocked down the defensive walls of occupied cities, and imposed the Akkadian language and cuneiform writing, uniform weights and measures, and standardized forms of command, thus boosting the flow of trade and creating an enormous system of government. He united Sumer and Akkad, founding a dynasty that lasted 120 years (c. 2371–2191 B.C.). Sargon founded a new capital, called Agade, in the far north of Sumer and made it the richest and most powerful city in the world.

The first great legend, the Gilgamesh epic, based on the life of one of Sumer's early kings, was recorded on twelve clay tablets in cuneiform about 2000 B.C. This poem is named for its hero, Gilgamesh, a tyrannical Babylonian king who ruled the city of Uruk, known in the Bible as Erech (now Al Warka', Iraq). Gilgamesh, hoping to achieve immortality, pursued immortality through plants and animals until he died.

The accounts of a world-destroying flood in the epic of Gilgamesh and the story of Noah and the Flood in Genesis chapters 6-8 are very similar. It is easy to understand how the mythological stories of the flood came from the real story. After the Flood people passed down the

Bible stories verbally. The record in Genesis would be the accurate record, whereas Gilgamesh would be a somewhat fictionalized record since it was based on oral traditions passed down over centuries. The epic of Gilgamesh included some of the main points, but altered many of the details. This is a perfect example of why writing is important. When an event is written down, the story remains the same. On the other hand, people passing on an event from one to another will tend to add or leave out sections.

Abraham lived in Sumer when he lived in the city of Ur. Ur is mentioned four times (Gen. 11:28,31; 15:7; Neh. 9:7), all as the home of the patriarch Abraham before his migration to Canaan.

Research Sumer and Akkad. Use any resource (an encyclopedia, non-fiction book, historical novel, or the Internet). We recommend the following:

Books

The Victor Journey through the Bible ♥
Read: "Abraham's Journeys" (18-19).

The Holman Bible Atlas ♥
Read: "The Rise and Decline of Early Civilizations: The Early Bronze Age" (35-40); "The World of the Patriarchs" (40-45).

The Student Bible Atlas ♥
View: Map 2 and Map 3.

First Civilizations (Cultural Atlas for Young People) ♦
Read: "Urik" and "Ur" (34, 35, 40-45).

Usborne's Book of the Ancient World ♥
Read: Use the index to find all entries about "Sumer" or "the Sumerians."

Ancient Civilizations (Exploring History) ★
Read: "The Sumerians" (8-9).

Genesis: Finding Our Roots ♦
Read: "The Religion of Sumer" (84). See description in the *Adam to Abraham Unit*.

Resources recommended in ♦several lessons, ★ several units, ☐♦other HOW Units. ◉—Key Resource (see beginning of unit or page 32).

Heart of Wisdom Publishing   131

The Bible Comes Alive Volume One, Creation to Abraham ◆
Read: "The Ancient Sumerian Civilizations" (44).

Kingfisher History Encyclopedia ♥
Read: "Sumer and Akkad 5000-1600 B.C."

Streams of Civilizations: Earliest Times to Discovery ★
Read: Use the index to find all entries about "Sumer" or "the Sumerians."

Internet Sources

The Armies of Sumer and Akkad, 3500-2200 BC
Description: Chapter from *A Short History of War.*

The Sumerians
Description: Brief survey of the Sumerians from *Ancient Peoples of the Bible.*

The Sumerians
Description: Details the beliefs of the Sumerians, their major cities, their division of power, and agricultural-based commerce.

Sumer, Akkad, Babylon, and Assyria
Description: Overview of Iraq - Ancient Mesopotamia, from About.com

The Sumerian City-State
Description: Good background information on this topic; middle-school level.

Ziggurats of Ur
Description: Details the various sizes and uses of ziggurats in the city of Ur, and provides illustrations.

Ziggurats
Description: Furnishes background and photos of the White Temple at Uruk, the ziggurat of Ur-Nammu, and Marduk or the Tower of Babel.

Step 3 Expand

Choose and complete one of the following activities:

Activity 1: Trace a Map
Trace the map showing the Akkadian dynasty. Color the water blue and shade the Akkadian dynasty area. Look for the journey of Abraham on this map from Ur to Canaan. Place this in your portfolio.

Activity 2: Find Illustrations
Find pictures of what was believed to be the armor of the Sumerians from the listed resources. Sketch or trace for your portfolio. Sumerians went to war in chariots, shielded with copper helmets and armed with copper spears. The ancient civilization of Sumer had no natural barriers, so the region became home to a variety of invading peoples, including Ubaidians, Semites, and the Sumerians themselves.

Activity 3: Build a Miniature Ziggurat
Look at pictures of a ziggurat. Make mud bricks by putting wet dirt into the flat part of egg cartons. (What did the Mesopotamians use to shape bricks?) Let the mud dry for at least a week. Build a miniature ziggurat. Imagine what it would be like to build a structure seventy feet high from mud bricks!

Activity 4 Make a Scrapbook Page
Create a scrapbook page or lapbook about Sumer. Ideas to get you started: law/government, transportation/trade, writing/literature, cities. Send us a photo or scan of your page to share with others. See sample pages at http://HeartofWisdom.com/studentswork.htm.

Activity 5: Copy Passages
Copy (by hand or typing) two or more paragraphs from your research, or have someone dictate the passage to you. Younger students can copy one or two sentences or narrate (tell back) what has been learned.

Activity 5: Write an Essay
Write a traditional essay about the early Sumerians. Include what they looked like, who and how they worshiped, marriage customs, approximate population, government, basic laws, monetary system, entertainment, clothing, food, what their homes were like, their educational system and written language, the roles of men and women, their weapons and scientific achievements, transportation, agriculture, etc. Refer to "Structure of the Traditional Essay" and "Sample of a Traditional Essay" in *Writers INC*, or "How to Write an Essay."

Step 4 Excel

Share your work from Step 3 with your family. Using information learned from this lesson, create a crossword puzzle with questions about the ancient Sumerians. Make copies and distribute them to your family members, then see if anyone can solve the puzzle.

Resources recommended in ◆several lessons, ★ several units, ▯▸other HOW Units. ☞Key Resource (see beginning of unit or page 32).

Heart of Wisdom Publishing   133

Cuneiform

Step 1 Excite

Cuneiform writing, which originated in southern Mesopotamia, was probably invented by the Sumerians, who used it to inscribe the Sumerian language. Originally, each sign stood for a word. Words were expressed by pictographs of related objects (for example, "god" by a star, "to stand" and "to go" by a foot). Some signs stood for several different words. The earliest ancient libraries were clay-tablet repositories in ancient Mesopotamia, and the later papyrus-scroll libraries in Egypt, Greece, and Rome.

Before writing, human knowledge was confined by the limits of memory—what one could learn for oneself or find out from talking to someone else. Brainstorm and make a list (or <u>mind map</u>) of the advantages of writing. Discuss how you would communicate with someone far away without the alphabet (if you could have something delivered to them but you could not use letters). Before you read any more of this lesson, try drawing a message on paper without using any letters. Give it to a friend to see if your friend can decipher it.

Step 2 Examine

Through research, trace the alphabet regressively from today's alphabet to cuneiform writing. Use any resource (an encyclopedia, non-fiction book, historical novel, or the Internet). We recommend any of the following:

Books

<u>Usborne Book of the Ancient World</u>★
Read: "Cuneiform" (10-11, 25).

<u>Genesis: Finding Our Roots</u> ◆
Read: "The History of Cuneiform" (95).

<u>First Civilizations (Cultural Atlas for Young People)</u> ◆
Read: "Writing" (38-39).

Kingfisher History Encyclopedia ♥
Read: "Cuneiform" (9, 41).

Kingfisher Illustrated History of the World ♥
Read: "Communications" (28-29).

Mesopotamia and the Fertile Crescent ♦
Read: "The Invention of Writing" (46-48).

The Birth of Writing by Robert Claiborne (The Emergence of Man Series)
Description: An easily readable, well-illustrated survey of the birth and development of writing in the ancient Near East, with information on writing as it appeared in the Far East and the Americas. (1974) Alexandria, Virginia: Time Life Books; ISBN: 0809412829.

The Beginning of Civilization in Sumer: The Advent of Written Communication by Joan Parrish
Description: A Unit of Study for Grades 5-8. A curriculum guide with information for teachers and activities for students. (1991) Los Angeles: National Center for History in the Schools, University of California at Los Angeles.

Cuneiform: Reading the Past by C.B.F. Walker
Description: A detailed discussion of cuneiform writing and information on how cuneiform symbols were used in mathematics. (1987) Berkeley, California: University of California Press.

Internet Sources

About Cuneiform Writing
Description: Article with illustrations from *About Cuneiform Writing*, University of Pennsylvania, Museum of Archaeology and Anthropology.

Alfabets
Description: Article explaining the history of writing.

Ancient Texts Relating to the Bible
Description: See different alphabets and writings from all over the world and different time periods.

Cuneiform Writing Tablet 2000 B.C. Sumeria
Description: View photos of tablet artifacts.

Resources recommended in ♦several lessons, ★ several units, ▯♦other HOW Units. ●━Key Resource (see beginning of unit or page 32).

Heart of Wisdom Publishing   135

Early Writing Materials
Description: An explanation of cuneiform, early writing materials, papyrus, vellum manuscripts, early parchment, rare books, rare prints, and much more, from The Foliophiles Collection.

Learning Family Learns about Cuneiform
Description: Overview of and links about cuneiform from a family that has dubbed itself "The Learning Family." Includes several topics and virtual field trips.

MSN Encarta "Cuneiform"
Description: Encyclopedia provides an article about the form of writing originated by the Sumerians. Also find links to related articles and premium resources.

Writing/Alphabet Quiz
Description: Weekly quiz from About.com.

Step 3 Expand

Choose and complete one of the following activities:

Activity 1: Write Like a Babylonian
Write like a Babylonian at the University of Pennsylvania Museum of Archaeology and Anthropology site. See your monogram in cuneiform, the way an ancient Babylonian might have written it.

Activity 2: Make and Write on Clay
You need: 2 cups salt , 2/3 cup water, 1 cup cornstarch, 1/2 cup water (cold). Stir salt and water over heat for about 5 minutes. Remove from heat and stir in cornstarch and cold water. Mix until smooth, return to heat and cook until thick. Cool before using. Store in plastic bag. Use clay or playdough to make a tablet. Then use a stick to write a message in code. Dry your tablet in the sun.

Activity 3: Make a Chart
Using the above resources as a reference, make and display a chart showing the history of the alphabet and writing. Include parchment, hieroglyphic, alphabet, library, Arabic numerals, printing press, Johann Gutenberg, rotary press, and the Linotype.

Step 4 Excel

Write another message without letters as you did in Step 1. Share your message with a friend. Did studying cuneiform help you learn to communicate better?

Underlined text refers to Internet link at http://Homeschool-Books.com

Assyria 1200–612 B.C.

752-775

The Narrated Bible
*See note on page 102

Note: You'll learn more about the Assyrian invasion of Judah in the *Ancient Israel Unit*.

Step 1 Excite

Do you know the story of Jonah running away from Nineveh? Where was Nineveh? Look on your ancient Near East map. You know Jonah's trip took him across a body of water because he was swallowed by a big fish. Take a guess where Jonah was when God told him to go to Nineveh and where Jonah went instead.

You probably know about Egypt holding Israel captive and Moses leading the Exodus through the Red Sea. But do you know that the Israelites were held captive by the Assyrians?

Step 2 Examine

Of Noah's three sons, Shem, Ham, and Japheth, the Assyrians came from Ham (Gen. 10:6-11), and thus were related to the Egyptians, Ethiopians, and Canaanites.

Assyria first ascended to world-power status in the twelfth century B.C. The fortunes of the Assyrian Empire, which was centered at Nineveh in the heart of Mesopotamia, rose and fell under numerous kings over a period of several centuries.

Around 700 B.C. (seven hundred years before Christ) the two greatest world powers were Egypt and Assyria. By the the seventh century B.C., the Assyrian Empire covered most of the Fertile Crescent, from Babylon to the Sinai.[1] Assyrian and Babylonian civilizations over-lapped, with Babylonia under Assyrian rule for long periods. King Nebuchadnezzar II (604-562 B.C.) is significant in Assyrian-Babylonian history.

The prophets Amos and Hosea predicted that Israel (the Northern Tribes) would be destroyed. The people had betrayed their faith, worshipping false gods and oppressing the poor of the land. They did not trust God, but instead relied on foreign alliances. Hosea had

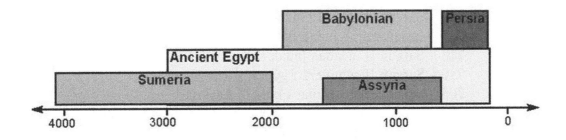

Resources recommended in ◆several lessons, ★ several units, ▷other HOW Units. Key Resource (see beginning of unit or page 32).

The Ministry of Jonah
About the Time of Jeroboam II

1. Jonah was a resident of Gath–hepher in Zebulun (2 Kings 14:25).

2. Ship (course unknown) bound for Tarshish, thought by many to be Tartessus in southern Spain, near Gibraltar, a Phoenician colony some 2,200 miles from Joppa, more than three times as far as Nineveh.

3. After his experience in the "great fish," Jonah probably followed the main trade route to Nineveh.

4. Nineveh

(Map from Logos Deluxe Map Set)

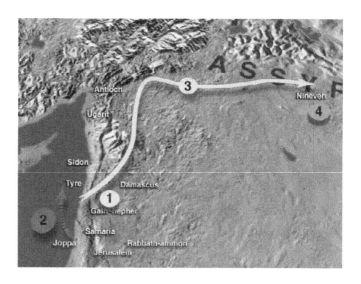

warned: "*Ephraim also is like a silly dove without heart: they call to Egypt, they go to Assyria. ..*" (Hosea 7:11). Ahaz disobeyed God by relying upon Assyria rather than upon God (2 Kings 16:5-9).

In 722 B.C., Assyrian records claim that 27,290 Israelites were taken into captivity. They were deported to the region of the river Habor and to Media. For those who were taken to Media, this meant a journey of over 800 miles on foot. Israel became a province of the Assyrian empire. The land was filled with foreign exiles forcibly removed from Babylon and Syria.[2] The people never returned (2 Kings 17:1–23), resulting in the "Lost Ten Tribes" of Israel.

Assyrian Time Line

933 – The Division of the Kingdom
900 – Assyria becomes a world power
820 – The Lord began to "cut off" Israel
734 – The captivity of Northern Israel by Tiglath-Pileser III
722 – The end of the Northern Kingdom by Sargon II
721 – 28,000 Israelites are deported
720 – Sargon invades Judah
713 – Sargon invades Philistia, Edom, and Moab
713 – Isaiah warns Judah not to ask Egypt for help
713 – Sargon II invades Judah again
710 – Sargon II conquers Egypt
705 – Sennacherib becomes king of Assyria
702 – Sennacherib devastates Northern Judah and Lachish
701 – Sennacherib attacks Jerusalem

Underlined text refers to Internet link at http://Homeschool-Books.com

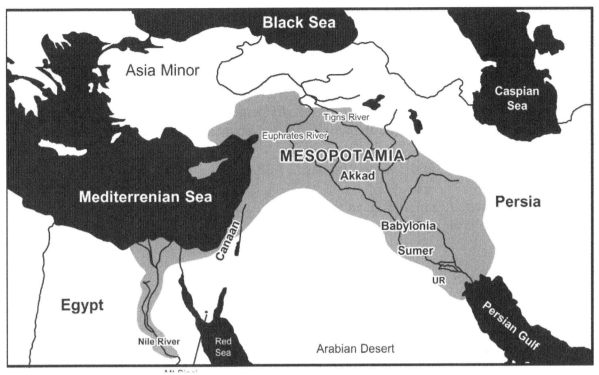

Assyria (1350–612 B.C.)

701 – The Assyrian Army is smote by God
612 – Assyria is destroyed by Babylon
609 – The Assyrian Empire comes to an end

Military strategists today study the tactics of the Assyrians and admire their skill more than that of Alexander the Great and the Roman legions. The Southern Hebrew Kingdom, Judah, survived the Assyrian invasion which swept away the Northern Kingdom, Israel.

The capital of Assyria from 1305-883 B.C. was Assur. From 883-824 it was Nimrud (also Kalhu or Calah). Nineveh, the site of the Temple of Ishtar, was capitol for most of the years between 705-627 B.C. Nineveh had a population of around 600,000. When Jonah went to Nineveh with his message of repentance, the king of Assyria was either Shalmanezer IV (783-773 B.C.) or Ashurdan III (773-755 B.C.). The prophets Elijah, Elisha, Isaiah, Jeremiah, Ezekiel, Hosea, Micah, Nahum, Zephaniah, and Zechariah all refer to Assyria.

The Assyrian empire eventually declined, and by 600 B.C. it was overcome by the Babylonians. In 623 B.C. a long and indecisive war begins between Assyria and Babylon. It is believed that Egypt may have been either supporting Assyria with a small force or protecting their interests in Syria.

Resources recommended in ◆several lessons, ★ several units, ▯▶other HOW Units. ●━Key Resource (see beginning of unit or page 32).

Heart of Wisdom Publishing   139

By 612 B.C. Babylon joins forces with the Medes and Scythians in an attempt to finally destroy Assyria. They lay siege to Nineveh, which falls within three months, and kill the Assyrian King within the burning capital. An Assyrian general, Assur-uballit, becomes King and forms a new stand at Harran. In 608 B.C. Assur-uballit fails to recapture Harran and fades out of the historical records. The victorious Medes in turn attack their own allies, the Scythians, who are forced to retire to their own homeland. In 604 B.C. the old Assyrian Empire accepts the Chaldean/Neo-Babylonian king, Nebuchadnezzar, as their ruler.

Read the Book of Jonah, and 2 Kings chapters 17-18.

Research the Assyrian Empire. Use an encyclopedia, a nonfiction book, or the Internet. We recommend the following:

Books

Exploring Ancient Cities of the Bible ❤
Read: "The Assyrian Empire" (23).

The Victor Journey through the Bible ❤
Read: "The Story of Jonah" (160-161); "Israel Taken into Captivity" (164-165); "Sennacherib Goes Against Hezekiah" (166-167); "The Story of Jeremiah" (170-171).

Encyclopedia of the Bible (Nelson's Illustrated) ❤
"The Rise of Assyria" (30-31), "The Assyrians" (60-61).

First Civilizations (Cultural Atlas for Young People) ◆
Read: "Mittani and the Rise of the Assyrians" (58-60); "The Late Assyrian Empire" (70-71); "Assyria Triumphant" (72-73).

Ancient Civilizations (Exploring History) ★
Read: "The Assyrians" (13-14).

The Usborne Book of the Ancient World ❤
Read: "The Assyrians" (74).

Kingfisher History Encyclopedia ❤
Read: "The Assyrians 1900-612 B.C." (22-23).

Kingfisher Illustrated History of the World ❤
Read: All index entries under "Assyrians" ("Origins," "Rise to Power," "War with Babylonians," and "Warfare").

Internet Sources

(i) Assyria (c. 1350-612 B.C.)
Description: This page contains dozens of local files as well as links to source texts throughout the Internet from the Internet Ancient History Sourcebook.

(i) Assyria
Description: Dictionary topic from M.G. Easton M.A., D.D., *Illustrated Bible Dictionary*, Third Edition.

(i) Old Testament History: Assyrian Dominance (745-640 B.C.)
Description: A brief summary of Old Testament history during the Assyrian era, 745 B.C.-605 B.C., organized around the reigns of Israel's kings.

(i) Revival of the Assyrian Empire under Tiglath-Pileser 745-730 B.C.
Description: Article from *Era of Small Civilizations*.

(i) Something Extra
Description: Achievements of the Sumerians and the Assyrians.

Step 3 Expand

Choose and complete one of the following activities:

Activity 1: Map Work
Make or trace a copy of the ancient Near East map. Shade the area of Assyria with a colored pencil and include in your portfolio. Find out about the geographical features.

Activity 2: Add to Your Time Line Book
Add the events from the Assyrian Time Line (Step 2) to your Time Line Book.

Activity 3: Make a Scrapbook Page
Create a scrapbook page or lapbook about Assyria. Ideas to get you started: law/government, transportation/trade, writing/literature, cities, Jonah.

Activity 4: Write a Summary
Choose one of the events from the Assyrian Time Line (Step 2) to study in detail. Write a summary paragraph about the event.

Activity 5: Copy Passages
Copy (by hand or typing) two or more paragraphs from your research, or have someone dictate the passage to you. Younger students can copy one or two sentences or narrate (tell back) what has been learned.

Activity 6: Expand Your Research
Find out about the Assyrian army. Look at the extent of the empire. Research how the army was organized. Find out how important the army was in the expansion of the empire.

Activity 7: Write a Summary
2 Chronicles 32:23 shows the effect of God's mighty work in saving Hezekiah and the inhabitants of Jerusalem from the hand of Sennacherib, king of Assyria. Read the story and write a summary of this event explaining how God's name was glorified and exalted in the sight of the nations.

Activity 8: Write an Essay
Write a traditional essay about the Assyrians. Include what they looked like, who and how they worshiped, marriage customs, approximate population, government, basic laws, monetary system, entertainment, clothing, food, what their homes were like, their educational system and written language, the roles of men and women, their weapons and scientific achievements, transportation, agriculture, etc. Refer to "Structure of the Traditional Essay" and "Sample of a Traditional Essay" in *Writers INC*, or "How to Write an Essay."

Step 4 Excel

Share your work from Step 3 with someone. Explain what you have learned in this lesson. Correct written work to demonstrate correct punctuation and spelling, and effective use of grammar. Add corrected written work or any illustrations to your portfolio.

Footnotes
1. Jenkins, S. 1997, c1985. *Nelson's 3-D Bible Mapbook* (electronic ed.). Thomas Nelson: Nashville
2. Karleen, P. S. 1987. *The Handbook to Bible Study.* Oxford University Press: New York

Underlined text refers to Internet link at http://Homeschool-Books.com

Babylonia 625–536 B. C.

1006-1242

The Narrated Bible
*See note on page 102

Step 1 Excite

Do you recall Bible stories about Daniel in the lion's den, or the writing on the wall? What about Daniel and his three friends taken captive? Or King Nebuchadnezzar's dreams? Do you know where they took place? Refresh your memory by reading the stories from Daniel chapters 1-6.

What famous building was supposedly built in Babylon? (Gen. 11:2, 4-5, 8-9) . What famous garden was build by a king for his wife?

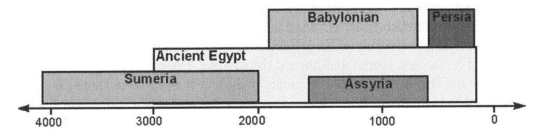

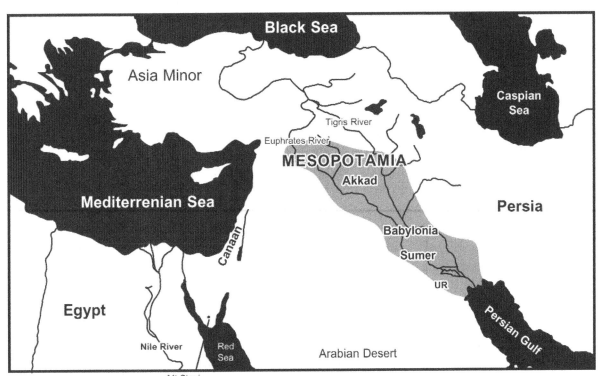

Babylonian Dynasty (2000 -323 BC)

Resources recommended in ♦several lessons, ★ several units, ▯▶other HOW Units. ●━Key Resource (see beginning of unit or page 32).

Heart of Wisdom Publishing   143

Babylon Time Line

- Before 2100 B.C.   Tower of Babel
- 1792-1760 B.C.   Hammurabi
- 625 B.C.   Beginnings of the Chaldean kingdom in Babylon
- 612 B.C.   Assyrian capital of Nineveh is destroyed by the Chaldeans
- 587 B.C.   Jerusalem is taken by Nebuchadnezzar II of Babylon

Step 2 Examine

According to Wayne Blank in *Ancient Empires: Babylon*[1],

> The New Babylonian Empire, which existed from 606 to 536 B.C., fully conquered the southern kingdom of Judah in 586 B.C. It was then that the Babylonians, under the rule of King Nebuchadnezzar, completely devastated the city of Jerusalem, looted and burned the original Temple of God (built by Solomon) and carried the people of Judah, including the prophets Daniel and Ezekiel, off into captivity.

> In 536 B.C., after 70 years of supremacy, the Babylonian empire (the "head of gold" on Daniel's statue) came to an end when it fell to the Persians. There is much more yet to come however. "Babylon" has many prophetic applications that have yet to be completed (Revelation 18:1-24).

The Teacher's Commentary further explains:

> It would be a mistake to imagine that the Babylonian Captivity was a time of continual hardship for the Jewish people. In fact, it was a time of relative peace and prosperity! The captives were taken to the capital city of Babylon itself. They were settled there in several districts. The best known of these was called Tel Aviv, by the river (actually the canal) Chebar. The typical exile very likely owned his own home, and had enough property to grow garden crops (cf. Jer. 29:4, 7; Ezek. 8:1; 12:1–7). The land they lived on was fertile, and under irrigation. In the early days many may even have sent money back to Jerusalem!

> Archeologists have found that the Babylonians recognized three classes of citizens. The first was Awelin, free men of the upper classes. Mushkenu were free men also, but of lower classes. The third class, Wardu, were slaves. The Jewish captives who settled in Babylon were probably Mushkenu; free, but not influential.

Underlined text refers to Internet link at http://Homeschool-Books.com

We do know that many of the Jews were prosperous. They worked on the king's building projects, and some at least entered business as merchants. The Babylonians kept careful records, and recovered records show Jewish names on copies of various business transactions. At least one trading house was owned and operated by Jews.

Another indication of the favored treatment given the Jews is that, by the time a return to Jerusalem was permitted by Cyrus the Persian, many Jews decided to stay in Babylon. They were unwilling to trade their material success for the risky business of settling in the now-empty and desolate land God had given their forefather, Abraham!

Finally, we know from Jeremiah and from Ezekiel's writings that the Jews were allowed much self-government. The community had its own elders, and in them priests and prophets continued to play an influential role.

But despite the material benefits of life in Babylon, those who loved God still experienced those decades as punishment. God's people were far away from the land of promise, uprooted from their past, and far from the place where the promised Messiah was to appear.

Babylon was the capital of Babylonia during biblical times, and it was one of the major cities of the ancient world. The Babylonians worshiped many gods, often of Sumerian origin. Their chief god was Marduk, whose cult center was located at Babylon.

The Captives

Because the Israelites did disobey
God sent a king to take them away.
Uprooted from family and kin that day;
Some were trained in the Babylonian way.

Far from their home, friends, and land,
Four brave men took their stand.
They would not take the king's own meat,
But asked for water and vegetables to eat.

Daniel and his friends purposed that day
That from their God, they would never stray.
These four friends who did obey
Prospered greatly in every way.

They were wiser and healthier than all
Because they did obey God's law.
King Nebuchadnezzar gave them a high position.
Daniel and his three friends helped rule the nation.

Based on the story in Daniel 1
By Rachel Keller 2000

Read the following verses about Babylon: Genesis 10:10; (In the land of Shinar) Genesis 11:2; (Tower of Babel) Genesis 11:1-9; (Capital of the kingdom of Babylon) Daniel 4:30; 2 Kings 25:13; 2 Chronicles 36:6,7,10,18,20; (Gates of) Isaiah 45:1,2; Jeremiah 51:58; (Walled) Jeremiah 51:44; (Splendor of) Isaiah 14:4.

Research Babylonia and Nebuchadnezzar. Use any resource (an encyclopedia, non-fiction book, historical novel, or the Internet). We recommend the following:

Resources recommended in ♦several lessons, ★ several units, ▯▸other HOW Units. ◉━Key Resource (see beginning of unit or page 32).

Heart of Wisdom Publishing   145

Books

Exploring Ancient Cities of the Bible ❤
"The Babylonian Empire(21-22).

The Victor Journey through the Bible ❤
Read: "Judah Falls, Jerusalem is Destroyed and Zedekah is Blinded" (172-173); "Daniel and the King's Food" (174); "The Fiery Furnace" (175); "The Handwriting on the Wall" (176-177).

Encyclopedia of the Bible (Nelson's Illustrated) ●—❤
"The Babylonian Invasion" (32-33), "The Babylonians" (62-63).Babylonians Religion" (64-65).

First Civilizations (Cultural Atlas for Young People) ◆
Read: "Babylon" (80-81); "The Kassite Empire" (60-61); "Everyday Life" (62-63); "Babylon Revival: 626-560" (78-79).

Ancient Civilizations (Exploring History) ★
Read: "Ancient Babylon" (10-11).

The Usborne Book of the Ancient World ❤
Read: "The Babylonians" (76); "Babylon Under Nebuchadnezzar II" (76).

Kingfisher History Encyclopedia ❤
Read: "Babylon Revival" (36-37).

Kingfisher Illustrated History of the World ❤
Read: Look under "Babylon" or "Babylonia" in the index. Read these entries about Babylon: "Hittites Conquer," "Origins of," "Rise of Empire," "Wars with Assyrians," and "Persians Conquer."

What in the World is Going On Here? A Judeo Christian Primer of World History by Diana Waring
Description: See description on page 38. Listen to and discuss the tapes "The Rise of Babylon to Jesus Christ."

Mesopotamia and the Fertile Crescent ◆
Read: "Babylon, A Chaldean City" (35-36).

Streams of Civilizations: Earliest Times to Discovery ★
Read: "Ancient Babylon," and "Babylon Fall."

The Gifts of the Jews
Read: Chapter 6, "Babylon: From Many to One." See description of this book in the *Ancient Israel Unit*.

Internet Sources

Babylon 580 B.C.
Description: A tour of the ancient world of Babylonia, featuring daily life, law, astronomy, culture, literature, and more. Includes a quiz.

Babylonia (c. 2000-1600 B.C.)
Description: This page contains dozens of local files as well as links to source texts throughout the Internet, from the Internet Ancient History Sourcebook.

Babylonian and Egyptian Mathematics
Description: Article, map, and graphics from *The MacTutor History of Mathematics* archive.

Babylonians
Description: Includes brief articles about the Babylonian civilization, Hammurabi, Hanging Gardens, and Babylonian legal concepts.

The Babylonians
Description: Offers explanations of technologies from *Ancient People of the Bible*.

General Knowledge: Babylonians
Description: Overview of Babylonians from Bible Tutor.

God Saves Daniel's Three Friends
Description: Online Bible study of Daniel 1-3.

Gods and Heroes of the Babylonians
Description: Offers the genealogy of the older and younger gods of Babylonian mythology.

Inscription of Nebuchadnezzar
Description: Offers transcriptions of the columns depicting Nebuchadnezzar's rise and establishment of Babylonia.

King Nebuchadnezzar
Description: An examination of the Babylonian King, from *Daily Bible Study*.

Resources recommended in ◆several lessons, ★ several units, �yseveral units, ◑other HOW Units. ●—Key Resource (see beginning of unit or page 32).

(i) <u>The Life and Times of the Babylonians</u>
Description: A document of the important aspects of the Babylonians. It covers mainly the Babylonia of the great Amorite King Hammurabi who ruled at about the time of Abraham's journey to Israel.

(i) <u>Nebuchadnezzar</u>
Description: Historical text accounts of Nebuchadnezzar.

(i) <u>Why Babylon?</u>
Description: Article from *Daily Bible Study*.

Step 3 Expand

Choose and complete one of the following activities:

Activity 1: Map Work
Make or trace a copy of the ancient Near East map. Shade the area of Babylonia with a colored pencil and include in your portfolio. Find out about the geographical features.

Activity 2: Add to Your Time Line Book
Add the Babylonian time line events (Step 1) to your Time Line Book. Refer to <u>Reproducible Maps, Charts, Timelines & Illustrations</u> (11, 41).

Activity 3: Write a Summary
Write a summary of the story of Nebuchadnezzar. Refer to "Writing About a Person" in *Writers INC*.

Activity 4: Write a Summary
Belshazzar, Nebuchadnezzar's grandson, became king of Babylonia. He was also full of pride and arrogance. The kingdom was very rich and there was much idleness. All these things helped to bring about the fall of Babylonia. Write a summary of the story of Belshazzar.

Activity 5: Make a Newspaper
Make a mock newspaper titled "The Babylonian Times." Include at least two short articles, illustrations, a few classified ads, and advertisements. Use butcher paper or tape two pieces of 8½" x 11" paper together to make 17" x 11" pages.

Activity 6: Copy Passages
Copy (by hand or typing) two or more paragraphs from your research, or have someone dictate the passage to you. Younger students can copy one or two sentences or narrate (tell back) what has been learned.

Activity 7: Write an Essay
Write a traditional essay about the Babylonians. Include what they looked like, who and how they worshiped, marriage customs, approximate population, government, basic laws, monetary system, entertainment, clothing, food, what their homes were like, their educational system and written language, the roles of men and women, their weapons and scientific achievements, transportation, agriculture, etc. Refer to "Structure of the Traditional Essay" and "Sample of a Traditional Essay" in *Writers INC*, or How to Write an Essay.

Step 4 Excel

Share what you have learned about Babylonia with a friend or family member. Correct all written work to demonstrate correct punctuation and spelling, and effective use of grammar. Add corrected written work or any illustrations to your portfolio.

Footnotes
1. Blank, Wayne. 1998. "Ancient Empires - Babylon," <http://www.execulink.com/~wblank/index.htm> (Accessed 1999).

Resources recommended in ♦several lessons, ★ several units, ◗▸ other HOW Units. ☞ Key Resource (see beginning of unit or page 32).

Heart of Wisdom Publishing   149

Hanging Gardens of Babylon

Step 1 Excite

Have you ever heard of the Seven Wonders of the Ancient World? Can you name any of them? The Hanging Gardens of Babylon are one of the Seven Wonders.

Step 2 Examine

King Nebuchadnezzar II built a palace on the banks of the Euphrates river which was home to these legendary gardens. In his books on history, Diodorius Siculus, a Greek historian, described the Gardens this way: "The approach to the Garden sloped like a hillside and the several parts of the structure rose from one another tier on tier . . . On all this, the earth had been piled . . . and was thickly planted with trees of every kind that, by their great size and other charm, gave pleasure to the beholder . . . The water machines [raised] the water in great abundance from the river, although no one outside could see it."

Research the Hanging Gardens of Babylon. Use any resource (an encyclopedia, non-fiction book, historical novel, or the Internet). We recommend any of the following:

Underlined text refers to Internet link at http://Homeschool-Books.com

Books

Kingfisher Illustrated History of the World ❤
Read: "The Hanging Gardens of Babylon" (71-73).

First Civilizations (Cultural Atlas for Young People) ◆
Read: "The Hanging Gardens" (80).

Kingfisher History Encyclopedia ❤
Read: "The Hanging Gardens of Babylon" (36-37).

Usborne's Illustrated Ancient World ❤
Read: "The Hanging Gardens of Babylon" (76).

Streams of Civilizations: Earliest Times to Discovery ★
Read: "The Hanging Gardens of Babylon" (101, 102, 133).

Internet Sources

Hanging Gardens of Babylon
Description: Text and illustrations describing the Hanging Gardens of Babylon.

Hanging Gardens of Babylon: The Seven Wonders of the Ancient World
Description: Text and illustrations describing the Hanging Gardens of Babylon, from the Seven Wonders Site.

The Hanging Gardens of Babylon
Description: A computer-generated image of the Gardens during the day and night.

The Hanging Gardens of Babylon
Description: An overview of one of the Seven Wonders of the Ancient World. Middle-school level.

The Hanging Gardens of Babylon: The Seven World Wonders
Description: Details the Seven Wonders of the Ancient World.

Resources recommended in ◆several lessons, ★ several units, ᒋ◆other HOW Units. ◉—Key Resource (see beginning of unit or page 32).

Step 3 Expand

Choose and complete one of the following activities:

Activity 1: Write a Description
Using the information from your research, try to describe the Gardens in your own words. Use neither less than fifty words nor more than 200. In your description, compare the vastness of the Hanging Gardens to the gardens of today. Refer to "Writing About a Thing" in *Writers INC*.

Activity 2: Find Illustrations
Print out, trace, sketch, or photocopy a picture of the Hanging Gardens from a book or the Internet.

Activity 3: Make a Display
Make a scrapbook page or lapbook showing all Seven Wonders of the world.

Activity 4: Expand Your Research
Diodorius Siculus said that "great water machines" brought water to the garden. Research water hydraulics and draw a water machine to raise water. For example, research ram pumps. A ram pump is a simple two-piece hydraulic pump used to raise water to great heights.

Step 4 Excel

Share what you have learned with a friend or family member. Correct written work to demonstrate correct punctuation and spelling, and effective use of grammar. Add corrected written work or any illustrations to your portfolio. Add any new words you learned in this lesson to your Vocabulary Notebook (see page 22).

Underlined text refers to Internet link at http://Homeschool-Books.com

Hammurabi Code

Step 1 Excite

Brainstorm and make a list of at least fifteen basic laws which you believe are found in most countries today.

Step 2 Examine

In smaller groups of early civilizations, everyone knew and trusted each other. The leaders could easily make decisions when problems arose. As cities grew larger, the people needed consistent and fair laws.

King Hammurabi of the Babylonian Empire reigned between 1800 B.C. and 1760 B.C. The Code of Hammurabi is a collection of the laws and edicts of this king. A copy of the code, etched on a block of black diorite nearly 2.4 m. (8 ft.) high, was discovered by a team of French archaeologist at Susa, Iraq, in 1902. The people of Babylonia believed that Hammurabi received the law from the sun god Shamash. The code itself, composed of twenty-eight paragraphs, seems to be a series of amendments to the common law of Babylonia, rather than a strict legal code.

> Some point to the law code of King Hammurabi of Babylonia as the actual source of the laws given by Moses. Hammurabi is believed to have lived about 150 years before Moses wrote the laws of Israel. Far from being merely copied from Hammurabi's code, the Mosaic law stands far superior to that of Hammurabi. Concerning this, the noted Joseph Plessis wrote: "It does not appear that the Hebrew legislator made any use of the various codes of Babylonia and Assyria. Nothing in his work can be proved to have been borrowed. Although there are interesting similarities, they are not such that they cannot be easily explained by the codifying of customs shared by people with a common origin." (*Supple'ment au Dictionnaire de la Bible*) Also, W. J. Martin tells us: "Despite many resemblances, there is no ground for assuming any direct borrowing by the Hebrew from the Babylonian. Even where the two sets of laws differ little in the letter, they differ much in the spirit. For example, in the Hammurabi Code, theft and receiving stolen goods were punished by the death penalty (Laws 6 and 22), but in Israel's laws the punishment was compensation (Exodus 22:1; Leviticus 6:1-5). Whereas the Mosaic law forbade handing over an escaped slave to his master (Deuteronomy 23:15,16), the Babylonian laws punished by death anyone taking in a fugitive slave. — Laws 15, 16, 19."[1]

Resources recommended in ◆several lessons, ★ several units, ◖►other HOW Units. ●━Key Resource (see beginning of unit or page 32).

The Code of Hammurabi would have one display a spirit of vengeance, whereas the Hebrew law tells us: *You must not hate your brother in your heart . . . You must not take vengeance, nor bear any grudge against the children of your people, but you must love your neighbor as yourself. I am Yahweh* (Leviticus 19:17,18).

Research Hammurabi's law. Use any resource (an encyclopedia, non-fiction book, historical novel, or the Internet). We recommend the following:

Books

First Civilizations (Cultural Atlas for Young People) ◆
Read: "Law and Society" (56-57).

Mesopotamia and the Fertile Crescent ◆
Read: "Government, Society, and Law" (26-31).

Daily Life in Ancient Mesopotamia ◆
Read: "Government."

Of Codes and Crowns: The Development of Law by Constitutional Rights Foundation (Law and World History Series)
Description: Background information and activities on the development of law and legal systems from ancient times to the Renaissance. An entire section is devoted to Hammurabi's Law Collection. (1983) Los Angeles: Constitutional Rights Foundation. Reading level: Ages 12 and up.

The Code of Hammurabi: Law of Mesopotamia: A Unit of Study for Grades 9-12 by Joann Woodard
Description: This curriculum guide contains good activity ideas that can readily be adapted for middle-school use. Some of the background information is dated and does not reflect the latest research. (1991) University of California at Los Angeles: National Center for History in the Schools.

Internet Sources

The Code of Hammurabi
Description: The Avalon Project of the Yale Law School has made available "The Code of Hammurabi" translation by L. W. King, with an introduction by Charles F. Horne, Ph.D. (1915) and commentary from The Eleventh Edition of the *Encyclopaedia Britannica*.

Hammurabi Code: You Be the Judge
Description: Interactive site with engaging graphics and humor.

(i) History Department Student Essay Page
Description: A collection of student essays from middle- and secondary-school history students. In response to the question "How do the laws of a society reflect its most important cultural values, as seen in the law codes and cultures of Hammurabi's Babylon and Moses' Hebrews?" are two student papers: Moses-Hammurabi Paper and The Laws of Ancient Society.

Step 3 Expand

Choose and complete one of the following activities:

Activity 1:Contrast and Compare
Make a contrast and compare graphic (see page 26) to compare the Code of Hammurabi and biblical law.

Activity 2: Make a List
Make a list of five laws that Hammurabi made which you think would be appropriate for today's society.

Activity 3: Copy Passages
Copy several rules about water from the Code of Hammurabi. Write a summary of what you learned from the Code of Hammurabi about the importance of water and the problems of irrigation.

Activity 4: Read and Copy
Law is useless without God, and Babylonia was cursed for its idolatry. Read Psalm 14:4-26. The law of God is: *perfect, converting the soul: the testimony of the LORD is sure, making wise the simple. The statutes of the LORD are right, rejoicing the heart: the commandment of the LORD is pure, enlightening the eyes. The fear of the LORD is clean, enduring for ever: the judgments of the LORD are true and righteous altogether* (Psalm 19:7-9). Read and copy the following Bible verses for your portfolio: Psalm 19:7-9; Psalm 119:1-8; and Proverbs 28:4-5.

Step 4 Excel

Share your work from Step 3 with someone. Explain what you have learned in this lesson. Correct all written work to demonstrate correct punctuation and spelling, and effective use of grammar. Add corrected written work or any illustrations to your portfolio. Add any new words you learned in this lesson to your Vocabulary Notebook (see page 22).

Footnote
1.. Thomas, D. Winton. 1958. *Documents from Old Testament Times*. Nelson, ISBN: 0061300853.

Resources recommended in ♦several lessons, ★ several units, ▯➤other HOW Units. ●━Key Resource (see beginning of unit or page 32).

Heart of Wisdom Publishing   155

Persia 612–330 B.C.

Note: You'll learn about the Hebrews under Persian rule in the <u>The Persian Period</u> lesson and about <u>Queen Esther</u> in the *Ancient Israel Unit*.

1233-1318

The Narrated Bible
*See note on page 102

Step 1 Excite

The Jews return from Babylonian captivity to Israel under Persian rule. Can you begin to imagine how the Jews felt? This was during the time of Ezra, Nehemiah, and the prophet Haggai, when the situation looked very bleak. How were they to bring about the fulfillment of God's promises to Abraham and Moses? Their position seemed completely hopeless. Persia had total control over Israel. The Temple was in shambles. The people were few and without many resources. What could they possibly do to turn things around? How could they possibly bring about the Kingdom that God had promised?

The Book of Ezra begins where 2 Chronicles left off. It tells the story of the return of the Jews from Babylon to the Promised Land. The return and building of the Temple is symbolic of the Hebrews' spiritual commitment. The Book of Nehemiah is about the building of the wall of Jerusalem. Nehemiah was cupbearer to the king of Persia. The Book of Esther explains how God saved His people through Esther (who was married to a king of Persia). Copy the chart below for your portfolio. Make the names Ezra, Nehemiah, and Esther a special bold color.

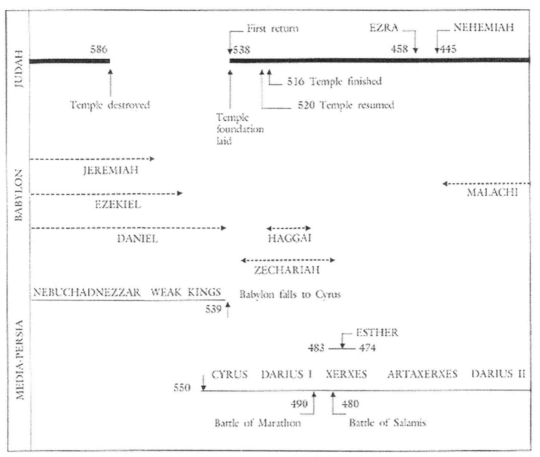

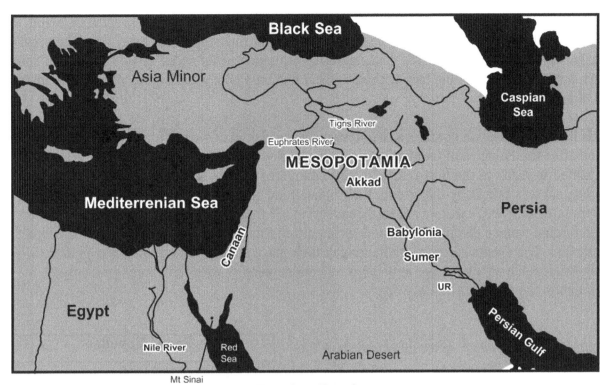

Persian Empire

Step 2 Examine

Most people today know Persia (modern-day Iran) through its carpets and the war with Iraq, or as one of the world's major oil-producing nations. Yet, Persia has one of the richest and oldest cultures in the world. We know much about the Persians because of their interaction with the Greeks, who wrote prolifically. It was the largest empire in history until it was over-run by Alexander the Great in 331 B.C.

Though the terms "Persia" or "Persian" occur only in Ezekiel, 2 Chronicles, Esther, Daniel, and Ezra, ancient Persia played an important role in the Old Testament books, including Nehemiah, Haggai, Zechariah, and Malachi. For more than 3,000 years, Persia was a melting pot of civilizations and demographic movements between Asia and Europe. Under Cyrus the Great, it became the center of the world's first empire. Successive invasions by the Greeks, Arabs, Mongols, and Turks developed the nation's culture through rich and diverse philo-sophical, artistic, scientific, and religious influences.

The ascendancy of the Medo-Persian Empire, which defeated Babylon in 539 B.C., is clearly connected with God's plan to bring the majority of Judeans back into the land. King Cyrus is portrayed as a beneficent instrument in the hand of God to enable Judah to return home after God's spiritual purposes had been accomplished (Isa. even refers to Cyrus as God's "messiah" or "anointed one" [45:1]). But in the meantime, the distress over absence from the land (as

---

Resources recommended in ♦several lessons, ★ several units, ▢▸other HOW Units. ◉━Key Resource (see beginning of unit or page 32).

in Ps.137) had served as part of the chastising instrument of God to bring repentance and remove idolatry. In this case then, being under an idolatrous oppressor away from the previously neglected land and Temple had caused a rethinking of the value of God's love and concern for Judah. This simple fact of geographical distance is of great significance in the history of Israel.[1]

The Book of Nehemiah continues the story of the Jewish exiles who returned to their homeland after the Babylonian Captivity. As told in the Book of Ezra, a group of about 50,000 returned to Judah in the first year of Cyrus, conquerer of Babylon (538 B.C.). The Temple at Jerusalem was rebuilt by this group. Ezra himself led about 1,500 more back some eighty years later (458 B.C.). Ezra's spiritual leadership led to a vital reform: Those who had married foreign women divorced them and recommitted themselves to their covenant relationship with God. The events recorded by Nehemiah took place some twelve years later (446 B.C.). Nehemiah came as a governor appointed to lead his people, with the express purpose of rebuilding the walls of the Holy City.[2]

Smith's Bible Dictionary[3] gives an overview of the Persians:

Persia Timeline	
715 B.C.	Medes conquer Persia
550	Persians overthrow Medes
539	Cyrus the Great of Persia captures Babylon
539-332	Judah becomes province of Persian empire
485-465	Reign of Xerxes
480	Esther becomes queen of Persia
465	Death of Xerxes
336-330	Reign of Darius Codomannus
330	Alexander the Great conquers Persian Empire

The Persians were a people of lively and impressible minds, brave and impetuous in war, witty, passionate, for Orientals truthful, not without some spirit of generosity: and of more intellectual capacity than the generality of Asiatics. In the times anterior to Cyrus they were noted for the simplicity of their habits, which offered a strong contrast to the luxuriousness of the Medes; but from the late of the Median overthrow this simplicity began to decline. Polygamy was commonly practiced among them. They were fond of the pleasures of the table. In war they fought bravely, but without discipline. The religion which the Persians brought with them into Persia proper seems to have been of a very simple character, differing from natural religion in little except that it was deeply tainted with Dualism. Like the other Aryans, the Persians worshiped one supreme God. They had few temples, and no altars or images.

Research Persia. Use any resource (an encyclopedia, non-fiction book, historical novel, or the Internet). We recommend the following:

Read the Books of Ezra, Nehemiah, and Esther in the Bible or in a Bible storybook.

Books

Exploring Ancient Cities of the Bible ☞ ♥
Read: "The Persian Empire" (24-25).

The Victor Journey through the Bible ☞ ♥
Read: "The Story of Queen Esther" (178-179); "Ezra and the People
Return" (180-181); "Nehemiah Prays for His Homeland" (182-183); "Nehemiah
Builds Jerusalem's Walls" (176-177); "Ezra Reads the Law" (186-187).

Encyclopedia of the Bible (Nelson's Illustrated) ♥
"The Persians" (66-67), "Esther" (215), "The Persian Empire" (35)

First Civilizations (Cultural Atlas for Young People) ♦
Read: "Rise of the Persian Empire" and "The Empire of Darius" (82-85).

The Usborne Book of the Ancient World ♥
Read: "The Persians" (77).

Kingfisher History Encyclopedia ♥
Read: "The Persian Empire" (40-41).

Ancient Civilizations (Exploring History) ★
Read: "The Persian Empire" (14-15).

Mesopotamia and the Fertile Crescent ♦
Read: "Persia: The Rising New Power" (58-59).

Internet Sources

Early Days of Persia
Description: A small time line from 2000 B.C. to A.D. 642.

The Persian Empire
Description: A list of important events of the Persian era to help one understand the significance of the Persian civilization's influence on future governments.

Step 3 Expand

Choose and complete one of the following activities:

Resources recommended in ♦several lessons, ★ several units, ♥other HOW Units. ☞—Key Resource (see beginning of unit or page 32).

Heart of Wisdom Publishing   159

Activity 1: Map Work
Make or trace a copy of the ancient Near East map. Shade the area of the Persian Empire with a colored pencil and include in your portfolio.

Activity 2: Add to Your Time Line Book
Add the building of the second Temple, the building of the wall of Jerusalem, the story of Esther, and the Persian kings to your Time Line Book.

Activity 3: Answer Questions
Answer the following:
1. In what modern-day country was the Persian Empire located?
2. Persia was the largest world empire until conquered by whom?
3. Who were the four "powerful" Persian kings?
4. What was it that motivated the Hebrews to return to building the second Temple? Who led the building?
5. Who led the building of the wall around Jerusalem?
6. What wife of a Persian king saved the Jewish people?

Activity 4: Make an Outline
Outline the Book of Ezra, Nehemiah, or Esther.

Activity 5: Write a Prayer
Rewrite Ezra 9:6–15 in your own words.

Activity 6: Expand Your Research
In writing, describe and assess the circumstances surrounding the Persians' defeat at Plataea by using the Internet and other resources. Explain the people involved and the repercussions.

Step 4 Excel

Explain orally to your parents what you've learned in this lesson. Correct all written work to demonstrate correct punctuation and spelling, and effective use of grammar. Include corrected written work in your portfolio.

Footnotes
1. Karleen, P. S. 1987. *The Handbook to Bible Study*. Oxford University Press: New York.
2. Richards, L. 1987. *The Teacher's Commentary*. Victor Books: Wheaton, Ill.
4. Smith, William, Dr. "Entry for 'Persia'" *Smith's Bible Dictionary*.

Underlined text refers to Internet link at http://Homeschool-Books.com

Art in Mesopotamia

Step 1 Excite

The lower parts of the Mesopotamian region encompassed a fertile plain, but its inhabitants perpetually faced the dangers of outside invaders, extremes in temperature, drought, violent thunderstorms and rainstorms, floods, and attacks by wild beasts. Their art reflects both their love and fear of these natural forces. Mesopotamian

civilizations are well known for their wonderful masterpieces of art, many of which can be seen in famous museums like the Louvre, the British Museum, and the Iraq Museum.

View and compare art from Mesopotamia with art from other ancient civilizations using library books or the site described below.

Timelines of Art History
Description: An outstanding site for the ancient civilizations of Egypt, Mesopotamia, Greece, Rome, India, Japan, and China. Each entry on the time line links to a page of narrative and a large gallery of images.

Step 2 Examine

Find examples of Mesopotamian art in a book from the library or using the Internet resources. One of the greatest qualities of art is the way it "speaks" to each of us. People may share opinions about a work of art, and even feel similar emotional responses, but ultimately our reactions to art and our interpretations of it are as individual and unique as we are. We recommend any of the following:

Books

Kingfisher History Encyclopedia ♥
Read: "Prehistoric Arts and Crafts." (15, 42).

First Civilizations (Cultural Atlas for Young People) ♦
Read: "The Art of Pottery" (26-27).

Mesopotamia and the Fertile Crescent ♦
Read: "Arts and Crafts" (46-53).

Resources recommended in ♦several lessons, ★ several units, ⬚▸other HOW Units. ●━Key Resource (see beginning of unit or page 32).

Internet Sources

The Detroit Institute of Arts
Description: Take a virtual tour of the DIA collection of ancient Mesopotamian art. Each image leads to further information and an enlarged view of the work.

The Fertile Crescent and the Eastern Aegean
Description: Illustrations from Assyrian, Babylonian, and Sumerian civilizations.

Mesopotamian Art 3500-331 B.C.
Description: Art History 101 from About.com.

Mesopotamian Art and Archaeology
Description: A well-organized collection of Mesopotamian art and archaeology links. Includes brief descriptions for each resource.

The Mesopotamian Collection of the Oriental Institute Museum
Description: An index of materials on Mesopotamian culture and history. Includes details of museums and archaeological digs from the University of Chicago.

University of Pennsylvania Museum of Archaeology and Anthropology
Description: A renowned collection from the Royal Cemetery at Ur (in modern-day Iraq).

Step 3 Expand

Choose and complete one of the following activities:

Activity 1: Write a Story
Express your responses to art by writing stories inspired by a particular piece of art. Examine a piece of art, then write a description to help others imagine what it looks like. Select the most important details to include in a descriptive paragraph: Distinguish between factual and judgmental language. Write a descriptive text using only facts; write a story using both facts and judgmental language.

Activity 2: Study Art
Find illustrations of Mesopotamian art in a book, on the Internet or at the library. Make a printout, sketch, or photocopy of the illustration to include in your portfolio.

Underlined text refers to Internet link at http://Homeschool-Books.com

Activity 3: Discuss and List
Discuss and make a list of what you can tell about a given civilization from its art.

Activity 4: Build a Miniature Ziggurat
Mud bricks were a cheap and abundant building material in Mesopotamia. Builders used pitch (oil) as mortar. Look at pictures of a ziggurat. Make mud bricks by putting wet dirt into the flat part of egg cartons. (What did the Mesopotamians use to shape bricks?) Let the mud dry for at least a week. Build a miniature ziggurat. Imagine what it would be like to build a structure seventy feet high from mud bricks!

Step 4 Excel

Share illustrations of Mesopotamian art with a friend or family member. Correct written work to demonstrate correct punctuation and spelling, and effective use of grammar. Add corrected written work and any illustrations to your portfolio. Add any new words you learned in this lesson to your Vocabulary Notebook (see page 22).

Resources recommended in ♦several lessons, ★ several units, ☐➧other HOW Units. ●━Key Resource (see beginning of unit or page 32).

Heart of Wisdom Publishing   163

Daily Life in Mesopotamia

Step 1 Excite

Brainstorm and discuss how you believe the first people farmed, and make a list including items involved in pest control, tools, watering, technology, etc. How did they cook their food? How did they carry water? How much time do you think was devoted to making the containers? How did they make tools?

Changes in food supply have caused many of the major changes in cultures and civilizations throughout history. Mesopotamia found itself rich in emmer wheat, einkorn wheat, barley, legumes, peas, and other high-carbohydrate foods which people needed. This allowed the people to settle down and turn to farming instead of looking for food by traveling from place to place. Brainstorm and discuss how you think the modern diet differs from the diet in ancient Mesopotamia. What are the results of straying from a natural diet?

Step 2 Examine

Most of daily life in Mesopotamia consisted of work. The majority of the people worked at farming. The most common implements of farming in ancient times were the plow, the hoe, the harrow, and the rake. Soon, farmers used yoked animals (camels, cattle, etc.) to power plows and harrows. Later, terrace agriculture was a common method of farming. Irrigated agriculture was prevalent in the river plains of Africa and Asia.

Other than farmers there were potters, builders, traders, slaves, servants, priests, kings, and elders. It has always been important for people to be able to carry things. There is a limit to what we can carry with our hands. Objects could be carried in hides, but hides were somewhat inconvenient because of their shapes. Gourds were probably used at first. Eventually, the Sumerians learned to weave twigs into baskets. These worked well for solid or dry objects, but they could not carry olive oil, flour, or (most importantly) water. The Sumerians probably dabbed clay over the baskets to make them solid. They discovered that if they baked the mud in the sun, it would become harder, hence the invention of pottery.

Read Daniel chapter 1. Describe what you think the "king's portion" was. This must have been the best of the land, yet Daniel rejected it. Read the Old Testament prohibitions against certain foods. You can find these in Leviticus and Deuteronomy. Why do you suppose that Daniel and the others rejected the king's portion? Why do you think God had placed certain types of food in a forbidden category?

Underlined text refers to Internet link at http://Homeschool-Books.com

Food in Bible times was prepared for use in various ways. The cereals were sometimes eaten raw (Lev. 23:14; Deut. 23:25; 2 Kings 4:42). Vegetables were cooked by boiling (Gen. 25:30,34; 2 Kings 4:38,39), and thus other articles of food were prepared for use (Gen. 27:4; Prov. 23:3; Ezek. 24:10; Luke 24:42; John 21:9). Food was also prepared by roasting (Ex. 12:8; Lev. 2:14).

Research daily life in Mesopotamia. Use any resource (an encyclopedia, non-fiction book, historical novel, or the Internet). We recommend the following:

Books

Encyclopedia of the Bible (Nelson's Illustrated) ❤
Skim Part 3 "The World of the Bible" (83-143).

Ancient Civilizations (Exploring History) ★
Read: "Introduction" (6-7).

First Civilizations (Cultural Atlas for Young People) ◆
Read: "First Farmers" (ignore the dates).

Kingfisher History Encyclopedia ❤
Read: "The First Farmers."

Kingfisher Illustrated History of the World ❤
Read: Use the index to look up entries about farming in ancient times.

Usborne's Illustrated Ancient World ★
Read: "Farming in Canaan"; "Farming in Sumer." Use the index to look up "farming."

First Civilizations (Cultural Atlas for Young People) ◆
Read: "Early Peoples (14-15); "Early Village Life" (18-19); "Everyday Life" (62-63).

Ancient Civilizations (Exploring History) ★
Read: Pages 6-15.

Mesopotamia and the Fertile Crescent ◆
Read: "Everyday Life" (42-45).

Daily Life in Ancient Mesopotamia ◆
Read: "Society, Part I: City Life, Country Life, Nomadic and Semi-Nomadic Life"; "Society, Part II: Private Life"; and "Recreation."

Internet Sources

Resources recommended in ◆several lessons, ★several units, ▯❤other HOW Units. ●—Key Resource (see beginning of unit or page 32).

Heart of Wisdom Publishing   165

Beginning and Development of Agriculture
Description: Overview of the history of food and agriculture from the Agropolis-Museum, with links to maps and further information.

Development of Agriculture
Description: Article with illustrations and maps explaining the transition from hunter/gatherers to settled gardeners (horticulturists and the development of agriculture).

Near East: Daily Life
Description: Overview of daily life from Odyssey Online. This site explores Near Eastern, Egyptian, Greek, Roman, and sub-Saharan African cultures.

World History 8000 B.C. to 3500 B.C.
Description: Map and overview of this period from *Poppa's Ancient World*.

Step 3 Expand

Choose and complete one of the following activities:

Activity 1: Contrast and Compare
Create a Venn diagram (see page 26) comparing life after the Flood in Bible times, in the Middle Ages, in your local area 100 years ago, and in your local area today. Refer to "Methods of Organization" in *Writers INC*. Share your diagram with a group or your family.

Activity 2: Write an Essay
Write an essay explaining how the Agricultural Revolution altered human history. Use materials from the resources to draw evidence for your presentation. Remember to focus on both the process and the impact of the event.

Activity 3: Make a Storyboard
Make and share a storyboard (see page 26). A storyboard is a graphic, sequential depiction of a narrative. Sketch or trace an example of each type of farmer throughout history, showing the farmer's technical progress from digging-stick to hoe and from the cattle-drawn wooden plow to the tractor-driven, steel-shared plow.

Activity 4: Make Lentil Soup
The following is a very easy recipe. To make it a bit more like that made in ancient times, begin with dried lentils (follow package directions). For easy lentil soup you need: 1-15 oz. can lentils, 1-14.5 oz. can stewed tomatoes (or diced tomatoes), 1 cup vegetable broth, 1 teaspoon minced garlic, 1/2 teaspoon oregano,

---

Underlined text refers to Internet link at http://Homeschool-Books.com

salt and pepper to taste, and 1 tablespoon extra-virgin olive oil (optional). Directions: Combine lentils, tomatoes, vegetable broth, garlic, oregano, and a dash of red pepper. Add salt and pepper to taste. Bring to a boil, then reduce heat and simmer, uncovered, for ten minutes. Just before serving, stir in the olive oil. If you want it thicker, leave out the vegetable broth. As you make the soup, discuss the modern conveniences we have that make cooking easier.

Activity 5: Create a Picture Book

Create a book of daily life in Mesopotamia for younger children in picture-book form. Explore a single activity over this time period (such as farming or entertainment), a single group of people (such as women or the military), or leisure time (such as leisure-time activities of common men). Title the book. Using pictures from the Internet, sketches, or photocopies from resource books, cut out images and paste them into the book.

Activity 6: Experiment

Use naturally occurring materials in your yard to see if you can make a watertight container out of natural resources. Drink from your container every time you get thirsty for at least one full day.

Activity 7: Write an Essay

Write a traditional essay about the people of early civilizations. Include what they looked like, who and how they worshiped, marriage customs, approximate population, government, basic laws, monetary systems, entertainment, clothing, food, what their homes were like, their educational system and written language, etc. Refer to "Structure of the Traditional Essay" and "Sample of a Traditional Essay" in *Writers INC,* or "How to Write an Essay."

Step 4 Excel

Serve lentil soup to your family. Discuss other meals that families in Mesopotamia ate. Explain orally to your parents what you've learned about farming and daily life in ancient times. Correct all written work to demonstrate correct punctuation and spelling, and effective use of grammar. Add corrected written work or any illustrations to your portfolio.

Resources recommended in ◆several lessons, ★ several units, ▷ other HOW Units. ●— Key Resource (see beginning of unit or page 32).

Heart of Wisdom Publishing   167

Religion in Mesopotamia

Step 1 Excite

There were a vast number of gods, spirits, and demons in Mesopotamian religion, reputedly nearly two thousand of them. In their normal, everyday life, most inhabitants of the region felt themselves to be surrounded by a host of supernatural forces, both good and bad; a belief that is revealed in a vast number of surviving incantations and counter-incantations.

Step 2 Examine

Research religion in ancient Mesopotamia. Use any resource (an encyclopedia, a non-fiction book, or the Internet). We recommend the following:

Books

Encyclopedia of the Bible (Nelson's Illustrated) ♥
"Ancient Beliefs" (146-147).

Kingfisher History Encyclopedia ☞ ♥
Read: "Religion in the Ancient World." Look in the index under "Religion."

Usborne's Illustrated Ancient World ☞ ★
Read: "Sumerian Religion"; "Canaan Religion"; "Assyrian Religion." Look up entries in the index under "Religion."

Mesopotamia and the Fertile Crescent ◆
Read: "Religion and Mythology" (37-41).

Streams of Civilizations: Earliest Times to Discovery ★
Read: "Sumerian Religion"; "Assyrian Religion"; "Babylonian Religion." Look up entries in the index under "Religion."

Internet Sources

Ancient Mesopotamia
Description: Overview of history of Mesopotamia, including religious practices.

Underlined text refers to Internet link at http://Homeschool-Books.com

(i) The Divine World
Description: Sketch of religion in Mesopotamia.

(i) Mesopotamian Deities
Description: About.com explores Mesopotamian, Sumerian, and Babylonian deities and mythology.

(i) Who Were the Gods and the Heroes of the Babylonians Then?
Description: Summaries of each of the following: the older gods, the younger Anunnaki and Igigi, the chthonic gods, the heroes, and monsters.

Step 3 Expand

Choose and complete one of the following activities:

Activity 1: Write an Essay
From your research of the religions of Assyria, Babylon, Canaan, and Sumeria, write an essay on the comparison of the roles which the four major gods played in each civilization.

Activity 2: Research and Discuss
The nation of Israel was often tempted and fell into the trap of worshipping these gods of Mesopotamia instead of the only Living True God. Molech, for example, is referred to in the Bible (Lev. chapters 8 and 20). Also, Baal and Ashtoroth are referenced in the Bible (Numbers, Judges, and Kings). Use the Bible Study Aids in the Research Area to study what God has to say about idolatry. What other gods are spoken about in the Bible? Discuss with your parents why you think that the Israelites were so tempted that they fell away from worshipping the True and Living God to worship idols and false gods.

Activity 3: Copy Passages
Copy (by hand or typing) two or more paragraphs from your research, or have someone dictate the passage to you. Younger students can copy one or two sentences or narrate (tell back) what has been learned.

Step 4 Excel

Share what you have learned in this lesson with a friend or family member. Correct written work to demonstrate correct punctuation and spelling, and effective use of grammar. Add corrected written work or any illustrations to your portfolio. Add any new words you learned in this lesson to your Vocabulary Notebook (see page 22).

Resources recommended in ◆several lessons, ★ several units, ⬡ other HOW Units. ●━ Key Resource (see beginning of unit or page 32).

Science and Technology in Mesopotamia

Step 1 Excite

Brainstorm and discuss the inventions and discoveries that may have come from ancient Mesopotamia. Think about daily life in this time period. It is said, "Necessity is the mother of invention." What problems occurred in daily life that triggered inventions? What do you think would happen if you were sick in ancient Mesopotamia? Could you go to a doctor? What if you broke your leg? What if you had a toothache? What remedies do you think were used for colds and the flu? Who attended the birth of babies?

Step 2 Examine

The first writing (a system of pictographs), a lunar calendar, the wheel, and early bronze work are all from ancient Mesopotamia. The use of the number 12 (and multiples of 12) as applied to time and degrees comes to us from the Sumerians, along with the dozen as a common measure.

Mathematics
We use a mathematical system based on 10, and we have a unit called zero. Try adding, subtracting, and multiplying with a zero. 10 times 10 equals 100. To the Babylonians math was much different. They had a base number of 60, but had no zero.

Calendar
Much of our calendar system is from the Babylonians. They were probably the first people after the Sumerians to have a calendar. This calendar was very important because without it agriculture could not be planned properly.

There were twelve lunar months in the year but as the months were shorter than our months often an extra month would have to be added. This was called the second Elul. Each week was divided into seven days. The day was divided into six parts each of two hours duration and containing thirty parts. The Babylonians measured time with a water or sun clock. One can see from this that the Babylonian calendar has marked similarities with our own: for instance the twelve months in the year and seven days in a week.[1]

Medicine:
Two kinds of specialists dealt with disease in ancient Mesopotamia: The ashipu practiced magic, and the asu was a physician who prescribed practical remedies.

Underlined text refers to Internet link at http://Homeschool-Books.com

Research the contributions of the Sumerians and science in Mesopotamia. Use any resource (an encyclopedia, a non-fiction book, or the Internet). We recommend the following:

Books

Encyclopedia of the Bible (Nelson's Illustrated) ❤
"Health and Healing" (138-139).

The Bible Comes Alive Volume One, Creation to Abraham ◆
Read: "Metallurgy in Ancient Civilizations" (24).

Usborne Book of Discovery: Inventors/Scientists/Explorers ❤
Read: "Early Inventions"(4-5), "Early Scientific Ideas" (51-52) .

Science in Ancient Mesopotamia (Science of the Past) by Carol Moss
Description: Outlines the enormous accomplishments of the Sumerians and Babylonians of ancient Mesopotamia in every scientific area, a heritage which affects our own everyday lives. School & Library Binding (September 1998) Franklin Watts, Incorporated; ISBN: 0531203646. Reading level: Ages 9-12.

Mesopotamia and the Fertile Crescent ◆
Read: "Science and Technology" (54-57); "Doctors and Medicine" (56).

Daily Life in Ancient Mesopotamia ◆
Read: "The Sciences."

Internet Sources

Medicine in Ancient Mesopotamia
Description: Includes information about concepts and understanding of disease and medicine

Medicine through Time
Description: This is a very informative site from the BBC. Read through the "Prehistory" and "Ancient World" sections: "Disease & its Treatment," "Anatomy & Surgery," "Hospitals & Training," "Public Health," and "Alternatives to Medicine."

Mesopotamian and Sumerian Inventions
Description: A sixth-grade class studies Mesopotamian inventions such as the wheel, sailboat, arch, cuneiform writing, music, games, mathematics, and cities.

Mesopotamian Industry
Description: Overview of Mesopotamian inventions.

Resources recommended in ◆several lessons, ★ several units, �COother HOW Units. ●━Key Resource (see beginning of unit or page 32).

Heart of Wisdom Publishing   171

Track Star: Mesopotamia
Description: This track is designed for students to learn more about some aspects of ancient Mesopotamia by following selected Web links. Topics include: artifacts, the wheel, chariots, sailboats, maps, and Hammurabi's Code.

Step 3 Expand

Choose and complete one of the following activities:

Activity 1: Write an Explanation
Choose one of the inventions discussed in the resources above, and write an explanation (minimum 200 words) showing how one of these led to devices we use today. Refer to "Writing an Explanation" in *Writers INC*. Younger child can explain orally.

Activity 2: Find Illustrations
Print out, trace, sketch, or photocopy pictures of inventions or discoveries from this time period, from a book or the Internet. Include several examples for your portfolio.

Activity 3: Make a Display
Make a display out of poster board, using colored pencils or markers to illustrate scientific and technological contributions of the Mesopotamians.

Activity 4: Make a Cartoon Strip
Draw a comic book page complete with conversations in "bubbles" showing the invention of the wheel. Show men talking about moving heavy objects, first attempts maybe using a tree log, etc.

Activity 5: Write a Short Story
Write a short story about someone ill or hurt in ancient Mesopotamia. Focus on the character. Include details of his disorder, and the remedy. Refer to "Writing a Short Story" in *Writers INC*. (Younger children can dictate a story.)

Activity 6: Contrast and Compare
Make a contrast and compare graphic (see page 26) to show the uses of the different forms of medicines in ancient Mesopotamia and in modern medicine.

Activity 7: Answer Questions
Answer the following:
1. What type of surgery was practiced in ancient Mesopotamia?

Underlined text refers to Internet link at http://Homeschool-Books.com

2. What are some of the herbs and plants used in making the medicines and cures for the common diseases experienced in the Mesopotamian civilizations?

3. What are some of the modern medicines that have come about because of Mesopotamian medicines?

Activity 8: Expand Your Research
Chariots and sailboats were invented by the Mesopotamian people. Do research to find out about the first chariots and sailboats.

Activity 9: Expand Your Research
Metallurgy is the science and technology of metals, including the extraction of metals from ores, and the preparation of metals for use. Find out more about metallurgy.

Step 4 Excel

Share what you have learned about discoveries and inventions with a friend or family member. Correct all written work to demonstrate correct punctuation and spelling, and effective use of grammar. Add corrected written work or any illustrations to your portfolio. Add any new words you learned in this lesson to your Vocabulary Notebook (see page 22).

Footnote
1. Butterley, Francis C.S. *The Life and Times of the Babylonians* <http://www.netcomuk.co.uk/~nynehead/babylon.html> [Accessed June 2000]

Resources recommended in ◆several lessons, ★ several units, ▯▶other HOW Units. ●━Key Resource (see beginning of unit or page 32).

Heart of Wisdom Publishing   173

Ancient Egypt Unit

Unit Overview

Ancient Egypt Overview 174
Ancient Egypt Objectives 176
Ancient Egypt Time Line 177
Ancient Egypt Vocabulary 178
Ancient Egypt Resources 179

Ancient Egypt Lessons

History of Ancient Egypt

Introduction 185
History of Ancient Egypt 187
Geography of Ancient Egypt 191
Egypt's Neighbors 193
Pyramids in Ancient Egypt 195
Ancient Egypt in the Bible 198
Joseph in Ancient Egypt (c. 1659) .202
Moses in Ancient Egypt (c. 1533) .206
The Plaques (c. 1454) 209
Passover (c. 1454) 214
The Exodus (c. 1454) 218
Pharaohs of Ancient Egypt 221
King Tutankhamen (1003-994) 224
Alliance with Israel 227

Life in Ancient Egypt

Agriculture in Ancient Egypt 229
Architecture in Ancient Egypt . . .231
Archaeology 234
Art in Ancient Egypt 236
Pottery in Ancient Egypt: 240
Cities in Ancient Egypt 242
Clothing in Ancient Egypt 244
Economy and Trade in Egypt . . .246
Daily Life in Ancient Egypt 248
Education in Ancient Egypt 252
Food in Ancient Egypt 254
Government in Ancient Egypt . . .256
Hieroglyphics 260
Language in Ancient Egypt 262
Literature in Ancient Egypt 265
Medicine in Ancient Egypt 267
Mummies in Ancient Egypt 270
The Nile River 273
Men in Ancient Egypt 277
Women in Ancient Egypt 279
Religion in Ancient Egypt 283
Science and Technology in Egypt .286
Slavery in Ancient Egypt 288

Bonus Lesson

Egypt Today 291

Related Lessons in Other Units

Egyptian Bondage (Israel) 325
Exodus and Passover (Israel) . . .328

Ancient Egypt Overview

It is impossible to properly understand the history of God's people without knowing something of ancient Egypt. The children of Israel were brought into Egypt and settled there for centuries before becoming an independent nation. Their removal from contact with the people of Canaan and their time of affliction prepared them for inheriting the land promised to their fathers. However historians may differ as to the periods when particular events have taken place, the land itself is full of reminiscences of Israel's story.

As Paul says about the Hebrews who were in the Exodus, *all these things happened to them as an example, and they were written for our admonition.* (1 Cor. 10:11). The Hebrews were enslaved by Egypt. How is that an example for us? We were enslaved by sin. God gave a deliverer to bring the Hebrews out of bondage to Egypt. God gave us a Deliverer to bring us out of bondage to sin. The Bible uses Egypt as a symbol of sin. Egypt is ancient, mysterious, and exotic. Jeremiah died there. Jesus lived there. Moses was educated there. Joseph ruled there.

What do we know of the people who inhabited the land; a people so cruel that they could murder infants, and yet so tenderhearted that they could adopt and raise a slave child? Who were the workers who did the backbreaking labor of moving barges and stones? Who were the artisans who painted murals, crafted jewelry, and carved magnificent sculptures? What kind of men and women spent hours getting dressed, pleating sheer linen fabric for their garments, applying cosmetics, arranging wigs? What kind of people served gods dedicated to frogs and flies?

Only in modern times have we re-learned to read the hieroglyphic inscriptions that tell of pharaohs, wars, conquests, and colonies. These have been brought to light by recent research projects that, almost year by year, add to our stock of knowledge. And it is especially remarkable that every fresh historical discovery tends to shed light upon—and to confirm—the biblical narratives.

Alfred Edersheim explains in *Bible History: Old Testament*:

> God marvelously uses natural means for supernatural ends, and maketh all things work together to His glory as well as for the good of His people. It was, indeed, as we now see it, most important that the children of Israel should have been brought into Egypt and settled there for centuries before becoming an independent nation. The early history of the sons of Jacob must have shown the need alike of their removal from contact with the people of Canaan and of their being fused in the furnace of affliction to prepare them for inheriting the

land promised unto their fathers. This, however, might have taken place in any other country than Egypt. Not so their training for [to be] a nation. For that, Egypt offered the best, or rather, at the time, the only suitable opportunities. True, the stay there involved also peculiar dangers, as their after-history proved. But these would have been equally encountered under any other circumstances, while the benefits they derived through interaction with the Egyptians were peculiar and unique. There is yet another aspect of the matter. When standing before King Agrippa, St. Paul could confidently appeal to the publicity of the history of Christ, as enacted not in some obscure corner of a barbarous land, but in full view of the Roman world. *For this thing was not done in a corner* (Acts 26:26). And so Israel's bondage also and God's marvelous deliverance took place on no less conspicuous a scene than that of the ancient world-empire of Egypt.

Israel as a nation was born of God, redeemed by God, brought forth by God victorious on the other side [of] the flood, taught of God, trained by God, and separated for the service of God. And this God was to be known to them as Jehovah, the living and the true God. The ideas they had gained, the knowledge they had acquired, the life they had learned, even the truths they had heard in Egypt might be taken with them, but, as it were, to be baptized in the Red Sea, and consecrated at the foot of Sinai.

As you study Egypt, try to put together the pieces. Learn how the time line of Egypt fits with Bible events. Learn how the Bible stories played out over the geography of the region.

Recommended Literature for this Unit

<u>Mara, Daughter of the Nile</u> by Eloise Jarvis McGraw ♦ Description on page 179.

<u>The Golden Goblet</u> (Puffin Newbery Library) by Eloise McGraw ♦ Description on page 179.

<u>The Midwife's Song</u> by Brenda Ray Description on page 179.

Resources recommended in ♦several lessons, ★ several units, ♥other HOW Units. ⚷━Key Resource (see beginning of unit or page 32).

Ancient Egypt Objectives

Upon completion of this unit your student should:

- Gain a closer relationship with God through study of His Word.
- Understand Egyptian culture.
- Understand Bible passages relating to Egypt.
- Understand the importance of the Nile River.
- Understand the interaction of Egypt and the nation of Israel during biblical times.
- Understand the tasks and functions of an archaeologist.
- Know and use the terminology of archaeology.
- Know about the traditions of Egyptian painting.
- Know the grandeur of ancient Egyptian architecture.
- Identify major exports of ancient Egypt.
- Understand daily life of ancient Egyptians.
- Understand how ancient Egyptians were educated.
- Have a general knowledge of famous ancient Egyptians.
- Have a general knowledge of ancient Egyptian food.
- Be familiar with the geography of Egypt and its neighbors.
- Have a grasp of the medical knowledge of ancient Egypt.
- Understand the character and life of Moses.
- Have a general knowledge of mummies.
- Know about the significance of the ten plagues.
- Understand the significance of the Passover event and celebration.
- Be familiar with the history of the Pharaohs.
- Have a general knowledge of the significance of pyramids.
- Understand the use of Egypt as a refuge in biblical times.
- Reflect on how the idolatry of the Israelites is an example for us.
- Learn how Egyptian religion influenced the rest of their culture.
- Know how idolatry was a temptation for the Hebrews.
- Understand the technology and scientific knowledge available to Egyptians.
- Reflect on the hardship of slavery.
- Appreciate the freedom we have.
- Identify Tutankhamen's contribution to our historical knowledge.
- Compare and contrast Egypt and Mesopotamia.
- Understand how God's Word uses Egypt as a symbol.
- Appreciate God's mercy and love towards Egyptians.
- Understand the life of Joseph and God's plan.
- Become familiar with the Exodus and how it relates to the plan of Salvation.
- Recognize, understand, and appreciate the function of ancient Egyptian hieroglyphs.

Ancient Egypt Time Line

Dates	Dynasty	Events & Kings	Bible
c. 2781-2662	1st Dynasty	Unification of all Egypt. Step Pyramids, Earliest evidence of hieroglyphic writing. Development of law, and religion.	
c. 2662-2511	2nd Dynasty	Papyrus used for writing paper. Ships made of planks. Physicians set broken arms using splints.	
c. 2511-2456	3rd Dynasty	Great sphinx at Gizeh is built.	
c. 2456-2346	4th Dynasty	The Great Pyramids of Giza are built	
c. 2346-2220	5th Dynasty	Worship of the sun god Re becomes state religion. First mummies.	
c. 2220-2054	6th Dynasty	Pepi I. Organizational military caste.	
c. 2054-2039	7th Dynasty		
c. 2067-1939	8th Dynasty	17 or 18 kings during 8th dynasty lasting about 20 years.	
not established	9th Dynasty	Rulers controlled from Herakleopolis.	
c. 1939-1839	10th Dynasty	House of Khety	
c. 1939-1796	11th Dynasty	Thebes - a nomarch and a priest.	
c. 1796-1632	12th Dynasty	Well developed calligraphy, papyrus, reed pens, soot ink	c. 1750 Abraham in Egypt?
c. 1632-1445	13th Dynasty	1674 Horse and chariot are introduced. 1567 Hyksos are driven out of Egypt by Egyptian military forces from Thebes. Medicine is taught in the temple schools.	From 1679 Joseph in Egypt. From 1659 Seven year Famine. From 1658 Jacob in Egypt.
not established	14th Dynasty	Ships are up to 50 metres long.	
c. 1445-1573	15th Dynasty	Scrolls made of papyrus. Two wheeled wooden chariot. Memphis replaces Thebes as capital.	c. 1533 Moses born in Egypt. c. 1454 Exodus
c. 1284-1194	16th Dynasty		
c. 1290-1183	17th Dynasty	Theban Dynasty	
c. 1194-960	18th Dynasty	1150-1085 King Thutmose I-III, 1131-1116 Hatshepsut, 1003-994 Tutankhamun	
963-854	19th Dynasty	Ramesses I-II. Water clocks. Book of the Dead.	
868-813	20th Dynasty	Ramesses III- IV, Amenemope's Book of Wisdom	
332 BC		Invasion of Egypt by Alexander the Great	

Resources recommended in ◆several lessons, ★ several units, ♥other HOW Units. ☛—Key Resource (see beginning of unit or page 32).

Ancient Egypt Vocabulary

See Vocabulary Instructions on page 22.

alabaster	faience	ostracon
Amarna	Giza	papyrus
Amenti	Hieratic	pylon
amulet	Hyksos	pyramid
ankh	inundation	relief
bas-relief	jackal	sarcophagus
Book of the Dead	Ka	Saqqara
canopic jars	Luxor	Scarab
cartonnage	mastaba	scribe
cartouche	mummification	shabi
cataracts	mummy	shaduf
cuneiform	natron	Sinai
delta	Necropolis	sphinx
demotic	nemes	stela
double crown	Nile	uraeus
dynasty	Nomarch	Via Maris
ebony	nome	Vizier
egyptologist	obelisk	
embalm	oracle	

Ancient Egypt Resources

The ❶ symbol indicates a resource appropriate for grades 4-12 or family read aloud. All other books are appropriate for young adults or adults.

Main Recommended Resources for this Unit

<u>Ancient Egypt (Eyewitness)</u> by George Hart ⊙— ◆
Eyewitness Books' *Ancient Egypt* continues the tradition of excellent, accurate, and beautiful reference works. This book is recommended in most of the "Life in Ancient Egypt" lessons. Ancient Egyptian civilization holds a special fascination for many, with its mummies, pyramids, and highly stylized artworks. Kids can explore a Pharaoh's tomb, see a mummy up close, and find out about Egyptian gods. A large number of archaeological relics show what life was like for the ancient Egyptians, from how they dressed to the games they played. Hardcover - 63 pages (August 1990) Knopf; ISBN: 067980742X. Reading level: Ages 9-12.

<u>The Golden Goblet</u> (Puffin Newbery Library) by Eloise McGraw ◆
Ranofer struggles to thwart the plottings of his evil uncle, Gebu, so that he can become a master goldsmith like his father in this exciting tale of ancient Egyptian mystery and intrigue. Newbery Honor Book. (October 1990) Viking Pr; ISBN: 0140303359. Reading level: Ages 9-12. Interest level: 9-young adult.

<u>Encyclopedia of the Bible</u> (Nelson's Illustrated) ⊙—♥
See description in the "Key Resources" section beginning on page 32.

<u>The Holman Bible Atlas</u> ⊙— ♥
See description in the "Key Resources" section beginning on page 32.

<u>Mara, Daughter of the Nile</u> by Eloise Jarvis McGraw ◆
The adventures of an ingenious Egyptian slave girl who undertakes a dangerous assignment as a spy in the royal palace of Thebes, in the days when Queen Hatshepsut ruled. Paperback - 279 pages Reissue edition (October 1990) Viking Pr; ISBN: 0140319298. Reading level: Ages 9-12.

<u>The Midwife's Song</u> by Brenda Ray
Biblical fiction. Under Pharaoh's ungodly decree, Puah, midwife to the Hebrew people, finds love, and sees her own vacillating faith grow in the fire of adversity. Utilizing biblical narrative, folklore, Ancient Near Eastern history, and imagination this story explains life in this time period and how an ordinary young woman can be used by God in an extraordinary way. Karmichael Press (2000). Paperback 256 pages. ISBN: 0965396681.

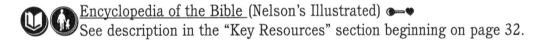

Resources recommended in ◆several lessons, ★several units, ♥other HOW Units. ⊙—Key Resource (see beginning of unit or page 32).

Pharaohs and Kings: A Biblical Quest by David M. Rohl ★
Little conclusive evidence for an historical Old Testament has come to light in two centuries of archaeological endeavor. Ever since excavations in the Lands of the Bible began at the beginning of the last century, biblical scholars have been systematically stripping out elements of the narratives - the stories of Joseph, Moses, Joshua, Saul, David and Solomon - and consigning them to the realms of myth and folklore. Egyptologist and ancient historian David Rohl has made a discovery which challenges the modern skeptical view of Old Testament history. His revolutionary theory demonstrates that archaeologists have been looking in the right places for evidence of the Israelites - but in completely the wrong time. The New Chronology reveals the true historical setting of the biblical epics, providing astonishing archaeological evidence for the existence of the Old Testament's most charismatic personalities. For the first time the lives of Joseph, Moses, Joshua, Saul, David and Solomon are examined from an historical perspective, as David Rohl explores their cities, palaces and tombs. Unveils such archaeological wonders as the desecrated statue of Joseph in his 'coat of many colors', the Israelite city of bondage in Egypt (including graphic evidence of the plagues), and letters from King Saul. Presents the most remarkable understanding of the Bible since archaeologists first began to recover the wonders of ancient times. Illustrations. Color photos. Paperback - 448 pages (July 1997) Crown Pub; ISBN: 0609801309. The video is listed later in this section.

Usborne Book of the Ancient World ★
See description in the "Key Resources" section beginning on page 32.

The Victor Journey through the Bible ●—❤
See description in the "Key Resources" section beginning on page 32.

Alternative Resources

Ancient Egypt (The Nature Company Discoveries) by George Hart
Ancient Egypt continues the tradition of excellent, accurate, and beautiful reference works for kids 9 to 12 years old. Ancient Egyptian civilization holds a special fascination for many, with its mummies, pyramids, and highly stylized artworks. Kids can explore a Pharaoh's tomb, see a mummy up close, and find out about Egyptian gods. A large number of archaeological relics show what life was like for the ancient Egyptians, from how they dressed to the games they played. Reading level: ages 9-12.

Ancient Egypt/Book and Treasure Chest by George Hart
Learn about the ancient Egyptians' mysterious art, science, beliefs, daily life, games, and practices. Includes a replica stone necklace, papyrus, hieroglyphic rubber stamp, and more. Full color. Hardcover (October 1994) Running Pr; ISBN: 1561384623. Reading level: Ages 9-12.

Ancient Egypt and the Old Testament by John D. Currid
The role of Egypt in the Old Testament, particularly the Pentateuch, is a significant one. John Currid's in-depth study of that role sheds valuable light on this important aspect of Israel's history and Scriptures. After surveying the scholarly interest in Egypt and the Bible and highlighting the uniqueness of the Hebrew worldview, Currid proceeds through the Old Testament canonically, showing Egyptian influences throughout. He explores the creation story, the Joseph narrative, serpent confrontation, ten plagues, route of the exodus, Solomon's contacts with Egypt, the relationship of Hebrew poetry to Egyptian wisdom literature, and the links between Hebrew prophecy and Egyptian magic and soothsaying. Paperback - 256 pages (October 1997) Baker Book House; ISBN: 0801021375. Reading level: Advanced (high school-adult).

An Egyptian Pyramid (Inside Story) by Jacqueline Morley
Text and illustrations depict the construction and uses of the pyramids in ancient Egypt and explore how people lived and worked in that time. Paperback Reissue edition (March 1993) Peter Bedrick Books; ISBN: 0872262553. Reading level: Young Adult.

The Greenleaf Guide to Ancient Egypt by Cyndy Shearer
Description: A study of Egypt, with readings and activities in ten lessons; each lesson takes one to two weeks. Includes vocabulary lists and discussion questions. (June 1989) Greenleaf Pr; ISBN: 1882514009. Reading level: Grades 2-7.

Israel in Egypt: The Evidence for the Authenticity of the Exodus Tradition by James K. Hoffmeier
Professor Hoffmeier's book constitutes one of the most recent additions to the ongoing debate on ancient Israel's origins. The author begins with the proposition that, while no direct archaeological evidence for the Exodus has been discovered to date, indirect indications show the events transcribed to be plausible and therefore potentially historical—not to be dismissed merely because the theme in which such stories are recorded emphasizes a religion which has many adherents even today. The book begins with a critique of currently fashionable scholarship which minimizes the historical relevance of any portions in the Hebrew Bible relating to periods prior to the return from Babylonian exile. Paperback - 280 pages (March 1999) Oxford Univ Press; ISBN: 019513088X.

Resources recommended in ◆several lessons, ★ several units, ◗other HOW Units. ⚷━Key Resource (see beginning of unit or page 32).

Heart of Wisdom Publishing   181

Pharaohs of Ancient Egypt (Landmark Books) by Elizabeth Payne Ruled by awesome god-kings called Pharaohs, ancient Egypt was a land of bustling cities, golden palaces, and huge stone monuments. This astonishing civilization endured for more than 3,000 years before it gradually vanished from the face of the earth. Beginning with the Rosetta Stone, author Elizabeth Payne examines archaeological studies that have helped unlock the incredible secrets of Egypt's first kings. Paperback - 192 pages Reissue edition (August 1998) Random House (Merchandising); ISBN: 0394846990. Reading level: Ages 9-12.

Senefer: A Young Genius in Old Egypt by Beatrice Lumpkin ◆ This is the exciting story of Senefer, an African child in ancient Egypt. Senefer was a carpenter's son who became a famous mathematician and engineer. The story of his adventures brings to life the rich culture of ancient Egypt and the African tradition of excellence in mathematics and science. Senefer's love of numbers shows young readers that mathematics can be fun. Other role models include Nefert, Senefer's mother who taught him how to value work, and the female Pharaoh of Egypt, Hatshepsut. (March 1997) Africa World Press; ISBN: 0865432457. Reading level: Ages 9-12.

Videos

Look for these at your local video stores or watch TV listings for showings (The Discovery Channel, The History Channel, A&E or PBS).

Egypt: Quest for Eternity (1982) Description: Explore the great temples of Luxor and Karnak. Cross the Nile to the Land of the Dead, and enter the elaborately decorated tombs where the kings and queens are buried. Join Egyptologists as they unravel and interpret the riddles of Egypt's intriguing past. Rated: NR ASIN: 6304474164.

Egypt-Secrets of the Pharaohs (1998) Description: *National Geographic* and a team of archaeologists explore the well-kept secrets of mummification and building of the pyramids in ancient Egypt. Features a scientific re-creation of mummification to discover how the bodies of the pharaohs were preserved, plus a look at the ancient underground vault that houses the ship of the Pharaoh Khufu. ASIN: 0792250982.

Joseph-Master of Dreams Description: Sold into slavery by his brothers because of his gift of prophesy, Joseph is finally rewarded with great political power when he uses his divine gift to help the pharaoh save Egypt from famine. Was there actually a terrible famine in Joseph's time? And does evidence exist to support the events described in his story? A&E probes the answers to these questions in this program, formerly part of the "Mysteries of the Bible Collection II." ASIN: 6303696619.

Pharaohs and Kings
Description: Controversial Egyptologist David Rohl takes you from the banks of the Nile to the Holy Land—and explores new archaeological evidence that he believes will unveil a compelling new version of the biblical past. You'll journey from Saul and David to Joshua and the Promised Land, from new evidence for the Exodus to new evidence of Solomon's wealth and the lineage of Joseph. And at journey's end you'll have a new—and controversial—insight into biblical history. 2 hours 30 minutes on two videocassettes.

Software

A Nile Passage to Egypt
Description: Samia, your Egyptian guide will help you explore the art, architecture, culture, and wildlife of the ancient and modern worlds. Cruise Lake Victoria, the legendary source of the Nile. Keep your personal diary. Plan your own trip. Or match minds with Ramses II, in a challenging game of Senet. Publisher: Discovery Channel.

Other

Mysteries of Egypt
Description: If there is an IMAX Screen in your area, look for the showing of *Mysteries of Egypt*. View the film clip from the Web site in Quicktime and RealPlayer formats. The first IMAX film from *National Geographic* unlocks the myths and reveals the masterpieces of this fascinating empire.

Magazines

Calliope: World History Magazine for Young People
Description: The September 1997 issue includes "Science and Medicine in Ancient Egypt" ISBN: 0382408934; the November/December 1991 issue includes "Queens of Egypt" ISBN: 0382405897; the September/October 1994 issue includes "Pharaohs of Egypt" ISBN: 0382406036.

Ancient Egypt Magazine
Description: This magazine is researched and written by experts in the field of Egyptology. Its lively and informed style appeals to the many thousands of ordinary people fascinated by this early civilization, and provides them with the latest news about their interest. Available online.

Resources recommended in ◆several lessons, ★ several units, ● other HOW Units. ●━Key Resource (see beginning of unit or page 32).

Heart of Wisdom Publishing   183

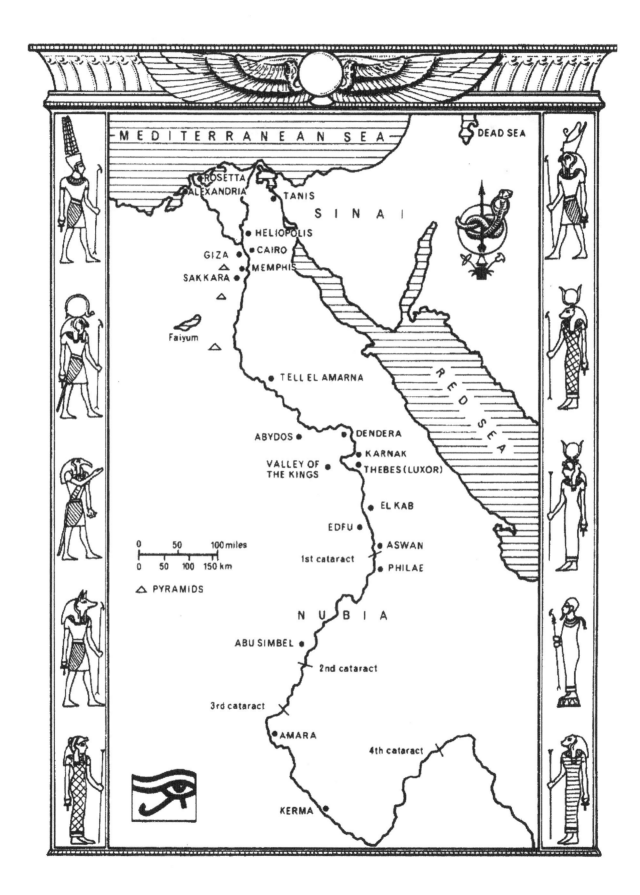

Introduction

Step 1 Excite

Make two lists, one of what you know and one of what you would like to know, about Egypt in biblical times. List any events you can think of in Egypt's history that affected its then-current population and culture.

Step 2 Examine

Browse through books in the resource section or one of these Internet sites:

Discovery Channel's Ancient Egypt
Description: An archive of stories, images, videos, links, and a video quiz. We recommend you take the quiz before and after studying this unit.

An Introduction to Ancient Egypt
Description: A tour though Internet sites, for an overview of ancient Egypt. Includes questions for each site.

Mark Millmore's Ancient Egypt
Description: Includes information about pyramids, temples, kings, and queens. Offers free screen savers, and a hieroglyphic made by the artist (write your name in the ancient script).

Exploring Ancient Egypt
Description: A sampling of some of the aspects of Egypt with many fun Internet activities!

History of Egypt
Description: An excellent historical reference on Pharaonic history.

Egypt's History
Description: An excellent summary of the history of Egypt from Countrywatch.com.

Step 3 Expand

Activity 1: Produce a Newspaper
This is an ongoing project you should work on as you study this unit. Prepare an outline to produce a newspaper that might have been published in

Resources recommended in ♦several lessons, ★ several units, ♥ other HOW Units. ●—Key Resource (see beginning of unit or page 32).

Heart of Wisdom Publishing   185

ancient Egypt. Keep a separate notepad to gather information for stories, advertising, editorials, etc. as you complete the lessons. Include feature story, journalistic reports, agricultural happenings (grain harvest), political stories, technological stories (inventions), weather reports, puzzles and cartoons, etc. Type articles and print them out in various sizes. Cut and paste the articles on 81/2" x 11" pieces of paper. Use empty space to put in ads. Put your newspaper together, then print the copies you need for distribution.

Activity 2: Create a Mind Map
This is an ongoing project you should work on as you study this unit. Use sheets of unlined paper and colored markers or pencils. Put an image or circle in the center along with the phrase "Ancient Egypt." As you study this unit, draw lines out from the center as you determine the major categories of information (hieroglyphic, pharaohs, etc.). Branch lines from the major categories will hold subtopics (look at the list of lessons for subtopic ideas). Use different colors for each cluster of information. Ask yourself, "Who?" "What?" "Where?" "When?" and "How?" Color and patterns will organize your ideas into meaningful groups that will make connections and relationships more clear. Also use symbols, numbers, arrows, or other "doodles" on your mind map (figures, etc.).

Step 4 Excel

Play the computer game Ancient Lands.

Description: You'll take an in-depth tour of ancient Egypt, among other empires, with this unique CD ROM. Learn about the lives and culture, battles and politics, and myths and legends of the people of the times. Over one thousand full-color photographs and illustrations, dozens of animations and videos, and hundreds of sound effects are integrated into the program for enjoyable learning. (MS-DOS, Windows; Microsoft Corp. Redmond, WA; (206) 882-8080.)

Underlined text refers to Internet link at http://Homeschool-Books.com

History of Ancient Egypt

Step 1 Excite

Brainstorm and discuss what you know about the people listed in the <u>Ancient Egypt Time Line</u>. Which one of these do you know the most about? Which one do you know the least about?

Step 2 Examine

Ancient Egypt is the longest-lived civilization of the ancient world (from about 3300 B.C. to 30 B.C.) About 3100 B.C., Egypt was united under a ruler known as Mena, or Menes, who inaugurated the 30 Pharaonic dynasties into which Egypt's ancient history is divided, the Old and the Middle Kingdoms and the New Kingdom. The pyramids at Giza (near Cairo) were built in the fourth dynasty, demonstrating the power of the Pharaonic religion and state. Ancient Egypt reached the peak of its power, wealth, and territorial extent in the period called the New Kingdom (1567-1085 B.C.). Authority was again centralized, and a number of military campaigns brought Palestine, Syria, and northern Iraq under Egyptian control.

The history of Ancient Egypt has been divided into eight or nine periods, sometimes called Dynasties (see Time Line on page 177). Scholars have grouped the dynasties into kingdoms (chart on this page is example note there are slight date differences).

3100-2686	The Early Dynastic Period
2686-2181	The Old Kingdom
2181-2050	The First Intermediate Period
2050-1786	The Middle Kingdom
1786-1567	The Second Intermediate Period
1567-1085	The New Kingdom
1085-322	The Late Period
332-30	Greek Rule

Research the history of ancient Egypt. Use any resource (an encyclopedia, Bible dictionary, nonfiction book, or the Internet). Look up ancient Egypt or Pharaonic dynasties. We recommend the following:

Books

<u>Encyclopedia of the Bible</u> (Nelson's Illustrated) ❤
"The Egyptians" (52-53), "Exodus from Egypt" (20-21).

<u>Exploring Ancient Cities of the Bible</u> ❤
Read: "The Egyptian Empire" (14-15).

Resources recommended in ◆several lessons, ★ several units, ❤other HOW Units. ☀━Key Resource (see beginning of unit or page 32).

The Holman Bible Atlas ☞ ♥
Read: "The Egyptian Experience" (52-62). This chapter gives an excellent overview of Egypt's history, a time line, and maps.

The Usborne Book of the Ancient World ☞ ★
Read: "Early Egypt" (9), "The Middle Kingdom" (26-27), "The Early New Kingdom" (46-47), "The Late Period" (78-79).

Pharaohs and Kings: A Biblical Quest ☞ ★
Read: "A Brief History of Pharaonic Egypt" (11-26) and "A Brief History of Israel" (an *excellent* summary of Israel's history) (26-38).

The Penguin Historical Atlas of Ancient Egypt ◆
Reviews: ". . . first-rate . . . Lavishly illustrated with well-chosen, -annotated, and -placed photographs, illustrations, maps, and timelines. Ms. Harris's smooth narrative is a pleasure to read and learn from." - The Kobrin Letter "Purchase this one where Egyptology is a popular topic, or to supplement more rudimentary texts with archaeological and geographical detail." - School Library Journal. Summary: This volume offers a vivid portrait of the history, people, customs, and institutions of this fascinating civilization and explores the sources of our modern-day knowledge of ancient Egypt. Full color maps and illustrations throughout. Paperback (January 1997) Penguin USA; ISBN: 0140513310.

A Short History of Ancient Egypt: From Predynastic to Roman Times by T. G. H. James
The former keeper of Egyptian antiquities at the British Museum provides a lively short history of ancient Egypt which examines the rise of cults, the development of power struggles among the elite and bureaucracies, and the behavior of commoners in a barter economy. Excellent color photos of relics and excavations provide the visual embellishment for a fine survey. (Midwest Book Review). 168 pages Reprint edition (May 1998) Johns Hopkins Univ Pr; ISBN: 0801859336.

Internet Sources

The History of Ancient Egypt
Description: A time line divided into eight periods helps you navigate through history and discover the formidable pharaohs of ancient Egypt.

The History of Egypt
Description: Information on this site is taken from a number of sources, including Sir Alan Gardiner's *Egypt of the Pharaohs*. Many sources are used so as to reflect a wide variety of theories and ideas about Egypt's history, particularly its early days.

The History of Ancient Egypt
Description: An extensive time line and history from the Egyptian Ministry of Tourism.

The History of Ancient Egypt
Description: A visit to an exhibit in the Minnesota State University EMuseum, which has information on the history of ancient Egypt, including Dynasties, significant people, time-frames, dates, and maps. The site gives a brief explanation of the political history for each time period.

The Pharaohs Network - Ancient Egypt
Description: Good overview of the history of ancient Egypt, with a few paragraphs for each time period.

Step 3 Expand

Activity 1: Write an Outline
Write an outline divided by ancient Egypt periods (see chart in step 2). Include one or two summary paragraphs for each period.

Activity 2: Add to Your Time Line Book
Add all major historical events that occurred in ancient Egypt to your Time Line Book. Add illustrations and summaries.

Activity 3: Write a Newspaper Article
Write a feature article (with a headline) that tells about an event in ancient Egypt's history. Make it appear as it might be found on the front page of a newspaper in the town where the story takes place.

Activity 4: Build a Set
Build a miniature stage setting of a scene from ancient Egypt's history. Include a written explanation of the scene.

Resources recommended in ◆several lessons, ★ several units, ♥ other HOW Units. ⌀━Key Resource (see beginning of unit or page 32).

Heart of Wisdom Publishing   189

Activity 5: Make a Storyboard
Create a storyboard divided by ancient Egypt periods (refer to the chart in step 2 and time line at the beginning of this unit). Include one or more significant events for each period.

Activity 6: Write Interview Questions
Pretend you are going to interview a character from ancient Egypt's history. Write at least ten questions that will prompt the character to discuss his/her thoughts and feelings about his/her role in history. Refer to "Preparing an Interview" in *Writers INC.*

Step 4 Excel

Present your work from Step 3 to someone and give a brief overview of Egypt's history. Correct written work to demonstrate correct punctuation and spelling, and effective use of grammar. Add corrected written work or illustrations to your portfolio. Add any new words (such as Pharaonic dynasties) which you learned in this lesson to your Vocabulary Notebook (see page 22).

Underlined text refers to Internet link at http://Homeschool-Books.com

Geography of Ancient Egypt

Step 1 Excite

Brainstorm and discuss: Is Egypt, as a nation, more flat or more mountainous? Is it arid or humid? What weather conditions, general climate, and natural disasters are prevalent for this geographical location? Would there ever be a tsunami? Are there volcanoes? Has Egypt experienced earthquakes or cyclones?

Step 2 Examine

Egypt is located on the northeastern portion of the African continent between Libya and the Gaza Strip/Israel.

Browse maps of and geography information on ancient Egypt. Use any resource (an encyclopedia, atlas, or the Internet). We recommend the following:

Books

Encyclopedia of the Bible (Nelson's Illustrated) ♥
"The Egyptians" (52-53), "Exodus from Egypt" (20-21).

Exploring Ancient Cities of the Bible ♥
Read: "The Egyptian Empire" (14-15).

Holman Bible Atlas ⚷ ★
Read: "Egypt: Land of Bondage" (6-7). Browse through "Chapter 6 (52-62) and Chapter 7 (63-74).

Internet Sources

Mustardseed Media's Virtual Multimedia Tour of the Holy Land
Description: This site includes geography from ancient Egypt to ancient Rome, including Israel and Jordan. The continually updated tour will take you to key biblical sites.

Egypt - National Geographic
Description: Satellite imaging and political map-making combine to create a zoomable map of this well-known African country.

Resources recommended in ♦several lessons, ★ several units, ♥other HOW Units. ⚷═Key Resource (see beginning of unit or page 32).

Heart of Wisdom Publishing   191

Egypt- Nova Online
Description: Indicates Giza's location in Africa with an inset overlay of the eastern Mediterranean.

Step 3 Expand

Choose and complete one of the following activities:

Activity 1: Answer Questions

1. What is the latitude and longitude of Egypt?
2. Which countries border it?
3. Which bodies of water are closest to it?
4. Which bodies of water are within its borders?
5. How much area does it cover?
6. On which continent is it?
7. Is it larger or smaller than the state in which you live?
8. Does it have mountain ranges, deserts or other geographic characteristics?

Activity 2: Create a Postcard
Note the terrain, vegetation, and the ancient monuments from the resources above. Illustrate a postcard of ancient Egypt (use an Internet printout or draw an illustration). Write a message on the card as if you were currently traveling in Egypt.

Activity 3: Create a Map
Make and display a detailed map of Egypt, labeling the following ancient landmarks: Valley of the Kings, Red Sea, Nubian Desert, Goshen, Lower Egypt, Upper Egypt, Giza, Nile River, Nile Valley, Kush, Libya, Phoenicia, Memphis, Thebes, and Alexandria.

Step 4 Excel

Share what you have learned about the geography of Egypt with a friend or family member. Correct written work to demonstrate correct punctuation and spelling, and effective use of grammar. Add corrected written work or illustrations to your portfolio. Add any new words you learned in this lesson into your Vocabulary Notebook (see page 22).

Underlined text refers to Internet link at http://Homeschool-Books.com

Egypt's Neighbors

Step 1 Excite

What was the homeland of the woman Moses married during the time that the Israelites wandered in the desert? (Numbers 12:1) What color of skin was she likely to have had? (Jeremiah 13:23) Look at 2 Chronicles 12:2-3 and Isaiah 20:3-4 to discover with whom the Ethiopians were allied. What other allies of Egypt are mentioned? Read Psalm 68:31. What does this prophecy say about Kush?

Step 2 Examine

Investigate Egypt's southern neighbors, the African kingdoms along the Nile River. Modern-day Sudan and Ethiopia are in the location of some rich and powerful African kingdoms of the past. The ancient Egyptian culture strongly influenced the people in this region. The area around the first cataract of the Nile River, called Nubia, was conquered and colonized by ancient Egypt. Kush was located at the third cataract of the Nile. Its capital city, Kerma, was an important trading city. The entire region is sometimes called Nubia, sometimes Kush, and sometimes Ethiopia, leading to confusion.

Find historical maps that show Nubia, Kush, and Ethiopia—the location of the ancient kingdom of Aksum (or Axum). Sort out where and when ancient kingdoms existed near the source of the Nile River. Find out the names of the capital cities. For a time, Kush ruled ancient Egypt. When did this happen and how was Egypt conquered? Kush ruled the largest empire along the River Nile. Identify the city called Jebel Barkal. How long did the Kushite culture exist? (two thousand years) When did the kingdom of Kush cease to exist, and why?

Read the following Bible verses: 2 Kings 19:9; 2 Chronicles14:9; Job 28:19; Psalm 68:31; Isaiah 11:11; 20:3; 20:5; 37:9; 43:3; 45:14; Jeremiah 38:7; 38:10; 38:12; 39:16; Ezekiel 30:4-5; 38:5; Nahum 3:9; Zephaniah 3:10.

Research Egypt's neighbors. Use any resource (an encyclopedia, a nonfiction book, or the Internet). We recommend the following:

Book

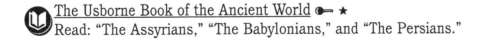

The Usborne Book of the Ancient World ●– ★
Read: "The Assyrians," "The Babylonians," and "The Persians."

Resources recommended in ◆several lessons, ★ several units, ◗ other HOW Units. ●– Key Resource (see beginning of unit or page 32).

Heart of Wisdom Publishing   193

Internet Source

Africa and Egypt, to 1750 B.C.
Description: Chapter 3 from "Antiquity Online." Includes: Early agriculture and herding across Africa, and Civilization along the Nile, to 1750 B.C.

Step 3 Expand

Choose and complete one of the following activities:

Activity 1: Make a List
Make a list of facts that you learn from the Bible about ancient Egypt's neighbors.

Activity 2: Write a Summary
Write a summary paragraph detailing what you learned about African kingdoms in the Upper Nile region. Add an introductory paragraph, a concluding paragraph, and a catchy title.

Activity 3: Listen to Music
Listen to the music from the opera, *Aïda*, which is based on a story of an Ethiopian slave.

Activity 4: Read a Story
Read the story of Aïda from a story book.

Aïda by Leontyne Price
Description: *Aïda* is one of the world's most famous—and tragic—operas. This tale of the Ethiopian princess-turned-slave, her soldier lover, and their inevitable tragedy is a favorite of Price, who reveals her feeling of sisterhood with the doomed Aïda in the book's afterword. (Amazon review) (October 1997) Harcourt Brace; ISBN: 0152015469MU-4. Reading level: Elementary.

Step 4 Excel

Share what you have learned about Egypt's neighbors with a friend or family member. If you read a book for this lesson, write a book review. Correct written work to demonstrate correct punctuation and spelling, and effective use of grammar. Add corrected written work or illustrations to your portfolio. Add new words you learned in this lesson into your Vocabulary Notebook (see page 22).

Underlined text refers to Internet link at http://Homeschool-Books.com

Pyramids in Ancient Egypt

Step 1 Excite

When Abram entered Egypt, his attention, like that of the modern traveler, must have been riveted on the Great Pyramids. Of these, about sixty have been counted, but the largest are those near ancient Memphis, which lay about ten miles above Cairo. It is scarcely possible to convey an adequate appreciation of the pyramids. Imagine a structure covering at the base an area of some 65,000 square feet, and slanting upwards for 600 feet; or, to give a better idea than these figures convey "more than half as long on every side as Westminster Abbey, eighty feet higher than the top of St. Paul's, covering thirteen acres of ground, and computed to have contained nearly seven million tons of solid masonry" (Canon Trevor, *Ancient Egypt*).

Watch a video.

Pyramid (1988)
Description: Illustrator David Macaulay hosts this highly praised PBS special about the great pyramid of Khufu at Giza, one of the seven wonders of the ancient world. King Khufu's tomb is the largest pyramid in the world, forty stories tall and covering thirteen acres! Animation and live-action sequences illustrate sites and artifacts, including the mummy of Ramses II, and tell the tales of kings, courts, heirs, and more. ASIN: B00000FAHI.

Mysteries of the Pyramids
Description: Travel back in time, and explore the secrets of ancient Egypt, as host Omar Sharif presents the latest scientific theories with state-of-the-art technology used to probe the many riddles that have perplexed the world for thousands of years.

Step 2 Examine

Do research about pyramids. Use any resource (an encyclopedia, a nonfiction book, or the Internet). We recommend the following:

Books

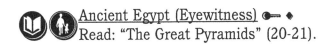
Ancient Egypt (Eyewitness) ⊶ ♦
Read: "The Great Pyramids" (20-21).

Resources recommended in ♦several lessons, ★several units, ♦other HOW Units. ⊶Key Resource (see beginning of unit or page 32).

Pyramid by David Macaulay
Description: Text and black-and-white illustrations follow the intricate step-by-step process of the building of an ancient Egyptian pyramid. (1982) Houghton Mifflin Co (Juv); ISBN: 0395321212.

Pyramid Eyewitness Book by James Putnam
Full-color photographs complement a detailed look at the secrets of these remarkable monuments of the ancient world, from the pyramid tombs of Egypt to Central America's majestic temples. Hardcover - 63 pages (October 1994) Knopf; ISBN: 067986170X. Reading level: Ages 9-12.

An Egyptian Pyramid (Inside Story) by Jacqueline Morley
Text and illustrations depict the construction and uses of the pyramids in ancient Egypt and explore how people lived and worked in that time. Paperback Reissue edition (March 1993) Peter Bedrick Books; ISBN: 0872262553. Reading level: Young Adult.

Internet Sources

NOVA Online/Pyramids -- The Inside Story
Description: This site has several pyramids for your viewing pleasure, including the "Sphinx." Each pyramid is cross-section optioned, and includes an "inside story" complete with historical information and updates.

Pyramid Dig - Nova Online
Description: Details current archaeological work and scientific reasoning behind the decisions made about where to dig and the items found at the excavation of Giza. Excellent site.

Who Built the Pyramids - Nova Online
Description: Discusses many popular theories of who built the pyramids and provides evidence to support Nova's claims of it being a local labor force.

How Old Are the Pyramids? - Nova Online
Description: Elaborates on how archaeologists assign dates to pyramids, including looking at inscriptions, concurrent artifacts, and carbon dating.

Giza Plateau Map - Nova Online
Details the relative positions of the three pyramids.

Palace Hypothesis - Nova Online
Description: Explains where the pyramid builders and their pharaohs may have lived, and how the excavation's location was chosen.

Step 3 Expand

Choose and complete one of the following activities:

⚫⚫ Activity 1: Make a Book
Use David Macaulay's book as a guide to make your own step-by-step illustrations for building a pyramid. See Creating Books.

⚫⚫ Activity 2: Do Further Research
The pyramids are one of the Seven Wonders of the Ancient World. What are the other six? Make a chart, painting, or collage depicting the Seven Wonders (using colored pencils, colored chalk, paints, or other media), and display it.

⚫⚫ Activity 3: Make a Pyramid
Materials needed: oaktag or other stiff paper, pencil or pen, ruler, scissors, glue, cardboard, sand (optional).

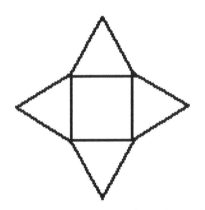

In the center of the paper draw a 7 1/2-inch square. Divide each side of the square in half and draw a line outward from each center point that extends 6 inches; this marks the center points of the triangles you will draw next. Draw lines from each point to the corners of the square closest to it (as shown in figure). This will make four triangles with sides of equal lengths. Fold along the borders between the square and the triangles. Decorate the outside and inside of your pyramid. To make base, cut a 12-inch square of cardboard, spread with glue, and sprinkle with sand. Glue bottom of pyramid to center of base.

Step 4 Excel

Write and perform an original soliloquy about life in ancient Egypt from the perspective of a person your age and gender. Imagine that King Zoser has just built the step pyramid. What do you think of it? What is it for? Look up information regarding this event to give historical basis to your acting. Then perform your soliloquy in front of family members, your church class, homeschool support group, etc. Add any new words you learned in this lesson into your Vocabulary Notebook (see page 22).

Resources recommended in ♦several lessons, ★ several units, ♥other HOW Units. ●—Key Resource (see beginning of unit or page 32).

Heart of Wisdom Publishing   197

Ancient Egypt in the Bible

Step 1 Excite

Write the following text on index cards or sticky notes: Moses, Abraham, Jesus, Exodus, Joseph. Line up the cards in chronological order. From memory, tell your parents the story of each and their relationship to Egypt. Include as many details as you can remember. When you are finished, compare your memory with the Ancient Egypt Time Line (page 173).

Step 2 Examine

Throughout the Bible, Egypt is a place of refuge and a place of oppression. The Hebrews relationship with Egypt begins with Abraham seeking refuge in Egypt because "there was a famine in the land" (Gen 12:10). Later, ,Jacob's son, Joseph is enslaved, imprisoned, and raised to be second in the land. The Hebrews population increases in Egypt to the point the Egyptian ruler feels threatened. They suffer great oppression from Pharaoh (Ex 1:8-10). Moses born in Goshen, first as a baby saved from death by the daughter of the Egyptian Pharaoh, who brought the infant up as her own child. When an adult, Moses killed an Egyptian who had murdered a Hebrew; he then fled from Egypt. Moses was a shepherd until he was 80 years of age when Yahweh appeared to him in a burning bush. Following God's direction, Moses returns to Egypt, delivers his people from their bondage by leading them out of Egypt to the land of Canaan (later Israel). By the time of Solomon (960-920 B.C.), Egypt is no longer an oppressor but a trading partner (1 Kings 10:28), diplomatic relation, and cultural influence. Egypt becomes a place of refuge after the Babylonian capture of Jerusalem in 587 B.C., although it was a false refuge, since the fleeing Hebrews placed their trust in a dying nation rather than in the living God. In the New Testament, Joseph was warned in a dream to take Jesus and his mother *and escape to Egypt* (Matt. 2:14). After the death of Herod, an angel tells Joseph to return to the land of Israel.[1]

We know all the Bible stories above are true because they are recorded in God's Word. But is is there historical evidence for these Bible events? How do secular historians view these spiritual events? Robert Steven Bianchi explains in the Forward to *Pharaohs and Kings: A Biblical Quest* by David Kohl:

> In recent years, a certain degree of skepticism has developed regarding the historicity of the Genesis, Exodus and Joshua narratives, and doubt is now even being expressed about the later books of the Old Testament, such as Judges, Samuel, and the early sections of Kings and Chronicles. Some contemporary scholars - even the occasional theologian - would today prefer to treat

---

Underlined text refers to Internet link at http://Homeschool-Books.com

the early books of the Bible as, for the most part, works of fiction. This is primarily because, in their view, these narratives are later compilations, prepared by post-exilic editors who had only an imperfect understanding of the more remote times about which they were attempting to narrate.

Clearly a wide philosophical schism has opened up between those who would accept the biblical narratives at face value and those who would entirely dismiss the historical accuracy of those accounts.

David Rohl re-examination produces some startling results. He notes the problems which have come to light over the last two centuries of archaeological endeavor in Egypt and the Holy Land, where little corroborative evidence for the biblical traditions has been unearthed His solution is simple: archaeologist have been looking in the right places for evidence to confirm the biblical stories but in entirely the wrong time. He thus relocates the events described at the end of Genesis and the beginning of Exodus to a quite different era than the received wisdom demands. Accordingly, the Sojourn in the land of Goshen and the Exodus from Egypt can be reasonably placed in the early second millennium BC - in Egyptian terms the time known as the Second Intermediate Period - when a large population of Asiatics resided in the eastern Nile delta.[2]

Examine how the Egyptian and Israelite timelines in this unit fit together. Research ancient Egypt and the Old Testament. Use any resource (an encyclopedia, nonfiction book, historical novel, or the Internet). We recommend the following:

Books

Encyclopedia of the Bible (Nelson's Illustrated) ♥
"The Egyptians" (52-53), "Exodus from Egypt" (20-21).

Exploring Ancient Cities of the Bible ♥
Read: "The Egyptian Empire" (14-15).

The Holman Bible Atlas ⌖ ♥
Read: "The Egyptian Experience" (52-62).

Ancient Israel: From Abraham to the Roman Destruction of the Temple ★
Read: Chapter 2 "Israel in Egypt: The Egyptian Sojourn and the Exodus." See description in Ancient Israel Unit.

Pharaohs and Kings: A Biblical Quest ⌖ ★
See description in the "Resources" section at the beginning of this unit.

Resources recommended in ♦several lessons, ★ several units, ♥other HOW Units. ⌖Key Resource (see beginning of unit or page 32).

Heart of Wisdom Publishing   199

Ⓤ Ancient Egypt and the Old Testament ◆
Read: Part One "Introduction" and Part Two "Egyptian Elements in the Pentateuch."

Ⓤ Israel in Egypt: The Evidence for the Authenticity of the Exodus Tradition ◆
See description in the "Resources" section at the beginning of this unit.

Internet Sources

ⓘ Is there evidence that the Israelites once lived in Egypt as the Bible says?
Description: Archaeological answers about the presence of Hebrews in ancient Egypt from ChristianAnswers.net

ⓘ Egyptian Reflections
Description: An article by Lloyd Thomas in "The Thomas Pages."

ⓘ A New Chronology
Description: A synopsis of David Rohl's Book Pharaohs and Kings: A Biblical Quest (also called "A Test of Time in The Historical Debate").

Video

📼 Pharaohs & Kings Video
Description: Is the Bible fact or faith? Controversial Egyptologist David Rohl takes you from the banks of the Nile to the Holy Land, and explores new archaeological evidence that he believes will unveil a compelling new version of the biblical past. You'll journey among sites dealing with topics from Saul and David to Joshua and the Promised Land, from new evidence for the Exodus to new evidence of Solomon's wealth and the lineage of Joseph. And at journey's end you'll have a new—and controversial—insight into biblical history. 2 hours 30 minutes on two videocassettes. Discovery Communications 1-800-889-9950.

Step 3 Expand

Choose and complete one of the following activities:

🗐👥 Activity 1: Fill Out a Worksheet
Fill out an Event Worksheet on one or more of the following:
- Abraham Lives in Egypt (Genesis 12:10-20; 13:1)
- Joseph's Early Years (Genesis 37:1-36)
- Joseph the Egyptian Ruler (Genesis 30:1-23)
- Egyptian Bondage (Exodus 12:40,41; Genesis 15:13; Acts 7:6; Galatians 3:17)

Underlined text refers to Internet link at http://Homeschool-Books.com

- Moses' Birth to Midian (Exodus 2)
- Moses' Emergence as Leader (Exodus 1)
- The Plagues on Egypt (Exodus 5-11)
- Passover and Exodus (Exodus 5-12)
- Jesus' Escape to Egypt (Matthew 2)

Activity 2: Answer Questions
Answer the following orally.
1. What were some of the products of ancient Egypt? (Numbers 11:5; Psalms 78:47; Proverbs 7:16; Isaiah 19:5-9)
2. What were some of the imports of ancient Egypt? (Genesis 37:25,36)
3. What were some of the exports of ancient Egypt? (Genesis 37:25,36; 1 Kings 10:28,29; Proverbs 7:16; Ezekiel 27:7)
4. What did God tell the Egyptians about their idols? (Ezekiel 20:7,8)
5. What were some of the prophecies against Egypt? (Genesis 15:13,14; Isaiah 19; 20:2-6; 45:14; Jeremiah 9:25,26; 43:8-13; 44:30; 46; Ezekiel 29; 30; 31; 32; Hosea 8:13; Joel 3:11; Zechariah 10:11)

Activity 3: Share with a Child
Fill out one or more of the following Internet worksheets with a child (elementary level). Jesus' Escape to Egypt; Israel Moves to Egypt; The Plagues on Egypt.

Activity 4: Add to Your Time Line Book
Add all major Bible events that occurred in ancient Egypt to your Time Line Book to get a feel of the chronological order. When you study each event (in other lessons in this book) add illustrations and summaries.

Step 4 Excel

Some Egyptians were at Pentecost. The Coptic Church is one of the oldest Christian churches in the world. Have you ever praised God for His mercy towards Egyptian people? Lead your family in praising God for His kindness, grace, and mercy towards Egyptians. Find out if there is something you can do to serve the brothers in Christ who are living in Egypt. See The Voice of the Martyrs.

Correct written work to demonstrate correct punctuation and spelling, and effective use of grammar. Add corrected written work or illustrations to your portfolio.Add any new words you learned in this lesson into your Vocabulary Notebook (see page 22).

Footnotes
1. Elwell, Walter A. "Entry for 'Egypt'". *Evangelical Dictionary of Theology*.
2. Bianchi, Professor Robert S. "Forward" to *A Test of Time: The Bible - From Myth to History*, now titled *Pharohs and Kings: A Biblical Quest*.

Resources recommended in ◆several lessons, ★ several units, ♥other HOW Units. ⌕—Key Resource (see beginning of unit or page 32).

Joseph in Ancient Egypt

Step 1 Excite

74-96

The Narrated Bible

Several themes flow throughout the story of Joseph:

1. God is present and involved in our lives even when He seems to have abandoned us. Through all Joseph's trials, he learned to trust; his faith reached a new level of maturity.
2. God's timing is perfect. Joseph is wrongly imprisoned. Instead of feeling sorry for himself he becomes diligent and self-disciplined.
3. God can help us forgive. Joseph forgives his brothers for selling him into slavery.
4. God can teach us to see good in everything. Joseph tells his brothers, *As far as I am concerned, God turned into good what you meant for evil. He brought me to the high position I have today so I could save the lives of many people.* (Genesis 50:20)

Read the entire account of Joseph's life in the Bible. Start by reading Acts 7:9, then read about his prophetic dreams in Genesis 37 up to his death in Genesis 50. Read Psalm 105:12-22. Take notes of new things you notice about Joseph.

Joseph's Life			
Early Life	Prisoner	Egyptian Ruler	Brother
Genesis 37:1-36	Genesis 37-40	Genesis 41-45	Genesis 46-50
With Family	Separated from Family	Reunited with Family	Dwells with Family

Step 2 Examine

The story of Joseph gives a detailed picture of Egypt and the ambiguity of its role. Egypt is a place of oppression, since Joseph is initially enslaved, eventually ending up in prison. Egypt is also a place of hope and refuge, since Joseph is raised to be second in the land. From this position of great power he is able to provide a refuge from famine for his family. One of the themes of the Joseph story is that God is not restricted by national boundaries.

Research Joseph. Use any resource (an encyclopedia, nonfiction book, historical novel, or the Internet). We recommend the following:

Books

Underlined text refers to Internet link at http://Homeschool-Books.com

The Victor Journey through the Bible ⌐◦─♥
Read: The stories about Joseph (40-51).

Encyclopedia of the Bible (Nelson's Illustrated) ♥
Read: "Genesis" (198-199).

Joseph (Young Reader's Christian Library Series) by Rex Williams
Description: Sold into slavery in a foreign land by his brothers, Joseph holds fast to the belief that God will deliver him. (1990) Barbour & Co; ISBN: 1557481164. Reading level: Ages 9-12.

Bible History: Old Testament ⌐◦─ ★
Read: Book 1, Chapters 21 and 22 "Departure of Jacob And His Family Into Egypt."

Joseph: A Man of Absolute Integrity by Charles R. Swindoll
Description: *Joseph* is the third in a multi-volume series exploring great lives from the Bible. Charles Swindoll shows us the heart and soul of a man shaped in the crucible of rejection, loneliness, deprivation, and false accusation, a man who learned patience and obedience by becoming totally dependent on God. Joseph's story gives us a heartening example of courage, integrity and forgiveness in the face of cruelty, temptation and hatred. Joseph's pardon of his cruel brothers demonstrates the depth of love God has for us all. (Editorial review) (August 1998) Word Books; ISBN: 084991342X.

The Bible Comes Alive: Volume One, Creation to Abraham ⌐◦─ ★
Read: Section IV "Joseph in Egypt."

Internet Sources

Joseph
Description: This Web page explains how this son of Jacob rose to prominence in Egypt.

Bible History: Old Testament
Read: Book 1, Ch. 22 "Departure Of Jacob And His Family Into Egypt."

The Historicity of the Joseph Story
Description: Charles F. Aling of Associates for Biblical Research wrote this discussion on the historicity of the Joseph story, brought to you by ChristianAnswers.net.

Resources recommended in ◆several lessons, ★several units, ♥other HOW Units. ⌐◦─Key Resource (see beginning of unit or page 32).

Heart of Wisdom Publishing   203

1754 B.C. - 1504 B.C. Joseph in Egypt
Description: A visual time line of Joseph in Egypt.

Videos

Joseph-Master of Dreams
Description: Examine the biblical story of Joseph, who was sold into slavery by his own brothers because of his prophetic abilities, only to rise to power when his gift saves Egypt from famine. *Mysteries of the Bible*, et al. ASIN: 6303696619.

Joseph - King of Dreams
Description: This stirring story of family and forgiveness, an inspiring musical adventure, retells the fascinating story of a boy whose extraordinary gift of seeing the future in his dreams sparks a deep division in his family. The jealousy of his brothers sends Joseph to faraway Egypt, where he is suddenly thrown into a world of high adventure, hidden intrigue, and blossoming romance. In this new land, the pharaoh enlists Joseph to interpret his dreams and save Egypt from disaster. Joseph is rewarded with honor and status, and as he rises to power, Joseph finds love and happiness. But when a sudden twist of fate reunites Joseph with his brothers, Joseph must face decisions of forgiveness. Animated. ASIN: B00004YNUH.

Step 3 Expand

Choose and complete one of the following activities:

Activity 1: Write and Act Out a Drama
Write a drama about Joseph's imprisonment, including several monologues. You might have Joseph reflecting to himself about his false accusation and his frustration about being thrown into prison, and have him speak of his determination to prove himself innocent. At the end of each monologue, have him lie down, as though it is night. After he arises, start a new monologue, perhaps after the passage of a few weeks or months. As you write the script, don't forget to include the setting and time so that the stage can be set for the scene. Include how he might feel about his brothers now, how he misses his father, his excitement at the prospect of being mentioned to the pharaoh by the released butler, what he sees while in prison, the caliber of people with whom he is forced to reside, etc.

Select a dramatic young man to act out the part of Joseph. Act as the director, ensuring that all the actors have the props and costumes that they need. Perhaps a few simple scenes can be staged. Arrange the set to fit the setting of each scene. Have the house lights go down at the end of each scene as Joseph lies down, and then bring the house lights up for the next scene. How can you quickly change the set? Your cast of actors should be given the opportunity to perform for an audience. You can be a blessing to an audience at a place such as an after-school day care or a retirement home.

Activity 2: Fill Out a Worksheet
Compile information from your research to fill out a Person Worksheet or an Event Worksheet on Joseph's Early Years (Genesis 37:1-36), on Joseph the Prisoner (Genesis 37-40), on Joseph the Egyptian Ruler (Genesis 41-45), and on Joseph the Brother (Genesis 46-50).

Activity 3: Create an Outline
Outline Joseph's life from Genesis 37 up to his death in Genesis 50. Refer to the Outline Example for help.

Activity 4: Sew a Quilt Block
Patchwork Partners provides quilt block directions and a brief Bible study relating to this lesson on the Internet at Bible Blocks: Joseph's Coat.

Activity 5: Teach a Child
Fill out the following Internet worksheets with a child (elementary level): "Joseph and His Brothers"; "Joseph in Egypt"; "Joseph's Family Reunion."

Activity 6: Read a Story to a Child
Read a story about Joseph to younger children. We recommend any of the following: Forgive, Joseph! (Follow the Leader Series) by Carolyn Nystrom, Sharon Dahl (Illustrator) (October 1998) Moody Press; ISBN: 0802422071. Joseph by Brian Wildsmith (Illustrator). Description: Wildsmith brings the story of Joseph to life for a new generation of readers. (October 1997) Wm. B. Eerdmans Publishing Co.; ISBN: 0802851614. The Story of Joseph Description: An online, illustrated slide show that tells the story of Joseph for children.

Step 4 Excel

Share what you have learned about Joseph in Egypt with a friend or family member. Correct all written work to demonstrate correct punctuation and spelling, and effective use of grammar. Add corrected written work or any illustrations to your portfolio.

Resources recommended in ◆several lessons, ★ several units, ♥ other HOW Units. ☛Key Resource (see beginning of unit or page 32).

Heart of Wisdom Publishing   205

Moses in Ancient Egypt

97-102, 203

The Narrated Bible

Step 1 Excite

Moses went from a prince to a shepherd to a slave then a hero. He grew up in the palace of Pharaoh where he would have received a first-class education, learning to read and write hieroglyphics and was possibly introduced to several other languages spoken by Egypt's neighbors. After killing the Egyptian overseer, he fled into Sinai where he was sheltered by the Midianite priest and settled down to the life of a shepherd. He returns to live among the Hebrew slaves and becomes their deliverer. Brainstorm with your family and contrast and compare the different periods of Moses' life. In which period of his life do you think he was content? Was it when he was rich? famous? a servant? a leader?

Step 2 Examine

"Moses the man of God" (Deuteronomy 33:1; Joshua 14:6) was distinguished for his meekness, patience, and firmness, and *he endured as seeing him who is invisible. There arose not a prophet since in Israel like unto Moses, whom the Lord knew face to face, in all the signs and the wonders, which the Lord sent him to do in the land of Egypt to Pharaoh, and to all his servants, and to all his land, and in all that mighty hand, and in all the great terror which Moses shewed in the sight of all Israel* (Deuteronomy 34:10-12).

Research Moses. Use any resource (Bible study tools, an encyclopedia, nonfiction book, historical novel, or the Internet). We recommend the following:

Books

The Victor Journey through the Bible ●—♥
Read: The stories about Moses (52-72).

Encyclopedia of the Bible (Nelson's Illustrated) ♥
Read: "Exodus" (200-201).

Who's Who in the Bible ●— ♥
Read: "Moses and the Israelites" (14-16).

Moses: A Man of Selfless Dedication by Charles R. Swindoll
Description: Charles Swindoll paints a portrait of the biblical Moses in this fascinating look into the heart and mind of Moses, "a man of selfless dedication." Swindoll gives us straight-from-the-shoulder facts based squarely on the truth revealed in God's Word. He also fills in the fine details of Moses' life with emotion

Underlined text refers to Internet link at http://Homeschool-Books.com

and feeling, because Moses, like all of us, was a human being with faults and frailties. Finally, Swindoll helps us apply the lessons of Moses' life to our own daily dilemmas. (April 1999) Word Books; ISBN: 0849913853.

Internet Sources

Prophet Unto Moses
Description: An article with a chart of scriptures comparing the life of Moses with that of Christ.

Project on Moses, Egypt and Current Events
Description: This project challenges students to study ancient Egypt, the lives of the Israelites, and how God is a part of history for people of yesterday and today.

Moses from BibleTutor
Description: A brief biography of Moses with related links.

Moses from Daily Bible Study
Description: Good overview of Moses' life with hyperlinks to related people, places, and events.

Bible Character Clues
Description: An online game. Read each rhyme and identify the person connected with it. Read the Bible verses if you need help.

Read passages about Moses that are outside of the Torah: Jeremiah 15:1; Matthew 17:3-4; John 1:17; 9:29; Acts 3:22; 6:11; 7:20; 7:22, 29, 31-32; 2 Corinthians 3:7; 1315; 2 Timothy 3:8; Hebrews 3:2-5; 9:19; 11:23-24; 12:21; Jude 1:9; Revelation 15:3.

Step 3 Expand

Choose and complete one of the following activities:

Activity 2: Fill out a Worksheet
Choose one of the events from the chart above. Fill out an Event Worksheet or a Person Worksheet about Moses.

Activity 3: Make a Chart
Make a list of the similarities between Moses and Jesus. Include Bible references. Transform this list into a chart.

Resources recommended in ◆several lessons, ★ several units, ● other HOW Units. ⊙━ Key Resource (see beginning of unit or page 32).

Heart of Wisdom Publishing   207

Activity 4: Write an Essay
Write an essay about the personal character of Moses. Use examples from his life and comments in the Bible to show the qualities that he had. Younger students can narrate (orally tell) what they have learned.

Activity 5: Make an Outline
Use the chart below to make an <u>outline</u> of the life of Moses. Include a summary under each major event.

Reference	Event	Summary
Exod. 2:1-10	Birth	
Exod. 3:1-22	Call	
Exod. 14:15-31	Exodus	
Exod. 34:27-35	Receives the Law	
Deut. 34:1-12	Death	

Activity 6: Write an Editorial
Write an editorial as if you are a time traveler writing for a newspaper during the Exodus. Try to persuade the Israelites to give Moses the respect that he is due. Because you are a time traveler, you can write in a modern style and use information that the people of the Exodus didn't have.

Step 4 Excel

Share what you have learned about Moses by filling out the following worksheets with a child (elementary level): <u>Baby Moses</u> and <u>The Burning Bush</u>. Correct written work to demonstrate correct punctuation and spelling, and effective use of grammar. Add corrected written work or illustrations to your portfolio.

Underlined text refers to Internet link at http://Homeschool-Books.com

The Plagues

Step 1 Excite

Make a list of the plagues, from memory if possible. Then read Psalm 78. Which plagues are mentioned?

Step 2 Examine

The Lord's purpose in the 10 plagues is to reveal himself. Four players or groups of players have the opportunity to know the Lord in the drama of the plagues: Moses, the Israelites, the Egyptians and Pharaoh. Ultimately, the Lord reveals himself by distinguishing between himself and everyone else. The difference between the Lord and everyone else is enhanced in the following ways, as seen in the plagues, which appear in three series of three, with the 10th and final plague standing alone. [1]

A Family Guide to the Biblical Holidays [2] explains that each plague that God put on the Egyptians related to an Egyptian idol as follows:

First Plague: The Nile Waters Turn to Blood—The Nile, the river of Egypt, was the Egyptians' idol. The Nile's waters nourished the land and determined the welfare of all the people. The Egyptians thirsted after blood when they slaughtered the Hebrews' children, and now God gave them blood to drink. Thus, the source that usually brought the Egyptians life brought death instead. (Exodus 7:14-25)

Second Plague: The Frogs—The frogs represented the fertility goddess, Isis, which was supposed to help women in childbirth. Frogs were everywhere: in their houses, in their beds, and at their tables. They could not eat, drink, or sleep without their precious god. The frog that symbolized life had to be raked into heaps of rotting death. (Exodus 8:1-15)

Third Plague: The Lice—The lice, which came up out of the dust of the earth, represented the Egyptians' god of the earth, Seth. Matthew Henry notes that lice were small, despicable, inconsiderable creatures, and yet, by their vast numbers, they rendered a sore plague to the Egyptians. God could have plagued them with lions, bears, wolves, vultures, or other birds of prey, but He chose to do it using these minuscule but contemptible instruments. (Exodus 8:16-19)

Resources recommended in ◆several lessons, ★several units, ●other HOW Units. ☞Key Resource (see beginning of unit or page 32).

Fourth Plague: The Flies—The stinging, disease-carrying flies ruined the land. Beelzebub, the prince of the power of the air, has been glorified as the god of flies, the god of Ekron. The fly was always present at idolatrous sacrifices. This fourth plague came upon the Egyptians only. It made Israel a separate and Holy People. (Exodus 8:20-32)

Fifth Plague: The Disease of Livestock—A great number of cattle died by a sort of pestilence. The Egyptians made the Hebrews poor, so God caused great loss to the Egyptians. The Egyptians believed that animals were possessed by the spirits of gods. The bull was sacred in Egypt, identified in its markings with their god Apis. As God's Word tells us, this disease afflicted only the Egyptian livestock, not the Hebrew livestock. (Exodus 9:1-7)

Sixth Plague: The Boils—Again God demonstrated His ability to control nature. When the death of their cattle didn't convince the Egyptians, God sent a plague that seized their own bodies. *And they took ashes of the furnace, and stood before Pharaoh; and Moses sprinkled it up toward heaven; and it became a boil breaking forth with blains upon man, and upon beast.* (Exodus 9:10) Sores in the body were looked upon as punishment for sin, a means by which to call one to repentance. None of the Hebrews had any boils. This plague was a direct attack on the shamanism of the medico-mystical processes in Egypt. (Exodus 9:8-12)

Seventh Plague: The Hailstorm—Moses gave the people a one-day warning before this plague. The notice was given because the sorcerers of Egypt were also agricultural shamans who supposedly controlled the weather. Those who feared the Lord took shelter (showing us that God had mercy on some of the Egyptians). Those who did not believe in God and took no shelter died in the fields. (Ex. 9:21) There was ice *and fire mingled with the hail, very grievous, such as there was none like it in all of the land of Egypt.* The hail killed both men and cattle, and battered down the herbs, vegetable gardens, fruit trees, and other plants. God, in His judgment, caused it to rain and hail on the Egyptians and not on the Hebrews. (Exodus 9:13-35)

Eighth Plague: The Locusts—By this time, Pharaoh's people, his magicians, and his advisors began to rebel. Pharaoh stood alone against God. *Moses stretched forth his rod over the land of Egypt, and the LORD brought an east wind upon the land all that day, and all that night; and when it was morning, the east wind brought the locusts. And the locusts went up over all the land of Egypt, and rested in all the coasts of Egypt: very grievous were they; before them there were no such locusts as they, neither after them shall be such.* This plague devastated the land and hence the power of the gods and shamans of agriculture. Pharaoh sent for Moses and pretended to repent. He asked Moses to pray to God to take the locusts away. *And the LORD turned a mighty strong west wind, which took away the locusts, and cast them into the Red Sea; there remained not one locust in all the coasts of Egypt.* (Exodus 10:13-14,19)

Underlined text refers to Internet link at http://Homeschool-Books.com

Ninth Plague: The Darkness—The Egyptians rebelled against the light of God's Word and they were justly punished with darkness. This thick darkness was over Egypt three days, but the people of Israel had light where they dwelt. What a picture of dark and light, of being lost and saved. The children of God walked in the light while Pharaoh and his people wandered in the darkness. Matthew Henry's Commentary states,

> The cloud of locusts, which had darkened the land (v. 15), was nothing to this. It was a total darkness. We have reason to think, not only that the lights of heaven were clouded, but that all their fires and candles were put out by the damp or clammy vapors which were the cause of this darkness; for it is said (v. 23), "They saw not one another." It is threatened to the wicked (Job 18:5-6) that the "spark of his fire shall not shine," even the sparks of his own kindling, as they are called (Isa. 50:11), and that the "light shall be dark in his tabernacle." Hell is utter darkness. The "light of a candle shall shine no more at all in thee" (Rev. 18:23).

This plague was an attack on the power of the supreme deity of Egypt, the sun god, Ra or Amun-Ra. The Egyptians could do nothing but stay in their homes and consider what they had experienced to that point regarding the power of the God of the Israelites. Even then, Pharaoh refused to yield. (Exodus 10:21-29)

Tenth Plague: The Death of the Firstborn—God said in Exodus 13:2, *Sanctify unto me all the firstborn, whatsoever openeth the womb among the children of Israel, both of man and of beast: it is mine.*

Nelson's *Illustrated Bible Dictionary* explains the importance of the firstborn:

> God placed a special claim on the firstborn of man and beast (Ex. 13:11-13). This meant that the nation of Israel attached unusual value to the eldest son and assigned special privileges and responsibilities to him. Because of God's claim on the first offspring, the firstborn sons of the Hebrews were presented to the Lord when they were a month old. Since the firstborn was regarded as God's property, it was necessary for the father to redeem, or buy back, the child from the priest. Early Hebrew laws also provided that the firstlings of beasts belonged to the Lord and were turned over to the sanctuary (Ex. 13:2; 34:19; Lev. 27:26). The firstborn's birthright was a double portion of the estate and leadership of the family. As head of the home after his father's death, the eldest son customarily cared for his mother until her death, and provided for his unmarried sisters until their marriages. He was the family's spiritual head and served as its priest. In figurative language, the term firstborn stands for that which is most excellent.

Resources recommended in ♦several lessons, ★ several units, ♥other HOW Units. ☞—Key Resource (see beginning of unit or page 32).

Heart of Wisdom Publishing   211

The significance of the death of every firstborn in Egypt, from the house of Pharaoh to the slaves and the livestock, was great. But Israel would be spared so that there would be an obvious distinction between those who belong to the YAWH and those who do not. (Exodus 11:1-10)

And it came to pass, that at midnight the Lord smote all the firstborn in the land of Egypt, from the firstborn of Pharaoh that sat on his throne unto the firstborn of the captive that was in the dungeon; and all the firstborn of cattle. And Pharaoh rose up in the night, he, and all his servants, and all the Egyptians; and there was a great cry in Egypt; for there was not a house where there was not one dead. And he called for Moses and Aaron by night, and said, Rise up, and get you forth from among my people, both ye and the children of Israel; and go, serve the Lord, as ye have said. Also take your flocks and your herds, as ye have said, and be gone; and bless me also. And the Egyptians were urgent upon the people, that they might send them out of the land in haste; for they said, We be all dead men. And the people took their dough before it was leavened, their kneading troughs being bound up in their clothes upon their shoulders. And the children of Israel did according to the word of Moses; and they borrowed of the Egyptians jewels of silver, and jewels of gold, and raiment: And the Lord gave the people favour in the sight of the Egyptians, so that they lent unto them such things as they required. And they spoiled the Egyptians. (Exodus 12:29-36)

Research the Plaugues. Use any resource (an encyclopedia, nonfiction book, historical novel, or the Internet). We recommend the following:

Books

Encyclopedia of the Bible (Nelson's Illustrated) ❤
Read: "The Exodus from Egypt" (20-21).

The Victor Journey through the Bible ◐—❤
Read: "The Plagues" (58-59).

Step 3 Expand

Activity 1: Write a Newspaper Story
Write a newspaper story as if you are a reporter summing up the Ten Plagues of Judgment on the Egyptians. Refer to the book of Exodus: 7:14-25 (plague of blood); 8:1-15 (frogs); 8:16-19 (lice); 8:20 (flies); 9:1-7 (murrain of cattle); 9:8-12 (boils and sores); 9:18-34 (hail); 10:1-20 (locusts); 10:21-23 (darkness); and 11:4-7; 12:17,29 and 30 (death of the firstborn). Read Psalm 105:23-38

to find out how the Egyptians felt about the Israelites. Include an imaginary interview with an Egyptian, describing how he feels about the events. Refer to "Writing about an Event" in *Writers INC*.

Activity 2: Copy a Passage
Copy a descriptive passage or interesting conversational passage from the Bible that discusses the plagues.

Step 4 Excel

Have your family join you in acting out the ten plagues in a ten-day period.

1. Water into blood: use red food coloring on all the water sources (drinking water, sinks, cat's bowl, etc.).
2. Frogs: put paper ones everywhere around the house, including on your plates of food and in beds.
3. Lice: slap at imaginary ones and scratch "itches."
4. Flies: go through the house swatting with fly swatters, and tape pepper to windows.
5. Livestock death: put stuffed animals belly-up around the house.
6. Boils: draw red spots all over your body with lipstick or face paint.
7. Hail: go outside and toss ice chips on each other.
8. Locusts: tape paper locusts on walls, clothing, etc.
9. Darkness: tape black paper over the windows.
10. Firstborn are killed: read the biblical account and put red electrical tape or crepe paper on the doors (sides and top) leading into the house.

Share what you have learned about the plagues by filling out the following Internet worksheet with a child (elementary level): The Plagues Upon Egypt.

Footnotes
1. Dolphin, Lambert. (1998). <http://searchpdf.adobe.com/proxies/2/51/50/56.html> (Accessed 2000)
2. Sampson, Robin Scarlata. (1997). *A Family Guide to the Biblical Holidays.* TN: Heart of Wisdom Publishing.

Resources recommended in ◆several lessons, ★ several units, ◖other HOW Units. ☞Key Resource (see beginning of unit or page 32).

Heart of Wisdom Publishing   213

Passover

110-112

The Narrated Bible

Step 1 Excite

The first Passover was kept while the Israelites were still in Egypt. Brainstorm and discuss the following: How do you think the common Egyptian felt about the Hebrews as he/she watched them brush blood on the lintels? Do you think any of them were afraid that perhaps the Hebrews knew something they didn't? What do you think they told their children when their children asked what was going on? On "the morning after," do you think any Egyptians were ready to convert?

Watch a video.

The Unleavened Messiah: A Portrait of Christ in the Passover Description: The Jewish feast of Passover was obviously important to our Lord; therefore it requires the attention of every believer. We can learn so much from the ancient customs and symbols of the Passover and how they were fulfilled 2,000 years ago in Christ. *The Unleavened Messiah* will not only change the way you view the Christian sacrament of Communion, it will revolutionize the way you look at out Savior, the holy Lamb of God. (review by Josh McDowell). Sojourner Ministries. Garland TX 972-226-SOJ4 (7654) View a video clip online.

Step 2 Examine

Research Passover. Use any resource (an encyclopedia, a nonfiction book, or the Internet). We recommend the following:

Books

Encyclopedia of the Bible (Nelson's Illustrated) ♥
Read: "Annual Festivals" (156-157), Jesus in Jerusalem (40-41)

The Victor Journey through the Bible ☗—♥
Read: "The Passover" (60-61).

Our Father Abraham ☗— ♥
Read: Chapter 12 (237-252).

A Family Guide to the Biblical Holidays ☗— ★
Read: Chapter on Passover.

The Web pages below are from the book <u>A Family Guide to the Biblical Holidays</u>.

(i) <u>Passover</u>
Description: An overview of the purpose of Passover.

(i) <u>Jewish Customs of Passover</u>
Description: An overview of the Jewish customs for celebrating Passover today.

(i) <u>Messiah in Passover</u>
Description: Find out how several symbolic clues during Passover are fulfilled in Christ.

(i) <u>Suggestions for Celebrating Passover</u>
Description: There are no set rules for the basic order of the seder; traditions vary among families. This page gives several suggestions for having a Messianic seder.

(i) <u>Matzah</u>
Description: Find out what matzah and afikoman are.

(i) <u>Traditional Seder</u>
Description: An outline of a traditional seder.

(i) <u>Simple Seder</u>
Description: Directions for a seder without all the fuss.

(i) <u>Seder Checklist</u>
Description: A checklist to gather everything you'll need for a seder.

(i) <u>Four Cups</u>
Description: An explanation of the four expressions of redemption that are mentioned in the Bible (Ex. 6:6-7).

(i) <u>Four Questions</u>
Description: The answers to these four questions remind us why Passover is different from all other nights.

(i) <u>Ten Plagues Activity</u>
Description: A fun activity to reenact the ten plagues.

Step 3 Expand

Choose and complete one of the following activities:

Resources recommended in ◆several lessons, ★ several units, ❤other HOW Units. ☛Key Resource (see beginning of unit or page 32).

Activity 1: Answer Questions
Answer the questions in Our Father Abraham (252-255) in writing.

Activity 2: Add to Your Time Line Book
Add the story of Passover to your Time Line Book. See a sample Passover page from a timeline book on page 21.

Activity 3: Celebrate Passover
Have a Seder dinner. Use A Family Guide to the Biblical Holidays (by this author) or a similar resource as a guide.

Activity 4: Copy Scripture
Copy (by hand or typing) three or more verses about Passover: Ex. 12:3-49; 13:3,6; 23:15-18; 34:18; Lev. 23:4-8; Num. 9:2-5,11,13,14; 28:16-25; Deut. 16:1-8,16; Joshua 5:10,11; 2 Kings 23:22-23; 2 Chron. 30:1; 35:1,18; Ezra 6:19-20; Ps. 81:3,5; Ezek. 45:21-24; Mat. 26:2,17-20,26-28; Mark 14:1-2,12-25; Luke 2:41-50; 22:7-20; John 2:13,23; 13; 18:28; Acts 12:3; and 1 Cor. 5:7-8.

Activity 5: Answer Questions

1. What was the Passover sacrifice? (2 Chronicles 30:17; 35:3-11; Ezra 6:20)
2. Did non-Jews celebrate Passover? (Exodus 12:48,49; Numbers 9:14)
3. Where did God designate Passover to be observed? (Deuteronomy 16:5-7)
4. What type of bread was to be used and why? (Exodus 12:8,15-20; 13:3,6; 23:15; Leviticus 23:6; Numbers 9:11; 28:17; Deuteronomy 16:3,4; Mark 14:12; Luke 22:7; Acts 12:3; 1 Corinthians 5:8)
5. What was the penalty for neglecting to observe Passover? (Numbers 9:13)
6. Did Jesus observe Passover? (Matthew 26:17-20; Luke 22:15; John 2:13,23; 13)
7. When was Jesus crucified? (Matthew 26:2; Mark 14:1,2; John 18:28)
8. What is another name for The Lord's Supper? (Matthew 26:26-28; Mark 14:12-25; Luke 22:7-20)

Activity 6: Find Out More
Research the times in history that the people of God renewed the observation of Passover:
1. Upon entering Canaan. (Joshua 5:10,11)
2. By Hezekiah. (2 Chronicles 30:1)
3. By Josiah. (2 Kings 23:22,23; 2 Chronicles 35:1,18)
4. After the return from Babylonian captivity. (Ezra 6:19,20)

Activity 7: Learn Hebrew Words

Look up each of these words in a Hebrew lexicon. Add the word, phonetic spelling, and meaning to your Hebrew Notebook. See The Old Testament Hebrew Lexicon. The Hebrew word for Passover is *Pecach* (phonetic - *peh'-sakh*). It means "to pass over" or "passover offering." It is used forty-six times in the KJV Old Testament. The Greek word *Pascha* is used twenty-seven times in the KJV New Testament twenty-six times it is translated correctly as Passover the twenty seventh time (in Acts 12:4) it is translated wrong as "Easter." (The Textus Receptus translates it as Passover.). Seder (pronounced *say-dur*) is the traditional ceremonial meal at Passover.

Step 4 Excel

Share with someone how Passover reveals Christ. Do you have a Jewish friend who does not embrace Christ? Speak with your pastor about the right and wrong ways to witness to a Jew, then humbly share Christ with that person. There are excellent guides available, written by messianic Jews, which teach how to share Christ with a Jew. Now that you have learned about our Passover, Jesus, you may wish to purchase a guide that you can use in the future for any "divine appointments" that God may set. We recommend the following:

Answering Jewish Objections to Jesus: by Michael Brown
Description: Michael Brown's thinking is incisive and to the point. His ability to explain so that anyone can understand is amazing. He will surely be acclaimed as the new expert in Jewish Christian apologetics. (January 2000) Baker Book House; ISBN: 080106063X.

You Bring the Bagels, I'll Bring the Gospel: Sharing the Messiah With Your Jewish Neighbor by Barry Rubin, Steffi Rubin (Illustrator)
Description: This user-friendly introduction to the minds and hearts of the Jewish people will teach you how to establish a foothold for the gospel on their turf. Special study questions help you to shift your mind into a messianic mode. (March 1999) Lederer Messianic Publications; ISBN: 1880226650.

Resources recommended in ♦several lessons, ★ several units, ♥ other HOW Units. ☜ Key Resource (see beginning of unit or page 32).

Heart of Wisdom Publishing   217

The Exodus

114-117

The Narrated Bible

Step 1 Excite

Read the biblical account of the Exodus, then watch the 1956 Cecil B. DeMille movie "The Ten Commandments" (available from video rental stores). Discuss with your parents how true-to-life you believe this account to be. Make a list of anything that contradicted scripture. (Check the Bible account of Moses' age.)

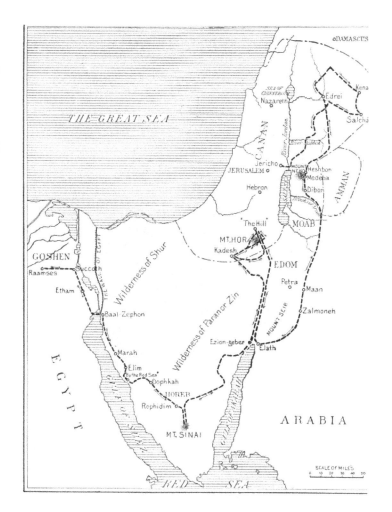

Step 2 Examine

Read the following New Testament passages that refer to the Exodus: Acts 7:9-40; 13:17; Hebrews 3:16; 8:9; Jude 1:5.

Do research about the Exodus. We recommend:

Books

Encyclopedia of the Bible
(Nelson's Illustrated) ♥
Read: "The Exodus from Egypt" (20-21).

The Victor Journey through the Bible ●━♥
Read: "The Exodus" (62-63).

Holman Bible Atlas ●━ ★
Read: Chapter 7 "The Exodus" (63-74).

Our Father Abraham ●━ ♥
Read: References to the Exodus, pages 161, 237, 238, 240, and 251.

Underlined text refers to Internet link at http://Homeschool-Books.com

Ancient Egypt and the Old Testament ♦
Read: Chapter 5 "The Egyptian Setting of the Serpent Confrontation," Chapter 6 "An Exegetical and Consideration of the Ten Plagues of Egypt," and Chapter 7 "The Travel Itinerary of the Hebrews from Egypt."

Exodus by Brian Wildsmith (Illustrator)
Description: The story of the Exodus and the rescue of the Hebrews from slavery in Egypt is a powerful and exciting tale which attests that God's guiding hand is always evident. (January 1999) Wm. B. Eerdmans Publishing Co.; ISBN: 0802851754. Reading level: Ages 4-8. Interest level: Ages 4-12.

Exodus (Jewish Children's Bible)
Description: Based on the original Hebrew text, *Exodus* presents all the major stories in the second book of the Bible in simple, easy-to-read prose that children can understand and follow. More than fifty original, full-color illustrations accompany the text and bring to life the traditional weekly reading of the Bible that takes place in the synagogue. The Children's Haggadah, written especially for young children, presents the fifteen sections of the Passover Haggadah in a very readable format. Reading level: Ages 4-8. Interest level: Ages 4-12.

Internet Sources

How Reliable Is Exodus?
Description: An article from the Biblical Archaeology Society.

1504 B.C. - 1254 B.C. Exodus
Description: A visual time line of the Exodus from Egypt.

Exodus
Description: Article from *Easton's Bible Dictionary*.

The Exodus
Description: Part of "God's Story: From Creation to Eternity" from ChristianAnswers.net. (Follow the "next" buttons on the bottom of each page.)

Step 3 Expand

Choose and complete one of the following activities:

Activity 1: Create a Map
Trace a map to show the Exodus from Egypt to the Promised Land. First was the journey from Egypt to Mount Sinai, where the law was given, and then on

Resources recommended in ♦several lessons, ★ several units, ♥other HOW Units. ⊙—Key Resource (see beginning of unit or page 32).

Heart of Wisdom Publishing   219

to Kadesh-Barnea, located at the southern end of Canaan. At Kadesh, the people, frightened by their spies, refused to invade Canaan and were condemned to forty years in the wilderness.

1600 BC   *1400 BC*

MOSES

Activity 2: Do Further Research
Investigate the modern exodus of Jews from former Soviet bloc countries and from Ethiopia to Israel. Do these modern pilgrims find it easy to leave Europe and Ethiopia? What modes of transportation do they use? Are they leaving behind a form of enslavement or oppression? In Israel, are they being taught God's law for the first time? Do they require special provisions for food and shelter? Write a comparison of the Exodus from enslavement in Egypt to the modern exodus to the state of Israel.

Activity 3: Make a Display
Use a combination of magazine photos, drawings, and Internet pictures to make a collage titled "Exodus." Your poster should be artistic. Strive to depict the feeling of journeying away from oppression and toward the unknown.

Activity 4: Add to Your Time Line Book
Add the story of Exodus to your Time Line Book. Here is a sample from Reproducible Maps, Charts, Time Lines and Illustrations (What the Bible Is All About Resources).

Step 4 Excel

Share what you have learned about the Exodus with a friend or family member. Correct written work to demonstrate correct punctuation and spelling, and effective use of grammar. Add corrected written work or any illustrations to your portfolio.

Underlined text refers to Internet link at http://Homeschool-Books.com

Pharaohs of Ancient Egypt

Step 1 Excite

Visit a Internet site or watch a video:

Pharaohs and Kings

Description: Controversial Egyptologist David Rohl takes you from the banks of the Nile to the Holy Land—and explores new archaeological evidence that he believes will unveil a compelling new version of the biblical past. You'll journey from Saul and David to Joshua and the Promised Land, from new evidence for the Exodus to new evidence of Solomon's wealth and the lineage of Joseph. And at journey's end you'll have a new—and controversial—insight into biblical history. 2 hours 30 minutes on two videocassettes.

Cleveland Museum of Art Pharaohs Exhibition

Description: The Louvre houses Egyptian art treasures. Many of them were on loan to the Cleveland Museum of Art, which produced this online exhibit. In addition to the artifacts, this site has a time line of the dynasties and rulers. A section on hieroglyphs will appeal to adults. A special section for kids, with "Rosetta Stone" as the tour guide, shows them how to build a paper model of a pharaoh's death mask.

The Great Pharaohs of Egypt

Description: Long before the birth of Christ, a great nation arose on the banks of the Nile. For 3,000 years, Egypt stood at the forefront of human achievement, blending creativity, intellect, and mysticism in a culture the likes of which had never been seen. And for all that time, the fate of the nation rested in the hands of its storied rulers, the pharaohs. *The Great Pharaohs of Egypt* uses expert interviews, computer re-creations, extensive location footage, and the latest archaeological and scientific evidence to tell the story of these ancient kings. See how the warrior Narmer first united Egypt. Explore the pharaohs' most famous legacy, the awe-inspiring pyramids. Discover how the pharaohs' age came to an end with the death of Cleopatra. A remarkable inquiry into the lives and legacy of the leaders who were worshiped as gods-on-earth. Four videos. A&E in the classroom. Check for airtime in your area.

Egypt-Secrets of the Pharaohs

Description: *National Geographic* and a team of archaeologists explore the well-kept secrets of mummification and the building of the pyramids in ancient

Resources recommended in ◆several lessons, ★ several units, ● other HOW Units. ●—Key Resource (see beginning of unit or page 32).

Heart of Wisdom Publishing   221

Egypt. Features a scientific re-creation of mummification to discover how the bodies of the pharaohs were preserved, plus a look at the ancient underground vault that houses the ship of the Pharaoh Khufu. ASIN: 0792250982.

Step 2 Examine

The Egyptian chronology and archaeology corroborates the biblical records if one correlate the archaeological ages, the Egyptian pharaonic chronology and the biblical chronology of early Israelite history with the absolute Christological timescale. In Pharaohs and Kings: A Biblical Quest, David M. Rohl explains:

> In order to integrate the knowledge gained from different civilizations into the timescale as a whole, we need to have common dates that can be used to link known events in two or more civilizations. Examples are battles or marriage alliances between kings. This done, the relation of these different nations can be ascertained.
>
> There were three basic cross-links made by 19th century Egyptologists to synchronize Israelite and Egyptian history.
>
> - The sacking of Thebes in 664 B.C. by the Assyrian king Ashurbanipal as punishment for a revolt led by Pharaoh Taharka of the 25th Dynasty of kings in Egypt. Assyrian, Babylonian, Egyptian and other sources make this a very firm date, fixing the history of Egypt after this time. This date is beyond contention.
> - The identification of Pharaoh Shishak (who is recorded in I Kings 14:25, 26 and II Chronicles 12:2-9 as having conquered Jerusalem when Rehoboam was king of Judah) with Pharaoh Shoshenk I of the 22nd Dynasty.
> - The identification of Ramesses II (Ramesses the Great, a 19th Dynasty ruler) as the pharaoh of the oppression of the Israelites in Egypt.
>
> The absolute dates for Shishak/Shoshenk I were calculated from the biblical chronology, i.e. counting back regnal years to Rehoboam, the son and successor of Solomon. From this date, the date for Ramesses II was calculated by counting back the regnal lengths of the pharaohs between Ramesses and Shoshenk I. Other Egyptian kings were spread to fill in the gaps between these dates and other data, e.g. from the Ebers Calendar and Leiden Papyrus used to support the chronology.

Underlined text refers to Internet link at http://Homeschool-Books.com

Look up as much information as you can find about King Khufu, Pepi II, Theban king Mentuhotep II, King Thutmose I, and King Tutankhamen, and read about these rulers. Use any resource (an encyclopedia, a nonfiction book, or the Internet). We recommend the following:

Books

Ancient Egypt (Eyewitness) ◉— ◆
Read: "Famous Pharaohs" (10-11), "The Royal Court" (12-13).

Kingfisher History Encyclopedia ◉— ♥
Read: All entries on individual pharaohs.

Kingfisher Illustrated History of the World ◉— ♥
Read: All entries on individual pharaohs, and page 26.

The Usborne Book of the Ancient World ◉— ★
Read: "Egyptian Kings," and "Ramesses" (82, 69-71).

Pharaohs of Ancient Egypt ◆
See description in the "Resources" section at the beginning of this unit.

Pharaohs and Kings: A Biblical Quest ◉— ★
See description in the "Resources" section at the beginning of this unit.

Internet Sources

King Tutankhamen
Description: Article and links from Brittanica.com.

Egyptian Kings
Description: A one-page time line of all the pharaohs, with almost every one linked to a separate biography page. Most biographies have interesting links, including recommended books and videos.

Pharaohs
Description: Chronological lists, time lines of dynasties and kingdoms, and information on individual pharaohs, from About.com.

Test Your Knowledge of the Pharaohs and Dynasties
Description: This site contains basic introductory information, a quiz with pages for reference, and pages on Akhenaten, Nefertiti, Aten (the sun disc), the city of Akhet-Aten, and the art of ancient Egypt.

Resources recommended in ◆several lessons, ★ several units, ♥other HOW Units. ◉—Key Resource (see beginning of unit or page 32).

Step 3 Expand

Choose and complete one of the following activities:

Activity 1: Write a Summary
Take notes on all of the above rulers as you read, then write a summary about each. Refer to "Summary Writing" in *Writers INC*. Younger students can narrate (orally tell) what they have learned.

Activity 2: Write a Poem
Thutmose III was the greatest of the Egyptian kings and reigned from 1504-1450 B.C. During his reign, he brought Egypt to the height of its power. Write a poem or song about his achievements from his viewpoint. Do you think he was humble or self-inflated about his success? Reflect in your writing your perception of his attitudes with regard to his accomplishments. Get background information from encyclopedias or other resources.

Activity 3: Add to Your Time Line Book
Add the Egyptian rulers from 3500 (Pharaoh Menes) to 1200 B.C. (Ramses III) to your Time Line Book. Illustrate your time line with pictures and symbols from ancient Egypt.

Activity 4: Create a Mural
Make a mural or collage of various rulers in ancient Egypt for display. Use library books to find paintings and other Egyptian art to help you draw authentically.

Activity 5: Expand your research
Raamses in the Bible is a city of the eastern delta of Egypt, built by Hebrew slave labor. It was rebuilt by Ramses II (also called Ramese the Great). The Ramses in the books of Genesis and Numbers is the region of the central eastern delta. When Jacob and his family migrated from Asia to Egypt, they were settled in "the land of Rameses" and that they became property owners there (Genesis 47:11, 27). Find out more about Ramses II. Refer to Pharaohs and Kings: A Biblical Quest Chapter 7, "The Historical Shishak."

Step 4 Excel

Read or perform what you have learned about the rulers in ancient Egypt with a friend or family member. Correct written work to demonstrate correct punctuation and spelling, and effective use of grammar. Add corrected written work or any illustrations to your portfolio.

King Tutankhamen

Step 1 Excite

Watch a video.

King Tut: Tomb of Treasure
Description: Archaeologist Howard Carter breaks through the burial chamber that was sealed for over 3,000 years. Check <u>PBS TV Schedule</u> for air time.

In Search of History: The Mysteries of King Tut
Description: In 1922, archaeologist Howard Carter unsealed Tut's grave, revealing a treasure that defied description. But did he uncover something else as well? *The Mysteries of King Tut* examines the extraordinary events that have led many to believe that an ancient curse protects the spirit of the boy king. It is a tale of death and destruction; it is a riveting look at a captivating legend that will not die. A&E in the classroom. <u>Check for air time in your area.</u>

Step 2 Examine

Research King Tutankhamen. Use any resource (an encyclopedia, a nonfiction book, or the Internet). We recommend the following:

Book

Ancient Egypt (Eyewitness) ●— ◆
Read: "The Valley of the Kings" (22-23).

The Usborne Book of the Ancient World ●— ★
Read: "Tutankhamen" (36, 38, 51, and 87).

Tutankhamen's Gift by Robert Sabuda
Description: This book portrays Tutankhamen as a small, frail boy whose greatest delight is watching the Egyptian artisans and crafts people build temples to the gods. What do you think of Tutankhamen's "gift"? What does the book tell you about that era in history? What was the attitude toward monotheism? Do you think *Tutankhamen's Gift* is suitable for young children, its intended audience? (1997) Aladdin Paperbacks; ISBN: 0689817304. Reading level: Elementary.

Internet Sources

Resources recommended in ◆several lessons, ★several units, ♥other HOW Units. ●—Key Resource (see beginning of unit or page 32).

Heart of Wisdom Publishing   225

At the Tomb of King Tutankhamen
Description: An exciting site from *National Geographic* which shows how the tomb was uncovered, and provides helpful facts.

King Tutankhamen
Description: This site gives a short history of Tut, and links to information about his early life, family tree, interests, etc.

Step 3 Expand

Choose and complete one of the following activities:

Activity 1: Answer Questions

1. When did King Tutankhamen live?
2. How old was he when he died?
3. Do we know of anything that was accomplished during his reign?
4. Why is he so famous?
5. How was his tomb discovered?
6. What made his tomb different from those of other pharaohs?
7. What objects were found in his tomb?
8. What object do you find the most beautiful? The most intriguing?

Activity 2: Prepare an Interview
Arrange a list of questions to ask Howard Carter after his discovery of King Tut's tomb. What would Mr. Carter's answers be?

Activity 3: Write a Newspaper Article
Write a newspaper article describing the discovery of King Tut's tomb.

Activity 4: Add to Your Time Line Book
Add King Tut to your Time Line Book.

Step 4 Excel

Publish your newspaper article in a family newspaper or revise your interview into a skit. Persuade another student to perform with you for an audience. Correct written work to demonstrate correct punctuation and spelling, and effective use of grammar. Add corrected written work or illustrations to your portfolio.

Underlined text refers to Internet link at http://Homeschool-Books.com

Egypt's Alliance with Israel

Step 1 Excite

Israel was located between two great empires: Egypt, and the empire which was ruling Mesopotamia at various times—Assyria, Babylon, Persia, or Greece. These empires traded with one another. Israel lay in the path of a major trading route called the Via Maris. This trading route provided an opportunity for Israelites to give witness to foreigners about the Lord God. And yet, the foreigners brought both temptation and war. Whoever controlled the trade route, controlled trade, so the land of Israel was a prize which the empires fought over. The Jews were often allied with Egypt, seeking Pharaoh's protection from their powerful northern neighbors.

Find a good topographic map of Israel. Find Mt. Carmel and the Valley of Megiddo, now called the Valley of Jezreel. Does this valley appear to be a good place for the trade route to go north and south? Why wouldn't traders want to go straight down the coastline? (Because of the presence of Mt. Carmel, which blocked their way.)

Can you find a map that shows the Via Maris? This route went along the coast of Palestine, and through the Valley of Jezreel. This is the path that traders took from Mesopotamia to Egypt. Do you think that the Valley of Jezreel was a valuable corridor to control? Megiddo was the doorway city to this valley. "Megiddo (me·GID·o), or Tel Megiddo (TEL-me·GID·o), an ancient fortified city, is one of the most famous battlegrounds in the world. Historians believe that more battles were fought at this location than anywhere else on earth." [1]

Step 2 Examine

Read 2 Kings 17:4. To whom had Israel paid tribute? Why was Hoshea considered a traitor? What reason did Assyria give for besieging and then deporting the residents of Samaria? God tells His reason why the Northern Kingdom of Israel was exiled in 2 Kings 17:7-23. After the Northern Kingdom was taken into captivity by Assyria, the godly king of Judah, Hezekiah, was threatened by Assyria. What was the king of Assyria saying about Egypt in 2 Kings 18:21? Was it true that Hezekiah was relying on Egypt for protection? Read 2 Kings 19:14-19 to find out.

The Holman Bible Atlas ⊶ ♥
Read: "The Egyptian Experience" (52-62).

Resources recommended in ♦several lessons, ★ several units, ♥other HOW Units. ⊶Key Resource (see beginning of unit or page 32).

Heart of Wisdom Publishing   227

Step 3 Expand

Choose and complete one of the following activities:

Activity 1: Paraphrase Verses
Prophets warned the Israelites not to trust in Egypt for protection. Read Isaiah 30:1-5; 31:1-3. Paraphrase these prophecies. What should we learn from the example of Israel? What does Egypt represent in your life? To whom or to what do you go for protection? Where does your confidence come from? Write a paragraph that explains what these verses mean to you personally.

Activity 2: Map Work
Find these cities on a map: Sidon, Tyre, Nazareth, Megiddo, and Caesarea. Would traders go near these places as they traveled between Mesopotamia and Egypt?

Activity 3: Read and Discuss
Examine the alliance between Israel and Egypt. Read 1 Kings 3:1. Why did Solomon marry Pharaoh's daughter? Read 1 Kings 9:16,24; 11:16. What does the Bible show about their marriage? Read 2 Chron. 12:1-11. Did the peaceful alliance that Solomon had made through marriage last very long?

Step 4 Excel

Tell your family what you have learned from studying the relationship between Israel and Egypt. How can you, as a family, avoid making "an alliance with Egypt"?

Correct all written work to demonstrate correct punctuation and spelling, and effective use of grammar. Add corrected written work or illustrations to your portfolio.

Footnotes
1. "Megiddo," Bib. Arch: The Premiere Biblical Archeology Web site, <http://www.bibarch.com/ArchaeologicalSites/Megiddo.htm> (Accessed May 23, 2000)

Agriculture in Ancient Egypt

Step 1 Excite

A bram was driven into Egypt by famine. The same cause also led the brothers of Joseph to seek Egyptian corn for their sustenance, for, from the earliest times, Egypt was the great granary of the ancient world. The exceptional fertility of the country depends on the annual overflow of the Nile, caused by rains in the highlands of Abyssinia and Central Africa.

Read Numbers 11:15 to learn what types of foods were eaten in ancient Egypt. Read what they exported in Proverbs 7:16 and Ezekiel 27:7. Read of their horses in 1 Kings 10:28 and 29. Find out other facts using the Bible. Make a list of your findings.

Step 2 Examine

The ancient Egyptians gave a great deal of attention to the fruit and flower gardens attached to their villas. Gardens adorned pavilions and colonnades; orchards were stocked with palms, figs, pomegranates, citrons, oranges, plums, mulberries, apricots, etc.[1]

Research ancient Egyptian agriculture. Use any resource (an encyclopedia, a nonfiction book, or the Internet). We recommend the following:

Books

The Usborne Book of the Ancient World ◑— ★
Read: Use the "Egypt" contents to find "Farming."

Kingfisher History Encyclopedia ◑— ♥
Read: Look for "Farming" in the index under "Egypt."

Internet Sources

Agriculture in Ancient Egypt
Description: Information on agriculture and irrigation in ancient Egypt.

The Grain Harvest in Ancient Egypt
Description: This site provides a description of, and pictures from, the tomb of Menna in ancient Egypt.

Resources recommended in ◆several lessons, ★ several units, ♥other HOW Units. ◑—Key Resource (see beginning of unit or page 32).

Domesticated Animals in Ancient Egypt
Description: This site describes the various animals used in farming, in transportation, and in the home in ancient Egypt.

A Taste of the Ancient World: Farming at Karanis
Description: Photos and descriptions of ancient farming tools and seeds, from Kelsey Museum.

Step 3 Expand

Choose and complete one of the following activities:

Activity 1: Plan a Project
Plan a project, such as a report, drawing, model, or mural. Use one format, or several, to compare what an Egyptian farmer's life was like when the Nile River was in flood stage and when it was not flooding. Add a dramatic depiction of life when the river failed to flood. Refer to Amos 8:8 and 9:5.

Activity 2: Copy a Passage
Copy (by hand or typing) two or more paragraphs from your research giving an overview of Egyptian agriculture. (Copying is a good exercise for teaching yourself accuracy and attention to detail, and you will probably discover things about the text you are copying that you would be unlikely to notice otherwise.)

Activity 3: Answer Questions
Answer the following: Where is arable land found in Egypt? Who owned this land in ancient times? How were fields irrigated? What crops were grown? What plant is used to make linen fabric? What growing conditions are required for flax and cotton? What tools did farmers use? What animals were used to work in the fields? What animals were raised for meat? What fruits were cultivated?

Step 4 Excel

Share your project on ancient Egyptian agriculture with a group, such as your family, your homeschool group, a 4-H club, or a church group. Add any new words you learned in this lesson into your Vocabulary Notebook (see page 22).

Footnotes
1. Canon, Trevor. *Ancient Egypt*, p. 40.

Underlined text refers to Internet link at http://Homeschool-Books.com

Architecture in Ancient Egypt

Note: This lesson is an overview of Egyptian temples and palaces. You'll learn more about Egyptian architecture in the Pyramid Lesson.

Step 1 Excite

What materials did Hebrew slaves sometimes use in building? What types of buildings do you think they were making at the time that they were forced to gather their own straw? Read Exodus 5.

Step 2 Examine

Research famous Egyptian temples and palaces. Use any resource (an encyclopedia, nonfiction book, historical novel, or the Internet). We recommend the following:

Books

The Usborne Book of the Ancient World ●― ★
Read: Use the "Egypt Contents" page to find "Pyramids and Tombs," "Egyptian Temples," and "Egyptian Building Methods."

Kingfisher History Encyclopedia ●― ♥
Read: Look in the index under "Egypt" for "Pyramids" and "Temples."

Internet Sources

Mysteries of the Nile
Description: This Nova online site leads you on a fascinating excursion through the wonders of ancient Egypt. To see for yourself the enormous energies the pharaohs devoted to erecting their soaring monuments—particularly obelisks—you will travel to Giza, site of the Pyramids and that enigmatic half-man, half-lion, the Sphinx, and to Luxor, site of the archaic capital of Thebes, to examine some of the great tombs and temples of the New Kingdom. You'll also visit Aswan, where a NOVA team tried to raise a 25-ton obelisk using tools and techniques the pharaohs themselves might have used. Finally, watch a new team working in a Massachusetts quarry succeed at last in raising an obelisk using an ingeniously simple technique.

Architectural Elements of Ancient Egypt
Description: Learn about foundations, arches, pillars, obelisks, stairs, and more, with excellent illustrations.

Resources recommended in ♦several lessons, ★ several units, ♥other HOW Units. ●―Key Resource (see beginning of unit or page 32).

Heart of Wisdom Publishing   231

Building in Ancient Egypt
Description: This site describes construction planning, building materials, and builders' tools in ancient Egypt.

Town Planning in Ancient Egypt
Description: Find out about town planning, or rather the lack of it, in ancient Egypt.

Egypt
Description: This site includes links to illustrations, with historical highlights featuring pyramids, tombs, and thrones.

Typical Country Estate in Ancient Egypt
Description: Picture and information from The Discovery Channel.

Ancient Egyptian Virtual Temple
Description: Embark on a journey to explore the realm known as ancient Egypt, or Kemet as it was known to the Egyptians themselves.

The Wonders of Ancient Egypt
Description: Take a journey into the world of the ancient Egyptians, the Great Pyramid, the Sphinx, and much more.

History of Egyptian Architecture
Description: A chronological timetable of Egyptian architecture.

Color Tour of Egypt
Description: Take a tour of over a dozen ancient Egyptian sites along the Nile River (from the University of Memphis Institute of Egyptian Art and Archaeology).

Ancient Egyptian Architecture
Description: This site is from Great Buildings Online. It includes links to several sites with information about temples and pyramids.

Egyptian Pyramids Index
Description: Observe data on pyramid construction, geometry, and statistics.

Videos

Ancient Egyptian Art and Architecture by Ann Campbell
Description: The *History Through Art and Architecture* videos were developed as a unique program to excite and stretch a student's interest in history. In learning about the art and architecture of a period, a student not only finds visual pegs on which to hang facts and dates, but often discovers, to his or her amazement, that today is merely a new twist on ancient history. Through watching and listening, and then participating in the learning activities that are included, every

Underlined text refers to Internet link at http://Homeschool-Books.com

student should have acquired a basic understanding of the art and architecture of ancient Egypt and be able to apply this knowledge to his or her present environment. Alarion Press, P.O. Box 1882, Boulder, CO ASIN: 80306-1882. (1993). Interest Level: Grades 5-12.

Step 3 Expand

Choose and complete one of the following activities:

Activity 1: Sketch
Draw sketches of Egyptian architecture. Choose one building to portray, or several. Try several sketches, some depicting a detail of the building, others showing the outlines of the building.

Activity 2: Make a Model
Create a model of an Egyptian building. You can use Make This Egyptian Temple by Iain Ashman (December 1999) E D C Publications; ISBN: 0746037813, or construct ideas of your own. Can you devise a simple method of assembling an obelisk? Exhibit your sketches and model(s).

Activity 3. Answer Questions

1. What materials did ancient Egyptians use in their architecture?
2. Where did they get the rocks that were used for building?
3. Were the buildings painted?
4. How large were they?
5. Where were they located?

Step 4 Excel

Share what you have learned about the Egyptian Architecture lesson with a friend or family member. Add any written work or illustrations to your portfolio. Include at least one picture (Internet print-out, photocopy, or illustration) of an Egyptian building.Add any new words you learned in this lesson into your Vocabulary Notebook (see page 22).

Resources recommended in ♦several lessons, ★ several units, ♥other HOW Units. ☛Key Resource (see beginning of unit or page 32).

Archaeology

Step 1 Excite

Work virtually with archaeologist on a real dig at:

(i) Odyssey in Egypt
Description: During a ten-week period, you can exchange e-mails with people on-site, see the objects uncovered, learn about Egyptian culture, and even help solve problems as they occur. Read about the unfolding excavation. Walk through the dig site in virtual reality. You can also view a QuickTime Movie of the excavation site. Sign up for the next project online.

Step 2 Examine

Research archaeology. Use any resource (an encyclopedia, a nonfiction book, or the Internet). We recommend the following:

Books

Kingfisher History Encyclopedia ●— ♥
Read: "What is History."

Kingfisher Illustrated History of the World ●— ♥
Read: Use the index to look up "Archaeology."

Streams of Civilizations: Earliest Times to Discovery ●— ★
Read: "Introducing History."

The Usborne Young Scientist Archaeology by Barbara Cork
Description: Usborne's colorful visual introductions to exciting topics and concepts use straightforward language and dramatic pictures to help explain archaeology. (January 1986) E D C Publications; ISBN: 0860208656

Internet Sources

(i) Ask Dr. Dig
Description: A site where you can ask an archaeologist, Caroline Nicholson, Ph.D., archaeology questions online! Read the other posts. Someone may have already gotten an answer to a question you have in mind.

 An Egyptian Scavenger Hunt and an Interactive Story
Description: Students from San Diego State University's Isis Productions in conjunction with a class of Grade 6 students have designed and published an elaborate adventure game about ancient Egypt.

The University of Memphis Institute of Egyptian Art and Archaeology
Description: This site has a wonderful exhibit of Egyptian artifacts from the Department of Art of the University of Memphis. It includes statues and mummies, with explanations, and a tour of the major archaeological sites in Egypt.

Step 3 Expand

Choose and complete one of the following activities:

Activity 1: Answer Questions

1. What is the purpose of archaeology?
2. What types of artifacts have archaeologists discovered?
3. What is a "tell"?
4. What types of information are archaeologists able to uncover about communities in history?
5. What types of information are archaeologists not able to document?
6. What kinds of medical examinations can be performed on human remains, and what kinds of information can be discovered?
7. Where are some active digs in the Middle East?
8. Who are some famous Egyptologists?

Activity 2: Go on an Archaeological Expedition
Arrange a location to host your expedition: a backyard, a park, a farm, a church, or a community center. You will need: a sheet of plastic, sand, a sand box or small plastic swimming pool, clay pots, acrylic non-toxic paints and small craft paintbrushes, clean bones from beef or chicken, cheap large paintbrushes, and pails. The project is best carried out in two sessions.

Participants in the first session will imitate ancient people. Dressing in costumes can add fun to your project. In the first session, lay the sheet of plastic down near where you will sit on the ground to work. Paint bright designs on the clay pots. When the paint is dry, "throw the pots in the garbage pile"—that is, smash them by throwing them onto the big sheet of plastic. Gather the shards of pottery by wrapping them up in the sheet of plastic. Select some broken pottery—those pieces that are the least sharp—to put in your archaeological dig. Set up the site by putting pottery and bones into the sandbox with sand. Create a mysterious map

Resources recommended in ◆several lessons, ★ several units, ♥other HOW Units. ●—Key Resource (see beginning of unit or page 32).

Heart of Wisdom Publishing   235

to lead the "archaeologist" to your "ancient village." Finish your session by having a feast fit for ancient people.

The second session is best for elementary-aged children. Give each child a copy of your map and play follow-the-leader as you explore the territory, looking for the site of the ancient village. When you come to your sandbox, hand out the large paintbrushes and show the children how to brush sand away to uncover "artifacts." Warn them to be careful of the sharp edges of the pottery. When "artifacts" are uncovered, collect them in pails. Can the children recognize who painted the pieces of pottery by looking at the artwork? Make sure everyone understands these terms: "artifact," "dig," and "archaeology."

Activity 3: Expand Your Research
Egypt was home to two of the Seven Wonders of the Ancient World: the Great Pyramid (the only one of the seven to survive) and the lighthouse at Alexandria. Research both. Write a summary (at least two paragraphs) of what you learned about each. Younger students can dictate or narrate.

Step 4 Excel

Share what you have learned about archaeology with a friend or family member. Correct all written work to demonstrate correct punctuation and spelling, and effective use of grammar. Add corrected written work and any illustrations to your portfolio. Add new words you learned in this lesson into your Vocabulary Notebook (see page 22).

Art in Ancient Egypt

Step 1 Excite

As you study artists, their work, and how that work communicates cultural values and beliefs, you'll gain vivid insight into the cultural and historical forces that shape an era.

God gave the Hebrews artistic skills and the ability to make beautiful objects for worship. Read Exodus 36 for a description of the work of Jewish artisans shortly after the giving of the Ten Commandments. Brainstorm and make a list of everything you learn from this passage about ancient art in this region.

Step 2 Examine

Much of Egyptian life and customs can be deduced from paintings on tomb walls. The pictures explain their life style, the varieties of foods and their preparation, the methods of caring for flocks and herds, the trapping of wild animals, the building of boats, and the processes of the other crafts. The illustrations were arranged on the wall in groups that can be read as continuing narratives. The sculptors acted as teams, with different stages of the work assigned to different members of the group. Egyptian sculptors worked with clay, wood, metal, ivory, and stone. An artist in ancient Egypt was proud to be part of a highly respected craft.

Research ancient Egyptian art. Look at paintings and relief sculptures of different pharaohs in books or on the Internet. We recommend the following:

Books

The Usborne Story of Painting by Anthea Peppin ♥
Read: The chapter on Egypt. Description: Gives a visual understanding of the various styles of art used through out history.(October 1980) E D C Publications; ISBN: 0860204413

The Usborne Book of the Ancient World ⊶ ★
Read: "Crafts and Trades" (66).

Kingfisher History Encyclopedia ⊶ ♥
Read: Look in the index under "Egypt" for "Prehistoric Art."

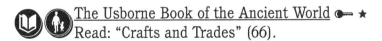

Resources recommended in ♦several lessons, ★several units, ♥other HOW Units. ⊶Key Resource (see beginning of unit or page 32).

Heart of Wisdom Publishing   237

Egyptian Art in the Days of the Pharaohs by Cyril Aldred
Description: An excellent chronological survey of Egyptian art. (February 1985) Thames & Hudson; ISBN: 0500201803.

Ancient Egyptian Art Postcards
Description: Full color/twenty-four ready-to-mail Cards by British Museum (July 1991) Dover Pubns; ISBN: 0486267032.

Internet Sources

Detroit Institute of the Arts: Ancient Egyptian Art
Description: The works here demonstrate the basic principles of Egyptian sculpture in its symbolic formality.

Institute of Egyptian Art and Archaeology
Description: A beautiful site by the Art Department of the University of Memphis. Browse online exhibits of artifacts; take a tour of ancient Egyptian monuments.

The Galleries of Egyptian Art
Description: This site includes photographs and paintings of ancient Egyptian art, archaeology, mythology, and dynastic history.

Egyptian Art and Archaeology
Description: This site will take you to its collection of mummies, religious and funerary items, jewelry, and objects from everyday life. This resource has been created to provide an understanding of ancient Egyptian art and its central role in Egyptian civilization. It is primarily organized around three themes—"Ancient Egyptian Beliefs," "Looking at Egyptian Art," and "The Story of the Collection"—that group objects and historical ideas into questions and answers. From the University of Memphis Institute.

Egyptian Art
Description: This site from NileRiver.com includes two excellent exhibitions: Papyrus Works of Art and Pharaoh's Art Gallery.

Step 3 Expand

Activity 1: Illustrate
Think about your personal beliefs and events in your life. List these items, then think of how you would illustrate them symbolically. Use markers,

charcoal, or paint to create a group of pictures in the Egyptian style that tell a story of an activity in your life (preparing a meal, making clothing, homeschooling, etc.).

Activity 2: Answer Questions
Select several works of art (paintings, sculpture, etc.) from your research, and answer the following:
1. What posture do the ancient Egyptians exhibit in their portraits?
2. Which parts of the body are in profile, and which are facing you?
3. The body profile to depict the pharaoh was used for 2,500 years. Why do you think that ancient Egyptian artists kept this tradition?
4. What kinds of postures do the figures have?
5. How did the artist decide what size to make the figures?
6. Is there any background scenery? Any writing? Are there any animals? Any objects?
7. Do any of the pictures look three-dimensional?
8. Can you tell where the figures are in relation to one another, or do they seem to float in thin air?
9. Look at sculptures of people. Were the sculptures painted?
10. How were the eyes made?
11. Do the figures seem real or symbolic?
12. How skillful were the sculptors?
13. What two plants are symbolic of upper and lower Egypt?
14. What types of paints or pigments did the ancient Egyptians use?
15. What types of homes did the workmen and their families live in?

Step 4 Excel

Add illustrations (photocopies from books or printouts from the Internet) of Egyptian art to your portfolio. Share your illustrations with a friend or family member. Add new words you learned in this lesson into your Vocabulary Notebook (see page 22).

Resources recommended in ◆several lessons, ★ several units, ♥other HOW Units. �—Key Resource (see beginning of unit or page 32).

Heart of Wisdom Publishing   239

Pottery in Ancient Egypt

Step 1 Excite

The Early Dynasties brought the development and use of the potter's wheel and the more extensive use of clay. Indicative of this time are large pottery storage jars, with conical clay sealings, some stamped with the royal seal at the top. The creation of these large vessels was made possible, in part, by the exquisite throwing techniques of the potters, but also by the extensive use of hand-building. The fine decorated pottery of ancient Egypt began to disappear toward the end of the Pre-dynastic Period. In its place, undercoated earthenware (a humble medium) was used for mostly utilitarian endeavors such as storage jars, grain bins, water and beer jars, cooking pots, and the like. (Minnesota State University EMuseum.)

Read the following verses, each of which uses potters and clay to illustrate a point: Isaiah 29:15-16; Jeremiah 18:1-15; Romans 9:18-24.

Step 2 Examine

Research the development of pottery in ancient Egypt. Use any resource (an encyclopedia, nonfiction book, historical novel, or the Internet). We recommend the following:

Kingfisher History Encyclopedia ●— ♥
Read: Look in the index under "Pottery."

Pottery, Stoneware and Ceramics
Description: A good overview of pottery, stoneware, and ceramics in ancient tomes, from the Minnesota State University EMuseum.

Pottery
Description: An article explaining how archaeologists can learn about a culture through its pottery.

Step 3 Expand

Choose and complete one of the following activities:

Activity 1: Discuss
Isaiah 64:8 says *But now, O LORD, thou art our father; we are the clay, and thou our potter; and we all are the work of thy hand.* We are the work of God's hand.

Underlined text refers to Internet link at http://Homeschool-Books.com

He is taking a worthless clump of clay and with the application of pressure, water, and a great deal of spinning, shaping us into a beautiful vessel. We will find that it is through the trials and the application of His truth in our lives that we will become a masterpiece. Brainstorm and discuss ways we can allow God to shape us into the image of His will.

Activity 2: Research How to Make Pottery
Do research to find out how you can make pottery today. Use any resource (a craft book or the Internet). We recommend the following:

Book

First Civilizations (Cultural Atlas for Young People) ○━ ◆
Read: "The Art of Pottery" (26-27). See description on page 106.

Internet Sources

Pottery Tutorial
Description: Designed for the beginner, this site contains a step-by-step guide to making ceramics.

Pottery Links and Resources
Description: Many links to pottery instruction and help.

Potter's Guide Basic Throwing
Description: An article which helps you become proficient on the potter's wheel.

Step 4 Excel

Use Play-Doh or clay to show a child how to make a simple pot. Ask, "How did a Hebrew slave use a clay pot?" See what the child can imagine. Add new words you learned in this lesson into your Vocabulary Notebook (see page 22).

The Transformation

To the Potter's house I went down one day,
And watched him while molding the vessels of clay,
And many a wonderful lesson I drew,
As I noted the process the clay went through.

Trampled and broken, down-trodden and rolled,
To render more plastic and fit for the mold
How like the clay that is human, I thought,
When in Heavenly hands to perfection brought!

For Self must be cast as the dust at His feet,
Before it is ready, for service made meet.
And Pride must be broken, and self-will lost –
All laid on the altar, whatever the cost.

But lo! Bye and by, a delicate vase
Of wonderful beauty and exquisite grace.
Was it once the vile clay? Ah! Yes; yet how strange,
The Potter hath wrought such a marvelous change!

Taken from "Poems of Dawn"

Resources recommended in ◆several lessons, ★ several units, ◆other HOW Units. ○━Key Resource (see beginning of unit or page 32).

Heart of Wisdom Publishing   241

Cities in Ancient Egypt

Step 1 Excite

Ancient Egypt's major cities were Memphis, Thebes (Luxor), and Alexandria. The Bible also mentions On, holy City of the Sun; in Egyptian it was called "Annu," in Greek, "Heliopolis." For many centuries, the capital of ancient Egypt was Thebes. It is the city identified in the Old Testament as No ("city") or No-Amon ("city of Amon"). Look in a Bible concordance for verses that mention these Egyptian cities.

Step 2 Examine

Research Egypt's major cities. Use any resource (an encyclopedia, a nonfiction book, or the Internet) to look up each of the following individually: Cairo, Giza, Philae, Luxor, Thebes, Alexandria, and Tanis. We recommend any of the following resources for this lesson:

Books

The Usborne Book of the Ancient World ● ★
Read: Use the index to look up each city. See the map of ancient Egypt.

The Holman Bible Atlas ● ♥
Read: "The Egyptian Experience" (52-62).

Internet Resources

Cities in Ancient Egypt
Description: A map of major cites from Odyssey Online. Click on the links for audio pronunciation.

Town Planning in Ancient Egypt
Description: Article explaining town planning, or rather the lack of it, in ancient Egypt.

A Guide to the Cities of Ancient Egypt
Description: Maps of upper and lower Egypt and links to charts showing the cities, the ancient Greek names, the temples, and modern sites.

Color Tour of Egypt
Description: From this hyperlinked map you can click on a city to find out a bit about it and see images. Includes Cairo, Giza, Saqqara, The West Bank, and more.

Underlined text refers to Internet link at http://Homeschool-Books.com

Step 3 Expand

Choose and complete one of the following activities:

Activity 1: Make a Map
Put a map in your portfolio with the major cities of ancient Egypt labeled.

Activity 2: Make a Chart
Make a chart of information about the ancient Egyptian cities of Cairo, Giza, Philae, Luxor, Thebes, Alexandria, and Tanis. Explain where they were located, when they were founded, how long Thebes was the capital, and who ruled there. Why was the capital changed?

Activity 3: Make a Brochure
Prepare a travel brochure of one of the cities you studied in this lesson, using pictures you have found or drawn. Decide on four places or topics to feature in your brochure. Be sure to include basic facts about the country as well as interesting and exciting places to visit.

Activity 4: Write Summaries
Retell what you have learned about ancient Egyptian cities in a written summary. Write a paragraph about each city: Cairo, Giza, Philae, Luxor, Thebes, Alexandria, and Tanis.

Step 4 Excel

Share what you have learned about the cities in ancient Egypt with a friend or family member. Correct all written work to demonstrate correct punctuation and spelling, and effective use of grammar. Add corrected written work or illustrations to your portfolio. Add new words you learned in this lesson into your Vocabulary Notebook (see page 22).

Resources recommended in ◆several lessons, ★ several units, ● other HOW Units. ●━Key Resource (see beginning of unit or page 32).

Heart of Wisdom Publishing   243

Clothing in Ancient Egypt

Step 1 Excite

L ook at pictures of ancient Egyptian clothing. Men usually wore short skins; women usually wore long, straight dresses. Both sexes wore jewelry and black wigs.

Step 2 Examine

Research the clothing, jewelry, and makeup in ancient Egypt. What fabrics were used? How were the clothes adapted for the climate? How often did fashions change? What kind of jewelry was worn? What were cosmetics made of? How were cosmetics applied?

Use any resource (an encyclopedia, a nonfiction book or the Internet). We recommend the following:

Books

Ancient Egypt (Eyewitness) ●— ♦
Read: "From Fabric to Finery" (14-15), "All that Glitters" (56-57), "Adorning the Body" (58-59).

The Usborne Book of the Ancient World ●—
★
Read: Use the "Egypt Contents" page.

Kingfisher History Encyclopedia ●— ♥
Read: Look in the index under "Egypt."

Internet Sources

Daily Life in Ancient Egypt
Description: Photos and information from Carnegie Museum of Natural History.

Garments in Ancient Egypt
Description: A description of garments and footwear, from the Pharaonic Egypt site.

Underlined text refers to Internet link at http://Homeschool-Books.com

ⓘ <u>Flax and Linen in Ancient Egypt</u>
Description: A description of the growing and use of flax, spinning and weaving linen, from the Pharaonic Egypt site.

ⓘ <u>Ancient Egyptian Garment Making</u>
Description: Article explaining textile manufacturing and garment making in ancient Egypt.

Step 3 Expand

Activity 1: Make a List
Read Exodus 12:35-36. Find out what happened to some of these clothing items in Exodus Chapters 35 and 36. Make a list of the skills that the Hebrews demonstrated in creating and using textiles.

Activity 2: Illustrate
Draw sketches or trace pictures of clothing in ancient Egypt. Pay attention to the edges and the folds of the cloth.

Step 4 Excel

Create and share paper dolls with a younger child. Create your own male and female paper dolls from this time period, and design a wardrobe for them, including "at home" clothes and attire for special events. Or, purchase Egyptian paper dolls, and help a younger student create new clothes for the dolls. Or use <u>Crayola Magic Wardrobe</u> (described below) to make ancient Egyptian paper-doll clothes. Tell the younger student how the Egyptians gave clothing and jewelry when the Hebrews asked for them. Why did the Hebrews ask for clothes and jewelry? Why did the Egyptians give these things away?

<u>Crayola Magic Wardrobe Demo</u>
Description: At this site, you can download a demo of Crayola Magic Wardrobe. You can print out some paper dolls and paper clothes. The clothing is representative of eras such as ancient Egypt, Imperial China, and Medieval France (to name a few). You can also read and put entries into diaries from girls in each time period.

Resources recommended in ◆several lessons, ★ several units, ◕other HOW Units. ⊶Key Resource (see beginning of unit or page 32).

Economy and Trade in Ancient Egypt

Step 1 Excite

Ancient Egyptian history includes examples of cultural continuity and change. For three thousand years there was stability of basic economic, religious, social, and political systems. But change also occurred in the face of expansion, trade, invasion, and technological innovation. As you study ancient Egypt, look for examples of change and continuity, tradition and innovation.

Read the story of Jacob's brothers going to Egypt to buy food. Brainstorm and discuss the traffic, the trade, and the businesses that supplied food to the region.

Step 2 Examine

Investigate the Via Maris that Egyptian traders used to reach Asian markets. Read Genesis 37:25-28. These traders were traveling from the northern part of Palestine south towards Egypt. Find on a map the locations mentioned in that chapter. Notice the trade goods they were carrying. Create a list entitled "Trade goods."

Read Isaiah 19:6-10 and 2 Chron.1:16-17 to find out the major industries in ancient Egypt. Add these to your Trade-Goods List.

Research ancient Egyptian trade and economy. Use any resource (an encyclopedia, a nonfiction book, or the Internet). We recommend the following:

Book

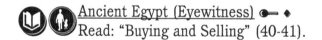Ancient Egypt (Eyewitness) ●━ ◆
Read: "Buying and Selling" (40-41).

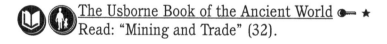The Usborne Book of the Ancient World ●━ ★
Read: "Mining and Trade" (32).

Internet Sources

The Ancient Egyptian Economy
Description: A description of Egyptian economy during the pharaonic period, from the Pharaonic Egypt site.

Underlined text refers to Internet link at http://Homeschool-Books.com

(i)(*) Ancient Egyptian Overseas Trade
Description: A description of the trade relations between ancient Egypt and its neighbors, and of the trading routes and goods.

(i)(*) Internal Trade in Ancient Egypt
Description: An overview of trading, bartering, market places, and merchants.

Step 3 Expand

Choose and complete one of the following activities:

(?)(*) Activity 1: Answer Questions
What exports or trade-goods from ancient Egypt are mentioned in the Bible? Gold and salt were important trade items in Africa. Where did Egyptians obtain these? What did ancient Egyptians have to trade?

(*)(*) Activity 2: Write a Summary
Write a summary of what you learned about the economy (minimum fifty words). Younger students can narrate (orally tell) what they have learned.

(*)(*) Activity 3: Create a Map
Draw or trace a map of trade routes from Africa to Europe and the Near East.

(*)(*) Activity 4: Create a Coloring Book
Design a coloring book that illustrates the economy of ancient Egypt. Use your list of trade goods to decide what to include. You can use Life in Ancient Egypt/Coloring Book by John Green (October 1989) Dover Pubns, ISBN: 0486261301 as a resource. Share the coloring book with children as you explain how ancient Egyptians traded goods with their neighbors.

Step 4 Excel

Share what you have learned about the economy in ancient Egypt with a friend or family member. Correct written work to demonstrate correct punctuation and spelling, and effective use of grammar. Add corrected written work or illustrations to your portfolio. Add new words you learned in this lesson into your Vocabulary Notebook (see page 22).

Resources recommended in ◆several lessons, ★ several units, ♥other HOW Units. ●━Key Resource (see beginning of unit or page 32).

Daily Life in Ancient Egypt

Step 1 Excite

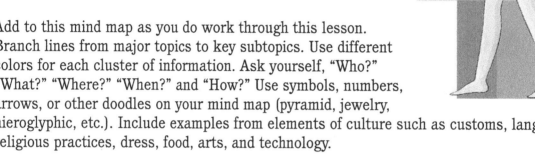

Brainstorm and make a <u>mind map</u> expressing items found in daily life for an average person in ancient Egypt. Use sheets of unlined paper and colored markers or pencils. Put an image or circle in the center and write in "A Day in Ancient Egypt." Draw lines out from the center as you determine the major "chunks" or categories of information.

Add to this mind map as you do work through this lesson. Branch lines from major topics to key subtopics. Use different colors for each cluster of information. Ask yourself, "Who?" "What?" "Where?" "When?" and "How?" Use symbols, numbers, arrows, or other doodles on your mind map (pyramid, jewelry, hieroglyphic, etc.). Include examples from elements of culture such as customs, language, religious practices, dress, food, arts, and technology.

Step 2 Examine

People in ancient Egypt used perfumes in their everyday life. Anointing someone else with perfume was a gracious act of kindness. In a hot climate, filled with sweat, spoiling meat and fish, and exotic fruits and spices, the smells would be very different from those we know in America. Imagine the spices, foods, and also the less-pleasant smells that filled the air.

Do research on daily life in ancient Egypt. Use any resource (an encyclopedia, nonfiction book, historical novel, or the Internet). We recommend the following:

Books

<u>Ancient Egypt (Eyewitness)</u> ⚷ ◆
Read: "An Egyptian Carpenter" (42-43), "Hunting Fishing and Fowling." (44-45), The Egyptians at Home" (46-47), "Song and Dance" (50-51), "Toys and Games" (52-53).

<u>The Usborne Book of the Ancient World</u> ⚷ ★
Read: "Egyptian Homes" (54) and "Women and Family Life" (58).

<u>Kingfisher History Encyclopedia</u> ⚷ ❤
Read: "Ancient Egypt 4000-1800 B.C."

Underlined text refers to Internet link at <u>http://Homeschool-Books.com</u>

Kingfisher Illustrated History of the World ⊶ ♥
Read: "Egypt the New Kingdom" (54-55).

Mara, Daughter of the Nile ♦
See description in the "Resources" section at the beginning of this unit.

The Golden Goblet ♦
See description in the "Resources" section at the beginning of this unit.

Internet Sources

Daily Life in Ancient Egypt
Description: This Web site was designed to introduce students to the civilization of the ancient Egyptians. It was developed by students and teachers at the University of Richmond, Department of Education, under the supervision of Dr. Patricia Stohr-Hunt. Topics include daily life, hieroglyphs, pharaohs, pyramids, religion, and the Sphinx. The units were written to satisfy Virginia social studies standards for 3rd grade, but can be easily used by teachers and students 3rd-10th. The site provides information, not lesson plans. It's perfect for a textbook supplement or to print out and hand to students along with a writing assignment. From the Department of Education, University of Richmond.

Life in Ancient Egypt
Description: The Walton Hall of Ancient Egypt explores one of the world's oldest civilizations. Inside "Life in Ancient Egypt," you will find many important objects—fragments of a three-thousand-year history left behind by a people determined to continue, after death, the life they had known on earth.

Everyday Life in Ancient Egypt
Description: This site includes a story of a fictional but plausible day in the life of two ancient Egyptian families, a chance to explore the world of an ancient Egyptian nobleman, and a challenge to play Senet, a popular ancient Egyptian game. From the British Museum.

The Ancient Egypt Site
Description: This site is dedicated to the history and culture of ancient Egypt. There is an overview of history, which can be searched chronologically or by keyword, and an explanation of the names of the Pharaohs (including an illustration of their names in hieroglyphs). It also includes an extensive bibliography and links to other sites.

Resources recommended in ♦several lessons, ★ several units, ♥other HOW Units. ⊶Key Resource (see beginning of unit or page 32).

Heart of Wisdom Publishing   249

Aspects of Life in Ancient Egypt
Description: An overview of various aspects of culture and society in ancient Egypt, from the Pharaonic Egypt site.

Egypt: Daily Life
Description: An overview of ancient Egypt's family life, marriage, housing and furniture, food and cooking, cosmetics, hairstyles, jewelry, and more.

Step 3 Expand

Choose and complete one of the following activities:

Activity 1: Make a Diorama
Discuss what is used to decorate houses today as compared to what was used during the ancient Egyptian period. Using pictures from a Web site and other sources, make a diorama/model of an ancient Egyptian home. Consider furniture, floor coverings, wall hangings, etc. Shoe boxes are wonderful for this. Refer to How to Build a Diorama.

Activity 2: Complete the Mind Map
Complete the mind map you began in Step 1.

Activity 3: Write a Journal Entry
Write a journal entry as if you were an ancient Egyptian. Use these questions to help you write: What kind of clothes do you wear? What do you look like? Describe your home. Do you have a job? If so, describe what you do and what conditions are like on the job. What do you do for fun? What kinds of foods do you eat? What hardships do you face? Which machines, conveniences, or technologies do you use every day? What are the major differences between your life and modern life? Describe how world, national, or local events have affected you. What do you hope for? What or whom do you fear? Whom do you admire? What are your beliefs (religious, political, personal, and so on)? Younger students can narrate (tell back) what has been learned.

Revise your journal entry into a monologue. Perform for an audience, depicting a normal day for an ancient Egyptian. Provide props to make your skit come alive.

Underlined text refers to Internet link at http://Homeschool-Books.com

Activity 4: Write a Short Story
Write a short story about a person who finds a time capsule created in ancient Egypt. What is in the time capsule, and what can the "finder" infer about the culture and time from which the capsule came by analyzing the contents?

Activity 5: Write an Essay
Write a traditional essay about the ancient Egyptians. Include the following: what they looked like, how they worshiped, marriage customs, approximate population, government, basic laws, what their homes were like, what they ate and wore, what they used for money, entertainment, educational system, scientific achievements, transportation, written language, roles of men and women, agriculture, weapons, etc. Refer to "Sample of a Traditional Essay" in *Writers INC*. Younger students can copy passages or narrate (tell back) what has been learned.

Activity 6: Create a Travel Brochure
Pretend you are a travel agent living in ancient Egypt. Items and information that may be included in the brochure are: Location, transportation, climate, type of clothing to take, currency, industry, etc.

Activity 7: Write a Book Review
Write a book review about a novel you have read that is set in ancient Egypt. Refer to "How to Write a Book Review" in *Writers INC*. Younger students can give an oral book review.

Activity 8: Expand Learning Through Historical Fiction
If you read *The Golden Goblet*, go to the following Web site and complete the related activities.

"Golden Goblet" Historical Fiction
Description: While participating in this unit, students will read the book *The Golden Goblet*, then do several related activities, all focused on increasing the understanding of the text and the student's knowledge level of ancient Egypt. Written for grades 5-9.

Step 4 Excel

Share what you have learned about daily life in ancient Egypt with a friend or family member. Correct written work to demonstrate correct punctuation and spelling, and effective use of grammar. Add corrected written work or illustrations to your portfolio. Add new words you learned in this lesson into your Vocabulary Notebook (see page 22)

Resources recommended in ◆several lessons, ★ several units, ♥other HOW Units. ⚬━Key Resource (see beginning of unit or page 32).

Education in Ancient Egypt

Step 1 Excite

Egyptians developed two types of formal schools for privileged youth under the supervision of governmental officials and priests: one for scribes and the other for priest trainees. At the age of five, pupils entered the writing school and continued their studies in reading and writing until the age of 16 or 17. At the age of 13 or 14, the schoolboys were also given practical training in offices for which they were being prepared. Priesthood training began at the temple college, which boys entered at the age of 17, the length of training depending upon the requirements for various priestly offices. It is not clear whether or not the practical sciences constituted a part of the systematically organized curriculum of the temple college.[1]

In comparison, the Hebrews' education was essentially familial; that is to say, the mother taught the very young and the girls, while the father assumed the responsibility of providing moral, religious, and handcraft instruction for the growing sons. This characteristic remained in Jewish education, for the relation of teacher to pupil was always expressed in terms of parenthood and filiation. Education, furthermore, was rigid and exacting; the Hebrew word *musar* signifies at the same time education and corporal punishment. Read Acts 20-22. What do you learn about ancient Egyptian education from this passage?

Step 2 Examine

In the pictographic ancient Egyptian language, part of the verb "to teach" is the picture of a man hitting with a stick. Research education in ancient Egypt. Use any resource (an encyclopedia, nonfiction book, historical novel, or the Internet). We recommend the following:

Books

Ancient Egypt (Eyewitness) ●— ◆
Read: "Scribes and Scholars" (32-33).

The Usborne Book of the Ancient World ●— ★
Read: "Education" (64).

Internet Sources

Education, Learning in Ancient Egypt
Description: An illustrated article explaining the education process in ancient Egypt.

Underlined text refers to Internet link at http://Homeschool-Books.com

(i) (person) <u>Scribe School</u>
Description: This article from "Ancient Egypt For Children" describes the education process boys had to go through to become scribes, and what that involved.

(i) <u>Education and Writing</u>
Description: An overview of education and writing in ancient Egypt, including a hieroglyphs chart.

Step 3 Expand

Choose and complete one of the following activities:

Activity 1: Fill out a Contrast-and-Compare Worksheet
Make a <u>contrast-and-compare</u> graphic (see page 26). Compare education in ancient Egypt to the Hebrews' education.

Activity 2: Fill out a Contrast-and-Compare Worksheet
Make a <u>contrast-and-compare</u> graphic (see page 26). Compare education in ancient Egypt to modern American education.

Activity 3: Write a Summary
Retell what you have learned about ancient Egyptian education in a written summary. Write at least two paragraphs. Younger students can copy one or two sentences or narrate (tell back) what has been learned.

Activity 4: Write Diary Entries
Write a week of diary entries as if you were a student in ancient Egypt. Demonstrate what you have learned about education in ancient Egypt.

Step 4 Excel

Share what you have learned about education in ancient Egypt with a friend or family member. Correct written work to demonstrate correct punctuation and spelling, and effective use of grammar. Add corrected written work and any illustrations to your portfolio. Add new words you learned in this lesson into your Vocabulary Notebook (see page 22).

Footnote
1. Britannica.com, *Encyclopaedia Britannica* History of Education.

Resources recommended in ♦several lessons, ★ several units, ♥other HOW Units. ☛Key Resource (see beginning of unit or page 32).

Food in Ancient Egypt

Step 1 Excite

Brainstorm and make a list of the foods you think were abundant in ancient Egypt.

Step 2 Examine

Major foods in ancient Egypt were fish (from the Nile), the fayum, marsh birds (geese etc.), meat from cattle and gazelles, bread and pastry, figs, grapes, vegetables, and spices.

Research food in ancient Egypt and the Old Testament. Use any resource (an encyclopedia, a book on manners and customs of the Bible, or the Internet). We recommend the following:

Books

Ancient Egypt (Eyewitness) ●— ◆
Read: "Food and Drink" (34-35).

The Usborne Book of the Ancient World ●— ★
Read: "Farming (14-15), "Bread, Beer, and Wine" (57).

Read a novel set in Egypt. Look for mention of foods and drinks. We recommend:

Mara, Daughter of the Nile ◆
See description in the "Resources" section at the beginning of this unit.

The Golden Goblet ◆
See description in the "Resources" section at the beginning of this unit.

Internet Sources

Food in Ancient Egypt
Description: You'll find a description of food, its preparation, and its consumption in ancient Egypt on this page from the Pharaonic Egypt site.

Ancient Egypt Food and Drink
Description: This article describes basic food and drink commonly consumed in ancient Egypt. It includes two ancient Egyptian recipes.

Underlined text refers to Internet link at http://Homeschool-Books.com

Step 3 Expand

Choose and complete one of the following activities:

Activity 1: Go on a Field Trip
If you live near a major city, visit an Egyptian market. Members of a Coptic church could help you locate one. Explore the foods that are available. Some items are foods that you might be familiar with, but they will have a distinctive flavor, such as olives, couscous, and feta cheese. Which of the groceries could have been found in an ancient market? (Remember: tomatoes, potatoes, cocoa, and corn are New World discoveries.) Take some ingredients home, and experiment with them.

Activity 2: Create a Menu
Create a menu with illustrations for an ancient Egyptian restaurant.

Activity 3: Make Bread
Make Wholemeal Bread: Ingredients: 4 cups of wholemeal flour, half a teaspoon of salt, 2 cups of warm water (optional dates). Mix together the salt, flour and water (add optional dates). Knead ingredients with your hands until dough forms. Shape the dough. Leave it on a greased baking tray overnight. The next day, bake it for about half an hour at 350. (Recipe from _Ancient Egypt For Children_ By Lucy Charlotte Acland Johnson.)

Activity 4: Write a Summary
Retell what you have learned about ancient Egyptian food in a summary. Write at least one paragraph. Younger students can copy one or two sentences or narrate (tell back) what has been learned.

Activity 5: Write a Book Review
Write and share a book review about a novel you read during this unit. Younger students can narrate (tell back) their view of the book.

Step 4 Excel

Make and serve an Egyptian meal for your family. Correct written work to demonstrate correct punctuation and spelling, and effective use of grammar. Add corrected written work or illustrations to your portfolio. Add new words you learned in this lesson into your Vocabulary Notebook (see page 22).

Resources recommended in ◆several lessons, ★ several units, ♥other HOW Units. ☞Key Resource (see beginning of unit or page 32).

Government in Ancient Egypt

Note: This lesson is an overview of political history in ancient Egypt. See the "Pharaohs of Ancient Egypt" lesson for more information on this topic.

Step 1 Excite

Ancient Egypt, called the Old Kingdom of Egypt, spanned five centuries of rule by the 3rd through the 6th dynasties. Ruling monarchs held absolute power over a strongly unified government. Religion played an important role. The Pharaohs, as the rulers were called, were honored both as absolute monarchs and as gods. Read Exodus 5:20,21 and 11:9. Why was the Pharaoh so angry?

Step 2 Examine

The Egyptian civilization began around 3200 B.C. During the Early Dynastic Period, the divine kingship became established as Egypt's form of government, and that would remain virtually unchanged for 3,000 or more years.

The ancient Egyptian territory was divided into the two kingdoms: Upper Egypt and Lower Egypt. The rivalry between these two regions erupted into war; Upper Egypt would emerge victorious and rule all of Egypt under one king. The kings were later called Pharaohs. The first king was Menes (also called Narmer). King Menes chose the city of Memphis to be the capital of his country.

Egypt was a theocratic state ("theo" = god and "cratic" = ruled by). A theocrata is a person who rules or governs as a representative of God or some other deity, or is a member of the ruling group in a theocracy, such as a divine king or a high priest. The king was considered a divine being, a living god incarnate in the king, who kept the Nile flowing and brought fertility and life to the people he ruled. Anyone who questioned the authority of the king was considered a blasphemer. The first kings built expensive tombs for themselves called "mastaba." When they died they were mummified and placed in the tombs with their clothing, jewelry, furniture, and food.

Research the political history of ancient Egypt. Use any resource (an encyclopedia, nonfiction book, historical novel, or the Internet). We recommend the following:
Books

Underlined text refers to Internet link at http://Homeschool-Books.com

The Usborne Book of the Ancient World ⊶ ★
Read: "The Government of Egypt" (34).

Kingfisher History Encyclopedia ⊶ ♥
Read: "Ancient Egypt 4000-1800 B.C." (10-11) and "Egypt, The New Kingdom 1550-1070 B.C." (26-27).

Kingfisher Illustrated History of the World ⊶ ♥
Read: "Old Kingdom," "Middle Kingdom," "New Kingdom," and "Dynasties."

Ancient Civilizations ⊶ ★
Read: "Rameses II"

Pharaohs of Ancient Egypt ♦
See description in the "Resources" section at the beginning of this unit.

Internet Sources

Mysteries of Ancient Egypt: Government
Description: A brief article about government in ancient Egypt, from the Canadian Museum of Civilization.

The History of Ancient Egypt
Description: This is a portion of the Ancient Egypt site. This history section includes a page on each major time period in ancient Egypt: Early Dynastic, Old Kingdom, 1st Intermediate, Middle Kingdom, 2nd Intermediate, New Kingdom, Late Dynastic, and Greek-Roman period. A time line helps you navigate through history and discover the formidable Pharaohs of ancient Egypt.

History of Egypt
Description: This is an excellent in-depth historical reference on Pharaonic history.

The Union of Two Lands
Description: This page is part of the Egypt Project. It explains Upper Egypt and Lower Egypt, both before and after they were united. Also see Egypt Before the Pharaohs and The Three Kingdoms on this site.

Egypt (Ancient Egypt)
Description: This encyclopedia article is an overview of Egypt's rulers, from the Electronic Library.

Resources recommended in ♦several lessons, ★ several units, ♥other HOW Units. ⊶Key Resource (see beginning of unit or page 32).

Mysteries of Ancient Egypt: Bureaucracy
Description: A brief article about bureaucracy in ancient Egypt, from the Canadian Museum of Civilization.

Rediscover Ancient Egypt: Democracy
Description: This article is from the Tehuti Research Foundation.

The Old Kingdom, Middle Kingdom, and Second Intermediate Period, 2686 to 1552 B.C.
Description: A bit of Egyptian history, from an About.com Guide.

Step 3 Expand

Choose and complete one of the following activities:

Activity 1: Make a Chart
The more than three-thousand-year history of ancient Egypt has been divided into eight or nine periods, sometimes called Kingdoms (see History of Ancient Egypt lesson). Make a chart similar to the one below. Write a summary about the main events in the Old, Middle, and New Kingdoms.

Year	Kingdom	Summary
2650 to 2140 B.C.	Old Kingdom	
2040 to 1640 B.C.	Middle Kingdom	
1570 to 1070 B.C.	New Kingdom	

Activity 2: Write a Summary

Read the poem "Ozymandias," by Percy Shelley. What did these words mean to Ozymandias? What did they mean to the traveler? How are the ruins of ancient Egypt like the ruin of the statue of Ozymandias? If you traveled to Egypt and saw the ancient ruins, what emotions might you feel? Write a summary explaining how you feel about the way that the power and might of the ancient Egyptian Empire has disappeared.

Ozymandias
by Percy Bysshe Shelley

I met a traveler from an antique land
Who said: Two vast and trunkless legs of stone
Stand in the desert. Near them, on the sand,
Half sunk, a shattered visage lies, whose frown,
And wrinkled lip, and sneer of cold command,
Tell that its sculptor well those passions read
Which yet survive, stamped on these lifeless things,
The hand that mocked them, and the heart that fed;
And on the pedestal these words appear:
"My name is Ozymandias, king of kings:
Look upon my works, ye Mighty, and despair!"
Nothing beside remains. Round the decay
Of that colossal wreck, boundless and bare
The lone and level sands stretch far away.

Step 4 Excel

Share what you have learned about the government of ancient Egypt with a friend or family member. Correct written work to demonstrate correct punctuation and spelling, and effective use of grammar. Add corrected written work or illustrations to your portfolio. Add new words you learned in this lesson into your Vocabulary Notebook (see page 22).

Resources recommended in ◆several lessons, ★ several units, ● other HOW Units. ●—Key Resource (see beginning of unit or page 32).

Heart of Wisdom Publishing   259

Hieroglyphics

Step 1 Excite

Egyptian hieroglyphic inscriptions are composed of two basic types of signs: ideograms and phonograms. Ideograms denote either the specific object drawn or something closely related to it. For example, a picture of the sun may mean "sun" or "day." Phonograms, or sound signs, were used purely for their phonetic value and have no relationship to the word they are used to spell, as when an owl represented the sign "m," because the word for owl had "m" as the principal consonant. There were basically 604 symbols that might be put to three uses. This rebus principle, when the picture of an object could stand not only for that object but also for a word with the same sound but a different meaning, made possible the writing of proper nouns, abstract ideas, and grammatical elements.

Brainstorm and make a list of ten ways hieroglyphic changed society.

Step 2 Examine

Find examples of hieroglyphic in an encyclopedia or one of the listed resources.

Books

Ancient Egypt (Eyewitness) ⊶ ♦
Read: "Writing" (34-35).

The Usborne Book of the Ancient World ⊶ ★
Read: "Writing" (10).

Kingfisher History Encyclopedia ⊶ ♥
Read: All entries for "hieroglyphic" in the index under "Egypt."

Kingfisher Illustrated History of the World ⊶ ♥
Read: All entries for "hieroglyphic" in the index under "Egypt."

Internet Sources

Hieroglyphs in Ancient Egypt
Description: Article with illustrations explaining hieroglyphic.

See Your Name in Hieroglyphic
Description: See your name in Egyptian hieroglyphic or print a personalized message in hieroglyphic from this site.

The Hieroglyphic Tutor
Description: A Java Applet that helps in the understanding and pronunciation of Egyptian Hieroglyphic.

Writing in Ancient Egypt
Description: On this site, you will learn about the different scripts used in ancient Egypt by reading a story, find out where writing was used in ancient Egypt by exploring, and play a hieroglyphic game. From the British Museum.

Education and Writing
Description: An overview of education and writing in ancient Egypt. Includes hieroglyphs chart.

Step 3 Expand

Choose and complete one of the following activities:

Activity 1: Send a Message
Make your own hieroglyphic symbols and write a message (minimum four sentences) using your "code." Give it to someone, and find out if he or she is able to interpret it.

Activity 2: Write a Speech
Write a short persuasive speech as if you were a person trying to convince the people of ancient Egypt of the advantages of the alphabet over ideographs. Describe where you think the Egyptian society is headed in the future and how the alphabet can help. Refer to "Writing a Speech" in *Writers INC*.

Step 4 Excel

Share what you have learned about hieroglyphics with a friend or family member. Correct written work to demonstrate correct punctuation and spelling, and effective use of grammar. Add corrected written work or illustrations to your portfolio.

Resources recommended in ◆several lessons, ★ several units, ♥other HOW Units. ☜—Key Resource (see beginning of unit or page 32).

Heart of Wisdom Publishing   261

Language in Ancient Egypt

Step 1 Excite

What languages did Moses know? Read Psalm 114:1 and Psalm 81:5. What kind of speech did the Hebrews hear the Egyptians using? The ancient Hebrew language is still in use. Is the language of the Pharaohs still spoken?

Have you noticed how foreign languages that are spoken where you live influence your language? Can you think of any foreign words that you use? Make a list. English has influenced how Spanish is used in the Americas. If you know any Spanish-speaking people, ask them what English words are used in Spanish. The language of Egypt influenced the language of the Hebrews. Why did this happen?

Step 2 Examine

Investigate how the language of ancient Egypt influenced Biblical Hebrew. Thomas explains in his article titled "Egyptian Reflections"[1]:

> An example of ancient Egyptian practice in the fabric of the Bible itself is the word used in Exodus 1:16 ('haobhnayim') for 'birthstool'. The Hebrew word literally means 'the two stone tablets'. These stone birth-blocks were used by the ancient Egyptians for a woman in labor. They were supports against which the woman pressed her feet or crouched during delivery.
>
> A dominant culture commonly influences the terminology of a subordinate group, which Israel certainly was during its centuries in Egypt. Egyptian influence can be found in the shared terms that are common to the Hebrew of the Bible and the language of the ancient Egyptians.

A significant exception here is the word for sea (yam) from the New Kingdom era of Egypt. The term, "ym" (sea), unlike other terms, is shown in hieroglyphic script as syllabic orthography; that is, it is an imported word. As "ym" is Semitic, this word was probably borrowed from the renowned sailors of the ancient world, the Phoenicians.

	Ancient Egyptian	Biblical Hebrew
sea	ym	ym
river	ye'or	ye'or
to die	mwt	mwt
bulrushes	gm'	gm'
trained person	hnkh	hnkh
magicians	hrtmm	htrmm
reeds	ahu	ahu
ark	tebah	tebah

Underlined text refers to Internet link at http://Homeschool-Books.com

This origin should therefore condition our understanding of "ym suf". Because "suf" may be translated as reeds, many scholars understand it to have been a fresh water lake or swamp. This ignores the origin of the term "yam". Sailing in a swamp, especially by these renowned sailors, is most unlikely. The same term "yam suf" is used later in the Bible for the Red Sea and the Gulf of Aqaba (an arm of the Red Sea) which contained enough sea-weed to feed large herds of dugong (sea cows) that were common in the area then and still exist there today.

Research the language in ancient Egypt. Use any resource (an encyclopedia, a nonfiction book or the Internet). We recommend the following:

Internet Sources

An Overview of Linguistic Features
Description: This is a portion of the Ancient Egypt site. This section includes an introduction to the general characteristics of the language of the ancient Egyptians and the linguistic relationship with other languages.

The Story of the Rosetta Stone, "Finding a Lost Language"
Description: The story of the Rosetta Stone is told here via a chapter from "Ancient Peoples: A Hypertext View."

Step 3 Expand

Activity 1: Expand Your Research
In 1799 near the town of Rashîd (Rosetta) in Lower Egypt, French troops found the Rosetta Stone. It is now in the British Museum, London. Investigate, in an encyclopedia or online, the story of the Rosetta Stone. We recommend the following:

Books

Kingfisher History Encyclopedia ⊶ ♥
Read: Look for "Rosetta Stone" in the index under "Egypt."

The Usborne Book of the Ancient World ⊶ ★
Read: Use the Egypt Contents to find "Writing," or look in the index for "Rosetta Stone."

Resources recommended in ◆several lessons, ★ several units, ♥other HOW Units. ⊶Key Resource (see beginning of unit or page 32).

Internet Sources

The Rosetta Stone Site
Description: A site for children, led by tour guide Rosetta Stone. It includes a lot of activities to help them learn about ancient Egypt, including pages to color, quizzes to take, and the opportunity to make a cutout figure of a pharaoh. The coloring book and kid quiz are about the story of the Rosetta Stone.

The Rosetta Stone
Description: The British Museum tells the story of the Rosetta Stone with illustrations.

Write a story about the finding of the Rosetta Stone (minimum two hundred words). Include names, dates, and the languages involved. What was this stone? Why was it an important discovery? Why is it on display at a museum?

Step 4 Excel

Share what you have learned in this lesson with a friend or family member. Correct written work to demonstrate correct punctuation and spelling, and effective use of grammar. Add corrected written work or illustrations to your portfolio. Add new words you learned in this lesson into your Vocabulary Notebook (see page 22).

Add the Rosetta Stone Coloring Pages to your portfolio or Time Line Book.

Footnotes
1. "Egyptian Reflections." The Thomas Pages. <http://users.iafrica.com/l/ll/lloyd/Egypta.htm> (Accessed May 22, 2000).

Literature in Ancient Egypt

Step 1 Excite

Brainstorm and discuss where the fairy tales *Cinderella* and *Little Red Riding Hood* come from.

Step 2 Examine

Egyptians wrote, read and possessed books. Their books were scientific, secular, and religious. The writings included moral and educational treatises; state-papers; works on geometry, medicine, astronomy, and magic; travels, tales, fables, heroic poems, love-songs, and essays in the form of letters; hymns, dirges, rituals; and that collection of prayers, invocations, and religious formula known as *The Book of the Dead.* Papyrus, (a reed like plant that grew in the marshes of the river Nile) was manufactured as paper about 3100 B.C. That biblical literature was originally written on papyrus (rather than on parchment).

Look in the library for examples of literature from ancient Egypt. Be aware that Egypt was a non-Christian culture, and its literature will reflect its enmity toward God. The safest place to look for inoffensive Egyptian literature is in the children's section of a library. Read a folk tale and a poem. We recommend the following:

Books

The Literature of Ancient Egypt by William Kelly Simpson
Description: Many narratives, stories, lamentations, and poems are included. Footnotes and commentaries attempt to explain the missing parts. Yale Univ Pr; ISBN: 0300017111.

The Usborne Book of the Ancient World ● ★
Read: "Myths and Legends" (92).

Internet Sources

World Cultures: Ancient Egypt
Description: An online research textbook of world cultures and history, the home page (click on the "contents" option) allows you to research the history and culture of ancient Egypt, read the literature of the time, look up terms in the glos-

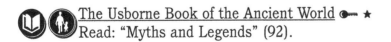
Resources recommended in ◆several lessons, ★ several units, ♥ other HOW Units. ●━Key Resource (see beginning of unit or page 32).

Heart of Wisdom Publishing   265

sary, look at maps, and find other Internet resources. In the ancient Egypt learning module, to which this link leads you (click on the "contents option"), you can get a good overview of the history of ancient Egypt, learn about its culture, read Egyptian literature, and more.

Ancient Egyptian Literature
Description: Folk stories from ancient Egypt; some are religious in nature.

Egyptian Stories
Description: Classic fairy tales told in ancient Egypt including *Croco'nile* and *Egyptian Cinderella*.

Step 3 Expand

Activity 1: Write a Folk Tale
Refer to "Writing About an Event" in *Writers INC*. You may choose to imitate the style of the ancient text, or use modern language. Younger students can narrate (orally tell) or dictate a tale.

Activity 2: Contrast and Compare
FIll out a contrast and compare graphic (see page 26) comparing the Mesopotamian's cuneiform written on tablets of clay with the Egyptian's hieroglyphics written on papyrus.

Activity 3: Illustrate a Story
Read a story from ancient Egyptian literature. Draw pictures to illustrate the story.

Activity 4: Do Further Research
Do research to find out how papyrus was made. find out what else the Ancient Egyptians made from the papyrus plant. Create a list and illustrate each item. Add papyrus to your Time Line Book.

Step 4 Excel

Share your creative writing or illustrations with your family, as well as the ancient literature that you discovered. Correct written work to demonstrate correct punctuation and spelling, and effective use of grammar. Add corrected written work or illustrations to your portfolio. Add new words you learned in this lesson into your Vocabulary Notebook (see page 22).

Underlined text refers to Internet link at http://Homeschool-Books.com

Medicine in Ancient Egypt

Step 1 Excite

Can you guess some of the disorders that have been found in the remains of ancient Egyptians?

- Tuberculosis
- Parasites
- Polio
- Dwarfism

Can you guess some of the diseases that physicians were able to diagnose?

- Diseases of the stomach
- Intestinal parasites
- Skin diseases
- Hair disorders
- Burns
- Flesh wounds
- Diseases of extremities such as toes, fingers, and legs
- Diseases of the tongue
- Dental conditions
- Diseases of the ear, nose, and throat
- Gynecological conditions

Step 2 Examine

Ancient Egyptian physicians had a remarkable knowledge of physiology, surgery, the circulatory system, and antiseptics. They didn't practice medicine by always praying to their gods for help; on the contrary, they had magical spells to keep supernatural forces from interfering with the diagnosis and treatment of their patients. Research medicine in ancient Egypt. Use any resource (an encyclopedia, a nonfiction book or the Internet). We recommend the following:

Books

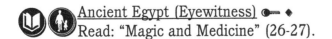
Ancient Egypt (Eyewitness) ⊙— ♦
Read: "Magic and Medicine" (26-27).

Resources recommended in ♦several lessons, ★ several units, ♥other HOW Units. ⊙—Key Resource (see beginning of unit or page 32).

The Usborne Book of the Ancient World ●— ★
Read: "Medicine" (41).

Ancient Egyptian Medicine by John F. Nunn
Description: Retired anesthesiologist and member of the Egypt Exploration Society, Nunn translates and reviews original Egyptian medical papyri; integrates evidence from skeletons, mummies, statues, tomb paintings, and coffins; and evaluates the medical practice of ancient Egypt in terms of modern medical thought. He also explores the role of spells, incantations, and other aspects of magic and religion. An extensive compilation and interpretation of material. (Review. by Book News, Inc.).

Internet Sources

Medicine in Ancient Egypt
Description: A good, comprehensive overview of medicine in ancient Egypt.

In Sickness and in Health
Description: This site explores the practice of medicine, physicians and their tools, and medicines in ancient Egypt.

Medicine Through Time
Description: This site, produced by the BBC for their education web, examines the practice of medicine from the ancient world to modern times. Five historical periods are each divided into five different topics: disease and its treatment, anatomy and surgery, hospitals and training, public health, and alternatives to medicine. Specific to the ancient world is information on: Egyptian, Greek, Indian and Chinese Medicine; the four humors; gods and spirits; Egyptian surgery and mummification; and more.

Ancient Egyptian Medicine
Description: This site includes general information about Egyptian medicine, including some common plants used.

Egyptian Herbal Medicine
Description: An article about herbs used in ancient Egypt, from PlanetHerbs Online.

The Egyptians
Description: This article from Nexus focuses on the history of ophthalmologic surgery and medicine. Includes information about Egyptian medicine and physicians gained from carvings on stones or inscriptions on papyrus scrolls.

History of Ancient Egyptian Medicine
Description: There are dozens of links about medicine in ancient Egypt on this page.

Step 3 Expand

Choose and complete one of the following activities:

Activity 1: Write a Summary
Write a summary about medical practices in ancient Egypt. Younger students can narrate (orally tell) what they have learned.

Activity 2: Copy a Passage
Copy two or more paragraphs from your research explaining how the ancient Egyptians practiced medicine.

Activity 3: Expand Your Research
The oldest known physician is Imhotep. Do research to find out more about him. Write a summary showing which discoveries made in ancient Egypt affect medicine today.

Step 4 Excel

Share with a friend or family member what you have learned about how the ancient Egyptians practiced medicine. Correct written work to demonstrate correct punctuation and spelling, and effective use of grammar. Add corrected written work or illustrations to your portfolio. Add new words you learned in this lesson into your Vocabulary Notebook (see page 22).

Resources recommended in ◆several lessons, ★ several units, ♥other HOW Units. ◉—Key Resource (see beginning of unit or page 32).

Heart of Wisdom Publishing   269

Mummies in Ancient Egypt

Step 1 Excite

Ancient Egyptian funeral rituals and materials are the most elaborate the world has ever known. Brainstorm and discuss, then make a list of why the ancient Egyptians used such elaborate methods to preserve the dead.

Step 2 Examine

The ancient Egyptians believed that the life force was composed of several psychic parts, of which the most important was the "ka." They believed that the ka, a copy of the body, accompanied the body throughout life and, after death, departed from the body to take its place in the kingdom of the dead. They believed the ka could not exist without the body; therefore, they tried to preserve the corpse. Bodies were embalmed and mummified according to a traditional method supposedly begun by Isis, who mummified her husband Osiris. Wood or stone replicas of the body were put into the tomb in the event that the mummy was destroyed. As a final protection, exceptionally elaborate tombs were erected to protect the corpse and its supplies.

The deceased was furnished with a copy of *The Book of the Dead*. Part of this book, a guide to the world of the dead, consists of charms designed to overcome the dangers that the deceased would face.

Research mummies. Use any resource (an encyclopedia, nonfiction book, historical novel, or the Internet). We recommend the following:

Books

Ancient Egypt (Eyewitness) ⊶ ◆
Read: "Preparing the Tomb" (14-15), "Everlasting Bodies" (16-17), "Journey to Afterlife" (18-19).

The Usborne Book of the Ancient World ⊶ ★
Read: Use the Egypt Contents to find "Mummies."

Kingfisher History Encyclopedia ⊶ ♥
Read: Look for "Mummies" in the index under "Egypt."

Internet Sources

Clickable Mummy
Description: Click on different parts of the Mummy to view interesting facts and information about the mummification process.

Mummification
Description: A short description of the process of mummification by the Carnegie Museum of Natural History.

The Virtual Mummy
Description: Unwrap a mummy by a mouse click. Learn about mummification using Quicktime VR! From the Institute of Mathematics and Computer Science in Medicine (IMCM).

Make a Mummy
Description: This site includes directions to make a miniature modern mummy.

How to Make A Mummy
Description: *National Geographic* presents this feature on mummies. Click to follow this interesting photographic tour.

CyberMummy Project
Description: Unlock the secrets of a mummy with the help of modern medical imagery, a supercomputer, and an archaeologist. Includes a QuickTime Mummy Movie.

Mummified - The Match Game
Description: A Discovery Online feature story includes a mummy game.

Resources recommended in ◆several lessons, ★ several units, ♥other HOW Units. ⊶Key Resource (see beginning of unit or page 32).

Heart of Wisdom Publishing   271

Mummies on the Web!
Description: Links to everything you've always wanted to know about ancient Egyptian mummies and mummification.

Step 3 Expand

Choose and complete one of the following activities:

Activity 1: Answer Questions
Answer these questions from your research: What methods were used for embalming? Who was mummified? How many mummies do you think were made over the years? Why did the ancient Egyptians mummify animals? Make a list of the animals that have been found mummified.

Activity 2: Write a Summary
Read what the Bible says about our bodies: 2 Cor. 5:1; Job 4:19; 1 Cor. 3:16; 6:15; 19:1. Write a summary comparing and contrasting ancient Egyptian beliefs with what the Bible says about receiving eternal life. Cite scripture references. Younger students can narrate (orally tell) what they have learned.

Activity 3: Mummify Fruit
Mummify fruit by following the directions from Newton's Apple. Click Mummies and look for the activity "Salt of the Earth."

Activity 4: Create a Mummy
Make a miniature mummy with aluminum foil, gauze strips, masking tape, newspaper, scrap cardboard, and white glue. Refer to the Internet site Make a Mummy or Make Your Own Mummy.

Step 4 Excel

Teach a younger student about mummies. Use your research above or the book, Tut's Mummy Lost — And Found by Judy Donnelly (May 1988) Random House (Merchandising); ISBN: 0394891899, to help you.

Correct written work to demonstrate correct punctuation and spelling, and effective use of grammar. Add corrected written work or illustrations to your portfolio. Add new words you learned in this lesson into your Vocabulary Notebook (see page 22).

Underlined text refers to Internet link at http://Homeschool-Books.com

The Nile River

Step 1 Excite

Use a map to examine the Nile River. Brainstorm and make a list of what the consequences would be if the Nile stopped flowing through Egypt. (Hints: food, drink, transportation, animals, clothing, electricity, etc.) Make a list of what the consequences would be if the Nile began to flow across the Sahara.

Read the following Scriptures about events that occurred on the Nile: Exodus 1:22; 2:3; 7:15,20; 8:3.

Step 2 Examine

The Nile River begins at Lake Victoria, on the border of the countries of Uganda and Tanzania. From there, the Nile goes north to the country of Egypt, where the Nile empties into the Mediterranean Sea.

> The fertility of the land [Egypt] depends on the overflowing of the Nile, which commences to rise about the middle of June and reaches its greatest height about the end of September, when it again begins to decrease. As measured at Cairo, if the Nile does not rise twenty-four feet, the harvest will not be very good; anything under eighteen threatens famine. About the middle of August the red, turbid waters of the rising river are distributed by canals over the country and carry fruitfulness with them. On receding, the Nile leaves behind it a thick red soil, which its waters carried from Central Africa, and over this rich deposit the seed is sown. Rain there is nil, nor is there need for it. Besides soaking and fertilizing the land, the Nile also furnishes the most pleasant and even nourishing water for drinking. Some physicians have ascribed to it healing virtues. It is scarcely necessary to add that the river teems with fish. Luxuriously rich and green, amidst surrounding desolation, the banks of the Nile and of its numerous canals are like a well-watered garden under a tropical sky. Where climate and soil are the best conceivable, the fertility must be unparalleled. [1]

Resources recommended in ♦several lessons, ★ several units, ● other HOW Units. ●—Key Resource (see beginning of unit or page 32).

Heart of Wisdom Publishing   273

Find pictures that depict the environment of the Nile Valley, including landforms, climate, flooding, and irrigation. Use the library or a search engine to find the information. We recommend the following resources:

Books

Ancient Egypt (Eyewitness) ⊶ ◆
Read: "On the Banks of the Nile" (8-9), "Sailing the Nile" (38-39).

Kingfisher History Encyclopedia ⊶ ♥
Read: All references to the Nile that you find in the index.

Kingfisher Illustrated History of the World ⊶ ♥
Read: All references to the Nile that you find in the index.

The Usborne Book of the Ancient World ⊶ ★
Read: All references to the Nile that you find in the index.

Usborne Book of Discovery: Inventors/Scientists/Explorers ⊶ ♥
Read: "The Source of the Nile" (106-107).

A Thousand Miles up the Nile
Description: A well-known work by Englishwoman Amelia Edwards, who travelled the famous river in 1873-4. Presents an unusual perspective on this classic river journey. ISBN: 071260037X. This book is available online.

Internet Sources

Mysteries of the Nile
Description: Explore the pyramids, temples, and other monumental architecture of ancient Egypt through riveting 360° photos shot during this NOVA/PBS online adventure. With real-time dispatches and digital photos filmed from the Nile in March 1999, and from a quarry in Massachusetts in August and September 1999, the adventure chronicles both NOVA's search for archaic clues to obelisk-raising and its attempt to erect one of these pillars of stone itself. Learn what happened, meet the team, and try to lever your own obelisk.

Nile River
Description: This article is part of A-Z Geography from Discovery Channel School, and powered by World Book Online.

Underlined text refers to Internet link at http://Homeschool-Books.com

The Nile River: Geography and Beyond
Description: This track is created as a supplement to a sixth-grade study of ancient Egypt and the Nile River. The track deals with the geography of the river as well as other subjects associated with the river.

Nile Activity Sheet
Description: This Acrobat (PDF) file includes activities related to the Nile at the six levels of Bloom's taxonomy.

Ancient Egypt - Introduction
Description: Examine how the Nile River influenced ancient Egyptian life.

Mysteries of the Nile
Description: This site provides support materials, maps, and lesson plans on the Nile River.

Wild Egypt; an Online Safari of the Nile River
Description: Contains some useful pictures and a description of the Nile River.

Institute of Egyptian Art and Archeology
Description: This site includes a colorful tour of monuments along the Nile River.

Geology and Geography of the Nile Basin
Description: View a comprehensive collection of pictures of the Nile River.

Step 3 Expand

Choose and complete one of the following activities:

Activity 1: Make a Relief Map
Use maps and atlases to make a relief map of the Nile region.

Activity 2: Write a Report
Research and write a report about papyrus. This sturdy reed was a product of the banks of the River Nile. It was made into a material that could be easily written on.

Activity 3: Answer Questions

Resources recommended in ◆several lessons, ★ several units, ♥other HOW Units. ◉━Key Resource (see beginning of unit or page 32).

1. How did the Nile River protect the people of Egypt from invaders?
2. What is the Nile called in the Bible? (Genesis 41:1; 3 Isaiah 11:15; 27:12; Joshua 13:3; Jeremiah 2:18.)
3. What kind of land surrounds the Nile River?
4. Why is Egypt called the "gift of the Nile"?
5. Where is the source of the Nile?
6. Why does it flood each year?
7. How does it deposit silt on the land?

Activity 4: Compare and Contrast
Make a compare-and-contrast graphic (see page 26) on the Nile River and the Mississippi River. Include the rivers' uses, deltas, and flow, as well as the farming cultures and traditions that have developed along each river.

Step 4 Excel

Make an educational home video or a display using three poster boards or foam boards to explain the geography of the Nile, as well as its importance to the Egyptians. Find an opportunity to share your exhibit or video, along with the relief map you made, with other students.

Correct written work to demonstrate correct punctuation and spelling, and effective use of grammar. Add corrected written work or illustrations to your portfolio. Add new words you learned in this lesson into your Vocabulary Notebook (see page 22).

Underlined text refers to Internet link at http://Homeschool-Books.com

Men in Ancient Egypt

Step 1 Excite

Who are some Egyptian men mentioned in the Bible? Use a <u>Bible concordance</u> to make a list of what the Bible tells us about these men. What guesses can you make about their status, their occupations, and their lives? (Example: Potiphar, the Egyptian slave who helped David.)

Brainstorm and list at least twenty duties of men in ancient Egypt.

What do you know about Aaron, the brother of Moses? What major events in his life does the Bible report? Use a <u>Bible concordance</u> to make a list of what the Bible tells us about Aaron and Moses in Egypt. (Hints: consecrated as high priest, the death of his sons, complaining about Moses in Numbers 12:1.)

Step 2 Examine

Men in ancient Egypt worked on farms, in workshops, in army units, on ships, in temple offices or departments of state, etc. Women bore and raised children and were responsible for the familiar, domestic relationships, while men related to society at large.

> The father headed the family in ancient Egypt. Upon his death, his oldest son became the head. But women, unlike most ancient civilizations, had almost as many rights as men. They could own and inherit property, buy and sell goods, and make a will. A wife could obtain a divorce. . . Kings commonly had several wives at the same time. In many cases, a kings' chief wife was a member of the royal family, such as his sister or half sister. [1]

Research men's roles in ancient Egypt. Use any resource (an encyclopedia, nonfiction book, historical novel, or the Internet). We recommend the following:

<u>Man and Wife in Ancient Egypt</u>
Description: Here you'll find statues of ancient Egyptian couples, love poems, and information about the status of the wife in ancient Egypt.

<u>Trades in Ancient Egypt</u>
Description: This site describes craftsmen and skilled laborers in ancient Egypt.

Resources recommended in ♦several lessons, ★ several units, ● other HOW Units. ⊶Key Resource (see beginning of unit or page 32).

Heart of Wisdom Publishing   277

Kinship & Marriage
Description: Marriage and family ties among the common ancient Egyptians are described.

Step 3 Expand

Choose and complete one of the following activities:

Activity 1: Write a Summary
Write a summary of what you have learned about the lives of Egyptian men. Younger students can copy one or two sentences or narrate (tell back) what has been learned.

Activity 2: Copy a Passage
Copy (by hand or typing) two or more paragraphs from your research. Younger students can copy one or two sentences or narrate (tell back) what has been learned.

Activity 3: Write a Dialogue
The Bible gives us glimpses into the lives of enslaved Hebrew men. Look in a concordance for Amram. Reread the stories of Hebrew male infants (Exodus 1), the slave who was beaten (Ex. 2:11), the quarreling Hebrews (Ex. 2:13,14), the elders (Ex. 4:29-31), and the Israelite foremen (Ex. 5:14-21). Write a dialogue, either between one of these men and you or between two Hebrew foremen. Try to portray the personalities and strengths of these men. Refer to "Dialogs" in *Writers INC*. Younger students can act out a conversation orally.

Activity 4: Prepare an Interview
Arrange a list of interview questions (minimum ten) that you would ask a 1) Farmer; 2) Builder; 3) Sailor, living in ancient Egypt.

Step 4 Excel

Share the Bible stories of Aaron with an older man whom you respect. What do these passages teach him? Ask him to tell you any insights he has into the lives of ancient Hebrew men. Correct written work to demonstrate correct punctuation and spelling, and effective use of grammar. Add corrected written work or illustrations to your portfolio.

Footnotes
1. Didier, Nikole (2000). "Life by the Nile." *Land of the Pharaohs*. <http://www.egypt.com/history/nile.html> (Accessed May 19, 2000).

Underlined text refers to Internet link at http://Homeschool-Books.com

Women in Ancient Egypt

Step 1 Excite

Some of the Egyptian women mentioned in the Bible are: Hagar, Potiphar's wife; Asenath, the daughter of Pharaoh who rescued Moses; the Egyptian women giving birth that the midwives refer to in Exodus 1; King Solomon's Egyptian wife. Use a <u>Bible concordance</u> to find what the Bible tells us about these women. What guesses can you make about their status, their occupations, and their lives? What do you know about Miriam, the sister of Moses? Read the following verses and make a list of everything these verses tell you about Miriam. Exodus 2:4-8; 15:20,21; Numbers 12:1-15; 20:1; 26:59; Micah 6:4; 1 Chronicles 6:3.

Famous Egyptian women include Cleopatra, Nefertiti, Hathor, and Hatshepsut.

Step 2 Examine

In *The Status of Women in Ancient Egyptian Society*, Peter Piccione, Professor of Comparative Ancient History, explains:

> The position of women in Egyptian society was unique in the ancient world. The Egyptian female enjoyed many of the same legal and economic rights as the Egyptian male—within the same social class. However, how their legal freedoms related to their status as defined by custom and folk tradition is more difficult to ascertain. In general, social position in Egypt was based, not on gender, but on social rank. On the other hand, the ability to move through the social classes did exist for the Egyptians. Ideally, the same would have been true for women. However, one private letter of the New Kingdom from a husband to his wife shows us that while a man could take his wife with him as he moved up in rank, it would not have been unusual for such a man to divorce her and take a new wife more in keeping with his new and higher social status. Still, self-made women certainly did exist in Egypt, and there are cases of women growing rich on their own resources through land speculation and the like. [1]

Resources recommended in ◆several lessons, ★ several units, ◗ other HOW Units. ◖—Key Resource (see beginning of unit or page 32).

Heart of Wisdom Publishing 279

Research women in ancient Egypt. Use any resource (an encyclopedia, nonfiction book, historical novel, or the Internet). We recommend the following:

Book

The Usborne Book of the Ancient World ⚷ ★
Read: "Women and Family Life" (58).

Internet Sources

Marriage, Standing of Women
Description: An account of the status of the wife in ancient Egypt.

Ancient Egyptian Hairstyles
Description: This site explains that the ancient Egyptians' appearance indicated a person's status, role in society, or political significance.

Men and Wife in Ancient Egypt
Description: Here you'll find statues of ancient Egyptian couples, love poems, and information about the status of the wife in ancient Egypt.

Women and Gender in Ancient Egypt
Description: This online exhibition and essay explores the interface between archaeology and the interpretation of gender relations and roles from artifacts.

Educating Women of Antiquity
Description: This essay focuses on the education of women of the middle and upper classes in ancient Greece, Egypt, and Italy.

Dress, Adornment, Body Care
Description: Illustrations and descriptions of makeup and dress in ancient Egypt.

Women in Ancient Egypt
Description: This article describes womens' roles and rights in ancient Egypt.

ⓘ <u>Royal Women</u>
Description: This page includes a brief article about royal women in ancient Egypt, from the Canadian Museum of Civilization.

Step 3 Expand

Choose and complete one of the following activities:

Activity 1: Add to Your Time Line Book
Add the women you studied in this lesson to your Time Line Book. You should include: Cleopatra, Nefertiti, Hathor, Hatshepsut; Hagar, Potiphar's wife; Asenath; the daughter of Pharaoh who rescued Moses; the Egyptian women giving birth that the midwives refer to in Exodus 1; King Solomon's Egyptian wife. Include summaries from the next activity in your Time Line Book.

Activity 2: Write a Summary
Write a summary of what you learned about each of the Egyptian or Hebrew women you have studied. Younger students can copy one or two sentences or narrate (tell back) what has been learned.

Activity 3: Write a Dialogue
The Bible gives us glimpses into the lives of enslaved Hebrew women. Reread the stories of the midwives (Exodus 1), Moses' mother (Exodus 2), and Miriam (Exodus 2,15;Numbers 12). Write a dialogue, either between one of these women and you or between Miriam and her mother. Try to portray the personalities and strengths of these women. Refer to "Dialogues" in *Writers INC*. Younger children can act out such a conversation orally.

Activity 4: Write Diary Entries
Write diary entries of a woman or girl in ancient Egypt. Include the events of three days. Demonstrate what you have learned about daily activities such as chores, school, and meals. Younger children can explain orally.

Activity 5: Write an Autobiography
Write an autobiography as if you were a woman in ancient Egypt. Answer the questions below. Younger children can explain orally. Look up verses for help.
  • What kind of clothes do you wear?
  • What do you look like?
  • What domestic duties do you perform?
  • Describe your home.
  • What holidays do you observe?

Resources recommended in ◆several lessons, ★ several units, ♥other HOW Units. ☞Key Resource (see beginning of unit or page 32).

Heart of Wisdom Publishing   281

- What do you do for fun?
- What hardships do you face?
- Describe how world, national, or local events have affected you.
- What do you hope for?
- What or whom do you fear?
- Whom do you admire?
- What are your beliefs (religious, political, personal, etc.)?

Step 4 Excel

Share the Bible stories of Miriam with an older woman whom you respect. What do these passages teach her? Ask her to tell you any insights she has into the lives of ancient Hebrew women.

Correct written work to demonstrate correct punctuation and spelling, and effective use of grammar. Add corrected written work or illustrations to your portfolio.

Religion in Ancient Egypt

Step 1 Excite

Brainstorm and make a list of questions you would like to have answered about religion in ancient Egypt. Think about the story of the Exodus. Why was Pharaoh so insistent to keep the Hebrew people in Egypt? Why didn't Pharaoh believe in the Hebrew God Yahweh? How did the Egyptian belief about the ka differ from what the Bible teaches about the soul? How did the Egyptian belief about life after death differ from what the Bible teaches? How did the Egyptian belief about the means of going to heaven differ from the truth? Did Egyptians believe in sin? Did they believe in a Creator?

Think about the household shrines of Buddhist, Hindu, and Shinto worship. How are household icons of Catholicism and Eastern Orthodoxy different from these? What percentage of people alive today would you guess have a religious shrine in their home that they use for worship?

Religion deeply dominated all aspects of the Egyptian culture, in art, science, government, and law. The average Egyptian citizen did not have access to the temples' shrines and gods. They could only approach the gods during the national festivals. But there were "household deities" that supposedly helped with everyday family life.

Are you surprised to learn that the Egyptians, who had so many expensive temples honoring the official gods, worshiped additional gods in family shrines in their homes? Why do you think that people throughout history have had household shrines?

Step 2 Examine

Why do you think that Rachel's father had household idols, and why did she steal them? (Genesis 31:19) While working in Egyptian households, do you think the Israelite slaves became familiar with household shrines? How did the Commandment against making images for worship seem to them? (Exodus 20:4,5) Look up Bible verses that show the Israelites falling into idol worship: Psalm 78; Joshua 24:14; Judges 2:12; 1 Samuel 8:8; 1 Kings 9:9; 1 Kings 12:28; 2 Kings 17:7; 2 Kings 21:15; 2 Chron. 7:22; Neh. 9:18. Is there a modern temptation to worship idols? What form might a modern idol take?

The Book of the Dead is the name generally given to a large collection of funerary texts of various dates, containing magic formulas, hymns, and prayers believed by the ancient Egyptians to guide and protect the ka in its journey into the region of the dead (Amenti). Ancient Egyptians believed that the knowledge of these texts enabled the ka to ward off

---

Resources recommended in ♦several lessons, ★ several units, ● other HOW Units. ☞—Key Resource (see beginning of unit or page 32).

demons attempting to impede its progress, and to pass the tests set by the forty-two judges in the hall of Osiris, god of the underworld. These texts also indicated that happiness in the afterlife was dependent on the deceased having led a virtuous life on earth. See the lesson on <u>Mummies</u> for more.

Egyptian gods were depicted with human bodies and human or animal heads. Sometimes the animal or bird expressed the characteristics of the god. Ra, for example, had the head of a hawk.

Research the religion in Egypt. Use any resource (an encyclopedia, nonfiction book, historical novel, or the Internet).We recommend the following:

Books

<u>Ancient Egypt (Eyewitness)</u> ●─ ◆
Read: "Gods and Goddesses" (25-26), "Priests and Temples" (28-29), "Sacred Rituals" (30-31).

<u>The Usborne Book of the Ancient World</u> ●─ ★
Read: "Egyptian Gods and Goddesses."

<u>Kingfisher History Encyclopedia</u> ●─ ♥
Read: Look for "Religion" in the index under "Egypt."

Internet Sources

<u>Egyptian Mythology</u>
Description: This page includes an overview of ancient Egyptian religion, with links to descriptions of several gods and several links to information for further research.

<u>The Religion of Ancient Egypt</u>
Description: This exhibit contains information on the Divine Ennead, Memphite Theology, the Priest Caste, and Egyptian astrology, as well as a list of gods.

Step 3 Expand

Choose and complete one of the following activities:

Activity 1: Answer Questions
James B. Walker made this comment about idol worship:
"Man is a religious being, he will worship. . .Man by worshipping, becomes assimilated to the moral character of the object which he worships. . .Without an exception, the character of every nation and tribe of the human history has been formed and modified, in a great degree, by the character attributed to their gods." [1]

Use focused free writing to explore these questions: Were any of the Israelites idol worshippers? Read Exodus 32:1-6; 1 Corinthians 10:7; and 1 Kings 12:28. Write a personal summary of these passages. What can you learn by their example that will help you stay away from temptation? How can you avoid the temptation to behave as the world does and to worship things that worldly people worship?

Activity 2: Write an Essay
Write a traditional essay comparing the worship of ancient Egyptians to the worship of the true God in Old Testament times. Give examples of Egyptian practices, as well as examples from the Old Testament of the worship that God commanded. Conclude your essay by stating your opinion about why some Israelites, like Aaron, fell prey to the temptation of idol worship, and some, such as the Levites, did not (Exodus 32). Refer to "Essay of Comparison" in *Writers Inc.*

Activity 3: Write a Summary
Read and copy verses that discuss the consequences of idolatry in Ezekiel 29:12-15, 30:23 and 26, then write a summary. Younger students can narrate (orally tell) what they have learned.

Activity 4: Write a Summary
Remember the symbolism of the Exodus. Egypt is a picture of sin. The deliverance from Egypt is a picture of God's deliverance of His people from their enslavement to sin. The passage through the Red Sea is compared to baptism in 1 Corinthians 10:2. Like the Israelites, we live amongst heathen people, though we are called to be separate and holy (1 Peter 2:9-12). The passage in 1 Corinthians 10:1-13 teaches us to see the experience of the Israelites as an example for us, to help us avoid temptation. Write a personal summary of Psalm 81. Younger students can narrate (orally tell) what Psalm 81 means.

Step 4 Excel

Share what you have learned about religion in ancient Egypt with a friend or family member. Correct written work to demonstrate correct punctuation and spelling, and effective use of grammar. Add corrected written work or illustrations to your portfolio.

Footnotes
1. Walker, James B. (1886) *The Philosophy of the Plan of Salvation.* Minneapolis, Minnesota: Bethany. (pp. 26-28.)

Resources recommended in ◆several lessons, ★ several units, ♥other HOW Units. ☛—Key Resource (see beginning of unit or page 32).

Heart of Wisdom Publishing   285

Science and Technology in Ancient Egypt

Step 1 Excite

One of the mysteries of Egyptian history is that the pyramids at Giza were built at the beginning of Egyptian civilization. No one knows how the sufficient technology and scientific knowledge was acquired at this early date in history. How do you think the ancient Egyptians learned the engineering necessary to construct the Great Pyramid?

Step 2 Examine

Research ancient Egypt's science and inventions. Look up ancient Egyptian knowledge about the following: paper and book making, irrigation techniques, engineering, metallurgy, plumbing, astronomy, glass making, chemistry, and chariot making. Use any resource (an encyclopedia, a nonfiction book, or the Internet). We recommend the following:

Books

Usborne Book of Discovery: Inventors/Scientists/Explorers
Read: All references to Egypt.

The Greenleaf Guide to Ancient Egypt ◆
Read: All references to discoveries and inventions in Egypt.

Ancient Inventions
Read: All references to Egypt.

Ancient Egyptian Materials and Industries by A. Lucas, J. R. Harris
Description: A detailed study of ancient Egyptian technology, documenting materials, and processes that were an integral part of ancient Egyptian daily life. Covers the use of animal products and building materials, manufacture of glass and fibers, use of metals and alloys, precious stones, distillation of alcoholic beverages, and the mummification process. Includes an appendix of chemical analysis. First published in 1926. (Book News, Inc., Portland, OR.)

Internet Sources

Ancient Egyptian Science
Description: Information on science, with a short section on technical arts related to alchemy.

(i) (person) Astronomy of Ancient Egypt
Description: Concise one-page article about ancient Egyptian astronomy.

(i) (person) Egyptian Glass Making
Description: Article explaining that some believe the Egyptians made the first glass. Some experts disagree with this theory.

(i) (person) Plumbing in Ancient Egypt
Description: Article found in *Plumbing and Mechanical Magazine* examines the innovations in transporting water in ancient Egypt.

(i) Ancient Egyptian Mining
Description: Divulges insights into the mining capabilities of early Egyptians. Findings stem from archaeological surveys.

(i) Pharaoh's Pump
Description: A Giza researcher reveals that the Great Pyramid was built to function as a water pump. Conveys a method of construction.

(i) Egyptian Invention of Chemistry
Description: Article from *Discover Magazine* reports that modern French research indicates that the ancient Egyptians invented chemistry while developing cosmetics.

Step 3 Expand

Choose and complete one of the following activities:

(icon) Activity 1: Write a Summary
Write a summary about ancient Egyptian technology and science. Write at least four paragraphs and add illustrations (sketches or printouts from Web sites including Web site credits). Younger students can narrate (orally tell) what they have learned.

(icon) (person) Activity 2: Make a Chart
Make a chart of science and technology discoveries in ancient Egypt. List the discoveries in one column and the descriptions in another column. Include: paper and book making, irrigation techniques, engineering, metallurgy, plumbing, astronomy, glass making, chemistry, and chariot making.

(icon) (person) Activity 3: Create a Model
Make a model of one ancient Egyptian technology in use. Examples: A book, an irrigation system, a plumbing fixture, a star map, or a chariot.

Resources recommended in ♦several lessons, ★ several units, ♥other HOW Units. ☞—Key Resource (see beginning of unit or page 32).

Activity 4: Add to Your Time Line Book
Add any science and technology discoveries in ancient Egypt to your Time Line Book.

Step 4 Excel

Share what you have learned about the science and technology in ancient Egypt with a friend or family member. Correct written work to demonstrate correct punctuation and spelling, and effective use of grammar. Add corrected written work or illustrations to your portfolio.

Slavery in Ancient Egypt

Step 1 Excite

Read Exodus 1:14. Enslaved African-Americans compared themselves to the Israelites in Egypt. What symbolism is used in the song "Go Down Moses"? God told Abraham his descendants would undergo Egyptian bondage. Read Genesis 15:13-14.

Step 2 Examine

Joseph was sold into slavery in Egypt by his brothers. The Hebrew children were in slavery in Egypt. The Pharaoh had purchased the Hebrews from the Egyptian people during a famine.

Research slavery in Egypt. Use any resource (an encyclopedia, a nonfiction book, or the Internet). We recommend the following:

Books

Ancient Israel: Its Life and Institutions ⚷– ★
Read: "Slaves" (80-88). See description is from the Israel Unit.

Ancient Israel: From Abraham to the Roman Destruction of the Temple ⚷– ★
Read: "Israel in Egypt." See description is from the Israel Unit.

The Bible Comes Alive: Volume One, Creation to Abraham ⚷– ★
Read: Section IV "Joseph in Egypt."

Escape from Egypt: A Novel by Sonia Levitin
Description: Sonia Levitin is a renowned author of young-adult stories who lives up to her reputation in this retelling of the story of the Exodus. Jesse, a Hebrew slave, is the main character, along with Jennat, a half-Egyptian, half-Syrian girl whom Jesse falls in love with. The story revolves around their adventures while leaving Egypt during the Ten Plagues. (March 1996) Puffin; ISBN: 0140375376. Reading level: Young adult. (This book includes a romance theme but is good background for this time period.)

Internet Source

Resources recommended in ◆several lessons, ★ several units, ● other HOW Units. ⚷– Key Resource (see beginning of unit or page 32).

Heart of Wisdom Publishing   289

(i) Egyptian Bondage
Description: A Bible study worksheet on Genesis 37-Exodus 14.

Step 3 Expand

Choose and complete one of the following activities:

Activity 1: Paraphrase a Bible Passage
Read Genesis 15:12-16. Paraphrase the prophecy in these verses.

Activity 2: Make a Mind Map
Make a mind map about the enslavement of the Hebrews. Use sheets of unlined paper and colored markers or pencils. Put a circle in the center and write in "Slavery in Egypt." As you reflect on what you have learned, draw lines out from the center for each main fact you have learned about what the Bible says about the Hebrew slaves. Branch lines from these will hold key subtopics. Continue branching until you are out of ideas. Use different colors for each cluster of information. Ask yourself, "Who?" "What?" "Where?" "When?" "Why?" and "How?" Use color and patterns; symbols, numbers, and arrows; and other doodles such as a drawing bricks. Add Bible verses and references.

Activity 3: Create an Art Project
Create an artistic project which expresses the emotions of enslavement. Remember, enslavement can be spiritual as well as physical. Your art can take the form of a song, a painting, a sculpture, or textile art. Next, create an artistic project expressing the emotions of freedom. Try to make this project in the same genre as the first, although if you feel strongly that you need to express freedom in another art medium, you should do so. Title your two pieces of artwork, and display them together.

Step 4 Excel

Celebrate the freedom we have in Christ. Prepare decorations and special food ahead of time. Then join with your family and friends in songs, prayer,s and family games. Correct written work to demonstrate correct punctuation and spelling, and effective use of grammar. Add corrected written work or illustrations to your portfolio.

Underlined text refers to Internet link at http://Homeschool-Books.com

Bonus Lesson: Egypt Today

Step 1 Excite

What do you know about modern-day Egypt? Where is this country located? What are the largest cities in this country? What are the major ethnic, religious, and linguistic groups in this country? When did this country gain independence? What type of government is in place? Who is the leader of this country? What is the state of the economy? What is the country's key industry? What environmental issues does the country face today? What are some of the current events in this country?

If you were to visit Egypt, what languages would you expect to hear, and what types of religious services would you expect the Egyptians to have? Would you expect to see much racial and ethnic diversity?

Step 2 Examine

Contrast and compare Egypt today with ancient Egypt. The information below summarizes a wealth of information from Countrywatch.com. Learn much more by visiting Countrywatch.com's section on Egypt.

Largest Cities		
City	*Population*	*Estimated*
Cairo	6,452,000	1990
Alexandria	3,170,000	1990
Giza (Al-Jizah)	2,156,000	1990

People

Egypt is the most populous country in the Arab world.

History

Archaeological findings show that primitive tribes lived along the Nile long before the dynastic history of the pharaohs began.

Economy

At the beginning of the 1990s, Egypt was plagued by continuing softness in world oil markets, and was struggling to serve a foreign debt totaling about $50 billion.

Agriculture

Resources recommended in ♦several lessons, ★ several units, ♥other HOW Units. ☞Key Resource (see beginning of unit or page 32).

Heart of Wisdom Publishing   291

The agriculture sector in Egypt contributes 17.7% of the GDP and employs an estimated 35.0% of the labor force.

Energy

Egypt produced an average 866,000 barrels per day (bbl/d) of crude oil during 1998.

Metals

In addition to hydrocarbons, Egypt produces a wide variety of metals and industrial minerals.

Environment

With the exception of its northern and eastern coastlines, as well as the Nile Valley, Egypt is predominantly desert.

Key Data

Region	Africa
Population	67,273,906 (July 1999 Estimate)
Area Total	1,001,450 km²
Area Land	995,450 km²
Coastline	2,450 km
Climate	Desert; hot, dry summers with moderate winters.
Languages	Arabic (official), English and French widely understood by educated classes.
Currency	1 Egyptian pound = 100 piasters
Holiday	Anniversary of the Revolution, 23 July (1952)

Boundaries

Sudan	1,273 km
Libya	1,150 km
Israel	255 km

Ethnic Divisions

Eastern	Hemitic stock 99%
Greek, Nubian, Armenian, and other Europeans	1%

Religions

Muslim	90%
Coptic Christian and other	10%

Underlined text refers to Internet link at http://Homeschool-Books.com

Step 3 Expand

Activity 1: Contrast and Compare

Make a contrast-and-compare graphic (see page 26). Choose one of the topics above. Contrast and compare ancient Egypt and modern Egypt.

Activity 2: Make a Travel Brochure

Make a travel brochure for Egypt. Use search engines (using keywords "Egypt" and "travel agencies") to gather information from travel agencies. Print out color pictures from the Internet, then cut and paste information into your brochure. List the country, its capital, and facts about its people. Write something about the country's geography and climate. Include the places or topics which interest you most, and why.

Step 4 Excel

Share what you have learned about modern-day Egypt with a friend or family member. Correct written work to demonstrate correct punctuation and spelling, and effective use of grammar. Add corrected written work or illustrations to your portfolio.

Resources recommended in ◆several lessons, ★ several units, ♥other HOW Units. ☞Key Resource (see beginning of unit or page 32).

Heart of Wisdom Publishing   293

Ancient Israel Unit

Unit Overview

Ancient Israel Overview 296
Ancient Israel Objectives 297
Ancient Israel Time Line 299
Ancient Israel Vocabulary 300
Ancient Israel Resources 302

History of Ancient Israel

Father Abraham 313
God's Covenant with Israel 316
The Patriarchs (2000-1700 B.C.) 322
Egyptian Bondage (1700-1275 B.C.) . .325
The Exodus and Passover 328
Wilderness Wanderings (1275-1235 B.C.)332
The Law 335
The Tabernacle 340
The Priesthood 343
The Twelve Spies 346
Occupation of Canaan (1250-1050 B.C.)348
The Twelve Tribes 353
Ancient Israel Geography 355
Period of the Judges (1235-1050 B.C.) 358
United Kingdom (1050-922 B.C.) 362
King Saul (1020-1000 B.C.) 364
King David (1000-960 B.C.) 367
Jerusalem 370
King Solomon (960-920 B.C.) 374
Solomon's Temple 378
Assyrian Captivity (721 B.C.) 382
Divided Kingdom 385
The Babylonian Exile (587-539 B.C.) .388

The Diaspora 393
Restoration and Second Temple . .396
The Persian Period (539-332 B.C.) . .398
Queen Esther 401
The Hellenistic Period (19 B.C.) . . .404
The Maccabean Period 406
The Roman Period 411
Herod's Temple 415
Israel History Review 418

Life in Ancient Israel

Agriculture in Ancient Israel 419
Archaeology in Ancient Israel . . .423
Clothing: the Tallit 428
Clothing: General 431
Education in Ancient Israel 434
Family Life in Ancient Israel 438
Food in Ancient Israel 441
Israel's Holidays 446
Prayer in Ancient Israel 450
The Sabbath 455
Women in Ancient Israel 458

Related Lessons in Other Units

Joseph (Ancient Egypt) 202
Moses (Ancient Egypt) 206
The Plagues (Ancient Egypt) 209
Passover (Ancient Egypt) 214
The Exodus (Ancient Egypt) 218
Hebrews (Ancient Greece) 504
Hanukkah (Ancient Greece) 517
Jewish Revolts (Ancient Rome) . .614

Ancient Israel Overview

Three things must be held in common by a society in order for it to be a people: religion, education, and law. In all history, there is only *one* civilization that bases its religion, education, and law on Scripture—Israel. Christians should understand the relationship between us, the Bible, Israel, and the Jewish people. In Jesus' life, death, and resurrection is the fulfillment of the Law and the prophets of the Hebrew Scriptures (the Old Testament). As we study how God has dealt redemptively with the Hebrews, our spiritual ancestors by faith, we gain insight into the plans and purposes of God. As we turn our attention to the Jewish roots of the Christian faith, we may reevaluate our beliefs and the realities of our faith for our every day life and deepen our personal walk and relationship with the Lord.

Since the days of Abraham, for the past 4,000 years, the Jewish people have had an inseparable relationship with God. Thirty-six books of the Bible tell the history of the children of Israel. Israel is mentioned in Scripture some 2,293 times with at least fifteen references to God's everlasting covenant with the children of Israel. There are only two chapters on Creation, in contrast with fourteen chapters about Abraham, the father of the Hebrew nation. Sixty-four of the sixty-six books of the Bible were written by Jewish writers! The people of Israel were to be the living testimony of God through their lifestyle and message. Israel was to be a light to the world—a light to the Gentiles (Isaiah 43).

Emil Schurer in his series of books, *A History of the Jewish People in the Time of Jesus Christ*, stated; "In the fullness of time the Christian religion sprang out of Judaism; as a fact, indeed, of divine revelation, but also inseparably joined by innumerable threads with the previous thousand years of Israel's history. No incident in the gospel story, no word in the preaching of Jesus Christ, is intelligible apart from its setting in Jewish history, and without a clear understanding of that world of thought - distinction of the Jewish people."

Joseph Teluskhin states in his book *Jewish Literacy*, "The New Testament depiction of Jesus suggests that he was largely a law-abiding and highly nationalistic Jew, and a man of strong ethical concerns. Like many of Judaism's great rabbis, he saw love of neighbor as religion's central demand. Though many Christians are under the impression that he opposed Judaism's emphasis on law, in actuality he criticized anyone who advocated dropping it ....almost no Jewish scholars believed Jesus intended to start a new religion. Were Jesus to return today, most Jews believe, he undoubtedly would feel more at home in a synagogue than a church."

We must focus on the language and thought-patterns found in the Scriptures so that we are able to penetrate the mind of the Hebrew people. When we enter their civilization and view it through their eyes, we find that the contour of their thought is vibrant, rich, and colorful. It has its own nuances and features. Indeed, the Hebraic background to Christian thought is at the heart of the rich spiritual legacy that the Jews have shared with Christians. [1]

Footnote:
1. Wilson, Marvin R. (1989) *Our Father Abraham: Jewish Roots of the Christian Faith*. Grand Rapids, MI: William B. Eerdmans Publishing Company, and Dayton, OH: Center For Judaic-Christian Studies; ISBN: 0802804233.

Underlined text refers to Internet link at http://Homeschool-Books.com

Ancient Israel Objectives

Upon completion of this unit your student should:

- Understand the key events, people, beliefs, and places of Judaism and Christianity, particularly those recorded in the Bible passages cited.

- Acquire a foundational basis for understanding the Old Testament as a whole.

- Be able to understand the highlights of biblical history with Israel as the centerpiece.

- Begin a process of interpreting the Old Testament.

- Have an understanding of the main Bible periods: 1. Creation; 2. Great Flood; 3. Patriarchs; 4. Egyptian Bondage; 5. Wilderness Wandering; 6. Conquest of Canaan; 7. Judges; 8. United Kingdom; 9. Divided Kingdom; 10. Babylonian Captivity; 11. Return from Captivity; 12. Between the Testaments; 13. Life of Christ.

- Have an understanding of the setting for important events such as Abraham's journey and Exodus, as well as other events mentioned in the Scripture passages from the Old and New Testaments.

- Understand that the Land of Canaan, renamed Israel by the Lord, was given by God to Abraham and his descendants as an everlasting possession.

- Understand that the gift of this Land to Abraham and his descendants was based on an unconditional covenant from God Himself.

- Understand that the Land of Israel was given to Abraham and his descendants as part of God's redemptive blessing to the world.

- Understand that the Land of Israel was not given to the descendants of Ishmael (one ancestor of the Arab peoples), but rather to the descendants of Isaac.

- Understand that Israel's sin and subsequent exile from the Land did not change their divine right to this Land which was given to them by the Lord in the covenant.

- Be able to explain the origins of the Jewish people.

- Recognize the importance of Abraham's rejection of paganism.

Resources recommended in ◆several lessons, ★ several units, ♥other HOW Units. ☛Key Resource (see beginning of unit or page 32).

Heart of Wisdom Publishing   297

- Understand the meaning of a covenant.
- Be able to describe the Israelites' experience in Egypt.
- Understand the significance of Moses as a leader.
- Be able to discuss the period of Israel's history covered in Judges, and to fit it into the chronology of Israel's entire history.
- Be able to explain who the Judges were, and to discuss the source and scope of their power.
- Be able to identify and discuss the Hebrews' schools of thought on education.
- Understand the causes leading to the division of the Divided Kingdom.
- Understand the roles played by the kings and prophets.
- Be able to gather and use information for research purposes.
- Be able to use a variety of resource materials to gather information for research topics.
- Be able to analyze the values held by specific people who influenced history and the role their values played in influencing history.
- Be able to analyze the influences that specific ideas and beliefs had on a period of history, and to specify how events might have been different in the absence of those ideas and beliefs.
- Be able to analyze how specific historical events would be interpreted differently based on newly uncovered records and/or information.
- Understand how to evaluate the credibility and authenticity of historical sources.
- Be able to write compositions that are focused for different audiences.
- Be able to write compositions that fulfill different purposes.
- Be able to write fictional, biographical, autobiographical, and observational narrative compositions.
- Be able to write in response to literature.
- Demonstrate competence in the stylistic and rhetorical aspects of writing.

Ancient Israel Timeline

	Period	People and Events
	Primeval Period	Creation to Abraham
2000-1700	Patriarchal Period	Abraham to Moses (Abraham, Isaac, Jacob, Joseph)
1700-1275	Egyptian Bondage	Slaves in Egypt
1275	Exodus	Moses' Leadership
1250-1050	Conquest of Canaan	Joshua's Leadership
1235-150	Period of Judges	No Leadership (Othniel, Deborah, Gideon, Abimelech, Jephthah, Samuel.)
1250-922	United Kingdom	Monarchy Established Establishment (David) c. 1000 Decline (Solomon) c. 960
922-587	Divided Kingdom	Two Kingdoms (Israel, Elijah, Elisha, Judah)
721	Assyrian Rule	(Hezekiah, Amos, Hosea, and Micah)
587-539	Babylonian Captivity Restoration	Torn from Land (Daniel, Ezekiel) The Jews Return
539-332	Persian Period	Dominated by Persian Empire.
332-363	Hellenistic period	Dominated by Greek Empires.
165-63	Maccabean revolt	Hasmoneans, under Juda Maccabee
63 B.C. onward	Roman Period	A.D. Jesus the Messiah, Paul, Jewish Revolts

Resources recommended in ◆several lessons, ★ several units, ♥ other HOW Units. ◉─Key Resource (see beginning of unit or page 32).

Ancient Israel Vocabulary

The vocabulary words for this unit aren't easily found in the dictionary, so we have included brief definitions. See Vocabulary Instructions on page 22.

C.E.

Common Era (same as A.D.; however, C.E. follows the date, whereas A.D. precedes it).

Covenant

1. A binding agreement; a compact. 2. Law. a. A formal sealed agreement or contract. b. A suit to recover damages for violation of such a contract. 3. In the Bible, God's promise.

God (names)

Adonai, Elohim, El Shaddai, YHVH, YHWH, Hakadosh Baruch Hu, Ribono shel Olam, Harachaman, Avinu Shebashamayim.

Diaspora

(Exile or Dispersion) - (Greek, dispersion), the Jewish communities outside Israel. It began with the exile of Judeans to Babylonia by Nebuchadnezzar in 586 B.C.

Haftorah

Selection from the Prophets read or chanted after the weekly Torah portion during the synagogue service on Sabbath and holidays. (al. Haftarah) pl. Haftarot.

Haggadah

Telling. 2. the prayer book used at the Seder, or ritual dinner observed at Passover. (al. Hagadah, Agada, Agadah, Aggadah) pl. Haggadot.

Hanukah

Literally: dedication; name of the winter holiday commemorating the Maccabean victory over the Syrians in 165 B.C. (al. Chanukah, Hanukkah)

Patriarch

A name employed in the New Testament with reference to Abraham (Heb. 7:4), to the sons of Jacob (Acts 7:8,9), and to David (2:29). This name is generally applied to the progenitors of families, or heads of the fathers (Josh. 14:1) mentioned in Scripture, and they are spoken of as antediluvian (from Adam to Noah) and post-diluvian (from Noah to Jacob) patriarchs. But the expression the patriarch, by way of eminence, is applied to the twelve sons of Jacob, or to Abraham, Isaac, and Jacob. (*Easton's Bible Dictionary*)

Pentateuch

The Greek word for the first five Books of the Bible, the Five Books of Moses.

Seder	Seder means order. The Seder invites each family to recount its own version of the great story of Passover, with each family member actively involved. The meal induces the experience of going from slavery to liberty through the food experiences and story, as the meal turns into an elaborate feast. The Seder is usually a family dinner but can also be held with your family or with a church group. During the Seder, the narrative of the exodus is related and prayers of thanksgiving are offered up to God for His loving protection.
Seder Plate	A special plate used during a Seder. The Seder consists of three directive foods listed in Exodus 12, and customary foods later added by the Rabbis. Each of the foods symbolizes some aspect of the ordeal undergone by the Israelites during their enslavement in Egypt.
Shabbat	The Sabbath; begins at sunset on Friday and lasts until sunset on Saturday.
Tallit	(al. Talit) Prayer shawl with ceremonial fringes on four corners. A four-cornered cloth used by Jewish men as a prayer shawl as mentioned in Numbers 15:38.
Talmud	Comprised of both the Mishnah and Gemara, the Talmud is the collected legal and ethical discussions of the rabbis, edited around the year 500 C.E. A Hebrew word meaning teaching, used as the title of this unique literary work containing the study and discussions of ancient scholars covering eight centuries, including the work passed down from the academies in Israel and Babylon.
Tanach	The Hebrew term for the Old Testament Scriptures, derived from the initial letters of Torah, Neviim, and Ketuvin, which corresponds to the Pentateuch, the Prophets, and Hagiographa.
Tetragrammaton	The four Hebrew letters usually transliterated YHWH or YHVH that form a biblical proper name of God.
Torah	The Hebrew word for the first five Books of the Bible, the Five Books of Moses.

Resources recommended in ◆several lessons, ★ several units, ♥other HOW Units. ☛Key Resource (see beginning of unit or page 32).

Heart of Wisdom Publishing   301

Ancient Israel Resources

The ❶ symbol indicates a resource appropriate for grades 4-12 or family read aloud. All other books are appropriate for young adults or adults.

Main Resources Suggested in this Unit

Ancient Israel: Its Life and Institutions by Roland De Vaux ⚷ ★
This book is recommended in most of the "Life in Ancient Israel" lessons. Now considered by many to be a modern classic, this book offers a fascinating, full-scale reconstruction of the social and religious life of Israel in Old Testament times. Drawing principally from the text of the Old Testament itself, as well as from archaeological evidence and information gathered from the historical study of Israel's neighbors, De Vaux first provides an extensive introduction to the nomadic nature of life in ancient Israel and then traces in detail the development of Israel's most important institutions - family, civil, military, and religious - and their influence on the nation's life and history. Paperback - 616 pages (March 1997) W. B. Eerdmans Publishing Co.; ISBN: 080284278X. Reading level: Advanced.

Encyclopedia of the Bible (Nelson's Illustrated) ⚷ ❤
See description in the "Key Resources" section beginning on page 32.

Exploring Ancient Cities of the Bible ❤
See description in the "Key Resources" section beginning on page 32.

The Holman Bible Atlas ⚷ ❤
See description in the "Key Resources" section beginning on page 32. This book is recommended in most of the "History of Ancient Israel" lessons.

Introducing the Old Testament ❤
See description in the "Key Resources" section beginning on page 32.

Our Father Abraham ⚷ ❤
See description in the "Key Resources" section beginning on page 32. This book is recommended in several of the "Life in Ancient Israel" lessons and in many lessons in many other units.

The Victor Journey through the Bible ⚷ ❤
See description in the "Key Resources" section beginning on page 32.

Underlined text refers to Internet link at http://Homeschool-Books.com

Alternative Resources for this Unit

365 Fascinating Facts About the Holy Land by Clarence M. Wagner
From general information about climate, culture, and customs, to concise information about Middle East politics, wars, and efforts for peace. (March 2000) New Leaf Pr; ISBN: 0892214899.

Ancient Israel: From Abraham to the Roman Destruction of the Temple by Hershel Shanks (Editor) ★
This is an excellent book for high school students and is recommended in most of the "History of Ancient Israel" lessons. Many prestigious colleges and universities have adopted *Ancient Israel* for classroom use, but it is written in an easy-to-understand language, easy enough for high school students. Chapters: The Patriarchal Age; Israel in Egypt; The Settlement in Canaan; The United Monarchy; The Divided Monarchy; Exile and Return; The Age of Hellenism; Roman Domination. 378 pp.; 34 illus.; 10 color plates; 16 maps and charts. (1999) ISBN 1-880317-53-2, hardcover. ISBN 1-880317-54-0, paper. Order from the Biblical Archaeology Society. 202-364-3300.

The Ancient Hebrews ◆
The perspective is a historical one; biblical events are labeled according to the Bible or "it is said." The author goes overboard to remain historical. This book explores the many journeys of the Hebrew people and their belief in one god. Many illustrations as well as clear maps, a time line, a glossary of Hebrew terms, and a bibliography help readers find their way through the complexities of Hebrew faith and history from Abraham to the present time. Library Binding - 80 pages (October 1999) Marshall Cavendish Corp.; ISBN: 076140302. Order from the publisher Marshall Cavendish 800-821-9881. Reading level: Grades 5-9.

The Atlas of Jewish History by Martin Gilbert
This atlas traces the history, the worldwide migrations, the achievements, and the lives of the Jewish people from ancient Mesopotamia to the present day. It is the product of remarkable research and sheds a vivid light on the role of the Jews in their different national settings, and on their complex history, their reaction to persecution—whether by dispersal, acceptance, or defense—and their enormous contribution to human experience in many fields over almost four thousand years. (January 1993) William Morrow & Co; ISBN: 0688122647.

Christianity and Rabbinic Judaism: A Parallel History of Their Origins Edited by Hershel Shanks with contributions by James H. Charlesworth ◆
This parallel history of Judaism and Christianity presents both separate and integral accounts of the first six centuries in the development of both religions, in one understandable volume. This book begins where its companion volume Ancient

---

Resources recommended in ◆several lessons, ★ several units, ♥ other HOW Units. ☛ Key Resource (see beginning of unit or page 32).

Heart of Wisdom Publishing   303

Israel ends. Chapters include: Palestinian and Diaspora Judaism in the First Century; The Life of Jesus; After the Crucifixion--Christianity through Paul; Judaism to the Mishnah: 135-220 C.E.; The World of the Talmud: From the Mishnah to the Arab Conquest; Christianity from Constantine to the Arab Conquest; Christians and Jews in the First Six Centuries. Hardcover - 380 pp.; 50 black-and-white photographs; 2 illus.; 11 color plates. (November 1992) Biblical Archaeology Society; ISBN: 1880317036. Reading level: Advanced.

Christianity Is Jewishby Edith Schaffer
Edith Schaeffer, wife of the late Francis Schaeffer, wrote that Christianity, no matter how un-Jewish some of its current forms of expression may be, has its roots in Judaism and in the Jewish people. The very concept of a Messiah is nothing but Jewish. Finally, Yeshua (Jesus) himself was Jewish - was then and apparently is still, since nowhere does Scripture say or suggest that he has ceased to be a Jew. (1977) Tyndale House Pub; ISBN: 0842302425

Chronicles of the King:The Lord Is My Strength by Lynn Austin
Book 1 in this series. Weaving a complex novel of suspense, action, inspiration, and God's enduring grace, Austin brings a new level to Biblical fiction.Beacon Hill Press (1995) ISBN: 0834115387.

Chronicles of the King: The Lord Is My Song by Lynn Austin
Book 2 in this series. With a new-found faith in the one true God, King Hezekiah brings reform to the nation, and that means revival and renewed prosperity. But not everyone is pleased with the king's "religious fanaticism," and Hezekiah soon finds himself besieged by these enemies. Can his faith hold a nation together? (1996) 288 pages, paper. ISBN: 0834116022.

Chronicles of the King: The Lord Is My Salvation by Lynn Austin
Book 3 in this series. God has rewarded King Hezekiah's faithfulness, but the king has no heir. In desperation, his wife makes a forbidden pact with the fertility goddess, Astarte, to bear him a son. When Hezekiah discovers her idolatry, he smashes her shrine and their love. In his final battles--to redeem a wife and save a nation--will Hezekiah stand firm and let the lord be his salvation?

Chronicles of the King: My Father's God by Lynn Austin
Book 4 in this series. Biblically based on verses from Kings, Chronicles and Isaiah, young King Manasseh has been appointed to the throne after his father's sudden death. Reared with his best friend, Joshua, and instructed in the beliefs of their fathers, the young men's lives are forever changed one fateful night, pitting them against one another and transforming the friends into mortal enemies. As Manasseh slides deeper into the dark world of pagan rituals and ancient evil, Joshua comes close to abandoning his hope and faith in the God of his fathers. (1997) ISBN: 0834116758

Underlined text refers to Internet link at http://Homeschool-Books.com

Chronicles of the King: Among the Gods by Lynn Austin
Book 5 in this series. Surrounded by pagan gods...far from home...can the Israelites cling to their faith and have hope for the future? A magnetic story of vengeance, loss, courage, love, and the all-encompassing grace of God. Can two men, both deeply entrenched in the pain of the past, reclaim the Heavenly Father they lost so many years ago? ISBN: 0834117339

First Light by Bodie and Brock Thoene
The first book in a new series by the Thoene duo (authors of the Zion Legacy and Zion Chronicles). Go back in time to first century Jerusalem--just after the massacre of Jews before Passover--a dark time in the nation's history. During the dark days of Herod's reign, there are many who pray for Light: Peniel, the blind beggar; Marcus, the Roman; Zadok, priest of Israel; Susanna and Manaen, lovers, yet worlds apart. When they meet Yeshua, their lives are transformed---and history is changed forever! 300 pages, hardcover from Tyndale Tyndale House Pub; (August 2003) ISBN: 0842375066

The Gifts of the Jews: How a Tribe of Desert Nomads Changed the Way Everyone Thinks and Feels by Thomas Cahill ◆
A light-handed, popular account of ancient Jewish culture, which is the culture of the Bible. The book is written from a decidedly modern point of view. It encourages us to see the Old Testament through ancient eyes—to see its characters not as our contemporaries but as those of Gilgamesh and Amenhotep. Cahill also lingers on often-overlooked books of the Bible, such as Ruth, to discuss changes in ancient sensibility. The result is a fine, speculative, eminently readable work of history. Note that Cahill's audience is secular society, not Biblical Christianity. (September 1999) Anchor Books; ISBN: 0385482493. Reading level: Adult.

God's Appointed Customs: A Practical Guide for Understanding & Observing the Biblical Customs by Barney Kasdan
Explains how biblical customs (like circumcision and the wedding) impact both Jews and Gentiles. Especially relevant to believers in the Messiah, since Yeshua (Jesus) observed them. It is divided into two sections: Biblical Lifecycle and Biblical Lifestyle; each chapter offers historical background, traditional Jewish observance, relevance to the New Testament, and a practical guide to help believers observe. Paperback - 160 pages (April 1998) Lederer Messianic Publications; ISBN: 1880226634.

God King: A Story in the Days of King Hezekiah by Joanne Williamson
This novel is inspired by research on the historical King Taharka and his period. By the author of the best-selling *Hittite Warrior*, carries the reader back to Ancient Egypt and to the biblical Jerusalem. Around 701 B.C. Egypt is being ruled by the Kushite dynasty. Young Prince Taharka, a very minor royal son, suc-

---

Resources recommended in ◆several lessons, ★ several units, ♥other HOW Units. ☞—Key Resource (see beginning of unit or page 32).

ceeds unexpectedly to the throne of Kush and Egypt -- a "divine" rulership. He begins to find his way. . .until a treacherous plot pushes him into sudden exile and into the hands of Amos, an emissary of King Hezekiah seeking help for Judea from the Egyptians against the Assyrians. Far from home, near Jerusalem, and found out in his disguise as a medical assistant, Taharka encounters two kings in conflict. One is the mighty Assyrian, Sennacherib, promising alliance; the other is Hezekiah, the Jew who trusts in Yahweh. Taharka must choose with whom to live or die. Bethlehem Books (2002) Reading level: Young Adult. ISBN: 1883937736

Hittite Warrior by Joanne Williamson
Judea has always been the crossroads and battlefield of contending nations. It is no less so in this biblical time of Barak and Deborah. Uriah Tarhund's Hititte home is destroyed by invading Greeks. His dying father tells him to go south to seek a Canaanite named Sisera. "He will help you. For my sake. . . ." Uriah is plunged into the tumult of an uneasy Judea. When he saves a young boy from being sacrificed to Moloch, he is given succor for a time by the Hebrews. Later, he finds Sisera and joins him in war against these same people. When the Canaanites are defeated, the young Hittite has the opportunity to come to a peace with himself, the Hebrew people and their God. This meticulously researched novel is set in the time of Judges, and incorporates Biblical facts with a gripping story, set against the wide background of ancient civilizations. Bethlehem Book (1999) Paperback. 264 pages. Reading level: Young Adult. ISBN: 1883937388.

A Historical Atlas of the Jewish People: From the Time of the Patriarchs to the Present by Eli Barnavi (Editor)
This is one of those rare books that can literally make a reader gasp with delight and horror. It may even be the best one-volume history of Judaism in print. Beginning with The Migrations of the Patriarchs, and continuing to the present day, the book's chapters include historical maps, time lines, illustrations and photographs, and narrative essays by leading historians that help readers not only understand but visualize the movements of the Jewish people. (January 1995) Schocken Books; ISBN: 0805241272.

History of the Jewish People Volume 1: Second Temple Era by Rabbi Hersh Goldwurm ◆
Based on a book that has become a standard text in Israel, it tells the story of the Jewish nation from the vantage point of the Jews themselves. This volume covers the period from the Destruction of the First Temple to the Destruction of the Second; the era of the Second Commonwealth. It is a fascinating story. It includes some of the great names, famous miracles, and heart-rending tragedies; Simeon the Just, the Maccabees, Yochanan ben Zakkai, Hillel; Alexander the Great, Julius Caesar, Vespasian; the heroic defense of Jerusalem and the heartbreak of its fall. It shows the Jewish people struggling to maintain its integrity in the face of for-

eign conquest and internal betrayal. It includes the development of the Oral Law and Rabbinic leadership. This book is a valuable contribution to an understanding of the Jewish people, and it is an exciting, inspiring, engrossing tale for every kind of reader. ISBN: 0-89906-455-8. Order from Eichlers 800-286-5157. Reading level: 7th grade and up.

History of the Jewish People Volume 2: From Yavneh To Pumbedisa by Meir Holder Price

Covers nine centuries, from the destruction of the Second Temple to the end of the Geonic period. Without a Temple and without sovereignty, Jewry fell back upon the soul of its nationhood, the Torah. In this volume, we find Romans, Babylonians, Christians, Byzantines, and Moslems dominating Israel, sometimes benignly, usually oppressively. But simultaneously, Israel produced the Mishnah, the Talmud, the Geonic responsa, and the institutions of learning and leadership. ISBN: 089906499X. Order from Eichlers 800-286-5157. Reading level: 7th grade and up.

A History of the Jews by Paul Johnson ★

A national bestseller, this brilliant 4,000-year survey covers not only Jewish history but the impact of Jewish genius and imagination on the world. The author (a Christian) delivers a brilliant and comprehensive one-volume survey covering 4,000 years of Jewish history. His book is a forceful and sustained analysis of Jewish emergence and an interpretation of how Jewish history, philosophy, ethics, and social and political notions interplay with world history. (September 1988) HarperCollins (paper); ISBN: 0060915331. Chapter One "Israelites" is available online.

Introduction to Jewish History: From Abraham to the Sages by Seymour Rossel ◆

Highly recommended for the Ancient Israel Unit. This book provides an effortless transition from childhood Bible tales to purposeful study of the Jewish past. Simple stories present the highlights of Jewish history from the age of the patriarchs to the destruction of the Second Temple, and from the Bar Kochba rebellion to the completion of the Talmud. Children will grasp the historical continuity essential to the development of a confident Jewish identity. Includes a handy, at-a-glance historical time line. Illustrated with photographs and artwork. Though this was written for grades 4-6, most adults don't know the basics which it covers. This is a much-needed, clear overview of ancient Israel's history, in chronological order. Reading level: 9-12.

Israel—The Land and the People: An Evangelical Affirmation of God's Promises

Israel . . . one word that brings with it a flood of images and emotions. This long-overdue book draws together the wisdom of twelve scholars (including a leader on

Resources recommended in ◆several lessons, ★ several units, ● other HOW Units. ●━Key Resource (see beginning of unit or page 32).

Heart of Wisdom Publishing   307

the Jews for Jesus staff) to answer the question Who is Israel today, and how is Israel different from the church? Chapters include: The Church's Appropriation of Israel's Blessings; A New Covenant—an Eternal People; The Land of Israel and the Future Return; A Celebration of the Lord our God's Role in the Future of Israel. 348 pp (December 1998) Kregel Publications; ISBN: 0825428793.

The Jews in the Time of Jesus: A History by Peter Connolly
The teachings of Jesus, his life story, his relationships, the things that were said of him by early Christians—all are best understood against the backdrop of Jesus' own time and place. Understanding Jewish life in the first century will help us better understand Jesus' mission and how it relates to our own religious concerns today. Ideal for anyone who is interested in understanding the Jewish roots of Christianity. A useful historical resource. Paperback Reprint edition (March 1995) Oxford Univ Pr (Trade); ISBN: 0199101620. Reading level: Ages 9-12.

Jerusalem in the Twentieth Century by Martin Gilbert
Travel back in history as *Jerusalem* takes you on a once-in-a-lifetime tour of this holy city. Renowned historian Martin Gilbert guides us through thirty centuries of incredible events, from the dawn of civilization to the latest developments in the Arab-Israeli peace talks. Hardcover - 412 pages (September 1996) John Wiley & Sons; ISBN: 0471163082 (see Video Resources for the video by this name).

Jerusalem: Footsteps Through Time by Ahron Horovits
This is a different kind of tour—a spectacular look at Jerusalem's old city that makes the words of Scripture come alive. Walk in the footsteps of Abraham, look in on the camp of David in his conquest of Yevus, build the Temple with King Solomon—it's all here. This is a book that you can take with you to the actual sites or read at your leisure. A much-appreciated gift for a special occasion. In attractive coffee-table format. Philipp Feldheim; ISBN: 1583303987.

Living Emblems: Ancient Symbols of Faith by Dr. John Garr
The ancient symbols are living emblems. They attest to a living faith in the God of Abraham, Isaac, and Jacob, a faith that came to include all Christians when Jesus brought God's light to the nations. For traditional Jewish people, the emblems of Judaism are vibrant reminders of their special election as covenant partners with God. For Christians, biblical emblems are living portraits of Jesus as Messiah and Lord. Chapters include: Vital Signs, The Shofar, The Menorah, The Mezuzah, The Tallit, The Tefillin, The Kiddush Cup, Passover Symbols, Sabbath Symbols, The Hanukkah, The Decalogue, and The Star of David. Available online.

Moses and the Law

A nondenominational book of twelve lesson packets designed to teach the Bible student about the life of Moses and his enduring contribution to our world. *Moses and the Law* provides both teacher and student with a valuable vehicle for study. Each chapter contains activity sheets which include charts, crossword puzzles, flash cards, and thought-provoking research questions or assignments encouraging the study of certain Bible passages in order to find answers. Chapters include: Origin of the Torah; Geography; People in Moses' Time; Bible Time Line; Hebrew Vocabulary; Life of Moses; The Ten Commandments; The Tabernacle. Order from Infinite Discovery 800-475-7308. Reading level: Grades 4-12.

Made According to Pattern by Charles W. Slemming ♦

This is the sixth edition of British pastor-author C.W. Slemming's standard study of the Old Testament tabernacle, first published in 1938 but still useful to today's Bible students. Paperback (October 1982) Christian Literature Crusade; ISBN: 0875085067.

Restoring of the Early Church by Mike and Sue Dowgiewicz ♥

This book's main purpose is to explain the Hebraic facets of the early church. It's an excellent book for Heart of Wisdom's "Early Church " unit study (not yet published) but it also includes excellent historical information about Israel and ancient Greece so it is referenced to in this unit and in the Ancient Greece Unit (Greek Philosophy) and the Ancient Rome Unit (Jewish Revolts). Restoration Ministries (888-229-3041).

Restoring Our Lost Legacy by Dr. John Garr

For the past nineteen centuries, millions of believers have been denied their biblical legacy, the riches of the Hebrew foundations of their faith. Christian Judaeophobia, anti-Judaism, and anti-Semitism have conspired to rob them of the treasures of their inheritance. This book presents selected essays and lectures in which Dr. Garr urges the church to recover its Hebrew heritage, its connection with the Jewish matrix from which it was produced. These pages call Christians back to the Bible, to the roots of faith that enrich lives and equip believers to achieve greater maturity through a more complete knowledge of Jesus, our Jewish Lord. Golden Key Books (423-472-7321). 0-9678279-2-2. Available online.

Sketches of Jewish Social Life by Alfred Edersheim ♦

Ever wonder what it would be like to have lived during the time of Jesus . . . to mingle with men and women of that period, see them in their homes and with their families, learn their habits and manners, and follow them in their ordinary life? Contains more than fifty illustrations, maps, and photos! Chapters include: Jews and Gentiles in 'the Land'; Mothers, Daughters and Wives in Israel; Relation

---

Resources recommended in ♦several lessons, ★ several units, ♥ other HOW Units. ●—Key Resource (see beginning of unit or page 32).

Heart of Wisdom Publishing   309

of the Pharisees to the Sadducees and the Essenes, and to the Gospel of Christ; The Worship of the Synagogue. (November 1994) Henderickson Publishers, Inc.; ISBN: 156563005X. Available online.

A Survey of Israel's History by Leon James Wood
Since its first publication in 1970, *A Survey of Israel's History* has established itself as a popular and useful text in Bible colleges and seminaries. Numerous line-maps, charts, and diagrams help to clarify details. An extensive chronological chart provides an overall summary of names and dates. (September 1986) Zondervan Publishing House; ISBN: 031034770X.

The Young Reader's Encyclopedia of Jewish History by Ilana Shamir (Editor) Shlomo Shavit (Editor) ♦
Currently out of print but worth a trip to the library. An excellent overview of Jewish history, beginning approximately 5,000 years before the birth of Christ and ending with the present time. A time line summarizes the text and places Jewish history in the context of general world history. Includes 300 photographs, maps, charts, and drawings. Reading level: Ages 10 and up.

Videos

Discovering Our Jewish Roots by Dwight A. Pryor, Marvin Wilson
Experience firsthand an exciting Jewish Roots conference. Each of the three videos in this set includes a one-hour teaching by Dwight Pryor and a one-hour teaching by Marvin Wilson. An especially good tool for use in introducing others to Jewish Roots teachings and for use in home group studies. Six 60-minute messages on three videos. Sessions include: Jewish Roots of Spiritual Living; Rediscovering the Historical Jesus; The Jewish Setting of the New Testament; Parable of the Merciful Father/Prodigal Son; Kingdom Confusion; Kingdom Challenge; Relevance of Jewish Roots for Our Times. Center for Judaic-Christian Studies 937-434-4550.

Jerusalem: City of Heaven
No place on Earth has inspired such love, conflict, and passion as Jerusalem—a city that's been conquered, destroyed, and rebuilt over twenty times in thirty centuries. Join narrator Liam Neeson to meet the Jews, Moslems, and Christians who, over the past 3,000 years, have struggled to build an enduring peace in the home they each consider their gateway to heaven. 1 hour 15 minutes.

Jesus In His Jewish World by Dwight A. Pryor
Drawing upon the very latest biblical research, Dwight opens up the Gospels to wonderfully new and inspiring insights into the life of our Lord. A picture is

drawn of the historical Jesus, living in the land of Israel and within the Jewish culture of the first century, that dramatically illuminates the method and meaning of his teachings. Filmed at an Anglican church near London, this series builds upon and extends the teachings found in the audio series, *Our Hebrew Lord*. Seven 60-minute messages on four videos. Center for Judaic-Christian Studies 937-434-4550.

Jerusalem in the Twentieth Century
See description of the book in the Book Resources. Available on home video in The History Channel Store 888-423-1212.

Jews and Christains: A Journey of Faith
A PBS Documentary Film Project based on the book *Our Father Abraham* by Dr. Marvin Wilson. Despite a shaky past, the potential for concord between Christians and Jews is far greater than that of conflict. Why? Both religious communities find their deepest roots in the same people through a common Jewish ancestor, one referred to in both parts of the Bible as "our father Abraham." Seeking to understand this family relationship is what this documentary series is all about. Due 2001. Copies of *Jews and Christians: A Journey of Faith* and the study guide are available through Auteur Productions Ltd. by calling 866.299.6554.

Magazines

Restore! Magazine
The Restoration Foundation is dedicated to research, development, and implementation of the church's Judaic heritage. They are committed to studying the Hebrew foundations of Christian faith and the profound implications that these historical and theological truths have for the church's life and renewal. *Restore!* is full of excellent teaching articles concerning Israel's history by authors such as: Dr. Marvin Wilson, Dr. Howard Morgan, Dr. Karl D. Coke, Dr. John D. Garr, Dwight Pryor; Robin Sampson (author of this book); Clarence Wagner, Jr., Dr. Douglas A. Wheeler, David Bivin, Rev. Robert S. Somerville, and more. Available online.

The Jerusalem Christian Review
For more information or questions, you may e-mail Edchr@Christian.edu. Telephone in US: 619-745-4000. Telephone in Jerusalem: (011) 972-2-532-2771. Fax: (011) 972-2-532-3028.

Jerusalem Perspective
Excellent teaching articles by authors such as: : William Bean, David Bivin, David Flusser, Robert Lindsey, Lenore Mullican, Dwight Pryor, Marvin Wilson and Brad Young. Focus on the Family (James Dobson) purchased the rights to fifty-seven articles that first appeared in Jerusalem Perspective magazine. Available online.

Resources recommended in ♦several lessons, ★ several units, ♥ other HOW Units. ☜—Key Resource (see beginning of unit or page 32).

Heart of Wisdom Publishing   311

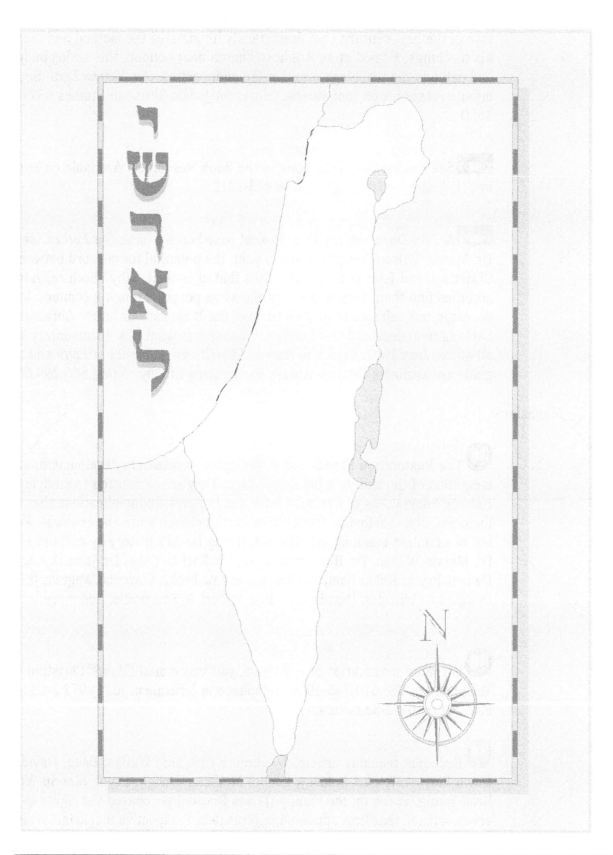

Father Abraham

29-32

The Narrated Bible

Step 1 Excite

The story of Abraham made a deep impression upon the ancient world. Almost all Eastern nations refer to Abraham (Abram). He is called the friend of God (James 2:23), and faithful Abraham (Galatians 3:9). Between the time of Adam and the time of Christ, God called Abram. The call separated him from his country and his family. Abram heard; he believed; he obeyed. His belief in God was counted to him for righteousness, and great promises were given him. He was a man of faith: when put to the test, he counted unwaveringly on God. Against hope, he believed in hope, that he might become the father of many nations (Romans 4:18), and thus the blessing of Abraham came on the Gentiles through Jesus Christ, and he became the father of the faithful in all generations, whether of Jewish or Gentile descent. Who is called our Father? (Romans 4:16).

Step 2 Examine

Read about Abraham's life: Marries Sarah (Gen. 11:29); Ishmael born to (Gen. 16:3, 15); Isaac born to (Gen. 21:2, 3); Lives in Ur (Gen. 11:31; Neh. 9:7; Acts 7:4); Moves to Canaan (Gen. 12:4, 5, 6; Acts 7:4); Call of (Gen. 12:1-3; Josh. 24:3; Neh. 9:7; Is. 51:2; Acts 7:2,3; Heb. 11:8); Canaan given to (Gen. 12:1,7; 15:7-21; Ezek. 33:24); Lives in Bethel (Gen. 12:8); Sojourns in Egypt (Gen. 12:10-20; 26:1); Defers land to Lot (Gen. 13; 14:13; 35:27); Blessed by Melchizedek (Gen. 14:18-20; Heb. 7:1-10); God's covenant with (Gen. 15; 17:1-22; Mic. 7:20; Luke 1:73; Rom. 4:13; 15:8; Heb. 6:13,14; Gal. 3:6-18, 29; 4:22-31); Name changed to Abraham (Gen. 17:5; Neh. 9:7); Circumcision (Gen. 17:10-14, 23-27); Angels appear to (Gen. 18-24:7); His questions about Sodom (Gen. 18:23-32); Witnesses the destruction of Sodom (Gen. 19:27, 28); Deceives Abimelech (Gen. 20); Sends Hagar and Ishmael away (Gen. 21:10-14; Gal. 4:22-30); Trial of his faith by offering Isaac (Gen. 22:1-19; Heb. 11:17; Jas. 2:21); Sarah, dies (Gen. 23:1-20); Marries Keturah (Gen. 25:1); Provides a wife for Isaac (Gen. 24); Death (Gen. 15:15; 25:8-10).

Research Israel's beginnings. Use any resource (an encyclopedia, nonfiction book, historical novel, or the Internet). We recommend the following:

Books

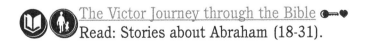
The Victor Journey through the Bible ●—♥
Read: Stories about Abraham (18-31).

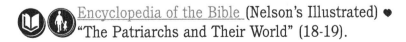
Encyclopedia of the Bible (Nelson's Illustrated) ♥
"The Patriarchs and Their World" (18-19).

Resources recommended in ♦several lessons, ★ several units, ♥other HOW Units. ●—Key Resource (see beginning of unit or page 32).

Heart of Wisdom Publishing   313

Who's Who in the Bible ❤
Read: "Abraham and His People" (8-9).

Introduction to Jewish History: From Abraham to the Sages ◆
Read: Chapter 1 "Jewish History Begins."

The Holman Bible Atlas ⚷ ❤
Read: "The World of the Patriarchs" (41-49).

The Young Reader's Encyclopedia of Jewish History ◆
Read: Chapters From Nomadic Tribes to a Nation and From the Babylonian Exile Through the Return to Zion.

Our Father Abraham ⚷ ❤
Read: Chapter 1 "The Root and Branches."

The Bible Comes Alive: Volume One, Creation to Abraham ★
Read: Section III Abraham: His Background and His Family.

Ancient Israel: From Abraham to the Roman Destruction of the Temple ★
Read "The Patriarchal Age: Abraham, Isaac, and Jacob" (1-32).

Videos

Abraham
Description: (from the back cover) Emmy winner Joseph Sargent brings us the first in a series of magnificent biblical epics from Turner Home Entertainment. *Abraham* is a powerful film, based on the most dramatic and moving tale from the Old Testament in which an ordinary shepherd is called upon by God to show his abiding faith in extraordinary ways. ASIN: 6303257828.

Internet Sources

Abraham, Man of Faith
Description: A Bible study on Abraham with hyper links to information about events and places, from the *Daily Bible Study*.

40 Significant Facts About Israel's History
Description: Article from the *Israel Teaching Letter* by Clarence H. Wagner, Jr.

Step 3 Expand

Choose and complete one of the following activities:

Activity 1: Answer Questions (See Genesis 12)
1. What did the Lord tell Abram to do? 2. What did the Lord promise to do for Abram? 3. What did Abram do? (12:4-5) 4. Whom did Abram take with him when he left home? (12:4-5) 5. What did the Lord tell Abram He would do, and how did Abram respond? 6. What did Abram do in Bethel? (12:8-9) 7. How did the Egyptians treat Abram? (12:16) 8. Why might it have been hard for Abram to leave his country, his people, and his father's household? 9. How did you feel when you left home for the first time for an extended period of time?

Activity 2: Add to Your Time Line Book
Include: Abram's Call, God's Promises, Abraham's Faith, The Binding of Isaac, and Abraham's Death. Refer to Reproducible Maps, Charts, Timelines & Illustrations ♥ (13).

Activity 3: Write a Paper
Read about Abraham's faith in the following verses. Romans 4:1-22; Galatians 3:6-9; Hebrews 11:8-10,17-19; James 2:21-24. Write a paper titled "Faith." Refer to "Writing an Explanation" in *Writers INC*. Younger students can narrate (orally tell) what they have learned.

Activity 4: Make a Map
Trace Abraham's journeys on a map. Abraham dwells in Ur, but removes to Haran (Gen. 11:31; Neh. 9:7; Acts 7:4) and Canaan (Gen. 12:4-6; Acts 7:4), dwells in Beth-el (Gen. 12:8), sojourns in Egypt (Gen. 12:10-20), deferring to Lot, chooses Hebron (Gen. 13; 14:13; 35:27), and dwells in Gerar (Gen. 20; 21:22-34). Refer to *The Holman Bible Atlas* (45-47).

Activity 5: Write a Summary
Choose one of the events in Abraham's life to write about. Younger students can narrate (tell back) one of the events. See Step 2.

Step 4 Excel

Share what you have learned about Abraham by filling out the following worksheets with a child (elementary level): The Call of Abram, Abram and Lot, Abram Rescues Lot, God Promises Abraham a Son, The Three Visitors, Sodom and Gomorrah, Abraham is Tested, God's Promise to Abraham.

Correct all written work to demonstrate correct punctuation and spelling, and effective use of grammar. Add corrected written work or any illustrations to your portfolio. Add new words you learned in this lesson into your Vocabulary Notebook (see page 22).

Resources recommended in ♦several lessons, ★ several units, ♥ other HOW Units. ☛―Key Resource (see beginning of unit or page 32).

Heart of Wisdom Publishing   315

God's Covenant with Israel

Step 1 Excite

29-34/121-126

The Narrated Bible

The Bible continually refers to the Covenant and the divine blessings for observing the Covenant and penalties for breaking it. So it is very important for us to clearly understand the actual nature and content of the Covenant. The Hebrew word *berith*, Covenant, occurs over 280 times in the Old Testament. Covenants generally can include treaties, alliances, agreements, compacts, pledges, mutual agreements, promises, and undertakings on behalf of another; covenants in the Bible can be agreements between two individuals, between a king or leader and his people; or between God and individuals, or God and groups of individuals. Covenants can be conditional or unconditional. Conditional covenants are forfeited if one party violates or defaults on his part of the agreement. Unconditional covenants are arrangements in which the default of one party does not negate the ultimate fulfillment and blessing of the Covenant. [1] The Bible gives three major Covenants between God and His people:

ABRAHAMIC COVENANT (unconditional)

And I will establish my covenant between me and thee and thy seed after thee in their generations for an EVERLASTING covenant, to be a God unto thee, and to thy seed after thee. And I will give unto thee, and to thy seed after thee, THE LAND wherein thou art a stranger, all the land of Canaan, for an everlasting possession; and I will be their God. (Genesis 17:7,8)

MOSAIC COVENANT (conditional)

And he was there with the LORD forty days and forty nights; he did neither eat bread, nor drink water. And he wrote upon the tables the words of the covenant, the ten commandments. (Exodus 34:28)

MESSIANIC COVENANT (Grace or the New Covenant)

For this is my blood of the new testament, which is shed for many for the remission of sins. (Matthew 26:28)

Read about God's covenant with Abraham in the following verses: Genesis 15; 17:1-22; Micah 7:20; Luke 1:73; Romans 4:13; 15:8; Hebrews 6:13,14; Galatians 3:6-18,29; 4:22-31.

Step 2 Examine

God made an everlasting and unconditional Covenant with Israel. The covenant with the Jews was for them to keep the Law of Moses as a lifestyle of the godly to set them apart from the other nations. Gentiles were invited into the new Covenant that Jesus made with Israel (Romans 9:22-33) as full fellow heirs of all the promises of God. The Gentile church is grafted in (Romans 11:17), brought near (Ephesians 2:13), Abraham's offspring (by faith) (Romans 4:16), and partakers (Romans 15:27) with Israel. The church never replaced Israel. Ephesians 2:12,13 and 18,19, explains *You [Gentiles] were excluded from God's people, Israel, and you did not know the promises God had made to them. You lived in this world without God and without hope. But now you belong to Christ Jesus. Though you once were far away from God, now you have been brought near to him because of the blood of Christ. (18) Now all of us, both Jews and Gentiles, may come to the Father through the same Holy Spirit because of what Christ has done for us. So now you Gentiles are no longer strangers and foreigners. You are citizens along with all of God's holy people. You are members of God's family.*

Read Romans 11. What does the root represent? The different branches? What is the wild olive tree? What condition causes a branch to be cut off? Romans 11:18 says, *Boast not against the branches. But if thou boast, thou bearest not the root, but the root thee.*

The olive-tree, wild by nature (Romans 11:24), is the shoot or cutting of the good olive-tree which, left ungrafted, grows up to be a wild olive. In Romans 11:17, Paul refers to the practice of grafting shoots of the wild olive into a "good" olive that has become unfruitful. By such a process the sap of the good olive, by pervading the branch that is grafted in, makes it a good branch, bearing good olives. Thus the Gentiles, being a wild olive, but now grafted in, yield fruit, but only through the sap of the tree into which they have been grafted. [2]

Genesis 12:3 says, *And I will bless them that bless thee, and curse him that curseth thee: and in thee shall all families of the earth be blessed.* (God speaking to Abraham, father of the Jewish people.)

Circumcision is a sign of the covenant God made with Abraham. Circumcision — cutting the foreskin — was a continuing reminder that God had cut a covenant with Abraham and his descendants. God commanded it to be performed on all males on the eighth day to be the special badge of his chosen people, an abiding sign of their consecration to him. It was established as a national ordinance (Genesis 17:10,11). It is interesting to note that medical science only recently realized the benefits of the eighth-day procedure: Prothrombin promotes coagulation of the blood, and the babies' natural supply of prothrombin on the eighth day is 110% of normal. When a baby is circumcised before the eighth day he is prone to excessive bleeding, and the doctor must first give the child an injection of vitamin K which helps produce prothrombin. In some circumcisions there is no bleeding when done on the eighth day.

Resources recommended in ◆several lessons, ★ several units, ♥ other HOW Units. ☀—Key Resource (see beginning of unit or page 32).

Heart of Wisdom Publishing   317

Research God's Covenant with Israel. Use any resource (Bible-study aids such as commentaries, dictionaries, encyclopedias, or the Internet). We recommend the following:

The Victor Journey through the Bible ●━♥
Read: "God's Covenant With Abraham" (21).

Encyclopedia of the Bible (Nelson's Illustrated) ♥
"Old Testament Overview" (204-205), "God's Law in Practice" (152-153).

Introduction to Jewish History: From Abraham to the Sages ♦
Read: Chapter 1 Jewish History Begins.

The Narrated Bible ●━ ♥
Read: Israel's Covenant with God (121).

Manners and Customs in the Bible ★
Read: Look up all entries to circumcision and covenant in the index.

Our Father Abraham: Jewish Roots of the Christian Faith ●━ ★
Read: The Olive Root and Branches and Grafted into Israel.

Yeshua: A Guide to the Real Jesus and the Original Church ●━ ♥
Read: "The Old and New" (49-66), "The New in the Old and the Old in the New" (67-86). See description in the Key Resources section beginning on page 32.

Ancient Israel: Its Life and Institutions ●━ ★
Read: "Circumcision" (466).

God's Plan for Israel: A Study of Romans 9-11 by Steven A. Kreloff
Description: This is a small, easy-to-read, much-needed book about a greatly misunderstood topic. It is an excellent, balanced explanation of God's mercy, grace, and faithfulness to the Jews and Gentiles. Kreloff, a saved Jew, shows how clearly the Scriptures distinguish between the church and Israel. Kreloff explains that God's sovereignty in election does not negate human responsibility in salvation. Packed with much more than the study of Romans 9-11, this book combats the false doctrines claiming that the church replaced Israel. Paul warns Gentiles who have come to faith not to boast or become arrogant against the olive root, which is the nation of Israel. Kreloff explains that we must combat Gentiles who consider themselves spiritually superior to Jews by focusing on God's grace. *God's Plan for Israel* is divided into three main sections: (1) How God Spared the Hebrew Nation in the Past; (2) The Reason He Continues to Preserve the Jewish People; (3) The Plan God Has to Restore Israel in the Future.

The Seed of Abraham by Robert Somerville
Description: Robert Somerville answers the question, Just what is the biblical distinction between the Jewish people, Israel, and the Christian church? This writing presents a complicated subject in very understandable terms and reconciles the seeming contradictions of Scripture in this area. This is a very significant publication on the subject of How We View the Jew for the purpose of bringing unity to the body of Christ. Available online.

The God Contracts by Robert Somerville
Description: An excellent summary of the seven main covenants that God has initiated with mankind. These Covenants include: (1) God's Eternal Covenant with Himself, (2) Adam's Covenant of Dominion, (3) Noah's Covenant of Preservation, (4) Moses' Covenant of the Law, (5) Abraham's Covenant of Real Estate, (6) David's Covenant of Government, and (7) Jesus' Covenant of Redemption. These earth-oriented Covenants are foundational for believers to understand their God-given inheritance.

The Miracle of the Scarlet Thread by Richard Booker
Description: This is one of the most profound books of the blood of Messiah ever written! Booker explains how the First and Second Testaments are woven together by the scarlet thread of the blood Covenant to tell one complete story throughout the Bible. Subjects explained are the blood Covenant ritual, the Covenant with Abraham, in the tabernacle, in the sacrifices, in the High Priest and Passover. This is a worldwide, best-selling classic. (December 1988) Destiny Image; ISBN: 0914903268.

Replacement Theology, Its Origin, History and Theology by Derek White
Description: So called Replacement Theology is still deeply entrenched in the church in various forms, with disastrous consequences for the relationship of the church with Israel. Few are aware of the roots and development of this teaching. This booklet will be of help to Christian leaders and teachers, bringing understanding and countering many of the present-day negative attitudes toward Israel. (1997) Teddington, Middlesex, U.K.: Christian Friends of Israel. Reading level: Adult.

Internet Sources

Abraham's Seed
Description: An article on the sensitive and misunderstood issues of Jews and Gentiles.

Resources recommended in ◆several lessons, ★ several units, ♥ other HOW Units. ●━Key Resource (see beginning of unit or page 32).

(i) Did God Break His Covenant With the Jews?
Description: Excellent article about the Covenant from *Bridges for Peace* by Clarence H. Wagner, Jr.

(i) What is A Covenant?
Description: This is a detailed article explaining Bible Covenants between God and man, by Lambert Dolphin.

(i) The Holy Root of the Olive Tree
Description: An article explaining that the Church and Israel are both supported by the root of the tree—the Messiah. By Jim Gerrish: Director, Galilee Study Center.

(i) The Everlasting Covenant
Description: An overview of the Covenant and the blessings associated with it.

(i) God's Covenant with Abraham
Description: An article by David Brewer explaining the provisions and promises.

(i) The Apple of His Eye, A Message for Israel
Description: A list of Bible verses of promises for Israel.

(i) Israel and the Church: the Differences
Description: Article by Dr. Thomas McCall, the Senior Theologian of Zola Levitt Ministries.

Step 3 Expand

Activity 1: Write Summaries
Write a summary of each of the everlasting Covenants in the Old Testament:
1. The Covenant with Noah (Gen. 9:16)
2. The Covenant with Abraham (Gen. 17:7,13,19)
3. The Covenant God made with David (2 Sam. 23:5)
4. The New Covenant (Is. 55:3; 61:8; Jer. 32:40; 50:5; Ezek. 16:60; 37:26)

Activity 2: Learn Hebrew Words

Look up each of the words below in a Hebrew lexicon. Add each word, and its phonetic spelling and meaning to your Hebrew notebook. See The Old Testament Hebrew Lexicon. The Hebrew word for covenant is *berit* (phonetic - bereeth') derived from a root which means "to cut" and hence a covenant is a "cutting." It appears more than 250 times in the Old Testament. The Hebrew word for circumcision is muwlah (phonetic - moo-law'), it comes from the word muwl which means "to be cut off."

Activity 3: Answer Questions

1. Isaiah 1:11 says *To what purpose is the multitude of your sacrifices unto me? saith the LORD: I am full of the burnt offerings of rams, and the fat of fed beasts; and I delight not in the blood of bullocks, or of lambs, or of he goats.* Why were the Old Testament sacrifices of animals only temporary? (Heb. 10:4)
2. What does the Bible say about religious ceremonies when our hearts are not toward God? (Matt. 15:8)
3. Why was the blood necessary in order for redemption to occur? (Heb. 9:22)
4. How was the blood of Jesus Christ different from the blood of the animal sacrifices? (1 Pet. 3:18; Heb. 9:12-14)
5. How does the redemption through Christ affect our ability to overcome Satan? (Rev. 5:9)

Activity 3: Write a Summary

Read Genesis 15:10 and Leviticus 17:11. Write about your perspective on the blood covenant. Explain: Why is the blood necessary for restoring a right relationship between God and man? Why is it foolish to attempt to approach God through our merits instead of the blood Covenant? (Heb. 9:22)

Step 4 Excel

Share what you have learned about the Covenants between God and His people with a friend or family member. Correct all written work to demonstrate correct punctuation and spelling, and effective use of grammar. Add corrected written work or any illustrations to your portfolio. Add new words you learned in this lesson into your Vocabulary Notebook (see page 22).

Footnotes

1. Dolphin, Lambert. (1993) What is a Covenant? <http://www.ldolphin.org/Covn.html> (Accessed September, 2000).
2. Easton, Matthew George. Entry for Olive-tree. *Easton's Bible Dictionary*.

Resources recommended in ◆several lessons, ★ several units, ♥ other HOW Units. ☞—Key Resource (see beginning of unit or page 32).

Heart of Wisdom Publishing   321

The Patriarchs 2000-1525 B.C.

23-96

The Narrated Bible

Step 1 Excite

Abraham, Isaac, and Jacob are known as the Patriarchs; their descendants are the Jewish people. They migrated through the Fertile Crescent (Babylonia, Mesopotamia, Syria, Canaan, Egypt). There is disagreement as to the exact period of the Patriarchal Age. Much evidence has also been put forward for a dating of 2000-1700 B.C. (realize that these are approximates).

Brainstorm and discuss what the following names mean to you: Abraham, Sarah, Isaac, Rebecca, Jacob, Leah, and Rachael.

Step 2 Examine

In the first unit "Adam to Abraham" you studied Genesis 1-12. Genesis 1-11 deals with the Creation, the Fall, the Flood, Babel, and the nations. The rest of Genesis consists of narratives of the patriarchal figures. Read about the four key Patriarchs:

The Narrated Bible
Abraham

The Narrated Bible
Isaac

The Narrated Bible
Jacob

The Narrated Bible
Joseph

A. Abraham (the father of faith and of the nation Israel) (Gen. 12-23)
B. Isaac (the beloved son of promise) (Gen. 24-26)
C. Jacob (scheming and chastening) (Gen. 27-36)
D. Joseph (suffering and glory) (Gen. 37-50)

Find out more about the Patriarchs. Use any resource (an encyclopedia, a nonfiction book, or the Internet). We recommend any of the following:

Books

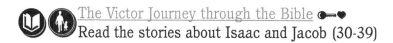
The Victor Journey through the Bible ●—♥
Read the stories about Isaac and Jacob (30-39)

Encyclopedia of the Bible (Nelson's Illustrated) ♥
"The Patriarchs and Their World" (18-19).

Who's Who in the Bible ♥
Read: "The Patriarchs" (10-13).

The Holman Bible Atlas ⊶ ♥
Read: "The World of the Patriarchs" (41-49).

The Young Reader's Encyclopedia of Jewish History ♦
Read: From Nomadic Tribes to a Nation (9-12).

Ancient Israel: From Abraham to the Roman Destruction of the Temple ★
Read: Chapter 1 The Patriarchal Age: Abraham, Isaac, and Jacob.

The Ancient Hebrews ♦
Read: The Patriarchs (11-12).

Bible History: Old Testament ★
Read: Chapter 7 The History of the Patriarchs.

Internet Sources

Hebrew History: The Age of the Patriarchs, 1950-1500 BC
Description: The Hebrews: A Learning Module from Washington State
University by Richard Hooker.

Judaism 101: The Patriarchs and the Origins of Judaism
Description: Highlights of the acts of Abraham, his son Isaac and grandson
Jacob, and how the latter's twelve sons were the fathers of the twelve tribes.

The Genealogy of The Patriarchs
Description: Interesting chart showing the ages at which men of the Bible
had a son; also, the number of years from Adam.

Step 3 Expand

Choose and complete one of the following activities:

Activity 1: Write a Summary
Choose at least one event in each of the Patriarchs'(Abraham, Isaac,
Jacob, and Joseph) lives to write about. Refer to the "Father Abraham" lesson
(page 313), "Joseph in Ancient Egypt" lesson (page 270) and text below:
Major events in Isaac's life: The miraculous son of Abraham (Genesis 17:15-19);
Offered in sacrifice by his father (Genesis 22:1-19; Hebrews 11:17); Is provided a
wife (Genesis 24); Esau and Jacob born to (Genesis 25:19-26); His old age, last
blessing upon his sons (Genesis 27:18-40).

Resources recommended in ♦several lessons, ★ several units, ♥other HOW Units. ⊶Key Resource (see beginning of unit or page 32).

Heart of Wisdom Publishing   323

Major events in Jacob's life: Obtains Esau's birthright (Genesis 25:29-34); Fraudulently obtains father's blessing (Genesis 27:1-29); His vision of the ladder (Genesis 28:10-22); Serves fourteen years for Leah and Rachel (Genesis 29:15-30; Hosea 12:12); Wrestles with an angel (Genesis 32); Name changed to "Israel" (Genesis 32:28; 35:10).

Activity 2: Create a Comic Strip
Draw a comic-book page complete with conversations in bubbles showing the stories of one of the patriarchs.

Activity 3: Make a Family Tree
Make and display a family tree showing the progression of Abram to the twelve tribes of Israel. Refer to Reproducible Maps, Charts, Timelines & Illustrations ❤ (17).

Activity 4: Add to Your Time Line Book
Create one page in your Time Line Book for each of the four key patriarchs: Abraham, Isaac, Jacob and Joseph. Include add illustrations and summaries for main events. Refer to Reproducible Maps, Charts, Timelines & Illustrations ☞ ❤ (11-13).

Activity 5: Write Biographies
Write a brief biography of Abraham, Isaac, Jacob, and Joseph. Include the time period in which they lived and a minimum of three facts about each. Refer to Writing About a Person in *Writers INC* or to the Biography Maker on the Internet. Younger students can narrate (tell back) what they remember about each man.

Activity 7: Write a Story
Write the story of the election of a nation and the preparation for the redeemer (Genesis 12-50) on the level a child can understand. Younger students can narrate (tell back) the story. Include a section for each of the four key patriarchs.

Step 4 Excel

Explain orally to your parents what you've learned in this lesson. Correct all written work to demonstrate correct punctuation and spelling, and effective use of grammar. Add corrected written work or any illustrations to your portfolio. Add new words you learned in this lesson into your Vocabulary Notebook (see page 22).

Underlined text refers to Internet link at http://Homeschool-Books.com

Egyptian Bondage 1700-1275 B.C.

Note: See these related lessons in the Ancient Egypt Unit: "The Plagues" (209), "Passover" (214), "The Exodus" (218).

97-110

The Narrated Bible

Step 1 Excite

In the Covenant God made with Abraham, God told Abraham that his descendants would undergo Egyptian bondage (Genesis 15:13-14). As promised, God did not leave the Israelites in bondage, but chose a deliverer, and He reminded the Israelites of His plans for them:

> Go, and gather the elders of Israel together, and say unto them, The Lord God of your fathers, the God of Abraham, of Isaac, and of Jacob, appeared unto me, saying, I have surely visited you, and seen that which is done to you in Egypt: And I have said, I will bring you up out of the affliction of Egypt unto the land of the Canaanites, and the Hittites, and the Amorites, and the Perizzites, and the Hivites, and the Jebusites, unto a land flowing with milk and honey. (Exodus 3:16,17)

Step 2 Examine

Previous to the deliverance from Egyptian bondage, the Hebrews had no experiential knowledge of redemption. Under Moses they were to experience such deliverance and have the redemptive power of God made real to them. The deliverance from Egyptian bondage was a portrait of the coming redemption through Christ.

Read about the Hebrews in Egypt in Exodus.
I.   The Hebrews in Egypt (1:1-12:36)
   A.   Progressive mistreatment of the Hebrew slaves (1:1-22)
   B.   Preparation for the deliverance of the Hebrew slaves (2:1-4:31)

Find out more about Israel in Egypt. Use any resource (an encyclopedia, a nonfiction book, or the Internet). We recommend any of the following:

Books

The Victor Journey through the Bible ●—♥
Read the stories about Joseph (40-50), "Hebrews Become Slaves" (51)

Encyclopedia of the Bible (Nelson's Illustrated) ♥
"The Egyptains" (52).

Resources recommended in ◆several lessons, ★ several units, ♥other HOW Units. ●—Key Resource (see beginning of unit or page 32).

Heart of Wisdom Publishing   325

The Holman Bible Atlas ⚷ ❤
Read: "The Egyptian Experience" (52-62).

Ancient Israel: From Abraham to the Roman Destruction of the Temple ★
Read: Chapter 2 Israel in Egypt: The Egyptian Sojourn and the Exodus.

Ancient Israel: Its Life and Institutions ★
Read: Slaves (80-88).

The Bible Comes Alive: Volume One, Creation to Abraham ★
Read: Section IV Joseph in Egypt.

Bible History: Old Testament ★
Read: Volume 2, Chapters 1 through 4. (Available online—see Internet Resources in this lesson.)

The Midwife's Song by Brenda Ray
Biblical fiction. Under Pharaoh's ungodly decree, Puah, midwife to the Hebrew people, finds love, and sees her own vacillating faith grow in the fire of adversity. Utilizing biblical narrative, folklore, Ancient Near Eastern history, and imagination this story explains life in this time period and how an ordinary young woman can be used by God in an extraordinary way. Karmichael Press (2000). Paperback 256 pages. ISBN: 0965396681.

Escape from Egypt: A Novel by Sonia Levitin
Description: It is the biblical tale of the Exodus—the Israelite flight from Egypt—here seen from the point of view of two teenagers: Jesse, a Hebrew slave, and Jennat, a half-Egyptian, half-Syrian girl. The pair meet when they work together learning jewelry-making, but their burgeoning relationship is dwarfed by momentous events. Moses has come to gather the Jewish people; he is going to make Pharaoh let them go. The biblical setting provides the wider context for a drama that is primarily a human one. Plagues and miracles swirl around real people who are so enmeshed in their own lives and passions that, at times, they seem almost oblivious to the spectacle threatening to engulf them. This human scale is the great strength of the novel. (Booklist review). (March 1996) Puffin; ISBN: 0140375376. This book includes a romance theme but is good background for this time period. Reading level: Young adult.

Ancient Egypt and the Old Testament ★
See description in the Ancient Egypt Resources section..

Internet Sources

ⓘ The Exodus: Volume 2 Chapters 1 through 4
Description: These chapters from *Bible History: Old Testament* by Alfred Edersheim address Egypt and its history during the stay of the children of Israel, the birth and the training of Moses, both in Egypt, and the Call of Moses.

ⓘ The Exodus
Description: Part II of "God's Story: From Creation to Eternity" from ChristiansAnswers.net. (Follow the next buttons on the bottom of each page.)

ⓘ Egyptian Bondage
Description: This is a Bible study worksheet on Genesis 37-Exodus 14.

Step 3 Expand

Choose and complete one of the following activities:

Activity 1: Outline Exodus 1-4
Refer to the outline example on the Heart of Wisdom Internet site, or to "Outlining" in *Writers INC*.

Activity 2: Prepare a Cartoon Strip
Choose a section of the story about the Hebrews' Egyptian bondage (Gen. 15:13-14) that includes a conversation between characters. Create a series of drawings with outlines of cartoon figures with blank bubbles over their heads. Fill in the bubbles with the characters' words.

Activity 3: Answer Questions
Write a summary answering these questions: Who are the key personalities discussed in this lesson? What are the important concepts? How does the material fit with what has been learned in previous lessons? How does this information relate to your Christian life?

Activity 4: Write a Book Review
Write a book review about a book that you read for this lesson. Refer to How to Write a Book Review or Writing a Book Review in *Writers INC*.

Step 4 Excel

Share with a friend or family member how the deliverance from Egyptian bondage was a portrait of the coming redemption through Christ. Correct all written work to demonstrate correct punctuation and spelling, and effective use of grammar. Add corrected written work or any illustrations to your portfolio. Add new words you learned in this lesson into your Vocabulary Notebook (see page 22).

Resources recommended in ♦several lessons, ★ several units, ♥ other HOW Units. ☛Key Resource (see beginning of unit or page 32).

Heart of Wisdom Publishing   327

The Exodus and Passover

110-117

The Narrated Bible

Note: See these related lessons in the Ancient Egypt Unit: "The Plagues" (209), "Passover" (214), "The Exodus" (218).

Step 1 Excite

At the beginning of the book of Exodus, the people of God were slaves in Egypt. When they left Egypt in 12:41, they were the Lord's warriors. The Passover and the Exodus provide the biblical paradigm for redemption. God wants us to remember the Exodus, and He commanded the Passover to be a memorial forever:

> *And ye shall observe the feast of unleavened bread* [Passover]; *for in this selfsame day have I brought your armies out of the land of Egypt: therefore shall ye observe this day in your generations by an ordinance for ever.* (Exodus 12:17)

> *And the LORD spake unto Moses in the wilderness of Sinai, in the first month of the second year after they were come out of the land of Egypt, saying, Let the children of Israel also keep the passover at his appointed season. In the fourteenth day of this month, at even, ye shall keep it in his appointed season: according to all the rites of it, and according to all the ceremonies thereof, shall ye keep it.* (Numbers 9:1-3)

Jesus set an example for us (I Pet. 2:21), observing the Passover once a year (Luke 2:41). The name of the festival, *Pesach* in Hebrew, means passing over or protection and is derived from the instructions given to Moses by God (Ex. 6:6-8). Moses was chosen by God to lead the Israelites out of Egypt. God commanded Moses to tell the children of Israel,

> *Wherefore say unto the children of Israel, I am the LORD, and I will bring you out from under the burdens of the Egyptians, and I will rid you out of their bondage, and I will redeem you with a stretched out arm, and with great judgments: And I will take you to me for a people, and I will be to you a God: and ye shall know that I am the LORD your God, which bringeth you out from under the burdens of the Egyptians. And I will bring you in unto the land, concerning the which I did swear to give it to Abraham, to Isaac, and to Jacob; and I will give it you for an heritage: I am the LORD.* (Ex. 6:6-8)

Make a mind map about the Exodus. Use sheets of unlined paper and colored markers or pencils. Put an image or circle in the center and write in the phrase Exodus. Draw lines out from the center as you determine the major categories of information (slavery, Moses, Pharaoh, plagues, Passover, Red Sea, etc.). Branch lines from these will hold subtopics. As

Underlined text refers to Internet link at http://Homeschool-Books.com

you study this lesson, continue branching. Use different colors for each cluster of information. Ask yourself, Who? What? Where? When? and How? Colors and patterns will organize your ideas into meaningful groups that will make connections and relationships more clear. Also use symbols, numbers, arrows, or other doodles on your mind map (slaves, lamb, unleavened bread, etc.).

Step 2 Examine

Read about the Hebrews' deliverance in Exodus. (You'll read about the wilderness wanderings in another lesson):

    A   The Israelites delivered from Egyptian bondage (5:1-15:21)

    B.   Israel redeemed by the blood of a lamb—Passover (12:1-13:16)

    C.   Israel crosses Red Sea, is saved from the Egyptian army (13:17-15:22)

Research the Passover and the Exodus (add notes to your mind map created in Step 1). Use any resource (an encyclopedia, non-fiction book, historical novel, or the Internet). We recommend the following:

Books

The Victor Journey through the Bible ⬤—❤
"The Plagues" (58-59), "Passover" (60-61), "The Exodus" (62-63). "Crossing the Red Sea" (64-65).

Encyclopedia of the Bible (Nelson's Illustrated) ❤
"The Exodus from Egypt" (20-21), "Exodus" (200-201).

Who's Who in the Bible ❤
Read: "Moses and the Israelites" (14-15).

The Holman Bible Atlas ⬤—❤
Read: "The Exodus" (63-74).

Introduction to Jewish History: From Abraham to the Sages ◆
Read: Chapter 2 God Remembers Israel.

A Family Guide to the Biblical Holidays ★
Read: "Feast of Passover" (111-162). (See links to the online pages below.)

Our Father Abraham: Jewish Roots of the Christian Faith ⬤—★
Read: Chapter 12 Passover and Last Supper.

Resources recommended in ◆several lessons, ★ several units, ❤ other HOW Units. ⬤—Key Resource (see beginning of unit or page 32).

Bible History: Old Testament ★
Read: Volume 2, Chapters 6 and 7 of The Exodus.

Ancient Israel: From Abraham to the Roman Destruction of the Temple ★
Read: Chapter 2 "Israel in Egypt: The Egyptian Sojourn and the Exodus."

The Bible Comes Alive: Volume Two, Moses to David ◆
Read: Section I: "Moses in Egypt...And that Code of Laws."

The Gifts of the Jews ◆
Read: Chapter 3 Egypt: From Slavery to Freedom.

The Midwife's Song by Brenda Ray
Description in previous lesson.

Internet Sources

Passover
Description: An overview of the purpose of Passover. Directions for a seder without all the fuss. A fun activity and crafts from A Family Guide to the Biblical Holidays.

Exodus: The Story of Redemption
Description: Overview of the Exodus from Egypt from Abiding in Christ.

The Exodus (Chapters Six and Seven)
Description: These chapters from *Bible History: Old Testament* by Alfred Edersheim address the oppression of Israel, analyze each of the ten plagues, and cover the Passover and its Ordinances, the children of Israel leaving Egypt, and the passage through the Red Sea.

The Exodus
Description: Part II of *God's Story: From Creation to Eternity* from ChristiansAnswers.net. (Follow the "next" buttons on the bottom of each page.)

Step 3 Expand

Choose and complete one of the following activities:

Activity 1: Answer Questions
Answer the questions in Our Father Abraham (252-255).

Underlined text refers to Internet link at http://Homeschool-Books.com

Activity 2: Have a Seder Dinner
Use A Family Guide to the Biblical Holidays or a similar resource as a guide.

Activity 3: Make a Map
Trace a map of the Exodus journey. Refer to the Holman Bible Atlas ☞ ♥ (66-72) or Reproducible Maps, Charts, Timelines & Illustrations ♥ (22).

Activity 4: Illustrate a Cartoon Strip
Choose a section of the story about the Exodus that includes a conversation between characters. Create a series of drawings with outlines of cartoon figures with blank bubbles over their heads. Fill in the bubbles with the characters' words.

Activity 5: Write a Summary
Write a summary explaining the first Passover. Younger students can narrate (tell back) their view of Passover.

Activity 6: Write a Story
Write an account of the Exodus from the viewpoint of Caleb. Write as if you were Caleb, telling the story to a group of Hebrew children.

Step 4 Excel

Share what you have learned about the Passover or the Exodus with a friend or family member. Correct all written work to demonstrate correct punctuation and spelling, and effective use of grammar. Add corrected written work or any illustrations to your portfolio. Add new words you learned in this lesson into your Vocabulary Notebook (see page 22).

Resources recommended in ♦several lessons, ★ several units, ♥other HOW Units. ☞Key Resource (see beginning of unit or page 32).

Heart of Wisdom Publishing   331

Wilderness Wanderings 1275-1235 B.C.

117-194

The Narrated Bible

Step 1 Excite

God's purpose was to deliver His people from Egypt and bring them right into Canaan. The trip from Egypt to the Promised Land was only an eleven-day journey, but because of the Israelites' lack of faith and trust in God, they spent their lives wandering in the wilderness. Forty years later, the Hebrews still had not arrived at the place God had wanted to give them at the beginning!

A few weeks after the children of Israel had left Egypt (the Exodus), atop Mt. Sinai God gave Moses two things for us: ten commandments (including judgments and ordinances—the Law) and the pattern of the tabernacle (detailed instructions about the layout, the materials, and its construction). We will study lessons on the Law and the Tabernacle later in this unit.

The Feast of Tabernacles is a week-long, autumn-harvest festival to be kept in remembrance of the forty-year period during which the children of Israel were wandering in the desert dwelling in tents. The Feast of Tabernacles is also known as the Feast of the Ingathering, Feast of the Booths, Sukkoth, Succoth, or Sukkot. The word Sukkoth means booths, and refers to the temporary dwellings. Jesus celebrated the Feast of Tabernacles. Read more about this holiday at BiblicalHolidays.com. See the section on Tabernacles.

Step 2 Examine

Read about the Hebrews' wilderness wanderings in Exodus.
I. The Hebrews in the Wilderness (15:23-18:27)
II. The Hebrews at Sinai (19:1-40:38)
      A. Revelation of the Covenant between God and Israel (19:1-25)
      B. Commandments (20:1-26)
      C. Various laws (21:1-23:33)
      D. Renewal of the Covenant (24:1-11)
      E. The Tabernacle (24:12-27:21)
      F. The Priests (28:1-29:46)
      G. Instructions (30:1-31:18)
Do more research about the wilderness wanderings. Use any resource (an encyclopedia, non-fiction book, historical novel, or the Internet). We recommend the following:

Underlined text refers to Internet link at http://Homeschool-Books.com

Books

The Victor Journey through the Bible ◉—♥
Read: "Food in the Wildreness" (66-67), "The Golden Calf" (70-71), "Twelve Spies" (74-75), "The Bronze Serpent" (76-77).

Encyclopedia of the Bible (Nelson's Illustrated) ♥
If you have not read "The Exodus from Egypt" do so now. (20-21).

Introduction to Jewish History: From Abraham to the Sages ◆
Read: Chapter 2 God Remembers Israel.

The Holman Bible Atlas ◉— ♥
Read: "The Route of the Exodus" (66-74).

The Bible Comes Alive: Volume Two, Moses to David ◆
Read: Section I "Moses in Egypt...And that Code of Laws."

Made According to Pattern ◆
See description in the Resource section.

Internet Sources

Exodus: The Story of Redemption
Description: Overview of the Exodus from Egypt, from Abiding in Christ.

Step 3 Expand

Choose and complete one of the following activities:

Activity 1: Build a Sukkoth
Remember the dwelling in tents for the forty-year period during which the children of Israel were wandering in the desert by building a Sukkoth (Leviticus 23:43). See ideas at Celebrating the Feast of Tabernacles.

Activity 2: Contrast and Compare
Make a contrast-and-compare graphic (see page 26) comparing the Hebrews' wandering in the wilderness with a Christian's spiritual wanderings.

Activity 3: Write a Summary
Write a summary about the wilderness wanderings answering these questions: Who are the key personalities discussed in this lesson? What are the

---

Resources recommended in ◆several lessons, ★ several units, ♥other HOW Units. ◉—Key Resource (see beginning of unit or page 32).

Heart of Wisdom Publishing   333

important concepts? How does the material fit with what has been learned in previous lessons? How does this information relate to your Christian life? Younger students can narrate (orally tell) what they have learned.

Activity 4: Outline Exodus 15-31
Refer to the outline example or "Outlining" in *Writers INC*.

Activity 5: Write a Letter
Write a letter to a friend explaining the Feast of Tabernacles.

Activity 6: Sew a Quilt Block
Patchwork Partners provides directions to sew a quilt block and a brief Bible study relating to this lesson on the Internet. See Bible Blocks: Hill and Valley.

Step 4 Excel

Share what you have learned about Israel's wilderness wanderings with a friend or family member. Correct all written work to demonstrate correct punctuation and spelling, and effective use of grammar. Add corrected written work or any illustrations to your portfolio.

The Law

Step 1 Excite

219-295

The Narrated Bible

Discuss what the term law means in the Bible (if you don't know the answer, guess). Does law refer to the Ten Commandments? Are there other laws? Have you ever heard of the 613 laws? What is the Mosaic Law? What is Ceremonial Law? What is the Judicial Law? What is the Moral Law? Brainstorm and discuss what type of society we would have without law.

Step 2 Examine

When the Hebrews referred to the Law, they were usually referring to the Torah (the first five books of the Bible) or to the Tanakh (the Torah, the Prophets, and the Old Testament writings). The Torah, meaning law or teaching in Hebrew, is the cornerstone of Jewish religion and law.

Americans usually think of the term law as a negative word. The word law in the Bible actually means instruction. It is something which teaches or instructs believers how to live in ethical and moral harmony with their fellow man and before God. The Jews believed in and practiced freedom and independence for all. In contrast, the Greeks organized their society around slavery.

The Law is a magnificent demonstration of God's grace. The Law is good, spiritual, and holy. The problem is, we have trouble keeping it. The Law is not weak; the Law is not imperfect. We are weak; we are imperfect. But, thanks be to God, we are declared to be righteous (that is, in a right relationship with God) based not upon what we do but upon what He is. Jesus' purpose was to establish God's Law among the Jews. Paul's purpose was to extend God's Law to embrace the non-Jews. For both Jesus and Paul, law was grace. Jesus said, *Think not that I am come to destroy the law, or the prophets: I am not come to destroy, but to fulfill.* (Matthew 5:17)

Torah

Dr. James Tabor[1] explains that Deuteronomy 4 is the key chapter for understanding the outline of ideas related to the Torah, and that Chapter 5, the Ten Commandments, is the core of Torah:

- 4:1-8. Torah consists of commandments, statutes, and judgments. If followed they will make the nation of Israel, in the Land of Israel, unique among all the nations of the world. No other nations will be as wise and as great, nor have a God so near/real to them.

Resources recommended in ♦several lessons, ★ several units, ♥ other HOW Units. ◉━Key Resource (see beginning of unit or page 32).

Heart of Wisdom Publishing   335

- 4:10-14. The Israelites have had an absolutely unique revelation of God at Sinai—He appeared to them and spoke the Ten Commandments (see Chapter 5). Verse 20—they are to become God's special or treasured people, among all the other nations.
- 4:25-31. If they forget and turn from God to idols, then they will be cast out of the Land, sent into exile, but even then not ultimately forgotten. Those who repent will be gathered back in the last days.

The Ten Commandments

1. You shall have no other gods.
2. You shall not make any graven images
3. You shall not take the name of the Lord your God in vain.
4. You shall remember and keep the Sabbath day holy.
5. Honor your father and your mother.
6. You shall not commit adultery.
7. You shall not comit murder.
8. You shall not steal.
9. You shall not bear false witness against your neighbor.
10. You shall not covet any thing that is your neighbor's.

613 Mitzvot (Commands)

According to the Talmud (body of Jewish civil and religious law, including commentaries on the Torah), there are 613 commands, including 248 positive commands and 365 negative ones. Some apply to the priesthood, the temple, and ritual purity, and are not possible to keep since the temple is not functional. Some laws apply exclusively to men, others to soldiers, others to women, and others to employers. There are only about 200 of these laws that can be kept during this present age. In actuality, the Torah contains thousands of rules, and the 613 mitzvot (commands) are only the broad classifications.

Noahhide Laws

The Rabbis understood that Seven Basic Categories (Seven Laws of Noah) of the Torah were of universal application, and were absolutely required of all humankind, whether Jews or Gentiles:

1. Idolatry/One True God
2. Blasphemy/Right Speech
3. Murder/Sanctity of Life
4. Stealing/Property Rights
5. Sexual Immorality/Marriage and Family
6. Eating Blood/Respect for Animal Life
7. Establishing Justice

Resources recommended in ◆ several lessons, ★ several units, ♥ other HOW Units. ☞—Key Resource (see beginning of unit or page 32).

Heart of Wisdom Publishing   336

The Nine-Fold Purpose of the Law below is from The Spirit of the Law by Dr. Ron Mosley[2]:

The Nine-Fold Purpose of the Law

First - To teach the believer how to serve, worship, and please God (Psalms 19:7-9; Acts 18:13,14).

Second - To instruct the believer how to treat his fellow man and to have healthy relationships with him (Leviticus 19:18; Galatians 5:14; 6:2).

Third - To teach believers how to be happy and prosper here on Earth by manifesting the power and authority of God's reign in their lives (Joshua 1:8; Psalms 1:1-3; Luke 12:32).

Fourth - The Law was given, not to save, but to measure man's deeds both toward his God and toward his fellow man, straightening out all matters contrary to sound doctrine (I Timothy 1:8-10; II Timothy 2:5; I Corinthians 6:1-12; 3:13; Romans 2:12; Revelation 20:12,13).

Fifth - The Law is a schoolmaster, showing that we are guilty and then leading us to Christ, our Messianic justification (Galatians 3:21-24; Romans 3:19).

Sixth - The Law gives us the knowledge and reveals the depth of our sin (Romans 3:20; 4:15; 7:7,8; Luke 20:47 - greater damnation).

Seventh - The Law reveals the good, holy, just, and perfect nature of God and serves as the visible standard for God's will (Romans 2:17; Psalms 19:7-9; Acts 18:13,18; Romans 7:12; II Peter 1:4).

Eighth - The Law is to be established or accomplished by our faith; therefore, it is called the Law of Faith (Romans 3:27,31).

Ninth - The same Law today is written on our hearts, and through God's Spirit we can delight in and serve the Law of God (Romans 7:6-25).

Research the law or Torah. Use any resource (an encyclopedia, nonfiction book, historical novel, or the Internet). We recommend the following:

Books

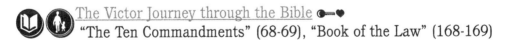
The Victor Journey through the Bible ●—♥
"The Ten Commandments" (68-69), "Book of the Law" (168-169)

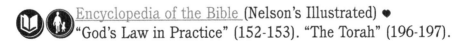
Encyclopedia of the Bible (Nelson's Illustrated) ♦
"God's Law in Practice" (152-153). "The Torah" (196-197).

The Spirit of the Law by Ron Mosley ♦
Description: A scholarly book on law and grace in the teachings of Jesus and Paul, which is a must for all Christians. Available online.

Resources recommended in ♦several lessons, ★ several units, ♥ other HOW Units. ●—Key Resource (see beginning of unit or page 32).

Heart of Wisdom Publishing   337

Yeshua: A Guide to the Real Jesus and the Original Church ○━ ♥
Read: "Misconceptions Concerning the Law" (29-48). See description in the Key Resources section beginning on page 32.

Our Father Abraham: Jewish Roots of the Christian Faith ○━ ★
Read: The Problem with Judaizing (24-26), Salvation: By Grace or Works (20-21), and Paul and the Law (27-28).

Ancient Israel: Its Life and Institutions ★
Read: Law and Justice (143-160).

Internet Sources

Summary of the Torah
Description: An overview of the Torah by James Tabor, author of The Jewish Roman World of Jesus.

Law Written on the Heart
Description: Article from *Bridges for Peace* by Jim Gerrish, explaining that divine intention is that the Law would be perfectly fulfilled in each individual's life.

The 248 Positive Mitzvot/Commandments: The Do's
Description: A list of positive commands.

The 365 Negative Mitzvot/Commandments: The Don'ts
Description: A list of the negative commands.

Proclamation of the Law
Description: Encyclopedia article explaining the Law, from *Condensed Biblical Cyclopedia*.

What Is Torah?
Description: Article expressing the Jewish love of Torah.

Other Laws
Description: Encyclopedia article explaining more about law, from *Condensed Biblical Cyclopedia*.

Step 3 Expand

Choose and complete one of the following activities:

Activity 1: Write a Summary
Write a summary explaining what Torah is. Younger students can narrate (orally tell) what they have learned.

Activity 2: Make an Outline
Outline The Spirit of the Law by Dr. Ron Mosley.

Activity 3: Copy Text
Copy (by hand or typing) "The Nine-Fold Purpose of the Law" (in Step 2).

Activity 4: Memorize
Memorize the Ten Commandments.

Step 4 Excel

Share what you have learned about the Law with a friend or family member. Correct all written work to demonstrate correct punctuation and spelling, and effective use of grammar. Add corrected written work or any illustrations to your portfolio. Add new words you learned in this lesson into your Vocabulary Notebook (see page 22).

Footnotes

1. Tabor, Dr. James. (1998) *The Jewish Roman World of Jesus*, Summary of the Torah
<http://www.uncc.edu/jdtabor/torah.html> (Accessed 2000)
2. Mosley, Ron. (1993) *The Spirit of the Law*, Mozark Research Foundation, 9700 Hwy. 107 Sherwood, AR 72120 (501) 835-1453.

Resources recommended in ◆several lessons, ★ several units, ♥ other HOW Units. ●━Key Resource (see beginning of unit or page 32).

Heart of Wisdom Publishing   339

The Tabernacle

Step 1 Excite

126-135

The Narrated Bible

The Tabernacle is full of fascinating symbols, pictures, and shadows of the Messiah. Atop Mount Sinai, a few weeks after the children of Israel had left Egypt (the Exodus), God gave Moses two things for us: ten Commandments (including judgments and ordinances—the Law) and the pattern of the Tabernacle (detailed instructions for the layout, the materials, and its construction). The Hebrews built the Tabernacle under the supervision of Moses. The Tabernacle was a portable structure, transported by the Levite tribe during the forty years in the desert wilderness.

Step 2 Examine

Research the Tabernacle. Use any resource (an encyclopedia, a nonfiction book, or the Internet). We recommend the following:

Books

The Victor Journey through the Bible ●━♥
"The Tabernacle" (72-73).

Encyclopedia of the Bible (Nelson's Illustrated) ♥
"The Tabernacle" (158-159).

Made According to Pattern ♦
See description in the Resource section.

The Tabernacle: Shadows of the Messiah (Its Sacrifices, Services, and Priesthood)
See description in the Ancient Israel Unit Resources section.

Gods Lamp, Mans Light - Mysteries of the Menorah by John Garr
Presents these vivid images of a rich biblically Hebraic tradition. As you read this volume, you'll be enriched by the amazing wealth of understanding manifest in the biblically Hebraic symbols designed by God and by his chosen people Israel. Chapters include: God's Lamp, Mans Light, Divine Design, Pure Gold, One Hammered Work, Clear Consecrated Oil, The Light Motif, Mans Soul-God's Torch, Israel-God's Menorah, You Are the Light of the World, The Tree of Life, A Messianic Portrait, Menorah Mystery Numbers, By My Spirit, Dedication Produces Light, Synagogue, and Church Aflame. Paperback - 160 pages (2001) Restoration Foundation; (678) 615-3568; ISBN: 0967827949. Great read aloud for the family.

Underlined text refers to Internet link at http://Homeschool-Books.com

The Tabernacle of Israel: Its Structure and Symbolism by James Strong
In this very detailed, thorough exposition o ft the Tabernacle, the author of *The Exhaustive Concordance of the Bible,* provides a rare insight into the spiritual symbols this elaborate structure displays. (April 1987) Kregel Publications; ISBN: 0825437458.

Tabernacle Model to Make by Marian Bennett, Tom Green
This book is out of print but is available through some bookstores and libraries. It's a ready-to assemble scale model tabernacle, printed in full color on heavy paper explaining the symbolism of the Tabernacle.

Internet Sources

What The Bible Says About The Tabernacle
Description: The Tabernacle, its blueprint, and its priesthood—taken from *What The Bible Says About The Tabernacle,* by Alpha-Omega Ministries, Inc.

Tabernacle Home Page
Description: Details the layout, structure, and furnishings of the Tabernacle and relates the pictures from the book of Exodus to Jesus Christ.

Tabernacle - MSN Encarta
Description: Brief encyclopedia article describing the Tabernacle.

Tabernacle or Tent of Meeting - Bible Tutor
Description: A detailed description and diagram of the size and contents of the Tabernacle.

Church Inside The Tabernacle
Description: Explains how the biblical types issuing forth from the Tabernacle of Moses are an exact typical prefiguration of the body of Christ.

The Tabernacle Revealed!
Description: Study guide explaining how life flows from the Holy of Holies (Spirit) into the Holy Place (Soul) and out to the Outer Court (Body), resulting in complete redemption.

The Tabernacle
Description: Ward R. Williams, Ph.D., from the University of Minnesota, explains the Tabernacle and its message.

The Lamp of God: Menorah by Robert Somerville
Description: A booklet presenting a study on the scriptural symbolism of the Menorah from both the Old and New testaments. You will discover that this lamp-stand symbolizes many things such as the Nation of Israel, the Church, the Holy

Resources recommended in ♦several lessons, ★ several units, ♥ other HOW Units. ☜—Key Resource (see beginning of unit or page 32).

Heart of Wisdom Publishing   341

Spirit, the Word of God, the Seven Spirits of God, even the Lord Jesus Christ himself as the light of the world. It is believed by many that a menorah was on public display in each of the first-century churches.

Step 3 Expand

Activity 1: Draw a Floor Plan
Draw a floor plan of the Tabernacle. Label the furniture. Refer to
Reproducible Maps, Charts, Timelines & Illustrations ❤ (25).

Furnishings	
Alter of Burnt Offering	
Alter of Incense	
Ark of The Covenant	
Aaron's Rod	
Curtains	
Door to the Outer Court	
Holy of Holies	
Inner Court	
Lampstand (Menorah)	
Laver	
Outer Court	
Pot of Manna	
Table of Showbread	
Tablets of Law	
Veil	

Activity 2: Make a Chart
Make a chart similar to the one below. Using your research, fill in the columns. Find a picture of each item (print out from the Internet or make copies from books) and paste each picture next to its corresponding description.

Step 4 Excel

Share the floor plan, description of furnishings, and offerings of the Tabernacle with a friend or family member. Correct all written work to demonstrate correct punctuation and spelling, and effective use of grammar. Add corrected written work and any illustrations to your portfolio. Add new words you learned in this lesson into your Vocabulary Notebook (see page 22).

The Priesthood

Step 1 Excite

248-250

The Narrated Bible

Brainstorm and discuss what you know about the priests in the Bible. What do you think their duties were in the Tabernacle in the wilderness? What do you think their duties were in Solomon's or Herod's temples? What tribe did the priests come from? How many priests where there at one time? What is the difference between a priest and a high priest? Why is Jesus referred to as our High Priest? What does holy mean? What is the Great Sanhedrin? What would qualify or disqualify a person to be a priest? What did the priests wear?

Step 2 Examine

Once a year, on the great Day of Atonement, the high priest would enter the Holy of Holies in the Tabernacle (later the Temple) where he would offer sacrifices for the nation of Israel (Ex. 30:10; Lev. 16; Num. 18:2,5,7; Heb. 8:3; 9:7). He would sprinkle blood on the Mercy Seat, which was actually a lid on top of the Ark of the Covenant. His garments were specially made (Ex. 28). He wore a breastplate of stones on his chest (Ex. 28:15-29). Each stone was named after a tribe of Israel. Everything connected with the priesthood was intended to be symbolical and typical—the office itself, its functions, even its dress and outward support. [1]

Aaron was the first person solemnly set apart to be a high priest (Ex. 29:7; 30:23; Lev. 8:12). He wore this peculiar dress, which on his death passed to his successor in office (Ex. 29:29,30). Initially, the duties of the Levites in assisting the priests focused on such tasks as the transportation of the Tabernacle (Num. 3-4; 1 Chron. 15:2) and guarding the doorway to the Tabernacle (1 Chron. 9:19,22-27). At the special festival times the priests had specific responsibilities in handling the offerings brought by the people (Lev. 23:9-21,25,36-38).

Jesus is now our high priest. He offered Himself on the altar of the cross once, for all (Heb. 2:17). Every year the high priest had to offer sin offerings for his own sins and the sins of the people. This annual repetition of the sacrifices served as a reminder that perfect atonement had not yet been provided. Jesus, however, through His own blood, effected eternal redemption for His people (Heb. 9:12). The Old Testament offerings served as a pattern and a prophecy of Jesus, who, through His better sacrifice, cleanses the conscience from dead works (Heb. 9:13-14). God always determined what was an acceptable offering and what was not. He finally provided His Son, the Lamb of God, as the sacrifice for the sins of the world (John 1:19; 3:16).

Do research about Israel's priests. Use any resource (an encyclopedia, nonfiction book, or the Internet). We recommend the following:

Resources recommended in ◆several lessons, ★ several units, ❤ other HOW Units. ●━Key Resource (see beginning of unit or page 32).

Books

The Victor Journey through the Bible ●—♥
"The Tabernacle" (72-73).

Encyclopedia of the Bible (Nelson's Illustrated) ♥
"Priest and Rituals" (158-159).

A Family Guide to the Biblical Holidays ★
Read: The Day of Atonement chapter (319-344).

The Temple: Its Ministry and Services ♦
Read: Chapter 4 The Officiating Priesthood.

Internet Sources

Priestly Garments for Glory & Beauty
Description: This is the detailed study guide for the Garments of the Priesthood.

The Officiating Priesthood
Description: Chapter 4 from The Temple: Its Ministry and Services.

The Breastplate
Description: A detailed study of the high priest's breastplate with its twelve stones representing the twelve tribes of Israel.

The Priesthood
Description: An overview of the priesthood from the Condensed Biblical Cyclopedia.

Garments for Priests
Description: Outline explaining the garments for the priests.

The Garments of the Priests, and of the High Priest
Description: Excerpt from The Life and Works of Flavius Josephus by William Whiston, Translator.

Step 3 Expand

Choose and complete one of the following activities:

Activity 1: Write a Summary

Write a summary about the Day of Atonement. Include a brief description for each of the headings: Purpose of Day of Atonement, Jewish Customs of Day of Atonement, Priestly Duties During the Day of Atonement, The Two Goats, Messianic Significance of Day of Atonement.

Activity 2: Create an Outline

Make an outline about the priesthood. Include the topics below:

- The Priesthood
- Duties of a Priest
- The Week's Service
- Training of a Priest
- Qualifications
- The Priestly Garments

Activity 3: Create a Chart

Make a chart titled "Priestly Garments." Include columns with these titles: Breastplate, Crown, Girdle, Linen Bonnet, Robe of the Ephod, Linen Coat, Ephod, Bells and pomegranates. Refer to the Web site Priestly Garments for Glory & Beauty.

Step 4 Excel

Print out the picture of the high priest in full garb from the Web site Priestly Garments for Glory & Beauty (or photocopy a picture from a book or draw your own illustration). Share the illustrations and chart with a friend or family member. Correct all written work to demonstrate correct punctuation and spelling, and effective use of grammar. Add corrected written work or any illustrations to your portfolio. Add new words you learned in this lesson into your Vocabulary Notebook (see page 22).

Footnotes
1. Sampson, Robin. (1998) *A Family Guide to the Biblical Holidays*, Woodbridge, VA.: Heart of Wisdom Publishing.

Resources recommended in ♦several lessons, ★ several units, ♥ other HOW Units. ●━Key Resource (see beginning of unit or page 32).

Heart of Wisdom Publishing   345

Twelve Spies

Step 1 Excite

171-174

The Narrated Bible

Have you ever heard the expression seeing the cup half full? Optimists view a half-filled cup as half full, while pessimists tend to view the same as half empty. The difference is a person's perspective.

The Israelites had just come out of Egyptian bondage. They were at the doorway to of a land flowing with milk and honey, which God had promised them, but unbelief blinded them. They focuses on the negative and fear. They took their eyes off the solution, off what they knew to be true, and dwelt on the problem. The more they focused on their circumstances, the easier it was to make a negative interpretation.

The way we respond to disappointment is extremely important. A wise person will face disappointments by asking God what He is trying to teach them and respond to the disappointments with new insight into God's plans and purposes.

As you read the story of the twelve spies think about how rewarding it would be have the faith and commitment Joseph and Calab had.

Step 2 Examine

Three months after leaving Egypt, God's people came to the Wilderness of Sinai and camped before the mountain of the Lord (Exodus 19:1-2). *God came down upon Mount Sinai in the sight of all the people* (Exodus 19:11) and made a Covenant with them. After reaching the border of Canaan, twelve men were sent into the promised land to *spy out the land of Canaan* (Numbers 13:2). When the twelve spies returned (forty days later) they brought glowing reports of the land, but ten of them felt that it was too strong to be conquered (Numbers 13:31-33). Joshua and Caleb were the only two who had confidence that God would give Israel the land of Canaan despite its formidable inhabitants. After the death of Moses, the servant of the Lord, Joshua, became the leader of God's people.

Read Numbers 13:1-3; 17-14:10.

Do research about The Twelve Spies. Use any resource (an encyclopedia, nonfiction book, historical novel, or the Internet). We recommend the following:

<u>Thoughts on The Twelve Spies</u>
Description: An article explaining that the story of The Twelve Spies stands forever as both an inspiration and a warning.

<u>Lessons from The Twelve Spies</u>
Description: An outline study of the story of The Twelve Spies.

<u>Giants in the Land</u>
Description: Bible study with test and answers by George Kirkpatrick.

Step 3 Expand

Choose and complete one of the following activities:

Activity 1: Prepare a Play
Write and act out a play showing the return of The Twelve Spies. Write a dialog for Joshua and Caleb. Emphasize why these two were not afraid to go into Canaan. Refer to <u>How to Write a Play</u> or Writing a Play in *Writers INC*.

Activity 2: Write a Letter
Read how Rahab assists the spies of the Israelites in Joshua 2 and how she is spared when the Israelites capture Jericho (Joshua 6:17-25). Rahab believed God and acted on it, then she came under the protection of the blood and experienced her salvation. Her faith was commended in Hebrews 11:31 and James 2:25. Write about Rahab's encounter with the spies as if you were Rahab telling the story in a letter.

Activity 2: Answer Questions
1. What was the mission of the spies? 2. What did they see? 3. What did they bring back? 4. Why were ten afraid? 5. What did Caleb and Joshua say? 6. What punishment did God give the people for their lack of faith?7. Why was Caleb and Joshua allowed to enter the land after forty years in the wilderness?

Activity 3: Add to Your Time Line Book
Add the story of the twelve spies to your Time Line Book. Refer to <u>Reproducible Maps, Charts, Timelines & Illustrations</u> ♥ (43).

Step 4 Excel

Share what you have learned about the twelve spies with a friend or family member. Correct all written work to demonstrate correct punctuation and spelling, and effective use of grammar. Add corrected written work or any illustrations to your portfolio. Add new words you learned in this lesson into your Vocabulary Notebook (see page 22).

Resources recommended in ♦several lessons, ★ several units, ♥ other HOW Units. ☞Key Resource (see beginning of unit or page 32).

Heart of Wisdom Publishing   347

Conquest and Occupation of Canaan

296-345

The Narrated Bible

Step 1 Excite

After forty years wandering in the wilderness under the leadership of Moses, the tribes were led by Joshua into the Promised Land, Canaan. Canaan was inhabited by the pagan Phoenicians and Amorites, who were called Canaanites. Canaan was a land made up of numerous small kingdoms. The first city to be attacked was Jericho; the walls came tumbling down when the trumpets were heard. The Hebrews took the rest of Canaan in a series of military campaigns. Various Canaanite kings joined their armies to stop the Hebrews, but on each occasion God gave His people victory. This period of conquest occupied between six and seven years (Joshua 14:7-11; cf. Deuteronomy 2:14), and by the close of this time, the basic occupation of the land was considered complete (Joshua 11:23; 14:5).

The Promised Land is a picture of God's grace. In Deuteronomy 7:6-9; 9:5 God assures His people that this privilege was not given to them because they were so numerous or righteous, for they were neither. He chose them and gave them the land that He had promised because of His love for them, His loyalty to the patriarchs, and His revulsion at the wickedness of that land's previous inhabitants (Deuteronomy 7:6-9; 9:4-6).

Much has been written about the Hebrews' conquest and settlement of Canaan. All accounts are based on two biblical books: Joshua and Judges. It is written that later Canaan became divided: the northern part was called Israel and the southern part was called Judah.

Read about the conquest and settlement of Canaan:

The conquest of Canaan	Josh. 1:1-12:24
The partition of the land	Josh. 13:1-22:34
Joshua's farewell address to Israel	Josh. 23:1-24:33

Step 2 Examine

Canaan (often called Israel or Palestine) is the name of what was the land that God promised to Abraham (Gen. 12:1-3). It extends along the coast of the eastern Mediterranean. Lebanon lies to the north, and Egypt is to the south. The eastern border is the Jordan River.

The pre-Israelite inhabitants of Canaan were called Canaanites. When the Hebrews left Mesopotamia and settled in Canaan, they became known as Israelites. Some of these Israelites later went to Egypt; then, in the 1200s B.C., Moses led the Israelites out of Egypt. After the Exodus, the Hebrews traveled to Canaan under Moses and reentered the promised land under Joshua.

The Canaanites were warlike people. They lived in walled cities built on hilltops for safety. These cities were easy to defend and difficult to attack. The Israelites were influenced by the Canaanites in both positive and negative ways. They learned new skills such as farming, weaving, pottery making, and building, but they were also influenced by the idol-worship of Baal and Astarte.

Research the conquest and settlement of Canaan. Use any resource (an encyclopedia, nonfiction book, historical novel, or the Internet). We recommend the following:

Books

The Victor Journey through the Bible ●—♥
Read: "The Twelve Spies" (74-75), "The Bronze Serpant" (76-77), "Crossing the Jordan" (78-79), "Jericho Captured" (80-81).

Encyclopedia of the Bible (Nelson's Illustrated) ♥
Read: "Joshua" (206), "The Canaanites" (56-57).

The Holman Bible Atlas ●— ♥
Read: "Conquest and Settlement" (75-88).

The The Ancient Hebrews ♦
Read: Chapter 1 In the Beginning (6-20).

Introduction to Jewish History: From Abraham to the Sages ♦
Read: Chapter 4 The Promised Land (28-33).

The Bible Comes Alive: Volume Two, Moses to David ♦
Read: "Joshua and the Conquest of Canaan" (79).

Sketches of Jewish Social Life ♦
Read: Chapter 1 Palestine Eighteen Centuries Ago.

Ancient Israel: From Abraham to the Roman Destruction of the Temple ★
Read: Chapter 3 "The Settlement in Canaan."

Bible History: Old Testament ★
Read: Volume III Israel in Canaan Under Joshua and the Judges.

Resources recommended in ♦several lessons, ★ several units, ♥other HOW Units. ●—Key Resource (see beginning of unit or page 32).

Heart of Wisdom Publishing   349

The Gifts of the Jews ◆
Read: Chapter 5 Canaan: From Tribe to Nation.

Joshua in the Promised Land by Miriam Chaikin
A vivid retelling of the Bible story of Joshua, who as the successor to Moses was commanded by God to lead the Israelites in their conquest of Canaan, the Promised Land. "A good starting point for a discussion of the Bible and biblical times." (Booklist review). (November 1990) Clarion Books; ISBN: 0395547970. Reading level: Ages 9-12.

The Promise of the Land: The Inheritance of the Land of Canaan by the Israelites by Moshe Weinfeld
Description: Weinfeld approaches his subject from three viewpoints: historical, using the Bible as a source; literary-comparatist, comparing Patriarchal stories of settlement with Greek and Roman foundation myths; exegetical, explaining that in Judaism, land is a gift from God. He emphasizes the ethical weight of God's Promise of the Land, and how failure to achieve it was seen as a reflection of sin and lack of faith; thus illustrating the importance of biblical tradition to one of the most troubled issues of modern history. (1993) University of California Press; ISBN: 0520075102.

Victorious Christian Living by Alan Redpath
Description: Using the Old Testament Book of Joshua as his launching pad, Alan Redpath shows his readers how to enter God's Promised Land and enjoy victorious Christian living. As Dr. Redpath goes through the exciting Book of Joshua chapter by chapter, he notes that the whole land of Canaan was given to the people of Israel, but they could possess only the portion they claimed. He then draws the parallel that the greatest of saints are the greatest receivers. (Review by Crosslife Books http://www.crosslifebooks.com/) Fleming H. Revell; ISBN: 0800754905.

Conquest of Canaan by Jessie Penn-Lewis
Description: The Christian experience is related to the crossing of the Jordan by Joshua and the Israelites. Christian Literature Crusade; ISBN: 0875089437.

Egypt, Canaan, and Israel in Ancient Times by Donald B. Redford
Description: Covering the time span from the Paleolithic Period to the destruction of Jerusalem in 586 B.C., the eminent Egyptologist Donald Redford explores 3,000 years of uninterrupted contact between Egypt and Western Asia across the Sinai land bridge. The first section deals with the history and prehistory of Egypt and the Levant down to the Hyksos, drawing on both archaeological and textual evidence. The second section deals with the Egyptian New Kingdom and its Asian Empire; only then do the characters and events of traditional biblical history make an appearance. Princeton Univ Pr; ISBN: 0691000867.

Internet Sources

The Occupation of Canaan 1250-1050
Description: The Hebrews: A Learning Module from Washington State University, by Richard Hooker.

Joshua and the Promised Land: An Interactive Multimedia Bible Study
Description: This exploration focuses on four stories from the biblical book of Joshua. In each story you can learn about Joshua and nurture your spiritual life.

Ancient Canaan
Description: An overview of daily life, government, social order, and industry in ancient Canaan.

Bible Study Lessons in the Book of Joshua
Description: Seventeen Bible lessons by Dr. Lester Hutson from Berean Baptist Church.

Book of Joshua: Setting the Scene
Description: Bible study from Joyful Heart Ministries.

Entering the Promised Land: Memorial & Dedication at the Jordan
Description: Bible study on Joshua 3:1-5:12 from Joyful Heart Ministries. Also see The Battle of Jericho.

The Conquest of Canaan
Description: Overview from Quartz Hill School of Theology.

The Settlement of Canaan by Gerald Larue
Description: Chapter 9 from *Old Testament Life and Literature*.

Ancient Canaan Unit
Description: Study unit from The William Penn Charter School.

Ancient Canaan/Israel/Palestine
Description: A learning module of the Middle East & Inner Asia from the Research Institute at Richard Stockton College of New Jersey. This section of the module pays close attention to Israel from ancient times through 1917.

Step 3 Expand

Choose and complete one of the following activities:

Activity 1: Write an Essay
Write a traditional essay about the Canaanites; include: what they looked like; who and how they worshiped; marriage customs; approximate population;

Resources recommended in ♦several lessons, ★ several units, ♥other HOW Units. ●━Key Resource (see beginning of unit or page 32).

Heart of Wisdom Publishing   351

government; basic laws; what they used for money; entertainment; clothing; food; what their homes were like; their educational system and written language; the roles of men and women; their weapons and scientific achievements; transportation; agriculture, etc. Refer to "Structure of the Traditional Essay" and "Sample of a Traditional Essay" in *Writers INC*, or How to Write an Essay. Younger students can copy one or two sentences or narrate (tell back) what has been learned.

Activity 2: Add to Your Time Line Book
Add the conquest of Canaan to your Time Line Book. Include Joshua, Jericho, Rahab, Gideon, Achan, Caleb, Ephraim, and Manasseh. Refer to Reproducible Maps, Charts, Timelines & Illustrations (43-44).

Activity 3: Create an Outline
Write an outline of the book of Joshua.

Activity 4: Contrast and Compare
From your research, make a contrast-and-compare graphic (see page 26) on Israelite and Canaanite warfare.

Activity 5: Fill Out Worksheets
Fill out the following worksheets with a child (elementary level):
Exploring Canaan, Crossing Jordan, The Fall of Jericho, Judges, Gideon.

Activity 6: Write a Description
Write about Gideon's surprise attack against the Midianites; minimum 100 words. Younger students can narrate (orally tell) the story.

Step 4 Excel

Discuss with your parents how the Canaanite's religion affected the other areas of their society. For example, how did their beliefs affect laws, government, and other aspects of their daily lives? Discuss how you think Christianity affects or has affected your society. Discuss the role of television, magazines, and fads in our culture today. How do they influence Christians? Is this similar to the Canaanite influence on the Israelites?

Explain orally to your parents what you've learned in this lesson about God's grace to the Hebrews. Correct all written work to demonstrate correct punctuation and spelling, and effective use of grammar. Add corrected written work or any illustrations to your portfolio. Add new words you learned in this lesson into your Vocabulary Notebook (see page 22).

The Twelve Tribes of Israel

185-166/194-198

The Narrated Bible

Step 1 Excite

God changed Jacob's name to Israel. Israel had twelve sons: Reuben, Simeon, Levi, Judah, Dan, Naphtali, Gad, Asher, Issachar, Zebulun, Joseph, and Benjamin. From these twelve sons of Israel came the twelve tribes of Israel. (The Levites were dispersed throughout the eleven tribes. Two of Jacob's grandsons, Ephraim and Manasseh, were designated as individual tribes.)

Read Gen. 29-31; 35:22-26; 49:3-27; Deut. 33:6-29; Num. 1:2; 26:5-50; Josh. 7:14.

Step 2 Examine

The tribes were united in one great kingdom until after the reign of David's son Solomon. After Solomon died a power struggle ensued, resulting in a division of the people. The northern ten tribes were still called Israel, but the southern two tribes, and the land which they occupied, were called Judea, after the name of the larger of the two tribes, Judah. This is the name from which the words "Jew" and "Jewish" were derived. The tribe of Levi formed the priesthood (Moses, Aaron, and John The Baptist are Levites). King David and Jesus Christ descended from the tribe of Judah.

In Matthew 19:28 Jesus prophesied that His twelve disciples would sit on twelve thrones judging the twelve tribes of Israel. The twelve gates surrounding the New Jerusalem, and guarded by twelve angels, are named after the twelve tribes of Israel (Revelation 21:12).

Research the tribes of Israel. Use any resource (an encyclopedia, nonfiction book, historical novel, or the Internet). We recommend the following:

Books

Encyclopedia of the Bible (Nelson's Illustrated) ♥
Read: Pages refering to the Tweleve Tribes" (23, 26, 28, 116, 150, 158-159, 162-163, see chart on page 198).

The Holman Bible Atlas ☞ ♥
Read: "The Tribes of Israel" (83-84).

Internet Sources

ⓘ Israel - God's Miracle Nation
Description: Details the deportation of Northern tribes to Assyria in 722 B.C., and suggests the reconvening of the tribes in Israel where they remain.

Resources recommended in ◆several lessons, ★several units, ♥other HOW Units. ☞Key Resource (see beginning of unit or page 32).

(i) The Tribes Of Israel
Description: Overview of the tribes from BibleStudy.com, with links to related articles.

(i) Israel - Twelve Tribes
Description: Furnishes an overview of the Twelve Tribes of Israel and offers a map representing the apportionment of land to Jacob's children.

(i) Ten Lost Tribes of Israel - PBS Nova
Description: PBS Nova guide examines the mystery of the ten lost tribes of Israel which were scattered into oblivion by the Assyrians in the 8th century B.C.

(i) Twelve Tribes of Israel
Description: Offers the twelve tribal emblems and brief biblical quotations suggesting their stories.

(i) Twelve Tribes of Israel - Encyclopedia Britannica
Description: Provides a history of the establishment of the twelve tribes of Israel and describes how the term Israelite came into common use.

Step 3 Expand

Activity 1: Make a Family Tree
Show the genealogy from Abraham to the twelve tribes. Refer to Reproducible Maps, Charts, Timelines & Illustrations ♥ (17).

Step 4 Excel

Share what you have learned about the twelve tribes with a friend or family member. Correct all written work to demonstrate correct punctuation and spelling, and effective use of grammar. Add corrected written work or any illustrations to your portfolio. Add new words you learned in this lesson into your Vocabulary Notebook (see page 22).

Ancient Israel Geography

Step 1 Excite

The stories of the Bible tell of great journeys, cities, battles, histories of whole nations, and the lives of individual people. The goal of this lesson is to help you acquire an appreciation of the physical world in which people lived, and ultimately to learn to think geographically. Maps, globes, and atlases should be daily resources available to answer questions about location, regions, climates, the movement of people, and the relationship between places and the characteristics of the people who live there.

The Holman Bible Atlas provides maps and factual information on all main historical periods of the Bible, plus geographical background, giving the reader an insight into the world of the Bible. Use *The Holman Bible Atlas* or another resource to trace or copy at least two copies of a map of the Old Testament World and the Roman Empire during the time of Christ.

Step 2 Examine

Today's Israel includes four general areas:

1. The Coastal Plain is a fertile, humid, and thickly populated area stretching along the Mediterranean Sea.
2. The Central Highlands include the Hills of Galilee in the north, with the country's highest elevation at Mt. Meron, and the arid Judean Hills to the south.
3. The Jordan Rift Valley, with the country's lowest point (399 meters below sea level) at the Dead Sea.
4. The Negev Desert, which accounts for about half of Israel's area.

Research the geography of ancient Israel. Use any resource (an atlas, or the Internet). We recommend the following:

Books

> The Victor Journey through the Bible ●—♥
> Browze Maps through out the book showing where the events took place.

> Encyclopedia of the Bible (Nelson's Illustrated) ♥
> Browze Maps in Section 1 (18-34) and Part 7 (274).

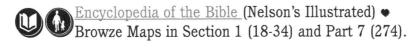

Resources recommended in ◆several lessons, ★ several units, ♥ other HOW Units. ●—Key Resource (see beginning of unit or page 32).

Heart of Wisdom Publishing   355

The Holy Land (The Ancient World Series) ♦
See description in the Resource section.

The Atlas of Jewish History by Martin Gilbert, Eli Barnavi (Editor)
Description: This atlas traces the history, the worldwide migrations, the achievements, and the lives of the Jewish people from ancient Mesopotamia to the present day. Filled with unusual facts and details, the atlas offers new appreciation and understanding of the crucial role played by a people in the making of the modern world. (January 1993) William Morrow & Co; ISBN: 0688122647.

A Historical Atlas of the Jewish People: From the Time of the Patriarchs to the Present by Eli Barnavi (Editor)
Description: Rich with chronologies and commentaries by leading experts and featuring hundreds of brilliantly detailed maps, photographs, and drawings, this beautifully designed volume sets forth this amazing saga pictorially in an authoritative work of scholarship. (January 1995) Schocken Books; ISBN: 0805241272.

Internet Sources

Daniel's Digs
Description: See the real beauty of the Sinai Desert and many other things that make the Sinai the special place that it is.

Videos

Land & Word: A Biblical Journey
Three videos. See description in the Ancient Israel Unit Resources section.

Step 3 Expand

Choose and complete one of the following activities:

Activity 1: Answer Questions
Answer the following questions about Israel:

1. What is the latitude and longitude?
2. Which countries border it?
3. Which bodies of water are closest to it?
4. Which bodies of water are within its borders?
5. How much area does it cover?
6. Which continent is it in?
7. Is it larger or smaller than the state you live in?

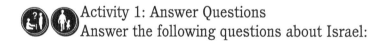

Underlined text refers to Internet link at http://Homeschool-Books.com

8. Does it have mountain ranges, deserts, or other geographical characteristics?

Activity 2: Map Work
Locate the following modern territories on a map of the eastern Mediterranean area: Jordan, Israel, West Bank, Gaza Strip, Syria, Lebanon, Saudi Arabia, Egypt, Cyprus, Turkey, and Sinai Peninsula.

Activity 3: Write a Description
Find a painting or drawing that depicts a place in Israel. Try to write a description of this place that is as faithful to the artist's rendering as possible. How hard was it to capture this picture in words? Younger students can narrate (orally tell) their description.

Activity 4: Make a Cookie Map
Make a cookie map of the Bible Lands. You will need: a Bible Atlas, a cookie recipe, a can of frosting, a variety of chocolate chips, mini fun chips, or candy dots, and several tubes of cake decorating gels in a variety of colors. Bake one large cookie that will be your map. Frost the cookie (this becomes the glue), and then use chocolate chips to locate selected cities or towns. Use the decorating gels to draw rivers, lakes, parks, or centers of mineral resources on the map. Take a photograph of your cookie map and include the photo in your portfolio.

Activity 5: Create Illustrations
Add map illustrations (create your own or make photo copies from books or print outs from the Internet) showing the journeys of Abraham, Paul, or Jesus.

Activity 6: Play a Game
You'll need a Bible, *The Holman Bible Atlas* (or a similar resource), and a timer. To play: A parent looks up a Bible story and calls out the title (Examples: Tower of Babel, Crossing the Red Sea, A Fiery Furnace) or a person's name (Examples: King David, Ruth, Paul). The student uses the index to find a map or illustration of the Bible story as the parent times the student. Do this for several different events.

Step 4 Excel

Share your work from Step 3 with someone. Explain what you have learned in this lesson. Correct all written work to demonstrate correct punctuation and spelling, and effective use of grammar. Add corrected written work or any illustrations to your portfolio. Add new words you learned in this lesson into your Vocabulary Notebook (see page 22).

Resources recommended in ◆several lessons, ★ several units, ♥ other HOW Units. ☞ Key Resource (see beginning of unit or page 32).

Heart of Wisdom Publishing   357

Period of the Judges 1235-1050 B.C.

346-383

The Narrated Bible

Step 1 Excite

During the period of the Judges, the Israelites were influenced by their Canaanite neighbors. They forgot God's past deliverance and began worshipping Ba'al (and the fertility gods). The Israelites never abandoned the worship of Yahweh; they simply added the worship of Ba'al to their worship of Yahweh. Because of this, the leaders were unable to bring unity to the people and could not provide any spiritual leadership.

Brainstorm and discuss: What is peer pressure? Why are we influenced by those with whom we associate? Is an act permissible because everybody else is doing it? If you were following a crowd whose collective thinking began to deteriorate (daring and risky—such as taking drugs, shoplifting, performing some act of violence), what would you do? Is it true that what we think and do affects others, either directly or indirectly? Do you need to be as careful about selecting television programs, movies, music, and books as you are about selecting friends?

The Bible speaks of choosing friends carefully: *Make no friendship with an angry man; and with a furious man thou shalt not go: Lest thou learn his ways, and get a snare to thy soul.* (Proverbs 22:24-25). Paul wrote in Romans 12:2: *And be not conformed to this world: but be ye transformed by the renewing of your mind, that ye may prove what is that good, and acceptable, and perfect, will of God.* The Bible says that those who compare themselves among themselves are not wise (2 Corinthians 10:12). It is better to trust in God than to put your confidence in man.

Step 2 Examine

The occupation of Canaan by the Hebrews was a gradual process (Judges 2:3). The preliminary conquest was completed within six or seven years after the crossing of the Jordan. The Israelites gained control by winning a series of battles at Jericho, Ai, and other places. Their control was far from complete, however, and other people sometimes dominated the area. During this period, after the death of Joshua, the Israelites were led by those who would later be called judges.

The historical time frame of the Judges was from the death of Joshua (about 1235 B.C.) until the establishment of the kingdom under David (about 1050 B.C.). The book of Judges takes its name from the title by which the men who governed Israel during this period were known. There was no permanent, central government, only the guidance of judges who were appointed by God (Judges 3:15; 4:6; 6:12; etc.). Gideon, Deborah, and Samson are judges who became national heroes. The last and most significant of the judges was Saul (who is usually considered the first King).

The Book of Judges asks why Israel failed to realize the prosperity promised under their Covenant with God. The answer is sounded clearly that Israel, due to disobedience, is at fault, and not God. He has remained faithful and merciful, but His people have not.

Read the book of Judges.

I. Background: Failure to drive out the Canaanites (1:1-2:5)
II. Introduction: Cycle of Apostasy (2:6-3:6)
III. Cycles: Israelites did evil in the eyes of the Lord (3:7-16)
    A. Othniel (3:7-11)
    B. Ehud (3:12-31)
    C. Deborah (4-5)
    D. Gideon (6-8)
    E. Minor Leaders (9-10:5)
    F. Jephthah (10:6-12:7)
    G. Other Minor Judges (12:8-12:15)
    H. Samson (13-16)
IV. Tribal Depravity: Everyone did as he saw fit (17-21)
    A. Danites (17-18)
    B. Benjamites (19-21)

Do more research about the period of the Judges. Use any resource (an encyclopedia, nonfiction book, historical novel, or the Internet). We recommend the following:

Books

The Victor Journey through the Bible ⊶♥
Read: "Gideon's Call" (86), "Judges of Israel" (87)"Gideon's 300" (88-89). Also see "The Story of Ruth" (94-95).

Encyclopedia of the Bible (Nelson's Illustrated) ♥
Read: "The Time of the Judges" (24-25). "Judges" (207). Also see "Ruth" (214).

Who's Who in the Bible ⊶ ♥
Read: "Time of the Judges" (18-21).

The Holman Bible Atlas ⊶ ♥
Read: "The Days of the Judges" (89-93).

Resources recommended in ◆several lessons, ★ several units, ♥ other HOW Units. ⊶ Key Resource (see beginning of unit or page 32).

The The Ancient Hebrews ♦
Read: Judges and Kings (14).

Judges and Ruth by Stephen Dray
Description: The Book of Judges describes a large period of internal troubles in the history of the children of Israel; a time when the Judges ruled. What a contrast, seen as all the more serious in light of the successful period under the leadership of Joshua. Stephen Dray points out the important lessons to be learned from this period. The book of Ruth is more than a love story; it shows God to have been at work, ensuring the continuation of the genealogical line from which the future Messiah would be born.

Internet Sources

The Occupation and Period of the Judges
Description: Overview of this period from BibleTutor.com.

Book of Joshua: Setting the Scene
Description: Bible study from Joyful Heart Ministries.

The Battle of Jericho
Description: Bible study on Joshua 5:13-6:27 from Joyful Heart Ministries.

Conquest or Settlement? History, Literary, and Theology Issues
Description: A survey of the historical problems encountered in comparing the biblical books of Joshua and Judges.

Introduction to Judges
Description: Outline from netbible.com.

Step 3 Expand

Choose and complete one of the following activities:

Activity 1: Make an Outline
Outline the Book of Judges. Refer to outline example.

Activity 2: Add to Your Time Line Book
Add the period of Judges to your Time Line Book. Include Othniel, Ehud, Deborah, Gideon, Jephthah, Samson, and Ruth. Refer to Reproducible Maps, Charts, Timelines & Illustrations ♥ (47-55).

Underlined text refers to Internet link at http://Homeschool-Books.com

Activity 3: Compare-and-Contrast
Create a contrast-and-compare graphic (see page 26) comparing and contrasting Samson's life with that of Israel as a people.

Activity 4: Write an Essay
Write an essay on peer pressure. Compare peer pressure in your life with the influence on the Israelites by their Canaanite neighbors. Younger students can narrate (orally tell) their thoughts on peer pressure.

Activity 5: Memorize Scripture Passages
Analyze and memorize Proverbs 22:24-25 and Romans 12:2.

Activity 6: Write a Biography
Write a biography (minimum 250 words) on one of the following: Deborah, Gideon, or Samson.

Activity 7: Write a Summary
The story of Ruth occurs during the reign of the Judges. Read the Book of Ruth. Write a condensed version of this story in your own words. Younger students can copy one or two sentences or narrate (tell back) the story.

Activity 8: Write an Essay
Write a brief essay on the role of a judge during this period in Israel's history.

Step 4 Excel

Share what you have learned about the Judges by filling out the following worksheet with a child (elementary level): Judges. Add new words you learned in this lesson into your Vocabulary Notebook (see page 22).

Resources recommended in ◆several lessons, ★ several units, ❤ other HOW Units. ●—Key Resource (see beginning of unit or page 32).

Heart of Wisdom Publishing   361

United Kingdom 1050-922 B.C.

384-392

Step 1 Excite

The Narrated Bible

Two hundred years after occupying and holding lands in Palestine, the Hebrews united to form a single state under a single monarch. During this period, Saul, David, and Solomon were kings and Jerusalem was the capital of the kingdom. In the previous years, the Hebrews had been ruled loosely by judges. In 961 B.C., King Solomon built the First Temple. After the reign of Solomon, the kingdom was divided into North and South.

Timeline

    c. 1050 B.C. Kingdom of Israel is established. Saul is Israel's first king.

    c. 1010 B.C. David becomes Israel's king.

    c. 970 B.C. David's son Solomon becomes Israel's king.

    c. 961 B.C. The Jerusalem Temple is completed by Solomon.

Saul, the first king of ancient Israel, reigned from about 1050-1010 B.C. David ruled from around the year 1010 until around 970 B.C. His son Solomon ruled from 970-920 B.C. The kingdom established by David and expanded by Solomon would see Israel at its greatest power and its greatest geographical control. Historians refer to this time period as the Middle Iron Age (1020-842 B.C.).

Step 2 Examine

Research the United Kingdom of Israel. Use any resource (an encyclopedia, non-fiction book, historical novel, or the Internet). We recommend the following:

Books

    The Victor Journey through the Bible ●—♥
    Read: Stories of Saul, David and Solomon (102-134).

    Encyclopedia of the Bible (Nelson's Illustrated) ♥
    Read: "The First Kings" (26-27), The Philistines (58-59), THree Temples" (160-161) 1and 2 Samual (208-209), 1 and 2 Kings (210-211).

    The Holman Bible Atlas ●—♥
    Read: "The Kingdom of David and Solomon" (102-114).

    Introduction to Jewish History: From Abraham to the Sages ♦
    Read: Chapter 2 God Remembers Israel.

Underlined text refers to Internet link at http://Homeschool-Books.com

Ancient Israel: From Abraham to the Roman Destruction of the Temple ★
Read: Chapter 4 The United Monarchy: Saul, David and Solomon.

Internet Sources

Kingdom Period
Description: Chronicles the emergence of Judah as the dominant tribe of Israel and the establishment of the royal line of David.

Monarchy, 1050 to 920 BC - Hebrew History
Description: A learning module detailing the Hebrews' establishment of a single monarchical state in Israel under kings Saul, David, and Solomon.

United Monarchy
Description: Briefly describes ancient Israel's shift to monarchy, beginning with the reign of Saul. Includes related archaeological and biblical readings.

Step 3 Expand

Activity 1: Write a Summary
Write a description of the united monarchy. Younger students can copy one or two sentences or narrate (tell back) what has been learned.

Activity 2: Contrast and Compare
Make a contrast-and-compare graphic (see page 26) for King Saul, King David, and King Solomon. You may prefer to do this after you complete the King Saul Lesson, King David Lesson, and King Solomon Lesson.

Activity 3: Make and Play a Game
Use your Bible or a Topical Bible to find at least five major events involving each king (King Saul, King David, and King Solomon). Write the events on index cards or slips of paper. Have each member of your family draw a card and identify the king associated with that card.

Step 4 Excel

Share with a friend or family member what you have learned about this time period in ancient Israel. Correct all written work to demonstrate correct punctuation and spelling, and effective use of grammar. Add corrected written work or any illustrations to your portfolio.

Resources recommended in ♦several lessons, ★ several units, ♥ other HOW Units. ●—Key Resource (see beginning of unit or page 32).

Heart of Wisdom Publishing   363

King Saul

Step 1 Excite

Brainstorm and discuss: Have you ever asked God for something without asking Him if it was His will? Would you really want something if it wasn't His will? Why or why not?

The Israelites originally consisted of many tribes, each having its own leader or king. After the Philistines attacked this, they established an organized form of government. There were three kings; Saul, David, and Solomon.

In Samuel Chapter 8, Israel demands a king (verses 4-9). Samuel tells the people what to expect from an earthly king in verses 10-22. Samuel opposed the kingship. God permitted the establishment of the monarchy, but in speaking to Samuel, The Lord said of it, *Listen to all that the people are saying to you; it is not you they have rejected, but they have rejected Me as their King. As they have done from the day I brought them up out of Egypt until this day, forsaking Me and serving other gods, so they are doing to you. Now listen to them; but warn them solemnly and let them know what the king who will reign over them will do.* (1 Samuel 8:7-9)

Step 2 Examine

Saul, a Benjamite, was a strong central military authority. He was both a warrior and a charismatic leader. He was also subject to fits of melancholy and jealousy. Saul was secretly anointed by Samuel before being publicly chosen by lot. He was anointed by Samuel to fight the Philistines in the name of Yahweh. His first success was against the Ammorites at Jabesh-gilead. For some years he defended the central hills from the Philistines, but he and several of his sons fell in the disastrous battle of Gilboa, and the Philistines once more occupied the hill country. Saul succeeded in uniting the Israelite tribes under one king. His son Jonathan was a very close friend of David. Saul reigned from about 1020-1000 B.C.

Before his fall, Saul made a series of grave mistakes, beginning with the offering of a sacrifice, which was to be performed only by the priests. His behavior degenerated from unwise to foolish, including ordering his military forces to go without food until they had defeated the enemy, and consulting with the witch of Endor to contact the dead. His jealousy over David's military success and popularity with the people resulted in Saul attempting to murder David. The last chapters of Samuel tell of the war with the Philistines that ended in disaster for both Israel and Saul: He committed suicide, his army was dispersed, and his sons were killed.

Underlined text refers to Internet link at http://Homeschool-Books.com

Read about the major events in Saul's life: Made king of Israel (1 Samuel 9; 10); Defeats the Philistines (1 Samuel 13; 14:46,52); Reproved by Samuel (1 Samuel 13:11-14); Tries to kill David (1 Samuel 19); His life spared by David (1 Samuel 24:5-8); His death (1 Samuel 31; 1 Chronicles 10:13).

Do more research about King Saul. Use any resource (an encyclopedia, non-fiction book, historical novel, or the Internet). We recommend the following:

Books

The Victor Journey through the Bible ●━♥
Read: "Saul is Made King" (102-103).

Encyclopedia of the Bible (Nelson's Illustrated) ♥
Read: "The First Kings" (26-27), (160-161).

The Holman Bible Atlas ●━ ♥
Read: "Saul: King of Israel" (97-101).

Pharaohs and Kings: A Biblical Quest ●━★
Read: "The Lion Man" (195-220). See description in the Ancient Egypt Key Resources.

Ancient Israel: From Abraham to the Roman Destruction of the Temple ★
Read "Saul" (92-100).

The Bible Comes Alive: Volume Two, Moses to David ◆
Read: "Saul and David in the Light of History" (123).

Internet Sources

Bible History: Old Testament
Read: Chapter 5 The Calling of Saul; Occasion of his Interview with Samuel; Samuel Communes with Saul; Saul is Anointed King; The Three 'Signs'; Their Deeper Significance.

Saul
Description: Overview of the first king of Israel, and links to passages from the Book of Samuel as well as relevant people and places. From BibleTutor.com.

Saul - Encyclopedia.com
Description: Thumbnail biography of the first king of the Hebrews.

Resources recommended in ◆several lessons, ★ several units, ♥ other HOW Units. ●━Key Resource (see beginning of unit or page 32).

Saul - MSN Encarta
Description: Brief description of the reign of the first king of ancient Israel who died during a battle with the Philistines in the 11th century B.C.

Second Part of Saul's Life
Description: Examines the latter half of Saul's life, which was marked by an overwhelming jealousy of King David.

Step 3 Expand

Choose and complete one of the following activities:

Activity 1: Write a Biography
Compile information from your research into a one-page biography of King Saul. Include the major events in his life (see previous page).

Activity 2: Add to Your Time Line Book
Add Saul to your Time Line Book. Include major events in his life (see previous page). Refer to Reproducible Maps, Charts, Timelines & Illustrations ◓━ ❤ (55, 87).

Activity 3: Fill Out a Person Worksheet
Compile information from your research to fill out a Person Worksheet about King Saul.

Activity 4: Write a Short Story
Recount an adventure of King Saul; this written account should include as much description of the character as possible, as well as dialogue with other characters.

Activity 5: Create a Cartoon Strip
Make a cartoon strip recounting an adventure of King Saul.

Activity 6: Sew a Quilt Block
Patchwork Partners provides directions and a brief Bible study relating to this lesson on the Internet. Click Bible Blocks: Coronation.

Step 4 Excel

Share what you have learned about King Saul with a friend or family member. Correct all written work to demonstrate correct punctuation and spelling, and effective use of grammar. Add corrected written work or any illustrations to your portfolio. Add new words you learned in this lesson into your Vocabulary Notebook (see page 22).

Underlined text refers to Internet link at http://Homeschool-Books.com

King David 1000-960 B.C.

Step 1 Excite

434-490

The Narrated Bible

David, the youngest son of Jessie and a shepherd, was anointed by Samuel to be successor to Saul. When Saul died, David rose to power by conquering the south and then Jerusalem. The northern tribes of Israel voluntarily submitted to David. David was the first king of a united Israel. David's rule began around the year 1050 B.C. and lasted until around 960 B.C. David was a valiant warrior and an outstanding leader. He was skillful at playing musical instruments and gifted in his ability to write Psalms (Tehilim) or songs of praise to God. He brought the Ark of the Covenant to Jerusalem Jerusalem and made it the capital. God promised David that one of his sons would always be on the throne, and the New Testament finds this promise fulfilled in Jesus. Several accounts of his accomplishments occur in the Old Testament, mainly in the books of Samuel, Kings, and Chronicles.

Brainstorm with your family and make a list of things you know about David's life.

Step 2 Examine

Read about the major events in David's life: A shepherd (1 Samuel 16:11); Kills a lion and a bear (1 Samuel 17:34-36); Anointed king by the prophet Samuel (I Samuel 16:1,13); Kills Goliath (1 Samuel 17); friend of Jonathan (1 Samuel 18:1-4); Popularity (1 Samuel 18); defeats the Philistines (1 Samuel 19:8); Refrains from killing Saul (1 Samuel 24); Assembles thirty-thousand men to escort the ark of the covenant to Jerusalem with music and thanksgiving (2 Samuel 6:1-5).

Research David's reign. Use any resource (an encyclopedia, nonfiction book, historical novel, or the Internet). We recommend the following:

Books

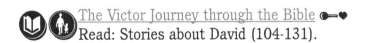

The Victor Journey through the Bible ⬤━❤
Read: Stories about David (104-131).

Encyclopedia of the Bible (Nelson's Illustrated) ❤
Read: "The First Kings" (26-27), (160-161) "1and 2 Samual" (208-209), "1 and 2 Kings" (210-211).

The Holman Bible Atlas ⬤━ ❤
Read: "The Reign of David" (102-106).

Introduction to Jewish History: From Abraham to the Sages ◆
Read: "King David" (102-108).

Pharaohs and Kings: A Biblical Quest ⊶★
Read: "The Beloved" (221-236). See description in Ancient Egypt Key Resources.

Ancient Israel: Its Life and Institutions ★
Read: The Kingdom of David (133).

Ancient Israel: From Abraham to the Roman Destruction of the Temple ★
Read: "David" (100-108).

Internet Sources

Davidic Covenant
Description: Examines the story of God's promise to David, an event as important as the covenants made with Abraham and Jeremiah.

Davidic Kingdom
Description: Overview of the Davidic kingdom of Israel and profiles of King David and King Saul.

History of the Davidic Monarchy
Description: Chronicles the reigns of King David, King Solomon, and the kings of Judah, from Rehoboam to Cyrus' edict of return from exile.

Reign of David
Description: Find out when the forty-year rule of the second Hebrew king began. Includes relevant links. From BibleTutor.com.

Special Status of the Davidic Monarchy
Description: Rav Mosheh Lichtenstein's essay distinguishes the Davidic monarchy from other Jewish/Israelite monarchies.

Story of Saul and David
Description: Chronicles the deuteronomic history of the Israelites as told through the story of the two kings of Israel; David and Saul.

Videos

Biography - King David
Description: This edition of *Biography*, the long-running documentary series from A&E, explores the life of King David.

King David (1985)

Description: Richard Gere plays the role of David, the shepherd boy who slew Goliath and later ascended to the throne of Israel. ASIN: 6300213927. PG-13 rating (some nudity).

Step 3 Expand

Choose and complete one of the following activities:

Activity 1: Write a Biography
Compile information from your research into a chronological biography of King David. Identify the parts of his life that show a character has changed his attitudes or ways of behavior. Younger students can dictate and/or illustrate their story.

Activity 2: Add to Your Time Line Book
Add David to your Time Line Book. Include major events in his life. Refer to Reproducible Maps, Charts, Timelines & Illustrations ♥ (61-65).

Activity 3: Create an Outline
Outline David's life and ministry from I Samuel 15-24. Refer to the Outline Example.

Activity 4: Write a Summary
First Chronicles 12 through 20 record the results of David's sin. Write a summary of David's failure and God's forgiveness.

Activity 5: Write a Story
Write as if you were David, telling the story of his life to young Solomon.

Activity 6: Sew a Quilt Block
Patchwork Partners provides directions and a brief Bible study relating to this lesson on the Internet. Click Bible Blocks: David's Crown.

Step 4 Excel

Share what you have learned about King David with a friend or family member. Correct all written work to demonstrate correct punctuation and spelling, and effective use of grammar. Add corrected written work or any illustrations to your portfolio. Add new words you learned in this lesson into your Vocabulary Notebook (see page 22).

Resources recommended in ◆several lessons, ★ several units, ♥ other HOW Units. ●━ Key Resource (see beginning of unit or page 32).

Heart of Wisdom Publishing   369

Jerusalem

Step 1 Excite

The Narrated Bible

By bringing the Ark of the Covenant to his city, David established Jerusalem, both symbolically and practically, as both a religious and political capital. Jerusalem is known as The City of David. God chose the city of Jerusalem as His own, and His claim is eternal and necessary for the outworking of His redemptive plan for the earth. God Himself refers to Jerusalem, and to no other place on earth, as My City (Isaiah 45:13) or more often, My Holy Mountain (Isaiah 11:9; 56:7; 57:13; Ezekiel 20:40; Joel 2:1; 3:17). Psalms 122:6, tells us to Pray for the peace of Jerusalem.

Jews were repeatedly persecuted, massacred, and subjected to exile. In spite of this, the Jewish presence in Jerusalem remained constant and enduring. Do you know who owns Jerusalem today?

Step 2 Examine

In the early Canaanite period, Jerusalem (known as Jebus) was one of many independent city-states that existed in the region; it was a Canaanite village. This was before the time of King David. David then selected the city to be the capital of Israel. Jerusalem became the religious center when David brought the Ark of the Covenant to the city and Solomon built the First Temple. In New Testament times, Jesus visited Jerusalem as a child (Luke 2). He also came to Jerusalem a number of times as an adult, teaching and working miracles. Jesus was crucified in Jerusalem and appeared to his disciples there after his resurrection (Luke 24; John 20). The disciples received the Holy Spirit in Jerusalem during the Feast of Weeks (Shavuot or Pentecost). Paul was arrested in Jerusalem (Acts 21:17-22:30), imprisoned in Caesarea, and finally sent to Rome. The Jerusalem Temple was destroyed in A.D. 70 in the Jewish Revolt against Rome.

Do research about Jerusalem in Bible times. Use any resource (an encyclopedia, nonfiction book, historical novel, or the Internet). We recommend the following:

Books

> The Victor Journey through the Bible ●━♥
> Read: David Captures Jerusalem" (122-123), "The Story of Jersusalem" (172-173).

> Encyclopedia of the Bible (Nelson's Illustrated) ♥
> Read: "A Brief History of Jersusalem" (38-39), "The Tree Temples" (160-161), "Trade and Commerce" (12-125). .

Underlined text refers to Internet link at http://Homeschool-Books.com

The Holman Bible Atlas ⊶ ♥
Read: Jerusalem: City of David and Solomon (110-112).

The Holy Land (The Ancient World Series) ◆
Read: Jerusalem at the Death of Herod (44-45), Woe to Thee Jerusalem (72-92).

The Young Reader's Encyclopedia of Jewish History ◆
Read: Look in the index for Jerusalem entries in different time periods.

The Kingfisher History Encyclopedia ⊶ ♥
Read: Look in the index for Jerusalem entries.

Ancient Israel: Its Life and Institutions ★
Read: The Temple at Jerusalem (312-329).

Step by Step to Jerusalem
Description: A Drawing, Coloring and Work Book For Children by Hersh Goldman. (47 pages) An enjoyable book that teaches children about going up Step by Step to Jerusalem. Fun-to-do projects to complete, and scenes of Jerusalem to color, with explanations of each scene. Available from Messengers of Truth.

Internet Sources

Jerusalem Time Travel
Description: Get ready for an incredible tour through one of the world's most fascinating cities—the Holy City of Jerusalem—from its ancient beginnings, through its golden glory, to its present splendor. This site's guides are King David, Herod the Great, and Tammar, a Jewish resident of modern-day Jerusalem. One by one, they will take you through the five most important periods in the history of this eternal city. In this amazing site you will be able to use your RealVideo and RealAudio plug-ins to their optimum. (If you do not have RealAudio/Video, you can download them from the site.) The characters are from the Pathways Through Jerusalem CD-ROM described in the Software section below.

Virtual Tour of Jerusalem
Description: This set of photographs contains scenes of the Walls of Jerusalem, people praying at the Wailing Wall, and the Dome of the Rock. You can also read an article on The Holy Land, reprinted from *Reflections on Truth*.

Ancient Sandals
Description: Here you will experience Israel as it was promised to Abraham, inhabited by his descendants, ruled over by Israel's judges and kings, lamented

Resources recommended in ◆several lessons, ★ several units, ♥ other HOW Units. ⊶ Key Resource (see beginning of unit or page 32).

Heart of Wisdom Publishing   371

for by the prophets, and traversed by Jesus and His disciples. Strap on your sandals and come tour through one hundred thirty locations, with some nine hundred color photographs covering every corner of the Land.

3-D Tour of the Western Wall
Description: Walk into the plaza adjacent to the Temple Mount. Navigate your way across the paving stones and down the steps, until you stand face-to-face with the great, golden stones of the Western Wall. Once there, you can write a prayer and virtually place it between the cracks, as hundreds of thousands of visitors do every year.

15 Keys to Understanding the Incomparable Jerusalem
Description: This excellent article is from *Bridges for Peace Israel Teaching Newsletter.* By Clarence H. Wagner, Jr.

Jerusalem: Three Religions One Holy City.
Description: Explore the sights, sounds, people, and time lines that created the Holy City Jerusalem, in a special exhibit from The History Channel.

The Jerusalem Mosaic
Description: Travel through Jerusalem while visiting this site, and follow the links from the Hebrew University of Jerusalem.

The History of Ancient Jerusalem (1070-607 B.C.E.)
Description: Charts the history of the city of Jerusalem from its capture by King David in 1070 B.C.E., down to the Babylonian army sacking it in 607 B.C.E.

Software

Pathways Through Jerusalem
Description: An excellent CD-ROM with a premium database for researching specific sites and topics. You'll find interesting interactive time lines, hyperlinked databases, and multimedia maps covering the city, its history, and its significance. The comprehensive two-disc title also presents nine guided video tours throughout the city. Browse through the time line for three thousand years of Jerusalem and world history at a glance. Search through the database for easy-to-read articles about important events, places, and personalities in Jerusalem's history. See a sample online—Jerusalem Time Travel. You will explore the drama of Jerusalem throughout history with five ancient-tour guides: 1.) King David, a shepherd who became the leader of his people; 2.) Dirk the Crusader, who marched across Europe to liberate the Holy Land; 3.) Herod the Great; 4.) Suleiman the Magnificent, Ottoman sultan; 5.) Queen Helena, who left the royal court to make a pilgrimage of faith.

Step 3 Expand

Activity 1: Trace a Map
Trace a map of Israel (showing the location of Jerusalem) and the map on this page for your portfolio. Refer to Reproducible Maps, Charts, Timelines & Illustrations ⚷— ♥ (75).

Activity 2: Create an Outline
Make an outline of Jerusalem's important characteristics using these fifteen key points. Include a summary paragraph and Bible references for each point:

- City of Many Names
- A Chosen City
- A City of Pilgrimage
- God's Dwelling Place
- A Protected City
- A City of Conflict
- A Capital of the Jews Alone
- Never Sacred for Moslems
- A City Important to Jesus
- The City of God's Redeemer
- Worthy of Praise and Exaltation
- Always Populated by Jews
- A Flash Point in Bible Prophecy
- The Focus of Our Prayers
- There Will Be a New Jerusalem

Activity 3: Add to Your Time Line Book
Add any significant events studied in this lesson to your Time Line Book.

Step 4 Excel

The Bible commands us to pray for the peace of Jerusalem (Psalms 122:6). Make a commitment to do so. Make a small sign to hang in your bedroom or other area of your home to serve as a reminder. Add new words you learned in this lesson into your Vocabulary Notebook (see page 22).

Resources recommended in ◆several lessons, ★ several units, ♥ other HOW Units. ⚷—Key Resource (see beginning of unit or page 32).

Heart of Wisdom Publishing   373

King Solomon 960-920 B. C.

Step 1 Excite

587-613/672-689

The Narrated Bible

Solomon was given great wisdom from God. What do you consider the most inspirational statement that you have read? Who wrote this statement? What lesson does this statement try to convey? How did this statement affect you personally? Brainstorm and list the characteristics or attributes that a wise man should possess.

Watch a Video

The Bible - Solomon
Description: Chronicles the period of Solomon's fight with Adonijah through to the split of the kingdom between Jeroboam and Rehoboam. Basically faithful to the Scriptures except for the Queen of Sheba legend. Two video tapes. ASIN: B00004VVP1.

Solomon and Sheba (1959)
Description: A Hollywood story about the famed reign of King Solomon over ancient Israel, and how the Queen of Sheba plots his overthrow. Starring Yul Brynner. This drama was the ninth in a series of made-for-TV features dramatizing famous stories from the Bible. ASIN: 6303050050

Step 2 Examine

Solomon ruled from 960-920 B.C. When Solomon became king he had a vision of God in which God asked him what his heart desired above everything else. Solomon asked that he be granted wisdom. Because he asked for this instead of riches or fame, God gave him all three. Many of the Proverbs were written by Solomon.

Solomon built a majestic Temple dedicated to God. The religious ritual in the Temple, together with the biblical pilgrimage festivals, transformed Jerusalem into an important political and commercial center during Solomon's reign. Read 1 Kings 2:12-11:43.

Do more research about King Solomon and Solomon's Temple. Use any resource (an encyclopedia, nonfiction book, historical novel, or the Internet). We recommend the following:

Books

The Victor Journey through the Bible
Read: "Solomon Builds the Temple" (132-133), S"Solomon's Glory" (134), Solomon Turns from God" (135).

Underlined text refers to Internet link at http://Homeschool-Books.com

Encyclopedia of the Bible (Nelson's Illustrated) ♥
Read: "The First Kings" (26-27), "1 and 2 Samuel" (208-209), "1 and 2 Kings" (212), "1 and 2 Chronicles" (212).

The Holman Bible Atlas ⊶ ♥
Read: "The Reign of Solomon" (107-110).

Ancient Israel: Its Life and Institutions ⊶ ★
Read: Administration under Solomon (133).

Pharaohs and Kings: A Biblical Quest ⊶★
Read: "The Age of Solomon" (173-194). See description in the Ancient Egypt Key Resources.

Ancient Israel: From Abraham to the Roman Destruction of the Temple ★
Read: "Solomon" (108-120).

King Solomon by Frederic Thieberger
Description: A fascinating portrait of the great biblical monarch within the historical framework of his time. The personality of King Solomon has intrigued countless generations. On the one hand, he has been accepted as a symbol of pomp, magnificence, and wisdom; on the other hand, in recent years there has been a tendency to trace the cause of the subsequent decay of the Jewish Kingdom to his autocratic rule. Thieberger has based his portrait of King Solomon on the Bible, the facts of archaeology and history, and our knowledge of philosophy and psychology to probe the character of the Wise King and to assess his contribution to Israel and to all mankind. Available from Messengers of Truth 502-222-5189.

Joseph's Wardrobe by Paul J. Citrin
King Solomon's fleet commander narrates the story of his mission to bring personal belongings of Joseph which were remaining in Egypt after his death to Israel where they can be enjoyed by Joseph's descendants. (November 1998) Union of American Hebrew Congregations; ISBN: 0807403199. Reading level: Ages 9-12.

Sayings of the Wise: The Legacy of King Solomon (Classic Bible Series) by Lawrence Boadt (Editor), Libby Purves
Description: From the time of King Solomon until after the exile of the Jews in Babylon, sages and scribes composed and collected the aphorisms and longer discourses that now constitute the Old Testament books of Proverbs and Ecclesiastes. The powerful phrases and images which they used have had a profound impact on subsequent conceptions of what it means to be wise or foolish. Even today, many of these sayings are a part of commonplace parlance. The com-

---

Resources recommended in ♦several lessons, ★ several units, ♥other HOW Units. ⊶Key Resource (see beginning of unit or page 32).

Heart of Wisdom Publishing 375

plete texts of the books of Proverbs and Ecclesiastes are reproduced here, along with helpful commentary on the literary influence of key images and quotations. (January 2000) St. Martin's Press; ISBN: 0312221053.

Internet Sources

King Solomon - 970-928 BC
Description: Chronicles the reign of ancient Israel's King Solomon and the magnificent temple he had built on the summit of Mount Moriah.

King Solomon Builds a Temple
Description: Read the story of the building of the first temple in Jerusalem by the construction-minded King Solomon.

King Solomon's Temple in 3-D Virtual Reality
Description: Download the provided plug-in and take a 3D tour of the famed Temple of Solomon. Includes biblical descriptions of this lost marvel.

Biblical History of King Solomon's Temple
Description: Furnishes the biblical accounts of the building and use of the Temple of Solomon and provides Masonic commentary.

Solomon's Temple - Great Buildings Online
Description: Details the ancient temple built by King Solomon in the 10th century and destroyed by Babylonian invaders in 586 B.C.

Solomon - Solomonic Era
Description: Studies the foreign and domestic policies of King Solomon whose reign brought prosperity to the kingdom of Israel. Details Solomon's Temple.

Analysis of David and Solomon's Accession Histories
Description: Examines the rise to power of King David and his son King Solomon.

Step 3 Expand

Choose and complete one of the following activities:

Activity 1: Write a Biography
Compile information from your research into a one-page biography of King Solomon. Younger students can narrate (tell back) what they remember about Solomon.

Activity 2: Add to Your Time Line Book
Add King Solomon to your Time Line Book. Include major events in his life. Refer to Reproducible Maps, Charts, Timelines & Illustrations ♥ (67-73, 87).

Activity 2: Answer Questions
Answer the following:
1. What command did Solomon ignore? (1 Kings 11:1-2)
2. How many wives and concubines did Solomon have? (1 Kings 11:3-8)
3. How did God decide to punish Solomon for ignoring his command? (1 Kings 11:9-13)

Activity 3: Fill out a Person or Event Worksheet
Compile information from your research to fill out a Person Worksheet about King Solomon or an Event Worksheet about the building of Solomon's Temple.

Activity 4: Write a Summary
Read 1 Kings 11:4-9. Write a summary explaining how Solomon's tolerance of his wives' pagan religions led to terrible sins against God. Read the passage aloud for younger students. Allow them to narrate (orally tell) what they have learned.

Activity 5: Write a Brief Essay
Choose the Proverbs passage written by Solomon that is most meaningful to you, and write a brief essay explaining the significance of the lesson it teaches to you and to others. Read the passage aloud for younger students. Allow them to narrate (orally tell) what they have learned.

Activity 6: Sew a Quilt Block
Patchwork Partners provides directions and a brief Bible study relating to this lesson on the Internet. See Bible Blocks: Solomon's Puzzle.

Step 4 Excel

Share what you have learned about King Solomon with a friend or family member. Correct all written work to demonstrate correct punctuation and spelling, and effective use of grammar. Add corrected written work or any illustrations to your portfolio. Add new words you learned in this lesson into your Vocabulary Notebook (see page 22).

Resources recommended in ◆several lessons, ★ several units, ♥ other HOW Units. ◉—Key Resource (see beginning of unit or page 32).

Heart of Wisdom Publishing   377

Solomon's Temple

596-608

The Narrated Bible

Step 1 Excite

Brainstorm and discuss where and how the Hebrews worshiped God before Solomon's Temple was built. How did they worship God in the Temple? Read 1 Chronicles 22, 28, 29; 2 Chronicles 2-7.

Step 2 Examine

Solomon's Temple was the first permanent structure built for Jewish worship. For the previous 480 years, the Israelites had worshiped God within a tent (1 Kings 6:1). According to biblical descriptions, the First Temple consisted of entrance pylons, courts, and a naos, a large rectangular chamber giving entrance to the holy of holies which housed the Ark of the Covenant. Its several destructions and reconstructions since the original edifice was destroyed by King Nebuchadnezzar of Babylon have rendered unrecognizable any remains of the First Temple. Seventy years after the destruction of the First Temple, it was rebuilt under Zerubbabel and Joshua; this Second Temple was then desecrated by Antiochus Epiphanes, a Greco-Syrian ruler. Herod the Great again rebuilt and also enlarged it around 20 B.C.

The Temple was not necessary because of God's nature (Acts 7:46-50). God is Spirit. The Temple was merely an accommodation to the limitations and needs of His people (1 Kings 8:27).

Building Materials

1 Chron. 29:2 describes the building materials of the Temple: *Gold for things to be made of gold; silver for things of silver; brass for things of brass; iron for things of iron; wood for things of wood; onyx stones and stones to be set, glistening stones of diverse colors, and all manner of precious stones, and marble stones in abundance. Nails of gold were used, and nails of brass and iron; chains of gold; ivory from Ophir; hewn stones, stones sawed with saws, great stones (granite), costly stones (marble of various colorings); cedar wood from Mt. Lebanon, algum wood from Mt. Lebanon and from Ophir, fir wood, sycamore, shittim wood or acacia, olive wood and palm, juniper, balsam, and mulberry wood.*

The First Temple was the result of the efforts of 153,000 workers. Leather came from ox skins and chamois, fur from goats and badgers, and wool from sheep. Fine (white) twined linen, goats' and camels' hair was used to make textile fabrics of purple, crimson, and blue. Varicolored dyes were produced from clays, stones, fish, and vegetation. Oils, spices, incense, myrtle, fitches, myrrh, sweet cinnamon, calamus, cassia, stacte, onycha, galbanum, and frankincense were furnished for the services.

Underlined text refers to Internet link at http://Homeschool-Books.com

Pillaged
The temple erected by Solomon was pillaged many times during the course of its history:
First: 1 Kings 14:25, 26; second: 2 Kings 14:14; third: 2 Kings 16:8, 17, 18; 2 Kings 18:15, 16.

Destruction
Solomon's Temple was completely destroyed in 587 B.C. by Nebuchadnezzar and the Babylonians when they captured Jerusalem (2 Kings 24:13; 2 Chronicles 36:7). When the Persian Empire took over from the Babylonian Empire, King Cyrus allowed the Hebrews to return to Jerusalem and build a Second Temple on the site of the first. King Herod the Great, who ruled from 37-4 B.C., restored the Second Temple.

Research Solomon's Temple. Use any resource (an encyclopedia, a nonfiction book, or the Internet). We recommend any of the following:

Books

The Victor Journey through the Bible
Read: "Solomon Builds the Temple" (132-133).

Encyclopedia of the Bible (Nelson's Illustrated)
Read: "Three Temples" (160-161).

The Holman Bible Atlas
Read: "Solomon's Temple" (113-114).

The Young Reader's Encyclopedia of Jewish History
Read: "The People of Israel Set Up a Kingdom" (13-16).

The Usborne Book of the Ancient World
Read: "Solomon's Temple" (73).

The Kingfisher History Encyclopedia
Read: "Solomon's Temple" (50-51).

The Kingfisher Illustrated History of the World
Read: "Solomon's Temple" (24).

The Temple: Its Ministry and Services
See description in the Ancient Israel Unit Resources section. Available online.

Resources recommended in ♦several lessons, ★ several units, ♥other HOW Units. ☞—Key Resource (see beginning of unit or page 32).

Heart of Wisdom Publishing 379

Craft Kit

Build The Temple (Scale Model of the Second Temple)
This exciting Model of the Second Beit HaMikdash or Second Temple is a fantastic fun way to learn about the Temple. This Model comes complete, no additional tools needed. No cutting - No gluing - No MESS! Instead, the precission die cut cardboard Temple parts fit together to produce a beautiful scale model of the Temple. All parts of the temple from Bricks to Gold Doors and Marble Pillars are beautifully detailed with accurate Graphics. This Model is an intricate, yet very rewarding project for classroom learning, school projects, or quality time at home.   Included with the Model is a Booklet in Hebrew and English which tells about the Temple and gives detailed building instruction. When completed you have a beautiful Model ready to be displayed and a nicely detailed display base. For ages 10 and up. Available from jewishsoftware.com (not software).

Internet Sources

Bible History: Old Testament
Read: Chapter 6, which describes the building of Solomon's Temple, preparations for it, the plan and structure of the Temple, internal fittings, history of the Temple, and Jewish traditions.

King Solomon's Temple in 3-D Virtual Reality
Description: This is a 3D virtual-reality self-guided tour of the likeness of a room in King Solomon's Temple.

The Temple
Description: Cyber encyclopedia of Jewish history and culture explaining the First and Second Temples.

Solomon's Temple
Description: A detailed, very personal vision of the temple, based on biblical analysis.

King Solomon's Astonishing Temple Secrets
Description: This illustrated site explains that the greatest secret of King Solomon's Temple is that it may have been constructed in the hidden form of a human body.

Do research to learn about the furniture in the Temple. Use any resource (an encyclopedia, a nonfiction book, or the Internet). We recommend the following:

The Lamp of God: Menorah by Robert Somerville
Description: A booklet presenting a study on the scriptural symbolism of the Menorah from both the Old and New testaments. You will discover that this lamp-

Underlined text refers to Internet link at http://Homeschool-Books.com

stand symbolizes many things such as the Nation of Israel, the Church, the Holy Spirit, the Word of God, the Seven Spirits of God, even the Lord Jesus Christ himself as the light of the world. It is believed by many that a menorah was on public display in each of the first-century churches. You can read this booklet online.

Step 3 Expand

Choose and complete one of the following activities:

Activity 1: Create a Chart
Make a chart showing the Temple furnishings from 1 Kings 7:41-45, 48-50.

Activity 2: Write a Summary
Write a summary of the building and the destruction of Solomon's Temple. Younger students can narrate (orally tell) what they have learned.

Activity 3: Add to Your Time Line Book
Add building of Solomon's Temple to your Time Line Book: Refer to Reproducible Maps, Charts, Timelines & Illustrations ♥ (67-73).

Activity 4: Gather Artwork
Find and gather illustrations (print outs from the Internet or photocopies from books) of Solomon's Temple.

Activity 5: Answer Questions
Answer the following:
1. Why wasn't the temple built under King David's rule? (2 Samuel 7:4-12; 1 Kings 5:3; 1 Chronicles 22:8; 28:3)
2. Was David able to contribute to the building of God's temple? (1 Chronicles 28:11-12; 22:5,14-16)
3. Was David eager to build the temple? (2 Samuel 7:2; 1 Chronicles 22:7; 29:3; Psalms 132:2-5)

Step 4 Excel

Share what you have learned about Solomon's Temple with a friend or family member. Correct all written work to demonstrate correct punctuation and spelling, and effective use of grammar. Add corrected written work or any illustrations to your portfolio. Add new words you learned in this lesson into your Vocabulary Notebook (see page 22).

Resources recommended in ◆several lessons, ★several units, ♥other HOW Units. ●—Key Resource (see beginning of unit or page 32).

Assyrian Captivity c. 721 B.C.

813-815/859-878

The Narrated Bible

Note For more about Assyria see the "Assyria" lesson in the Mesopotamia Unit. For more about the lost tribes see "The Twelve Tribes" in this Unit.

Step 1 Excite

God oversees the rise and fall of nations, according to their moral standards. Deuteronomy 28 explains the blessings which the people of Israel would enjoy if they were obedient and the troubles which God would bring upon them if they failed to honor their promise.

Amos, Hosea, and Micah all date to the Assyrian Period. These books do not extensively deal with Assyria. Rather, they address the moral and spiritual condition of Israel and Judah in the middle of the eighth century B.C.

Read the story of the Assyrian invasion in 2 Kings 15-17; I Chronicles 5:26; II Chronicles 32.

Step 2 Examine

After Solomon's death, the ten northern tribes set up a separate kingdom (Israel) under King Jeroboam, who was not of the House of David (1 Kings 12:20). However, during the time of the divided kingdom, many Israelites in the Northern Kingdom identified themselves with the House of David (2 Chronicles 11:14-17; 15:9; 19:4). The terms Israel, Judah, and Jacob became interchangeable (Isaiah 1:1-3; 48:1; 2 Chronicles 19:1; 21:2).

The Assyrians took the Northern Kingdom captive in 722 B.C., and the Southern Kingdom was captured by Babylon in 586 B.C. Following both invasions, the Jews were deported to the same general geographical area (modern-day Iraq and Iran). Since Babylon and Assyria ruled largely the same territory, the Israelite and Judean captives commingled. Both groups lived as captives under similar conditions. During this time, the divisions, enmity, and rivalry between Judah and Israel ended. Jeremiah says the captors made no distinction between Israel and Judah (Jer. 50:33). [2]

The Assyrian invasions are said to be the most traumatic political events in the history of Israel. The Assyrians were brutal, stacking heads in heaps and skinning men alive. The prophet Amos was active during the reigns of King Uzziah (c. 783-742 B.C.) of Judah (the Southern Kingdom) and King Jeroboam II (c. 786-746 B.C.) of Israel. He foretold the destruction of the Northern Kingdom of Israel.

Underlined text refers to Internet link at http://Homeschool-Books.com

Moses warned the Hebrews in Deut. 28:64, *And the LORD shall scatter thee among all people, from the one end of the earth even unto the other. . .*

The prophet Ezekiel foretold of Israel being reunited in Ezekiel 37:21-22: *And say unto them, Thus saith the Lord GOD; Behold, I will take the children of Israel from among the heathen, whither they be gone, and will gather them on every side, and bring them into their own land: And I will make them one nation in the land upon the mountains of Israel; and one king shall be king to them all: and they shall be no more two nations, neither shall they be divided into two kingdoms any more at all.* The prophecies of Ezekiel 37 will be complete when the Jews are unified in faith under the Messiah Jesus Christ. Ezekiel 39:7 says that when this happens, the eyes of the Israelites will be opened so that they might know God again.

Research the Assyrian conquest of Judah and the prophets Hosea, Amos, Isaiah, and Micah. Use any resource (an encyclopedia, nonfiction book, historical novel, or the Internet). We recommend the following:

Books

Chronicles of the King Series by Lynn Austin
See description of these five books on page 304.

The Victor Journey through the Bible ○—♥
Read: "The Story of Isaiah" (162-163), "Israel Taken into Captivity" (164-165), Sennacherib Goes Against Hezekiah" (166-167).

Encyclopedia of the Bible (Nelson's Illustrated) ♥
Read: "The Assyrians" (60-61), "The Rise of Assyria" (30-31), "1 and 2 Kings" (210-211), "Isaiah" {226-227).

The Holman Bible Atlas ○— ♥
Read: "The Rise of the Neo-Assyrian Empire" (131-139) and "Judah Alone Among International Powers" (152).

Bible History: Old Testament ★
Read: Volume VII From the Decline of the Two Kingdoms to the Assyrian and Babylonian Captivity. This book is available online.

Ancient Israel: From Abraham to the Roman Destruction of the Temple ★
Read: "Israel and Judah Under the Assyrian Empire" (165-199)

Internet Sources

Primary Source: The Bible 2 Kings Chap. 15-17
Description: The destruction of Israel at the hands of the Assyrians.

Resources recommended in ◆several lessons, ★ several units, ♥other HOW Units. ○—Key Resource (see beginning of unit or page 32).

From the Decline of the Two Kingdoms to the Assyrian and Babylonian Captivity
Description: Volume II of *Bible History: Old Testament.*

Mystery of the Myth: The Ten Lost Tribes
Description: Chuck Missler explores the legend of the Ten Lost Tribes of Israel, the Northern and Southern Kingdoms, and what they might mean to modern Israel.

Step 3 Expand

Activity 1: Add to Your Time Line Book
Add the Assyrian invasions and the main people from this period to your Time Line Book. Also add the prophets during this period:Hosea, Amos, Isaiah and Micah. Also add the Assyrian kings Sargon, Shalmaneser, Pul, and Sennacherib. Refer to Reproducible Maps, Charts, Timelines & Illustrations ◉➡ ❤(115-117).

Activity 2: Fill out a Person Worksheet
Compile information from your research to fill out a Person Worksheet about Amos.

Activity 3: Fill out an Event Worksheet
Document the Assyrian invasion by filling out an Event Worksheet.

Activity 4: Write a Story
Write a story from a first-person point of view, as if you were a Hebrew in the northern tribe during the Assyrian invasion. Younger students can narrate (orally tell) the story.

Step 4 Excel

Explain orally to your parents what you've learned about Israel's time line of events from Egyptian bondage to the Assyrian invasion. Correct all written work to demonstrate correct punctuation and spelling, and effective use of grammar. Add corrected written work or any illustrations to your portfolio. Add new words you learned in this lesson into your Vocabulary Notebook (see page 22).

Footnotes
1.Halff, Dr. Charles (2000) Are the Ten Tribes Really Lost? The Christian Jew Foundation, San Antonio, Texas.

Divided Kingdom 922-587 B.C.

690-803

The Narrated Bible

Step 1 Excite

When Solomon died, the kingdom was divided. Ten tribes formed a northern kingdom called Israel. The remaining two tribes created a southern kingdom, Judah. In approximately 722 B.C., the Assyrians invaded the kingdom of Israel and destroyed it. In ancient times, the practice was to relocate defeated populations. The Assyrians carried the ten northern tribes into exile; they were scattered over the world, and came to be known as the Ten Lost Tribes of Israel. In about 597 B.C., the Babylonians attacked the kingdom of Judah, which was home to the remaining two tribes. Most Judeans were taken to Babylon, where they lived in exile.

Step 2 Examine

There are many groups which believe that the northern tribes, separated during the rift between Rehoboam and Jeroboam after the death of Solomon (and subsequently taken captive by Assyria in 722 B.C.), later migrated to Europe and elsewhere. The myth of the Ten Lost Tribes is the basis for British-Israelism and other colorful legends, but these stories have no real biblical basis. They are based upon misconceptions derived from the misreading of various Bible passages[1]. Read about the division between Israel and Judah in 1 Kings 12:1-5.

Research the divided-kingdom period. Use any resource (an encyclopedia, nonfiction book, historical novel, or the Internet). We recommend the following:

Books

The Victor Journey through the Bible ●—♥
Read: "The Kingdom Divides" (136-137).

Encyclopedia of the Bible (Nelson's Illustrated) ♥
Read: "Two Kingdoms" (28-29), "The Prophets (166-167, "1 and 2 Kings" (210-211), "1 and 2 Chronicles" {212-213).

Who's Who in the Bible ●— ♥
Read: "Kings of Israel" (30-31), "Kings of Judah" (32-33).

The Holman Bible Atlas ●— ♥
Read: "The Kingdoms of Israel and Judah" (115-139).

Ancient Israel: From Abraham to the Roman Destruction of the Temple ★
Read: Chapter 5 The Divided Monarchy: The Kingdoms of Judah and Israel.

Resources recommended in ◆several lessons, ★several units, ♥other HOW Units. ●—Key Resource (see beginning of unit or page 32).

Introduction to Jewish History: From Abraham to the Sages ◆
Read: Chapters 7 & 8 "The Northern Kingdom" and "The Kingdom of Judah."

Software

Beyond the Sambatyon: The Myth of the Ten Lost Tribes
Description: Compelling narration, museum-quality paintings, powerful music, and more, contained on a multimedia CD-ROM created in conjunction with The Museum of the Jewish Diaspora in Tel Aviv. The quest to find these tribes has unearthed Jewish groups, or groups whose customs mirror Judaism, all over the world, from Chiang Min, China, to Lemba, South Africa, to Japan, to the Mormons of Utah. *Beyond the Sambatyon: The Myth of the Ten Lost Tribes* details the discovery of these groups, including the story of the people who sought them out, and offers explanations for the true origins of these groups. Its documentary style and good use of photographs, engravings, letters, travelogues, and interviews from the original exhibit make this a worthwhile addition to any library. The CD works on both Windows and Macintosh systems. Level: Grade 5 to adult.

Internet Sources

The Two Kingdoms
Description: The Hebrews: A Learning Module from Washington State University, by Richard Hooker.

Mystery of the Myth: The Ten Lost Tribes
Description: Article by Chuck Missler from Koinonia House.

Israel - Northern Kingdom
Description: Kent Kershenski briefly describes the Northern Kingdom of Israel as a rebel state which existed for roughly two centuries.

Kingdom Divides into North and South
Description: Reveals that the time during the harsh rule of David's grandson Rehoboam caused the kingdom to split into Israel in the north and Judah in the south. From BibleTutor.com, with links.

The Northern Kingdom, Israel
Description: Background on the state, formed under Jeroboam, which was an eventual casualty of Assyrian expansion. From BibleTutor.com, with a map and links to famous figures.

End of Judah - History of Ancient Israel
Describes the Hebrew monarchy under Egyptian and Babylonian control, the fall of Jerusalem, and the end of the monarchy.

Step 3 Expand

Choose and complete one of the following activities:

Activity 1: Write a Paper
Explain the causes leading to the division of the Kingdom of Israel. Younger students can narrate (orally tell) what they have learned.

Activity 2: Write a Play
Tell the story of Naboth's vineyard from I Kings 21. Younger students can narrate (orally tell) the story.

Activity 3: Sew a Quilt Block
Sew a Divided Kingdom quilt block. Patchwork Partners provides directions and a brief Bible study on the Internet at Bible Blocks: Divided Kingdom.

Activity 4: Do Further Research
Replacement Theology is unscriptural, but accepted in some Churches and taught to the extreme in some cults. One such theology, the Christian Identity view, is espoused by those who believe that there is a difference between true Israel and those who call themselves Jews; they think that the true Israelites are today's white Christians, descendants of white Europeans. Some of those in the Christian Identity include Aryan Nations, White Supremacists, the Ku Klux Klan, Christian Patriots, and other related groups. A few of these groups are heavily involved with gun ownership, self-defense, and paranoid conspiracy theories. Research Replacement Theology. Write a summary paragraph explaining the dangers of Replacement Theology. Use some of the following verses to support your argument: Genesis 12:1-3; Galatians 3:16; 3:28-29; Romans 8:18; 9:6-8; Deuteronomy 5:3; Hebrews 2:16-17.

Step 4 Excel

Share what you have learned about the Divided Kingdom by filling out the following worksheet with a child (elementary level): The Divided Kingdom. Add new words you learned in this lesson into your Vocabulary Notebook (see page 22).

Footnotes
1. Missler, Chuck. *Mystery of the Myth: The Ten Lost Tribes*, Koinonia House.
<http://www.khouse.org/articles/biblestudy/19950601-40.html> (Accessed September 2000)

Resources recommended in ◆several lessons, ★ several units, ♥ other HOW Units. ◉—Key Resource (see beginning of unit or page 32).

Babylonian Exile 587-539 B. C.

999-1010

The Narrated Bible

Note: This period is referred to as the Babylonian Exile or Babylonian Captivity. See the Babylonia Lesson in the Mesopotamia Unit.

Step 1 Excite

The Jews were taken into Babylonian captivity because of their departure from the laws of the Lord and their consequent idolatry (1 Kings 14:21-24; 15:1-3; 16:1-20; 1:1-24; 23:31-37; 2 Chronicles 36:1-21). Isaiah 13:17-22 described Babylon *as fairest of kingdoms, proud beauty of the Chaldeans.*

In ancient times, the practice was to relocate defeated peoples. Daniel, Esther, and others were carried away into exile by the Babylonians. There were several possible advantages to this practice: (1) the ability to utilize the skill of the craftsmen, (2) the fact that the mixing of several different populations diluted political, racial, and cultural power. The prophets Ezekiel and Daniel flourished during the Babylonian captivity. While Daniel spent the captivity with the kings and was involved in government, Ezekiel was with the Jewish captives in the colonies in Babylon, teaching and revealing visions to them of their return to Israel.

Imagine that you and three friends were taken captive (without your families) to another country. Your captors hope to break your commitment of devotion to God. They change your names and force you to learn a new language. Do you think you could stand your ground and refuse to compromise your beliefs? Read about Daniel and his friends Hananiah, Mishael, and Azariah (Shadrach, Meshach and Abednego) in Daniel 1:3-20.

> *Do not join a crowd that intends to do evil. When you are on the witness stand, do not be swayed in your testimony by the opinion of the majority.* (Exodus 23:2)

Read about the seventy years of captivity in 2 Chronicles 36; Jeremiah 25,29; Daniel 1,9.

Step 2 Examine

After Solomon's death, Israel split up into the northern and southern Kingdoms of Israel and Judah. In approximately 597 B.C., King Nebuchadnezzar and the Babylonians captured Jerusalem after a siege. Several thousand Jews were taken into exile in Babylonia (some died on the way). The Jews lived as slaves for seventy years, until King Cyrus and the Persians released them. This period, from 597 to 538 B.C., is referred to as the time of Babylonian Captivity. However, the first captives were taken much earlier than this time, making the duration of slavery seventy years.

Underlined text refers to Internet link at http://Homeschool-Books.com

The books of Samuel, Kings, and Chronicles, and most of the prophets of Israel, give us information about Israel being taken into exile in Babylon, and why the First Temple was destroyed. Jeremiah sent a letter to the Jews to advise them on how to live their lives in Babylon. He urges them to accept their lives there, to raise their households and families, and to live in peace. If they are faithful to God, He will bring their families back to Jerusalem. Jeremiah sent this letter to the captives to show that Hehad not forsaken them, though he was displeased, and corrected them, and that they may live comfortably in Babylon. Jeremiah 29:13 says, *And ye shall seek me, and find me, when ye shall search for me with all your heart.*

After the Babylonians were themselves conquered by the Persians, the Jews were allowed to return to Jerusalem, where they were conquered in turn by the Greeks and Romans. It was the King of Persia (Cyrus the Great) who freed the Israelites from Babylonian captivity. (II Chronicles 36; Ezra 1)

Daniel predicted, in about 538 B.C. (Daniel 9:24-27), that Christ would come as Israel's promised Savior 483 years after the Persian emperor would give the Jews authority to rebuild Jerusalem, which was then in ruins. This was clearly and definitely fulfilled, hundreds of years later. The seventy weeks in Daniel 9:24-27 are in prophetic time, and as such, each day represents a year (Ezekiel 4:6). So, the seventy weeks would be a literal period of 490 years, which takes us to the time of Christ. Methodius, one of the early church fathers, said: "...none of the prophets has so clearly spoken concerning Christ as has this prophet Daniel. For not only did he assert that he (the Messiah) would come, a prediction common to the other prophets as well, but also he set forth the very time at which he would come. Moreover he went through the various kings in order, stated the actual number of years involved, and announced beforehand the clearest signs of events to come. ..."

Research the Babylonian Captivity, Daniel, and Ezekiel. Use any resource (an encyclopedia, a nonfiction book, or the Internet). We recommend the any of the following:

Books

The Victor Journey through the Bible ●—❤
Read: "Judah Falls," "Jerusalem is Destroyed" (172-173), "Daniel and the Kings Food" (174), "The Fiery Furnace" (175), "The Handwriting on the Wall" (176-177).

Encyclopedia of the Bible (Nelson's Illustrated) ❤
Read: "The Babylonians" (62-63), "The Babylonian Invasion" (32-33), "1 and 2 Kings" (210-211).

Who's Who in the Bible ●— ❤
Read: "Jewish Nation in Exile" (32-33).

Resources recommended in ◆several lessons, ★ several units, ❤ other HOW Units. ●—Key Resource (see beginning of unit or page 32).

The Holman Bible Atlas ⌐ ♥
Read: "The Exile" (158-163).

History of the Jewish People Volume 1: Second Temple Era ♦
Read: Chapter 1 The Babylonian Exile.

The The Ancient Hebrews ♦
Read: Return from Exile (18-19).

The Young Reader's Encyclopedia of Jewish History ♦
Read: From the Babylonian Exile to the Return to Zion (17-20).

Ancient Israel: Its Life and Institutions ★
Read: Slaves (80-88).

Bible History: Old Testament ★
Read: Volume VII From the Decline of the Two Kingdoms to the Assyrian and
Babylonian Captivity.

Ancient Israel: From Abraham to the Roman Destruction of the Temple ★
Read: Exile and Return.

Internet Sources

When Was Judah's 70-Year Babylonian Captivity?
Description: An excellent article that will help you understand this time period. Most encyclopedia entries give the duration of the Babylonian Captivity as fifty
to sixty-eight years. Jeremiah prophesied that Judah's captivity in Babylon would
last seventy years.

The Assault on Jerusalem
Description: This commentary on the Book of Daniel begins by retelling the
events leading to the destruction of Jerusalem in 586 B.C. Also see the lessons:
Exile of the Four Hebrew Children, Daniel's Moral Dilemma, Daniel's Conduct,
and Daniel's Vindication.

The Babylonian Captivity
Description: Overview in outline form tells the story of the Babylonian
Captivity, from *Condensed Biblical Cyclopedia*.

Babylonian Captivity
Description: Recounts the story of the Israelite's period of captivity in
Babylon under the rule of king Nebuchadnezzar, and their later release. From MSN
Encarta.

(i) The Prayer of a Prophet
Description: Bible study from In Touch Ministries.

(i) The Babylonian Captivity
Description: A time line of Bible events explaining the details of the Babylonian Captivity. The dates are approximate.

(i) First Things First
Description: The story of Judah's exile and the period following from *Discovery Publishing*, a ministry of Peninsula Bible Church.

Step 3 Expand

Choose and complete one of the following activities:

Activity 1. Add to Your Time Line Book
Add the Daniel, Ezekiel, Nebuchadnezzar, Belshazzar and others studied in this lesson to your Time Line Book. Refer to Reproducible Maps, Charts, Timelines & Illustrations ♥ (131-133).

Activity 2: Write a Letter
Imagine that you were living in Judah in 587 B.C., and your family was taken into slavery to live in Babylonia. Write a letter to Jeremiah in response to his letter in Jeremiah 29. Explain your feelings and your hopes for the future.

Activity 3: Create a Chart
Make a chart showing the countries that ruled Israel in different time periods (Assyria, Babylon, Persia, Greece, Syria, Rome). Fill in the columns with a description of and the major events under each rule. Keep adding to this chart as you complete the appropriate lessons. Columns should include: Ruling Power, Year, Description, and Events.

Activity 4: Fill out a Person Worksheet
Compile information from your research to fill out a Person Worksheet for Ezekiel and Daniel.

Activity 5: Answer Questions
A: Answer the following questions about Ezekiel:
1. What did Ezekiel predict would happen to Jerusalem and his subjects at the hands of the Babylonians? (Ezekiel 4:1-5:17; 12:8-20)
2. What did he predict about Israel? (Ezekiel 6:1-15; 11:17-20; 16:60-62; 34:12-16)
3. What did he predict about the Pharaoh and Egypt? (Ezekiel 29:1-10)

Resources recommended in ♦several lessons, ★ several units, ♥ other HOW Units. ●—Key Resource (see beginning of unit or page 32).

Heart of Wisdom Publishing   391

4. What did he predict about the coming of the good Shepherd? (Ezekiel 34:23,24)

B. Answer the following questions about Daniel:

1. What did Daniel refuse to do? (Daniel 1:5-16)

2. What did God give Daniel? (Daniel 1:17-20)

3. What famous dream did Daniel interpret? (Daniel 2:48,49; 4:1-37)

4. What did Nebuchadnezzar do to Daniel, Hananiah, Mishael, and Azariah (Belteshazzar, Shadrach, Meshach and Abednego)? (Daniel 2:49-3:30)

5. What did Daniel have to do with the handwriting upon the wall? (Daniel 5:1-30)

6. What did Darius do to to Daniel? (Daniel 6:1-4)

7. What happened when Daniel was cast into a den of lions? (Daniel 6:4-23)

Activity 6: Fill out a Worksheet
Share what you have learned about Daniel with a child (elementary level). Then fill out the following worksheet with him or her: Daniel in the Lion's Den.

Activity 7: Write Summaries
Write a summary paragraph for each Bible story: 1.) King Nebuchadnezzar's Dream; 2.) Daniel's Three Friends and the Fiery Furnace; 3.) Nebuchadnezzar's Madness; 4.) Handwriting on the Wall; 5.) Daniel in the Lion's Den. Younger students can narrate (orally tell) the stories.

Step 4 Excel

Share your work from Step 3 with someone. Discuss how the seventy-year Babylonian Captivity affected the Jews. Correct all written work to demonstrate correct punctuation and spelling, and effective use of grammar. Add corrected written work or any illustrations to your portfolio. Add new words you learned in this lesson into your Vocabulary Notebook (see page 22).

The Diaspora

The Narrated Bible

Note: The Diaspora can refer to the dispersion of Jews among the Gentiles after the Babylonian Exile or to Jewish communities scattered "in exile" outside present-day Israel. This lesson refers to the first significant Jewish Diaspora as the result of the Babylonian Exile of 586 B.C.

Step 1 Excite

Imagine and discuss how you might feel if your family had to leave your county. What thing would you miss the most? Now imagine that many years later you were able to come back to your country. You endured the long journey home, but once you got to your homeland you weren't able to visit your relatives because they were scattered throughout different countries. How would you feel?

Step 2 Examine

After the Babylonians conquered the Kingdom of Judah, part of the Jewish population was deported into slavery. Cyrus the Great, the Persian conqueror of Babylonia, permitted the Jews to return to their homeland in 538 B.C.; a group of about 50,000 decided to return. But many Jews remained in Babylon constituting the first of numerous Jewish communities living permanently in the Diaspora. After 597, there were three distinct groups of Hebrews: a group in Babylon and other parts of the Middle East, a group in Judaea, and another group in Egypt. The Jews were scattered once more among all nations, where they have remained until this day. Some scholars believe that Daniel's prophecy follows the Jews who returned from Babylon, rebuilt Jerusalem and its walls, and rejected the Messiah, while Ezekiel's prophecy concerns those who did not return.

> The drama of the Jewish people during their Diaspora is little known to most Christians. It is fascinating reading because it soon becomes clear that God has in fact protected the Jewish people, their religion, values and culture against the great pressures to assimilate, against almost constant terrible anti-Semitism, against horrendous persecution down through the ages. The very existence of the Jews today, the recovery of their language, their regathering to the land of their fathers, and the clear signs of their Messianic expectations, are surely among the greatest miracles one can find on the pages of human history.
>
> In exile, the Jews gathered their traditions together into a single collection and developed a kind of religious life independent of the Temple. This kind of religious life revered the Temple and preserved its emphasis on ethics, purity, Sabbath and festivals, and food taboos, but it did not involve sacrifice, since

Resources recommended in ◆several lessons, ★ several units, ● other HOW Units. ●━Key Resource (see beginning of unit or page 32).

Heart of Wisdom Publishing   393

the Temple was in ruins. It engaged in religious practices that were most relevant to the institution of the Temple but whose meaning did not require the Temple to be standing. The leadership of this kind of Judaism expanded to include lay people who knew and understood the traditions collected to preserve a national memory. [2] This period is explained in the books of Ezra and Nehemiah. The timing of the events is vague because they are not in chronological order and they are intermixed between the two books.[1]

Research Babylonian Exile (the Diaspora). Use any resource (an encyclopedia, a nonfiction book, or the Internet). We recommend any of the following:

Books

Encyclopedia of the Bible (Nelson's Illustrated) ♥
Read: "From Exile to Return" (34-35).

The Holman Bible Atlas ⚷ ♥
Read: "The Exile" (158-163).

The Young Reader's Encyclopedia of Jewish History ♦
Read: From the Babylonian Exile to the Return to Zion (17-20).

History of the Jewish People Volume 1: Second Temple Era ♦
Read: Chapter 1 The Babylonian Exile.

Introduction to Jewish History: From Abraham to the Sages ♦
Read: Chapter 10 The Return to Jerusalem.

Ancient Israel: From Abraham to the Roman Destruction of the Temple ★
Read: Chapter 6 Exile and Return: From the Babylonian Destruction to the Reconstruction of the Jewish State.

Internet Sources

Diaspora - Hebrew History
Description: Reviews the history of the Jewish Diaspora beginning with the Assyrian conquest of Israel and moving through the Greek and Roman periods.

The Diaspora
Description: The Hebrews: A Learning Module from Washington State University, by Richard Hooker.

Underlined text refers to Internet link at http://Homeschool-Books.com

(i) Diaspora - Jewish Student Online Research Center
Description: JSOURCE provides this essay detailing the history of the Jewish Diaspora beginning with the Assyrian conquest of ancient Israel in 722 B.C.

(i) Jewish Diaspora
Description: The history of the Jewish Diaspora from the Babylonian exile to the 20th century.

(i) Outline of the Jewish Diaspora
Description: An outline of the history of the Jewish Diaspora beginning with the scattering of the ten tribes of Israel in 722 B.C.

Step 3 Expand

Activity 1. Add to Your Time Line Book
Add the Babylonian Exile to your Time Line Book. Refer to Reproducible Maps, Charts, Timelines & Illustrations ⚷ ❤ (89-95).

Activity 2: Write a Letter
Write a letter to a friend as if you were living during the time of the Diaspora. Explain that you have just returned to your homeland, and how you feel about leaving Babylon; your journey to a home you've never known (but heard about all your life); the excitement of your people to get home; and plans to rebuild the Temple. Include the differences between Persian and Babylonian rule.

Activity 3: Copy Passages
Copy (by hand or typing) two or more paragraphs from your research. Or have someone dictate the passage to you. Younger students can copy one or two sentences or narrate (tell back) what has been learned.

Step 4 Excel

Share what you have learned about the Diaspora after the Babylonian Captivity with a friend or family member. Correct all written work to demonstrate correct punctuation and spelling, and effective use of grammar. Add corrected written work or any illustrations to your portfolio. Add new words you learned in this lesson into your Vocabulary Notebook (see page 22).

Footnotes
1. Dolphin, Lambert and Graff, Ron. *The Chosen People* <http://www.ldolphin.org/kingdom/ch1.html> (Accessed May 2000).
2. PBS Online, *Echoes from the Ancients, History* <http://www.pbs.org/echoes/rel01.html> (Accessed September 2000).

Resources recommended in ◆several lessons, ★ several units, ❤ other HOW Units. ⚷Key Resource (see beginning of unit or page 32).

Restoration and the Second Temple

1233-1257

The Narrated Bible

Step 1 Excite

The exiles returned to their land under Zerubbabel in 537 B.C. and after urging from Haggai and Zechariah completed the rebuilding of Solomon's Temple 516 B.C. After they completed the Temple they celebrated the Passover. The seventy years of captivity had finally come to an end. Read some of the prophecies concerning the Temple's restoration: Isaiah 44:28; Daniel 8:13,14; Haggai 1; 2; Zechariah 1:16; 4:8-10; 6:12-15; 8:9-15; Malachi 3:1.

Step 2 Examine

The books of Ezra and Nehemiah tell the story of the return of a Jewish remnant from Persia and the rebuilding of the Temple and the city of Jerusalem. The Second Temple was smaller than the original. Those who remembered the original temple wept when they saw it (Ezra 3:12). This Second Temple was desecrated by Antiochus IV (Epiphanes), the Seleucid ruler, who had a pig slaughtered on the altar and set up an image of a pagan god in the Holy of Holies. This is the event that triggered the rise of the Hasmonean family of the Maccabees. The Jewish celebration of Hanukah comes from this time of restoration and renewal in their national history. This Temple was built by Zerubbabel, with the encouragement of the prophets Haggai and Zechariah, near the end of the 6th century B.C.

Do research about the Second Temple. Use any resource (an encyclopedia, nonfiction book, historical novel, or the Internet). We recommend the following:

Books

The Victor Journey through the Bible ●━♥
Read: "Ezra and the People Return" (180-181), "Nehemiah Prays for His Homeland" (182-183), "Nehemiah Builds Jersulam's Walls," (184-185). "Ezra Reads the Law" (186-187).

Encyclopedia of the Bible (Nelson's Illustrated) ♥
Read: "From Exile to Return" (34-35)."Ezra, Nehemiah" (213), "The Three Temples" 160-161).

The Holman Bible Atlas ●━ ♥
Read: "Zerubbabel and Joshua" (169).

History of the Jewish People Volume 1: Second Temple Era ◆
Read: Chapter 2 Building of the Second Temple.

Underlined text refers to Internet link at http://Homeschool-Books.com

Internet Sources

(i) Solomon's Temple Rebuilt!
Description: Historical study about the rebuilding of Solomon's Temple from BibleStudent.com.

(i) The Rebuilt Temple
Description: Chapter 9 from the book Thy Kingdom Come, Thy Will Be Done... by Ron Graff and Lambert Dolphin.

(i) The Destruction of the Second Temple
Description: Relates the accounts by Flavius Josephus of the Roman capture of Jerusalem and the burning of the Second Temple.

(i) The Second Temple
Description: A physical description of the Second Temple, from *Easton's Bible Dictionary.*

Step 3 Expand

Choose and complete one of the following activities:

Activity 1: Write a Summary
Write a summary of the building and the destruction of the Second Temple.

Activity 2 Add to Your Time Line Book
Add the Second Temple to your Time Line Book. Refer to Reproducible Maps, Charts, Timelines & Illustrations ☞ ♥(91-94).

Activity 3: Make a Table
Make a table comparing the three temples: First Temple, Second Temple, and Herod's Temple. Include dates, who ordered the construction, notes, etc.

Step 4 Excel

Share what you have learned about the Second Temple with a friend or family member. Correct all written work to demonstrate correct punctuation and spelling, and effective use of grammar. Add corrected written work or any illustrations to your portfolio. Add new words you learned in this lesson into your Vocabulary Notebook (see page 22).

Resources recommended in ◆several lessons, ★ several units, ♥ other HOW Units. ☞Key Resource (see beginning of unit or page 32).

Heart of Wisdom Publishing   397

The Persian Period 539-332 B.C.

1233-1254/ 1297-1304

The Narrated Bible

Note: There is a lesson on the Persian Empire from 612-330 B.C. in the Mesopotamia Unit and a lesson on the Persian Wars in the Ancient Greece Unit.

Step 1 Excite

The Hebrews were under Persian rule from approximately 539-332 B.C. In 538 B.C., the Persians defeated the Babylonians and Cyrus permitted the Jews to return to their homeland. One hundred sixty years earlier, when Jerusalem was prospering (about one hundred years before the Babylonian captivity), God told Isaiah that He would raise up a man (Cyrus), His shepherd, to rebuild His city. He told this to Isaiah,

> *That saith of Cyrus, He is my shepherd, and shall perform all my pleasure: even saying to Jerusalem, Thou shalt be built; and to the temple, Thy foundation shall be laid.* (Isaiah 44:28)

Step 2 Examine

Upon the return from Babylon, the Jews set up an altar to the God of Israel, and reorganized His sacrificial worship. Over a period of years they rebuilt the Jerusalem Temple which the Babylonians had destroyed (Ezra 1-6).

Do research about Israel under Persian rule. Use any resource (an encyclopedia, a nonfiction book, or the Internet). We recommend the any of the following:

Books

The Victor Journey through the Bible ⚫━❤
Read: "The Handwriting on the Wall" (176-177).

Encyclopedia of the Bible (Nelson's Illustrated) ❤
Read: "The Persians" (66-67), "From Exile to Return" (34-35). "Ancient Beliefs" (146-147).

The Holman Bible Atlas ⚫━ ❤
Read: "The Persian Period" (164-173)

The Kingfisher History Encyclopedia ⚫━ ❤
Read: The Persian Empire (40-41).

The Usborne Book of the Ancient World ★
Read: Persian Empire (137).

History of the Jewish People Volume 1: Second Temple Era ◆
Read: Persia Rules Far and Wide (26-29), Wars with Persia (44-51).

The Young Reader's Encyclopedia of Jewish History ◆
Read: From the Babylonian Exile to the Return to Zion (17-20). This book is out of print but available at many libraries.

Introduction to Jewish History: From Abraham to the Sages ◆
Read: Chapter 10 The Return to Jerusalem.

Ancient Israel: From Abraham to the Roman Destruction of the Temple ★
Read: Exile and Return.

Internet Sources

After the Exile 538-332
Description: The Hebrews: A Learning Module from Washington State University, by Richard Hooker.

The Persian Period and Return from Exile (538-323)
Description: A brief summary of Old Testament history during the Persian era, 538 BC-323 B.C., noting important developments during and after the exile.

King Cyrus of Persia in Ancient History
Description: Article revealing evidence which supports the biblical prophecy of Cyrus.

Step 3 Expand

Choose and complete one of the following activities:

Activity 1: Write a Description
Pretend you are a screenwriter who is writing a short description of Israel under Persian rule, thinking about how it could be made into a film that movie goers would flock to see. What scenes would you dramatize? What genre of film would it be? What conflict or pivotal event would drive the plot? Who would star in it?

Resources recommended in ◆several lessons, ★ several units, ♥other HOW Units. ☀—Key Resource (see beginning of unit or page 32).

Activity 2: Add to Your Time Line Book
Add the Persian Period to your Time Line Book. Include: Esther (see next lesson), Ezra, Nehemiah, Cyrus, and other people from this period. Refer to Reproducible Maps, Charts, Timelines & Illustrations ❤ (101).

Activity 3: Create a Chart
Make a chart with the following headings: Assyria, Babylon, Persia, Greece, Syria, Rome. Fill in the cells with a description of and the major events under each rule. Keep adding to this chart as you complete the appropriate lessons.

Activity 5: Write a Story
Driven by his passion for God's glory and honor, Nehemiah led a diverse group of people to accomplish a seemingly impossible task. Rewrite the inspiring story of Nehemiah building the wall for a child. Younger students can narrate (orally tell) the story.

Activity 4: Write an Explanation
Write to explain Isaiah's prophecy and its fulfillment through King Cyrus. Refer to "Writing an Explanation" in *Writers INC*.

Step 4 Excel

Share what you have learned about Israel under Persian rule with a friend or family member. Correct all written work to demonstrate correct punctuation and spelling, and effective use of grammar. Add corrected written work or any illustrations to your portfolio. Add new words you learned in this lesson into your Vocabulary Notebook (see page 22).

Queen Esther

1276-1285

The Narrated Bible

Step 1 Excite

Imagine that the nation which you live in decided that all Christians should be persecuted because they live differently from normal people due to their radical religious beliefs. Imagine that you were persecuted because you remain part of a different, distinct group, with morals and values that are not in line with the world's standards. Imagine that the nation which you live in decided that all Christians should be put to death. Then, imagine one day going through your normal daily routines, and a few hours later finding out that your entire religion is being persecuted to the point of death. Does this sound far fetched? It happened (more than once) to the Jewish people.

Step 2 Examine

The book of Esther in the Old Testament tells the story of how the beautiful Jewish woman Hadassah[1] (Esther) and her cousin Mordecai save the Persian Jews, overcoming one of the most dastardly plots to exterminate the Jewish people in history. This story is remembered today through the celebration of the holiday, Purim.

The Book of Esther has been referred to as a monument in the history of anti-Semitism. The anti-Semitism shown in the book of Esther is religiously based. The anti-Semitism shown in later Hellenistic-Roman literature through today is pure ethnic hatred. The Jewish people have faced elimination as a group many times throughout ancient, medieval, and modern societies.

When the Hebrew people lived under Persian rule, many of the Jews socialized with the Persians and became more and more worldly. They were accepted, integrated citizens who blended into Persian life. In fact, a Jewish woman became the Queen. Imagine their shock when, in a moment, their lives were drastically changed: The Prime Minister convinced the King to destroy the entire Jewish nation.

The Jews had a rude awakening! In a brief instant, they went from their normal daily routines to persecution to the point of death. They were hated, and on the verge of destruction because of their race.

Research the story of Esther. Use any resource (an encyclopedia, a nonfiction book, or the Internet). We recommend the any of the following:

Resources recommended in ◆several lessons, ★ several units, ♥ other HOW Units. ●━Key Resource (see beginning of unit or page 32).

Books

The Victor Journey through the Bible ⬤━❤
Read: "The Story of Queen Esther" (178-179).

Encyclopedia of the Bible (Nelson's Illustrated) ❤
Read: "Esther" (215).

A Family Guide to the Biblical Holidays ★
Read: "Purim" (417-427).

Reproducible Maps, Charts, Timelines & Illustrations ❤
Read: "Esther" (101).

History of the Jewish People Volume 1: Second Temple Era ◆
Read: "Purim" (27-28).

Esther
Description: Esther, a beautiful young Jewish woman, is made queen of the Persian Empire. The problem: No one knows she is Jewish! Here is a nonstop story of faith and loyalty despite the overwhelming evil of persecution. (October 1998) Barbour & Co; ISBN: 1557482608. Reading level: Young adult.

Internet Sources

BiblicalHolidays.com Purim
Description: An overview of the purpose of Purim., the story of Esther, overview of the Jewish customs of Purim today, symbolic pictures of Christ in Purim, ideas for a family Purim party and Purim links.

The Story of Purim (audio file)
Description: The beautiful Purim story, as read every Purim from the *Megillah*. The story of Esther is retold by eleven-year-old Rochel Posner in two parts.

Step 3 Expand

Choose and complete one of the following activities:

Activity 1: Add to Your Time Line Book
Add the story of Purim and people involved (Esther, Mordecai, Ahashverosh, Vashti, and Haman) to your Time Line Book. Refer to Reproducible Maps, Charts, Timelines & Illustrations (101).

Activity 2: Celebrate Purim
Refer to Suggestions for Celebrating Purim from A Family Guide to the Biblical Holidays.

Activity 3: Make an Outline
Make an outline of the book of Esther.

Activity 4: Write a Description
Write a description of the celebration of Purim. Younger students can narrate (orally tell) the story.

Activity 5: Write a Biography
Compile information from your research into a one-page biography of Queen Esther. Younger students can narrate (orally tell) the story.

Activity 6: Fill out a Person Worksheet
Compile information from your research to fill out a Person Worksheet about Queen Esther.

Step 4 Excel

Celebrate Purim to share what you have learned about Queen Esther with others. Correct all written work to demonstrate correct punctuation and spelling, and effective use of grammar. Add corrected written work or any illustrations to your portfolio.

Footnotes
1. Esther's Jewish name Hadassah means myrtle; the Persian name Esther means star.

Resources recommended in ◆several lessons, ★ several units, ♥ other HOW Units. ●—Key Resource (see beginning of unit or page 32).

Heart of Wisdom Publishing   403

The Hellenistic Period

1345-1346

The Narrated Bible

Step 1 Excite

The Hellenistic era began when Alexander the Great conquered Judea and, soon after that, Egypt and the ancient Near East. Alexander was a student of Aristotle, who was a student of Plato. Alexander caused the spread of Plato's ideas in the nations he conquered (see the Greek Philosophers lesson in the Ancient Greece Unit). Alexander attempted to unite the cultures and religions of those nations by blending their culture with Greek culture. He called his plan omonia, which can be translated as like-mindedness.

After two centuries of serving as a slave state to Persia, Israel fell under Greek rule. After Alexander's death, Judah was ruled by Egypt and later by Syria. Traditional Jews gave the name Hellenist to those Jews who adopted customs and attitudes derived from Hellenistic culture. There was tension between the Greeks and Hellenistic Jews as well as between the traditionalist Jews and Hellenistic Jews.

Step 2 Examine

Do research about the Jews under Greek rule. Use any resource (an encyclopedia, nonfiction book, historical novel, or the Internet). We recommend the following:

Books

The Victor Journey through the Bible
Read: "Great Empires of the Bible" (171). "Empires of the Ancient World," (maps 176-177).

Encyclopedia of the Bible (Nelson's Illustrated) ♥
Read: "The Greeks" (69-70), "Greek and Roman Empires" (36-37).

The Holman Bible Atlas
Read: "The Hellenistic Period" (174-182).

History of the Jewish People Volume 1: Second Temple Era ♦
Read: Chapter 5 "The Rise of Greece," and Chapter 6 "Alexander the Great."

Ancient Israel: From Abraham to the Roman Destruction of the Temple ★
Read: Chapter 7 "The Age of Hellenism: Alexander the Great and the Fall of the Hasmonean Kingdom."

Underlined text refers to Internet link at http://Homeschool-Books.com

From Mesopotamia to Modernity: Ten Introductions to Jewish History Literature ♥
Read: "Jewish History and Culture in the Hellenstic Period" (37-56). See description on page 39.

Internet Sources

Hellenistic World
Description: This page is an index to chapters in the Internet Ancient History Sourcebook (contains hundreds of local files as well as links to source texts throughout the Internet). The Hellenistic World section includes: The Hellenistic World, Alexander (356-323 B.C.E.), The Hellenistic States, Art and Architecture, Literature, Religion, Science and Medicine, Critical Thought, and much more.

Hellenistic Period
Description: Brief overview of the Hellenistic period from BibleTutor.com.

The Greek Period (332-63 B.C.)
Description: *Encyclopedia Britannica* article: Origin of Christianity: the Early Christians and the Jewish Community.

Step 3 Expand

Choose and complete one of the following activities:

Activity 1: Write a Letter
Write a letter as if you were a Hebrew living during the Hellenistic era.

Activity 2: Make a Test
Develop a Bible study test about the Hellenistic period. Include ten true-false, ten multiple choice, and ten short essay questions.

Activity # Add to Your Time Line Book
Add the Hellenistic period to your Time Line Book. Refer to Reproducible Maps, Charts, Timelines & Illustrations ●━♥(167).

Step 4 Excel

Share what you have learned about the Hellenistic Period in Judea with a friend or family member. Correct all written work to demonstrate correct punctuation and spelling, and effective use of grammar. Add corrected written work or any illustrations to your portfolio. Add new words you learned in this lesson into your Vocabulary Notebook (see page 22).

Resources recommended in ◆several lessons, ★ several units, ♥ other HOW Units. ●━Key Resource (see beginning of unit or page 32).

Heart of Wisdom Publishing   405

The Maccabean Period 166-63 B.C.

Step 1 Excite

Imagine and discuss what it would be like if America was taken over by another country and forced into a dictatorship. Under this new rule, you and your family are not allowed to attend church, read a Bible, or practice baptism. Imagine that soldiers came into your church, removed your Bibles, and replaced your altar with an altar to Satan, then forced you to bow down before this satanic altar.

Brainstorm and discuss why Americans celebrate Independence Day on the Fourth of July.

The Fourth of July celebrations in America are an annual reminder of the liberty we received with the Declaration of Independence on July 4, 1776. Hanukkah[1] is an annual festival to commemorate the rededication of the Temple of Jerusalem by Judas Maccabee in 165 B.C., after the temple had been profaned by Antiochus IV Epiphanes.

Step 2 Examine

The Jewish people had returned to the Land of Israel from the Babylonian Exile, and had rebuilt the Holy Temple, but they remained subject to the reigning powers: first, the Persian Empire, then later, the conquering armies of Alexander the Great. After the death of Alexander, his kingdom was divided among his generals. Judea was caught in the middle and ended up under the system of the Seleucid Dynasty, Greek kings who reigned from Syria. A Syrian tyrant, Antiochus IV, was the new king who ruled Judea in 167 B.C.E.

King Antiochus forced the Jews to bow down to false gods, and did not allow them to worship Yahweh. Antiochus went into Jerusalem, took the treasures from the temple, and forbid the Jews from keeping their holy traditions; such as the Sabbath, kosher laws, studying their holy books, and the practice of circumcision. To prove his point, he desecrated the Holy Altar by sacrificing a forbidden, unclean pig upon it. The Holy Temple was then dedicated to the worship of Zeus Olympus. An altar to Zeus was set up on the high altar, and the Jews were forced to bow down before it under penalty of death. The Holy Temple was invaded, and pillaged of all its treasures. Many innocent people were massacred, and the survivors were heavily taxed. Antiochus went so far as to proclaim himself a god, taking the name Epiphanes—God manifest.

Flavius Josephus, a renowned historian who lived at the time of the Apostles, recorded the horrifying event of that time: (*Antiquities of the Jews* Book 12, Chapter 5)

And when the king had built an idol altar upon God's Altar, he slew swine upon it, and so offered a sacrifice neither according to the law, nor the Jewish religious worship in that country. He also compelled them to forsake the worship which they paid their own God, and to adore those whom he took to be gods; and made them build temples, and raise idol altars, in every city and village, and offer swine upon them every day (254). He also commanded them not to circumcise their sons, and threatened to punish any that should be found to have transgressed his injunction. He also appointed overseers, who should compel them to do what he commanded (255). And indeed many Jews there were who complied with the king's commands either voluntarily, or out of fear of the penalty that was denounced; but the best men, and those of the noblest souls, did not regard him, but did pay a greater respect to the customs of their country than concern as to the punishment which he threatened to the disobedient; on which account they every day underwent great miseries and bitter torments (256). For they were whipped with rods and their bodies were torn to pieces, and were crucified while they were still alive and breathed: they also strangled those women and their sons whom they had circumcised, as the king had appointed, hanging their sons about their necks as they were upon the crosses. And if there were any sacred book of the law found, it was destroyed; and those with whom they were found miserably perished also.

Revolt

Many Jews resisted, and refused to follow pagan practices, and would not bow down to the pagan idols. The Syrians attempted to force Jews to abandon the Torah and commandments, but God was in charge. Many times God had fought the Jewish battles, against all odds, delivering the evil to the righteous and the outnumbered. God helped the Jews to organize the common people, farmers, workers, and servants, and they began to fight their Syrian persecutors.

The Maccabees

This small group of Hasmoneans, under the leadership of Judas Maccabee, employed guerrilla warfare and drove the Syrians out. The Maccabees regained control of the Holy Temple, and began the task of purifying it. The altar which had been defiled by the sacrifice of a pig upon it was torn down and rebuilt. All new holy vessels were crafted. A date for the rededication of the Temple was set—the twenty-fifth day of the Hebrew month of Kislev, which occurs approximately in the Roman month of December.

Taking unhewn stones, as the law commands, they built a new altar on the model of the previous one. They rebuilt the Temple and restored its interior, and consecrated the Temple courts. They renewed the sacred vessels and the lampstand, and brought the altar of incense and the table into the Temple. They burnt incense on the altar and lit the lamps on the lampstand to shine within the Temple. They decorated the front of the Temple with golden

Resources recommended in ◆several lessons, ★ several units, ◗ other HOW Units. ◗—Key Resource (see beginning of unit or page 32).

Heart of Wisdom Publishing 407

wreaths and ornamental shields. They renewed the gates and the priest's rooms, and fitted them with doors. When they had put the Bread of the Presence on the table and hung the curtains, all their work was completed (Killian 1996). The Temple was then rededicated to God with festivities that lasted eight days.

The Miracle

When the Jews cleaned out the temple idols, they found only one small cruse of oil containing only enough oil to light their holy lamps for one day. They decided to light the Menorah (the Temple candelabra) even with this small amount of oil. To everyone's amazement, the menorah miraculously burned for eight days until new oil was available!

Celebration

The congregation of Israel decreed that the rededication of the Temple should be observed with joy and gladness at the same season each year, for eight days, beginning on the twenty-fifth of Kislev. The light of the menorah is the symbol of the light of Yahweh. The fact that the light burned even when no supply was left is a perfect symbol of the eternity of God's Word. The heart of the celebration called Hanukkah is not only the Rabbis' retelling of the saga of revolt and renewal, but also the retelling of the divine experience of the miracle of the oil.

It is the practice, in Jewish tradition, to have festive meals for the eight days of Hanukkah, in addition to Latkes—jelly doughnuts fried in oil. (Both symbolize the miracle of the oil.) Other popular sources of joy are the Hanukkah gifts and Hanukkah gelt (money). The major ritual ceremony of the holiday is the lighting of the Hanukkah menorah. The eight days are marked by prayers of thanksgiving, special songs of praise (for the miracles and redemption), the Shmoneh Esrei (the central silent prayer) three times a day, and grace after meals.

Do more research about Hanukkah. Use any resource (an encyclopedia, nonfiction book, historical novel, or the Internet). If you do an Internet search, try several different spellings (Channuka, Channukah, Chanuka, Chanukah, Chanuko, Hannuka, Hannukah). We recommend the following:

Books

Encyclopedia of the Bible (Nelson's Illustrated) ♥
Read: "Between the Testaments" (238-239). "1-2, 3--4 Maccabees" (241).

The Holman Bible Atlas ♥
Read: "The Maccaabean Revolt" (183-189).

History of the Jewish People Volume 1: Second Temple Era ♦
Read: Chapter 8 Antiochus Epiphanes and His Decrees, and Chapter 9 The Hasmonean Wars and the Miracle of Chanukkah.

Underlined text refers to Internet link at http://Homeschool-Books.com

A Family Guide to the Biblical Holidays ★
Read: "Hanukkah" (381-403).

Ancient Israel: From Abraham to the Roman Destruction of the Temple ★
Read: The Age of Hellenism.

Internet Sources

The Internet pages below are from the book A Family Guide to the Biblical Holidays ★.

Purpose of Hanukkah
Description: An overview of the purpose of Hanukkah.

Hanukkah in Bible Times
Description: The inter-testamental story of Hanukkah.

Jewish Customs of Hanukkah
Description: An overview of the Jewish Customs of Hanukkah today.

Messianic Significance of Hanukkah
Description: Reveals the symbolic picture of Christ in Hanukkah.

Eight Hanukkah Readings
Description: Bible devotions for the eight nights of Hanukkah.

Hanukkah Internet Sites
Description: Jewish and Messianic links focusing on Hanukkah.

Step 3 Expand

Choose and complete one of the following activities:

Activity 1: Celebrate and Write About Hanukkah
Celebrate Hanukkah with your family. Write a diary or journal entry explaining the celebration and what it meant to you.

Activity 2: Create a Storyboard
A storyboard is a graphic, sequential depiction of a narrative. Gather the materials you would need to tell the story of Hanukkah on a storyboard. You can either draw this story or cut out pictures to tell this story to your family and friends. Refer to Storyboard directions (see page 26).

Resources recommended in ◆several lessons, ★ several units, ♥ other HOW Units. ◉—Key Resource (see beginning of unit or page 32).

Heart of Wisdom Publishing   409

Activity 3: Play a Game

Play the traditional Chanukah game, Dreidel, with your family. Refer to Make Your Own Dreidel and How to Play Dreidel. You can also Play Virtual Dreidel online.

Step 4 Excel

Share what you have learned about Hanukkah with a friend or family member. Correct all written work to demonstrate correct punctuation and spelling, and effective use of grammar. Add corrected written work or any illustrations to your portfolio. Add new words you learned in this lesson into your Vocabulary Notebook (see page 22).

Footnotes
1. Hanukkah (rededication) has only five letters in the original Hebrew. In English, there are at least seventeen ways to spell it, including: Channuka, Channukah, Chanuka, Chanukah, Chanuko, Hannuka, Hannukah, Hanuka, Hanukah, Hanukkah, Kanukkah, Khannuka, Khannukah, Khanuka, Khanukah, Khanukkah, and Xanuka.

The Roman Period 63 B.C. onward

Note: This lesson is an overview of Israel under Roman rule. The Christianity and Constantine lessons in the Ancient Rome Unit includes more on this topic. The Early Church Unit (in our next set of history unit studies) will include more about Israel under Rome in Paul's time.

Step 1 Excite

Rome was the most-celebrated city in the world at the time of Christ, and her occupation of Israel began in 63 B.C. To appease the Jews, the Roman Senate, with the approval of Octavian and Mark Antony, made the local leader, Herod the Great (73-74 B.C.), the king of Judaea (37-4 B.C.). Herod tried to win the support of his Jewish subjects by renovating the Temple in Jerusalem.

What do you remember about the mention of King Herod in the Bible? Read about Herod the King of Judah (Herod the Great) in Matthew 2, and about his son Herod Antipas, the Tetrarch of Galilee, in Luke 3:1; 23:7. Read the following as well: Incest of Herod in Matthew 14:3,4; Mark 6:17-19; beheads John the Baptist in Mark 6:16-28; Matthew 14:3-11; desires to see Jesus in Luke 9:7,9; 23:8; tyranny of in Luke 13:31,32; Jesus tried by in Luke 23:6-12,15; Acts 4:27. As you read, make a list of the character traits of each man.

Step 2 Examine

Herod was half Edomite and hated by the Jews because he tried to Romanize Judea. He was devoted to the Hellenistic culture, he disregarded the welfare of the Jewish people, and he murdered forty-five Hasmonean leaders upon gaining power. He placed a Roman eagle on the Temple gate, built a Roman theater and temple for the worship of the Roman emperor, murdered his Hasmonean wife and their sons, and basically neglected all things Jewish. He also slew all the children who were two years old or under that lived in Bethlehem, and in all the coasts thereof. (Matthew 2:16)

Herod accomplished much in the way of architecture. He rebuilt much of Jerusalem, including the Temple (a nine-year project); he expanded the boundaries of Judea; he built an aqueduct system, the desert fortress of Masada, and amphitheaters; and he created a new port in Caesarea.

After Herod's death, Judea became a Roman province (c. 4 B.C.). The territory that he ruled, which included almost all of Israel, was divided among his three sons: Herod Archelaus, Herod Philip, and Herod Antipas (see chart). This pattern of organization continued through Jesus's lifetime.

Resources recommended in ◆several lessons, ★ several units, ♥ other HOW Units. ☛ Key Resource (see beginning of unit or page 32).

Herod's son with his Samaritan wife Malthacewas was Herod Antipas. He was tetrarch of Galilee and Peraea during the time of Christ's life on earth (Luke 23:7). He was a vain man charged with many infamous crimes (Mark 8:15; Luke 3:19; 13:31,32), among which was the beheading of John the Baptist (Matthew 14:1-12). Pilate sent Christ to him when he was in Jerusalem at the Passover (Luke 23:7). Herod Antipas asked some idle questions of Him, and after causing Him to be mocked, sent Him back again to Pilate.

The Roman domination of the Western world continued to grow and stabilize throughout the first century A.D. The First Jewish Revolt occurred during 66-70; the Romans then destroyed the Second Temple. Afterwards, the area was organized as an imperial province, Palaestina, and governed by a legate from Caesarea.

The Second Jewish Revolt, led by Bar Kochba, occurred from 132-135. After that revolt, Jews were banished from Jerusalem and the area became the Roman colony Aelia Capitolinia.

After the second Revolt, serious Roman persecution of the Jews began. They were forbidden, upon pain of death, from practicing circumcision, reading the Torah, eating unleavened bread at Passover, etc. A temple dedicated to the pagan Roman god Jupiter was erected on Temple Mountain in Jerusalem. A temple to Venus was built on Golgotha, just outside the city.

From the early 4th century, when Christianity became legal in the Roman Empire, Jerusalem developed as a center of Christian pilgrimage.

Find out more about the Hebrews under the rule of Rome. Use any resource (an encyclopedia, nonfiction book, historical novel, or the Internet). We recommend the following:

Books

The Victor Journey through the Bible ●— ♥
Read: "Great Empires of the Bible" (171). "Empires of the Ancient World," (maps 176-177).

Encyclopedia of the Bible (Nelson's Illustrated) ●— ♥
Read: "The Romans" (72-73), "Greek and Roman Empires" (36-37), "Kings and Rulers" (116-117).

The Holman Bible Atlas ♥
Read: "Rome's Emergence as a World Power" (190-197) and "The Romans, Palestine and Herod the Great" (198-206).

History of the Jewish People Volume 1: Second Temple Era ♦
Read: Chapters 16-29.

Our Father Abraham: Jewish Roots of the Christian Faith ⊶ ★
Read: "First Jewish Revolt" (58-60, 74-77, 88, 93-95) "The Second Jewish Revolt" (69, 81-83, 88, 93).

Ancient Israel: From Abraham to the Roman Destruction of the Temple ★
Read: Chapter 8 Roman Domination: The Jewish Revolt and the Destruction of the Second Temple.

From Mesopotamia to Modernity: Ten Introductions to Jewish History Literature ❤
Read: "Judasim Under Roman Domination: From Hasmoneans Through the Destruction of the Second Temple" (57-70). See description on page 39.

The Jewish Roman World of Jesus by James Tabor
Description: Provides a cultural background of Judaism, Hellenism, the Roman world, and related matters. It is important to become familiar with the political, social, cultural, and religious ideas and realities of the mighty Roman Empire to gain an understanding of Jesus as a Jew in Palestine in his time.

Caesar and Christ: A History of Roman Civilization and of Christianity from Their Beginnings to A.D. 325 (Story of Civilization III) ★
Description: See description in the Ancient Rome Resource Section.

Internet Sources

The Roman World of Jesus: An Overview
Description: An explanation of the importance of understanding this time, by James Tabor, author of The Jewish Roman World of Jesus.

Palestine Under the Herods: New Testament Era
Description: A chart and brief history of the rule of the various Herods over Palestine during the New Testament era, by Dennis Bratcher of the Christian Resource Institute.

The Roman-Byzantine Period (135-638 C.E.)
Description: An overview of this period with links to information about food, costumes, sites, and the water systems during the Roman-Byzantine Period. Prepared for the Hebrew University of Jerusalem.

Herod the Great 37-4 BC
Description: Article about the Herodian family's rule from 40 B.C. until around A.D. 100.

Resources recommended in ◆several lessons, ★ several units, ❤ other HOW Units. ⊶Key Resource (see beginning of unit or page 32).

Rome and the Jews, Part I
Description: Overview of the Jews in Rome, by David L. Silverman.

Roman Rule (63 B.C.E.-313 C.E.)
Description: Overview of the Jews in Rome, from the Israeli Foreign Ministry.

Wars Between the Romans and the Jews
Description: Article with links describing the military engagements between the Jews and the Romans.

Step 3 Expand

Choose and complete one of the following activities:

Activity 1: Add to Your Time Line Book
Add Israel under Roman rule to your Time Line Book. Include King Herod, Pontius Pilate, and Paul. Refer to Reproducible Maps, Charts, Timelines & Illustrations ☛ ♥ (167, 231).

Activity 2: Write a Biography
Write a brief biography of King Herod, Pontius Pilate, and the Emperor Constantine. Younger students can narrate (orally tell) what they have learned.

Activity 3: Make a Chart
Make a chart of the Political Rulers of Judea. Use the following Scripture references: Matthew 2:1; Luke 3:1; Mark 6:17-29; 8:15; Matthew 2:22; Luke 3:1; Acts 12:1-3,21-23; Acts 25:13-26:32.

Activity 4: Write a Summary
Write a summary of the life of a Hebrew living under Roman rule.

Step 4 Excel

Share what you have learned about the Hebrews under Roman rule with a friend or family member. Correct all written work to demonstrate correct punctuation and spelling, and effective use of grammar. Add corrected written work or any illustrations to your portfolio. Add new words you learned in this lesson into your Vocabulary Notebook (see page 22).

Herod's Temple

Step 1 Excite

Review and recall what you learned from studying the Solomon's Temple Lesson. Read some of the Bible references to Herod's Temple: Forty-six years in building (John 2:20), very beautiful stones (Mark 13:1; Luke 21:5), magnificent structure (Matthew 24:1), the Beautiful Gate (Acts 3:10), and Solomon's Porch (John 10:23; Acts 3:11; 5:12).

Step 2 Examine

Herod the Great began the reconstruction of what some call the Second Temple in about 20 B.C.; it was really just an enhancement of the Second Temple. Herod was an ungodly foreigner, an Edomite (Idumean), who had been given the kingship by the Romans. He was the greatest builder in the world during that period of time. Herod built seven palaces and forts, and the work on the Temple was truly magnificent. The stones (ashlars) were huge, and every one had a border (embossing) carved around it. The work on the Temple and courts continued long after his death, until it was finished in A.D. 63. It was about twice the size of the Second Temple. Though some call it the Third Temple, but Jews do not think of it as other than their Second Temple. It had already been 46 years in the rebuilding process when Jesus ministered there (John 2:19). Neither Herod nor most of the Jewish leaders were at all godly during this period. The Temple was built for show and for political reasons, but a faithful remnant of priests and Jews worshiped Yahweh there nevertheless, in accordance with the teachings of the Torah. (Graff & Dolphin 1998).

According to the Gospels, Jesus participated fully in the practices and ethos of the temple. Jesus' birth was announced in the temple (Luke 1:17; 2:27-32), where he also was circumcised and studied with the rabbis as a lad (Luke 2:46). Later, of course, Jesus himself taught in the temple (John 7:14). It is not without significance that while Jesus was teaching in the temple precincts, He said, *If anyone is thirsty, let him come to me* (John 7:37), and the next day offered forgiveness to the woman taken in adultery (John 8:1-11). Blessing and forgiveness, which are priestly functions, were pronounced by Jesus in the shadow of the temple. (*Baker's Evangelical Dictionary of Biblical Theology*).

Do research about Herod's Temple. Use any resource (an encyclopedia, nonfiction book, historical novel, or the Internet). We recommend the following:

Resources recommended in ♦several lessons, ★ several units, ♥other HOW Units. �;— Key Resource (see beginning of unit or page 32).

Books

The Victor Journey through the Bible ○— ♥
Read: "Great Empires of the Bible" (171). "Empires of the Ancient World," (maps 176-177).

Encyclopedia of the Bible (Nelson's Illustrated) ○— ♥
Read: "The Romans" (72-73), "Greek and Roman Empires" (36-37), "Kings and Rulers" (116-117).

The Holman Bible Atlas ○— ♥
Read: "Herod the Great" (199-206).

History of the Jewish People Volume 1: Second Temple Era ♦
Read: Chapter 19 Herod's Rise to Power.

Ancient Israel: Its Life and Institutions ★
Read: The Position of Women, Widows (39-41).

The Temple and the Rock Study Booklet
Description: Within its sixty pages, you will find details of the most recent discoveries by Dr. Leen Ritmeyer on the Temple platform which for so long has been a scholarly terra incognita. These discoveries took place at the end of twenty-two years of intensive research, commencing with a study of the outer walls and ways of access to Herod's Temple Mount revealed in the excavations that followed the Six Day War.

The Splendor of the Temple: A Pictorial Guide to Herod's Temple and Its Ceremonies by Alec Garrard
Description: Contains a magnificent model of the Temple built in Jerusalem in the first century, which has been crafted exclusively for Ritmeyer Archaeological Design. Garrard has taken still shots of this enormous model to illustrate his book. Includes information on the services, functions of the temple, and sacrifices. (November 2000) Kregel Publications; ISBN: 0825426979.

Internet Sources

The Rebuilt Temple
Description: Chapter 9 from the book Thy Kingdom Come, Thy Will Be Done... by Ron Graff and Lambert Dolphin.

Herod's Temple Where Jesus Preached, Taught and Healed
Description: Brief overview of Jesus at Herod's Temple from BibleStudent.com.

Herod's Temple in Miniature
Description: A magnificent model of the Temple built in Jerusalem in the first century, crafted for Ritmeyer Archaeological Design.

Step 3 Expand

Choose and complete one of the following activities:

Activity 1: Write a Summary
Write a summary of the building and the destruction of Herod's Temple. Younger students can narrate (orally tell) what they have learned.

Activity 2: Add to Your Time Line Book
Add the building and the destruction of Herod's Temple to your Time Line Book. Refer to Reproducible Maps, Charts, Timelines & Illustrations ♥ (185).

Activity 3: Answer Questions
Answer the following:
1. How is it possible to enter the Most Holy Place? (Hebrews 9:6-8,11-12,26b)
2. When did this happen? (Matthew 27:50-51)
3. Why don't we offer sacrifices on the altar any more? (Hebrews 10:11-14)
4. What did Jesus say about the destruction of the temple? (Matthew 24:2; Mark 13:2; Luke 21:6)
5. How does the temple illustrate Christ? (Matthew 26:61; 27:40; John 2:19)
6. How does the temple illustrate the indwelling of God? (1 Corinthians 3:16,17; 2 Corinthians 6:16)
7. How does the temple illustrate the body of Christ? (Ephesians 2:21; 2 Thessalonians 2:4; Revelation 3:12)
8. How does the temple illustrate the kingdom of Christ? (Revelation 11; 14:15,17)
9. How does the temple illustrate the spiritual church? (1 Corinthians 3:16; 2 Corinthians 6:16; Ephesians 2:20-22)

Activity 4: Gather Illustrations
Find and gather illustrations (print outs from the Internet or photocopies from books) of Herod's Temple.

Step 4 Excel

Share what you have learned about Herod's Temple with a friend or family member. Add corrected written work or any illustrations to your portfolio.

Resources recommended in ♦several lessons, ★ several units, ♥ other HOW Units. ☞ Key Resource (see beginning of unit or page 32).

Heart of Wisdom Publishing   417

Israel History Review

Look over the events in Israel's history. Be sure all major events are recorded in your Time Line Book.

- God calls Abram to leave Ur and travel to the Promised Land. Abraham begets Isaac who begats Jacob, who begats Joseph from whom, the 12 tribes of Israel descended.

- The Israelites were enslaved by the Pharaohs of Egypt.

- Moses led them out of Egypt.

- After the forty years of wandering, the Israelites took over the land of Canaan.

- They were ruled by Judges for five hundred years.

- The Hebrews united to form a single state under a single monarch—the time of their early kings, David and Solomon. Their devotion to the Lord and their obedience to His law had brought about the blessings promised by Moses. As time passed, they drifted away from God. They imported the worship of foreign gods from the nations around them. Outwardly they observed the festivals and sacrifices of the Law, but neglected to care for the poor and oppressed.

- After the death of King Solomon, Israel split into 2 kingdoms—the southern kingdom of Judah and the northern kingdom of Israel.

- Neighboring peoples like the Syrians and Edomites encroached upon their territory.

- In 721 B.C., the Assyrians attacked and devastated Israel. Ten of the twelve tribes were taken to Mesopotamia, mixed with the population, and became the Ten Lost Tribes of Israel.

- Around 587 B.C., the Babylonians captured Jerusalem and exiled the other two tribes (Judah and Benjamin).

- After seventy years, a portion were allowed to return from Babylon.

- The Israelites were subject to the rule of the Persians, Greeks, and Romans.

Agriculture in Ancient Israel

The farmer knows just what to do, for God has given him understanding. (Isaiah 28:26)

Step 1 Excite

Brainstorm and discuss how your days would be different if you were a farmer totally dependent on your harvest to feed your family. (Read Deut 8:7-9.) What kinds of crops were grown in Bible times? What are some of the foods that were popular? What is gleaning? Were crops grown for things other than food? In what ways did farmers redirect rainwater into fields? Did God tell man how to farm? How do we know this?

Step 2 Examine

The sin committed by Adam and Eve in the Garden of Eden had catastrophic consequences for the human race. Since then, creation has been subject to decay. Adam and Eve could no longer dwell in a distinguished, blessed paradise, but were removed to cursed ground. The curse upon the ground, which made it barren and produced thorns and thistles, made man's employment with it much more difficult and toilsome.

. . . cursed is the ground for thy sake; in sorrow shalt thou eat of it all the days of thy life; Thorns also and thistles shall it bring forth to thee; and thou shalt eat the herb of the field. (Genesis 3:17-18)

Agriculture in ancient Israel was the basis of the economy, and the nation's wealth and welfare were tied to the land. The major crops of the land are listed in Deuteronomy 8:8: wheat, barley, grapes, figs, pomegranates, olives, and honey. Barley and wheat were the main food staples of the ancient Israelite. The primary harvest season in ancient Israel extended from April to November. This harvest period can be subdivided into three seasons and three major crops: the spring grain harvest, the summer grape harvest, and the autumn olive harvest.

Irrigation

To preserve water, the Hebrews devised elaborate systems of conduits and check-dams to capture and redirect rainwater into fields. Deep cisterns were also dug into the ground to catch and store rainwater. 2 Kings 2:19-22 tells about a town that had polluted water. The water was unfit to drink and could not even be used for irrigating crops. The people asked the prophet Elisha to do something about this problem. Elisha, who knew how to hear from

---

Resources recommended in ♦several lessons, ★ several units, ♥other HOW Units. ◉─Key Resource (see beginning of unit or page 32).

Heart of Wisdom Publishing   419

God, asked the people for some salt. He threw the salt into the water and said, This is what the Lord says: 'I have healed this water. Never again will it cause death or make the land unproductive.' The Bible says that, to this day, that water is still clean.

Commands

Various biblical laws and stories refer to ancient Israelite crops and harvests. One example is known as the Sabbatical Year. They were to sow their fields, prune their vineyards, and enjoy the fruits of their labors for six years, but in the seventh year, the land and the people were to rest (Leviticus 25:1-7). During the seventh year they subsisted upon the spontaneous accumulation of the excessive crops of the sixth year (Leviticus 25:6,7,20-22).

Another example is in Leviticus 19:9-10: *And when ye reap the harvest of your land, thou shalt not wholly reap the corners of thy field, neither shalt thou gather the gleanings of thy harvest. And thou shalt not glean thy vineyard, neither shalt thou gather every grape of thy vineyard; thou shalt leave them for the poor and stranger: I am the LORD your God.* The poor were allowed to glean the fields for food; farmers were not allowed to harvest the edges of their fields or go over them a second time, as that was reserved for the poor (Leviticus 19:9-10). Ruth gleaned from Boaz's fields in the story of Ruth.

Festivals

The Harvest seasons of ancient Israel were very important since they corresponded with the biblical festivals. The feast of Firstfruits was a time for the presentation to God of the first fruits of the barley harvest; Pentecost was a celebration of the wheat harvest; the Feast of Tabernacles was, in part, a time of thanksgiving for the harvest of olives, dates, and figs.

Figurative Bible References

The ancient Hebrews were involved with agriculture on a daily basis. Many Bible stories and parables use farming terms such as:

- Grafting (Romans 11:17-24)
- Fallow ground (Jeremiah 4:3)
- Sowing wheat, but reaping thorns (Jeremiah 12:13)
- Parable of the sower (Matthew 13:3-8,19-23; Luke 8:5-15)
- Parable of the tares (Matthew 13:24-30,36-43)
- Gleaning (Judges 8:2; Isaiah 17:6; Jeremiah 49:9; Micah 7:1)
- Sowing (Mark 4:3-20; Ecclesiastes 11:4; Isaiah 28:25; Psalms 126:5; Proverbs 11:18; Isaiah 32:20; Hosea 8:7; 10:12; Galatians 6:7,8)

Use one of the research resources to investigate ancient Israel's agriculture. Find out: Who owned the land? How were fields irrigated? What crops were grown? What plant is used to make linen fabric? What growing conditions are required for flax and cotton? What tools did farmers use? What fruits were cultivated? Use any resource (an encyclopedia, nonfiction book, historical novel, or the Internet). We recommend the following:

Books

The Victor Journey through the Bible ⊶ ♥
Read: "Planting and Harvesting (47), "Importance of Rain (143), "Rain and Harvest" (144), "Plowing and Plows" (145), "The Sower" (253).

Encyclopedia of the Bible (Nelson's Illustrated) ♥
Read: "The Farming Year" (104-105), "Feasts and Holy Days" (154-155), "Clothes Making" (136-137), "Food and Drink" (106-107). .

The Holman Bible Atlas ⊶ ♥
Read: Basic Economy and Food Supplies" (26-27), "The Agriculture Year" (27-29), "Agriculture and Israel's Pilgrim Feasts" (29).

The Usborne Book of the Ancient World ★
Read: Farming in Canaan (25).

Ancient Israel: Its Life and Institutions ★
Read: The Sabbatical Year (173-174).

Internet Sources

Agriculture in Ancient Israel
Description: Contains a discussion of aspects of culture, mainly those concerning agriculture and climate, which are useful for Bible study.

Thorns, Thistles, Briers, and Brambles
Description: A study of how plants and farming can be used to tell the good seed from the evil.

Agriculture - Easton's Bible Dictionary
Description: Explains the six agricultural periods and more.

The Ecology of Israel's Festivals
Description: Many of the Jewish holidays have a basis in nature. These pages provide a glimpse into some of the unknown history of the Jewish holiday cycle.

Resources recommended in ♦several lessons, ★ several units, ♥ other HOW Units. ⊶ Key Resource (see beginning of unit or page 32).

Heart of Wisdom Publishing   421

Plant List
Description: A listing of over two hundred plants, flowers, and trees mentioned in the biblical sources.

Farming in the Bible
Description: Explanation of the cessation of agriculture during the seventh year.

Sabbatical Year
Description: Explanation of the cessation of agriculture during the seventh year.

The History of Gardening
Description: A time line from ancient times to 1700, and more.

Step 3 Expand

Choose and complete one of the following activities:

Activity 1: Rewrite a Parable
Choose one of the Bible references using farming terms (in Step 2 above) to write about. Rewrite the referenced parable in your own words. Younger students can narrate (orally tell) the parable.

Activity 2: Define Terms
Look up and define the following farming terms: threshing, winnowing, terracing, plowing, gleaning, grafting, irrigation, reaping, pruning, and sower.

Activity 3: Expand Research
Today, much of the world's land is degraded due to erosion and poor farming practices. Do research to find out if allowing the land to rest in the seventh year makes the land more productive.

Activity 4: Expand Research
Look up a few verses containing farming laws, and discuss why these laws might have been commanded. The farming laws are found in: Exodus 20:9; 22:5,6; 23:10-12; 34:21,22; Leviticus 19:9,10,19,23-25; 25:2-12,15,16,19-28; Deuteronomy 5:13,14; 22:9,10; 23:24,25; 24:19-21; Proverbs 3:9,10; Ecclesiastes 5:9; Proverbs 27:23-27.

Step 4 Excel

Share what you have learned about the Hebrews in Egypt with a friend or family member. Correct all written work to demonstrate correct punctuation and spelling, and effective use of grammar. Add corrected written work or any illustrations to your portfolio. Add new words you learned in this lesson into your Vocabulary Notebook (see page 22).

Underlined text refers to Internet link at http://Homeschool-Books.com

Archaeology in Israel

Step 1 Excite

Archaeology in Israel has provided a valuable link between the country's present and past, with thousands of years of history unearthed at some 3,400 sites. Many finds attest to the long connection of the Jewish people with the land of Israel, including Solomon's stables at Jezreel Valley, houses of the Israelite period in Jerusalem, ritual baths at Masada, numerous synagogues, and the Dead Sea scrolls, containing the earliest extant copy of the Book of Isaiah in still-readable Hebrew script. Excavations have also revealed vestiges of other civilizations that left their imprint on the land over the centuries. All finds are recorded, and historical sites are carefully preserved and marked for scholar and visitor alike. [1]

Archaeologists have discovered evidence which proves that some of the Bible's stories are based firmly on real people and events. Although archaeologists, religious scholars, and historians vigorously debate the meaning of archaeological discoveries, on some conclusions almost everyone agrees. For instance, it is generally believed that the Bible version of Israelite history after the reign of King Solomon is based on historical fact because it is corroborated by independent accounts of Kings and battles in both Egyptian and Assyrian inscriptions of the time. Prior to that, however—before about 930 B.C.—the experts disagree on almost everything. [2]

In the1990s archaeologists in Israel unearthed amazing artifacts pertaining to two important figures from the Bible: a ninth-century B.C. stone inscription bearing the name of David—the ancient Israelite warrior-king who killed the giant Goliath—and a first-century A.D. tomb believed to be that of Caiaphas, the Jerusalem high priest who presided over the trial of Jesus. In both cases, it was the first archaeological evidence ever discovered suggesting that the two existed beyond the pages of the Bible. These are tremendously important finds, says James K. Hoffmeier, chairman of archaeology and biblical studies at Wheaton College in Illinois. They will certainly cause anxiety for the skeptics. Some have even hailed the discoveries as the beginning of a new golden age of biblical archaeology. [3]

The Bible tells us, . . . *faith is the substance of things hoped for, the evidence of things not seen.* (Hebrews 11:1)

Faith always has been the mark of God's servants, from the beginning of the world. Faith proves to the mind the reality of things that cannot be seen by the bodily eye. The Bible gives the most true and exact account of the origin of all things, and we are to believe it. The fact that it does not suit the imaginations of men is no reason to discount Scripture.

Resources recommended in ◆several lessons, ★ several units, ♥ other HOW Units. ●—Key Resource (see beginning of unit or page 32).

Heart of Wisdom Publishing   423

Step 2 Examine

Most biblical archaeologists and historians are decidedly post modern and secular in their thinking. They do not believe in the divine inspiration of the Bible. However, there are other scholars—men and women of faith—who view the Bible as the inspired Word of God even in regard to its historical details. Most of these traditional biblical scholars, including Christian evangelicals, are known as conservatives, fundamentalists, or maximalists.

Biblical archaeologists, historians, and theologians commonly hold four core perspectives toward the Bible and its historical content. Table below from Biblical Archaeology, (1999) High Top Media, http://www.bibarch.com/.

Unconcerned	Minimalists		Maximalists
Scholars in the Social Sciences (anthropology, political science, sociology, and the like)	Scholars in the Humanities (history, philosophy, religion, theology, and the like)		
Scientists	Critical Scholars	Liberal Scholars	Traditional Biblical Scholars
The historical inspiration of the Bible is a non-issue	The Bible is not an inspired historical account	The Bible is not an inspired historical account	The Bible is an inspired historical account containing trustworthy historical data
Need not look for correspondence between biblical account and archaeological record.	Need not look for correspondence between biblical account and archaeological record.	Need not look for correspondence between biblical account and archaeological record.	Must look for correspondence between biblical account and archaeological record.
Not disturbed when chronological placement of a biblical period reveals discrepancies between biblical account and archaeological record.	Not disturbed when chronological placement of a biblical period reveals discrepancies between biblical account and archaeological record.	Not disturbed when chronological placement of a biblical period reveals discrepancies between biblical account and archaeological record.	Disturbed when chronological placement of a biblical period reveals discrepancies between biblical account and archaeological record.
Willing to make chronological placement only in light of objective evidence (artifacts or inscriptions).	Willing to make chronological placement only in light of objective evidence (artifacts or inscriptions).	Willing to make chronological placement only in light of objective evidence (artifacts or inscriptions).	In light of such discrepancies, must seek a new chronological placement that demonstrates harmony between biblical account and archaeological record.
			This must be done if no evidence outside the Bible justifies the new chronological placement.

Pharaohs and Kings: A Biblical Quest ●━★
Originally titled "A Test of Time in The Historical Debate." See description in the Ancient Egypt Unit (181).

Pharaohs and Kings See description in the Ancient Egypt Unit (182).

Internet Sources

Bible Believers Archaeology: Historical Evidence That Proves the Bible
Description: An online book by John Argubright.

Biblical Archaeology - BibArch
Description: Explore the world of biblical archaeology with this comprehensive guide that features articles, research tools, glossaries, and bibliographies.

MSN Encarta - Biblical Archaeology
Description: This encyclopedic resource presents an abstract and reports on the history of the research of biblical antiquities and artifacts.

Biblical Archaeology
Description: A collection of links related to biblical archaeology.

Biblical Archaeology
Description: From the Mining Co.'s Israeli Culture page, a continually updated site regarding the ongoing discoveries in biblical archaeology.

Mysteries of the Bible
Description: Dedicated to the study and discussion of such Bible-related issues as Torah codes, the Dead Sea scrolls, and biblical archaeology.

Biblical Archaeology Review
Description: BAR provides information about its publications, travel and study programs, and educational seminars.

Foundation for Biblical Archaeology
Description: The Foundation for Biblical Archaeology organization promotes the science of biblical archaeology by providing funding and support for expeditions, publication, research, and education.

Are The Bible's Stories True?
Description: *Time Magazine* cover story, December 18, 1995, Volume 146, No. 25. A flood of archaeological discoveries in the Holy Land is separating fact from

Resources recommended in ◆several lessons, ★ several units, ♥ other HOW Units. ●━Key Resource (see beginning of unit or page 32).

Heart of Wisdom Publishing   425

fiction, casting new light on the questions of whether Abraham, Moses, and King David really existed, whether the Exodus took place, and whether Joshua actually fit the Battle of Jericho.

Step 3 Expand

Choose and complete one of the following activities:

Activity 1: Fill out a Contrast-and-Compare Sheet
Make a contrast-and-compare graphic (see page 26) to compare some-one who believes the accounts in the Bible without archaeological evidence with someone who believes the accounts in the Bible because of archaeological evidence. Refer to Hebrews 11:1. What NT Bible character does this assignment remind you of?

Activity 2: Create a Model
Create a superposition model (instructions below) to demonstrate what an archaeologist must uncover (dig through) in order to reveal several layers of artifacts. You will need:

- One-gallon plastic milk jug
- Artifacts (coins, seeds, buttons, etc.)
- Sand or fine soil (colored sand preferred)
- Resin (to glue the project so it will stay together)
- Newspapers
- Small knife

1. Spread out newspapers.
2. Cut the uppermost part of the milk jug off so that only the bottom six inches are left.
3. Place artifacts such as buttons, twigs, coins, beads, etc. on the bottom of the jug.
4. Add a 1-centimeter layer of sand, fine dirt, or clay over the artifacts.
5. Repeat the process using different artifacts and different colors of clay or sand (soil).
6. After the assemblage has been completed, use the resin to bind the different items together so that the model will be stable enough to view after the jug is taken away.
7. Wait twenty-four hours. Cut the milk jug from around the model.
8. Label the model as to each stratigraphic layer so that each of the 1-centimeter layers can be differentiated as to age, color, etc.

Activity 3: Write a Report
Write a report about archaeological discoveries made in Israel. Include a bibliography.

Step 4 Excel

Share what you have learned about archaeology in Israel with a friend or family member. Correct all written work to demonstrate correct punctuation and spelling, and effective use of grammar. Add corrected written work or any illustrations to your portfolio. Add new words you learned in this lesson into your Vocabulary Notebook (see page 22).

Footnotes
1. (Focus MultiMedia).
2. Adapted from *Time Magazine* cover story December 18, 1995.
3. Sheler, Jeffery L. *U.S. News & World Report*, April 17, 1995, pp. 60-68.

Resources recommended in ◆several lessons, ★ several units, ♥ other HOW Units. ☀—Key Resource (see beginning of unit or page 32).

Clothing in Ancient Israel: The Tallit

Step 1 Excite

There are familiar expressions, or sayings, in the English language that we often use without knowing where they come from. For example, you may know what the phrases *goody two-shoes* and the *whole nine yards* mean, but do you know the origins of those expressions?

Read Matthew 9:20-23. What part of Jesus did the woman touch? What does that mean to you (today in America)?

Step 2 Examine

The tallit or prayer shawl is a long rectangle of cloth mostly worn by men. It is used most often during morning prayer. On each of the four corners of the tallit are tzitzit (tassels), each of which has five knots and eight threads. *Make tassels on the corners of your garments and put a blue cord on each tassel. You are to do this for all time to come. The tassels will serve as reminders, and each time you see them you will remember all my commands and obey them; then you will not turn away from me and follow your own wishes and desires. The tassels will remind you to keep all my commands, and you will belong completely to me.* (Numbers 15:38-40) The tassels on the tallit represent the 613 commandments given by God to Moses. When we look at customs such as this, we can better appreciate stories in the Bible.

In *The Hem of His Garment,* Dr. John Garr[1] explains:

> The story in Matthew 9 is not just an isolated, one-of-a-kind event in the life of Jesus, a time when one lone woman reached out and touched the hem of his garment to be healed. In Matthew 14:35,36, this story is reported: And when the men of [Gennesaret] had knowledge of him, they sent out into all that country round about, and brought unto him all that were diseased; and besought him that they might only touch the hem of his garment: and as many as touched were made perfectly whole. Could it be that touching the hem of Jesus' garment became a common practice, with untold numbers of people—not just one woman or the diseased of one region—healed by such a simple touch? What was it about the hem of his garment that was so important that it should become a point of contact for the expression of faith that brought deliverance to all who touched it?

Underlined text refers to Internet link at http://Homeschool-Books.com

Hidden from the eye of the reader of these stories is an enriching key to understanding what actually happened on these days of deliverance. Virtually all of the translations of these passages of Holy Scripture render an incomplete portrayal of the actual object of the desperate woman's determined hand and of the touch of the diseased of Gennesaret. Most Christians imagine Jesus wearing a sumptuous robe and the woman touching the broad decorative band that was the hem of his robe. After all, as one person was heard to remark, That's the way he looked in all the photos we have of him!

Most versions of the Bible tell us that she touched the hem of his garment (2 Luke 8:44) or the border of his garment (3 Matthew 9:20, NIV.) or the edge of his cloak (Matthew 9:20, NRV.) or the fringe of his cloak (Luke 2:39). None of these translations, however, adequately conveys one important detail of the event. Without this detail, we simply miss the richness of this event and of an entire tradition in biblical history.

The word in the Greek text for hem is kravspedon (kraspedon), which means the extremity or prominent part of a thing, edge, skirt, margin; the fringe of a garment; the appendage hanging down from the edge of the mantle or cloak, made of twisted wool; a tassel or tuft. Kravspedon (kraspedon) is the Greek word that was used to translate the Hebrew word (tzitzit) in the Septuagint Version of the Hebrew Scriptures. (Scholars in Alexandria in the fourth century B.C.E. rendered this version in order to provide the Scriptures in the lingua franca of the Mediterranean Basin.) What the woman touched, then, was not a broad decorative band at the skirt of Jesus' garment, but the fringe, the twisted woolen tassel hanging from the edge of his mantle or cloak.

Do research about the Hebrew prayer shawl. Use any resource (an encyclopedia, nonfiction book, historical novel, or the Internet). We recommend the following:

Books

The Hem of His Garment by Dr. John Garr ★
As you read this volume, you'll be simply amazed at just how Jewish Jesus really was! You'll also be enriched by a comprehensive understanding of spiritual lessons found in biblically Hebraic dress. The story in Matthew 9 is not just an isolated, one-of-a-kind event in the life of Jesus, a time when one lone woman reached out and touched the hem of his garment to be healed. Hidden from the eye of the reader of these stories is an enriching key to understanding what actually happened in these days of deliverance. Most versions of the Bible tell us that she touched the "hem of his garment" or the "border of his garment" or the "edge of his cloak" or the "fringe of his cloak." None of these translations, however, adequately conveys one important detail of the event. Without this detail (which you

---

Resources recommended in ♦several lessons, ★ several units, ♥other HOW Units. ☞—Key Resource (see beginning of unit or page 32).

Heart of Wisdom Publishing   429

will learn about in this book), we simply miss the richness of this event and of an entire tradition in biblical history. Golden Key Books (423-472-7321). ISBN: 0-9678279-0-6

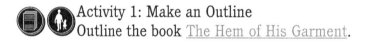 The Always Prayer Shawl by Sheldon Oberman, Ted Lewin (Illustrator) One thing that never changes is the beauty and tradition of Jewish family's prayer shawl. Young Adam is given his grandfather's prayer shawl when he leaves Czarist Russia for the U.S. Wrapped in the warmth of this special shawl each generation of Adams remembers the traditions and heritage that permeates the shawl. Lewin's enchanting pictures capture the passage of time in black & white and then color. The panorama of the historic scenes vividly recreate the time period while the color and intimacy of the contemporary period presents characters out of a family's photo album. Watercolor pictures. Paperback 40 pages. Puffin; Reprint edition (March 1997) ISBN: 0140561579 .

Internet Sources

The Hem of His Garment
Description: The book described above in online format.

Prayer Shawl History
Description: Article explaining that the prayer shawl is symbolic of something that God is doing on the earth.

Step 3 Expand

Choose and complete one of the following activities:

Activity 1: Make an Outline
Outline the book The Hem of His Garment.

Activity 2: Find a Picture
Find a picture of a tallit to add to your portfolio.

Step 4 Excel

Share what you have learned about the tallit with a friend or family member. Correct all written work to demonstrate correct punctuation and spelling, and effective use of grammar. Add corrected written work or any illustrations to your portfolio. Add new words you learned in this lesson into your Vocabulary Notebook (see page 22).

Footnotes
1. Garr, John, Dr. (2000) *The Hem of His Garment* Atlanta, GA: Golden Key Books (423-472-7321).

Underlined text refers to Internet link at http://Homeschool-Books.com

Clothing in Ancient Israel: General

Step 1 Excite

Brainstorm and discuss: what type of clothing did the Hebrews wear? How did their clothes differ from the clothing of the ancient Egyptians, Greeks, and Romans? What were the clothes made from? Who made them?

Step 2 Examine

What we know about clothing in ancient Israel comes from the Bible. *Easton's Bible Dictionary* explains,

> The earliest and simplest dress was an apron of fig-leaves sewed together (Genesis 3:7); then skins of animals (3:21). Elijah's dress was probably the skin of a sheep (2 Kings 1:8). The Hebrews were early acquainted with the art of weaving hair into cloth (Exodus 26:7; 35:6), which formed the sackcloth of mourners. This was the material of John the Baptist's robe (Matthew 3:4). Wool was also woven into garments (Leviticus 13:47; Deuteronomy 22:11; Ezekiel 34:3; Job 31:20; Proverbs 27:26). The Israelites probably learned the art of weaving linen when they were in Egypt (1 Chronicles 4:21). Fine linen was used in the vestments of the high priest (Exodus 28:5), as well as by the rich (Genesis 41:42; Proverbs 31:22; Luke 16:19). The use of mixed material, as wool and flax, was forbidden (Leviticus 19:19; Deuteronomy 22:11).

The robes of men and women were not very much different in form from each other. The description of biblical clothing below is from Daily Bible Study Web Site by Wayne Blank.

> The Inner Tunic: A long piece of plain cotton or linen cloth as an undergarment primarily for the upper body, but sometimes reaching all the way down to the ankles. It was usually not worn when the weather was very warm.

> The Tunic or coat or Ketonet: A shirt-like garment worn over the inner tunic in cool weather, or next to the body without the inner tunic when warm. It usually had long sleeves and extended down to the ankles.

> The Belt, or Girdle: Made of leather, from 2 to 6 inches wide, sometimes with a shoulder strap when heavier articles were being carried from it.
> The Cloak, or Mantle a robe worn over all of the other items of clothing as an outer garment for warmth and appearance.

Resources recommended in ◆several lessons, ★ several units, ❤ other HOW Units. ◉—Key Resource (see beginning of unit or page 32).

The Headdress: worn chiefly as protection against the sun. The Hebrew version could, depending upon circumstances, be a cap, a turban, or a head scarf.

Shoes or Sandals: shoes were made from soft leather, sandals from harder leather.

Tefillin (also called Phylacteries) Tefillin are black leather boxes with straps. Wearing tefillin was an observance of the commandment to bind the commandments as a sign on your arm and as a symbol on your forehead. The Rabbis interpreted the words in Deuteronomy 6:4-9; 11:18-21 literally. The arm phylactery had two strips of parchment folded up in a case of black calfskin. On the parchments were written four Scriptures: Exodus 13:1-10 and 11-16; and Deuteronomy 6:4-9 and 11:13-21. The arm phylactery was fastened with a long narrow strap to the arm and fingers so that when the arm touched the body the Law would be near the heart. The forehead phylactery or frontlet had the same four Scriptures placed in four divided compartments in a case fastened to the forehead with leather straps. In the first century, tefillin were part of ordinary Jewish dress.

Yarmulkes: Many modern Jews males wear a skullcap called a yarmulke (usually, but not really correctly, pronounced yah-mi-cah). It is the most recognized piece of Jewish garb, but the one with the least religious significance. In ancient Rome, servants were required to cover their heads while free men were not; thus, Jews covered their heads to show that they were servants of God. In medieval times, Jews covered their heads as a reminder that God is always above them. Whatever the reason given, however, covering the head has always been regarded as a custom (not a commandment).

Do research about the Hebrew s clothing. Use any resource (an encyclopedia, nonfiction book, historical novel, or the Internet). We recommend the following:

Books

The Victor Journey through the Bible ○━♥
Read: "Weaving on a Loom" (93), "Purple Cloth" (375).

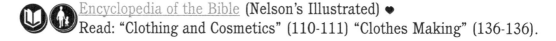
Encyclopedia of the Bible (Nelson's Illustrated) ♥
Read: "Clothing and Cosmetics" (110-111) "Clothes Making" (136-136).

Internet Sources

First Temple Period Costume
Description: Illustration of male attire from the First Temple period.

Second Temple Period Costume
Description: Illustration of usual attire of the upper class in the Kingdom of Judah (Roman toga).

Step 3 Expand

Choose and complete one of the following activities:

Activity 1: Make a Costume
Create a costume (for a male or female) using traditional styles listed above.

Activity 2: Create Illustrations
Create illustrations of biblical clothing.

Activity 3: Make Paper Dolls
Make paper dolls wearing Bible attire, with a younger child. See Bible Friends Paper Dolls or Bible Action Figures for ideas and patterns.

Step 4 Excel

Share your work by putting it on display. Include photos of displays or illustrations in your portfolio. Add new words you learned in this lesson into your Vocabulary Notebook (see page 22).

Resources recommended in ♦several lessons, ★ several units, ♥ other HOW Units. ●━ Key Resource (see beginning of unit or page 32).

Heart of Wisdom Publishing   433

Education in Ancient Israel

Step 1 Excite

Brainstorm, discuss, and make a list of the subjects that you study in your schoolwork. What subject do you focus on the most? Why? Make another list of the subjects that you think a boy living in ancient Israel would have studied. What subject do you think was his primary focus? Why?

Step 2 Examine

The Hebrew Bible does not give a detailed picture of formal education in ancient Israel, but it is clear that education was fundamental to the health and spiritual vitality of the community. The traditional importance that the Jewish people have placed upon education is based on Judaism's holistic view of life. Jews have long viewed all of life as a continuum in which each part of the human experience shares equal importance with every other aspect of life. Jews do not embrace dualism; for them there is no such thing as a difference between the spiritual and the material aspects of life; all of life is spiritual and good. God is the Creator of all things, and he declared all the things that he had created to be good and very good. (Genesis 1:31)

> Because of their holistic view of life, Jews do not make a vast distinction between spiritual and secular knowledge, for all knowledge is from God and is designed for the human good. The truth about the origin of knowledge can be found in Job 32:8:*There is a spirit in man: and the inspiration of the Almighty giveth them understanding*. All knowledge is the product of divine inspiration, often received by men as a flash of insight. Most of the great inventions and discoveries of history have not been merely the product of accumulated empirical evidence. They have come as a flash of inspiration. Both spiritual understanding and secular knowledge come from the inspiration or breath of the Almighty. (Dr. John Garr)

According to Duncan Ferguson there are four highlights of education in ancient Israel:

1. It was very practical in nature, often passed on in the home by the parents or acquired in guilds. It provided basic instruction in crafts and vocational pursuits (Exodus 35-36).
2. It gave guidance in worldly wisdom. The wisdom literature (Proverbs, Job, and Ecclesiastes) provides direction for coping with life, especially in social and economic relations (Proverbs 1:2-3).

3. It provided instruction in an ethical way of life. The emphasis is often on learning the law of the Lord (Exodus 20: 1-17).
4. It was a vehicle to pass on the traditions that bind the community together, give it a common language, and provide the symbols for the celebration of a good and meaningful life. There is a special emphasis on remembrance of what God has done (Deuteronomy 26:8-9).

The text below is from Our Father Abraham Study Guide:

Education with a Difference
1. All education was directed to this end: to be different was the law of existence . . . 'You shall be different, for I the Lord your God am different.' - Leo Baeck, *The Essence of Judaism* (New York: Schocken Books, 1948), p.261.
2. The ancient Greek world's view of teaching was that it primarily involved the transference of knowledge in the intellectual and technical areas, such as music, art, reading, or athletics.
3. In ancient Greek society, only the wealthy and leisure classes were enlightened through education. Indeed, our English words school and scholar derive from the Greek verb scholazo, to have leisure, to have spare time, to have nothing to do.
4. In contrast, Jewish education was for all people and concerned the whole person. Teaching had to do primarily with the communication of the Law or will of the Lord and was done by God himself, by the father of the family, or by a religious leader within the community.
5. In summary, the Greeks learned in order to comprehend, while the Hebrews learned in order to revere.

Biblical Education
1. The primary purpose of education in Bible times was to train the whole person for life-long, obedient service in the knowledge of God (Proverbs 1:7; Ecclesiastes 12:13).
2. The aim of learning was holiness in living—to be set apart unto God in every dimension of life. This holiness required a knowledge of God's acts in history and a commitment to observe his mitzvot (commandments), which instructed one how to live.
3. The center of education was the home.
4. Education is a matter which rests primarily with the parent, with the father. The teacher is but a representative of the father, according to Jewish tradition. Thou shalt teach them diligently, not vicariously. Now parents act as they please—commercialism and vulgarity blare from the loudspeakers—and little children are expected to listen to the voice of the Spirit. Religious instruction, like charity, begins at home. -- Heschel, *The Insecurity of Freedom* (New York: Schocken Books, 1972), pp. 54-55.
5. In the Hebrew Bible, teachers (priests) are called father (Judges 17:10; 18:19), and the relationship between teacher and student (e.g., Elijah and Elisha) is expressed as father and son (11 Kings 2:3,12).

Resources recommended in ◆several lessons, ★ several units, ● other HOW Units. ●— Key Resource (see beginning of unit or page 32).

Heart of Wisdom Publishing   435

6. In traditional Jewish homes today, when a child prays for his parents, he refers to them as my father, my teacher; my mother, my teacher.

7. The Bible teaches that study ought to be, above everything else, an act of worship, one of the highest ways by which a person can glorify God.

8. Paul makes no distinction between the so-called sacred and secular areas of life. He taught that all of life was God's domain. Every detail of life, therefore, must be set aside and consecrated to the glory of God.

9. Study is not an ordeal but an act of edification; the school is a sanctuary, not a factory; study is a form of worship. -- Heschel, p. 42.

Research education in ancient Israel. Use any resource (an encyclopedia, nonfiction book, historical novel, or the Internet). We recommend the following:

Books

The Victor Journey through the Bible
Read: "A Jewish Boy's Education" (212), "The Synagogue" (226).

Encyclopedia of the Bible (Nelson's Illustrated)
Read: "Education" (100-102) "Groups and Sects" (168-169), "In the Synagogue" (171).

Our Father Abraham: Jewish Roots of the Christian Faith
Read: A Life of Learning: The Heart of the Jewish Heritage.

Ancient Israel: Its Life and Institutions
Read: Children (41-51).

Sketches of Jewish Social Life
Read: Chapter 8 Subjects of Study; Home Education in Israel; Female Education; Schools and Schoolmasters.

Restoring of the Early Church
Read: Chapter 6 Greek Philosophy in the Church: How Did Plato Displace God?

Far Above Rubies: Wisdom in the Christian Community
Read: Part III The Wisdom Setting.

Education in Ancient Israel
See description in the Israel Resource section.

Internet Sources

Jewish Education in Ancient Times
Description: Article from *Restore!* magazine by Dr. Ron Mosley explaining that from the most ancient of times, the Jewish people were concerned with the education of their children.

A Life of Learning - The Heart of Jewish Heritage
Description: *Our Father Abraham Study Guide* Outline Part 7.

Beit Midrash–Learning How to Learn Together
Description: Article by Dr. Howard Morgan. One of the great advantages of the Judaic heritage that has been lost to the church is the art of the Beit Midrash, the House of Study, which has been so prominent in Jewish life. What can we learn about this art of interactive study that promotes maturity?

Step 3 Expand

Choose and complete one of the following activities:

Activity 1: Write a Story
Use your research to write a fictional story of a school day in the life of a young boy in ancient Israel.

Activity 2: Make an Outline
Outline the article Jewish Education in Ancient Times.

Activity 3: Contrast and Compare
Contrast and compare education in ancient Israel with education in ancient Greece, make a contrast-and-compare graphic (see page 26). Refer to the Education lesson in the Ancient Greece Unit.

Step 4 Excel

Share what you have learned about the ancient Hebrews' education with a friend or family member. Correct all written work to demonstrate correct punctuation and spelling, and effective use of grammar. Add corrected written work or any illustrations to your portfolio. Add new words you learned in this lesson into your Vocabulary Notebook (see page 22).

Resources recommended in ◆several lessons, ★ several units, ♥other HOW Units. ◐—Key Resource (see beginning of unit or page 32).

Heart of Wisdom Publishing   437

Family Life in Ancient Israel

Step 1 Excite

Brainstorm and discuss what you already know about family life in ancient Israel. Think of Bible stories.

Watch a video

Fiddler on the Roof
Description: A story about a poor Russian Jewish family at the turn of the century (not in ancient Israel). Ukrainian milkman Tevye clings desperately to the old Jewish traditions while all around him the world changes, day by day. His three daughters marry men whom he considers more and more unacceptable, and the ruling Russian government's anti-Semitism threatens to drive him from his home.

Step 2 Examine

Research family life in ancient Israel. Use any resource (an encyclopedia, nonfiction book, historical novel, or the Internet). We recommend the following:

Books

Encyclopedia of the Bible (Nelson's Illustrated) ♥
Read: "The Family" (94-95) "Marriage and Weddings" (96-97), " A New Baby" (98-99), "Daily Work" (102-103), "Tents and Houses" (112-113), "Inside the ome" (114), "God's Laws in Practice" (152-153).

The Victor Journey through the Bible ⚷ ♥
Read: "Children's Importance to Family" (26), "Birthright" (32).

Our Father Abraham: Jewish Roots of the Christian Faith ⚷ ★
Read: Marriage and the Family Through Hebrew Eyes.

Ancient Israel: Its Life and Institutions ★
Read: The Family (19-22).

Sketches of Jewish Social Life ◆
Read: Chapter 6 Jewish Homes and Chapter 7 The Upbringing of Jewish Children.

Underlined text refers to Internet link at http://Homeschool-Books.com

Sketches of Jewish Social Life ◆
Read: Chapter 8 Mothers, Daughters, and Wives in Israel.

Families in Ancient Israel by Leo G. Perdue, Joseph Blenkinsopp (Editor), John J. Collins, Carol L. Meyers
Description: The authors strive to show how biblical perspectives should influence the structure and functioning of actual modern families by demonstrating how social, cultural, and economic factors shaped the lives of actual ancient families and, in turn, how the realities of life in ancient families contributed to the various theological perspectives that come to expression in the Bible. The household was the theological lens, the ethical paradigm, the human context for understanding the character and activity of God and for living out moral responsibilities to others. Thus the household provided a crucial model or template for reflecting about God and God's relationship to His people. (May 1997) Westminster John Knox Pr; ISBN: 0664255671.

Families in the New Testament World: Households and House Churches
Description: Billed as 'the most comprehensive discussion of the family in early Christianity in any language,' this study explores the transformation that Christianity effected on the Greco-Roman family using everything from floor plans to classical references. The coverage includes the different systems of honor and shame for men and women in that culture. (May 1997) Westminster John Knox Pr; ISBN: 0664255469.

Internet Sources

Family and Society in Ancient Israel
Description: Brian Schwimmer at the University of Manitoba details ancient Hebrew customs, lineage, marriage, and social structure.

Home & Family
Description: Overview of home and family in Canaan and ancient Israel, from the University of Pennsylvania Museum of Archaeology and Anthropology.

Ancient Israelite Marriage Customs
Description: Lecture by a professor of Bible Studies at Quartz Hill School of Theology.

Marriage
Description: Discussion of Jewish weddings, the process of acquiring a spouse, and the marital relationship.

Resources recommended in ◆several lessons, ★ several units, ♥ other HOW Units. ☞—Key Resource (see beginning of unit or page 32).

Heart of Wisdom Publishing   439

(i) Birth and the First Month of Life
Description: Discusses Jewish customs relating to birth, naming, circumcision, adoption, and redemption of the firstborn.

(i) Love and Brotherhood
Description: Explains the importance of love, brotherhood, and the proper treatment of your fellow man in Judaism.

Step 3 Expand

Choose and complete one of the following activities:

Activity 1: Write a Summary
Write a summary about family life in ancient Israel. Minimum one hundred words. Younger students can narrate (orally tell) what they have learned.

Activity 2: Write a Description
Write a description of Jewish family life based on the movie Fiddler on the Roof. Younger students can narrate (orally tell) what they have learned.

Activity 3: Copy Paragraphs
Choose three paragraphs from one of the suggested resources. Have someone dictate each passage to you as you write it, or copy the section. Younger students can copy key sentences.

Step 4 Excel

Share what you have learned about family life in ancient Israel with a friend or family member. Correct all written work to demonstrate correct punctuation and spelling, and effective use of grammar. Add corrected written work or any illustrations to your portfolio. Add new words you learned in this lesson into your Vocabulary Notebook (see page 22).

Food in Ancient Israel

285-288

The Narrated Bible

He [God] made him ride on the high places of the earth, that he might eat the increase of the fields; and he made him to suck honey out of the rock, and oil out of the flinty rock; Butter of kine, and milk of sheep, with fat of lambs, and rams of the breed of Bashan, and goats, with the fat of kidneys of wheat; and thou didst drink the pure blood of the grape. (Deuteronomy 32:13-14)

Step 1 Excite

Brainstorm and discuss the kinds of foods eaten during Bible times. What are some of the foods that were popular? How do we know this?

Step 2 Examine

The Hebrew University of Jerusalem explains:

> During biblical times it was customary to have a late-morning meal, while the main meal was taken before dark. The most basic food, which constituted the staple of the common people, was bread. Wheat, barley, buckwheat, millet of lentils - these were eaten fresh, toasted over fire, or ground and crushed into flour. Bread was baked on hot stones covered with cinders, fried in a pan, or prepared in a twig-heated oven.
>
> One of the features that set apart the affluent in the ancient world was their frequent consumption of meat. The common people could not afford that luxury other than at the Passover sacrifice or on rare festive occasions. The description of the supplies for Solomon's kitchen brings the point home: Solomon's daily provisions consisted of 30 kors of semolina and 60 kors of [ordinary] flour, 10 fatted oxen, 20 pasture-fed oxen, and 100 sheep and goats, besides deer and gazelles, roebucks and fatted geese (1 Kings 5:2-3). Various types of food are mentioned: hunting meat, meat of domesticated and fatted pasture animals, meat imported from east of the Jordan River (cattle), and Egyptian foods (fatted geese).
>
> The picture also shows a selection of fruits and spices that could be gathered in the fields: hyssop, coriander, mallow leaves, mint, and thyme. Also visible are eggs of wild fowl, butter, and cheeses made of sheep's milk. Some scholars

---

Resources recommended in ◆several lessons, ★ several units, ♥ other HOW Units. ☞ Key Resource (see beginning of unit or page 32).

Heart of Wisdom Publishing   441

think that sugar cane reached the region in this period. Cooking oil, vinegar, and wine were foods in their own right and were also used as seasoning and toppings.

Kosher Foods

The Hebrew word kosher means fit or proper as it relates to dietary (kosher) laws. The word kosher itself means right, proper, fit to eat according to biblical law. There are two kinds of Kosher: Biblical Kosher and Rabbinic Kosher. A kosher label assures us that a food is biblically clean and fit for consumption; but food can meet the biblical standards without a kosher label.

Biblical Kosher

Biblical kosher refers to the dietary laws as outlined in the Scriptures, forbidding the eating of (1) animals that God calls unclean (Lev. 11:47), (2) animal fat (Lev. 3:17), or (3) animals that still have the blood in them (Lev. 17:12-14) as food.

Lev. 11 talks about clean and unclean foods. Clean animals include cows, sheep, goats, and deer. Unclean animals include pigs, horses, camels, rats, cats, dogs, snakes, raccoons, squirrels, and most insects. Clean birds include chicken, turkeys, geese, ducks, and doves. Unclean birds include eagles, sparrows, and crows. Clean seafood includes salmon, trout, and other fish with fins and scales. Unclean seafood includes catfish, sharks, shrimp, eel, octopus, squid, shellfish, and whales.

The story of Noah shows that the distinction between clean and unclean foods existed early in human history, long before God ratified His covenant with Israel. Almost a thousand years before there was a covenant with the nation of Israel, God told Noah to take two pairs of unclean animals and seven pairs of clean animals into the ark (Gen. 6:19-7:2).

Jesus knew these biblical dietary laws and obeyed them. But, He often came into conflict with the Pharisees over the traditions that they had added to God's law over the years. This brings us to Rabbinic Kosher.

Rabbinic Kosher

Rabbinic kosher is much more complicated and includes a whole body of tradition that distinguishes it from biblical kosher. The sources for the laws of kashruth are of biblical origin and expounded in Rabbinic legislation, through which the Rabbis interpreted, or added preventative measures to, the biblical regulations. The *Jewish Festival Cookbook* tells how the Jewish family is to make their kitchen kosher or ritually correct: All animals and poultry are to be slaughtered according to ritual by a highly trained man known as a schochet or kosher butcher. The animal must be of the clean variety, not being mutilated nor having signs of disease or lesions. First the animal must be killed a certain way; then only the forequarters may be used. After the meat is brought home, further koshering is necessary: soak for twelve hours, then drain and rinse. Next, sprinkle with coarse salt, let lay on a slanted board for one hour, and then wash the meat. Afterward, the book lists the different things to be done if the meat is organ meat or poultry. Then it goes into the restrictions in regard to eating milk and meat products together. This is carried to the extreme of separate utensils, dishes, silverware, pots and pans, dishtowels, washbasins, and even separate cupboards.

The selection and preparation of food according to the dietary laws, observed in kosher homes, have served to protect the health and welfare of the Jewish people since very early days.

Jesus Christ and his disciples obeyed the dietary laws of Leviticus 11 and Deuteronomy 14. But Jesus taught against the tacked on "fence" that the ancient sages had placed around Torah (Mark 7:1-23). The Pharisees and scribes taught that if you did not run flowing water over each hand, one at a time, and over the pots and cups then you were ceremonially defiled and when you touched the food it was also defiled. Jesus told the Pharisees that failure to observe all the ritualistic "Jewish traditions" was not a violation of God's law. He said, *"There is nothing from without a man, that entering into him can defile him: but the things which come out of him, those are they that defile the man."*

The Pharisees were fiercely proud of the righteousness they felt they had earned because of their meticulous obedience to all the regulations. But Jesus publicly rebuked them for putting their laws and regulations above the people. Jesus pointed out that washing cups and pots or hands was not the issue—it was what was in a man's heart—which defiled the man, not having his hands unwashed. Jesus affirmed the necessity of putting God's laws paramount above any tradition or requirement of any man or group of men. Insufficient hand-washing was not the point. What really matters is what comes out of one's mouth (our words and speech), which indicates what is going on in our heart. This message is found throughout Jesus' teachings—The attitude of the heart is the important thing.

Research food in ancient Israel or biblical dietary laws. Use any resource (an encyclopedia, nonfiction book, historical novel, or the Internet). We recommend the following:

A Word to Parents: This is a controversial subject. In the Old Testament, the issue was clear: God said to avoid eating the flesh of certain animals. It is in New Testament times that the issue has become blurred. In the modern world, Christians consume unclean meats because of a belief that New Testament scriptures permit them to do so. Some of the resources below promote following the biblical dietary laws for today (not as legalistic rules but as God's instruction for health). We urge you to look at both sides of this issue to understand both views. Utilize the controversy (iron sharpeneth iron) to prompt your student into deeper Bible study. *Study to show thyself approved unto God...* (2 Timothy 2:15) Discuss with your family your beliefs as a family about dietary laws, and why you believe as you do. *...be ready always to give an answer.* (1 Peter 3:15).

Resources recommended in ◆several lessons, ★ several units, ♥ other HOW Units. ☞—Key Resource (see beginning of unit or page 32).

Heart of Wisdom Publishing   443

Books

Encyclopedia of the Bible (Nelson's Illustrated) ●
Read: "Food and Drink" (106-107), "Food Laws and Customs" (108-109), God's Laws in Practice" (152-153), "Animals and Birds" (92-93).

The Victor Journey through the Bible ●—●
Read: "Manna" (66), "Passover Meal" (316).

Israel (Food and Festivals Series) by Ronne Randall
Description: Features some ink-and-watercolor maps and illustrations as well as many colorful photographs of people celebrating holidays and growing, preparing, and eating foods. (October 1999) Raintree/Steck-Vaughn; ISBN: 0739809598. Reading level: Ages 8 to 10.

God's Key to Health and Happiness by Elmer Josephson
Description: This remarkable study of nutrition is based on the oldest dietary laws known to mankind. Learn how good food, properly prepared, will bring you a healthy life, filled with glowing radiant personal happiness. The author is an ordained Baptist minister. ISBN: 0800708415.

Something Better, God's Original Design, Live Foods
Description: This book exposes some of the myths and prejudices against a high live-food diet. Better overall health, more energy, and clearer minds can be achieved when following God's Original Design—Live Foods. 175 pages. Order from Freedom of Health.

Internet Sources

Eating in Jerusalem of the First Temple Period
Description: Excellent article discussing foods in Bible times, from the Hebrew University of Jerusalem.

Eating in Jerusalem in the Byzantine Period
Description: Another article which discusses foods in Bible times, from the Hebrew University of Jerusalem.

Bread: the Daily Grind
Description: An explanation of the importance and making of bread in ancient Israel, from the University of Pennsylvania Museum of Archaeology and Anthropology.

Animals
Description: An overview of animals used for food and clothing in ancient Israel, from the University of Pennsylvania Museum of Archaeology .

(i) Clean Animals and Fat
Description: Dr. Gordon Tessler shows us that God's time-tested commandments in Scripture are a safer guide for food selection than a USDA stamp of approval.

(i) There is Nothing Unclean—or is There?
Description: Article by Dr. Gordan Tessler from *First Fruits of Zion Magazine.*

(i) To Market to Market to Buy...a Fat Hog?
Description: An article exposing the risks of eating pork.

(i) Unclean Meats of the Bible
Description: A list of foods which, according to the Bible, are fit or unfit to eat, including creatures of the air, sea, and land.

Step 3 Expand

Choose and complete one of the following activities:

Activity 1: Make Bread
Make bread from scratch. Bake a bread similar in style to that which ancient Canaanite and Israelite families would have eaten.

Activity 2: Create a Menu
Create a menu with illustrations for a restaurant in ancient Israel.

Activity 3: Create a Chart
Make a chart of the foods which God said were clean and unclean (Leviticus 11; Deuteronomy 14:3-21; Exodus 22:31;23:19; 29:13-22; 34:15; Leviticus 3:4-9; 9:18,19; 22:8). Were non-Jews (foreigners or strangers) commanded to keep the dietary laws? (Leviticus 17:12-15; 18:26; 20:2).

Step 4 Excel

Share your work from Step 3 with someone. Explain what you have learned in this lesson. Correct all written work to demonstrate correct punctuation and spelling, and effective use of grammar. Add corrected written work or any illustrations to your portfolio. Add new words you learned in this lesson into your Vocabulary Notebook (see page 22).

Resources recommended in ♦several lessons, ★ several units, ♥ other HOW Units. ☛—Key Resource (see beginning of unit or page 32).

Israel's Holidays

Step 1 Excite

Brainstorm and make a list of at lease five reasons why people celebrate annual festivals such as anniversaries, birthdays, July 4th, etc. Does your family observe any of the holidays listed in the Bible? Which ones? Think about the celebration of Thanksgiving. How much do you think you would remember about the pilgrims, Plymouth Rock, the Indians, and the Mayflower without the annual reminder?

Step 2 Examine

God told his people to set apart special days to remember Him. There are seven annual holy days listed in Leviticus: Passover, Unleavened Bread, Firstfruits, Pentecost, Trumpets (Rosh Hashanah), the Day of Atonement (Yom Kippur), and Tabernacles (Succoth). There are two other holidays mentioned in the Bible: Hanukkah (Chanukah or the Feast of Dedication) and Purim. The Sabbath is a weekly holy day. All of these holy days or Sabbaths are a beautiful picture of the Messiah's first and second coming!

The Biblical holidays contain more divine information of spiritual and prophetic value than any subject of scripture. Paul wrote to the Gentile believers in Colossians 2:16-17 that the holidays are a shadow of things to come. Each of the spring holidays is a picture of Christ's first coming. The fall holidays are a picture of His second coming and the beginning of the Messianic reign. Read the chart on the next page.

Read more about the Bible holidays. Use any resource (an encyclopedia, nonfiction book, historical novel, or the Internet). We recommend the following:

Books

Encyclopedia of the Bible (Nelson's Illustrated) ♥
Read: "Food and Drink" (106-107), "Food Laws and Customs" (108-109), God's Laws in Practice" (152-153), "Animals and Birds" (92-93).

The Victor Journey through the Bible ⚬––♥
Read: "Manna" (66), "Passover Meal" (316).

The Holman Bible Atlas ⚬––♥
Read: "Agriculture and Israel's Pilgrim Feasts" (29).

A Family Guide to the Biblical Holidays ★
See description in the "Resources Recommended in all Units."

Underlined text refers to Internet link at http://Homeschool-Books.com

Quick Overview of the Biblical Holidays

	FESTIVAL	PURPOSE	MESSIANIC SIGNIFICANCE
Spring Holidays	**Passover** Pesach Nisan 14 ❖	Remembering the deliverance from Egyptian bondage. An unblemished firstborn male lamb was sacrificed and its blood poured on the altar. A lamb was selected for each family, and four days before the lamb was to be slain it was brought into the home for a four-day examination period.	Jesus is the sacrificial lamb who died for our sins. On Nisan 15 at the exact time the lamb was to be slain, Jesus was slain. Jesus also had a four-day examination period before the religious leaders—and was found without blemish.
	Unleavened Bread Nisan 15	Leaven symbolizes sin. Unleavened Bread speaks of sanctification. God told the Jews to cleanse all leaven from their homes and eat only unleavened bread, matzah, for seven days, symbolizing a holy walk with Him.	Jesus is the "Bread of Life" without sin, born in Bethlehem. In Hebrew, Bethlehem means "house of bread." Just as matzah is striped and pierced, so was the Messiah. This Feast falls on the day Jesus was buried.
	Day of Firstfruits Nisan 16	The first of the barley harvest was brought as an offering to the priest in the Tabernacle/Temple. The priest would present the first of the harvest unto the Lord by waving them back and forth. This reminded the Hebrews that God gave them the land, and that the harvest belonged to Him.	Jesus is the Firstfruits (1 Cor. 15:20-23). Jesus' resurrection marked the beginning of the harvest of souls. John 12:23-24,32 shows Jesus was likened to a grain of wheat falling to the ground and dying to produce a great harvest. Jesus arose on Firstfruits.
	Feast of Weeks Shavuot 50 Days after Firstfruits ❖	Fifty days after the Feast of Firstfruits, a remembrance of the giving of the Torah (law) on Sinai took place.—Three thousand were killed that day. Also a reminder that the Jews were slaves to Egypt (Deut. 16:9-17). Two loaves of leavened bread are presented to God.	Fifty days after Jesus arose, a group of Messianic Jews received the Holy Spirit. Jesus said "Unless I go, the Holy Spirit will not come. But when I go (Firstfruits- His resurrection) I will send the Holy Spirit unto you." God wrote the law (Torah) on the hearts of the believers. Three thousand souls were saved.
Fall Holidays	**Feast of Trumpets** Rosh Hashanah Tishri 1	The Jewish New Year begins the high Holy Days in the Jewish month of Tishri (corresponding to September or October). A celebration of the spiritual birthday of the world or creation. Blowing of the trumpets and coronation of the King.	Possibly depicts the rapture of the church, a regathering of believers at the sound of the trumpet (1 Thes. 4:16-18; Rev. 19) and judgment of the wicked, or it is possible that this is the day of the second coming. Jesus will be King of Earth.
	Day of Atonement Yom Kippur Tishri 10	The holiest day in the Jewish year is spent in fasting, prayer, and confession. This was one gracious day a year given by God on which each individual could receive forgiveness. The high priest entered the holy of holies to make atonement for the nation by sacrificing animals.	Christ our Messiah was displayed as our sacrifice. We can use this as a time of self-searching, repentance, and recommitment to God. The goats represent Jews and Gentiles. Possibly points to the day of the Messiah's physically returning to earth. Or it is possible that this is the Judgment Day.
	Feast of Tabernacles Sukkoth Tishri 15 ❖	God told the people that they should live in booths for seven days so that the generations would know that His people lived in booths when He brought them out of Egypt. Each Sukkoth, the Jews build and dwell or eat in booths or temporary dwellings for seven days. A joyful celebration!	Christ is our tabernacle or dwelling place (John 14:14). May represent the 1000-year reign of Christ on Earth. Many believe that Jesus was born during this Feast because He was born in the late fall in a "booth." Or, this is possibly when we tabernacle (dwell) with God in heaven.

Internet Sources

Unless indicated otherwise the pages below are from the book A Family Guide to the Biblical Holidays ★.

Why Celebrate the Holidays?
Description: An explanation of how the festivals of God are blueprints for the plan of God.

What Happened to the Holidays?
Description: A brief history of the first- through fourth-century church.

Holiday Parable
Description: A modern parable about two kingdoms and two types of holiday celebrations.

Passover (Pesach)
Description: The Passover chapter from A Family Guide to the Biblical Holidays.

Step 3 Expand

Choose and complete two of the following activities concerning the seven holidays: Passover, Unleavened Bread, Firstfruits, Pentecost, Trumpets (Rosh Hashanah), the Day of Atonement (Yom Kippur), and Tabernacles (Succoth).

Activity 1: Write a Summary
Use your research to write a summary paragraph about each holiday. Refer to Writing a Summary in *Writers INC*.

Activity 2: Fill out an Event Worksheet
Fill out an Event Worksheet for each of the seven holidays.

Activity 3: Write a Poem or Song
Write a poem or song about one of the holidays.

Activity 4: Examine Scripture
Examine the verses about Jesus observing the holidays in Matthew 26:17-20; Luke 2:41,42; 22:15; John 2:13,23; 5:1; 7:10; 10:22. Examine the verses about Paul observing the holidays in Acts 18:21; 19:21; 20:6,16; 24:11,17.

Underlined text refers to Internet link at http://Homeschool-Books.com

Activity 5: Answer Questions

1. What are four words the Bible uses to describe the feast days? (Numbers 15:3; 2 Chronicles 8:13; Numbers 29:39; Isaiah 1:14; Leviticus 23:4)
2. With what emotion are these days to be kept? (Leviticus 23:40; Deuteronomy 16:11-14; Psalms 42:4; 122:4; Isaiah 30:29)
3. Does the Bible record non-Jews (foreigners or strangers) observing these days? (Exodus 12:19; 12:43-48; Leviticus 17:8,12; John 12:20; Acts 2:1-11)
4. When should Passover no longer be observed? (Exodus12:14)

Activity 6: Write Summaries
Read the verses explaining the times in history during which the people of God renewed the observation of God's holy days. Write a summary paragraph of each: Upon entering Canaan (Joshua 5:10,11), by Hezekiah (2 Chronicles 30:1), by Josiah (2 Kings 23:22,23; 2 Chronicles 35:1,18), after the return from Babylonian captivity (Ezra 6:19,20).

Step 4 Excel

Share what you have learned with a friend or family members by celebrating one or all of the biblical holidays. Correct all written work to demonstrate correct punctuation and spelling, and effective use of grammar. Add corrected written work or any illustrations to your portfolio. Add new words you learned in this lesson into your Vocabulary Notebook (see page 22) or Hebrew Notebook.

Footnote:
1. Sampson, Robin (1998) *A Family Guide to the Biblical Holidays*, Woodbridge, VA.: Heart of Wisdom Publishing.

Resources recommended in ◆several lessons, ★ several units, ● other HOW Units. ●—Key Resource (see beginning of unit or page 32).

Prayer in Ancient Israel

Step 1 Excite

The ancient Jewish people considered prayer to be equally important as Torah (Bible) study and charity. Prayer recurs in almost every book of the Old Testament (especially in Jeremiah). In the New Testament, Jesus, a Jew, taught his Hebrew followers how to approach God in prayer during the difficult days of the Roman occupation of Israel. Studying the patterns and principles of Jewish prayer can help Christians to pray more effectively and earnestly.

Watch a video

Jewish Roots, Jewish Prayer by Dwight Pryor
Description: This video is divided into two segments. First, Derek White of Christian Friends of Israel-UK conducts a discussion with Pryor on the importance of Jewish roots to the Christian life. Pryor then shares how Jewish roots have impacted his personal life and ministry. During the lecture portion of the video, Pryor discusses patterns and principles of Jewish prayer and shows how they relate to the Lord's Prayer. His lecture was delivered from the historical pulpit from which John Wesley and George Whitfield preached. Available from Jerusalem Perspective.

Step 2 Examine

Dr. Marvin Wilson explains:

> Prayer is the means by which Jews–both ancient and modern–have stayed attuned to the concept that all of life is sacred. Jewish prayers tend to be short because the entire working day of an observant Jew is punctuated with sentence prayers. More than one hundred of these berakhot, blessings, are recited throughout the day (cf. Mishnah, Berakhot 9:1-5). They customarily begin, Barukh attah adonai, Blessed are you, O LORD. As King and Creator of the universe, God's presence is acknowledged at all times and in every sphere of activity with his world. Moses commanded the Israelites to bless the Lord for his goodness (Deuteronomy 8:10). Building on this and other texts, the rabbis taught, It is forbidden to a man to enjoy anything of this world without a benediction, and if anyone enjoys anything of this world without a benediction, he commits sacrilege (Babylonian Talmud, Berakhot 35a). Abraham Heschel poignantly describes this Jewish mind-set as follows: Saintliness was not thought to consist in specific acts, such as excessive prayer . . . but was an atti-

tude bound up with all actions, concomitant with all doings, accompanying and shaping all life's activities. Indeed, today's Christians will fail to grasp Paul's admonition to Pray without ceasing, that is, Pray continually (I Thessalonians 5:17), unless they understand that a main feature of Jewish prayer is its persuasiveness.[1]

Prayer was of such great importance that, in Exodus 30:1-10, God commanded Aaron to offer up incense twice daily, once in the morning and once in the evening. These two occasions became known as the hours of prayer, from 9 until 10 a.m. and from 3 until 4 p.m. In the days of King David (Psalms 55:17) and in the days of Daniel the prophet (Daniel 6:10), we find that God actually gave Israel three hours of prayer—morning, noon, and evening. [2]

When Jesus' disciples asked Him how to pray, Jesus explained it to them with the example of the Lord's Prayer. The prayer that He offered as a model was a simple, condensed version of the rich Judaic prayer tradition that Jesus had practiced throughout His lifetime. Each phrase of the prayer model that Jesus taught His disciples was condensed from fundamental principles of the Judaic world view and mindset.

Our Father, who art in Heaven
(Communicating with God)
God is the Father of His people (as compared to the Greco-Roman view of god as an abstraction, the impersonal force of nature).

Hallowed be thy Name; Thy Kingdom come; Thy Will be done on Earth, as it is in Heaven
Praising and glorifying God
The coming of the kingdom clearly distinguishes Judaism from Gentile religions, the ultimate expectation of which is to escape the material earth to be absorbed into the spiritual, the realm of ideas (Platonism), or to escape the wheel of reincarnation into nothingness (Hinduism). Judaism anticipates and prays for the coming of the kingdom of God on earth and for the resurrection.

Give us this day our daily bread
Modestly asking for favors
A simple paraphrasing of Proverbs 30:8.

And forgive us our trespasses as we forgive those who trespass against us
Asking for forgiveness
There is a strong belief in Judaism that men cannot be at peace with God without first having been reconciled with their neighbors, as seen in the traditional Jewish Day of Atonement.

And lead us not into temptation; But deliver us from evil
Asking to help keep us good people

Resources recommended in ◆several lessons, ★ several units, ● other HOW Units. ●━ Key Resource (see beginning of unit or page 32).

Heart of Wisdom Publishing   451

Judaism recognizes God's allowing temptation to come into the lives of His chosen so as to test their faith.

The final part of the Lord's Prayer, which again praises God: "For thine is the Kingdom and the Power and the Glory for ever and ever" was added years later as a poetic finish to the prayer.[3]

Read more about prayer in Israel. Use any resource (an encyclopedia, nonfiction book, historical novel, or the Internet). We recommend the following:

Books

The Victor Journey through the Bible ☞ ♥
Read: "Prayer Times" (346), "The Synagogue" (226).

Encyclopedia of the Bible (Nelson's Illustrated) ♥
Read: "The Practice of Prayer" (174) "Psalms" (200-221), "Jesus the Teacher" (182-883). "The Earliest Christians" (172-173).

Our Father Abraham: Jewish Roots of the Christian Faith ☞ ★
Read: Pages 157-158, 187, 209-210, 248, 308.

Sketches of Jewish Social Life ◆
Read: Chapter 17 The Worship of the Synagogue.

The Jewish Background to the Lord's Prayer by Brad H. Young
Description: By examining the mindset of first-century Judaism, in which Jesus lived and spoke, the author shows the Disciples' Prayer to be a striking composite of Jesus' major teaching themes, serving to orient us toward God, self, others, the world, and evil. Can the timeworn and perhaps overly familiar words of the Lord's Prayer be more than a kind of spiritual pacifier for us today? Are there hidden in these simple words concepts that can stimulate and challenge us? The answer to both questions is yes, as the reader of this booklet will discover (Gospel Research Foundation, Tulsa, OK 1999). A teaching on this topic by Brad Young is available in an audio file from HaKesher Fellowship Series.

The Hours of Prayer by Robert Somerville
Description: Somerville writes on an aspect of prayer that is seldom considered: although the three daily hours of prayer are not mandatory for the believer, these prayer patterns established in the Scriptures are worth re-visiting and can bring a rich truth into the order of our prayer lives.

Biblical Prose Prayer: As a Window to the Popular Religion of Ancient Israel
Description: The Psalms are the best-known and most widely used prayer texts of the Bible. But the prayers of the Israelite took another form: the prose

prayers that we find embedded in biblical narrative. Contents: Lecture 1: The uniqueness of prose prayer as a humanly instituted mode of communication between man and God; the relation of form and content in petitionary prayers; Lecture 2: The social analogy; confessing guilt and confessionary prayer; thanksgiving; Lecture 3: Spontaneity vs. prescription in prayer; the validity of the evidence; lines of further inquiry; implications for the higher religion of the Hebrew Scriptures.

Internet Sources

Patterns and Principles of Jewish Prayer
Description: Judaism has a rich tradition of prayer that has been practiced in synagogues and in individual lives for centuries. Christians can gain a new respect for the dedication to God that devout Jews manifest, and they can learn lessons for more effective service to God.

Hebrew Foundations of New Testament Prayer
Description: Article by John D. Garr, Ph.D. A study of New Testament prayer reveals the earliest church's extensive Jewish roots. The Lord's Prayer is a condensed version of many synagogue prayers; apostolic instruction on prayer is based on the apostles' understanding of Jewish traditions.

The Lord's Prayer
Description: This series of nine articles by Brad Young rediscovers something of the original Jewish atmosphere in which Jesus taught his followers how to approach God in prayer. Young explains, It is difficult to grasp the full impact of the Lord's Prayer without an appreciation of its Jewish background. From JerusalemPerspective.com.

Prayer Lessons from Jewish Culture
Description: Article by Karl D. Coke, Ph.D., explaining the many features of prayer in the Jewish culture from which Christians can draw valuable insights that can make their own prayer life more complete and effective.

Software

First Steps in Hebrew Prayer
Description: This book provides an easy introduction to the first steps of Jewish prayer, bringing to you the most important prayers and blessings. It features the Hebrew text in bold letters, matched line-for-line with English translation and transliteration, and is illustrated with a selection of graphics and photos. You can order a book and a CD or tape together. See a sample page.

Resources recommended in ♦several lessons, ★ several units, ♥ other HOW Units. ◉—Key Resource (see beginning of unit or page 32).

Heart of Wisdom Publishing   453

Step 3 Expand

Choose and complete one of the following activities:

Activity 1: Make an Outline
Create an outline from the book The Jewish Background to the Lord's Prayer or one of the other resources listed.

Activity 2: Write a Prayer
Write a prayer for meals based on Deuteronomy 8:10. Jews do not bless their food. A Jew would not bless the object rather than the Creator; Jewish scholars used to hold that the object of the blessing was not the food but God. The Jews bless God after eating their meals.

Activity 3: Share with a Child
Visit the Torah Tots Internet Site and print out some of the prayer coloring pages. Share and discuss them with younger children.

Activity 4: Think about and Discuss
Use the following list to explain the twelve principles of Jewish prayer from the article Patterns and Principles of Jewish Prayer. Place a descriptive sentence after each principle.

1. In Jewish prayer there is no trace of vain repetition.
2. Jewish prayer is an outpouring of the soul.
3. Jewish prayers are congregational and community oriented.
4. Jewish prayer focuses on the Kingdom of God.
5. In Jewish prayer, God is acknowledged as personal.
6. In Jewish prayer, God is acknowledged as powerful.
7. Jewish prayer reminds us of great truths about God.
8. Jewish prayer references many biblical texts and allusions.
9. Jewish prayer is a daily duty.
10. Jewish prayer is a disciplined activity.
11. Jewish prayer is a focused devotion.
12. Jewish prayers are spoken in Hebrew.

Step 4 Excel

Share what you have learned about the Hebrews' prayer life with a friend or family member. Add corrected written work or any illustrations to your portfolio.

Footnotes
1. Wilson, Marvin R. (1989) *Our Father Abraham: Jewish Roots of the Christian Faith*. Grand Rapids, MI: William B. Eerdmans Publishing Company, and Dayton, OH: Center For Judaic-Christian Studies; ISBN: 0802804233.
2. Looper, Dr. John A. A House of Prayer for All People, *Restore Magazine*, RestorationFoundation@csi.com.

The Sabbath

Step 1 Excite

Brainstorm (for at least ten minutes) and make a mind map (or a list of words) about the Sabbath. Keep the list to compare your current feelings about the Sabbath with those you have after studying this lesson. Complete this step before going to Step 2.

Step 2 Examine

The Hebrews call the Sabbath "Shabbat." It is one of the best known, but least understood, of all Jewish observances. Many think of the Sabbath negatively, associating it with killjoys who want a day filled with suppressing restrictions. To appreciate the Sabbath day with God, we need to get rid of this negative image. To those who observe Shabbat, it is a precious gift from God, a day of great joy eagerly awaited throughout the week, a time when one can set aside all weekday concerns and concentrate on spiritual enrichment.

Observant Jews translate this command into practical observance by refraining from any act of creation or destruction on the Sabbath. Shabbat is a day devoted to rest, reflection, prayer, and Torah study. The order of the activities varies, especially among non-Orthodox communities—just as Thanksgiving varies in American homes. The Sabbath in Judaism is not just a day of rest, but a day on which to experience life in conformity with God's holy pattern.

The Roman Empire changed the Sabbath from Saturday to Sunday as a method of bringing sun worshippers into the church as well as separating Christianity from Judaism and furthering persecution of the Jews. Anyone found worshipping on the Saturday Sabbath was punished and sometimes killed. (See the Constantine and Christianity lessons in the Ancient Rome Unit.)

Research the Sabbath. Use any resource (an encyclopedia, nonfiction book, historical novel, or the Internet). We recommend the following:

Books

The Victor Journey through the Bible ●—♥
Read: "Sabbath Call to Worship" (227), "Pharisees' Rules About" (244), "Sabbath day's Journey" (245).

A Family Guide to the Biblical Holidays ★
Read: "Sabbath" (449-480). (See links to the online pages below.)

Resources recommended in ♦several lessons, ★ several units, ♥ other HOW Units. ●— Key Resource (see beginning of unit or page 32).

Heart of Wisdom Publishing   455

Our Father Abraham: Jewish Roots of the Christian Faith ◉— ★
Read: From Sabbath to the Lord's Day (79-80), Sabbath Observance (223-224).

Sketches of Jewish Social Life ◆
Read: Chapter 17 The Worship of the Synagogue.

Shabbat Shalom by Richard Booker
Description: For centuries the Jewish people have greeted each other with this wonderful phrase on their special day of rest—the Sabbath. In this book, you will learn what the Bible says about the Sabbath, and how Christians can celebrate the Sabbath from a Christian perspective in their own homes. You'll learn about the following topics: The Sabbath in the First Testament; The Sabbath Between the Testaments; Jews and the Sabbath; Sha'ul (Paul) in the Sabbath; The Church and the Sabbath; Celebrating the Sabbath in the Christian Home. While the Sabbath is central only in Jewish life, many Christians are being called by God to discover the Jewish roots of their Faith. The result is that a growing number of Believers around the world want to learn about the Sabbath. Sounds of the Trumpet, Inc.; ISBN: 096153026X.

Sabbath: The Light is Messiah by Cheryle Holeman
Written to the beginner interested in observing the Sabbath. Includes: Friday Night: Why do the Sabbath? Friday: Let's Begin the Sabbath; Challah Bread Recipe; Saturday and Havdalah Service. Available online.

Internet Sources

Pages below are from A Family Guide to the Biblical Holidays ★.

Sabbath in Bible Times
Description: An overview of Sabbath in Bible times, Jewish customs of Sabbath today, explanation of several symbolic clues in the Sabbath that are fulfilled in Christ, and suggestions for observing the Sabbath.

Step 3 Expand

Activity 1: Answer Questions

1. Who instituted the Sabbath? (Genesis 2:3)
2. On which day is the Sabbath to occur? (Exodus 20:9-11)
3. Why was the Sabbath made? (Mark 2:27)
4. What are the blessings for honoring the Sabbath? (Isaiah 56:2,6; 58:13,14)
5. Who is to honor the Sabbath? (Exodus 20:10; Deuteronomy 5:14)
6. What is God's instruction concerning the Sabbath (Leviticus 19:3,30; Exodus 20:8).
7. What is forbidden on the Sabbath? (Exodus 20:10; Leviticus 23:3; Nehemiah 10:31; 13:15-17,19; Jeremiah 17:21)
8. What is to be done on the Sabbath? List at least five things. (Ezekiel 46:3; Acts 13:14,15,27,44; 15:21; 16:13; 17:2; 18:4; Numbers 28:9; Matthew 12:5; John 7:23; Matthew 12:1,12; 13:16; John 9:14; Luke 13:15; 14:1)
9. What are four names for the Sabbath in Scripture? (Exodus 20:10; 31:15; Isaiah 58:13; Revelation 1:10).
10. Were non-Jews (foreigners or strangers) commanded to observe the Sabbath? (Exodus 20:10; Deuteronomy 5:14)
11. What does the Bible say about the wicked and the Sabbath? (Isaiah 56:2; 58:13; Nehemiah 13:15,17; Lamentations 1:7; Ezekiel 20:13,16; 22:8)
12. What is the punishment for those who profane the Sabbath? (Exodus 31:14,15; Numbers 15:32-36)
13. Did Jesus observe or teach on the Sabbath? (Matthew 5:17,18; Luke 4:16-31; 6:6)

Step 4 Excel

Share what you have learned about the Sabbath with a friend or family member. Correct all written work to demonstrate correct punctuation and spelling, and effective use of grammar. Add corrected written work or any illustrations to your portfolio. Add new words you learned in this lesson into your Vocabulary Notebook (see page 22).

Resources recommended in ♦several lessons, ★ several units, ♥other HOW Units. ☞—Key Resource (see beginning of unit or page 32).

Women in Ancient Israel

Step 1 Excite

Brainstorm and discuss what life was like for women in ancient Israel. How did others treat them? Were they educated? What did a typical day consist of? Was religion important to Jewish women? What were their primary roles? How did Jesus treat women? Did women teach, preach, pray, or prophesy?

Step 2 Examine

Many believe that women in ancient Israel were treated as possessions. This myth stems from the treatment of women in ancient Greece and Rome. In reality, Jewish women were honored.

The primary role of the Jewish woman in the first century was that of wife and mother; this was considered a position of prestige and honor; she was not looked upon as being inferior to man. The Lord anointed women and then gave them opportunities to serve His purposes. Women took an active role in religious life, in the home, and in the community. Miriam, Moses' sister, was a prophetess (Exodus 15:20). She was co-leader along with Moses and Aaron (Micah 6:4). Deborah (Judges 4:4) was a judge and leader in Israel. The *Wycliffe Bible Commentary* states, concerning this subject, "Discrimination on the grounds of sex was foreign to the spirit of the Old Testament. In her study of the role of women in the Old Testament period, Rachel Levine writes that woman was respected, her personhood was equivalent to that of a man, and she was considered to be a co-worker with the Lord in the creation of new life."

The examples of women in the Bible clearly show how the Lord anointed women and then gave them opportunities to serve His purposes. The Bible is full of stories of women of great faith and wisdom, like Jochebed (mother of Moses, Aaron, and Miriam), Abigail, Ruth, and Esther. The first promise of redemption was given to a woman (Genesis 3:15). Jesus encouraged the woman at the well to evangelize her whole town (John 4:7-42). Women such as the Virgin-mother, Elisabeth, and Anna enjoyed the privilege of ministering to Jesus. There were three women at the cross (John 19:25,26), and two women at the tomb who were the first to see the resurrected Savior and the first to proclaim the good news of His resurrection (Matthew 28:1,10). There were women who were preaching the gospel to such an extent that they were persecuted by Saul (Acts 8:3,4). The evangelist Philip had four daughters who were prophetesses (Acts 21:8-9). There were Jewish women in the Upper Room (Acts 1:14; 2:4). Women in the Old and New testaments did preach, pray, and prophesy.

A woman's family responsibilities exempted her from many commands, the observances of which depend upon a definite point in time. The demands of motherhood took precedence over religious observances outside the home; therefore, while permitted these religious observances, she was not required to observe them as was the man.

Mothers had the responsibility for the education of both boys and girls in the primary years. Rabbinic writings show that several women were considered scholars. (Rabbis were not averse to women studying as has been commonly supposed.) Excavations of first-century synagogues found no evidence for a separate women's gallery; on the contrary, archaeological evidence shows a common meeting room for both men and women. Three of the women prophets mentioned in the Old Testament are: Miriam (Exodus 15:20), Deborah (Judges 4:4), and Huldah (2 Kings 22:14). The rabbis add Sarah, Hannah, Abigail, and Esther (Meg. 14a) according to the *Encyclopedia Judaica*, Volume 13.

The obligations of husband and wife are explained by Alfred Edersheim in Sketches of Jewish Social Life:

> According to Jewish law, there were four obligations incumbent on a wife towards her husband, and ten by which he was bound. Of the latter, three are referred to in Exodus 21:9,10; the other seven include her settlement, medical treatment in case of sickness, redemption from captivity, a respectable funeral, provision in his house so long as she remained a widow and had not been paid her dowry, the support of her daughters till they were married, and a provision that her sons should, besides receiving their portion of the father's inheritance, also share in what had been settled upon her. The obligations upon the wife were, that all her gains should belong to her husband, as also what came to her after marriage by inheritance; that the husband should have her dowry, and of any gains by it, provided he had the administration of it, in which case, however, he was also responsible for any loss; and that he should be considered her heir-at-law.

Do research about women in ancient Israel. Use any resource (an encyclopedia, nonfiction book, historical novel, or the Internet). We recommend the following:

Books

Encyclopedia of the Bible (Nelson's Illustrated) ♥
Look up references to women in the index.

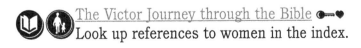
The Victor Journey through the Bible ●━♥
Look up references to women in the index.

Resources recommended in ◆several lessons, ★ several units, ♥ other HOW Units. ●━Key Resource (see beginning of unit or page 32).

Heart of Wisdom Publishing   459

Our Father Abraham: Jewish Roots of the Christian Faith ☞ ★
Read: Marriage and Family Through Hebrew Eyes.

Sketches of Jewish Social Life ◆
Read: Chapter 8 Mothers, Daughters, and Wives in Israel.

Ancient Israel: Its Life and Institutions ★
Read: The Position of Women, Widows (39-41).

A Novel Idea

The Midwife's Song by Brenda Ray
Biblical fiction. Under Pharaoh's ungodly decree, Puah, midwife to the Hebrew people, finds love, and sees her own vacillating faith grow in the fire of adversity. Utilizing biblical narrative, folklore, Ancient Near Eastern history, and imagination this story explains life in this time period and how an ordinary young woman can be used by God in an extraordinary way. Karmichael Press (2000). Paperback 256 pages. ISBN: 0965396681.

All the Women of the Bible by Herbert Lockyer
Description: Dr. Herbert Lockyer provides a convenient commentary on all the named and unnamed women of the Bible from Abi to Zipporah. (September 1988) Zondervan Publishing House; ISBN: 0310281512.

Paul, Women & Wives, Marriage and Women's Ministry in the Letters of Paul by Craig S. Keener
Description: Paul's letters stand at the center of the dispute over women, the church, and the home, with each side championing passages from the apostle. Now, in a challenging new attempt to wrestle with these thorny texts, Craig Keener delves as deeply into the world of Paul and the apostles as anyone thus far. Acknowledging that we must take the biblical text seriously, and recognizing that Paul's letters arose in a specific time and place for a specific purpose, Keener mines the historical, lexical, cultural, and exegetical details behind Paul's words about women in the home and ministry to give one of the most insightful expositions of the key Pauline passages in years. 350 pages (1992) Peabody, MA: Hendrickson. Reading level: Adult.

Private Women; Public Meals, Social Conflict in the Synoptic Tradition by Kathleen E. Corley
Description: This work, a revision of the author's Claremont dissertation, examines how women's differing roles in the ancient Greco-Roman world are reflected in the Gospel portraits of women. Focusing on women's varying portrayals in meal or banquet settings, Corley uncovers evidence that women's roles were undergoing radical social change throughout the Greco-Roman world—both in moving toward equality and in returning to a more traditional role. Such spadework helps us in analyzing

the conflicting portrayals of women in the New Testament gospels of Matthew, Mark, and Luke. Bibliography, notes and an index of ancient sources render this an invaluable tool for studying women in the Synoptics and ancient social attitudes toward women. This volume should be of particular interest to pastors and teachers and college, university, and seminary students, as well as informed laypeople. 217 pages (1993) Peabody, MA: Hendrickson. Reading level: Adult.

Women, Class, and Society in Early Christianity, Models from Luke-Acts by James Malcolm Arlandson
Description: Often scholars and students of the New Testament view women homogeneously, as if all women in antiquity existed at the same social, political, and economic level. Rather, women in antiquity, just as women of today, can be found anywhere along the spectrum of society, from voiceless slave to wealthy landowner. Anyone interested in women's studies will find this work indispensable in understanding the variegated nature of women in the ancient world and the Gospel's impact upon them. 238 pages (1997) Peabody, MA: Hendrickson. Reading level: Adult.

Missing Persons & Mistaken Identities: Women & Gender in Ancient Israel by Phyllis A. Bird
Description: This study retrieves the identities of women in ancient Israel through penetrating investigations of the Israelite religion, the creation stories in Genesis, harlots and hierodules, and the interpretation and authority of the Bible.

Internet Sources

The Biblical Woman
Description: Article by Dr. John D. Garr explaining that to understand proper roles for women in the church, we must return to the Hebrew Scriptures' patterns.

The Role of Women
Description: Article explaining that the role of women in traditional Judaism has been grossly misrepresented and misunderstood. From JewFAQ.org.

Women in Judaism
Description: An online course from Project Genesis covering a broad range of topics on women and Jewish spirituality, law, and philosophy. Archives include over twenty lessons such as: Men and Women in Judaism, The Eternal Jewish Bride: A Survey of Jewish Marriage Customs, and Women & Shabbat Candles.

Resources recommended in ◆several lessons, ★ several units, ● other HOW Units. ●—Key Resource (see beginning of unit or page 32).

Heart of Wisdom Publishing   461

Step 3 Expand

Activity 1: Write an autobiography as if you were a woman in ancient Israel. Answer the questions below; look up verses for help.

- What kind of clothes do you wear? (Deuteronomy 22:5; 1 Timothy 2:9,10; 1 Peter 3:3,4)
- What do you look like? (1 Corinthians 11:5-15)
- What domestic duties do you perform? (Genesis 18:6; Proverbs 31:15-19; Matthew 24:41)
- Describe your home.
- What holidays do you observe? (Leviticus 23)
- What do you do for fun?
- What hardships do you face?
- What are the major differences between your life and that of a modern American woman?
- Describe how world, national, or local events have affected you.
- What do you hope for?
- What or whom do you fear?
- Whom do you admire?
- What are your beliefs (religious, political, personal, etc.)?

Activity 2: Write a Poem
Several Hebrew women were poets: Miriam (Exodus 15:21), Deborah (Judges 5) Hannah (1 Samuel 2:1-10), Elisabeth (Luke 1:42-45), Mary (Luke 1:46-55). Write a poem about women's roles in the Bible.

Activity 3: Write a Book Report
Write a book review on a book you read during this unit. Focus on the women in the sotry.

Step 4 Excel

Share what you have learned about the women in ancient Israel with a friend or family member. Correct all written work to demonstrate correct punctuation and spelling, and effective use of grammar. Add corrected written work or any illustrations to your portfolio. Add new words you learned in this lesson into your Vocabulary Notebook (see page 22).

Resources recommended in ◆several lessons, ★ several units, ♥ other HOW Units. ☛ Key Resource (see beginning of unit or page 32).

Heart of Wisdom Publishing   463

Ancient Greece Unit

Unit Overview

Ancient Greece Overview 464

Ancient Greece Objectives 466

Ancient Greece Time Line 467

Ancient Greece Vocabulary 468

Ancient Greece Resources 469

Ancient Greece Lessons

History of Ancient Greece

Geography of Ancient Greece 474

Trojan War 1200 B.C. 477

Government of Ancient Greece . . .480

Greek Mythology (c. 1200-800 B.C.) . .482

The Olympics(first 776 B.C.) 485

Ancient Greek Astronomy (585 B.C.)488

Greek Philosophers (c. 550-250 B.C.) 491

Pythagoras (569-475 B.C.) 496

Persian Wars (497-490 B.C.) 499

Peloponnesian War (431-404 B.C.) . .502

Alexander the Great (356-323 B.C.) .504

Hebrews in Greece (332-363 B.C.) . . .508

Archimedes (287-212 B.C.) 511

Archimedes' Principle 514

Hanukkah (165 B.C.) 517

Life in Ancient Greece

Ancient Greek Architecture 520

Art in Ancient Greece 524

Cities: Athens 526

Cities: Sparta 529

Funerals in Ancient Greece 531

Weddings in Ancient Greece 533

Drama in Ancient Greece 535

Education in Ancient Greece . . .537

Daily Life in Ancient Greece 542

Food in Ancient Greece 545

Men in Ancient Greece 547

Women in Ancient Greece 549

Literature: Fables 552

Medicine in Ancient Greece 554

Religion in Ancient Greece 557

Science in Ancient Greece 560

Ancient Greece Overview

What does a group of people who lived before Christ have to do with your life today? Each of us has a worldview or a framework within which we think—a philosophy. The term "philosophy" means a set of basic values and attitudes toward life, nature, and society—thus the phrase "philosophy of life." The American, non-Christian worldview (secular Western philosophy) is generally considered to have begun in ancient Greece as a theory of the physical world. In its earliest form it was the same as natural science. Greek philosophy formed the basis of all later philosophical speculation in the Western world.

Our worldview is deeply affected by our culture. The intuitive hypotheses of the ancient Greeks foreshadowed many theories of modern science, and many of the moral ideas of pagan Greek philosophers have been incorporated into Christian moral doctrine. Christians need to be able to recognize Greek influence (Hellenism). We need to learn to think like Christians, not like the pagan Greeks. The Bible commands it.
Romans 12:2 cautions, *...be not fashioned according to this world, but be transformed by the renewing of your mind...* Philippians 2:5 encourages, *Have this mind in you, which was also in Christ Jesus...* And Corinthians 2:16 asserts, *But we have the mind of Christ.*

Christians are living in mindless times, days in which millions of people are drifting along through life, manipulated by the pagan influence of mass media (particularly television), though few realize it. Christians must swim against the tide by disciplining themselves to think—and, as a result, act—along biblical lines, obeying Paul's exhortation to the Romans to *be transformed by the renewing of your mind* (Rom. 12:2). There can be no neutrality in thinking. Jesus said, *No man can serve two masters....* Thought patterns are never truly "objective." At the root they reflect what we think about ourselves, the world, and God. In the way we think, we either serve the true God in Jesus Christ, or we serve some false god, some idol that has taken the place of God.

These lessons will address the key events, ideas, aspects, and issues of culture in ancient Greece in an effort to enhance your overall understanding. Through these lessons, you will learn about Greece's political history, social systems, cultural achievements, and economic conditions. Most importantly, you will see how the Greeks affected the view of Scripture and the church in ancient times, and how this effect is felt today. You will research concepts which have practical applications in the lives of individuals, for without such practical applications, these concepts remain little more than academic exercises.

During its time of greatness, the Greek Empire encompassed not only the southeastern region of the European continent, where we find it today, but also much of the land surrounding the Mediterranean and Black seas. Some scholars believe that it reached as far as India.

Greece originally consisted of the four provinces of Macedonia, Epirus, Achaia, and Peloponnesus. Acts 20:2 designates only the Roman province of Macedonia. The Romans conquered Greece in 146 B.C.

Moses makes mention of Greece under the name of "Javan" (Genesis 10:2-5); this name does not again occur in the Old Testament until the time of Joel (Joel 3:6). It was then that the Greeks and Hebrews first came into contact, in the Tyrian slave-market. Only prophetic notice is taken of Greece in Daniel 8:21, but the cities of Greece were the special recipients of the labors of the apostle Paul.

Much of today's culture—both good and evil—is influenced by ancient Greece's contribution to history, including botanical studies, free-standing statues, democratic government structures, advanced mathematics, humanism, and the Olympics. Sorting out the differences between a worthwhile contribution and idol worship requires prayerful study.

It would be a great help for you to read the following before you begin this unit:

The Greco-Roman World of the New Testament Era ●━ ♥
Read: "A Summary of Greco-Roman History" (293-320). See description on page 32.

Time Period Overview

Grecian history may be divided into four different ages that, together, span 2,200 years.

- The first age extends from the foundation of the several petty kingdoms of Greece, beginning with the most ancient, Sicyon, to the siege of Troy. It comprehends about 1,000 years, from 2200 B.C. to 1300 B.C.
- The second age reaches to the reign of Darius, the son of Hystaspes, at which point Grecian history begins to intermix with that of the Persians (approximately 1300 B.C. to 500 B.C.).
- The third age—the finest part of Grecian history—dates to the death of Alexander the Great, and spans the years from 500 B.C. to 300 B.C.
- The fourth, and last, age (which completes what is today referred to as the Hellenistic Age) commences at Alexander's death, at which time the Grecian Empire began to decline, leading to their final subjection by the Romans in 200 B.C.

Resources recommended in ◆several lessons, ★ several units, ♥other HOW Units. ●━Key Resource (see beginning of unit or page 32).

Ancient Greece Objectives

Upon completion of this unit your student should:

- Understand how ancient Greece's well-known and documented history intertwines with biblical time lines.
- Appreciate the pressures to succumb to idolatry which ancient Greece's culture placed on Jews then and still places on Christians today.
- Be familiar with the major events and understand the significance of the Persian Wars.
- Understand how Aegean civilization emerged and how interrelations developed among peoples of the eastern Mediterranean and southwest Asia from 600 to 200 B.C.
- Be able to name the major scientific and artistic achievements of Hellenistic society, and the Seven Wonders of the Ancient World.
- Understand culture in ancient Greece, including beliefs, rules of behavior, language, rituals, art, technology, styles of dress, ways of producing and cooking food, religion, and political and economic systems.
- Understand the significance of Alexander's achievements as a military and political leader (e.g., reasons for the disintegration of the empire into smaller areas after his rule; the campaigns, battles, and cities founded in Alexander's imperial conquests).
- Understand elements of Alexander of Macedon's legacy (e.g., the scope and success of his imperial conquests; his rise to power; methods used to unite the empire).
- Understand the major events and the significance of the Persian Wars (e.g., the long-term effects of the Persian Wars upon Greece; how the internal political and military structure of the two antagonists in the Persian Wars dictated their strategies; how the Greek city-states were able to defeat the "monolithic" Persian armies and navies; and Herodotus' version of the key events of the Persian Wars and how reliable this account might be).
- Understand how ancient Greece's geography influenced its governmental structures.
- Be able to explain why Greece is considered the birthplace of democracy.
- Understand the basis of ancient Greece's educational system and its influence on American schools.
- Understand ancient Greek advancements in the fields of science and math.
- Recognize artistic influences in statues, drawings, and pottery.
- Be able to draw parallels between the initial Olympics and today's games.
- Have the ability to point out ancient Greece's geographical coverage.
- Be able to explain how different ways of knowing and believing have influenced human history and culture.
- Have the ability to analyze the cultural characteristics that make specific regions of the world distinctive.
- Be able to explain factors that shape regions and places over time.

Underlined text refers to Internet link at http://HomeSchoolUnitStudies.com

Ancient Greece Timeline

Ancient Greece	The Hebrews
The Bronze Age (3000-1100 B.C.)	
c. 1500-1120 Mycenaean Civilization c. 1200 Fall of Troy	1200 Moses leads the Hebrews out of Egypt
The Dark Ages (1100-800 B.C.)	
c. 1100 Doric Invasion of Greece c. 1050-950 Greek colonization of Asia Minor (western coast of Turkey) c. 900 Beginning of the rise of the polis (city-state) 1000 King David takes Jerusalem	1000 King David takes Jerusalem 961 Solomon crowned King 942 Solomon starts construction on First Jewish Temple in Jerusalem 961 After Solomon's death Israel is split into two kingdoms, Judah and Israel 869 King Ahab reigns in Israel
Archaic Period (800-500 B.C.)	
c. 800-700 Rise of the aristocracies 776 Olympic Games established c. 750 Greek colonization of southern Italy and Sicily begins c. 720 Homer, *Iliad* c. 700 Hesiod, *Theogony* and *Works and Days* c. 680 Homer, *Odyssey*; Archilochus (lyric poet) c. 650 Greek colonization around the Black Sea 621 Draco's code of law in Athens c. 600 Sappho (poet); Thales (philosopher) 594-593 Archonship of Solon in Athens 545-510 Tyranny of the Peisistratids in Athens	701 King Hezekiah stops idol worship 586 Nebuchadnezzar burns the Temple 516 King Cyrus allows Hebrews to return to Jerusalem 516 Nehemiah begins second Temple
Classical Greece (500-323 B.C.)	
490-479 Persian War 431-404 Peloponnesian War 399 Trial and death of Socrates 399-347 Plato writes his dialogues 384 Aristotle born 387 Plato founds Academy at Athens 355-338 Sacred Wars	
Hellenistic Period (336-146 B.C.)	
335 Lyceum is opened by Aristotle 334-324 Alexander the Great rules 214-148 B.C. Macedonian War; Greece is reduced to province of Roman Empire	333 Israel under Greek rule 331 Alexander marches through Jerusalem on his way to conquer Persia 323 Ptolemies rule Jerusalem and Judea 204 Seleucid Kings rule Jerusalem and Judea 200 Dead Sea Scrolls 165 Maccabean revolt begins (Hanukkah)

Ancient Greece Vocabulary

See Vocabulary Instructions on page 22.

Acropolis

ambrosia

assuage

city-state

colonies

creature

cyclops

democracy

Dorians

drama

epic

fresco

god/goddess

helots

Homer
Ionia

laurel

lyre

metics

Minoan (Min-O-Un)

Mt. Olympus

mythology

Myths

narcissism

nectar

oligarchy

oracle

ostracized

Pantheon

Pegasus

Peloponnesus
Pericles

phalanx

philosophy

polytheism

precedent

realm

sacrifice

scythe

Sophocles

Styx

temple

thwart

titan

tunic

tyrant

vengeance

Ancient Greece Resources

The ❹ symbol indicates a resource appropriate for grades 4-12 or family read aloud. All other books are appropriate for young adults or adults.

Key Resources for this Unit

Ancient Greece (Eyewitness) by Anne Pearson ⚷— ♦
Full-color photographs of the artifacts, artwork, and architectural monuments of ancient Greece provide an informative look at the culture whose influential legacy—in science, medicine, art, and philosophy—shaped Western civilization. This book is recommended in most of the "Life in Ancient Greece" lessons. Hardcover— 63 pages (October 1992) Knopf; ISBN: 0679816828. Reading level: Ages 9-12.

The Holman Bible Atlas ⚷— ♥
See description in the "Key Resources" section beginning on page 32.

The Greco-Roman World of the New Testament Era ⚷— ♥
See description in the "Key Resources" section beginning on page 32.

Our Father Abraham ⚷— ♥
See description in the "Key Resources" section beginning on page 32.

Usborne Book of the Ancient World ⚷— ★
See description in the "Key Resources" section beginning on page 32.

Alternative Resources

Alexander the Great by Ulrich Wilcken
Provides a look into the life of one of the greatest conquerors of the ancient world and demonstrates the new trade and cultural routes that were created through Alexander's vast conquests in the East. Reissue edition (March 1997) W.W. Norton & Company; ISBN: 0393003817. Reading level: Young adult to adult.

Ancient City: Life in Classical Athens by Peter Connolly, Hazel Dodge
In this superbly illustrated volume, Athens and Rome, the greatest cities of antiquity, spring to life. By recreating the public buildings, temples, shops, and houses of these mighty civilizations, Connolly reveals every aspect of an ordinary person's life in glorious detail, including food, drama, religion, games, and the baths. 500 color illustrations. Hardcover— 256 pages (June 1998) Oxford Univ Pr (Trade); ISBN: 0199172420. Reading level: Young adult.

Resources recommended in ♦several lessons, ★ several units, ♥other HOW Units. ⚷—Key Resource (see beginning of unit or page 32).

Heart of Wisdom Publishing   469

Ancient Greece (Living History) by John D. Clare (Editor)
This book uses quotations, artifacts, and date charts to build informative portraits of people for young readers. It covers all areas of life in ancient Greece and emphasizes the importance of ancient Greek achievements to modern life. Includes index and glossary. Hardcover— 64 pages (March 1994) Gulliver Books; ISBN: 0152005161. Reading level: Ages 9-12.

The Ancient Greeks (Spotlights) by Charles Freeman
Now young people can investigate and understand ancient history in these handy and inviting surveys of days gone by. The text is concise yet packed with information to pique a child's curiosity and keep the pages turning. The full-color illustrations of people and activities, cutaways, and floor plans are fun to look at and make the basic ideas in the text crystal clear. Each page also features a series of captioned photographs of artifacts relevant to the subject. Expert captioning helps make learning about early civilizations interesting and fun. Spotlights on ancient civilizations are the perfect introductions to the fascinating world of history. Reading level: Ages 8-10.

Classical Kids: An Activity Guide to Life in Ancient Greece and Rome by Laurie Carlson
Travel back in time to see what life was like in ancient Greece and Rome while having fun with such hands-on activities as making a star gazer, chiseling a clay tablet, weaving Roman sandals, and making a Greek mosaic. 100+ line drawings. Paperback— 184 pages Chicago Review Pr; ISBN: 1556522908. Reading level: Ages 9-12.

A Coloring Book of Ancient Greece by Bellerophon Books, Nancy Conkle
Paperback (September 1985) Bellerophon Books; ISBN: 0883880008.

The Greeks
Examine the everyday lives of the world's oldest cultures and civilizations. Each book is filled with colorful pictures, maps, and diagrams. World History Dates covers 9000 B.C. to the present day. Usborne Books are educational children's books that make reading and learning FUN. Each includes a high ratio of illustrations to text. The illustrations alone are worth the cost of the book. (April 1991) E D C Publications; ISBN: 0746003420. Reading level: Young adult.

The Greek News by Anton Powell (Editor), Philip Steele (Editor)
Description: Designed to look like a full-color tabloid newspaper (though on glossy stock), with headlines, boxes, subheadings, columns, and illustrations, this book has a small news section, with stories on a few major events in Greek history, and a larger lifestyle section, with information on clothing, trade, health,

and more. Also included are advertisements for local shops and real estate, a quiz on how to be a good Greek, and numerous maps. Candlewick Pr; ISBN: 1564028747. Reading level: Ages 9-12.

The Groovy Greeks (Horrible Histories) by Terry Deary
A lively portrait of life in Greece more than two thousand years ago describes the origins of the Greek Olympic games, the highly revered god who ate his own children, the people who had the first flushing toilet, and more. Paperback (March 1997) Scholastic Paperbacks; ISBN: 0590031554. Reading level: Ages 9-12.

Handbook to Life in Ancient Greece ♦
This handy reference is recommended in most of the "Life in Ancient Greece" lessons. provides comprehensive access to over three millennia of ancient Greek history and archaeology, from the beginning of the Minoan civilization to the fall of the Greek city-states to the Romans by 30 B.C. Arranged thematically into ten chapters with titles such as "Economy, Trade and Transport" and "Religion and Mythology," the work is then subdivided by topics pertinent to each chapter, with further subdivisions as needed. The thematic arrangement of this volume makes it very useful for anyone desiring a brief overview of a specific aspect of Greek life all in one place. 179 halftones and linecuts. (December 1998) Oxford Univ Pr (Trade); ISBN: 019512491X.

How We Know About the Greeks by John James (Illustrator), Louise James
Looks at some of the evidence of the ancient Greek way of life, including archaeological research and the works of philosophers and playwrights. Library Binding - 32 pages 1 Ed edition (December 1997) Peter Bedrick Books; ISBN: 0872265374. Reading level: Young adult.

Jewish Women in Greco-Roman Palestine by Tal Ilan
This study explores the real—as opposed to the ideal—social, political, and religious status of women in Palestinian Judaism of the Hellenistic and Roman periods. This investigation concludes that extreme religious groups in Judaism of the period influenced other groups, classes, and factions to tighten their control of women. They also encouraged an understanding of ideal relationships between men and women, represented in the literature and the legal codes of the time, which required increasing chastity. Despite this, the lives of real women and their relationships to men continued to be varied and nuanced. This book integrates both Jewish and Early Christian sources, together with a feminist critique. It is the most comprehensive work of this sort published thus far and offers a vast repository of relevant material, as well as a fresh interpretation. Paperback— 270 pages (April 1996) Hendrickson Publishers, Inc.; ISBN: 156563240.

Resources recommended in ♦several lessons, ★ several units, ● other HOW Units. ●—Key Resource (see beginning of unit or page 32).

The Librarian Who Measured the Earth by Kathryn Lasky
The imaginative prose and bright, lively illustrations of the ancient land-scape tell the story of how Eratosthenes, the Greek mathematician and librarian, accurately measured the circumference of the earth more than two thousand years ago. (September 1994) Little Brown & Co (Juv Trd); ISBN: 0316515264. Reading level: Ages 4-8.

The Life of Greece (The Story of Civilization II) by Will Durant ♦
Volume 2 of *The Story of Civilization*, the Durants' dynamic synthesis of world history, deals with Greek civilization. *The Life of Greece* tells the whole story of Hellas, from the days of Crete's vast Aegean empire to the Roman conquest. The Durants' picture of 5th-century Athens is a masterpiece of compression, synthesizing the high points and highlighting the significance of what many consider the most fruitful epoch in history. "Tribute must be paid not merely to the immense learning which has gone into the making of the book but to the ease of its style and particularly the Durants' gift of concise, epigrammatic statement." (The New Yorker). (July 1997) Fine Communications; ISBN: 1567310133. You can buy or rent this book on tape from Books on Tape 1-800-88-BOOKS. You can listen to a sample reading from this book online. Note that this popular historian, Will Durant, was not a Christian. However, he does use the Bible as a historical record. See Caesar and Christ: A History of Roman Civilization and of Christianity from Their Beginnings to A.D. 325 (Story of Civilization III) in the Ancient Rome resources. Reading level: Advanced (high school to adult).

The Penguin Historical Atlas of Ancient Greece by Robert Morkot ♦
This book is recommended in most of the "History of Ancient Greece" lessons. This well-illustrated volume is just the thing to have on hand while working your way through the pages of Xenophon, Herodotus, and Thucydides. Robert Morkot traces the growth of Greece from a series of often-conflicting city-states—each with its own colonial outposts, which could be as far from home as Spain and Tunisia—to loosely knit alliances that waged huge conflicts against the Persian empire, and, as in the case of the Peloponnesian War, against each other. (January 1997) Penguin USA (Paper); ISBN: 0140513353. Reading level: Young adult to adult.

Software

The Civilization of Ancient Greece
Publisher: Florix Multimedia / Bonechi Multimedia
You'll find all the fascination of ancient Greece and of its refined culture, in five different interactive itineraries for a discovery tour of ancient Greece. Places: an archaeological excursion through the temples, the ruins, and the museums, all in

the evocative setting of the Mediterranean landscape. History: an overview of the course taken by Greek civilization, aided by twelve slide-shows complete with spoken commentary, reference maps, and animated sequences. Culture: an in-depth perspective on the art, literature, religion, and philosophy of the ancient Greeks, as well as detailed explanations of many aspects of their daily life, society, and political and economic organization.Florix Multimedia / Bonechi Multimedia.

History Through Art: Ancient Greece
Discover the Roots of Western Civilization, and learn how the architecture and sculpture of ancient Greece expressed the belief that humankind "is the measure of all things." A continuous multimedia overture (over forty minutes in length) dramatically illustrates the history and art of ancient Greece from 800 B.C. to 146 B.C. Witness the changes that occurred in the art of ancient Greece, from the vision of immortality and strength found in the Archaic Period, to the individuality and logic-tempered emotion reflected in the Classical Period, to the unrestrained emotionalism characteristic of the Hellenistic Period. Zane Publishing (972-488-9263).

Resources recommended in ◆several lessons, ★ several units, ❤ other HOW Units. ❂▬Key Resource (see beginning of unit or page 32).

Geography of Ancient Greece

Step 1 Excite

Ancient Greece consisted of numerous independent city-states populated by several ethnic groups. Greece is divided into three main regions:

- Peloponnese peninsula to the south; home of Sparta and Corinth.
- Attica in the middle; a plains area and home of Athens, Thebes, and Delphi.
- Macedonia to the north; a rough and rugged area that connects via the Hellespont to Asia Minor.

Step 2 Examine

The geography focus of this book, until this unit, has been on the Fertile Crescent area. Now we'll look at a bigger area. The Old Testament ends a few hundred years before the New Testament begins. This period had huge changes for the ancient Persians, Greeks, and Romans.

Use a globe to compare the modern boundries with those from ancient days. Research the geography of ancient Greece. Use any resource (an encyclopedia, nonfiction book, historical novel, or the Internet). We recommend the following:

Books

The Victor Journey through the Bible ●—❤
Read: "Great Empires ofthe Bible" (177). .

Encyclopedia of the Bible (Nelson's Illustrated) ●— ❤
"The Greek and Roman Empires" (36-37), "The Greeks (68-69).

Exploring Ancient Cities of the Bible ❤
Read: "New Testament Greece" (40-41).

The Holman Bible Atlas ●— ❤
See: "The Hellenistic Period" (174-189).

Handbook to Life in Ancient Greece ●— ◆
Read: Chapter 3 "Geography of the Greek World" (123-170). Topics include: Landscape, City-States and Colonies, Regions and Alliances, Place-Names, and Reading.

The Barrington Atlas of the Greek and Roman World
Description: The folio volume offers 99 maps in color extending over 175 map pages (mostly double spreads), and ranging from the British Isles to the Indian subcontinent and far up the Nile Valley. To be issued both in print and on CD-ROM. (September 15, 2000) Princeton Univ Pr; ISBN: 069103169X. Examples available online.

Internet Sources

Greek Geography
Description: A good overview explaining: the obstacles in the way of studying the geography, the various landscapes, cities, houses, towns and roads of ancient Greece.

Resources recommended in ◆several lessons, ★ several units, ● other HOW Units. ●━Key Resource (see beginning of unit or page 32).

Heart of Wisdom Publishing   475

Greek Geography
Description: A good overview explaining: the obstacles in the way of studying the geography, the various landscapes, cities, houses, towns, and roads of ancient Greece.

Outline of Greek Civilization
Description: Includes maps for each of the Greek historical periods.

Step 3 Expand

Choose and complete one of the following activities:

Activity 1:Make a Map
Trace or print out a map of ancient Greece to use during this unit. As you go through the units find and label each area mentioned. See http://heartofwisdom.com/maps.htm for Internet links.

Activity 2: Make a Cookie Map
Make a "cookie map" of ancient Greece. You'll need: a Bible Atlas, a cookie recipe, a can of frosting,a variety of chocolate chips, mini fun chips, or candy dots, and several tubes of cake-decorating gels in a variety of colors. Make a large cookie, then frost it (this becomes the "glue"), and use chocolate chips to locate selected cites or towns. Use the decorating gels to draw rivers, lakes, parks, or centers of mineral resources on the "map" using the symbols and the map key in the atlas.

Activity 3: Make a Salt-Dough Map
Make a salt-dough map of ancient Greece. You will need: 2 level cups plain flour, 1 level cup cooking salt, 3/4 cup water, 2 tsp cooking oil, food coloring (optional). Mix the ingredients together and then add the water and oil. Turn out onto a work surface and knead for 10 minutes, or until a small amount of the dough can be rolled into a ball without cracking. Divide the dough into parts and add food coloring (blue for water, green for land, etc.) or paint it with poster paints when dry. Draw an outline of ancient Greece on a sheet of poster board or other smooth card board. Spread the salt dough onto the outline, making mountains and other geographical features. Allow the map to dry thoroughly.

Step 4 Excel

Share your work from Step 3 with someone. Explain what you have learned in this lesson. Correct all written work to demonstrate correct punctuation and spelling, and effective use of grammar. Add corrected written work or any illustrations to your portfolio. Add new words you learned in this lesson into your Vocabulary Notebook (see page 22).

Underlined text refers to Internet link at http://Homeschool-Books.com

The Trojan War c. 1200 B.C.

Step 1 Excite

The Trojan War, arguably a mythical war, is described in the *Iliad* by Homer, and spoken of in the *Aeneid* by Virgil. This story is a major part of ancient Greek history. As the story goes, a war began between the Greeks and Trojans when Paris, a Greek, abducted Helen, wife of Menelaus, the king of Sparta. The Greeks pretended to depart, leaving the gift of a wooden horse for the Trojans. The Trojans, ignoring the warnings of Cassandra and Laocoön, took the horse into the city. Warriors hidden inside the horse opened the city gates to the Greek army, which destroyed Troy.

The Trojan War probably reflected a real war c.1200 B.C. over control of trade in the Dardanelles. Watch The History Channel program or the video below.

Ancient Mysteries: The Odyssey of Troy
Description: In the more than 3,000 years since Troy's fabled fall, its mysteries have yet to be unraveled. The legends of the Trojan horse, Helen of Troy, and Achilles have fueled some of archaeology's most celebrated expeditions, yet continue to baffle scholars and ignite controversy. *The Odyssey of Troy* is an exhaustive exploration of the legendary city. Travel to the site of Troy in modern-day Turkey, and visit the scientists and archaeologists who are probing its secrets. Search for answers to the central questions of this eternal mystery: Did the Trojan War really occur? Was the abduction of Helen its cause? And what do we know of Homer, the poet whose *Iliad* immortalized Troy's contentious history? The astonishing findings add a new and intriguing chapter to this legendary story. (Watch The History Channel local listings or call 1-800-408-4842.)

Step 2 Examine

Research the Trojan War. Use any resource (an encyclopedia, nonfiction book, or the Internet). We recommend the following:

Books

Resources recommended in ♦several lessons, ★ several units, ♥other HOW Units. ☢══Key Resource (see beginning of unit or page 32).

Heart of Wisdom Publishing   477

The Usborne Book of the Ancient World ★
Read: "The Trojan War" (110).

Kingfisher Illustrated History of the World ♥
Read: "Trojan Wars" (69).

Ancient Greece (Eyewitness) ♦
Read: "To Troy and Back" (12-13).

Kingfisher History Encyclopedia ♥
Read: "Trojan Wars" (38).

The Penguin Historical Atlas of Ancient Greece ♦
Read: "The Trojan Wars" (34-35).

The Life of Greece (The Story of Civilization II) ♦
Read: "The Siege of Troy" (55-59).

In Search of Troy by Piero Ventura and Gian Paolo Ceserani
Description: This easy-to-read adventure story is full of interesting
details tracing the story of the search for Troy. Described as an archaeological
detective story. ASIN: 0606012850. Reading level: Ages 9-12.

The Trojan Horse: How the Greeks Won the War by Emily Little, Michael
Eagle (Illustrator)
An ancient history lesson emerges from this account of the way the Greeks
tricked the Trojans and rescued Helen of Troy. The book is well tailored to
younger readers with careful explanations and short sentences; a pronunciation
guide is appended. Drawings portray the story's main events. A nice supplement
to units on ancient Greece. Full color illustrations. Paperback— 48 pages Random
House; ISBN: 0394896742. Reading level: Ages 9-12.

Inside the Walls of Troy: A Novel of the Women Who Lived the Trojan War by
Clemence McLaren
Helen is renowned as the most beautiful woman in the world. Her divine beauty
will lead her to a lifetime of adventure—from her kidnapping at age 12, through
an arranged marriage, to a passionate affair that will ultimately bring about the
Trojan War. Cassandra, the sister of Helen's true love, has the gift, or curse, to
predict the future. When she foresees the ruin of her family and city, caused by
Helen's arrival in Troy, she is outraged. Reading level: Young adult.

Internet Sources

ⓘ The Legend of the Trojan War
Description: Prepared for students in Classics 101 and Liberal Studies, this is a brief account of a number of different, ancient stories about the Trojan War.

ⓘ The Trojan War
Description: Includes images from the University of Haifa of the abduction, Briseis and Achilles, Achilles and Hector, Troy burning, Cassandra, Aeneas, and the wooden horse.

ⓘ Trojan War Images from Princeton
Description: Ancient artifacts depicting 19 characters from The Trojan War.

Step 3 Expand

Choose and complete one of the following activities:

Activity 1: Expand your Research
Find out if "Hellenistic" civilization received its name from the fact that its mythology centered on Helen of Troy, or if there is another reason. Support your answer with specific examples.

Activity 2: Look for Images
Find and copy, sketch, or print out pictures (from the library or Internet sites) to add to your portfolio.

Activity 3: Write Summary
Write a summary of the events of the Trojan War. Refer to "Writing Summaries" in *Writers INC*. Younger students can narrate or dictate their summary.

Step 4 Excel

Share what you have learned about the Trojan War with a friend or family member. Correct written work to demonstrate correct punctuation and spelling, and effective use of grammar. Add written work or any illustrations to your portfolio. Add new words you learned in this lesson into your Vocabulary Notebook (see page 22).

Resources recommended in ◆several lessons, ★ several units, ● other HOW Units. ●—Key Resource (see beginning of unit or page 32).

Heart of Wisdom Publishing   479

Government of Ancient Greece
Step 1 Excite

Originally the Greeks had no law. They took care of their legal problems themselves, including killing each other. The end of the Persian Wars marked the beginning of the Classical period. Then Greeks were taught to consider themselves and their families as part of a greater body, which was the state. Fathers brought up their children in this opinion; and the children were taught from their cradles to look upon their country as their common mother, to whom they strictly adhered even more than to their parents. Discuss this with your parents. Is this the governmental system God planned?

Step 2 Examine

The Greeks' ideal way of life was an integrated democratic social unit called a "polis." The polis was also the place where the community resided; a community or city. The polis affected all areas of their lives: social, spiritual, and intellectual; as well as their art. It was a commitment to an idea. The Acropolis was the center of the polis ("acro" meaning "high," and "polis" meaning "city"). Over the several thousand years of its history, five main forms of government existed in ancient Greece.

- Monarchy
- Tyranny
- Chiefdom
- Oligarchy
- Democracy

Monarchy, chiefdom, and tyranny depended on a strong central authority. Oligarchy and democracy depended on shared authority. Research ancient Greek government. Use any resource (an encyclopedia, nonfiction book, historical novel, or the Internet). We recommend the following:

Books

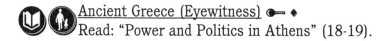
Ancient Greece (Eyewitness) ●▬ ♦
Read: "Power and Politics in Athens" (18-19).

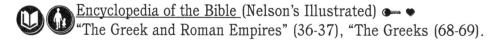
Encyclopedia of the Bible (Nelson's Illustrated) ●▬ ♥
"The Greek and Roman Empires" (36-37), "The Greeks (68-69).

Underlined text refers to Internet link at http://Homeschool-Books.com

The Usborne Book of the Ancient World ☞ ★
Read: "Democracy" (156), "Social Structure and Government" (116).

Kingfisher Illustrated History of the World ☞ ♥
Read: "City States" (84-85). Also see "Greek Government" entries in the timeline section on pages 70-75.

Kingfisher History Encyclopedia ☞ ♥
Read: "Greek Dark Age" (38), "Greek City States (54).

The Penguin Historical Atlas of Ancient Greece ☞ ♦
Read: "Dark Age to Athenian Ascendancy" (38-61).

Internet Sources

Government in Greece
Description: Brief synopsis of ancient Greek government from HistoryforKids.com.

Christian View of Government and Law by Kerby Anderson,
Description: A Christian view of government, political theory, and law in comparison to Greek government (including comments on Plato's *Republic*.).

Step 3 Expand

Choose and complete one of the following activities:

Activity 1: Write Summaries
Write a few paragraphs (minimum 50 words) describing a polis. Include the normal size, spirit, rituals, attitudes, etc. Write a summary for each of the five forms of government.

Activity 2: Find Articles
Examine newspaper articles for one week, cutting out examples of how the ancient Greeks' governmental structure and laws have been passed down to our society.

Step 4 Excel

Explain orally to your parents what you've learned in this lesson. Correct all written work to demonstrate correct punctuation and spelling, and effective use of grammar. Add corrected written work or any illustrations to your portfolio. Add new words you learned in this lesson into your Vocabulary Notebook (see page 22).

Resources recommended in ♦several lessons, ★ several units, ♥ other HOW Units. ☞ Key Resource (see beginning of unit or page 32).

Heart of Wisdom Publishing   481

Greek Mythology c. 1200-800 B.C.

Step 1 Excite

What are itching ears? (2Tim 4:4) When a person prefers "myths" to "the truth" as some today turn away to "humanism," "bolshevism," "new thought" or any other fad that will give a new momentary thrill to their itching ears and morbid minds.

Greek mythology includes a body of diverse stories and legends about a variety of gods. These stories comprise a religion which is essentially idol worship. The Greek gods resembled humans in form and showed human feelings. Greek mythology has no formal structure, sacred book, or spiritual teachings, unlike other religions, such as Hinduism or Judaism. Read the following Bible verse and the accompanying passage by Henry Ward Beecher with your parents.

> *Finally, brethren, whatsoever things are true, whatsoever things are honest, whatsoever things are just, whatsoever things are pure, whatsoever things are lovely, whatsoever things are of good report; if there be any virtue, and if there be any praise, think on these things.* (Phil. 4:8)

Henry Ward Beecher, (1813-1887) author, clergyman, and abolitionist wrote:

> Books are the windows through which the soul looks out. A home without good books is like a room without windows. No man has a right to bring up his children without surrounding them with books, if he has the means to buy them. It is a wrong to his family. He cheats them. Children learn to read by being in the presence of books. The love of knowledge comes with reading and grows upon it, and the love of knowledge in a young mind is almost a warrant against the inferior excitement of passions and vices. But to select the books—that is the difficulty. Their number is legion.
>
> Here is an opportunity to exercise judgment, wise discrimination, and criticism, supplemented by all the good advice parents, guardians, and other friends can bestow. Under these circumstances the choice of books is not easy, but is one of the most important and difficult duties imposed upon the young or old. Yet it must be done, or reading will prove a curse.[1]

Have a discussion with your parents about studying mythology. Should a Christian read spend time reading and studying stories about Greek gods?

Step 2 Examine

Jesus taught using examples and parables from everyday life and the culture of His day. Yet He never mentions the Greek myths. Paul, writing to Greeks, consistently appeals to the Old Testament Scriptures in his arguments, never mentioning Aristotle, Plato or others. Like Jesus, he never names Greek or Roman idols by name. Some of Paul's letters deal with prevailing non-Biblical philosophies, but always by emphasizing the truth, never by teaching the opposing philosophy.[2]

We believe that you gain an overview and understanding of this period without reading the mythology stories or memorizing the gods and goddesses. To obtain a general understanding of the literature of this time period and to have a core knowledge of the subject, students should know the basics of mythology and understand fables. (Core Knowledge examples include important events of world history, essential elements of mathematics and of oral and written expression, widely acknowledged masterpieces of art, etc.)

The Classics
There are three classical collections of myths:
- *Theogony* by the poet Hesiod
- *The Iliad* by the poet Homer
- *The Odyssey* by the poet Homer

The Greeks believed that the gods chose Mount Olympus, in a region of Greece called Thessaly (Thessalia), as their home. On Olympus, the gods formed a society that ranked them in terms of authority and powers. However, the gods could roam freely, and individual gods became associated with three main domains—the sky or heaven, the sea, and earth. The twelve chief gods, usually called the Olympians, were Zeus, Hera, Hephaestus, Athena, Apollo, Artemis, Ares, Aphrodite, Hestia, Hermes, Demeter, and Poseidon.

Browse through books to get an overview of mythology in ancient Greece. Use any Christian resource or reference books. We recommend the following:

Encyclopedia of the Bible (Nelson's Illustrated) ●━ ♥
"Greeak and Roman gods" (75), "The Greeks" (68-69), "Hellenistic Civilization" (70-71).

The Usborne Book of the Ancient World ●━ ★
Read: "Greek Myths and Legends" (178-182).

Handbook to Life in Ancient Greece ●━ ♦
Read: Chapter 8 "Religion and Mythology" (283-361).

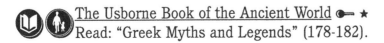
Resources recommended in ♦several lessons, ★ several units, ♥other HOW Units. ●━Key Resource (see beginning of unit or page 32).

The Life of Greece (The Story of Civilization II) ♦
Read: Chapter XIV "The Literature of the Golden Age" (374-414).

Step 3 Expand

Choose and complete one of the following activities:

Activity 1: Write a Sumary Paragraph
Some Christian try to justify reading stories about false gods by saying Paul read these writings. There is no such evidence. In fact, it is well documented that Paul was taught by Rabbis that preached against learning the Greek myths.[3] There is no need for any Christian to immerse themseves in mythology to understand it. We can understand history and culture (like theory of evolution) as Paul did by examining God's Word and recognizing deception. As Paul to Timothy some will *turn away their ears from the truth, and shall be tuned unto fables.*

Explain in writing the meaning of 2 Timothy 4:2-4 "*Preach the word; be instant in season, out of season: reprove, rebuke, exhort with all long-suffering and doctrine. For the time will come when they will not endure sound doctrine; but after their own lusts shall they heap to themselves teachers, having itching ears; And they shall turn away their ears from the truth, and shall be tuned unto fables.*"

Activity 2: Copy a Passage
Copy (by hand or typing) the passage by Henry Ward Beecher from Step 1. Place it in your portfolio.

Step 4 Excel

Discuss your family's decisions about studying Mythology of ancient Greece with with another homeschool family. Add new words you learned in this lesson into your Vocabulary Notebook (see page 22).

Footnotes
1. Beecher, Henry Ward. (1844). *Seven Lectures to Young Men.*
2. Rodd, Earl & Diane. (1998)"Questioning Secular Classical Education," *Homeschool Digest*, Wisdom's Gate. P.O. Box 374- wwwCovert, MI 49043, WisGate@characterlink.net.<http://www.homeschooldigest.com/ERodd.htm>
3. Hegg, Tim. (2002) The Letter Writer: Paul's Background and Torah Perspective, First Fruits of Zion; ISBN: 1892124165.

Underlined text refers to Internet link at http://Homeschool-Books.com

The Olympics (First 776 B.C.)

Step 1 Excite

Watch the video below (available at most video rental stores). Summarize ways in which you face the same choices in your daily life.

<u>Chariots of Fire</u>

This story strikes you as either a cold exercise in mechanical manipulation or as a tale of true determination and inspiration. The heroes are an unlikely pair of young athletes who ran for Great Britain in the 1924 Paris Olympics: devout Protestant Eric Liddell (Ian Charleson), a divinity student whose running makes him feel closer to God, and Jewish Harold Abrahams (Ben Cross), a highly competitive Cambridge student who has to surmount the institutional hurdles of class prejudice and anti-Semitism. There's delicious support from Ian Holm (as Abrahams's coach) and John Gielgud and Lindsay Anderson as a couple of Cambridge fogies. Vangelis's soaring synthesized score, which seemed to be everywhere in the early 1980s, also won an Oscar. *Chariots of Fire* was the debut film of British television commercial director Hugh Hudson (Greystoke) and was produced by David Puttnam. (Review by Jim Emerson— Amazon).

Step 2 Examine

The ancient Olympic games were first recorded in 776 B.C. They were held every four years in honor of Zeus, the king of the mythical Greek gods. Politics, nationalism, commercialism, and athletics were intimately related in the ancient Olympic Games. The Olympic festival was basically a religious gathering, with thousands of spectators traveling to the Games from across the Greek world. The Olympics began with a single foot race, and as time went on other events such as wrestling, the pentathlon, boxing, and chariot racing were added. Athletes usually competed nude.

The Greek word for "education" meant "the development of the entire human being," and could not be divided into physical and mental education. The ancient Greeks believed in educating children with gymnastics and music.

Research the Olympics. Use any resource (an encyclopedia, a nonfiction book, or the Internet). We recommend any of the following:

Books

<u>Encyclopedia of the Bible</u> (Nelson's Illustrated) ●— ♥
"Olympic Games" (68).

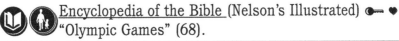

Resources recommended in ♦several lessons, ★ several units, ♥ other HOW Units. ●—Key Resource (see beginning of unit or page 32).

The Usborne Book of the Ancient World ●— ★
Read: "Athletics and Sport" (154).

Kingfisher Illustrated History of the World ●— ♥
Read: "Olympic Games"(64).

The Life of Greece (The Story of Civilization II) ♦
Read: "Games" (211-217).

Internet Sources

Ancient Olympics
Description: This site offers a comparison of ancient and modern Olympic sports. Tour the site of Olympia as it looks today, or read about the athletes who were famous in ancient times.

Ancient Olympics: The Real Story
Description: Visit the online exhibit from the University of Pennsylvania's Museum of Archaeology and Anthropology.

History of the Olympic Games
Description: Here you'll find reports on such topics as the importance of the games, the prehistory of them, and a schedule of what occurred during the games.

Step 3 Expand

Choose and complete one of the following activities:

Activity 1: Examine Scripture
Discuss this verse with your parents: 1 Corinthians 9:24, *Know ye not that they which run in a race run all, but one receiveth the prize? So run, that ye may obtain.* The word "prize" as used here is the Greek word *brabeion* {brab-i'-on} from *brabeus* (an umpire of uncertain derivation), which means 1). The award to the victor in the games, a prize; 2). Metaphor of the heavenly reward for Christian character.

Activity 2: Answer Questions
Politics, history, and race relations are topics you wouldn't necessarily link with sports. But studying the Olympics is useful in showing how the world's alliances have shifted. Use a search engine to find the answers to the following:
1. What was the motivation for the Arab terrorist raid on the Israeli Olympics compound at Munich in 1972?

Underlined text refers to Internet link at http://Homeschool-Books.com

2. What statement were black runners Tommie Smith and John Carlos making to America, and the world, with their medal-stand salute at Mexico City in 1968?
3. What made Jesse Owens' four gold medals, awarded in front of Hitler in 1936, so significant?
4. Why was the United States' victory over the Soviets at Lake Placid in 1980 (and also at Squaw Valley in 1960) so dramatic?

Activity 3: Write a Biography
Choose an Olympic athlete to study. Browse the Internet site <u>Olympic Heroes: Then and Now</u>. Write your chosen athlete's biography using questions such as:
1. What kind of clothes do you wear?
2. What country are you from?
3. Describe your home.
4. What kinds of foods do you eat?
5. What hardships do you face?
6. Which machines, conveniences, or technologies do you use every day?
7. What are the major differences between your life and an American life?
8. Describe how world, national, and local events have affected you.
9. What or whom do you fear?
10. What are your beliefs (religious, political, personal, and so on)?

Activity 4: Make an Award
Develop an award certificate which you can bestow upon someone in your life who has excelled in Christian spirit. Be sure to detail why this person is winning this particular "race."

Activity 5: Add to Your Vocabulary Notebook (see page 22)
Look up and define the following art terms: altis, athlete:, athlon, athlos, Amazons, arete:, diaulos, dolichos, drachma, dromos, gymnasium:, halteres, hellanodikai:, hippodromos, hoplitodromos, keles, palaistra, pankration, pentathlon, , periodonikes, stadion, tethrippon.

Step 4 Excel

Share your work from Step 3 with someone. Explain what you have learned in this lesson. Correct written work to demonstrate correct punctuation and spelling, and effective use of grammar. Add corrected written work or any illustrations to your portfolio.

Resources recommended in ♦several lessons, ★ several units, ♥other HOW Units. ☛Key Resource (see beginning of unit or page 32).

Heart of Wisdom Publishing   487

Ancient Greek Astronomy

Step 1 Excite

Greek Astronomers Time Line	
624-546 B.C.	Thales
611-545 B.C.	Anaximander
572-497 B.C.	Pythagoras
540-480 B.C.	Heraclitus
512-450 B.C.	Parmenides
500-428 B.C.	Anaxagoras
408-? B.C.	Eudoxus
310-230 B.C.	Aristarchus
240-194 B.C.	Eratosthenes
180-125 B.C.	Hipparchus
A.D. 85-165	Ptolemy

What are the astronomical objects that dominate our lives? Brainstorm and make a list of all the astronomy-related words you can think of. Make a <u>mind map</u> of the constellations you are familiar with. Include their names, their locations in the sky, and when they are visible. Discuss how we came to know about these things.

Step 2 Examine

One of the most important contributions the Greeks made to astronomy was the development of the celestial sphere. The Greeks thought that the stars were stationary around the earth, and that only half of them could be seen at any one time.

The author of Psalm 19 states that the heavens reveal God. Read Psalm 19:1-6:

The heavens declare the glory of God, And the firmament showeth His handiwork; Day unto day uttereth speech, And night unto night revealeth knowledge; There is no speech, there are no words, Neither is their voice heard. Their line is gone out through all the earth, And their words to the end of the world.

In them He has set a tent for the sun, Which is like a bridegroom coming out of his chamber; And rejoiceth as a strong man to run his course. His going forth is from the end of the heaven, And his circuit unto the ends of it; And there is nothing hid from the heat thereof.

Research Greek astronomy. Use any resource (an encyclopedia, a nonfiction book, or the Internet). We recommend the following:

Books

<u>Usborne Book of Discovery: Inventors/Scientists/Explorers</u> ●━ ❤
Read: "Science in Ancient Greece" (54-55).

<u>The Life of Greece (The Story of Civilization II)</u> ◆
Read: All references to astronomy in the index.

Handbook to Life in Ancient Greece ⚷— ◆
Read: References to astronomy and astronomers (490-491, 408).

The Usborne Internet-linked Science Encyclopedia ⚷— ♥
Read 154-165. See description of this book on the General Science Resources page of our site.

The Great Copernicus Chase: And Other Adventures in Astronomical History by Owen Gingerich
Description: A selection of Professor Gingerich's articles, from *Sky and Telescope* magazine, dealing with interesting episodes in the history of astronomy. Chapters range from Stonehenge and ancient Egypt to the Great Comet of 1965, and include Albert Einstein. In this series of articles, arranged roughly chronologically, the author covers the important periods and developments in astronomy. (September 1992) Cambridge Univ Pr (Trd); ISBN: 0521326885.

Greek Astronomy by Thomas L. Heath
Description: Heath discusses the ideas of Pythagoras, Eratosthenes, and many others, offering an outline of the foundations of scientific astronomy. (March 1991) Dover Publication; ISBN: 0486266206.

Internet Sources

Portland State University Greek Civilization for Kids Site: Science
Description: Written by college students to assist middle-school students in research reports. Covers astronomy, biology, boats and ships, mathematics, numbers, metal, water supply, and medicine.

Development of Modern Astrophysics
Description: Summaries of the work of: Nicolaus Copernicus (1473-1543), Tycho Brahe (1546-1601), Johannes Kepler (1571-1630), and Isaac Newton (1643-1727).

Ptolemy
Description: This site includes illustrations of the geocentric model.

Eratosthenes -
A brief biography of the Greek astronomer and mathematician who first measured the world, from PBS.

How the Greeks Used Geometry to Understand the Stars
Description: A lecture from the University of Virginia, with illustrations.

Resources recommended in ◆several lessons, ★ several units, ♥other HOW Units. ⚷—Key Resource (see beginning of unit or page 32).

Heart of Wisdom Publishing   489

(i) Early Greek Scientists Struggle to Explain How the Heavens Move
Description: An in-depth look at the interaction between Egypt, the Near-Eastern Greeks, and the Ionian Greeks, in the understanding of the workings of the solar system.

(i) How the Greeks Used Astronomy
Description: University of Virginia's Michael Fowler explains how Plato, Aristotle, Eudoxus, and others used circular paths (orbits) to explain observed phenomena.

(i) Measuring the Solar System
Description: This Michael Fowler lecture includes Eratosthenes' measurement of Earth's diameter and Aristarchus' theories on the distance to the moon and the distance to the sun.

Step 3 Expand

Choose and complete one of the following activities:

Activity 1: Add to Your Time Line Book
Add the Greek astronomers to your Time Line Book. Include a summary paragraph for each.

Activity 2: Contrast and Compare
Make a contrast-and-compare graphic (see page 26) to compare the above Greek astronomers and their discoveries.

Activity 3: Make a Mind Map
Make a mind map of one or more of the scientists in the list, with branches explaining the discoveries of each.

Activity 4: Write an Article
Write a newspaper article about the scientist you chose above as if you were writing for the "Greek Times."

Activity 5: Write a Classified Ad
Using other studies from this unit, add a "classified" section and "help wanted" section to your newspaper story.

Step 4 Excel

Share what you have learned about ancient Greek astronomy with a friend or family member. Correct written work to demonstrate correct punctuation and spelling, and effective use of grammar. Add corrected written work or any illustrations to your portfolio.

Underlined text refers to Internet link at http://Homeschool-Books.com

Greek Philosophers

1598

The Narrated Bible

Note: This lesson is appropriate for older students (grades 7 and up).

Step 1 Excite

Ancient Philosophy is usually divided into three periods: the Pre-Socratic period, from Thales to Socrates; the Classical Period, from Socrates to Plato and Aristotle; and the period of Hellenistic Philosophy, which lasts until Medieval Philosophy begins. The ancient philosophers believed, quite simply, that philosophy should in some way help to change one's life for the better. The Greeks believed that God was inherently "unknowable." However, a glimpse of God could be attained through rational thinking and deep meditation. They believed that man is the measure of all things, based on the idea that man is capable of self-fulfillment without God.

The Golden Age of classical Greek philosophy begins about 550 B.C., and lasts for over 200 years, well into the 4th century. The classical Greek philosophers include Socrates, Plato, and Aristotle the latter two of whom were each a student of the elder, and all of whom were to some degree indebted to Thales, the first of the Greek philosophers.

Read and memorize Colossians 2:4-8:

> *And this I say, lest any man should beguile you with enticing words. For though I be absent in the flesh, yet am I with you in the spirit, joying and beholding your order, and the stedfastness of your faith in Christ. As ye have therefore received Christ Jesus the Lord, so walk ye in him: Rooted and built up in him, and stablished in the faith, as ye have been taught, abounding therein with thanksgiving. Beware lest any man spoil you through philosophy and vain deceit, after the tradition of men, after the rudiments of the world, and not after Christ.*

Step 2 Examine

In Western culture, the lens through which we view the world has been colored by nearly three thousand years of Greek thought. You know the names. Homer. Thales. Socrates. Plato. Aristotle. What they thought and taught has had a profound impact on how we think. From these Greek thinkers came much that is good, including mathematics, the sci-

Greek Philosophers	
624-546 B.C.	Thales
?- 515 B.C.	Pythagoras
469-399 B.C.	Socrates
427?-347 B.C.	Plato
384-322 B.C.	Aristotle
372-287 B.C.	Theophrastus
365-300 B.C.	Euclid
341-270 B.C.	Epicurus

Resources recommended in ◆several lessons, ★ several units, ♥other HOW Units. ◕—Key Resource (see beginning of unit or page 32).

entific method ...But our inheritance from the Greeks also came with some serious baggage. The Greek thinkers, shunning the God of the Hebrews, came up with man-centered and mystical notions to define the world around them.[1]

The Greek philosopher Plato is said to be one of the most creative and influential thinkers in Western philosophy. His beliefs were the most popular in Greece and Rome when Christianity made its debut in those regions. Christianity achieved a substantial following from the followers of Plato, who influenced many doctrines that are taught in churches today. (Note that this lesson points out the Greek influence on the church, not the Bible.) Marvin Wilson explains in *Our Father Abraham: Jewish Roots of the Christian Faith* [2],

> As students of Western Civilization and the history of Ideas, we stand in awe of Plato and other Greek philosophers. Their impact has been great not only upon the thought of the ancient world, but also upon our world, today. We owe much to Plato and his later disciples for what they have taught us through their penetrating insights about reason, truth, wisdom, beauty, and the good life. Nevertheless, another side of Plato and other Greek thinkers has manifested itself through a dualistic kind of thinking that has largely negative consequences for the Church. We must therefore briefly note what this Greek dualism was, and how the Hebrew view of mankind and the world differed from it.

> Platonism holds that there are two worlds: the visible, material world and the invisible spiritual world. The visible or phenomenal world is in tension with the invisible or conceptual world. Because it is imperfect and the source of evil, the material world is inferior to that of the spiritual. In this view, the human soul originates in the heavenly realm from which it fell into the realm of matter. Though human beings find themselves related to both these worlds, they long for release from their physical bodies so that their true selves (their souls) might take flight back to the permanent world at the celestial and divine.

> Related to Plato's dualistic view of the cosmos, then, is a dualistic view of man. Plato likens the body to a prison for the soul. The immortal— pure spirit— is incarcerated in a defective body of crumbling clay. Salvation comes at death, when the soul escapes the body and soars heavenward to the invisible realm of the pure and eternal spirit. The widespread influence of Plato upon the history of Christian thought can hardly be overestimated. Accordingly, Warner Jaeger states that "The most important fact in the history of Christian doctrine was that the father of Christian theology, Origen, was a platonic philosopher at the school of Alexandria." Furthermore, he points out that "he [Origen] built into Christian doctrine the whole cosmic drama of the soul,

which he took from Plato and although later Christian fathers decided that he took over too much that which they kept was still the essence of Plato's philosophy of the soul".

Unlike the ancient Greeks, the Hebrew viewed the world as good. Though fallen and unredeemed, it was created by a God who designed it with humanity's best interest at heart. So instead of fleeing from the world, human beings experienced God's fellowship, love, and saving activity in historical order within the world. According to Hebrew thought there was neither cosmological dualism (the belief that the created world was evil, set apart from and opposed to the spiritual world) nor anthropological dualism (soul versus body). To the Hebrew mind a human being was a dynamic body— soul unity, called to serve God has created passionately with his whole being within the physical world.

Men still look back on the "Golden Days"of Greece for personal and cultural inspiration, but they fail to realize that the true nobility that they aspired to was never obtainable on any humanistic premise. True nobility, which the Greek and Roman ideal correctly identified, to some extent, is only available through the obedience to the Gospel of Christ, with its insistence on our recognition and confession of sin and its promise of containing sanctification. This is never attainable though education, but only through the free mercies of Christ our Savior.[3]

There were many who profoundly objected to the influence which this new and alien element began to exert on Christian theology. Tertullian wrote, "It is this philosophy which is the subject-matter of this world's wisdom, that rash interpreter of the divine nature and order ... What is there in common between Athens and Jerusalem? What between the Academy and the Church? What between heretics and Christians? ... Away with all projects for a 'Stoic' a 'Platonic' or a 'dialectic' Christianity! After Jesus Christ we desire no subtle theories, no acute enquires after the gospel ..." (Tertullian, *De praescriphene haeveticonum* c. 200).

Do more research about Greek philosophy. Use any resource (an encyclopedia, nonfiction book, or the Internet). We recommend the following:

Books

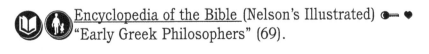
Encyclopedia of the Bible (Nelson's Illustrated) ☞ ♥
"Early Greek Philosophers" (69).

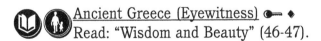
Ancient Greece (Eyewitness) ☞ ♦
Read: "Wisdom and Beauty" (46-47).

Resources recommended in ♦several lessons, ★ several units, ♥other HOW Units. ☞Key Resource (see beginning of unit or page 32).

Heart of Wisdom Publishing   493

The Usborne Book of the Ancient World ●— ★
Read: "Political and Moral Philosophers" (175). Also see "Who was Who in Ancient Greece" (183-185).

Our Father Abraham: Jewish Roots of the Christian Faith ●— ♥
Read: Pages 5-9, 8-11, 24, 44, 52, 90, 109, 150-153, 166-167. Also see references to Dualism and Gnosticism on pages 8, 90, 109, 156, and 167-185.

Restoring of the Early Church ♥
Read: Chapter 6 "Greek Philosophy in the Early Church: How Did Plato Displace God?" (See description in the Ancient Israel Unit Resources Section page 308).

The Life of Greece (The Story of Civilization II) ♦
Read: "Miletus and the Birth of Greek Philosophy" (134-140), Chapter XIV "The Conflict of Philosophy and Religion" (349-373), Chapter XXI "The Zenith of Philosophy" (500-535).

Assumptions That Affect Our Lives by Christian Overman
Description: This book examines the two major roots of Western thought--the ancient Greeks and the ancient Hebrews. It takes the reader back to the roots of the modern conflict between Christianity and secular humanism through a comparison of ancient Greek and Hebrew culture. The reader will discover the current tension between evangelical Christians and the non-biblical ideas with which they are surrounded is an age old conflict. By viewing the current situation in the context of the ancient Greeks and Hebrews, contemporary Christians can be better equipped to deal with the challenges of living in a predominately Greek-based culture today. Paperback - 273 pages (November 27, 1996) Micah 6:8; ISBN: 1883035503.

Internet Sources

A Greek Legacy by John D. Beckett
Description: An excerpt from the book Loving Monday.

A Different Window by John D. Beckett
Description: An excerpt from the book Loving Monday.

Influence of Greek Philosophy
Description: Encyclopedia article on the aspects of the Christian religion from Britannica.com.

Christian View of Government and Law
Description: Provides a Christian view of government, political theory, and law. Also gives a practical look at how Christians can be involved in social action.

ⓘ Hellenistic Dualism by James Tabor
Description: An overview of dualism.

ⓘ Early Heretical Movements in Christianity
Description: An encyclopedia article giving an
overview of dualism and gnosticism from Britannica.com.

Step 3 Expand

Choose and complete one of the following activities:

Activity 1: Write a Summary
Many colleges teach that the New Testament was heavily influenced by pagan philosophical systems. Prominent among such claims are the following: (1) elements of Plato's philosophy appear in the New Testament; (2) the New Testament reflects the influence of Stoicism; and (3) the ancient Jewish philosopher Philo was a source of John's use of the Greek word "logos" as a description of Jesus. Each of these claims may be easily refuted, a fact which challenges the badly outdated scholarship that continues to circulate these allegations in books and lectures. Read the online article below, and write a summary.

ⓘ Was the New Testament Influenced by Pagan Philosophy?
Description: An excellent article from Summit Ministries by Dr. Ronald H. Nash, explaining that Greek philosophy did not have an effect on our Bible, as some have claimed. He also briefly discusses the Greek influence on the Greek philosophy of the church.

Activity 2: Write an Essay
Write an essay on Dualism and Gnosticism. The essay should be at least 100 words, but not more than 500 words. Refer to "Structure of the Traditional Essay" and "Sample of a Traditional Essay" in *Writers INC*, or "How to Write an Essay."

Step 4 Excel

Share what you have learned about the influence of Greek philosophy on America with a friend or family member. Correct all written work to demonstrate correct punctuation and spelling, and effective use of grammar. Add corrected written work or any illustrations to your portfolio.

Footnotes
1. Beckett, John D. (1998) Loving Monday, Intervarsity Press.
2. Wilson, Marvin R. (1989). Our Father Abraham: Jewish Roots of the Christian Faith. Grand Rapids, MI: William B. Eerdmans Publishing Company; Dayton, OH: Center For Judaic-Christian Studies. ISBN: 0802804233.
2. Mulligan, David. (1994). Far Above Rubies: Wisdom in the Christian Community. VT: Messenger Publishing. 284 pages.

Resources recommended in ♦several lessons, ★ several units, ♥ other HOW Units. ☞ Key Resource (see beginning of unit or page 32).

Heart of Wisdom Publishing   495

Pythagoras 569-475 B.C.

Step 1 Excite

Pythagoras of Samos was a Greek philosopher responsible for important developments in mathematics, astronomy, and the theory of music. He is famous for his Pythagorean Theorem: the square of the length of the hypotenuse of a right triangle is equal to the sum of the squares of the lengths of the other two sides.

Watch the video of the NASA program below.

> The Theorem of Pythagoras
> Description: An excellent program which explains the Pythagorean Theorem using computer animation. It shows real-life problems that can be solved using the Pythagorean Theorem, illustrates several animated proofs, and weaves a historical perspective. Program schedules can be found on NASA's Educational Site (type in "Pythagoras" in the search box).

Step 2 Examine

Modern Christian scientist H. M. Morris explains,

> Since ancient times, people have been fascinated by the stars, and many astronomers have tried to count them. Yet, the Bible had said that 'the host of heaven cannot be numbered' (Jeremiah 33:22), while also comparing 'the sand which is upon the sea shore' to [the] 'stars of the heaven' in multitude (Genesis 22:17). Before the invention of the telescope, this must have seemed like a serious scientific mistake in the Bible. Now, however, it must be recognized as a supernatural scientific insight. Astronomers estimate that there are at least 10 raised to 26 stars (that is, a hundred-million-billion-billion stars), which reflects the same order of magnitude as the number of grains of sand on the earth. Truly, the stars cannot be numbered. If one could count 10 numbers per second, it would take him at least a thousand-million-billion years to count up to 10 raised to 26.[1]

The Greeks knew that the Evening Star appeared in the western sky after sunset, and the Morning Star appeared in the eastern sky before sunrise. Pythagoras was the first Greek to realize that the two were the same.

Underlined text refers to Internet link at http://Homeschool-Books.com

Research Pythagoras. Use any resource (an encyclopedia, nonfiction book, or the Internet).
We recommend the following:
Books

Usborne Book of Discovery: Inventors/Scientists/Explorers ⚷— ♥
Read: "Pythagoras" (53).

The Usborne Book of the Ancient World ⚷— ★
Read: See entry in "Who was Who in Ancient Greece" (185).

Kingfisher Illustrated History of the World ⚷— ♥
Read: References to Pythagoras (82, 88-89).

Handbook to Life in Ancient Greece ⚷— ◆
Read: "Pythagoras" (387, 401).

The Life of Greece (The Story of Civilization II) ◆
Read: References to Pythagoras (68-69, 131, 136, 142, 144, 161-167, 191, 202, 204, 303, 338, 355, 357, 500).

Internet Sources

Pythagoras— The School of Pythagoras
Description: This site includes a collection of book reviews, bibliographies, videos, and commentary related to Pythagorean theories of numbers.

Pythagoras— Mathematicians
Description: A study of the Greek philosopher responsible for developments in mathematics, astronomy, and music theory. References to and demonstration of his famous theorem.

Pythagoras of Samos— Early Greek Philosophy
Description: John Burnet provides a detailed chronology of the ancient Greek, pre-Socratic philosopher's life and contributions to cosmology and mathematics.

Pythagoras and His Theorem
Description: LookSmart Live resources which let you follow a detailed biography of this mathematician and philosopher, and learn how his theorem was developed.

Pythagoras— Funk and Wagnalls
Description: Summarizes the life and doctrines of the Neoplatonic philosopher/mathematician. Details his studies in numbers theory and astronomy.

Resources recommended in ◆several lessons, ★ several units, ♥other HOW Units. ⚷—Key Resource (see beginning of unit or page 32).

(i) Pythagoras and the Pythagoreans
Description: Anthony Beavers presents a biography of the philosopher/mathematician and details the principles of his cosmological school.

Step 3 Expand

Choose and complete one of the following activities:

Activity 1: Add to Your Time Line Book
Add Pythagoras to your Time Line Book. Include a summary paragraph.

Activity 2: Rewrite a Passage
When a ruler asked him, "What is philosophy?", Pythagoras reportedly gave the following answer: "Life is like a gathering at the Olympic festival, to which, having set forth from different lives and backgrounds, people flock for three motives: to compete for the glory of the crown, to buy and sell, or as spectators [to observe]. So in life, some enter the services of fame and others of money, but the best choice is that of these few who spend their time in the contemplation of nature, and as lovers of wisdom" (i.e., philosophers). Rewrite Pythagoras' answer in your own words.

Activity 3: Do an Experiment
Look up "Pythagorean Theorem" in your math book or click here. Complete the online lessons. Then, draw a right triangle and, using a ruler, measure the legs and hypotenuse, then use the Pythagorean Theorem to test your measurements. How many different proofs of the theorem can you find? Click here to see a geometrical proof of Pythagoras' Theorem.

Step 4 Excel

Share what you have learned about Pythagoras with a friend or family member. Correct all written work to demonstrate correct punctuation and spelling, and effective use of grammar. Add corrected written work or any illustrations to your portfolio.

Footnotes
1. Morris, Henry M. (1951). *Science and the Bible*. Renewal 1979, 1986; Moody Press.

Underlined text refers to Internet link at http://Homeschool-Books.com

The Persian Wars 499-479 B.C.

Step 1 Excite

The Persian Empire attempted to conquer Greece in the first decades of the 5th century B.C. (499-479). The outcome of these wars had long-lasting effects on the ancient Greek world. Brainstorm and make of list of what you know about the Persian Wars.

Step 2 Examine

The Persian Wars were several battles, in which Greek citizens fought against Persian invaders. The Greeks won and maintained the Greek culture and political structures long after the fall of the Persian empire.

Research the Persian Wars or "Greco-Persian Wars." During your study take notes. Include the causes and the major phases (four main battles) of the Persian Wars. Use any resource (an encyclopedia, nonfiction book, or the Internet). We recommend the following:

Books

The Usborne Book of the Ancient World ☞ ★
Read: "Persian Wars" (136-137).

Kingfisher History Encyclopedia ☞ ♥
Read: "Alexander the Great" (56-57).

Kingfisher Illustrated History of the World ☞ ♥
Read: "Persian Wars" (82).

The Penguin Historical Atlas of Ancient Greece ☞ ♦
Read: "The Persian Rival" (62-85).

Handbook to Life in Ancient Greece ☞ ♦
Read: References to Persian Wars (94, 137, 139, 146, 148, 151, 273).

The Life of Greece (The Story of Civilization II) ♦
Read: All references to the Persian Wars.

History of the Jewish People Volume 1: Second Temple Era ★
Read: "Wars with Persia" (44-51). (See description in the Ancient Israel Unit Resources Section.)

Resources recommended in ♦several lessons, ★ several units, ♥other HOW Units. ☞―Key Resource (see beginning of unit or page 32).

Internet Sources

(i) Persian War— Greek History
Description: This site records the growth and organization of the Persian Empire and their military campaigns in Asia Minor and Greece.

(i) Mardonius— Persian General of the Ionian Revolt Era
Description: Contains information about the Persian general who put down the Ionian revolt and led the first invasion of Greece, and describes his building programs in Asia Minor.

(i) Persian Conquest
Description: Learn about the 165-year rule of the Persians in ancient Anatolia before their defeat by the forces of Alexander the Great in 333 B.C.

(i) Persian Invasions— 560-360 B.C.
Description: An overview of the Persian Wars.

Step 3 Expand

Choose and complete two of the following activities:

Activity 1: Make a List
Make a list of the causes of the Persian Wars. During the First Persian War, the Ionians revolted against Persia, and King Darius tried to conquer Greece. This war included the battle of Marathon. During the Second Persian War, King Xerxes of Persia tried to succeed where Darius had failed. This war included the battles of Thermopylae, Salamis, and Plataea.

Activity 2: Add to Your Time Line Book
Add the Persian Wars to your Time Line Book. Include summaries and illustrations of key players from these wars: Aristides, Artabanus, Artemisia, Cyrus, Croesus (King of Ionia), Darius (King of Persia), Delphi, Eurybiades, Hoplites, Leonidas, Mardonius, Megistias, Pythius, Themistocles, and Xerxes (King of Persia, invader of Greece, and son of Darius).

Activity 3: Write a Report
Write a report titled "The Persian Wars: A Turning Point for Athens." Include an explanation of the ways in which the Persian Wars were pivotal in the evolution of Athenian politics, foreign relations, intellectual endeavors, and artistic achievements. Refer to "Writing an Explanation" in *Writers INC*. Younger students can narrate (orally tell) what they have learned.

Activity 4: Contrast and Compare
Fill in a contrast-and-compare graphic (see page 26) comparing the battles from these wars: Marathon, Thermopylae, Plataea, and Salamis. For each battle, include who was involved, where it was fought, dates fought, details, and who won.

Activity 5: Map Work
Obtain a map showing the Persian Empire, Macedonia, Thessaly, Peloponnese, Messenia, Laconia, Sparta, Corinth, Thebes, and Athens as they were in 477 B.C. Then, illustrate your findings by color-coding the map showing the neutral states, Athens and her allies, and Sparta and her allies. Include the map in your portfolio.

Step 4 Excel

Explain orally to your parents what you've learned in this lesson. Correct written work to demonstrate correct punctuation and spelling, and effective use of grammar. Add corrected written work or any illustrations to your portfolio.

Resources recommended in ◆several lessons, ★ several units, ● other HOW Units. ●━Key Resource (see beginning of unit or page 32).

Heart of Wisdom Publishing   501

The Peloponnesian War

Step 1 Excite

The Peloponnesian War (431-404 B.C.) was fought between the two leading city-states in ancient Greece; Athens and Sparta. Locate Athens and Sparta on a map of ancient Greece.

Step 2 Examine

Athens and Sparta had cooperated during the Persian Wars, but relations between these two most powerful states in mainland Greece deteriorated in the decades following the Greek victories of 479 B.C. This deterioration had progressed to open hostilities by the middle of the century. The peace struck in 446/445 formally ended the fighting, supposedly for thirty years. However, new disagreements that arose in the 430s, over the manner in which each of the two states should treat the allies of the other, led to the collapse of the peace. When negotiations to settle the disagreements collapsed, the result was the devastating war of twenty-seven years that modern historians call the Peloponnesian War, after the location of Sparta and most of its allies in the Peloponnese (the large peninsula that forms the southernmost part of mainland Greece). The war dragged on from 431 to 404 B.C., and engulfed almost the entire Greek world. This bitter conflict, extraordinary in Greek classical history for its protracted length, wreaked havoc on Athens' social and political harmony, its economic strength, and the day-to-day existence of many of its citizens.[1]

Research the Peloponnesian War. Use any resource (an encyclopedia, nonfiction book, or the Internet). We recommend the following:

Books

The Usborne Book of the Ancient World o— ★
Read: "The Golden Age and the Peloponnesian War" (158-159).

Kingfisher Illustrated History of the World o— ♥
Read: References to the Peloponnesian War (82-85, 90).

Kingfisher History Encyclopedia o— ♥
Read: References to the Peloponnesian War (53-56).

Underlined text refers to Internet link at http://Homeschool-Books.com

The Penguin Historical Atlas of Ancient Greece ◕━ ◆
Read: "Peloponnesian War- the Aegean" (96-97). "Peloponnesian War- Sicily" (98-99).

Handbook to Life in Ancient Greece ◕━ ◆
Read: References to the Peloponnesian War (134-135, 143).

The Life of Greece (The Story of Civilization II) ◆
Read: References to the Peloponnesian War.

Internet Sources

Peloponnesian War
Description: An outline of the major events and figures that led to the Peloponnesian War; and links to profiles by Thucydides.

Interactive Peloponnesian War
Description: A list of battles and related links concerning this famous war between Athens and Sparta.

Step 3 Expand

Choose and complete one of the following activities:

Activity 1: Copy Passages
Copy (by hand or typing) a passage from your research that gives an overview of this war.

Activity 2: Add to Your Time Line Book
Add the Peloponnesian War to your Time Line Book.

Activity 2: Write an Essay
Write an essay about this famous war between Athens and Sparta. What were the main causes of the Peloponnesian War? Was the war inevitable? Refer to "Structure of the Traditional Essay" in *Writers INC*, or "How to Write an Essay."

Step 4 Excel

Share what you have learned about this war with a friend or family member. Correct written work to demonstrate correct punctuation and spelling, and effective use of grammar. Add corrected written work or any illustrations to your portfolio.

Footnote: 1. Martin, Thomas. *Overview of Archaic and Classical Greek History.* Yale University Press. <http://www.perseus.tufts.edu> (Accessed March 1999).

Resources recommended in ◆several lessons, ★ several units, ●other HOW Units. ◕━Key Resource (see beginning of unit or page 32).

Alexander the Great

Step 1 Excite

Watch one of these videos or programs about Alexander the Great. (See TV schedules for The Discovery Channel and PBS programs or check your local video rental store).

<u>In The Footsteps of Alexander the Great</u>
Description: A four-hour series from PBS. As an educator, you may tape the series when it airs, for use in the classroom for up to one year from the date of the broadcast. Each episode is one hour long; shorter segments, which you can use to underscore activities and discussion questions, are listed in each core unit.

<u>Alexander the Great</u>
Description: A Discovery Channel program. Alexander's triumphs over the Persian Empire remain one of history's greatest campaigns of conquest. What inner conflicts drove this great military leader, student of Aristotle, and ruler at twenty-one? Follow the story of a man who ruled the world stage for a brief time, yet whose influence was felt years after his death. Check viewing times in The Discovery Channel's TV schedule.

<u>Alexander the Great: Ruler of the World</u>
Description: Alexander III, King of Macedonia, conquered the Persian Empire and annexed it to Macedonia. He was taught for a time by Aristotle and acquired a love for Homer and an infatuation with the heroic age, which he sought to duplicate in his reign. Alexander was twenty years old when he was presented to the army as king. He won their support, eliminated all potential rivals, gained the allegiance of the Macedonian nobles and the Greeks, and conquered the neighboring barbarians. From the History Makers.

Discuss the unique qualities of Alexander's personality and heritage that contributed to his "greatness" and popularity.

Step 2 Examine

Research Alexander the Great. Use any resource (an encyclopedia, nonfiction book, or the Internet). We recommend any of the following:

Books

Ancient Greece (Eyewitness) ⊶ ◆
Read: "Alexander and the Hellenistic Age" (62-63).

The Usborne Book of the Ancient World ⊶ ★
Read: "Alexander the Great" (170-171).

Kingfisher Illustrated History of the World ⊶ ♥
Read: References to Alexander the Great (77-79, 90-91, 138, 154, 155).

Kingfisher History Encyclopedia ⊶ ♥
Read: References to Alexander the Great (41, 50-51, 56, 74-75, 90).

The Penguin Historical Atlas of Ancient Greece ⊶ ◆
Read: "Alexander and After" (110-132).

Handbook to Life in Ancient Greece ⊶ ◆
Read: "Alexander the Great." (42-44).

History of the Jewish People Volume 1: Second Temple Era ◆
Read: Chapter 6 "Alexander the Great." (See description in the Ancient Israel Unit Resources Section.)

The Life of Greece (The Story of Civilization II) ◆
Read: Chapter XXII "Alexander" (538-554).

Streams of Civilization: Earliest Times to Discovery ★
Read: "Alexander the Great" (132).

Alexander the Great by Robert Green
Description: Provides a look into the life of one of the greatest conquerors of the ancient world, and demonstrates the new trade and cultural routes that were created through Alexander's vast conquests in the East. Franklin Watts, Incorporated; ISBN: 0531157997.

Alexander the Great
See description in the Resources section of this unit.

Alexander the Great by Robin Lane Fox
Description: Probably the best recent biography of Alexander the Great. Literate, accurate, and full of detail not found in other works on the great Macedonian. Fox is quite careful and analytical when using the minimal ancient sources from which Alexander's life has been pieced together. He shows great

Resources recommended in ◆several lessons, ★ several units, ♥other HOW Units. ⊶Key Resource (see beginning of unit or page 32).

Heart of Wisdom Publishing   505

knowledge of the time, terrain, and human psychology. A must for anyone interested in Alexander the Great and/or ancient Greece. (September 1994) Penguin USA (Paper); ISBN: 0140088784.

In the Footsteps of Alexander the Great
Description: Between 334 and 324 B.C., the Macedonian army, led by Alexander the Great, marched relentlessly across Asia. Historian Michael Wood actually retraced Alexander's 22,000-mile epic journey, and in an exciting blend of history, travel, and adventure, he recounts the Macedonian conquest as recorded in many ancient documents. 56 full-color illustrations, 56 b & w illustrations, and 8 maps. University of California Press; ISBN: 0520213076.

Internet Sources

Alexander the Great on the Web
Description: More than 350 pages relating to Alexander the Great.

Alexander the Great
Description: A teacher's guide to the Discovery Channel program. What inner conflicts drove this great military leader, student of Aristotle, and ruler at twenty-one? Follow the story of a man who ruled the world stage for a brief time, yet whose influence was still felt years after his death.

In the Footsteps of Alexander the Great
Description: From PBS Online: Michael Wood helps you retrace the steps of Alexander the Great.

Software

Great Battles of Alexander
Description: In-depth military-strategy game puts the emphasis on game play and strategy. Take control of Alexander's forces, or attempt to rewrite history by assuming the role of one of his rivals. The scenarios recreate the main battles of Alexander the Great's career, from Chaeronea in Greece to the Battle of the Hydaspes in India.

Step 3 Expand

Choose and complete one of the following activities:

Activity 1:Prepare an Interview
Write a list of questions and answers as if Alexander had conducted an empire-wide televised news conference. What questions might reporters have asked? How would Alexander have responded?

Activity 2: Write an Essay
Write and present a paper titled "Alexander the Great." Include a bibliography. Refer to "Structure of the Traditional Essay" and "Sample of a Traditional Essay" in *Writers INC*, or "How to Write an Essay." Younger students can narrate (orally tell) what they have learned.

Activity 3: Trace a Map
Trace a map showing Alexander's empire. A map of Alexander's empire can be found in most encyclopedias, or at one of the Internet sources.

Activity 4: Answer Questions
Answer the following questions about Alexander the Great, from The Discovery Channel.
1. What was the military goal that Alexander inherited from his father, Philip of Macedon?
2. How did Alexander's exposure to Aristotle shape the young man's future as a military leader?
3. What proposition did Alexander offer upon his arrival in Athens?
4. What is the phalanx strategy, and how did Alexander apply it in battle?
5. Why was the battle at Gaugamela, between Alexander and Darius, a significant turning point for Alexander?
6. What did Alexander do with the massive wealth he acquired from his victories? How did this make him popular among his soldiers?
7. What unfinished business did Alexander leave behind at the time of his death?
8. How did Alexander's accomplishments leave an important military legacy for future leaders?

Activity 5: Add to Your Time Line Book
Add Alexander the Great to your Time Line Book.

Step 4 Excel

Share your work from Step 3 with someone. Explain what you have learned in this lesson. Correct written work to demonstrate correct punctuation and spelling, and effective use of grammar. Add corrected written work or any illustrations to your portfolio.

Resources recommended in ◆several lessons, ★ several units, ●other HOW Units. ●━Key Resource (see beginning of unit or page 32).

Hebrews in Ancient Greece

Step 1 Excite

The Narrated Bible

1345-1346

Several portions of the Bible were written in ancient Greece. Masterpieces such as Ecclesiastes, Daniel, parts of Psalms and Proverbs—histories like Chronicles, and novels like Esther were written in Hebrew, Aramaic, or Greek[1]. Paul wrote First and Second Thessalonians in Athens around A.D. 50-52, and Romans in Corinth or Philippi about A.D. 55-59.

Alexander the Great's capture of Jerusalem in 332 B.C. is a turning point in the history of Israel. Trace or print out a map showing Alexander's empire. Israel's location between Egypt and Syria is directly in the path of Alexander's warring successors. Find a map of Alexander's empire. See the sources below:

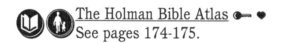
The Holman Bible Atlas
See pages 174-175.

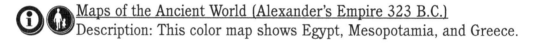
Maps of the Ancient World (Alexander's Empire 323 B.C.)
Description: This color map shows Egypt, Mesopotamia, and Greece.

Step 2 Examine

In 539 the king of Persia conquered Babylonia. This allowed the Jews of Babylonia to return to Jerusalem to rebuild the temple, and to practice their religion. In 333 B.C. Alexander the Great defeated the Persians at the battle of Issus, and from 333 to 142 B.C. the Jews were under Hellenistic power. While Alexander allowed the Jews to practice their religion, Alexander's successors, the Ptolemies, who ruled Israel for most of the third century A.D., placed the Jewish people under the domination of the Greco-Egyptians and their culture and beliefs. In *The Light of Two Faiths*, Susan Perlman gives an overview of the pressure for the Hebrews to conform to Greek ways:

> With the Persians, a foreign governor had been installed, but not so with the Ptolemies. Instead, the High Priest of Israel served as both political ruler and religious representative. This gave rise to political factions in Judea, some more disposed to the Greco-Syrians and others to the Greco-Egyptians. Wars were frequent, and eventually the Syrians conquered the Jewish land.
>
> Along with this greater degree of self-rule came pressure to conform to Greek ways. This gave rise to political factions in Judea; some were more disposed to the Greco-Syrians, others to the Greco-Egyptians. The Seleucids were even

Underlined text refers to Internet link at http://Homeschool-Books.com

more dedicated to inculcating Greek culture and customs on the people than the Egyptians. In order to conform, Jews adopted Greek names, wore Greek-style garments, and adopted Greek ways. This situation created tension between the Greeks and Hellenistic Jews and between the Hellenistic and the traditionalist Jews. Antiochus IV, the Syrian ruler, called himself "Epiphanes" (the visible god). A Hellenized Jew named Jason, formerly called Joshua, had assumed the corrupted position of High Priest.

The Persians had only wanted tribute from the Jewish people, but the Greek successors to Alexander, especially Antiochus IV, held to a belief in the superiority of "the Greek way of life" and wanted much more. Hellenism encouraged intellectual pursuits and a polite, highly civilized society, but it also involved idolatry and exalted human wisdom. The Hellenists hated the Jewish religion and the Jewish way of life, and they set about to "civilize" the people of Judea by forcing them into the Greek mold.[1]

Do research about the Hebrews in ancient Greece. Use any resource (an encyclopedia, nonfiction book, or the Internet). We recommend the following:

Books

Encyclopedia of the Bible (Nelson's Illustrated) ☻– ♥
"The Greek and Roman Empires" (36-37), "The Greeks (68-69).

The Holman Bible Atlas ☻– ♥
Read: "The Hellenistic Period" (174-182).

History of the Jewish People Volume 1: Second Temple Era ◆
Read: Chapter 5 "The Rise of Greece," and Chapter 6 "Alexander the Great." (See description in the Ancient Israel Unit Resources section.)

Our Father Abraham ☻– ♥
Read "Athens or Jerusalem" (5-9), "Education with a Difference" (291).

The Life of Greece (The Story of Civilization II) ◆
Read: "Hellenism and the Jews" (579-584), "Books of the Jews" (603-606).

Ancient Israel: From Abraham to the Roman Destruction of the Temple ☻– ★
Read: Chapter 7 "The Age of Hellenism: Alexander the Great and the Fall of the Hasmonean Kingdom."

The Jews in the Greek Age by Elias J. Bickerman
Description: This book "deals with stability and change in Jewish society during the first centuries of the Greek age, i.e., from Alexander's conquest of the

Resources recommended in ◆several lessons, ★ several units, ♥ other HOW Units. ☻– Key Resource (see beginning of unit or page 32).

Heart of Wisdom Publishing   509

Middle East until approximately 175 B.C. The Greek dynasties did introduce welcome technological innovations (the potter's wheel, the rotary mill, the oil press, and Archimedes' screw for lifting water), but their emphasis on athletics, nakedness, and widespread secular beliefs made some Jews fear that their traditions, diet habits, and monotheistic religion were at risk." Harvard University Press; ISBN: 0674474910. Reading level: High school-adult.

Internet Sources

The Hebrews in Greece
Description: An overview of Greek rulership over Jerusalem.

A Short History of the Jews of Greece
Description: Excerpts from the book *A Short History of the Jews in Greece*, which was written by Errikos Sevillias (a survivor of the Nazi death camps) and translated by Nikos Stavrolakis, director of the Jewish Museum in Greece.

Step 3 Expand

Choose and complete one of the following activities:

Activity 1: Write a Letter
Write a letter as if you are a traditional Jew under Greek power who is writing to a relative. Explain how many of the Jews have given way to Hellenistic dress and customs and your feelings about this.

Activity 2: Contrast and Compare
Make a contrast-and-compare graphic (see page 26). Compare the traditional Jews and Hellenistic Jews to devoted Christians and worldly Christians.

Activity 3: Add to Your Time Line Book
Add the period of Hebrews in ancient Greece to your Time Line Book.

Step 4 Excel

Share what you have learned about the Hebrews in ancient Greece with a friend or family member. Correct written work to demonstrate correct punctuation and spelling, and effective use of grammar. Add corrected written work or any illustrations to your portfolio.

Footnote
1. Perlman, Susan. *The Light of Two Faiths.* Jews for Jesus, 60 Haight Street, San Francisco CA 94102. <http://www.jewsfor-jesus.org>

Archimedes

Step 1 Excite

Archimedes (287-212 B.C.), a native of Syracuse, Sicily, was a Greek mathematician and inventor who wrote important works on plane and solid geometry, arithmetic, and mechanics.

Step 2 Examine

Read the following fascinating facts about Archimedes' discoveries:

Archimedes' Screw

Archimedes invented the screw in the third century B.C. Ancient screws were large wood contraptions, capable of raising water. Wood screws launched in the sixteenth century, but were not widely available until after 1850. (New York Times Magazine)

Levers

Archimedes understood levers well enough to claim, "Give me a lever long enough and a place to stand, and I could lift the world."

The Archimedes Principle

According to the story, Archimedes, as he was washing, thought of a way to compute the proportion of gold in King Hiero's crown by observing how much water "flowed over the bathing-stool." He leapt up as one possessed, crying Eureka! ("I've found it"). After repeating this several times, he went his way. You will learn more about this story in the next lesson.

Solar Energy

During a battle between the Greeks and Romans, Archimedes was credited with the defeat of the Roman fleet that was attacking Syracuse harbor. Using four thousand gold and bronze shields, he reflected the sun's rays onto the ships' sails and set them on fire. This became a popular war tactic.

Archimedes' Death

Resources recommended in ◆several lessons, ★ several units, ●other HOW Units. ●━Key Resource (see beginning of unit or page 32).

Heart of Wisdom Publishing   511

Archimedes had spent his life in Syracuse, studying mathematics in relative tranquility, but when he was in his late seventies, the invading Roman army shattered his peace. Legend has it that, during the invasion, Archimedes was so engrossed in the study of a geometric figure in the sand that he failed to respond to the questioning of a Roman soldier. As a result, he was speared to death.[1]

Research Archimedes. Use any resource (an encyclopedia, nonfiction book, or the Internet). We recommend the following:

Books

The Usborne Book of the Ancient World ●— ★
Read: "Archimedes" (174, 181, 191).

Usborne Book of Discovery: Inventors/Scientists/Explorers ●— ♥
Read: "Archimedes' Screw" (55).

The Life of Greece (The Story of Civilization II) ♦
Read: References to Archimedes.

Archimedes and the Door of Science (Living History Library) by Jeanne Bendick, Laura M. Berquist
A fantastic introduction to math and science! "Jeanne Bendick has succeeded in creating a book that is interesting in itself, as well as helpful in any history or science curriculum."—Laura Berquist. Against the backdrop of Archimedes' life and the culture of ancient Greece, the author discusses the man's work and discoveries, and the knowledge later based upon them. Includes some experiments to try at home! (April 1997) Bethlehem Books; ISBN: 1883937124. Reading level: Young adult.

Internet Sources

Archimedes Page
Description: An overview of his life and the Archimedes Principal.

Archimedes of Syracuse: The Father of Buoyancy
Description: See how Archimedes developed principles relating to how objects float or sink in liquids.

Underlined text refers to Internet link at http://Homeschool-Books.com

Archimedes Home Page
Description: A collection of Archimedean miscellanea, containing descriptions, sources, and illustrations of all aspects of Archimedes' life, including the siege of Syracuse, the death of Archimedes, Archimedes' tomb, Archimedes' screw, and much more.

Archimedes
Description: A collection of Archimedean miscellany under continual development. Includes off-site links to basic information about Archimedes.

Archimedes - MSN Encarta
Description: Offers links, an image, and an overview of the life of this ancient Greek inventor.

Step 3 Expand

Choose and complete one of the following activities:

Activity 1: Prepare an Interview
Pretend you are a reporter. Organize your questions and "interview" Archimedes. Ask about his discoveries and inventions; and his observations about interactions and changes in nature. Ask questions like: What do you mean by "a lever long enough"? Where would you place the fulcrum? Refer to "Writing an Interview" in *Writers INC*.

Activity 2: Write an Article
Write a newspaper story about Archimedes. Include his method for developing and understanding scientific principles. Add illustrations. Younger students can narrate (orally tell) what they have learned.

Step 4 Excel

Share your work from Step 3 with someone. Explain what you have learned in this lesson. Correct all written work to demonstrate correct punctuation and spelling, and effective use of grammar. Add written work or any illustrations to your portfolio.

Footnotes
1. Singh, Simon. (1997). *Fermat's Enigma: The Epic Quest to Solve the World's Greatest Mathematical Problem.* Walker and Company; ISBN 0-8027-1331-9.

Resources recommended in ◆several lessons, ★ several units, ● other HOW Units. ●—Key Resource (see beginning of unit or page 32).

Archimedes' Principle

Step 1 Excite

When you are in a swimming pool, you probably have noticed you do not weigh as much as you do when out of the water. It is easy to lift a small child with one hand when you are both in the pool, but it would be more difficult to do so if you were out of the water. Have you ever noticed that when wood is placed in water, there is a force that keeps it from sinking? Both these examples are a result of what is known as the buoyant force. Archimedes' Principle (buoyant force), which states that a body immersed in a fluid is buoyed up by a force equal to the weight of the displaced fluid, applies to both floating and submerged bodies.

Legend has it that the king of Syracuse suspected that the royal goldsmith had been substituting quantities of silver for gold in creating royal crowns. The irregular shape of the crown posed a problem in detecting the deception. Archimedes solved the problem by comparing the volume of the crown with the volume of a piece of pure gold that had the same mass as the crown. Since gold is more dense than silver, Archimedes figured that an ounce of gold would have less volume than an ounce of silver. If the goldsmith were cheating the king, it could be proven: a crown of pure gold would have less volume than a crown with the same mass that was made of both gold and silver.

When Archimedes placed the suspect crown in the water, it displaced more water than the equal mass of pure gold, indicating that the goldsmith had been cheating King Hiero. Legend says that Archimedes went running down the street shouting "Eureka!"

Step 2 Examine

Research the Archimedes Principle. Use any resource (an encyclopedia, nonfiction book, historical novel, or the Internet). We recommend the resources in the previous lesson and/or following:

Books

Underlined text refers to Internet link at http://Homeschool-Books.com

Usborne Book of Discovery: Inventors/Scientists/Explorers ●— ♥
Read: "Archimedes Principle" (55).

The Usborne Internet-linked Science Encyclopedia ●— ♥
Read "Achimedes" (136-138, 409, 412). See description of this book on
the General Science Resources page of our site.

Floating and Sinking (Start-Up Science) by Jack Challoner
Description: A pleasant mixture of illustrations, full-color photographs.
The content ranges from a simple explanation of why fish need to stay in water to
interesting trivia on how many gallons of water a camel drinks. Conversational
texts speak directly to readers, often in question form. Experiments are primarily
hands-on investigations of the concepts presented. Many are simple enough for
kindergartners, while others would challenge fourth graders. Paperback - 32
pages (April 1998) Raintree/Steck-Vaughn; ISBN: 0817264868 Reading level:
Ages 4-8.

Archimedes : What Did He Do Beside Cry Eureka? (Classroom Resource
Materials) by Sherman Stein
Description: Many people have heard only two things about Archimedes: He was
the greatest mathematician of antiquity, and he ran naked from his bath crying,
"Eureka, eureka!" Few of us, layperson or mathematician, are familiar with the
accomplishments on which his reputation rests. This book answers those questions by describing in detail his astonishing accomplishments: how he developed
the theory of the lever and the center of gravity; how he used the center of gravity
to study whether a floating object would tip over; how he summed a geometric
series and the squares; and how he found the volume and surface area of a
sphere. His ability to do so much with so few tools at his disposal is astonishing.
Paperback - 168 pages (June 15, 1999) Mathematical Assn of Amer; ISBN:
0883857189.High school-level mathematics.

Internet Sources

Mr. Archimedes' Bath: Floating and Sinking
Description: An experiment for elementary-age students, with displace-
ment by dropping objects in a container.

More Than Meets the Eye
Description: Demonstrates scientific principles behind observations using
the Archimedes Method.

The Golden Crown
Description: The story of how Archimedes discovered buoyancy.

Resources recommended in ◆several lessons, ★ several units, ♥other HOW Units. ●—Key Resource (see beginning of unit or page 32).

Buoyancy: Archimedes' Principle
Description: An overview of the principle of buoyancy.

Bathtub Physics - Density, Buoyancy and Flotation-
Description: Explains the Archimedes Principle, flotation and the reaction of buoyant forces. Explain the relationship between density and flotation.

BrainPop: Buoyancy
Description: Watch a cartoon on buoyancys, take quizzes, and try experiments to learn about what makes boats float.

Buoyancy Brainteasers -
Description: basics on buoyancy with puzzles to help you test your knowledge.

Step 3 Expand

Choose and complete one of the following activities:

Activity 1: Experiment
Compare a cup of puffed rice with a cup of salt. The volume is the same but the mass is different. Look up and discuss the terms "volume," "mass," and "density" in a dictionary. Add the three words to your Vocabulary Notebook.

Activity 2: Experiment
Objects float when they displace enough water to create a buoyant force greater than the force of gravity. Do an experiment. Construct a modeling-clay "boat" and other designs to test their buoyancy. Or, do the experiment found on this Internet site: Buoyancy Lesson.

Activity 3: Write a Summary
Explain, in writing, what you have learned about the Archimedes Principle (minimum 150 words). Younger students can narrate (orally tell) what they have learned.

Step 4 Excel

Share what you have learned about the Archimedes Principle with a friend or family member. Correct all written work to demonstrate correct punctuation and spelling, and effective use of grammar. Add corrected written work or any illustrations to your portfolio.

Underlined text refers to Internet link at http://Homeschool-Books.com

Hanukkah

Note: For more about Hanukkah see <u>The Maccabean Period</u> in the Ancient Israel Unit (page 406).

Step 1 Excite

Make a list of what you know about Hanukkah (the Feast of Dedication). Ask at least five people what they know about Hanukkah. Record your answers. (It is not the Jewish replacement for Christmas.)

Step 2 Examine

Hanukkah (also spelled Chanukah or Hanukah), is the celebration of the Jews' victory over the Hellenistic Syrians in 165 B.C. It is an annual festival of the Jews, celebrated on eight successive days to honor the restoration of divine worship in the Temple after it had been defiled by heathens. The return of their religious liberty was to them as life from the dead and, in remembrance of it, they kept an annual holiday on the twenty-fifth day of Kislev. Kislev is the third month of the Jewish calendar, corresponding approximately to early December in the Gregorian calendar. Jesus kept this festival (John 10:22).

The biggest lesson of Hanukkah was the power of the spirit, the ability of God's people to live by God's commands. ...*Not by might, nor by power, but by my spirit, saith the LORD of hosts* (Zech. 4:6). In between the Testaments, around 164 B.C., the Maccabees (or Hasmoneans), led by Judah Maccabee, wrested Judea from the rule of the Seleucids–Syrian rulers who supported the spread of Greek religion and culture. Hanukkah commemorates the recapture of Jerusalem by the Maccabees and the establishment of the Temple. The Temple had been profaned by Antiochus IV Epiphanes, king of Syria and overlord of Palestine. The Maccabees ruled Judea until Herod took power in 37 B.C.

Hanukkah centers around a menorah. The Hanukkah menorah has nine branches; eight to remember the eight days of Hanukkah, and one "shamus," the candle used to light the other candles (this is usually either higher or separate from the other eight branches). The Temple menorah has seven branches.

Research Hanukkah. Use any resource (an encyclopedia, nonfiction book, historical novel, or the Internet). We recommend the following:

Books

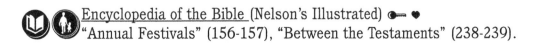 <u>Encyclopedia of the Bible</u> (Nelson's Illustrated) ⬤━ ♥
"Annual Festivals" (156-157), "Between the Testaments" (238-239).

Resources recommended in ♦several lessons, ★ several units, ♥ other HOW Units. ⬤━ Key Resource (see beginning of unit or page 32).

Heart of Wisdom Publishing   517

A Family Guide to the Biblical Holidays ★
Read: "Hanukkah" (381-403).

The Holman Bible Atlas ⊙— ❤
Read: "The Maccabean Revolt" (183-189).

History of the Jewish People Volume 1: Second Temple Era ⊙— ◆
Read: Chapter 8 "Antiochus Epiphanes and His Decrees," and Chapter 9 "The Hasmonean Wars and the Miracle of Chanukkah." (See description in the Ancient Israel Unit Resources Section.)

Alexandra's Scroll: The Story of the First Hanukkah by Miriam Chaikin and Stephen Fieser.
Description: A young girl's account of life in Jerusalem in 165 B.C. When the hated Syrian-Greek king fills ancient Jerusalem with statues of Greek gods and destroys the Jewish temple, feisty Alexandra takes up reed pen, ink, and sheet of papyrus and turns "scribe." In her scroll Alexandra records the everyday happenings of her life, as well as the events of the Jewish rebellion led by the Maccabees. When her father joins the resistance against the Greek authorities, Alexandra must leave her friends and the city she loves. The victory of the Maccabees three years later returns the family to Jerusalem—to old friends, new ones and, for Alexandra, a new life. Place and time are recreated in this story of a girl caught up in the events that led to the rebuilding of the temple, the miracle of oil that burns eight days, and the celebration of the first Hanukkah. Hardcover: 128 pages, Henry Holt & Company (2002) ISBN: 0805063846. Reading level: Ages 9-12.

The Life of Greece (The Story of Civilization II) ◆
Read: "Hellenism and the Jews" (579-584).

See list of Internet sites in The Maccabean Period in the Ancient Israel Unit (page 406).

Step 3 Expand

Choose and complete one of the following activities:

Activity 1: Make a List
Make a list of the traits of the Jews and the ancient Greeks that were pointed out by this lesson.

Activity 2: Play a Game
Play JCN's Great Computerized Dreidel Game (maintained by the Jewish Communication Network).

Activity 3: Answer Questions

1. What happened to the menorah and oil when enemy soldiers took over the Temple?
2. Why did Mattathias want to drive the enemy out of Jerusalem?
3. How long did the Jews fight the Greeks?
4. After the Jews conquered their enemy, how much oil did they find in the Temple?
5. What was the "miracle of the oil"?

Activity 4: Write a Story
Write a story titled "The Revolt of the Maccabees." Decide how you want to present the information; as a basic report or something more imaginative. Collect as much information as possible. Review your notes, and identify your main idea. Balance historical fact with the emotions and feelings of the Jews. Then re-create the events leading to The Feast of Dedication. Refer to "Point of View," "Feature Story," "Writing About an Event," and "Evidence" in *Writers INC*. Younger students can narrate (orally tell) what they have learned.

Activity 5: Celebrate
Celebrate Hanukkah this year using the information you gathered during this lesson.

Step 4 Excel

Share what you have learned about Hanukkah with a friend or family member. Correct all written work to demonstrate correct punctuation and spelling, and effective use of grammar. Add corrected written work or any illustrations to your portfolio.

Resources recommended in ◆several lessons, ★ several units, ♥other HOW Units. ◉━Key Resource (see beginning of unit or page 32).

Ancient Greek Architecture

Step 1 Excite

Architecture expresses man's innermost feelings and reflects the distinctive character of given periods of time. The Greeks developed three architectural systems (also called orders), each with its own distinguishing details. The Greek orders are: Doric, Ionic, and Corinthian.

The Greeks used the column as a pillar to support a building, and occasionally as a free-standing monument. In classical architecture, a column is a shaft that usually rests on a base and is topped by an enlarged section called a "capital." You can recognize the style of architecture by the columns and capitals. Find samples of each architectural system in a library book or by following these links:

The Doric Column
Description: An explanation of the characteristics of the Doric column: it has no base and a heavy shaft; its capital is an undecorated, square slab resting on a disc.

The Acropolis
Description: A sample of Doric columns in various structures. The architect Mnesicles directed the construction of a monumental entrance gateway to the Athenian Acropolis, the steep ramp of which is in the Doric style of western Greece.

The Parthenon
Description: A sample of Doric columns in various monuments. The Parthenon—temple of the goddess Athena—is considered to be the greatest of the Greek temples designed in the Doric style.

Ionic Column
Description: Contains details of the characteristics of the Ionic column, which is distinguished by its volute or scroll capital. More slender than the Doric

column, its height is eight or nine times the diameter of the shaft. Normally the Ionic column has twenty-four flutes, which are separated by "fillets" or soft edges; some examples have as many as forty-eight flutes.

Sample of Ionic Columns
Description: An explanation of the characteristics of the Ionic column, which is distinguished by its volute or scroll capital. More slender than the Doric column, its height is eight or nine times the diameter of the shaft.

The Corinthian Column
Description: Contains details of the characteristics of the Corinthian column, which is the most decorative and usually the most appealing to the modern eye.

Sample of a Corinthian Column
Description: A detailed description of the Corinthian capital, which is decorated with flowering, leaf-like structures below a lesser scroll design than that of Ionian capitals. The shaft has indented sides and the base is a more refined version of the Ionic. Unlike the Doric and Ionic roofs, which are at a slant, the Corinthian roofs are flat. The Corinthian frieze is the same as the Ionic frieze, but on a smaller scale.

Corinthian Sample
Description: A picture and description of the Choragic Monument of Lysicrates built in the Corinthian style. The Corinthian shaft is slender, and the ornately decorated capital is carved in the shape of an inverted bell.

Step 2. Examine

Go for a drive to the nearest city. Study local buildings and churches that copy Greek architecture, specifically columns. Make brief sketches and, if possible, take photographs.

Research Greek architecture. Use any resource (an encyclopedia, nonfiction book, or the Internet). We recommend the following:

Books

Resources recommended in ♦several lessons, ★ several units, ● other HOW Units. ●━ Key Resource (see beginning of unit or page 32).

Heart of Wisdom Publishing   521

The Usborne Book of the Ancient World ☞ ★
Read: "Architecture" (140), "The Greek House" (122).

The Penguin Historical Atlas of Ancient Greece ☞ ♦
Read: "Architecture of Ancient Greece" (134-135).

Handbook to Life in Ancient Greece ☞ ♦
Read: References to architecture and architects.

The Life of Greece (The Story of Civilization II) ♦
Read: "Architecture" (223-225). Also see references to architecture in different periods in the index.

Internet Sources

The Buildings of the Acropolis
Description: A portion of the site is based on the PBS series "The Greeks: Crucible of Civilization."

The History of Greek Architecture
Description: An excellent site which helps the non-professional understand and enjoy architecture. Click on the monument for details.

Foundations of Western Architecture
Description: This site is from Tulane University. Each link explores architectural, decorating, and furniture styles.

The Houses of Athens
Description: A portion of the site is based on the PBS series "The Greeks: Crucible of Civilization."

Preserving Jewish Heritage in Greece
Description: Article from *Archaeology Magazine*. Portions of Greek monuments remain today, but most of the Jewish architecture had been lost by the end of World War II. You'll find a few photos of the remains of Jewish architecture on this site.

The Parthenon
Description: A complete look at the Temple of Athena Parthenos, the Parthenon.

Great Buildings Online: Ancient Greek Architecture
Description: Click on a link to see individual Greek monuments. You'll see a photo or drawing of each and details including the architect, the location, date, building type, climate, style, notes, etc.

History of Greek Architecture
Description: This excellent site will help the non-professional understand and enjoy architecture. Click on each monument for details.

Greek Architecture Site
Description: Includes graphics and illustrations of famous buildings, both past and present. Read biographies of famous architects, see the different types of materials used in the construction of buildings, and learn how architecture progressed from the ancient Greeks and Romans, right up to the 21st century.

Step 3. Expand

Choose and complete one of the following activities:

Activity 1: Create Art
Produce a piece of artwork showing examples of ancient Greek architecture. This may include detailed drawing, modeling with clay or other appropriate materials, making junk models, drawing with chalk and charcoal, etc.

Activity 2: Find Illustrations
Print out or photocopy examples of Greek architecture and columns to add to your portfolio. Look at the different styles of classic architecture in each century and place them on a time line.

Step 4. Excel

Explain orally to your parents what you've learned in this lesson. Add any illustrations to your portfolio. Add new words you learned in this lesson into your Vocabulary Notebook (see page 22).

Resources recommended in ◆several lessons, ★ several units, ● other HOW Units. ●—Key Resource (see beginning of unit or page 32).

Art in Ancient Greece

Step 1 Excite

Discuss how art has influenced your life. What is your favorite painting/poster? Favorite song? Favorite book, essay, or poem? Think of places in which you have observed public art. What were the purposes for each work of art? Discuss art for pleasure; for decoration; for economic worth; for political power or importance; to record history; and for functional purposes.

Step 2 Examine

Greek art included Greek gods, goddesses, and myths, illustrated in paintings and marvelous statues. Find examples of art from ancient Greece. Use any resource (an encyclopedia, nonfiction book, or the Internet). We recommend the following:

Books

The Usborne Book of the Ancient World ●— ★
Read: "Pottery" (126) and "Sculpture" (142).

Handbook to Life in Ancient Greece ●— ◆
Read: Chapter 9 "Art" (363-380)

Ancient Greece (Eyewitness) ●— ◆
Read: "Vases and Vessels" (48-49).

History of Art for Young People by H. W. Janson
Description: This book surveys the history of art, including painting, sculpture, architecture, and photography, from cave paintings to modern art. ISBN: 0810941503.

Software

History Through Art: Ancient Greece CD-ROM
Description: See description in the Resources section.

Internet Sources

Greek Art and Architecture
Description: Dedicated to images and information on the art and architecture of ancient Greece, Crete, and the Cycladic Islands, this site is sponsored by the University of Colorado at Colorado Springs.

The New Greek Galleries
Description: Details of a section of the Metropolitan Museum of Art in New York City.

Girl with Doves
Description: Information about a work on display at the Metropolitan Museum of Art in New York City.

Step 3 Expand

Choose and complete one of the following activities:

Activity 1: Add to Your Vocabulary Notebook (see page 22)
Look up and define the following art terms: alloy, attribute, bronze, chiton, colonnade, corybant, dinos, excavation, engraving, kore, marble, patina, Polychromy, Praxiteles, relief.

Activity 2: Find Illustrations
Make color copies of your favorite artwork from library books or Internet sites to add to your portfolio.

Activity 3: Make an Art Time Line
Using photocopies from art books, or printouts from Internet sites, make a display of the art from the Archaic Period through the Classical Period to the Hellenistic Period. Present your display to your family or a homeschool group.

Step 4 Excel

Share your work from Step 3 with someone. Explain what you have learned in this lesson. Correct all written work to demonstrate correct punctuation and spelling, and effective use of grammar. Add corrected written work or any illustrations to your portfolio.

Resources recommended in ♦several lessons, ★ several units, ♥ other HOW Units. ☞—Key Resource (see beginning of unit or page 32).

Cities: Athens

Step 1 Excite

Athens was the most celebrated city of the ancient world and the seat of Greek literature and art during the golden period of Grecian history. Its inhabitants were fond of novelty (Acts 17:21) and were remarkable for their zeal in their worship of the gods. A Roman satirist said sarcastically that it was "easier to find a god at Athens than a man."

On his second missionary journey, Paul visited this city (Acts 17:15; Compare 1 Thessalonians 3:1), and delivered, in the Areopagus, his famous speech (17:22-31). The altar there, of which Paul speaks as dedicated "to the unknown God" (23), was probably one of several that bore the same inscription. It is supposed that these altars originated from the practice of letting loose a flock of sheep and goats in the streets of Athens on the occasion of a plague and then, at the spot where they lay down, offering them up in sacrifice "to the god concerned." (Easton)

Athens is best known for its temples and public buildings of antiquity.

Step 2 Examine

Research Athens. Use any resource (an encyclopedia, nonfiction book, or the Internet). We recommend the following:

Books

> The Usborne Book of the Ancient World ⟟— ★
> Read: "The City of Athens" (138).

> Ancient Greece (Eyewitness) ⟟— ◆
> Read: "Athens, city of Athena" (16-17).

> The Penguin Historical Atlas of Ancient Greece ⟟— ◆
> Read: 'Dark Age to Athenian Ascendancy" (38-61).

Underlined text refers to Internet link at http://Homeschool-Books.com

The Life of Greece (The Story of Civilization II) ◆
Read: Chapter V. "Athens" (98-126).

Internet Sources

Two Faces of Greece: Athens & Sparta
Description: This lesson was created by PBS to help students explore
and understand the ancient Greek world.

The Daily Athenian: A Greek Newspaper Project
Description: A site created by PBS to help students learn more about
daily life in ancient Athens through a group newspaper project.

Greek Life: Some Details
Description: A glance at the physical environment of the peninsula at the
time when the Greeks invaded it, and the results of its destruction particularly by
the ancient Athenians.

Athens
Description: An overview of the history, people, and economy of Athens
from Britannica.com.

Athens
Description: Brief overview of the city of ancient Athens from a
ThinkQuest project.

The Ancient City of Athens
Description: A photographic archive of the archaeological and architectural remains of ancient Athens.

The Ancient City of Athens: Sites & Monuments
Description: View images of the Acropolis, Philopappos Monument, the
Pnyx, Agora, and Library of Hadrian.

Athens Virtual Tour
Description: A theme-based interactive community, this site includes
images from various Athens sites. Download and view movies of ancient cities
rebuilt, take a virtual walking tour, or play the classic Web game, S.P.Q.R.

Perseus Project
Description: The definitive gateway to all things Athenian, this site
includes a vast array of resource materials. Here you'll find information on the art,

Resources recommended in ◆several lessons, ★ several units, ♥ other HOW Units. ◉━Key Resource (see beginning of unit or page 32).

Heart of Wisdom Publishing   527

architecture, texts, and history of ancient Greece from about 1200-323 B.C., including an atlas that uses Java and requires Internet Explorer 4, or Netscape 4 or above.

<u>Ancient Greece</u>
Description: This site gives the fine points of the council of nobles behind the Areopagus and its nine archons, as well as a description of the reforms of Solon, and Pesistratus' rebellion.

<u>Print Your Own Coloring Page</u>
Description: Includes a coloring page of the Parthenon in Athens.

Step 3 Expand

Choose and complete one of the following activities:

Activity 1: Create a Brochure
Prepare a travel brochure for Athens. Use pictures you have found or drawn. Decide on four places or topics to feature in your brochure. Be sure to include basic facts about the city as well as interesting and exciting places to visit there.

Activity 2: Prepare a Lesson
Imagine you are going to teach a younger student about ancient Athens. Create an outline as a teaching guide. Include entries such as: people, location, land, climate, transportation, trade, art, Athenian myths and legends, sites, and monuments. Create a map to refer to during your teaching.

Activity 3: Teach a Child
Teach a younger child about Athens using your prepared resources. When you complete the lesson, have the child tell you what he or she has learned (narration). Correct any errors.

Step 4 Excel

Share what you have learned about Athens with a friend or family member. Add any written work or illustrations to your portfolio.

Cities: Sparta

Step 1 Excite

What do you know about the Greek city of Sparta? Find a travel agency on the Internet that has information on modern-day Sparta. Brainstorm and discuss what ancient Sparta might have been like, based on your findings.

Step 2 Examine

Research ancient Sparta. Use any resource (an encyclopedia, nonfiction book, or the Internet). We recommend the following:
Books

Ancient Greece (Eyewitness) ⊶ ♦
Read: "The State of Sparta" (56-57).

The Penguin Historical Atlas of Ancient Greece ⊶ ♦
Read: "The Rise of Sparta (80-81), "Sparta and Thebes" (100-101).

The Life of Greece (The Story of Civilization II) ♦
Read: Chapter IV. "Sparta" (67-97).

Internet Sources

Two Faces of Greece: Athens & Sparta
Description: This lesson was created by PBS to help students explore and understand the ancient Greek world.

The Greeks: Crucible of Empire
Description: Learn about ancient Greek city-states and their lasting influence on Western civilization.

Ancient Greece: Sparta
Description: Historical background on the ancient Greek city-state.

Some Spartan Stories
Description: Passages from antiquity revealing Spartan character.
Anecdotes about Archidamus, Lycurgus, and Agesilaus.

Resources recommended in ♦several lessons, ★ several units, ♥other HOW Units. ⊶Key Resource (see beginning of unit or page 32).

Heart of Wisdom Publishing   529

Sparta
Description: Introduction to important Spartans and the significance of the city in history.

Sparta 800-500 B.C.
Description: A study page with course notes and links on many aspects of Spartan history. Most of the links other than those that go to Perseus are dead. Study test for philolaconians.

Sparta: A Bibliography
Description: Major ancient sources, a long list of books on history and society, and a collection of archaeological works on Sparta.

Timeline of Sparta
Description: A comparison of Spartan events to those of the rest of Greece, from 1550-222 B.C.

Step 3 Expand

Choose and complete one of the following activities:

Activity 1: Write a Story
Write a story as if you are a person living in ancient Sparta. You can choose to bea citizen, merchant, or slave. Younger students can narrate (orally tell) their story.

Activity 2: Create a Brochure
Prepare a travel brochure for Sparta. Use pictures you have found or drawn. Decide on four places or topics to feature in your brochure. Be sure to include basic facts about the city as well as interesting and exciting places to visit there.

Activity 1: Contrast and Compare
Make a contrast-and-compare graphic (see page 26) comparing Spartan government with Athenian government.

Step 4 Excel

Include your work from the above activities and a map of Greece (with Athens, Sparta, and Troy labeled) in your portfolio.

Funerals in Ancient Greece

Step 1 Excite

Brainstorm and discuss how funeral rituals reflect the people of the time and their religious beliefs. Do you know how funerals were held in ancient Greece?

Step 2 Examine

Research ancient Greek funerals. Use any resource (an encyclopedia, nonfiction book, or the Internet). We recommend the following:

Books

Ancient Greece (Eyewitness) ⌾▬ ♦
Read: "Death and the Afterlife" (62-63).

The Usborne Book of the Ancient World ⌾▬ ★
Read: "Death and the Underworld" (166). Also see pages 106-108).

Handbook to Life in Ancient Greece ⌾▬ ♦
Read: "Death and Afterlife" (420-425).

Internet Sources

Ancient Greek Burials
Description: Concise overview of burials in ancient Greece.

Burial
Description: By the University of Pennsylvania Museum of Archaeology and Anthropology, this site offers a description of the burial rituals of the ancient Greeks.

The Greek Cemetery
Description: A look at burial urns and symbols, and their meaning in ancient Greek culture, displayed by the University of Pennsylvania Museum of Archaeology and Anthropology.

Death and Burial
Description: From Odyssey Online: Emory University and Memorial Art Gallery, University of Rochester.

Resources recommended in ♦several lessons, ★ several units, ● other HOW Units. ⌾▬Key Resource (see beginning of unit or page 32).

Ⓘ Ancient Greek Religion: Burial
Description: University of Pennsylvania Museum describes the basic burial practices, funeral rituals, and cemetery designs of the ancient Greek culture.

Step 3 Expand

Choose and complete one of the following activities:

Activity 1: Answer Questions
Answer these questions about ancient Greek funerals: What happened to the spirit of a dead man, according to Greek belief? How were funeral announcements made? How did women participate in a funeral ceremony? Was the corpse displayed? What types of funeral rites were practiced in ancient Greece? Compare funeral ceremonies of a rich man and a poor man.

Activity 2: Write a Summary
Write at least two paragraphs retelling what you have learned about ancient Greek funerals. Younger students can narrate (orally tell) what they have learned.

Step 4 Excel

Explain orally to your parents what you've learned in this lesson. Correct all written work to demonstrate correct punctuation and spelling, and effective use of grammar. Add corrected written work or any illustrations to your portfolio.

Weddings in Ancient Greece

Step 1 Excite

Wedding ceremonies are an important feature of any culture. They mark the beginning of a new life; the joining of two families. Funeral rituals also reflect the people of the time. Both reflect religious beliefs. Brainstorm and discuss how weddings and funerals were held in ancient Greece.

Step 2 Examine

Research ancient Greek weddings. Use any resource (an encyclopedia, nonfiction book, or the Internet). We recommend the following:
Books

The Usborne Book of the Ancient World
Read: "Role of Women: Marriage" (146).

The Life of Greece (The Story of Civilization II) ◆
Read: "Love and Marriage" (302-304). Also see references to marriage (36, 40, 51, 81-82, 84-85, 117, 250).

Handbook to Life in Ancient Greece ●— ◆
Read: All references to weddings and marriage.

Internet Sources

Ancient Greek Marriage
Description: This site includes descriptions of the customs of ancient weddings, both Greek and Latin, as described in the poetry of Sappho and Catullus.

Ancient Greek Wedding
Description: Good overview of pre- and post- wedding ceremonies.

Resources recommended in ◆several lessons, ★ several units, ●other HOW Units. ●—Key Resource (see beginning of unit or page 32).

CLASS 220: The Greek and Roman Wedding
Terms, relevant links, and bibliography for course lectures on the Greek and Roman wedding.

Step 3 Expand

Choose and complete one of the following activities:

Activity 1: Answer Questions
Answer these questions about ancient weddings: Why, in Athens, were wedding ceremonies started after dark? Why did friends and family carry torches and play music? Why did the bride eat an apple during the wedding ceremony? What types of gifts would the couple receive? Why, in ancient Sparta, did the groom tussle and toss his bride over his shoulder?

Activity 2: Create an Invitation
Make an invitation to an ancient Greek wedding.

Step 4 Excel

Share your work from Step 3 with someone. Explain what you have learned in this lesson. Correct all written work to demonstrate correct punctuation and spelling, and effective use of grammar. Add corrected written work or any illustrations to your portfolio.

Drama in Ancient Greece

Step 1 Excite

Brainstorm and discuss types of entertainment before television. What did people do after work in their free time?

Step 2 Examine

The theater tradition grew out of religious rituals. The followers of Dionysus, the god of wine, enjoyed frenzied ceremonies filled with drunkenness. Through their singing and dancing, the people of the Dionysian cult would tell stories. Thespis pretended to be one of the characters and became the first actor and the first playwright. From that point on, physically enacting the story became popular. In 534 B.C., theater was integrated into a festival that was influenced by the followers of Dionysus.

Three of the most influential ancient Greek writers were Homer, Aeschylus, and Sophocles. Three types of drama were composed in Athens: tragedy, comedy, and satyr plays. There were three types of theaters: Athenian, Hellenistic, and Graeco-Roman, each distinctly different from the others.

Tragedy is not only a literary and theatrical practice, but also constitutes an object of contemplation, which has served as an intellectual touchstone for many philosophers and artists. Among the most influential theorists are Plato, Aristotle, Hegel, Schopenhauer, Nietzsche, and Brecht. Greek tragedy represents the output of a very short period of history, from about 480 B.C., when Aeschylus's early plays were performed, to the last plays of Sophocles and Euripides at the end of the fifth century. The two later tragedians wrote their early plays in the fifty years from 480, the end of the wars with Persia, to 430, the start of the Peloponnesian War with Sparta which was to destroy Athens as an independent city-state.

Research Greek drama and theaters. Use any resource (an encyclopedia, nonfiction book, or the Internet). We recommend the following:

Books

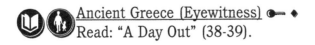
Ancient Greece (Eyewitness) ◉— ♦
Read: "A Day Out" (38-39).

The Usborne Book of the Ancient World ☞ ★
Read: "The Theatre" (152-153).

Handbook to Life in Ancient Greece ☞ ◆
Read: "Entertainment" (419-420), "Music and Dance" (263-264).

The Life of Greece (The Story of Civilization II) ◆
Read: "The Beginnings odf Drama" (230-232), "The Literature of the Golden Age" (230, 374-412).

Internet Sources

Introduction to Ancient Theater
Description: Includes images and links to Greek theatre sites; from Didaskalia.

Ancient Greek Theater
Description: A brief introduction to ancient Greek theater, with tools for further research. Includes a time line of Greek drama, origins, and more.

Step 3 Expand

Choose and complete one of the following activities:

Activity 1: Add to Your Vocabulary Notebook (see page 22)
From your research above, define each of the following: crane, logeion, paraskenia, skene, orchestra, ekkuklema.

Activity 2: Write a Summary
Write a brief summary of the Greek tragedies. Include those of Sophocles, Euripides, and Aeschylus.

Activity 3: Write a Play
Write and share a play that could have been written in ancient Greece. Refer to "Plays, Drama, and Dialog" in *Writers INC*. Consider entering your play in a play-writing contest at the Christians In The Theatre Arts site.

Step 4 Excel

Explain orally to your parents what you've learned in this lesson. Correct all written work to demonstrate correct punctuation and spelling, and effective use of grammar. Add corrected written work or any illustrations to your portfolio.

Underlined text refers to Internet link at http://Homeschool-Books.com

Education in Ancient Greece

Step 1 Excite

Aristotle said, "Virtue, like any art or faculty, can only be acquired by education. Education must be regulated by the State. For as the end of the State as a whole is one, the education of all the citizens must be one and the same, and must therefore be an affair of the State. Every citizen should remember that he is not his own master but a part of the State." This is the opposite of what most homeschoolers believe.

Review and update your family's homeschooling goals in writing.

Step 2 Examine

Two contrasting types of education appeared early in ancient Greece: that of Sparta, wholly controlled by the state, and that of Athens, left almost entirely to the home and to private schools. Up to the age of seven, the education of both boys and girls was accomplished at home; at the age of seven, boys were gathered in barracks, where emphasis was placed upon physical development through games, exercises, and the pentathlon (running, jumping, throwing the discuss, casting the javelin, and wrestling) and upon memorizing the laws of the Spartan lawgiver Lycurgus, and selections from Homer. The whole process was designed to develop endurance, resourcefulness, and discipline. At eighteen, definite training in the use of arms and warfare began; from twenty to thirty, service in the army and guarding the borders of the state were required, and even after thirty, men were required to live in barracks and assist in the training of the boys. Physical training was also emphasized in the education of girls and women, so that they might bear sturdy children. The whole purpose of education was to subordinate the individual to the needs of the state.

Education in general was considered a leisure pursuit only available to the privileged few. The majority of the population received no education. Girls in ancient Greece received no formal education in the literary arts, though many of them were taught to read and write informally, in the home. The pursuit of literature was considered the ultimate goal—an idle life of leisure devoid of manual labor. (This pagan goal of the idle rich exists in America today.)

The ancient Greeks' interest in learning is evident in their art, politics, and philosophy. Teachers lived in their households; these teachers were often slaves from conquered states. Later, when the Roman Empire was at its height, its citizens also followed the practice of

Resources recommended in ◆several lessons, ★ several units, ●other HOW Units. ●━Key Resource (see beginning of unit or page 32).

Heart of Wisdom Publishing   537

having teacher-slaves, usually Greeks, attached to their households. The work of several Greek writers served as the model for the educational systems of ancient Rome, which stressed gymnastics as well as mathematics and music.

The basic divisions of knowledge were: Grammar, Rhetoric, Dialectic— these were meant to help students communicate effectively, and included a study of literature and language— and Arithmetic, Music, Geometry, and Astronomy. These seven subjects later became known as the Liberal Arts. They survive in one form or another in many universities today. Anatomy, Biology, and Botany were also considered valid fields of study.

By the 4th century B.C., aristocratic 18-year-old males spent two years in a gymnasium, a state school devoted to the overall physical and intellectual development of young men. More advanced education in philosophy, mathematics, logic, and rhetoric was available to the aristocracy in highly select gymnasia, like the Academy of Plato and the Lyceum of Aristotle.

Socrates, Plato, Aristotle, and Isocrates were the influential thinkers on education. The Greeks were history's first humanists, believing that man was the measure of all things. The Greek aim was to prepare intellectually well-rounded young people to take leading roles in the activities of the state and of society. (By contrast, the Hebrews' primary purpose for education was to train for lifelong obedient service to God.)

> The classical schools, with their intention to produce perfect citizens through education, produced only an artificial and cruel society. Men still look back on the "golden Days" of Greece for personal and cultural inspiration, but they fail to realize that the true nobility that they aspired to was never obtainable on any humanistic premise. True nobility, which the Greek and Roman ideal correctly identified, to some extent, is only available through the obedience to the Gospel of Christ, with its insistence on our recognition and confession of sin and its promise of containing sanctification. This is never attainable though education, but only through the free mercies of Christ our Savior. [1]

Compare ancient Greek and Hebrew (biblical) education. The text below is from *Our Father Abraham Study Guide.*

Education with a Difference

1. "All education was directed to this end: to be different was the law of existence . . . 'You shall be different, for I the Lord your God am different.'"— Leo Baeck, *The Essence of Judaism* (New York: Schocken Books, 1948), p.261.
2. The Greek world's view of teaching was that it primarily involved the transference of knowledge in the intellectual and technical areas, such as music, art, reading, or athletics.

Underlined text refers to Internet link at http://Homeschool-Books.com

3. In ancient Greek society, only the wealthy and leisure classes were enlightened through education. Indeed, our English words school and scholar derive from the Greek verb scholazo, "to have leisure," "to have spare time," "to have nothing to do."

4. In contrast, Jewish education was for all people and concerned the whole person. Teaching had to do primarily with the communication of the Law or will of the Lord and was done by God himself, by the father of the family, or by a religious leader within the community.

5. To summarize, the Greeks learned in order to comprehend. The Hebrews learned in order to revere.

Biblical Education

1. The primary purpose of education in Bible times was to train the whole person for lifelong, obedient service in the knowledge of God (Proverbs 1:7; Ecclesiastes 12:13).

2. The aim of learning was holiness in living—to be set apart unto God in every dimension of life. This holiness required a knowledge of God's acts in history and a commitment to observe his mitzvot (commandments), which instructed one how to live.

3. The center of education was the home.

4. "Education is a matter which rests primarily with the parent, with the father. The teacher is but a representative of the father, according to Jewish tradition. Thou shalt teach them diligently, not vicariously. Now parents act as they please—commercialism and vulgarity blare from the loudspeakers—and little children are expected to listen to the voice of the Spirit. Religious instruction, like charity, begins at home." — Heschel, *The Insecurity of Freedom* (New York: Schocken Books, 1972), pp. 54-55.

5. In the Hebrew Bible, teachers (priests) are called "father" (Judges 17:10; 18:19), and the relationship between teacher and student (e.g., Elijah and Elisha) is expressed as "father" and "son" (11 Kings 2:3,12).

6. In traditional Jewish homes today, when a child prays for his parents he refers to them as "my father, my teacher; my mother, my teacher."

7. The Bible teaches that study ought to be, above everything else, an act of worship, one of the highest ways by which a person can glorify God.

8. Paul makes no distinction between the so-called "sacred" and "secular" areas of life. He taught that all of life was God's domain. Every detail of life, therefore, must be set aside and consecrated to the glory of God.

9. "Study is not an ordeal but an act of edification; the school is a sanctuary, not a factory; study is a form of worship." — Heschel, *The Insecurity of Freedom* (New York: Schocken Books, 1972).

Resources recommended in ♦several lessons, ★ several units, ♥other HOW Units. ☞—Key Resource (see beginning of unit or page 32).

Heart of Wisdom Publishing   539

Do research to compare the differences between ancient Greek and Hebrew education. Use any resource (an encyclopedia, nonfiction book, or the Internet). We recommend the following:

Books

Encyclopedia of the Bible (Nelson's Illustrated) ⊷ ♥
"Greek Education" (101).

The Usborne Book of the Ancient World ⊷ ★
Read: "Children and Education" (148), "Learning" (174).

Our Father Abraham ⊷ ♥
Read: "A Life of Learning."

Sketches of Jewish Social Life by Alfred Edersheim (1876)
Read "Subjects of Study"; "Home Education in Israel"; "Female Education"; "Elementary Schools"; "Schoolmasters"; and "School Arrangements." Available online (see Internet Sources).

Far Above Rubies: Wisdom in the Christian Community ⊷ ★
Read "Christianity, Classicism, and Chaos"; "Greeks, Romans, and a Paradox"; "The Greek Roman World as the City of Man"; and "The Greek Paideia."

Handbook to Life in Ancient Greece ⊷ ♦
Read: "Education" (253-254).

Internet Sources

Home Education in Israel
Description: Chapter 8 from Sketches of Jewish Social Life by Alfred Edersheim. (Also see "Female Education"; "Elementary Schools"; "Schoolmasters"; and "School Arrangements.")

The Greek Foundation of Modern Education
Description: An article illustrating how the roots of modern America's educational system and traditions reach back to the Greeks.

Step 3 Expand

Choose and complete one of the following activities:

Activity 1: Contrast and Compare
Make a <u>contrast-and-compare graphic</u> (see page 26) comparing the definition of education according to: Greek philosopher, Aristotle; the faithful Christian, Noah Webster; and a modern dictionary. Each is noted below:

> Education according to Aristotle: The ordinary branches of education are: 1. Reading and Writing, 2. Gymnastics, 3. Music, and 4. The Art of Design. Of these, reading/writing and design are taught for their practical utility. Gymnastics promotes valor.

> Webster's 1828 Dictionary: The bringing up, as of a child; instruction; formation of manners. Education comprehends all that series of instruction and discipline which is intended to: 1. Enlighten the understanding, 2. Correct the temper, 3. Form the manners and habits of youth, and 4. Fit them [youth] for usefulness in their future stations. To give a child an education in manners, arts, and science is important; to give them [children] a religious education is indispensable: an immense responsibility rests on the parents and guardians who neglect these duties.

> American Heritage Dictionary: 1. The act or process of educating or being educated. 2. The knowledge or skill obtained or developed by a learning process. 3. A program of instruction of a specified kind or level: driver education; a college education. 4. The field of study that is concerned with the pedagogy of teaching and learning. 5. An instructive or enlightening experience.

Activity 2: Write a Letter
Write a letter to your parents and other adult instructors, thanking them for their dedication to Christian education. Be sure to include why this is important.

Step 4 Excel

Share your work from Step 3 with someone. Explain what you have learned in this lesson. Correct all written work to demonstrate correct punctuation and spelling, and effective use of grammar. Add corrected written work or any illustrations to your portfolio.

Footnotes
1. Kandel, Gary H. (1996). *The Demonic Roots of Globalism: En Route to Spiritual Deception.* Huntington House Publishers.
2. Mulligan, David. (1994). *Far Above Rubies: Wisdom in the Christian Community.* VT: Messenger Publishing. 284 pages.
3. Wilson, Marvin R. (1989). *Our Father Abraham: Jewish Roots of the Christian Faith.* Grand Rapids, MI: William B. Eerdmans Publishing Company; Dayton, OH: Center For Judaic-Christian Studies. ISBN: 0802804233.

Resources recommended in ◆several lessons, ★ several units, ♥other HOW Units. ◑—Key Resource (see beginning of unit or page 32).

Daily Life in Ancient Greece

Step 1 Excite

Brainstorm and discuss the differences between a day in the life of people who are stereotyped as middle class, upper class, lower class, white-collar worker, or blue-collar worker in modern America.

Step 2 Examine

Between 650 and 500 B.C. a leader, the Tyrant, began to challenge for political power in the polis (city-state). Class, economic, and political warfare broke out between the rising aristocracy and the general population. Rigid social classes soon developed in Sparta in order to control the lives of the people. The descendants of the Dorians, who possessed all the property and money but were a minority, became known as Spartiates (citizens). Descendants of the Ionians became known as Perioeci (free people) who moved from the farms into the city and formed a large merchant class. They were free but were not citizens. Descendants of the Laconians, who made up the largest segment of the population, were enslaved and were called Helots (slaves).

Research the different classes in ancient Greece. Use any resource (an encyclopedia, nonfiction book, or the Internet).We recommend any of the following:

Books

    Ancient Greece (Eyewitness) ⊶ ◆
Read: "At Home" (28-29), "Growing Up in Greece" (32-34), "Fun and Games" (34-35) ""Crafts, Travel and Trade" (52-53).

    The Usborne Book of the Ancient World ⊶ ★
Read: "Social Structure" (116), "A Greek House" (122), "Markets, Money and Trade" (128), Farming and Food" (120-121).

Handbook to Life in Ancient Greece ⊙━ ◆
Read: Chapter 10 "Everyday Life" (405-427). Topics include: Calendars, the Family, Slaves, Food and Drink, Personal Appearance, Entertainment, Death and After Life.

The Life of Greece (The Story of Civilization II) ★
Read: Chapter IX. "Common Culture" (98-126), Chapter XII "Work and Wealth in Athens" (268-286).

Daily Life of the Ancient Greeks by Robert Garland Daily (Life Through History Series)
Description: Ancient Greece comes alive for students and other interested readers in this re-creation of the daily lives of ordinary people—men and women, children and the elderly, slaves and foreigners, rich and poor. Taking account of the most up-to-date discoveries, the author provides a wealth of information on such varied subjects as food and drink, dress, housing, literacy, juvenile delinquency, the plight of the elderly, the treatment of slaves, and much more. Greenwood Press; ISBN: 0313303835.

Internet Sources

Greek Life: Some Details
Description: A glance at the physical environment of the peninsula when the Greeks invaded it, and the results of their destruction of it, in particular by the ancient Athenians.

Where did the Greeks live?
Description: A section of a presentation from Odyssey Online exploring Greek cultures.

What did the Greeks like to do?
Description: Another section of a presentation from Odyssey Online which explores Greek cultures.

Step 3 Expand

Choose an activity below to expand your knowledge of life in ancient Greece:

Resources recommended in ◆several lessons, ★ several units, ◆other HOW Units. ⊙━Key Resource (see beginning of unit or page 32).

Heart of Wisdom Publishing   543

Activity 1: Contrast and Compare
Make a <u>contrast-and compare-graphic</u> (see page 26) showing the differences in the lives of a Spartan, an Athenian, a Corinthian, an Argive, a Megarian, and a Greek slave: include daily life activities, types of achievements, type of education, how they observed the Olympic Games, etc.

Activity 2: Make a Diorama
Using pictures from the Internet and other sources, make a diorama/model of an ancient Greek home.

Activity 3: Find Illustrations
Print out, trace, sketch or photocopy, from a book or the Internet, examples of fashions popular in ancient Greece (men, women, and children from various social classes). Include several examples for your portfolio.

Activity 4: Write a Report
Write and present an oral report about class structure in ancient Greece. Review your notes, and identify your main idea. Balance historical fact with your own emotions and feelings. For assistance, refer to "Point of View" or "Feature Story" in *Writers INC*. Younger students can narrate (orally tell) what they have learned.

Step 4 Excel

Share your work from Step 3 with someone. Explain what you have learned in this lesson. Correct all written work to demonstrate correct punctuation and spelling, and effective use of grammar. Add corrected written work or any illustrations to your portfolio.

Food in Ancient Greece

Step 1 Excite

Many of the "food-related" objects from ancient Greece are physically on display in the Kelsey Museum. This electronic exhibit is designed to showcase items that are kept in storage and to expand the range of artifacts we can study to explore the significance of food in the ancient world. The exhibit is divided into two parts: "Feeding Karanis" and "More Food for Thought." Take an Internet tour through the Museum.

Step 2 Examine

Eat a meal at a Greek restaurant. Notice what is available on the menu. Take notes.

Research the types of foods the Greeks ate for breakfast, lunch, and dinner. What was the most popular food? Use any resource (an encyclopedia, nonfiction book, or the Internet). We recommend the following:

Books

> Ancient Greece (Eyewitness) ⌐ ◆
> Read: "Wining and Dining" (36-37), "Farmiong, Fishing, and Food" (50-51).

> The Usborne Book of the Ancient World ⌐ ★
> Read: "Farming and Food" (120).

Internet Sources

> Food in Ancient Greece
> Description: Concise overview of food in ancient Greece including feasts, crops, meals, and land.

> What foods did the Greeks eat?
> Description: Another section of a presentation from Odyssey Online exploring Greek cultures.

Resources recommended in ◆several lessons, ★ several units, ● other HOW Units. ⌐ Key Resource (see beginning of unit or page 32).

Heart of Wisdom Publishing   545

A Taste of the Ancient World
Pictures and descriptions of food and food technology used in ancient Greece.

GreekCuisine.com
Traditional recipes which will help you enrich your knowledge of Greek cooking. Among these recipes are main courses, appetizers, desserts, and salads.

Step 3 Expand

Choose and complete one of the following activities:

Activity 1: Make A Salad
Prepare a Greek Salad. Ingredients: 1 head of Romaine Lettuce, 2 Tomatoes cut in wedges, 1 sliced Cucumber, 1 Sliced Onion, 1 Green Pepper cut in rings, 1/3 lb. Feta Cheese, 2 Dozen Black Olives, crumbled dried Oregano, Parsley. Dressing: 6 Tablespoons Olive Oil, 2 tablespoons Vinegar, Salt, and Pepper. Directions: Wash the lettuce and cut in pieces. Place the lettuce, tomatoes, cucumber, onion, and peppers in a large salad bowl. Shake together the olive oil, vinegar, salt, and pepper. Pour the dressing over the salad, then crumble the feta cheese over it. Add olives. Sprinkle with parsley or oregano. Enjoy!

Activity 2: Make a Dinner
Demonstrate your findings by making a full Greek dinner for your family. Design a decorated card explaining each course you served, including the recipes, and place the card in your portfolio.

Step 4 Excel

Share what you have learned about ancient Greek food with a friend or family member. Correct all written work to demonstrate correct punctuation and spelling, and effective use of grammar. Add corrected written work or any illustrations to your portfolio.

Men in Ancient Greece

Step 1 Excite

M en's activities encompassed politics, arts and crafts, construction, agriculture, seafaring, manufacturing, and trade. Their pastimes were hunting and horseback riding. The majority of Greek citizens relied on farming for their basic income. The rich did not labor in the fields, but would oversee the farming.

Watch a video from the Video Resource section.

Step 2 Examine

Research the lives of men in ancient Greece. Find information on the lives of a politician, a soldier, a farmer, a sailor, and a construction worker. Use any resource (an encyclopedia, nonfiction book, or the Internet). We recommend the following:

See books recommended in the Daily Life in Ancient Greece lesson (page 542).

Internet Sources

The Ancient Greek World: Men's Life
Description: An overview of the lives of men in ancient Greece, and links to schooling, hunting, warfare, horses, etc.

Daily Life in Ancient Greece
Description: A comparison of life in ancient Sparta, Athens, Corinth, Argos, and Megara.

Roles of Men, Women, and Children in Ancient Greece
Description: A summary of basic daily life in ancient Greece.

Step 3 Expand

Choose and complete one of the following activities:

Activity 1: Make a Chart
Make a chart with the following headings:

Resources recommended in ◆several lessons, ★ several units, ● other HOW Units. ●—Key Resource (see beginning of unit or page 32).

Heart of Wisdom Publishing   547

- Politician
- Soldier
- Farmer
- Sailor
- Construction worker

Answer these questions under each heading:

- What kind of clothes does he wear?
- What kind of home does he live in?
- What does he do for a hobby or pastime?
- What hardships does he face?
- What are the major differences between his life and modern-day American life?
- What or whom does he fear?

Activity 2: Write a Letter

Choose one of the men above to study in detail. Write a letter from your chosen man to a family member in another part of Greece. Explain the conditions of daily life. Add this to your portfolio.

Step 4 Excel

Explain orally to your parents what you've learned in this lesson. Correct all written work to demonstrate correct punctuation and spelling, and effective use of grammar. Add corrected written work or any illustrations to your portfolio.

Women in Ancient Greece

Step 1 Excite

Brainstorm and discuss the lives of women in ancient Greece. Make a list of daily duties, problems, responsibilities, dress, etc. What character traits would differ between a Jewish woman and a Greek woman?

Step 2 Examine

The ancient Greeks viewed women as wild animals needing to be tamed. Greek myth dramatizes the anxiety and apprehension which ancient Greek men felt regarding the taming of women.

Research women's lives in ancient Greece. Use any resource (an encyclopedia, nonfiction book, or the Internet). We recommend any of the following:

Books

Ancient Greece (Eyewitness) ☞ ◆
Read: "Woman's World" (30-31).

The Usborne Book of the Ancient World ☞ ★
Read: "The Role of Women" (146).

The Life of Greece (The Story of Civilization II) ◆
Read: "Women" (305-306).

Jewish Women in Greco-Roman Palestine
Description: This study explores the real—as opposed to the ideal—social, political, and religious status of women in Palestinian Judaism during the Hellenistic and Roman periods. This investigation concludes that extreme religious groups in Judaism of the period influenced other groups, classes, and factions to tighten their control of women. They also encouraged an understanding of ideal relationships between men and women as requiring increasing chastity, represented in the literature and the legal codes of the time. Despite this, the lives of real women and their relationships to men continued to be varied and nuanced. This book integrates both Jewish and early Christian sources, together with a fem-

Resources recommended in ◆several lessons, ★ several units, ●other HOW Units. ☞Key Resource (see beginning of unit or page 32).

Heart of Wisdom Publishing   549

inist critique. It is the most comprehensive work of this sort published thus far and offers a vast repository of relevant material, as well as a fresh interpretation. Hendrickson Publishers, Inc.; ISBN: 1565632400.

Women in Greece and Rome by Mary R. Lefkowitz, Maureen B. Fant
Description: This book reveals the state of women in a world dominated by men, and shows how the pattern was set in early society for the treatment of women. It is a collection of translations showing what life was like for a woman in the ancient world, including women as seen by both women and men, women in law and politics, the daily lives of women, women's sexuality, women and medicine, and women and religion.

Internet Sources

The Biblical Woman by Dr. John D. Garr
Description: An article from *Restore!* magazine which states that in order to understand proper roles for women in the church, we must return to the Hebrew Scriptures for our patterns rather than being reactive against the Greek's perceived evil. Then we will discover the biblical woman.

First Century Woman: Hellenic and Latin Influences on Western Views of Women
Description: In order to understand attitudes toward women in today's society, we must review the history of the Greco-Roman society on which Western civilization was founded. When we do, we will be resolved to embrace fully the Hebraic models for women's ministry.

Women's Life in Ancient Greece
Description: An overview of the lives of women in ancient Greece from the University of Pennsylvania Museum site.

Women in Ancient Greece and Rome
Description: A comprehensive index to several links, including famous women, legal status, men's opinions, and more.

Step 3 Expand

Choose an activity below:

Activity 1: Write an Autobiography
Write an autobiography as if you were a woman in ancient Greece. Ask yourself the following questions:
- What kind of clothes do you wear?
- What do you look like?
- What country are you from?
- Describe your home.
- What do you do for fun?
- What hardships do you face?
- Which machines, conveniences, or technologies do you use every day?
- What are the major differences between your life and that of a modern American woman?
- Describe how world, national, or local events have affected you.
- What do you hope for?
- What are your beliefs (religious, political, personal, and so on)?

Activity 2: Contrast and Compare
Make a contrast-and-compare graphic (see page 26) to compare traits of a Jewish woman and a Greek woman. Discuss which type of woman most closely resembles today's American women. This article will help you: First Century Woman: Hellenic and Latin Influences on Western Views of Women.

Step 4 Excel

Share what you have learned about ancient Greek women with a friend or family member. Correct all written work to demonstrate correct punctuation and spelling, and effective use of grammar. Add corrected written work or any illustrations to your portfolio.

Resources recommended in ◆several lessons, ★ several units, ●other HOW Units. ●—Key Resource (see beginning of unit or page 32).

Heart of Wisdom Publishing   551

Literature in Ancient Greece: Fables

Step 1 Excite

Brainstorm and discuss: What is a fable? What is the difference between fable and parable? Who was Aesop? What does the term "sour grapes" mean?

Step 2 Examine

A fable is a brief, imaginary tale which teaches a lesson, or moral, about real life. The moral may or may not be stated at the end of the fable. A fable has an intro-
duction, a problem, and an outcome. The characters are usually animals, which talk and act like human beings. Aesop, who was a slave in ancient Greece about 620 B.C., is famous for his clever animal fables through which he showed the wide and foolish behavior of men. Aesop's fables have become a part of American's daily language with phrases such as "sour grapes" or "not counting chickens until they are hatched."

Read a few fables from a book, or visit one of the following sites:

ⓘ Aesop— Collection of Fables
Description: An extensive collection of more than six hundred of Aesop's fables, including text and Real Audio files of selected tales and morals.

ⓘ Aesop— Aesop's Fables
Description: University of Massachusetts at Amherst students present illustrated versions of these classic tales. The site includes original texts.

Research the author, Aesop. Use any resource (an encyclopedia, nonfiction book, historical novel, or the Internet). We recommend the following:

📖🧍 Ancient Greece (Eyewitness) ⚷— ◆
Read: "Gods, Goddesses and Heros" (20-21).

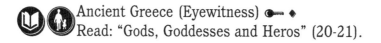

Underlined text refers to Internet link at http://Homeschool-Books.com

The Penguin Historical Atlas of Ancient Greece ☞ ♦
Read: "Greek Literature and Thought" (84-85).

The Life of Greece (The Story of Civilization II) ♦
Read: References to Aesop (104, 142, 315).

Handbook to Life in Ancient Greece ☞ ♦
Read: "Aesop" (265).

Step 3 Expand

Activity 1: Write a Fable
Write a fable about an animal. Make a list of the animal's qualities; is it:
Quick or slow? Clever? Strong? Will your fable teach a lesson? Will the animals
act like humans? Your fable might explain how the animal came to possess its
qualities, or it might illustrate how the animal uses the qualities. Refer to
"Writing a Fable" in *Writers INC*.

Activity 2: Copy Passages
Copy (by hand or typing) two or more paragraphs from a fable.

Activity 3: Find Illustrations
From a book or the Internet, print out, trace, sketch, or photocopy illustrations for one of the above activities.

Step 4

Share what you have learned about ancient Greek fables with a friend or family member.
Correct written work to demonstrate correct punctuation and spelling, and effective use of
grammar. Add corrected written work or any illustrations to your portfolio. Add new words
you learned in this lesson into your Vocabulary Notebook (see page 22).

Resources recommended in ♦several lessons, ★ several units, ♥other HOW Units. ☞Key Resource (see beginning of unit or page 32).

Heart of Wisdom Publishing   553

Medicine in Ancient Greece

Step 1 Excite

Discuss: How long, do you think, was the average life span during this period? What was the mortality rate? How did you come to these conclusions? What do you know about the Hippocratic oath?

Step 2 Examine

Greek medicine was quite advanced for its time. The works of Homer, Aristotle, Hippocrates, and Alcaemon show an advanced knowledge of physiology and of surgical and medicinal practices. The Greeks believed that the god Apollo invented healing and that his knowledge was passed on to Asclepius, the god of healing. The Greeks' worship of Asclepius began about the same time that Hippocrates of Cos (c. 460-380 B.C.) wrote the first of his famous books. Hippocrates is considered to be the "Father of Medicine" but little is known about him. He believed that disease had a rational basis. Hippocrates and his followers wrote over sixty medical books advising doctors how to examine patients for symptoms, provide simple treatments, and observe and record the development of diseases.

The Hippocratic oath,sworn by doctors in America today, originally began"I swear by Apollo the physician and AEsculapius, and Health, and All-heal, and all the gods and goddesses..." Click to read the complete original Hippocratic Oath. In 1995, a group of doctors changed the oath to begin "I swear in the presence of the Almighty..." Click to read the 1995 Oath.

Medicine in ancient Greece combined the scientific approach of Hippocrates with the super-natural beliefs of the followers of Asclepius, the god of healing. Many Greek doctors were priests of Asclepius. There were temples to this god all over Greece. Ill people would visit these temples, give sacrifices, and often sleep in the temples, hoping for healing.

Research Asclepius, Hippocrates, and Greek medicine. Use any resource (an encyclopedia, nonfiction book, historical novel, or the Internet). We recommend the following:

Books

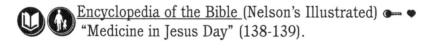 Encyclopedia of the Bible (Nelson's Illustrated) ⊶ ♥ "Medicine in Jesus Day" (138-139).

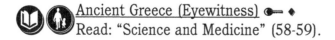 Ancient Greece (Eyewitness) ⊶ ♦ Read: "Science and Medicine" (58-59).

Underlined text refers to Internet link at http://Homeschool-Books.com

The Usborne Book of the Ancient World ☜ ★
Read: "Medicine" (176).

Usborne Book of Discovery: Inventors/Scientists/Explorers ☜ ❤
Read: "Greek Medicine" (57).

The Life of Greece (The Story of Civilization II) ◆
Read: References to Greek medicine (15, 96, 342-348, 638-639).

Internet Sources

Hippocrates Texts— Ancient/Classical History
Description: English translations of Hippocrates' writings.

Hippocratic Oath Online- Ancient/Classical History
Description: Information about the oath that was created about the fourth century B.C. and is still taken by modern doctors.

Medicine of Ancient Greece
One page summary BBC Education with links to other ancient cultures.

Medicine Through Time : Prehistory & the Ancient World
This site was produced by the BBC . It examines the practice of medicine in historical periods are each divided into five different topics: disease & its treatment, anatomy & surgery, hospitals & training, public health, and alternatives to medicine. Includes Hippocrates and the Greek god of health and more.

Step 3 Expand

Choose and complete one of the following activities:

Activity 1: Answer Questions
Use your research to answer the following. Where did ancient Greek doctors receive most of their knowledge? When were the first medical schools opened? What subjects did students learn? What medical instruments did doctors use? What methods of curing diseases did they practice? What gods, according to their belief, could help with healing? Where was the first public hospital? Were there female doctors? How many different specialties did the doctors have? What methods of treatment do we still use? What were the Greeks' birth customs? What was Hippocrates' contribution to medicine? How did Hippocrates change medicine?

Resources recommended in ◆several lessons, ★ several units, ❤other HOW Units. ☜Key Resource (see beginning of unit or page 32).

Heart of Wisdom Publishing   555

Activity 2: Interview a Doctor/Write a Report
Interview a Christian doctor to find out if a doctor can refuse to take the Hippocratic oath. Write a report about the evolution of medicine in ancient Greece.

Step 4 Excel

Share your work from Step 3 with someone. Correct written work to demonstrate correct punctuation and spelling, and effective use of grammar. Add corrected written work or any illustrations to your portfolio. Add new words you learned in this lesson into your Vocabulary Notebook (see page 22).

Religion in Ancient Greece

Step 1 Excite

The Olympian Zeus (also called Jupiter) was the national god of the Hellenic race, as well as the supreme ruler of the heathen world, and as such formed the true opposite to Jehovah. Jupiter or Zeus is mentioned in two passages of the New Testament. On the occasion of St. Paul's visit to Lystra (Acts 14:12,13), the expression "Jupiter, which was before their city," means that his temple was outside the city. Also see Acts 19:35.

Read Acts 14:8-18.

Step 2 Examine

Research ancient Greek religion. Use any resource (an encyclopedia, nonfiction book, or the Internet). We recommend the any of the following:

Books

      Ancient Greece (Eyewitness) ⌐ ♦
      Read: "Gods, Goddesses, and Heros" (20-23), "Festivals and Oracles" (24-25), "Temples" (26-27).

      The Usborne Book of the Ancient World ⌐ ★
      Read: "Minoan Religion" (104), "Gods and Goddesses" (160).

      Kingfisher Illustrated History of the World ⌐ ♥
      Read: "Religion" (124).

      Kingfisher History Encyclopedia ⌐ ♥
      Read: "Religion" (54, 92).

      The Greco-Roman World of the New Testament Era ⌐ ♥
      Read: "Religion in the Greco-Roman World" (89-109).

Resources recommended in ♦several lessons, ★ several units, ♥other HOW Units. ⌐ Key Resource (see beginning of unit or page 32).

The Life of Greece (The Story of Civilization II) ◆
Read: Chapter VIII, "Gods of Greece" (175-202).

Internet Sources

Mount Olympus. Acts 14:12,13
Description: This Bible passage mentions Zeus.

The Unknown God
Description: A discussion of Paul's address to the Greeks on Mars' Hill (a limestone hill in Athens situated between the Acropolis and the Agora). Note verse 23: Paul speaks of God as the "Unknown God."

What the Bible Says About Idolatry
Description: Explains that the Bible gives specific references to, warnings against, and punishments of idolatry.

Athens Versus Paul by Ray C. Stedman
Description: An article about Paul's speech on Mars' Hill, from Peninsula Bible Church.

Greek Religion
Description: High school class outline defines the characteristics of Greek religious practices and beliefs.

Ancient Greek Religion
Description: This site from the University of Pennsylvania provides a short summary of the importance of religion to the ancient Greeks and describes their principal gods and festivals.

The Olympians
Description: Explains the ancient Greek belief that the Olympians were a group of twelve gods who ruled after the overthrow of the Titans. All the Olympians were related in some way. They are named after their dwelling place, Mount Olympus.

How the Greeks Worshipped Their Gods
Description: Scholarly essay looks at the ritualistic practices of the ancient Greeks and the origins of their pantheon of deities.

Step 3 Expand

Activity 1: Write a Summary

Unlike the Egyptians, the Greeks were more interested in life than death. They were more concerned with reason and their superhuman false gods (no other civilization believed in human-like gods). Read Acts 17:16-34, in which Paul addresses the Greeks on Mars' Hill. Summarize what Paul was saying in your own words. (Minimum 100 words.) Younger students can narrate (orally tell) what they have learned.

Activity 2: Examine a Site

There are areas of the world where Christians could be killed for worshipping God (for instance, China). Browse through stories from The Voice of the Martyrs Web site.

Activity 3: Write a Newspaper Story

Write a series of newspaper stories contrasting and comparing the dedicated Jews trying to worship God in ancient Greece with Christians worshipping God today. Include an editorial that sums up your opinions of today's worship.

Step 4 Excel

Share what you have learned about religion in ancient Greece with a friend or family member. Correct all written work to demonstrate correct punctuation and spelling, and effective use of grammar. Add corrected written work or any illustrations to your portfolio.

Resources recommended in ♦several lessons, ★ several units, ● other HOW Units. ●━Key Resource (see beginning of unit or page 32).

Science in Ancient Greece

Step 1 Excite

The majority of people today hail the Greeks for their scientific achievements. However, trusting exclusively in science can encourage an atheistic belief (or at least an agnostic one). Job 28 insists that wisdom is hidden from humans and known only to God; wisdom is the key to the meaning and order of creation, valuable beyond sapphires and pearls, but humans cannot find her dwelling place.

Science is simply the process of discovering the mechanisms of nature, which God has put in place to make our universe work as it does. Science has opened up some of the secrets and meanings of nature, the creation of God.

The Greek philosopher Thales (624-546 B.C.) was the first person recorded to ask what things were made of and to seek an answer that did not depend on gods or the supernatural. He decided that the entire universe was made of water, even though it didn't look like water. He was wrong, but by asking the right questions, he made a contribution to our understanding of the world. Develop a list of questions which you would assume that scientific approaches could answer.

The Greek scholar Theophrastus was a student of Aristotle's. He wrote a book around 320 B.C. that included descriptions of 550 plant species. It was the first real book on botany. Brainstorm and make a list of why it would be important to have plants classified and documented.

Step 2 Examine

The ancient Greeks excelled in several areas of science, making contributions that we, today, recognize as very important, including: astronomy, baths and showers, beekeeping, boats, irrigation, lavatories, locks, magnetism, magnifying glasses, mining, sewers and plumbing and more. The city of Alexandria was known as the scientific center of the ancient

Research Greek scientists and their significant accomplishments. Use any resource (an encyclopedia, nonfiction book, or the Internet). We recommend the following:

Books

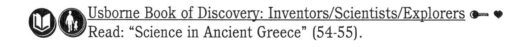 Usborne Book of Discovery: Inventors/Scientists/Explorers ⚷ ♥
Read: "Science in Ancient Greece" (54-55).

Underlined text refers to Internet link at http://Homeschool-Books.com

Handbook to Life in Ancient Greece ☞ ◆
Read: "Science" (390-393), "Scientist Biographies" (394-403).

The Life of Greece (The Story of Civilization II) ◆
Read: Chapter XXVIII, "The Climax of Greek Science" (627-658).

Internet Sources

Jason's Web Site on Ancient Greek Science
Description: An explanation of the many ways in which ancient Greece has influenced the Western World.

Presentations for Greek Science
Description: Student papers from Tufts University. Topics include: "The Golden Section," "Inventing the Solar System," "Thales," and "Categories of Greek Mathematics."

Ancient Greek Science Resources
Description: A list of links to ancient Greek science and technology resources, including information about philosophers, astronomers, and mathematicians.

Step 3 Expand

Choose and complete one of the following activities:

Activity 1: Add to Your Time Line Book
Add all scientific inventions and discoveries between 1400 B.C. and 150 B.C. Add Greek scientists: Anaxagoras, Anaximander, Archimedes, Aristarchus, Aristotle, Ctesibius, Democritus, Erasistratus, Eratosthenes, Euclid, Eudoxus, Galen, Hecataeus, Heron, Herophilus, Hipparchus, Hippocrates, Philon, Pollonius, Ptolemy, Pythagoras, Strabon, Thales, Theophrastus.

Activity 2: Exhibit a Project
Design and exhibit a visual presentation to explain contributions made by one of the scientists of ancient Greece.

Activity 3: Write a Letter
Write a letter to the Greek philosopher Thales or another scientist in this unit. Explain your beliefs based on Job 28. Refer to "Writing an Explanation" and "Writing to Persuade" in Writers INC, or read the online article "Writing to Persuade." Remember:
  • Clearly state your opinion.

Resources recommended in ◆several lessons, ★ several units, ♥other HOW Units. ☞Key Resource (see beginning of unit or page 32).

Heart of Wisdom Publishing   561

- Support the opinion with at least three specific facts or reasons.
- Support the facts or reasons with important details.
- Organize the information in logical order.
- Connect ideas with transition (linking) words or phrases.
- Restate the topic sentence in the conclusion.

Activity 4: Make a chart similar to the following, to show the Greek scientist their contributions, theories, whether their theories have been proven true.

Scientist	Contributions	Theories	Proven true?

Activity 5: Write a Summary
Both science and religion deal with the same universe; one part is physical and the other invisible. Write a summary (minimum 100 words) of your feelings about true wisdom and science.

Step 4 Excel

Share what you have learned about the ancient Greek scientists with a homeschool group. Correct written work to demonstrate correct punctuation and spelling, and effective use of grammar. Add corrected written work or any illustrations to your portfolio.

Ancient Rome Unit

Unit Overview

Ancient Rome Overview 564
Ancient Rome Objectives 566
Ancient Rome Vocabulary 568
Ancient Rome Time Line 569
Ancient Rome Resources 570

Ancient Rome Lessons

History of Ancient Rome

Geography 579
Founding of Rome (753 B.C.) 583
The Etruscan Dynasty (800-B.C.) . . .586
The Roman Republic (508-27 B.C.). . .589
The Punic Wars (264-146 B.C.) 593
Julius Caesar (100-44 B.C.) 597
Julius Caesar: The Play 602
Antony & Octavian (44-30 B.C.) 605
The Roman Empire (27 B.C.-A.D.-410) 609
The Jewish Revolts (A.D. 132-135) . .614
Barbarian Invasions (A.D. 235) 618
Constantine A.D. (361-395) 622
Birth of Christianity (A.D. 379) 627
The Fall of the Roman Empire . .633
Science in Ancient Rome 637

Life in Ancient Rome

Agriculture in Ancient Rome 639
Architecture in Ancient Rome . . .641
Art in Ancient Rome 644
Calendars in Ancient Rome 648
Citizenship in Ancient Rome 650
Clothing in Ancient Rome 652
Customs in Ancient Rome 655
Daily Life in Ancient Rome 657
Men in Ancient Rome 660
Women in Ancient Rome 662
Economy in Ancient Rome 666
Education in Ancient Rome 668
Famous Romans 670
Food in Ancient Rome 673
Gladiators and the Colosseum . . .675
Language in Ancient Rome 678
Laws in Ancient Rome 681
Literature in Ancient Rome 683
Medicine in Ancient Rome 687
Military in Ancient Rome 690
Money in Ancient Rome 694
Philosophy in Ancient Rome 696
Religion in Ancient Rome 698

Ancient Rome-Overview

The history of Rome covers a massive empire, a rich culture, a profound philosophical legacy, and a lengthy era. In studying this unit, you cannot possibly cover every fascinating and valuable facet of Roman history. The aspects of the life in the Greco-Roman world will help you place the New Testament in its original historical setting and consequently understand it better. The New Testament era was a society influenced by Hellenistic ideas, customs, religion and language but dominated by Roman law, governmental forms, ideas of class and the military.

Shadows of Rome appear in unexpected places: in advertisements and speeches, in books on government and art, in classes on church history and economics. To be well educated is to be acquainted with ancient Roman civilization. Rome's language, legal system, and architecture were some of the foundations for Western civilization.

A study of ancient Rome will give you a better understanding of Jesus and the early church. Jesus Christ lived His entire human life under the Roman empire, the first half under Caesar Augustus (Luke 2:1), who reigned when He was born in Bethlehem, the second half under Tiberius (Luke 3:1) when He still lived at Nazareth in Galilee, before moving to Capernaum on the shore of the Sea of Galilee, until His Crucifixion at Calvary in Jerusalem.

Paul was a Jew in under the Roman authorities in Jerusalem. He was sent to Rome after he exercised his legal right as a Roman citizen to appeal his case to Caesar (Acts 26:32). After an extremely dangerous voyage across The Mediterranean Sea that included a shipwreck on Malta , Paul arrived in Rome (Acts 28:16)around 61 A.D.

Wayne Blank explains in the Daily Bible Study,

> Rome was then the center of a vast and powerful empire that spanned from Britain, throughout southern and central Europe, northern Africa, and deep into the Middle East, measuring about 3,000 miles / 4,900 kilometers east to west and 2,000 miles / 3,200 kilometers north to south (see Ancient Empires - Rome). The population of the city at that time has been estimated to be 1,500,000 - a very large percentage of which were slaves.

> Paul remained in Rome for at least two years (Acts 28:30), where, despite being a prisoner, he wrote a very large part of what we now have as the New Testament epistles to the Ephesians, Philippians, Colossians, Philemon, and possibly Hebrews. Although the Bible record does not include his fate, most scholars believe that he was eventually acquitted of the charges and released in 63 or 64 A.D., upon which he made his way back through Greece and Asia

Minor (i.e. Turkey) before again being arrested and returned to Rome where he was martyred, by beheading, or torn apart by wild animals in the arena before a cheering crowd, about 67 A.D., during the time of Emperor Nero.[1]

Rome had two great eras: the Republic and the Empire. The transition from one era to the other is intriguing. In the early years of Rome, the people valued discipline, hard work, and respect for authority. The government that arose reflected those values. The Republic was based on a checks-and-balances system that ensured fairness to all. As the Romans became selfish, indulgent, and self-absorbed, their political system changed. As you investigate, you should form your own opinion as to whether the same problems that afflicted Rome will also bring America to poverty, ruin, and war.

People have compared America with ancient Rome. "John Adams wrote that whenever he read Thucydides and Tacitus, 'I seem to be only reading the History of my own times and my own life'"(Kopel, p.47). Would you make such a comparison? As you study, discover whether you seem to be "only reading the history" of your own times.

To place the New Testament in its original historical setting and consequently understand it better, it would be a great help for you to read the following before you begin this unit:

The Greco-Roman World of the New Testament Era ●━ ♥
Read: "Historical Background to the New Testament Era" (15-18). The first chapter serves as a warm-up for the chapters that follow. It describes a fictive dinner at the home of a member of the ruling class of first-century Jerusalem. Also see "A Summary of Greco-Roman History" (293-320). See description on page 32.

Discuss with your parents your plans for studying ancient Rome. You are investigating a civilization that warred against God's people for centuries. Some of the events and people are decidedly un-Christian. You must choose how well you want to be acquainted with them.

Recommended Literature for this Unit

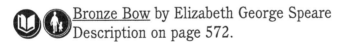
Bronze Bow by Elizabeth George Speare
Description on page 572.

All God's Children: The Tumultuous Story of A.D. 31-71 by James D. Snyder.
Description on page 572.

Footnote
Blank, Wayne (2000), Daily Bible Study, A freely-provided non-denominational Christian ministry.
http://www.execulink.com/~wblank/index.htm Email: wblank@execulink.com

---

Resources recommended in ♦several lessons, ★ several units, ♥ other HOW Units. ●━Key Resource (see beginning of unit or page 32).

Ancient Rome Objectives

Upon completion of this unit, your student should:

- Gain a knowledge of Greco-Roman societies and cultures and their impact on the New Testament era.
- Understand how the peoples in the Roman Empire organization affected the early Christian congregations.
- Understand the development of large regional empires (e.g., What was the significance of military power, state bureaucracy, legal codes, belief systems, written languages, and communications and trade networks, and how did trade networks, merchant communities, state power, and other factors contribute to the economic integration of large regions of Afro-Eurasia?).
- Understand political and social elements during the decline of the Roman Empire, the impact of barbarian movements on the regions of Europe, and the links between military, social, and economic causes for the decline of the Roman Empire.
- Understand how ancient Rome's history intertwines with biblical time lines.
- Analyze and evaluate the uses of evidence and data in conflicting interpretations.
- Develop a mental framework within which to process new information about ancient Rome.
- Appreciate the pressures to succumb to idolatry which ancient Rome's culture placed on Jews and Christians.
- Understand the major events and the significance of the Punic Wars.
- Recognize ancient Roman influences in today's culture.
- Understand farming practices.
- Appreciate architectural achievements.
- Understand the layout of an ancient Roman city.
- Identify significant buildings in a typical ancient Roman community.
- Enjoy ancient Roman art.
- Explore biblical teachings about idols.
- Be acquainted with the names of barbarian tribes.
- Develop a heart of gratitude toward God for the grace and mercy He showed to ancient European tribes.
- Understand how our calendar developed.
- Understand and value the Hebrew calendar.
- Connect ancient Roman citizenship to the life of Paul.

Underlined text refers to Internet link at http://Homeschool-Books.com

- Explore ancient Roman fashions.
- Reflect on proper Christian attire.
- View ancient Roman coins found in Bible stories.
- Understand the significance of Constantine.
- Develop a mental image of the type of daily life people led.
- Understand the ancient Roman economy.
- Understand ancient Roman education.
- Master a basic outline of the history of the Roman Empire.
- Investigate reasons for ancient Rome's downfall.
- Experiment with ancient Roman cuisine.
- Explore gender roles.
- Learn the geography of the Mediterranean region.
- Understand the government of the Roman Republic.
- Understand Polybius's idea of anacyclosis.
- Appreciate the importance of separation of powers.
- Learn about ancient Roman laws.
- Know what happened at Masada.
- Comprehend the devastation of Jerusalem in A.D. 70.
- Be familiar with the biography of Julius Caesar.
- Explore the literature of ancient Rome.
- Discover how the ancient Romans understood and practiced medicine.
- Grasp the realities of ancient Roman army life.
- Be acquainted with the basic teachings of Stoicism, Neoplatonism, and Epicureanism.
- Consider how to witness to a pagan.
- Understand biblical teachings regarding pagan worship.
- Appreciate martyrdom in ancient Rome.
- Comprehend the slavery system in ancient Rome.
- Grasp the basic history of the Roman Republic.
- Become familiar with ancient Roman technological achievements.
- Learn how ancient Romans used their technology.
- Understand the major events and the significance of the conflict between Julius Caesar and Pompey.
- Understand the major events and the significance of the conflict between Octavian and Antony.
- Be aware of the significant events that occurred throughout the world during the existence of the Roman Empire.

Resources recommended in ♦several lessons, ★ several units, ♥other HOW Units. ◉—Key Resource (see beginning of unit or page 32).

Heart of Wisdom Publishing   567

Ancient Rome Vocabulary

See Vocabulary Instructions on page 22.

Aeneas	emperor	magistrates	prefectures
anarchy	encaustic	maniple	proscriptions
aristocracy	Epicurean	Mars	redda
amphitheatre	façade	Mercury	relief sculpture
Apollo	felicitas	Minerva	sagitarii
aqueduct	First Triumvirate	mural	sarcophagus
carpentum	Franks	Neptune	Scholae Palatinae
carruca	frieze	Neoplatonism	Senate
castellum	forum	Notitia Dignitatum	Stoicism
castra	Gauls	patriarch	stucco
centurion	gladiator	patrician	tesserae
century	Goths	patron	testudo
cilent	gravitas	peristilios	thermae
cohort	imperators	plebeians	trompe l'oeil
Colosseum	incumbent	plebs rustica	Venus
Consul	insula	plebs urbana	Vesta
comitatenses	Janus	Pluto	veto
Comitia Centuriata	Juno	pomerium	villas
consolidate	Jupiter	pontifex maximus	Visigoths
consistory	keystone arch	pontiffs	voussoir
cursus publicus	Lares	portraiture	Vulcan
democracy	latifundia	pozzolana	
dictator	legion	praetorian prefect	
empire	limitanei	praetorian guard	

Ancient Rome Timeline

		Ancient Rome	Hebrews/Early Church
Founding		800-700 B.C. Italy inhabited by Hellenic and Etruscan people. The land is undeveloped.	722/721 B.C. Northern Kingdom (Israel) destroyed
		753 B.C. Romulus founds Roman culture at the Palatine.	587/586 B.C. Southern Kingdom (Judah) and Temple destroyed -- Babylonian exile
Etruscan Dynasty		524 B.C. Greeks stop the southward Etruscan migration at Cumae.	538-333 B.C. Persian Period 520-515 B.C. Jerusalem temple rebuilt
		509 B.C. Romans overthrow tyrant Tarquinius Superbus, ending the Etruscan dynasty.	
The Roman Republic 508-27 B.C.		450 B.C. Twelve Tables of Roman law published.	450-400 B.C. Reforms by Ezra and Nehemiah
		396 B.C. The city of Veii is conquered.	
		340 B.C. The Latin War begins.	333-63 B.C. Hellenistic (Greek) period - Alexander the Great conquers Palestine (333/331).
		264 B.C. First Punic War	
		241 B.C. Romans win Sicily.	
		221 B.C. The structure Circus Flaminius is built.	
		218-201 B.C. Second Punic War	
		179 B.C. The structure Basilica Aemilia is built.	168/167-63 B.C. Jewish Maccabean revolt
		149-146 B.C. Third Punic War ends with the Roman capture of Carthage.	
		63 Rome B.C. (Pompey) annexes Palestine.	
		44 B.C. The assassination of Julius Caesar marks the end of the Roman Republic.	
The Roman Empire 27 B.C. - A.D. 410		37-4 B.C. Herod the Great, King of Judæa, ruled for 33 years.	
		31 B.C. Octavian Caesar defeats Mark Antony and becomes emperor of Rome (given title Augustus).	
		Before 4 B.C.-c A.D. 30 Jesus	
		A.D. 36-64 Paul, 37-100 Josephus	
		A.D. 41 Gaius Julius, the emperor Caligula, is murdered.	
		A.D. 43 Claudius wins victories in Britain.	
		A.D. 64 Rome is burnt.	
		A.D. 66-73 First Jewish Revolt against Rome	
		A.D. 70 Capture of Jerusalem and the destruction of the Temple by the Romans	
		A.D. 114-117 Jewish Revolts against Rome outside Palestine	
		A.D. 249-51 Christians are persecuted throughout Roman Empire under Emperor Decius.	
		A.D. 235-284 Germans, Goths, and Persians attack Rome.	
		A.D. 284 Diocletian restores order to Rome.	
		A.D. 302 Diocletian bans Christians from the Roman Army.	
		A.D. 312 Constantine defeats Maxentius to become absolute ruler of Rome.	
		A.D. 312/313 Constantine embraces Christianity.	

Resources recommended in ◆several lessons, ★ several units, ♥other HOW Units. ☞—Key Resource (see beginning of unit or page 32).

Ancient Rome Resources

Resources with a ❶ symbol are appropriate for grades 4-12 or family read aloud. All other books are appropriate for young adults or adults.

Key Resources

All God's Children: The Tumultuous Story of A.D. 31-71 by James D. Snyder

The years A.D. 31-71 were both the most tumultuous and least understood period in the history of western civilization. How did a small band of Jesus followers spring from Judaism and expand across the Roman World? What made the Jews rebel against Roman rule despite impossible odds? And why did Rome itself almost self-destruct just a few years after reaching the height of its glory? And how did this upheaval set the stage for more than 2000 years of history to follow? Using the historical novel as its rostrum and a Greek ex-slave as its narrator, All God's Children compresses the works of ancient writers into a factual history that is at the same time riveting and inspiring. These critical-but-confusing 40 years -- from the crucifixion of Jesus to the destruction of the mighty temple at Jerusalem -- are explained in chronological order as you come to understand how people and events in the Roman, Jewish and Christian worlds all shaped each other's destinies. And through these pages you'll come to know such powerful personages as Caesar Augustus, Herod the Great, Herod Agrippa, Tiberius, Caligula, Nero, Seneca, Peter, Paul, Mark and John. Along the way, you'll learn about how the first churches were formed and the earliest New Testament works compiled. You'll begin to understand the efficiency of travel in the ancient Mediterranean and how people of all nationalities traded news and impacted on one another's lives. Most of all, you'll gain insight into why ordinary people were driven to embrace a message that spoke of God's grace and man's worth. Paperback, (1999) ISBN: 0967520002.

Ancient Rome (Eyewitness) ❍▬ ◆
Ancient Rome is another in the superb Eyewitness Books reference series for young people. This book is recommended in most of the "Life in Ancient Rome" lessons. Interesting, informative text, combined with many great color photos, brings the Roman Empire to life. Artifacts from the daily lives of slaves and emperors alike make the people seem real, their activities immediate. Special treats are the glass marbles—just like kids play with today—and centurion armor. A wonderful addition to a young historian's bookshelf. Hardcover - 62 pages (August 1990) Knopf; ISBN: 0679807411. Reading level: Ages 9-12.

Daily Life at the Time of Jesus by Miriam Feinberg Vamosh ❍▬ ◆
See description in the "Key Resources" section beginning on page 32.

The Greco-Roman World of The New Testament Era: Exploring the Background of Early Christianity ●— ❤
See description in the "Key Resources" section beginning on page 32. This book is recommended in most of the "Life of Rome" lessons.

Our Father Abraham ●— ❤
See description in the "Key Resources" section beginning on page 32.

The Penguin Historical Atlas of Ancient Rome by Christopher Scarre ●— ◆
This book is recommended in most of the "History of Rome" lessons. Matching clear graphics with informative text, Christopher Scarre's atlas gives a fine overview of Roman history from the emergence of the first city-state in the eighth century B.C. to the rise of Christian theocracy a millennium later. *The Penguin Historical Atlas of Ancient Rome* is especially helpful in showing the growth of the Roman Empire through successive centuries of military campaigning from Scotland to Arabia, and in delineating the networks of trade, transit, and communication that bound the far-flung outposts to the imperial capital. Paperback Reprint edition (September 1995) Penguin USA; ISBN: 0140513299.

Usborne Book of the Ancient World ●— ★
See description in the "Key Resources" section beginning on page 32.

Alternative Resources

Ancient Romans (Worldwise) by Daisy Kerr, John James (Illustrator)
Describes daily life in ancient Rome whose civilization lasted from about 500 B.C. to A.D. 400 and even then did not disappear completely. Paperback - 40 pages Reprint edition (March 1997) Franklin Watts, Incorporated; ISBN: 0531152952. Reading level: Ages 9-12.

Ancient Rome (Crash Course Series) by Christoph Umocker
A good supplement for college students as well as a superb handbook for amateur historians, this illustrated summary of Roman history is complemented with maps and chronologically divided into eight major sections, covering the rise of ancient Rome from 1000 B.C. through its decline in A.D. 480. Glossary. Index. More than 400 photos and illustrations, most in color. Paperback 1 Us Ed edition (October 1997) Barrons Educational Series; ISBN: 0764102443.

Ancient Rome (DK Pockets) by Susan McKeever
What did Roman nobles eat for dinner? Where did gladiators fight to the death? How did the Romans heat their baths? The answers to these questions and many more are packed within the pages of *DK Pockets: Ancient Rome*. Paperback - 160 pages Pocket edition (May 1995) DK Pub Merchandise; ISBN: 1564588882. Reading level: Young adult.

Resources recommended in ◆several lessons, ★ several units, ❤ other HOW Units. ●—Key Resource (see beginning of unit or page 32).

Ancient Rome (Nature Company Discoveries) by Judith Simpson
A portrait of ancient Rome, divided into four sections: "The Roman World," "Living in the Empire," "Expansion and Empire," and "The Fall of Rome." Along the way it covers the usual topics for this type of book—family life, education, farming—as well as more unusual topics, including the siege of Masada, appearing in a beautifully done four-page fold-out. Following The Nature Company Discoveries Library format, this book is lavishly illustrated, both with full-color reproductions of original paintings and with photographs of Roman antiquities (though a few are too small to view well). Hardcover - 64 pages (August 1997) Time Life; ISBN: 078354909. Reading level: Ages 9-12.

Ancient Rome, How it Affects You Today by Richard J. Maybury
An "Uncle Eric book." Uses historical events to explain current events. From the back cover: "Why is ancient history important to us today? To build a better future we need to know how we got where we are today. The political trend that has dominated the world for 2000 years ... remains almost unrecognized. Author Richard Maybury calls it the Roman Disease. Does America have the disease? Is there a cure? Or will America repeat the mistake of Ancient Rome and collapse into poverty, decay, ruin, and war?" See a collection of articles from Mr. Maybury's newsletter, U.S. & World Early Warning Report. An interesting and informative little book, whose ideas you will not find repeated elsewhere. (August 1995) Bluestocking Pr; ISBN: 0942617223. Recommended for grades 7 and up.

Ben Hur by Lew Wallace
A spiritual tale of the quest for love, and the recovery of identity and patrimony, *Ben-Hur* never fails to delight in its detail and realism. It is twenty years after the birth of Christ. Judah Ben-Hur, a wealthy young Jew, makes an enemy of a powerful Roman, Messala, who hungers to topple him. An "accident" sends Ben-Hur to the galleys. Stripped of his fortune, he works as a slave; meanwhile Messala prospers. But Ben-Hur finds a benefactor in Quintus Arrius, whose life he saves in a shipwreck. Under Quintus's tutelage, Ben-Hur learns the skills of a Roman warrior and the faith of a Christian. Both help him recover what he lost and underpin his emergence as one of the most powerful and respected men of the new Christian faith. "Among other things, this classic reminds us that most of the early Christians were Jews torn in their faith between two competing religions." (B-O-T Editorial Review Board). (July 2000) Barbour & Co; ISBN: 1577487761. You can buy or rent this book on tape from Books on Tape 1-800-88-BOOKS.

The Book of Acts in its Graeco-Roman Setting by Conrad Gempf (Editor), David W. Gill (Editor)
A better title would be "Understanding Ancient Rome: Crucial to Bible Study." This book describes the geographical, social, and cultural milieus of the Roman Empire that form the backdrop for the Book of Acts. Eight chapters provide a

comprehensive overview of the provinces and regions within which the early church fought for a foothold. Seven chapters offer thorough analysis of key social and cultural issues in the eastern provinces of the Roman Empire, including such topics as travel and maritime transport, the Roman roads of Asia, food shortages, Roman religion, the urban elite, and the house churches in which the first Christian communities met. Hardcover - 627 pages Vol 002 (May 1994) Wm. B. Eerdmans Publishing Co.; ISBN: 080282434X.

Bronze Bow by Elizabeth George Speare
Set in Galilee in the time of Jesus, this is the story of a young Jewish rebel who is won over to the gentle teachings of Jesus. "A dramatic, deeply felt narrative whose characters and message will long be remembered." — Booklist Horn Book Fanfare Selection. Paperback - 254 pages (September 1, 1997) Houghton Mifflin Co (Juv); ISBN: 0395137195. Reading level: Ages 9-12. Interest level: all ages.

Caesar and Christ: A History of Roman Civilization and of Christianity from Their Beginnings to A.D. 325 by Will Durant (Story of Civilization III) ♦ Description: Amazon customers rave about this book. It's written in a vivid and colorful style, giving an overview of all aspects of this time period. Includes wars, heroes and politicians of the epoch, way of living, arts, medicine, customs, family, etc. Durant wrote not merely a history of events and dates, but let the peoples of the nations come alive. He relates how the common, ordinary person lived and died, laughed and cried, worked and played. Mores, lifestyles, trends, and beliefs are all documented. Durant approaches the controversial topic of Jesus' historicity carefully and scientifically, with insight that will leave both the discriminating scientist and the pious believer satisfied.

Please note that this popular historian, Will Durant, was not a Christian. I don't agree with all his writings (especially his writings about Paul). However, he does use the Bible as a historical record and show evidence concerning Christ's historical validity, "The denial of that existence seems never to have occurred even to the bitterest gentile or Jewish opponents of nascent Christianity" (Durant, *The Story of Civilization*, vol. 3, p. 555). And again, "That a few simple men should in one generation have invented so powerful and appealing a personality, so lofty an ethic and so inspiring a vision of human brotherhood, would be a miracle far more incredible than any recorded in the Gospels" (Ibid., p. 557). It is a substantial thing that a historian who spends his life considering historical facts should affirm the reality of Christ's existence as well as the rapid growth of the early movement. (July 1994) Fine Communications; ISBN: 1567310141. You can buy or rent this book on tape from Books on Tape 1-800-88-BOOKS. You can also listen to a sample reading from this book online.

Resources recommended in ♦several lessons, ★ several units, ● other HOW Units. ●—Key Resource (see beginning of unit or page 32).

Heart of Wisdom Publishing   573

Classical Kids: An Activity Guide to Life in Ancient Greece and Rome by Laurie Carlson
Travel back in time to see what life was like in ancient Greece and Rome while having fun with such hands-on activities as making a star gazer, chiseling a clay tablet, weaving Roman sandals, and making a Greek mosaic. 100+ line drawings. Paperback - 184 pages (July 1998) Chicago Review Pr; ISBN: 1556522908. Reading level: Ages 9-12.

The Decline and Fall of the Roman Empire: An Abridged Version (Penguin Classics) by Edward Gibbon, Dero A. Saunders (Editor)
A clear view of the march of Rome's empire into anarchy and ruin. Concentrating on the centuries from the rule of Antoninus Pius (A.D. 138-161) to the fall of the Empire in the west, this abridged volume chronicles "the triumph of barbarism and religion" in the disruption of the united Empire, the rise of Christianity, the progress of the Asiatic Huns, and the revolt of the Goths. Penguin USA (Paper); ISBN: 0140431896. You can buy or rent an unabridged version of this book on tape from Books on Tape 1-800-88-BOOKS. You can also listen to a sample reading from this book online.

For the Temple, A Tale of the Fall of Jerusalem by G.A Henty, Preston/Speed Publications (Illustrator)
A stirring tale of the last days of the Temple at Jerusalem. Robber bands and political infighting set the stage for the Roman destruction of Jerusalem in A.D. 70. In the face of overwhelming odds, John of Gamala does his best to save God's Temple, harassing Roman work parties, burning Roman camps, defending Jerusalem during the Roman siege, and even fighting Titus himself in hand-to-hand combat—forging a relationship with the Roman leader that lasts until after the war. In spite of fighting a losing battle, John keeps his integrity and honor intact. —11 illustrations with map/plan of the siege of Jerusalem. Includes a Build-Your-Vocabulary Glossary of 460 words. 333 pages Preston/Speed Publications; ISBN: 1887159002.

Greek and Roman Science (World History Series) by Don Nardo
Examines the efforts of Greeks and Romans to study and understand the underlying principles of nature, and discusses their development of a more systematic approach to science. Hardcover - 128 pages (January 1998) Lucent Books; ISBN: 1560063173.

The Greenleaf Guide to Famous Men of Rome by Cynthia Shearer
The *Guide to Rome* sets the study of Rome in a biblical context, examining various figures to see if they match up to God's standards of justice or righteousness. Paperback (June 1989) Greenleaf Pr; ISBN: 1882514041.

Herod: King of the Jews and Friend of the Romans by Peter Richardson
This book provides a stunning look at the king who had an extraordinary impact on Roman-era Palestine. The author integrates historical, archaeological, and social analysis, writing with clarity and enthusiasm for his subject. The charts, maps, and diagrams make this a very accessible tool. From the Back Cover: "Herod the Great is one of the most fascinating and appalling figures of the ancient world. Peter Richardson's monumental study provides as thorough and as authoritative a documentation and analysis as one could wish for." —James D. G. Dunn, University of Durham. Paperback - 400 pages (June 1999) Fortress Pr; ISBN: 0800631641.

Judaism and Christianity in First-Century Rome by Karl P. Donfried ♦
Rome, as the center of the first-century world, was home to numerous ethnic groups, among which were both Jews and Christians. The dealings of the Roman government with these two groups, and their dealings with each other, are the focus of this engaging book. Archaeological and epigraphic, social-historical, and developmental studies targeted to a scholarly audience. Paperback - 289 pages (August 1998) Wm. B. Eerdmans Publishing Co.; ISBN: 0802842658. Reading level: Advanced.

Mark of the Lion 1: A Voice in the Wind by Francine Rivers
A.D. 70 Rome comes alive in this tale in which Hadassah, a young Jewess who watched her brother and sister die at the hands of Roman soldiers, her mother starve, and her father killed as he witnessed for Christ, is taken as a slave and sold into the Valerian family, an extremely wealthy Roman family. Torn between a desire to witness and her fear of persecution, she encourages readers to represent Christ in their world. Book 1 in the "Mark of the Lion Trilogy." 515 pages (March 1, 1998) Tyndale House Pub; ISBN: 0842377506.

Mark of the Lion 2: An Echo in the Darkness by Francine Rivers
The story of Hadassah continues in Volume 2, as she serves as an aide to a struggling physician who cannot see the spiritual aspect of the healings that she seems to perform and the effect she seems to have on their patients. Having escaped death, Hadassah conceals her scars and her identity with veils. Now she faces her greatest trial: being called to risk her life for the woman who would have destroyed her. Book 2 in the "Mark of the Lion Trilogy." 461 pages (March 1, 1998) Tyndale House Pub; ISBN: 0842313079.

Mark of the Lion 3: As Sure as the Dawn by Francine Rivers
Book 3 in the "Mark of the Lion Trilogy". Atretes, a German barbarian who has won his freedom in the Roman arena, finds his life changed forever by an encounter with a young Christian woman. Atretes vows to move heaven and earth

Resources recommended in ♦several lessons, ★several units, ●other HOW Units. ●—Key Resource (see beginning of unit or page 32).

Heart of Wisdom Publishing   575

to find his son—the baby he thought was dead—and take him back to Germany. Only one thing stands in his way: Rizpah, the Christian widow who has cared for the child since his birth. (July 1995) Tyndale House Pub; ISBN: 0842339760.

Palestine in the Time of Jesus: Social Structures & Social Conflicts by K. C. Hanson, Douglas E. Oakman
An excellent book for this unit. The core of the book systematically presents major domains and institutions of family, politics, and economy in Roman Palestine. Begins with an overview of social analysis and of the ancient Mediterranean worldview. Concludes with Palestine's religious institutions, especially Herod's Temple system and Jesus' relation to it. The wealth of archaeological data, documentary data, and analysis is enhanced by extensive charts, diagrams, study questions, glossaries, and suggested readings. "This book has been admirably conceived and developed to assist the ordinary Bible reader in narrowing the cultural distance between the world of Jesus and our own. Both authors are expert teachers, proven researchers, and clear articulators of what they know so well: the society of Palestine in the time of Jesus, its social institutions, cultural values, daily experiences, and elite and non-elite approaches to the God of Israel. A careful reading will . . . make the pages of the Gospels come alive. . ." — Bruce J. Malina, Creighton University. 256 pages (September 1998) Fortress Pr; ISBN: 080062808X.

Pompeii by Peter Connolly (Illustrator)
This extremely detailed archaeological description of the ruins of Pompeii has drawings, photographs, plans, and reconstructions of life in the ancient Roman city. Quite fascinating, but probably limited to those interested in ancient Roman life or archaeology. Paperback - 80 pages (September 1994) Oxford Univ Pr Childrens' Books; ISBN: 0199171580. Reading level: Ages 9-12.

The Roman Empire and the Dark Ages (The History of Everyday Things) by Giovanni Caselli
Traces the history of the Roman Empire and the Dark Ages which followed through a description of common objects, tools, clothes, dwellings, food, and day-to-day activities of the people in both the cities and the country. Paperback - 48 pages (September 1998) Peter Bedrick Books; ISBN: 0872265633. Reading level: Ages 9-12.

The Romans by Roy Burrell
Through engrossing essays and fictional "eyewitness" accounts, Roy Burrell vividly recreates 2,000 years of stormy Roman history for young readers. Accompanied by Peter Connolly's remarkable maps, cross-sections, detailed drawings, and even a complete scale model of what Rome may have looked like at the

---

height of its glory, *The Romans* is sure to pique a young student's interest. Color illustrations. Paperback - 112 pages Reprint edition (May 1998) Oxford Univ Pr (Trade); ISBN: 0199171025. Reading level: Ages 9-12.

The Romans
Traces the history of ancient Rome, discussing the development of the Roman Empire and providing a fascinating glimpse of Roman life, homes, food, entertainment, travel, armies, towns, and more. Hardcover (July 1996) Oxford Univ Pr (Trade); ISBN: 0195212401. Reading level: Ages 9-12.

The Rotten Romans (Horrible Histories) by Terry Deary, Martin Brown (Illustrator)
A fact-filled treasury on ancient Rome that celebrates the lesser-known daily realities of the period, such as what the Britons used to make their hair spiky and why rich Romans needed vomitoriums. Paperback (March 1997) Scholastic Paperbacks; ISBN: 059003152X. Reading level: Ages 9-12.

Videos

Ancient Rome: The Story of an Empire That Ruled the World ⊶ ◆
Description: The History Channel's four-part overview of the Roman Empire spans more than 3,000 years, from Rome's mythologized founding by Mars's twin sons Remus and Romulus, to Latium's expansion and domination of the Mediterranean world, to the rise of Christianity and Rome's ensuing fall. Volume 1: *The Republic of Rome*; Volume 2: *The Age of Emperors*; Volume 3: *Building an Empire;* Volume 4: *The Enduring Legacy.*

Hail Caesar ⊶ ◆
Six videos that chart the making and breaking of an empire, profiling the dynamic leaders who reigned in ancient Rome. *Hail Caesar* spans three continents and seven centuries to tell the saga of the Roman Empire and the men who shaped it. Its army dominated the known world and its culture forms the heart of Western civilization. At its peak, the Roman Empire extended from Persia to England, and from the Black Sea to the Atlantic Ocean, and throughout its history, its fate rested in the hands of individuals—men of genius and courage, madness and ambition. Includes: Volume. 1: *Julius Caesar: Master of the Roman World*; Volume 2: *Augustus: First of the Emperors*; Volume 3: *Nero: The Power and the Madness*; Volume 4: *Hadrian: Emperor of the Golden Age*; Volume 5: *Constantine: The Christian Emperor*; Volume 6: *Justinian: Last of the Romans*. Originally seen on A&E's "Biography." ASIN: 0767007751.

Learning About the Ancient World
A chronological overview of ancient Greece and Rome using artwork and background music. This two-part program covers food, shelter, clothing, worship,

---

Resources recommended in ◆several lessons, ★ several units, ♥ other HOW Units. ⊶Key Resource (see beginning of unit or page 32).

Heart of Wisdom Publishing   577

schools, recreation, philosophy, the gods, important leaders, politics, and wars. The narrator helps students experience what daily life was like for young people in Athens and Rome. Includes a mini-guide with comprehension questions, projects, and activities. Color. 30 minutes. Social Studies School Service (800-421-4246). Grades 4-9.

The Legions of Rome
Description: The History Channel's definitive look at these storied soldiers, their epic campaigns, and Julius Caesar, the man who left his mark on history as their greatest commander. Combining spectacular re-creations and battle re-enactments with location footage, brilliant scholarship, and period art and artifacts, the four videos in this collector's set bring the world of the Roman soldier to life. From the three wars fought and won against Carthage, through the brutal campaigns against the Celtic tribes of Gaul, to the bloody conquest of the mysterious island of Britain, this is the story of a fighting machine the likes of which the world had never seen. Also follows Julius Caesar's meteoric rise from civil servant to general to emperor. ASIN: 6305534632.

Roman City (1994) by David Macaulay
In this Emmy Award-winning production, illustrator David Macaulay examines how the Roman Empire linked Europe, the Middle East, and Africa into a political unit. Live-action segments visit sites throughout the once-great empire, and reveal how the structures were built and used. Animated segments tell the story of the construction and conflicts of a fictitious Roman city in the territory of Gaul. One in a multi-volume series based on Macaulay's books. ASIN: B00000FAHH.

Rome: Power and Glory ●— ◆
Experience the majesty and power of the Roman Empire as only The Learning Channel can bring it to you. *Rome: Power and Glory* charts the epic rise and fall of the Roman Empire in a six-volume set which-covers the political, military, and social history of the empire from its miraculous engineering feats to the exorbitant taxation that contributed to its downfall. Learn about ancient sporting events and Roman opinions on sex, fashions, slavery, and taxes. The series covers many of Rome's most famous, and in many cases infamous, figures, including Julius Caesar, Augustus, Nero, and Caligula. Volume I: *The Rise*; Volume II: *Legions of Conquest*;Volume III: *Seduction of Power*; Volume IV: *Grasp of Empire*; Volume V: *The Cult of Order*; Volume VI: *The Fall*. See video clips online. ASIN B00001TZ51.

Geography of Ancient Rome

Step 1 Examine

Look at a map of the Eastern Hemisphere. Why did one of the greatest civilizations in the world—ancient Rome—appear on the Italian peninsula? Did its geographical location help Rome to become one of the most powerful cities in the world? Why is Rome called "The City on Seven Hills"? Compare the maps from the Mesopotamia and Greece units to this map of the Roman Empire. Did you recognize Israel, the Red Sea, and the Nile River? Where is Mesopotamia from this map?

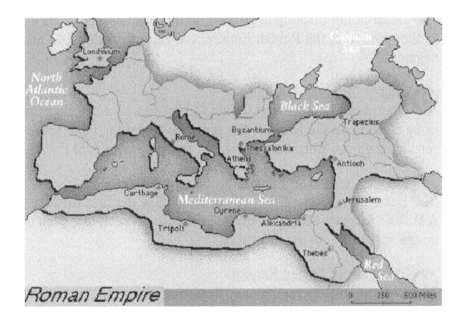

Step 2 Examine

The Roman Empire began in the city of Rome, Italy; progressively, over hundreds of years, the empire expanded to include what are today known as southern England, Spain, Switzerland, Austria, North Africa, the Middle East, and parts of Germany and France.

Research the geography of ancient Rome. Use any resource (an encyclopedia, nonfiction book, historical novel, or the Internet). We recommend the following:

Books

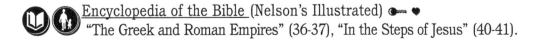

Encyclopedia of the Bible (Nelson's Illustrated) ●━ ♥
"The Greek and Roman Empires" (36-37), "In the Steps of Jesus" (40-41).

Resources recommended in ◆several lessons, ★ several units, ♥other HOW Units. ●━Key Resource (see beginning of unit or page 32).

The Usborne Book of the Ancient World ●━ ★
Browse: Pages 196-272. There are maps on several pages which show when certain events took place.

The Holman Bible Atlas ●━ ♥
Browse: Part Three "The New Testament Era" (190-276).

The Penguin Historical Atlas of Ancient Rome ●━ ♦
Read: From City to Empire. Browse the maps throughout the book.▯

Internet Sources

The Roman Empire at its Greatest Extent
Description: Clicking anywhere on this map will give you a more detailed look at that portion of the Roman Empire; the map is divided into nine roughly equal segments.

Map of the Roman Empire
Description: By clicking within the borders of a certain province on the map, or by clicking on the name of the province below the map, you can link to resources on the Web that are related to that province of the Roman Empire.

Map of the Roman Empire
Description: Map of the Roman Empire in the first-through-third centuries A.D. This interactive map is divided into eleven sections, each of which is an image supplied with overlaid texts.

Trade in the Roman Empire
Description: Interactive map depicting major trading centers throughout the Roman Mediterranean, with lists of the goods traded for each location.

Atlas of the Greek and Roman World
Description: The APA Classical Atlas Project home page. Contains ninety-eight maps, plus links to other sites of interest.

Maps of the Roman World in the First Century C.E.
Description: Includes maps of the Roman World during the reign of Augustus Caesar, during the reign of Claudius, and at the end of the reign of Trajan.

Step 3 Expand

Choose and complete one of the following activities:

Activity 1: Compare Maps
Compare a map of the Roman Republic with a map of the Roman Empire. Compare these with a map of today's United States.

Activity 2: Expand Your Research
Ancient Greeks and Romans agreed that humans had created seven great wonders in their ancient world. Since these observers never traveled to India, China, or America, their list included only the wonders of their own "world." Find out what the Romans labeled "The Seven Wonders of the World."

Activity 3: Make a Salt-Dough Map
Make a salt-dough map of ancient Rome. You will need: 2 level cups plain flour, 1 level cup cooking salt, 3/4 cup water, 2 tsp cooking oil, food coloring (optional). Mix the dry ingredients together and then add the water and oil. Turn out onto a work surface and knead for 10 minutes, or until a small amount of the dough can be rolled into a ball without cracking. Divide the dough into parts and add food coloring (blue for water, green for land, etc.) or paint it with poster paints when dry. Draw an outline of ancient Greece on a sheet of poster board or other smooth card board. Spread the salt dough onto the outline, making mountains and other geographical features. Allow the map to dry thoroughly. Label the following features:

- Cities: Rome, Byzantium, Londinium, Carthage, Athens, Jerusalem, Alexandria.
- Bodies of Water: Ionian Sea, Black Sea, Aegean Sea, Adriatic Sea, Mediterranean Sea.
- Mountains: Pyrenees, Alps, Atlas, Apennines, Caucasus, Urals.
- Provinces: Gaul (France), Hispania (Spain), Greece, Macedonia, Asia (Minor), Egypt, Britannia, Gaul (France).
- Rivers: Tigris, Nile, Po, Tiber, Euphrates, Thames, Danube.
- Islands: Sicily, Crete, Cyprus, Corsica, Sardinia, Britannia.

Activity 4: Make a Map
Using colored pencils, mark the countries from which people moved to Italy. Draw arrows from these countries to the areas in which these people settled, then write their names—Etruscans, Greeks, migrants from northern Africa and central Europe, including Latin tribes, etc.

Activity 5: Make a Cookie Map
With your family, make a "cookie map" of the Roman Empire during the time of Christ. You will need: a Bible Atlas, a cookie recipe, a can of frosting, and a variety of chocolate chips, mini fun chips, or candy dots, and several tubes of cake-decorating gels in a variety of colors. Bake a large cookie, frost it (this

Resources recommended in ◆several lessons, ★ several units, ● other HOW Units. ●—Key Resource (see beginning of unit or page 32).

Heart of Wisdom Publishing   581

becomes the "glue"), then use chocolate chips to locate selected cites or towns. Use the decorating gels to "draw" rivers, lakes, parks, or centers of mineral resources on the "map," using the symbols and the map key in the atlas.

Activity 6: Create a Worksheet
Develop a worksheet for elementary-aged students. Draw a blank map outline of Europe and the Mediterranean area. Make a list of geographical features of the Roman Empire that the students should know. Make blanks on the map for the students to fill in with names from a list. Share this worksheet with some younger students.

Activity 7: Expand Your Research
Investigate ancient Roman transportation. Travelers on horseback established some extraordinary records. Julius Caesar covered 800 miles, from the Rhone River in France to Rome, in eight days. Tiberius raced 500 miles in three days to reach his mortally wounded brother Drusus. The official messenger system, the Cursus Publicus, used couriers who changed horses at stations every 10 miles or at mansiones every 20 to 30 miles. They were expected to cover 50 miles per day. The same messenger (rather than a relay of messengers) carried such important tidings as the death or accession of an emperor. A courier could travel from Rome to Palestine in 46 days, and from Rome to Egypt in 64 days. Those who traveled by carriage could cover between 25 and 50 miles per day. Roman vehicles had no springs, so the passengers felt every bump on the road. The Romans had such vehicles as the "carpentum," a two-wheeled deluxe carriage; the "redda," a four-wheeled wagon; and the "carruca," a covered wagon. Wealthy individuals, like the Ethiopian treasurer of Queen Candace of Meroe, could afford a chauffeur-driven chariot. Read Acts 8:28,38.

Step 4 Excel

Share what you have learned in this lesson with a friend or family member. Add any illustrations to your portfolio.

Founding of Rome c. 753 B.C.

Step 1 Excite

The early history of Rome is a mixture of legend and fact. According to the tradition, Rome was founded by the Etruscans and ruled by Etruscan kings. Most history records seven kings of Rome between 753 B.C. and the founding of the Republic in 509 B.C. The legend of the first king, Romulus, is the most fictitious story. There is no archaeological evidence or contemporary written legend to indicate that a real king named Romulus actually lived.

Find a map of the Early Roman Civilization (around 753-509 B.C.).

Step 2 Examine

The famous legend of Romulus and Remus explains that in 753 B.C., Numitor, King of Alba Longa had a daughter, Rhea Silvia. Rhea conceived twin brothers by Mars, the god of war. Amulius, the king's wicked brother, took over the throne. To make sure that Numitor would have no heirs, King Amulius ordered the twin brothers killed. The twins were thrown into the Tiber River, but their basket washed up on the river bank where they were found by a she-wolf who suckled them with her milk.

The wolf looked after them until they were found by one of the king's shepherds, who adopted them; he and his wife raised the babies as their own. Romulus and Remus grew up and helped overthrow the king who had ordered their death.

They wanted to build their own city along the Tiber River where their basket had washed ashore. They disagreed about where it should be, and Romulus killed Remus during their quarrels. Romulus built the city of Rome on one of the seven hills along the Tiber—the Palatine Hill—and lived a long life as king of Rome.

Research the founding of Rome. Use any resource (an encyclopedia, nonfiction book, historical novel, or the Internet). We recommend the following:

Books

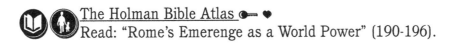 The Holman Bible Atlas ☛ ♥
Read: "Rome's Emerenge as a World Power" (190-196).

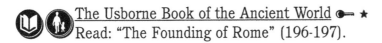 The Usborne Book of the Ancient World ☛ ★
Read: "The Founding of Rome" (196-197).

Resources recommended in ♦several lessons, ★ several units, ♥other HOW Units. ☛Key Resource (see beginning of unit or page 32).

Kingfisher History Encyclopedia ⊶ ♥
Read: "The Founding of Rome: 753-510 B.C." (34).

Kingfisher Illustrated History of the World ⊶ ♥
Read: "The Founding of Rome" (66).

Ancient Rome (Eyewitness) ⊶ ♦
Read: "City State to Super Power" (6-7).

The Greco-Roman World of the New Testament Era ⊶ ♥
Read: "Early Rome" (295-302).

The Penguin Historical Atlas of Ancient Rome ⊶ ♦
Read: "The Origins of Rome" (20-22). ▯

Internet Sources

The Founding of Rome
Description: An *Encarta* encyclopedia article.

The Founding of Rome
Description: Article from *Mr. Deutsch's Virtual Textbook*.

Step 3 Expand

Choose and complete one of the following activities:

Activity 1: Rewrite a Legend
Rewrite the legend of Romulus and Remus in your own words. Younger students can narrate (orally tell) the story.

Activity 2: Illustrate a Story
Illustrate a scene from the legend of Romulus and Remus.

Activity 3: Add to Your Time Line Book
Add the legend of of Romulus and Remus to your Time Line Book.

Activity 4: Do Further Research
The *Aeneid* is a legend (twelve books describing the seven-year wanderings of Aeneas) by the poet Virgil that tells the story of the founding of Rome. In writing the poem, Virgil used the old legends and the Greek *Iliad* and *Odyssey* to explain what happened between the Trojan War and the founding of Rome. Find a short description of this and make a list of the principal characters.

Underlined text refers to Internet link at http://Homeschool-Books.com

Step 4 Excel

Share what you have learned about the the founding of Rome with a friend or family member. Correct all written work to demonstrate correct punctuation and spelling, and effective use of grammar. Add corrected written work or any illustrations to your portfolio.

Resources recommended in ◆several lessons, ★ several units, ♥ other HOW Units. ☞ Key Resource (see beginning of unit or page 32).

Heart of Wisdom Publishing   585

The Etruscan Dynasty 800-508 B.C.

Step 1 Excite

In the Ancient Greece unit, you studied the Persian wars and the Peloponnesian War. This same period is referred to as the "early years" of Rome—the Etruscans were rising to power on the Italian peninsula. The Etruscans originated from Etruria, a country in the North. Several Etruscan princes conquered Rome around 600 B.C. Under the rule of the Etruscans, Rome grew in importance and power. Great temples and public works were constructed.

Brainstorm ways in which the Etruscan influence might be seen in later Roman culture.

Step 2 Examine

Research the Etruscans. Use any resource (an encyclopedia, nonfiction book, historical novel, or the Internet). We recommend the following:
Books

The Greco-Roman World of the New Testament Era ●━ ♥
Read: "Early Rome" (295-302).

Caesar and Christ (Story of Civilization III) ♦
Read: Chapter I "Etruscan Prelude: 800-508" (3-19).

Internet Sources

Rome - The Etruscans
Description: Details the emergence of the Etruscans on the Italian peninsula, and their influence on the native populations of Rome in 800 B.C.

Etruscans
Description: "A Mystery Disclosed" studies the origins, civilization, maritime ventures, religion, and daily life of the Etruscans of pre-Roman Italy.

Etruscans
Description: Includes: "Origins," "Etruscan Alphabet," "Etruscan Language," "Epigraphic Material," and more.

Underlined text refers to Internet link at http://Homeschool-Books.com

Step 3 Expand

Complete the following activity:

Write a Summary
Write a summary of what you have learned about the Etruscans.
Record main facts about the Etruscans including:

- Where they came from
- How they received their name
- Government
- Periods of prosperity in their civilization
- Towns
- Alphabet
- Professions
- Trade partners
- Favorite entertainment
- Clothing
- Art
- Religion

Step 4 Excel

Discuss with a friend or family member the ways in which you found the Etruscan culture to resemble later Roman culture, then share what you have learned with him/her. Correct written work to demonstrate correct punctuation and spelling, and effective use of grammar. Add corrected written work or any illustrations to your portfolio.

Resources recommended in ◆several lessons, ★ several units, ♥ other HOW Units. ◐—Key Resource (see beginning of unit or page 32).

Heart of Wisdom Publishing   587

The Roman Republic 508-27 B.C.

Step 1 Excite

Ancient Rome experienced several forms of government throughout the course of its history. In the years leading up to 510 B.C., Rome was ruled by kings. In 509 B.C. Rome became a republic, governed by elected consuls who were advised by a senate. In 27 B.C., after a civil war, Rome became an empire, and Augustus became the first emperor. This lesson is about the Republican Era (509-27 B.C.).

The Roman Republic that replaced the monarchy is similar to how the United States is governed today at the federal level. This democracy was founded on the principles of justice and fair treatment. Ancient-Roman justice was based upon the proper application of evidence. The Roman Republican Constitution is a model for many democracies. (Note: the terms "republic" and "democracy" have multiple meanings some overlapping, some diametrically opposed.)

Watch a video. (Look for the videos below at your local video store, or watch television schedules for local listings.) Take notes to define the following terms: citizen, plebeian, patrician, praetor, senate, and slave.

Ancient Rome: The Story of an Empire That Ruled the World ◆
Volume 1, "The Republic of Rome," examines the overthrow of the Etruscan monarchy and the conquest of Carthage and establishment of the two-class, plebeian-patrician republican system. See description of this four-volume set in the Resources Section.

Rome: Power and Glory, Volume I: The Rise ◆
Volume I: *The Rise* examines how Rome grows from a backwater village into a democratic republic. This episode sorts the myth from the reality in everything from the legends of Romulus and Remus to the attack on the Sabine women. See description of this six-volume set in the Resources section.

The Legions of Rome
See description of this four-volume set in the Resources Section.

Underlined text refers to Internet link at http://Homeschool-Books.com

Period	Dates	Events
The Roman Monarchy	753-509 B.C.E.	753 B.C.E. Traditional date for the founding of Rome.
The Early Roman Republic	509-264 B.C.E.	506 B.C.E. The last Tarquin king is overthrown and the Republic is founded. 494 B.C.E. The plebeians and patricians agree to give plebeians some political power. 450 B.C.E. The Law of the Twelve Tables gives plebeians a knowledge of their legal rights. 496 B.C.E. Romans defeat neighboring tribe at battle of Lake Regillus. Rome's territorial expansion begins. 390 B.C.E. Invading Gauls sack Rome. Romans quickly rebuild city, surrounding it with defensive wall that keeps Rome safe for centuries. 312 B.C.E. Roman officials begin construction of the first stone aqueduct, Aqua Appia (over 10 miles long). 265 B.C.E. Romans gain control of the entire Italian peninsula.
The Middle Roman Republic	264-134 B.C.E.	264 B.C.E. First Punic War results in Carthage giving up control of western Sicily. 218 B.C.E. Second Punic War: Carthage gives over all its territory to Rome except the capital city itself. 146 B.C.E. Third Punic War: Carthage is burned, and Carthaginians are sold into slavery. 146-130 B.C.E. Class conflicts, slave retaliation, and the Gracchi brothers strive for reforms of the Republic.
The Roman Republic: The Gracchan Period	133-111 B.C.E.	
The Roman Republic: Marius and Sulla	110-80 B.C.E.	107 B.C.E. Marius is appointed to rule. 82 B.C.E. Sulla is appointed dictator and grants all power to the aristocracy; Julius Caesar and Pompey defend the common people.
The Late Roman Republic	79-60 B.C.E.	
The Roman Republic: Caesar	60-44 B.C.E.	
Roman Empire	27 B.C.	

Resources recommended in ◆several lessons, ★ several units, ● other HOW Units. ●—Key Resource (see beginning of unit or page 32).

Heart of Wisdom Publishing   589

Brainstorm and discuss the differences between the ancient-Roman government and the American government. Could the history of Rome have influenced the creators of our Constitution? How did ancient Rome change from a Republic to a Dictatorship? Where did the power of the government lie in the Roman Republic? In the Roman Empire? Where does the power rest in our government?

Step 2 Examine

Research government in ancient Rome. Find out specific characteristics of the Roman Senate of the Republican Period. Why has it been called "the most distinguished and important political body that has ever existed in the world"? Use any resource (an encyclopedia, nonfiction book, historical novel, or the Internet). We recommend the following:

Encyclopedia of the Bible (Nelson's Illustrated) •— ♥
"Early Roman History" (72-73),

The Usborne Book of the Ancient World •— ★
Read: "The Early Republic" (198-199), "The End of the Roman Republic" (248).

The Holman Bible Atlas •— ♥
Read: "The Republican Period" (190-194).

Ancient Civilizations •— ★
Read: "Ancient Rome" (42-43).

Kingfisher History Encyclopedia •— ♥
Read: "Foundation of Rome" (34-35), "Rise of Rome" (44), "Society and Government" (62, 64, 66).

Kingfisher Illustrated History of the World •— ♥
Read: "The Rise of Rome" (104).

The Greco-Roman World of the New Testament Era •— ♥
Read: "Rome as Conqueror" (302-308), "Social Revolution in Rome" (308-314).

The Penguin Historical Atlas of Ancient Rome ♦
Read: "The Unification of Italy" (22-23). ⬜

Internet Sources

🛈 The Roman Republican Constitution
Description: This article explains how the Roman form of government roughly parallels the modern American division of executive, legislative, and judicial branches.

🛈 Ancient Roman History
Description: This site explains that ancient-Roman history is usually divided into three main periods: before the rise of Rome, the Roman Republic, and the Roman Empire. The Imperial Period is usually divided according to who was emperor. Links to each topic are included.

🛈 A Brief History of Ancient Rome
Description: This informative site, divided into the different political phases of ancient Rome, describes the evolution of a small tribe growing to its peak, then experiencing its downfall.

Step 3 Expand

Choose and complete at least one of the following activities:

Activity 1: Answer Questions
How did the Roman Republic begin? Why was it successful? What caused the economic struggle between rich and poor in the Republican period? What were the main reforms listed in the Licinian Laws of 367 B.C.? Learn about the patriotic statesmen, the Gracchi brothers. What problems did the government have at the time of Caesar? How did the republic become a dictatorship?

Activity 2: Copy Passages
Copy (by hand or typing) two or more paragraphs from your research giving an overview of the Roman Republic. (Copying is a good exercise for teaching yourself accuracy and attention to detail, and you will probably discover things about the text you are copying that you would be unlikely to notice otherwise.)

Activity 3: Make a Map
Starting with a map of Italy, make your own map, tracing battles using different-colored pencils for Roman allies and foes. What was the purpose of the Latin League? When and where was the decisive battle that made Rome supreme over all central and northern Italy? Show on a map which part of Italy still remained independent in 284 B.C., and write the name of the people who lived there.

Resources recommended in ◆several lessons, ★ several units, ♥ other HOW Units. ◐—Key Resource (see beginning of unit or page 32).

Heart of Wisdom Publishing   591

Activity 4: Write a Summary

Retell what you learned about the Roman Republic using the narration method. You should write, in one sitting, everything that you remember in chronological order. Younger students can narrate (orally tell) what they have learned.

Activity 5: Write an Essay

Write an essay about any event that happened between 506 B.C. and A.D. 31. Begin by writing what happened at the conclusion of the event. Then, working backward, explain the event's origins and its development over time.

Activity 6: Make a Chart

Make a chart comparing the Roman Senate and the American Senate: who can be elected, for what period of time, what are the main duties of senators, etc. Is each an advisory body, or does it have the power to administer?

Activity 7: Contrast and Compare

After the overthrow of the Tarquin monarchy by Junius Brutus in 509 B.C., Rome does not revert to a monarchy for the rest of its history. The history of the Republic is a history of continuous warfare; all of the historical stories which the Romans will use as stories of Roman virtue and values date from this tumultuous period of defense and invasion. Make a contrast-and-compare graphic (see page 26) to show how the way in which the Romans rid themselves of their king is similar to (or different from) the way that Americans rid themselves of King George III.

Step 4 Excel

Share your work from Step 3 with someone. Explain what you have learned in this lesson. Correct written work to demonstrate correct punctuation and spelling, and effective use of grammar. Add corrected written work or any illustrations to your portfolio.

Underlined text refers to Internet link at http://Homeschool-Books.com

The Punic Wars 264-146 B.C.

Step 1 Excite

Brainstorm and discuss how elephants could be used in war. What made the Roman army that fought in the Punic Wars different from armies of other nations?
Watch a video. (Look for the video below at your local video store, or watch television schedules for local listings.)

Hannibal

Rome: Power and Glory, Volume II: Legions of Conquest ♦
Spectacular wars transform the amateur Roman army into a vast legion that conquers the Western world. Included are Scipio's armies facing Hannibal's elephants and Julius Caesar's decade-long onslaught against Gaul. See description of this six-volume set in the Resources Section.

Step 2 Examine

The First Punic War broke out in 264 B.C.; it was concentrated entirely on the island of Sicily. Rome besieged many of the Carthaginian cities on Sicily, and when Carthage attempted to raise the siege with its navy, the Romans utterly destroyed that navy. For the first time since the rise of the Carthaginian empire, they had lost power over the sea-ways. The war ended with no particular side winning over the other.[1]

The Second Punic War began in 218 B.C. A young Carthaginian general named Hannibal nearly captured Rome in this war. The Romans expected Carthage to attack from the sea, but Hannibal attacked from the north by land. Hannibal led his army in a daring and difficult journey over the Alps while riding on elephants. Hannibal defeated the Roman army but was unable to take the walled city. The two sides fought for fifteen years, but Carthage recalled Hannibal to repel a Roman invasion, and the Romans defeated him there in 202 B.C. [2]

Find out more about the Punic (or Carthaginian) Wars. Use any resource (an encyclopedia, nonfiction book, historical novel, or the Internet). We recommend the following:

Books

Resources recommended in ♦several lessons, ★ several units, ● other HOW Units. ●—Key Resource (see beginning of unit or page 32).

Heart of Wisdom Publishing   593

The Usborne Book of the Ancient World ☞ ★
Read: "Punic Wars" (200-201, 212, 275).

Kingfisher History Encyclopedia ☞ ♥
Read: "The Punic Wars" (62-65).

Kingfisher Illustrated History of the World ☞ ♥
Read: "The Punic Wars" (106-107).

The Penguin Historical Atlas of Ancient Rome ☞ ♦
Read: "The Wars with Carthage" (24-25).

Caesar and Christ (Story of Civilization III) ♦
Read: Chapter III "Hannibal Against Rome" (39-55).

History of the Jewish People Volume 1: Second Temple Era ♦
Read: "The Punic Wars" (111-116). See the Ancient Israel Resource Section for a description of this book.

Far Above Rubies: Wisdom in the Christian Community ♥
Read: "Shades of Hannibal" (239-240). See Resources Recommended in all Units for a description of this book.

The Young Carthaginian by G. A. Henty
Description: A historical novel set during the times of Hannibal and the Punic Wars between Carthage and Rome. This adventure story describes the campaigns of Hannibal in Iberia, Gaul, Cisalpine Gaul, and at Rome's doorstep, through the experiences of a young Carthaginian noble. (June 1, 1998) Lost Classics Book Company; ISBN: 1890623016.

Internet Sources

The Punic Wars
Description: This site is a slide-show presentation by a world-history teacher from Williston Senior High School. An excellent site which gives a good chronological overview of events during this period.

The Punic Wars
Description: The seventh chapter of the learning module, "Rome"; this chapter narrates the history of the three conflicts between Rome and Carthage which left Rome in control of the Carthaginian Empire.

Punic Wars
Description: Concise article from the Ancient Rome site.

Underlined text refers to Internet link at http://Homeschool-Books.com

(i) (♦) Punic Wars
Description: Chronological studies of the Punic Wars from the *History of Western Civilization* by Boise State University.

Step 3 Expand

Choose and complete one of the following activities:

(↩) (♦) Activity 1: Add to Your Time Line Book
Add the Punic Wars to your Time Line Book. See a sample on page 23.

(▦) (♦) Activity 2: Make a Chart
Sum up in a chart what you have learned: dates of each of the three Punic Wars, how each was started, main battles, main leaders, results, and new boundaries of Rome after each.

(?) (♦) Activity 3: Answer Questions
Answer the following about the Punic Wars:
- What Phoenician colony in the western Mediterranean was the main rival of Rome after it gained control of the Italian Peninsula? (Carthage)
- Look at a map of ancient Carthage and its boundaries.
- When did the conflict for Mediterranean supremacy begin?
- Why were these wars called the Punic Wars?
- How did the First Punic War begin?
- How was the Second Punic War started?
- Why did one historian say that it was "a trial such as no people has ever gone through before or since, and survived"?
- How was the Third Punic War started?
- What politician was persistent in saying that "Carthage must be destroyed"?
- When and where was a Roman army completely destroyed?
- When and where did a battle take place after which Carthage was reduced to the position of a vassal state?
- When was Carthage finally destroyed?
- What happened to its territory?
- Where on a map are sites of main battles?
- Who were the great leaders of Carthage and Rome during these wars?
- What might have happened to the balance of power in the Mediterranean if Hannibal had conquered the city of Rome?

Resources recommended in ♦several lessons, ★ several units, ●other HOW Units. ●—Key Resource (see beginning of unit or page 32).

Heart of Wisdom Publishing   595

Activity 4: Draw a Map
Draw and mark a map to show the geographic location of Rome, the territorial expansion of the republic, and the route of Hannibal. After victories in the Punic Wars, Rome conquered upper Italy, Sicily, Macedonia, Greece, and Asia Minor and made them Roman provinces. Find all these lands on a map and mark their territories with colored pencils.

Activity 5: Appreciate Art
Joseph Mallord Turner (1775-1851) was an English painter, a celebrated watercolorist. A famous painting entitled *Hannibal Crossing the Alps* shows Hannibal crossing the Alps with Carthage's army. Find this picture in an art book or on the Web. Use the painting as an inspiration for a work of visual art in which you express the adventure and hardship of traveling from North Africa, over the Alps, and into enemy territory.

Activity 6: Write a Soliloquy
Imagine that you were participating in this most daring march of history. Write a dramatic soliloquy in which you are an African helping to care for one of the elephants on the way over the Alps. Tell about the hardships, the food you eat, the clothes you wear, and the people with whom you travel. Dramatize your feelings about the deaths that occur along the journey. Wear a costume as you perform your drama for your family.

Activity 7: Write a Book Review
Write a review of the book The Young Carthaginian by G. A. Henty. Discuss the quote, "I swear that so soon as age will permit . . . I will use fire and steel to arrest the destiny of Rome." The boy Hannibal said this as he stood at the altar beside his father. Was he loyal to his vow? What "destiny of Rome" was he trying to thwart?

Step 4 Excel

Share what you have learned about the Punic Wars with a friend or family member. Correct all written work to demonstrate correct punctuation and spelling, and effective use of grammar. Add corrected written work or any illustrations to your portfolio.

Footnotes
1. Hooker, Richard. (1996). "Rome: The Punic Wars" <http://www.wsu.edu:8080/~dee/rome/punicwars.htm> (Accessed May 2000).
2. Dowling, Mike. "The Electronic Passport to the Punic Wars" <http://www.mrdowling.com/702-punic.html> (Accessed May 2000).

Underlined text refers to Internet link at http://Homeschool-Books.com

Julius Caesar 100-44 B.C.

Note: In this lesson you will learn historical information about Caesar. In the next lesson you will study Shakespeare's play about Caesar.

Step 1 Excite

Brainstorm and make a list of words that define the word "leader." Make a list of good qualities (adjectives) which you think a good leader should have. Do the same for qualities that make a bad leader. What was the role of oratory in ancient Rome? What is the role of oratory in today's world?

Watch a video. (Look for the videos below at your local video store, or watch television schedules for local listings.)

Julius Caesar Time Line

100 B.C. July 13 - Caesar's Birth
84 Marries Cornelia, daughter of L. Cornelius Cinna
75 Captured by Pirates
73 Elected Pontifex
69 Cornelia dies
67 Marries Pompeia
65 Elected Aedile
63 Elected Pontifex Maximus
62 Divorces Pompeia
61 Governor of Further Spain
60 Becomes Consul and forms the Triumvirate
59 Consul
58 Defeats Helvetii and Germans
55 Crosses the Rhine; Invades Britain
54 His daughter, Pompey's wife, dies
53 Crassus killed
52 Clodius murdered; Caesar defeats Vercingetorix
49 Crosses the Rubicon - Civil War begins
48 Pompey murdered
45 Declared dictator for life
44 Ides of March, assassinated

Rome: Power and Glory, Volume III: Seduction of Power ◆
Bloody power struggles shape Rome's leadership as the Republic gradually transforms into an Empire. Included are Julius Caesar's rise from soldier to dictator and Augustus taking the throne as Rome's first Emperor. See description of this six-volume set in the Resources Section.

Hail Caesar Volume I: Julius Caesar (1997) ◆
Julius Caesar turned military victories into political power. His ambition created a colossal empire, and he gave his name to the rulers who succeeded him. He has been a symbol of power and majesty for 2,000 years. But to his countrymen, Caesar was an upstart, a gambler, and a tyrant who destroyed the Roman Republic and paved the way for the rule of emperors. (A&E Biography 888-423-1212).

The Great Commanders: Julius Caesar
Description: Julius Caesar, a scheming politician, used military power to dominate Rome. Massively in debt, he led his armies through a decade of conquest in a bid for wealth, glory, and power. In the process, he conquered Gaul and pre-

Resources recommended in ◆several lessons, ★ several units, ● other HOW Units. ●—Key Resource (see beginning of unit or page 32).

cipitated the downfall of the Celts. At the Battle of Alesia he brilliantly used technological superiority and tactical cunning against a force who outnumbered him more than five to one.(A&E Biography 888-423-1212).

Julius Caesar: Master of the Roman World

Description: Julius Caesar is one of the towering figures of human history. He gave his name to the rulers that followed him, and passed down a vast empire carved from his determination and military genius. This definitive portrait uses countless ancient artifacts, texts, commentary from leading experts, and dramatic re-enactments to explore his life and legacy. Follow his meteoric rise to power and his brilliant military conquests. Hear his own descriptions of some of his greatest battles, and visit the sites of these legendary engagements. Also investigate the controversy surrounding his legacy: was he an ambitious demagogue, as his detractors claim, or a defender of the people's rights against the vested powers of a controlling oligarchy? (A&E Biography 888-423-1212).

Step 2 Examine

Julius Caesar was one of the most successful military leaders of all time. He was one of ancient Rome's greatest generals and also an orator, politician, and writer. His victories in civil war helped him become dictator of the Roman people and made Rome the center of an empire that stretched across Europe. His power became so great that many were frightened by it, and a group of his political opponents assassinated him.

Research Julius Caesar. Use any resource (an encyclopedia, nonfiction book, historical novel, or the Internet). We recommend the following:

Books

The Usborne Book of the Ancient World ●— ★
Read: "Caesar's Rule" (205).

Kingfisher History Encyclopedia ●— ♥
Read: "The Roman Republic" (62), "The Roman Empire" (64).

Kingfisher Illustrated History of the World ●━ ♥
Read: "The Roman Empire" (118), "Julius Caesar" (time line page 115).

The Penguin Historical Atlas of Ancient Rome ●━ ♦
Read: "Caesar's Conquest of Gaul" (31-32), "Crossing the 'Rubicon'" (32-33), "The Civil Wars" (34-35), other references (18, 19, 42, 48, 50).

Caesar and Christ (Story of Civilization III) ♦
Read: Chapter IX "Caesar: 100-44 B.C." (167-197).

The Conquest of Gaul by Julius Caesar
Description: This translation chronicles Caesar's military adventures in Gaul (modern France), Germany, and Britain. (February 1983) Viking Pr; ISBN: 0140444335.

Internet Sources

Great Caesar Timeline
Description: A list of twenty major events in Caesar's life, from About.com.

Gaius Julius Caesar (100-44 B.C.)
Description: A biography of this famous Roman general and statesman.

Gaius Julius Caesar
Description: Links on this site include information about Caesar the Roman, and Caesar, the subject of drama.

May You Live in Interesting Times
Description: An account of Caesar's political life and a challenge to the claim that he was the greatest man in history.

Caesar
Description: An article on Caesar, the civil wars, and his policies; with evaluation and sources.

Step 3 Expand

Choose and complete one of the following activities:

Activity 1: Add to Your Time Line Book
Add Julius Caesar to your Time Line Book. Include a summary and illustration.

Resources recommended in ♦several lessons, ★ several units, ♥other HOW Units. ●━Key Resource (see beginning of unit or page 32).

Heart of Wisdom Publishing   599

Activity 2: Write a Paper

Write a paper titled "Julius Caesar." Include a bibliography. Collect as much information as possible, taking careful notes that include where you found your information. Before writing, review all of your notes and identify a main idea to keep in focus. For assistance, refer to "Bibliographies" and "Writing About a Person" in *Writers INC*.

Activity 3: Answer Questions

Answer the following about Julius Caesar: What book did he author? What is the highest political office he attained? Who was the mother of his only son? Why was he assassinated? Who warned him of the impending assassination? What part of Caesar's body was stabbed? How many conspirators were against him?

Activity 4: Fill Out an Event Worksheet

Choose an event from the time line of Caesar's life to focus on. Fill out an Event Worksheet.

Activity 5: Draw a Map

Draw a map of the Roman Empire at the time of Julius Caesar's birth (100 B.C.) and death (44 B.C.) to see his influence in the expansion of the empire. How did this expansion cause political instability?

Activity 6: Write a Review

Write a review of a video or book. Comment on the effect of setting the story in different time periods (i.e. 1953 & 1970).

Activity 7: Contrast and Compare

Create a contrast-and-compare graphic (see page 26) on the leadership qualities held by Caesar and Brutus.

Activity 8: Think and Discuss

Augustus was Julius Caesar's nephew and adopted son. Discuss the relationship between the two men and how it influenced Augustus' rise to power.

Activity 9: Answer Questions

The following discussion questions are recommended by A&E in the Classroom to use before and after watching the video *Hail Caesar Volume I: Julius Caesar*:

1. After 2,000 years, the name Caesar still is symbolic. What does this name represent? What is the symbolic value of this name in Western Civilization?

Underlined text refers to Internet link at http://Homeschool-Books.com

2. Julius Caesar's status at his birth influenced his later life. What was the station of his family at his birth? How did his position enable him to reach the heights of power in his later life?

3. How was Julius Caesar trained for greatness from the time he was a young boy?

4. During Julius Caesar's lifetime, the Roman Empire was expanding its territories. How did this expansion cause political instability?

5. In ancient Rome, a leader needed great speaking skills to be successful. What was the role of oratory in ancient Rome? What is the role of oratory in today's world?

6. Julius Caesar's toga was streaked with purple. What was the symbolic value of the color purple? Why was it a status symbol?

7. How did Julius Caesar's marriages help his career?

8. Julius Caesar was a member of Rome's aristocracy, yet he chose to court the urban poor. Why did he try to garner the affection and loyalty of the urban poor? How did this help him in his quest for power?

9. Discuss the role of women in the Roman Empire. How were women used as tools to gain political power through marriage alliances? What does this say about the way women were viewed?

10. Why did the Senate make Julius Caesar dictator?

11. Why was Caesar murdered?

Step 4 Excel

Share what you have learned about Julius Caesar with a friend or family member. Correct written work to demonstrate correct punctuation and spelling, and effective use of grammar. Add corrected written work or any illustrations to your portfolio.

Resources recommended in ◆several lessons, ★ several units, ◗ other HOW Units. ◗━Key Resource (see beginning of unit or page 32).

Heart of Wisdom Publishing   601

Julius Caesar: The Play

Step 1 Excite

Shakespeare wrote *The Tragedy of Julius Caesar* in 1599. The play opens in Rome, 44 B.C. Caesar is at the height of his career, ruler of most of the known world. As an introduction to this play, watch a video based upon it. We recommend either of the following:

Julius Caesar (1953)
Description: Appalled by the murder of his mentor, Julius Caesar, Mark Antony declares war on his assassins—especially Gaius Cassius and "the honorable" Brutus, who only reluctantly took part in the crime. Marlon Brando received an Academy Award nomination for his unorthodox portrayal of the impetuous Mark Antony in this adaptation of the William Shakespeare classic.

Julius Caesar (1970)
Description: William Shakespeare's timeless classic is brought to the screen with an all-star cast, with a brilliant performance by John Gielgud as the ill-fated Caesar. Charlton Heston plays Marc Antony.

Step 2 Examine

Read Shakespeare's play, *Julius Caesar*. This is one of his most famous historical plays, dealing with the downfall of Caesar and the subsequent power struggle between the factions representing monarchy and a republic. Reading Shakespeare can be difficult; a good copy of the play will have footnote references to unknown words and phrases. Try reading this play aloud with your family, pausing often for clarity and questions.

Research Shakespeare's play, *Julius Caesar*. Use any resource (an encyclopedia, nonfiction book, historical novel, or the Internet). We recommend the following:

Books

Julius Caesar (Cambridge School Shakespeare Series) by Tim Seward One of Shakespeare's best works, revised and repackaged for younger students. Includes an updated bibliography, suggested references, stage and film history, and an overview of Shakespeare's life. (July 1992). Cambridge Univ Pr (Trd); ISBN: 0521409039. Reading level: Ages 9-12.

Julius Caesar by William Shakespeare, Alan Durband (Editor)
Description: From the "Shakespeare Made Easy" series. The most famous of Shakespeare's Roman tragedies, *Julius Caesar* was written and first performed in 1599, and was apparently one of the plays his contemporaries enjoyed most. Recounting the death of Caesar on the steps of the Senate house, the play offers some of Shakespeare's finest scenes: Antony's skillful speech at Caesar's funeral, and the quarrel and reconciliation between Brutus and Cassius with the news of Portia's death. This edition includes a fresh consideration of the play's date and its place in the Shakespeare canon, and examines how Shakespeare reshaped his sources.

Internet Sources

The Life and Death of Julius Caesar
Description: The text of Shakespeare's play from *The Complete Works of William Shakespeare* site.

Julius Caesar Summary and Study Assistant
Description: A study guide created by a 10th-grade Literature class at Sprayberry High School. Select an act, which will take you to scene-by-scene summaries and commentaries.

Introduction to The Tragedy of Julius Caesar by William Shakespeare
Description: This is a brief introduction to *Julius Caesar*. It concentrates mainly on historical information on Caesar and his times and career. A second emphasis is on the nature of the play as a tragedy (not a history), and Shakespeare's effort to stay within the bounds of well-known legend and history.

Julius Caesar an Adaptation of Shakespeare's Classic
Description: A light-hearted approach to the play, emphasizing the motives of the characters and mischief worked by the politicians to achieve their ultimate aim.

Step 3 Expand

Choose and complete one of the following activities:

Activity 1: Narrate
Tell the story of Shakespeare's play, *Julius Caesar*, to your family.

Activity 2: Write a Review
Write a review of the video/s viewed. Comment on the effect of setting the play in different time periods (i.e. 1953 & 1970).

Resources recommended in ◆several lessons, ★ several units, ● other HOW Units. ●—Key Resource (see beginning of unit or page 32).

Activity 3: Write a Diary Entry
Write several entries from a diary that one of the story's main characters might have kept before, during, or after the main events. Remember that the character's thoughts and feelings are very important in a diary.

Activity 4: Write an Essay
Write a brief essay on which character is considered to be the tragic hero of Shakespeare's play, *Julius Caesar*, and why.

Activity 5: Write a Scene
Rewrite a scene of Shakespeare's play, *Julius Caesar*, using President Clinton and Vice President Gore (or the current president and vice president) as the main characters.

Step 4 Excel

Share the play *Julius Caesar* by William Shakespeare with someone. Use two or more readers for the speaking parts. Read at least one exciting passage such as Act III, scenes 1 and 2, when Caesar is assassinated and Marc Antony speaks at his funeral.

Antony & Octavian (Augustus) 44-30 B.C.

Step 1 Excite

After Julius Caesar's death, his grandnephew, Octavian (63 B.C.-A.D. 14), and Mark Antony (83?-30 B.C.), became consuls. They divided the empire between them. Antony ruled from Egypt (to be near Cleopatra) and Octavian ruled from Rome. In 27 B.C. the Roman Senate gave Octavian the title Augustus ("consecrated," or "holy").

Watch a video.(Look for the videos below at your local video store, or watch television schedules for local listings.)

Hail Caesar Volume II: Augustus Caesar (1997) ◆▯
Augustus Caesar was the nephew and adopted heir of the great Julius Caesar, and was responsible for the great consolidation of power that formed the Roman Empire. Take a look at his life from his childhood to his assumption of power as a young man, to the formation of Imperial Rome itself. Originally seen on A&E's "Biography." See full description of the six-video series in the Resources Section.

Cleopatra (1934)
Description: Claudette Colbert stars as the captivating and powerful queen of Egypt in this classic Hollywood film. When Julius Caesar, the leader of the Roman Empire, succumbs to the charms of the sultry Cleopatra, he creates a scandal big enough to shake the marble pillars of Rome. The ruler pays dearly for his romance, for the outraged Roman Senate repudiates him—and the fickle Cleopatra decides to protect her interests by bestowing her affections on her former lover's rival, Marc Antony.

Step 2 Examine

The Roman Empire was ruled jointly by Mark Antony and Octavian. Octavian befriended the senate and was made a consul; Antony fell in love with Cleopatra, the queen of Egypt. Rapidly, Octavian and Mark Antony became rivals, and in 31 B.C. Octavian's navy destroyed Antony's forces at the sea battle of Actium. Jay King explains in The Battle of Actium,

> In 31 B.C. the outcome of a sea battle off the West coast of Greece forever changed Roman history. As a result, the young and ambitious Octavian would become Rome's first emperor, Augustus. Octavian's victory firmly established his military power and dealt Marc Antony a serious defeat from which he would never recover. This battle took place between Octavian's fleet on one

---

Resources recommended in ◆several lessons, ★ several units, ● other HOW Units. ●—Key Resource (see beginning of unit or page 32).

side and the combined naval forces of Marc Antony and Cleopatra VII on the other. The battle is considered a major turning point in the history of Egypt and marked the beginning of Octavian's complete takeover of the rich North African kingdom. Octavian was given the title of Augustus by the Roman Senate four years later.

The struggle between Antony and Octavian was actually about the question of who would rule the Roman World. Antony had allied himself with Cleopatra, queen of Egypt, a descendent of the Ptolemaic Greek kings. Antony and the foreign queen were lovers, even having gone through an Egyptian wedding ceremony. Most Romans disliked such a close relationship between an important governing Roman and a foreign queen. They suspected that he would either give her a large area of Roman territory for her own kingdom, or, worse yet, make her queen over the Romans and himself king in the process. Octavian played on the Romans' intense dislike of the idea of being ruled by a king and denounced Antony's supposed plans.[1]

Research Antony, Octavian, the Second Triumvirate, and Battle of Actium. Use any resource (an encyclopedia, nonfiction book, historical novel, or the Internet). We recommend the following:

Books

The Usborne Book of the Ancient World ✏— ★
Read: "Octavian Takes Power" (214), "The Rule of Augustus 27 B.C.-A.D. 14" (215), and "Warships and Naval Tactics" (212).

The Penguin Historical Atlas of Ancient Rome ✏— ◆
Read: Part II "The Imperial Regime" (38-63).

Caesar and Christ (Story of Civilization III) ◆
Read: Chapter X "Antony: 44-30 B.C." (198-207).

Judaism and Christianity in First-Century Rome ◆
Read: "Augustan -Era Synagogue" (17-29). See description in the Resource section.

Internet Sources

Octavian (Caesar Augustus) Becomes Ruler of Rome
Description: This site is a slide-show presentation by a world-history teacher from Williston Senior High School. Also see The Birth of the Roman Empire, and The Triumvirate to get a good chronological overview of events during this period.

Underlined text refers to Internet link at http://Homeschool-Books.com

The Battle of Actium
Description: An account of the naval battle of Actium of 31 B.C., one of the "turning points" of ancient history.

Battle of Actium
Description: Encyclopedia article from Britannica.com.

Step 3 Expand

Choose and complete one of the following activities:

Activity 1: Add to Your Time Line Book
Add Mark Antony and Octavian to your Time Line Book. Include summary paragraphs about each.

Activity 2: Write a Report
Write a summary of what you have learned about the conflict between Antony and Octavian. Briefly explain the sequence of events from the assassination of Julius Caesar to the defeat of Antony by Octavian in 31 B.C. Minimum 150 words. Younger students can narrate (orally tell) the story.

Activity 3: Write a Letter
Imagine what would have happened if Marc Antony and Cleopatra had continued to rule Egypt as a province of the Roman Empire. Do you think Egypt could have become a rival to Rome? Write a letter to Marc Antony to persuade him not to give Roman provinces to Cleopatra's children. Write as if you were a close friend. Remind him of the reasons why he should try to live peacefully with the Roman leaders.

Activity 4: Answer Questions
Augustus Caesar is translated "exalted king." What was his original name? What was his family relationship to Julius Caesar? What was Octavian's family relationship to Mark Antony? What event prompted Octavian to declare war on Antony? What was the purpose of the Second Triumvirate? What was the result of the battle of Philippi? Show this place on a map. What caused the rivalry between Octavian and Antony? What was the result of the sea battle of Actium?

Activity 5: Answer Questions
The following questions are recommended by A&E in the Classroom to use before and after watching the video *Hail Caesar Volume II: Augustus Caesar*:
1. Augustus was Julius Caesar's nephew and adopted son. Discuss the relationship between the two men and how it influenced Augustus' rise to power.

Resources recommended in ◆several lessons, ★ several units, ● other HOW Units. ◉▬Key Resource (see beginning of unit or page 32).

2. Members of the Senate assassinated Julius Caesar on the steps of the Senate. How did Augustus react to the assassination of his uncle?
3. Roman politics involved a good deal of mud slinging and intrigue. Compare the politics of ancient Rome with politics today.
4. Julius Caesar had a son, Caesarian, with Cleopatra, queen of Egypt. Why did Caesar choose Augustus as his heir instead of Caesarian?
5. Although Augustus and Marc Antony were rivals, they forged an alliance. How did their common interests necessitate a temporary alliance?
6. Despite their temporary alliance, the time came when Augustus challenged the power of Marc Antony. What finally forced Augustus to challenge Marc Antony?
7. How did Augustus solidify his popularity with the Roman armies and the people?
8. What were some of the improvements Augustus made in Rome? How were these improvements symbolic gestures?
9. Augustus boasted that he "found Rome brick and left it marble." What did Augustus mean by this?

Step 4 Excel

Share what you have learned about Antony, Octavian, and the Battle of Actium with a friend or family member. Correct written work to demonstrate correct punctuation and spelling, and effective use of grammar. Add corrected written work or any illustrations to your portfolio.

Footnote
1. King, Jay. (1999). *The Mighty Roman Legions,* "The Battle of Actium."

Underlined text refers to Internet link at http://Homeschool-Books.com

The Roman Empire 27 B.C. 410A.D.

Step 1 Excite

Early Rome was governed by kings. Later, a council known as the "senate" ruled over Rome; this period is known as the Roman Republic. The Roman Republic lasted from 510 B.C. until 27 B.C. It was a time of many wars: the first, the second and the third Punic War and the civil wars. (See the Roman Republic lesson.)

The political system of the Roman Empire established c. 27 B.C.,lasted for nearly five centuries. The Roman Senate gave Gaius Octavius the name Augustus (see previous lesson) and he became the undisputed emperor after years of bitter civil war. At its peak the empire included lands throughout the Mediterranean world. Rome had first expanded into other parts of Italy and neighboring territories during the Roman Republic (509-27 B.C.), but made wider conquests and solidified political control of these lands during the empire. The empire lasted until Germanic invasions, economic decline, and internal unrest in the 4th and 5th centuries A.D. ended Rome's ability to dominate such a large territory. The Romans and their empire gave cultural and political shape to the subsequent history of Europe from the Middle Ages and the Renaissance to the present day.[1]

Find a map of the Roman Empire to refer to as you study this lesson.

Watch a video. (Look for the videos below at your local video store, or watch television schedules for local listings.)

> Rome: Power and Glory, Volumes III and IV ◆
> Volume III - *Seduction of Power*: Bloody power struggles shape Rome's leadership as the republic gradually transforms into an empire. Volume IV - *Grasp of Empire*: Rome expands her boundaries across the Western world, bringing stability to the nations she conquers. But problems accompany this growth, including crippling taxes, slavery, disease, and a growing air of decadence. See description of this six-volume set in the Resources Section.

> Ancient Rome: The Story of an Empire That Ruled the World ◆
> (Volumes 2 and 3)
> Description: Volume 2: *The Age of Emperors* is a history of the end of the republic and Augustus's defeat of Marc Antony, as well as a biography of Julius Caesar. Volume 3: *Building an Empire* focuses on Rome's golden age and its still-visible heritage—including art and science, and the systems of laws and roads that still connect and direct Europeans' lives. See description of the four-volume set in the Resources Section.

Resources recommended in ◆several lessons, ★ several units, ● other HOW Units. ●—Key Resource (see beginning of unit or page 32).

The Roman Empire		
Period	**Dates**	**Events**
Republic to Empire	63-27 B.C.E.	60 Caesar, Marcus Crassus, and Pompey form first Triumvirate, in which three consuls share power. 52 Pompey is elected by the Senate to be sole consul; Caesar is declared an enemy of the Republic. 48 Caesar defeats Pompey at Pharsalus. 46 Caesar is made dictator of Rome. The Julian calendar was also introduced this year. 44 Caesar is assassinated by personal friend Marcus Brutus, Cassius, and others. 30 Octavian defeats Antony and Cleopatra; A New Roman era called the Principate or Early Empire begins.
The Founding of the Empire	27 B.C.	27 B.C.-A.D. 14 The Emperor Augustus 70-19 B.C.: Vergil 65-8 B.C.: Horace 43 B.C. to A.D. 18: Ovid 59 B.C. to A.D. 17: Livy
The Roman Empire		A.D. 13 Augustus consecrates altar to gods of state A.D. 14 Augustus' death A.D. 54 Nero becomes emperor A.D. 64 Rome burns, Nero blames Christians A.D. 70 Jerusalem destroyed A.D. 80 Colosseum completed A.D. 96 Nerva becomes emperor A.D. 180 Death of Marcus Aurelius A.D. 203 Arch of Septimus Severus constructed A.D. 211 Death of Septimus Severus A.D. 235 Maximinus becomes emperor A.D. 284 Diocletian becomes emperor A.D. 305 Diocletian retires A.D. 324 Constantine becomes sole emperor

Underlined text refers to Internet link at http://Homeschool-Books.com

To fully understand the magnitude of the Roman Empire, compare a map of the Roman Empire with a current map of Europe.

Step 2 Examine

Read Matthew 22:21; Mark 12:14,16-17; Luke 20:22,24-25; John 19:12; Acts 25:10 and Philippians 4:22.

Research the Roman Empire. Use any resource (an encyclopedia, nonfiction book, historical novel, or the Internet). We recommend the following:

Books

The Holman Bible Atlas ●— ♥
Read: "The Age of Augustus: Foundation of an Empire" (195-197).

The Usborne Book of the Ancient World ●— ★
Read: "The Expansion of Rome" (200-201).

Kingfisher History Encyclopedia ●— ♥
Read: All references to the Roman Empire in the index.

Kingfisher Illustrated History of the World ●— ♥
Read: "The Roman Empire" (118-119).

Ancient Rome (Eyewitness) ●— ♦
Read: "The Emperors" (8-9), "The Legionary" (10-11), "Battle and Defense" (12-13), "Soldiers in Society" (14-15), "Senators, Citizens, Subjects, Slaves" (16-17).

Ancient Civilizations ★
Read: "Ancient Rome" (42-43).

The Penguin Historical Atlas of Ancient Rome ●— ♦
Read: "From City to Empire" (12-13), "The Imperial Regime" (38-63). ▯

Caesar and Christ (Story of Civilization III) ♦
Read: Book III "The Principate" (210-318).

Streams of Civilizations: Earliest Times to Discovery ★
Read: "The Roman Empire" (157-177).

Resources recommended in ♦several lessons, ★ several units, ♥other HOW Units. ●—Key Resource (see beginning of unit or page 32).

Heart of Wisdom Publishing   611

The Roman Empire and the Dark Ages by Giovanni Caselli
Traces the history of the Roman Empire and the Dark Ages which followed through a description of common objects, tools, clothes, dwellings, food, and day-to-day activities of the people in both the cities and in the country. 48 pages (September 1998) Peter Bedrick Books; ISBN: 0872265633. Reading level: Ages 9-12.

Internet Sources

Roman History and Government
Description: Article from SPQR Online (a premier Web resource concerning ancient Rome) explaining Rome's history and leadership through its three political stages.

The Romans
Description: Excellent resource from the BBC for investigation of key aspects of Roman history. Outlines most areas of life and culture in ancient Rome. Read articles on the government, the army, and the empire.

The Birth of the Roman Empire
Description: This site is a slide-show presentation by a word-history teacher from Williston Senior High School. An excellent site for a good chronological overview of events during this period.

Ancient Roman Empire Timeline
Description: Time line of significant events in the formation and evolution of the Roman Empire, covering the period from 2000 B.C.E. to 568 C.E.

Step 3 Expand

Choose and complete one of the following activities:

Activity 1: Add to Your Time Line Book
The first five Roman emperors were Augustus, Tiberius, Caligula, Claudius I, and Nero. Write a summary for each emperor and add them to your Time Line Book. Tell of the struggles for the throne between rival military commanders.

Activity 2: Write a Synopsis
Write a synopsis of the imperial history of Rome. Answer these questions:
- How did all power become concentrated in the hands of a single ruler?
- How did the rulers keep the support of the Roman legions?

Underlined text refers to Internet link at http://Homeschool-Books.com

Activity 3: Answer Questions
Answer the following about the Roman Empire:
- How many men did the Senate recognize as emperors from A.D. 180 to 284?
- Who finally stopped the succession of short terms and abolished the last Republican liberties?
- How was the first step made toward dividing the Empire?
- What was the new role of the Senate?

Activity 4: Create a Web Site
Create a Web site about the imperial history of Rome. Limit the scope of what you try to cover. Include either the influence of Roman history on the writers of the Constitution or the relationship of Roman Christians to the cruel pagan government that controlled their world.

Activity 5: Think and Discuss
If Christians considered Christ king, could they be loyal to the emperor of the Roman State? Read and discuss the online article Kingdoms in Conflict.

Activity 6: Do Further Research
When did the Roman Senate confirm Octavian's powers to rule "imperium"? Octavian was the Roman ruler when Jesus was born in a province of the empire (Luke 2:1). Later he was granted new tribunician powers. List these powers. Octavian had taken the name "Caesar," which then came to be used as a title for the emperor. From the word "Caesar" were derived the titles "czar," applied to all the Russian emperors ("czar" was first spelled "tsesar") and "kaiser," applied to the German emperors. Learn how the Roman emperor and his family were identified with the majesty of the Roman state, and deified. Where else were rulers deified?

Step 4 Excel

Explain orally to your parents what you've learned in this lesson. Correct all written work to demonstrate correct punctuation and spelling, and effective use of grammar. Add corrected written work or any illustrations to your portfolio.

Footnotes
1. "Roman Empire." (1997-2001). Microsoft® Encarta® Online Encyclopedia 200.1 <http://encarta.msn.com> Microsoft Corporation.
2. Richard, Carl J. (1995). *The Founders and the Classics: Greece, Rome, and the American Enlightenment.* Belknap Press; ISBN: 0674314263.

Resources recommended in ◆several lessons, ★ several units, ♥other HOW Units. ●—Key Resource (see beginning of unit or page 32).

Heart of Wisdom Publishing   613

The Jewish Revolts A.D. 132-135

Step 1 Excite

By the time of Christ, Jews were widely dispersed throughout the cities and countryside of the Empire and beyond. In A.D. 66, the First Jewish Revolt against Rome broke out. The Roman army destroyed Jerusalem, killed over 1 million Jews, took about 100,000 into slavery, and destroyed the Temple in A.D. 70.

The Second Jewish Revolt took place between A.D. 132 and 135. A half-million Jews were killed; thousands were sold into slavery or taken into captivity. The rest were exiled from Palestine and scattered throughout the known world in what is called the "Diaspora."

Watch a video. (Look for the videos below at your local video store, or watch television schedules for local listings.)

Mysteries of the Bible: The Last Revolt
Description: Six hundred years after its construction, the Temple was the scene of an unlikely battle for freedom, as Jews fought impossible odds to repel legions of Roman soldiers. Of all of the peoples of the Near East, why did the Jews alone dare challenge the greatest imperial power the world had ever known? Why was Rome determined to prevail at any cost? And what happened to the sacred Temple when the siege finally broke through Jerusalem's walls? Join the world's leading archaeologists and scholars as they unravel the riddles of the Holy Temple—and the great Jewish revolt that destroyed it. (1995) ASIN: 6304340109.

Masada - The Complete Mini-Series
Description: This television miniseries, based on Ernest K. Gann's historical novel *The Antagonists*, is a dramatization of a documented revolt by nearly a thousand Jerusalem Jews against Roman oppressors in A.D. 72 to 73. Following a city-wide siege by Rome's soldiers, Jewish Zealots move into a fortress in the mountains of Masada, from which they present a defense strong enough to convince the enemy to negotiate. Peter O'Toole, in all his golden dignity, plays Cornelius Flavius Silva, commander of the Roman legions, and Peter Strauss is Zealot leader Eleazar ben Yair. Both are outstanding as representatives from each side trying, in good faith, to find a way out of the deadlocked situation. Unfortunately, neither realizes that Rome has no intention of yielding, resulting in one of the greatest tragedies in Jewish history (Tom Keogh, Amazon reviewer) ASIN: 0783222823.

Underlined text refers to Internet link at http://Homeschool-Books.com

Read Luke 19:41-44 and 21:20-24 to learn how Jesus had warned of the city's destruction during His ministry.

Step 2 Examine

> The second revolt was around 133 C.E. Simon Bar-Kosiba arose as a champion of Jewish nationalism, and was heralded by Rabbi Akiva as the Messiah, who renamed him Simon Bar-Kochba, "Simon Son of the Star." Bar-Kochba led the Jews in a revolt against Rome after Hadrian forbade circumcision, Torah study and observance of the Sabbath and Jewish holidays. The 3½-year rebellion cost many lives, and the Romans eventually won only by cutting off supplies to one stronghold after another until the Jews could no longer hold out. Bar-Kochba himself was finally taken with the last stronghold and Roman suspicion of the Jews and their religion was intensified, so the end result was a worsening of the Jewish condition.[1]

The earliest followers of Jesus were all Jewish and worshiped in the synagogues alongside those who did not follow Jesus. Tensions gradually increased between these two groups. A final blow to the relationship between these two groups within Judaism was the Bar Kochba rebellion in A.D. 132. Messianic Jewish believers (believers in Jesus), fought alongside their Jewish brethren during the first year of the revolt. But then, Rabbi Akiva declared Bar Kochba the Messiah. The Jewish believers in Jesus could no longer support this war since it would involve denying Jesus as Messiah. This was an enormous step in the gradual growing-apart of these two groups within Judaism.

After the Jewish revolt of A.D. 135, the Romans replaced the Latin name "Judea" with the Latin "Palaestina" as their name for this province.

Research the Jewish Revolts against Rome. Use any resource (an encyclopedia, nonfiction book, historical novel, or the Internet). We recommend the following:

Books

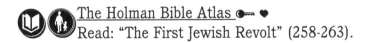
The Holman Bible Atlas ●— ♥
Read: "The First Jewish Revolt" (258-263).

History of the Jewish People Volume 1: Second Temple Era ★
Read: "From War Against Florus to War Against Rome" (165-171), "The War in Gallilee" (172-178), "Civil War in Besieged Jerusalem" (179-185), "Siege and Destruction" (186-194). See description in the Ancient Israel Resources Section.

Resources recommended in ♦several lessons, ★ several units, ♥other HOW Units. ●—Key Resource (see beginning of unit or page 32).

Heart of Wisdom Publishing   615

The Young Reader's Encyclopedia of Jewish History ★
Read: "Under the Yoke of Rome" (26-36). See description in the Ancient Israel Resources Section.

The Greco-Roman World of the New Testament Era ●– ♥
Read: "The Jewish Revolts" (139-140), "The Jews in the Cities" (211-219).

Our Father Abraham ●– ♥
Read: Chapter 6 "The Jewish Revolts and the Parting of the Way," and Chapter 7 "A History of Contempt, Anti-Semitism in the Church."

The Penguin Historical Atlas of Ancient Rome ●– ◆
Read: "Vespasian and the Jewish War" (58-59).

Ancient Israel: From Abraham to the Roman Destruction of the Temple ★
Read: Chapter 8 Roman Domination: The Jewish Revolt and the Destruction of the Second Temple. See description in the Ancient Israel Resources. []

Caesar and Christ (Story of Civilization III) ◆
Read: "The Rebellion" (543-545).

Restoring of the Early Church ●– ♥
Read: Chapter 5 "The Loss of Our Hebraic Roots." Includes details about the first and second Jewish Revolts. See description in the Ancient Israel Resources Section.

The Jewish War (The Penguin Classics) by Flavius Josephus
Description: Crossing from the Old Testament to the New Testament, *The Jewish War* covers what happened in the Intertestamental Period, such as the domination by the Greeks, the Maccabean revolt, and the destruction of Jerusalem in A.D. 70.

Internet Sources

The Great Revolt 66-73 C.E.
Description: Overview of the Second Jewish Revolt, and link to events that led up to this revolt.

Jewish Revolts (66-70 A.D. & 132-135 A.D.)
Description: Article explaining both revolts against Rome.

ⓘ Jewish Bar Kochba Revolt
Description: Article explaining the second revolt against Rome.

Step 3 Expand

Choose and complete one of the following activities:

Activity 1: Add to Your Time Line Book
Add the first and second Jewish Revolts to your Time Line Book. Include a summary of each revolt.

Activity 2: Answer Questions
From your research, answer the following: How many Roman legions were sent to bring the city back under Roman control? Who was the leader of the Roman army? When was the city captured and destroyed? What had happened to the rebels? After putting down the revolt, the emperors Vespasian and Titus authorized commemorative coins with the Latin inscription "judaea capta," meaning "Judah is captured."

Activity 3: Sketch a Picture
Look at a picture of the Titus Arch, which was built by Romans to commemorate the destruction of Jerusalem. Sketch a copy of a part of it.

Activity 4: Write an Essay
After you have read the historical narrative by Josephus, analyze the assumptions and prejudices he had when he wrote. Whom did the author blame for the revolt? Did he show sympathy for his people or for the Romans? Assess the strength of the evidence presented. Compare the differences between historical facts and historical interpretations. Consider multiple perspectives. Look up and compare the historical event in another source. Document your findings in a summary paragraph, and in an essay. Refer to "Contrasting and Comparing" in *Writers INC*.

Step 4 Excel

Share what you have learned about the the Jewish Revolts with a friend or family member. Correct all written work to demonstrate correct punctuation and spelling, and effective use of grammar. Add corrected written work or any illustrations to your portfolio.

Footnotes
1. Brown, David W. "Messianic Hope and Disappointment" <http://www.amfi.org/mhope.htm> (Accessed June, 2000)

Resources recommended in ◆several lessons, ★ several units, ♥other HOW Units. ◉━Key Resource (see beginning of unit or page 32).

Heart of Wisdom Publishing   617

Barbarian Invasions A.D. 235

Step 1 Excite

Are you, or anyone you know, descended from the barbarians of northern Europe? Have you ever considered God's mercy and power in how He transformed the cultures of the ancient tribes in northern Europe? Have you ever praised and thanked God for his goodness and love towards these "barbarian" tribes, in bringing to them the Gospel? Take time now to thank God for His mighty work of salvation in the tribes of northern Europe during the time of the Roman Empire.

Read a story about this time period. We recommend the following:

Beric the Briton, A Story of the Roman Invasion by G.A. Henty
Description: The invasion of Britain by the Roman legionaries is the setting for this story. Beric, a boy-chief of a British tribe, takes a prominent part in the insurrection against Rome under Boadicea. These efforts are useless against the might of the Roman army. For a short time, Beric and his companions continue the fight, but are ultimately defeated and taken as prisoners to Rome. Through the eyes of Beric, the reader will learn of life in Rome, the gladiatorial schools, the great fire, and life in Nero's court. (July 18, 1999) PrestonSpeed Publications; ISBN: 1887159363.

Outcast by Rosemary Sutcliff
Description: A fictional story of a young boy named Beric, who is raised in the village of a Celtic tribe living in Britain at the time of the Roman conquest. (October 1995) Sunburst; ISBN: 0374456739. Reading level: Young adult.

Step 2 Examine

Barbarian tribes who lived in what is now Europe poured into the Roman Empire after A.D. 200. The term "barbarians" was used by the Romans to describe uncivilized people living outside their empire. Historians use the term "barbarians" to describe the native tribes of Europe before their culture was significantly modified by contact with classical/Christian civilization. There are three main groups of barbarians:

1. Celtic peoples: Original homeland was central Europe. As Greek and Roman power spread, they either lost their identity or clung to it and migrated farther west.

---

2. Germanic peoples: A large family of tribes including Vandals, Goths, Burgundians, and numerous others.

3. Slavic peoples: The native tribes of Eastern Europe, whose descendants today live in Russia, the Czech Republic and Slovakia, Poland, the Balkans (Serbian areas of Yugoslavia, etc.), and elsewhere in Eastern Europe.

Famous barbarians include Alaric, Boadicea, Theodoric, Attila the Hun, Clovis, and Charlemagne. Attila the Hun was known as the Scourge of God, led various tribes of Mongoloid peoples, and invaded the Roman Empire from A.D. 436 to 453. Attila murdered his brother in A.D. 436 to gain sole control over the Hunnish Empire.

Do more research about the barbarians who inhabited Europe during the rule of the Roman Empire. Use any resource (an encyclopedia, non-fiction book, historical novel, or the Internet). *Be careful using search engines for this topic.* Many of the "Barbarian" sites on the Internet are full of explicit art, fantasy games, witchcraft, and other things objectionable to Christians. We recommend the following:

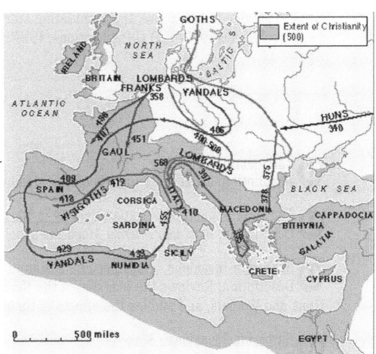

Books

The Usborne Book of the Ancient World ●— ★
Read: "Barbarians" (219).

Kingfisher History Encyclopedia ●— ♥
Read: "Barbarians" (82-83).

Kingfisher Illustrated History of the World ●— ♥
Read: "The Barbarians" (143-146).

Streams of Civilizations: Earliest Times to Discovery ★
Read: "German Life" (172-175).

Resources recommended in ◆several lessons, ★ several units, ♥other HOW Units. ●—Key Resource (see beginning of unit or page 32).

Heart of Wisdom Publishing   619

The Penguin Historical Atlas of Ancient Rome ●━ ◆
Read: "The Inheritors" (134-135). ⬚

Caesar and Christ (Story of Civilization III) ◆
Read: "The Barbarians" (478-481).

Usborne's Empires and Barbarians
Description: A book from the Usborne Picture World History series. Clear text and lively, labeled illustrations introduce children to the history of the world. Prepared with the help of experts in each period, each book has lots of illustrations to provide an attractive and stimulating starting point to each subject. Paperback (June 1979) E D C Publications; ISBN: 0860201430. Reading Level: Ages 8-12.

Internet Sources

Early Germanic States
Description: Online reference book for Medieval Studies.

The Development of Christian Society in Early England
Description: Britannia Internet Magazine article.

Barbarian Invasions - Encyclopedia Britannica
Description: Reviews the invasion of the Roman Empire by barbarian Goths, Huns and Vandals, and studies the effects of their expansion into Roman territory.

Barbarian Invasions - Map
Description: Color map depicting the migratory expansion of the barbarian Goths, Huns, and Vandals into the Roman Empire.

Barbarian Invasions - Timeline
Description: Time line chronicles the tumultuous barbarian invasions into the Roman Empire and Medieval Europe from A.D. 200 to 1000.

Barbarian Invasions into the Later Roman Empire - Map
Description: Two-color map showing the migratory routes of the Vandals, Visigoths, Ostrogoths, and Huns into the Roman empire.

Barbarian Invasions of the 5th and 6th Centuries - Map
Description: Map depicts the invasion routes of the expansionist barbarian tribes of the Huns, Goths, and Vandals during the 5th and 6th centuries A.D.

Step 3 Expand

Choose and complete one of the following activities:

Activity 1: Make a Chart
Record main facts about barbarian tribes in the form of a chart on poster board. Include a row for each: the Celts (the people of eastern and northern Europe), the Franks, the Goths, the Saxons, and the Visigoths. Include columns explaining: Where each tribe came from; How they received their names; What kind of governments they had; Periods of prosperity in their civilizations; Towns they built; Art; Technology; Professions; Trade partners; Favorite entertainment; Clothing; Religion.

Activity 2: Make a Map
Learn how the northern barbarians came down to Italy to invade the Empire. Write down the names of the tribes: Goths, Huns, Lombards, and Vandals. Draw arrows on a map of Europe, showing where each came from.

Activity 3: Write a Report
Write a report about your celebration of God's salvation of barbarian people. Explain how you celebrated, who participated, and what the celebration meant to the participants.

Activity 4: Read a Story
Find a translation of *Beowulf* to read aloud. The story is set before Christian missionaries came to the barbarians, but the storytellers are Christians and so glory is given to God throughout the tale. Prepare a short introduction about original storytellers long ago, and present *Beowulf* to an adventurous audience. To make it even more fun, dress as a barbarian! You can read *Beowulf* online at http://www.lone-star.net/literature/beowulf/beowulf.html

Step 4 Excel

Share what you have learned about the Barbarians with a friend or family member. Correct all written work to demonstrate correct punctuation and spelling, and effective use of grammar. Add corrected written work or any illustrations to your portfolio.

Resources recommended in ◆several lessons, ★ several units, ♥ other HOW Units. ●━Key Resource (see beginning of unit or page 32).

Heart of Wisdom Publishing   621

Constantine A.D. 361-395

Step 1 Excite

There are many conflicting views about Constantine, an Emperor of Rome. Catholics see him as the Messiah for the church. Historians call him a magnificent ruler endowed by God. Jews and Messianics see him as an anti-Semite on the level of Hitler. Idolaters of his time gave him honor as a pagan god on his deathbed. Eusebius viewed him as a quasi-divine figure.

Constantine claimed conversion to Christianity, and considered himself the leader in the Christian church at the time of the Council of Nicaea (A.D. 325). Christians in Rome were persecuted (See the Christianity Lesson in this unit) until Constantine's conversion; then it became an economic advantage to be a Christian.

Constantine and his mother, Helen, made a pilgrimage to Jerusalem and began excavations to recover artifacts in the city. This popularized the tradition of pilgrimages in Christianity. In 314 he placed the symbol of the cross on his coins along with the marks of Roman gods, Sol Invictus and Mars Conservator. Constantine retained the title of chief priest of the state cult until he died, although he was baptized on his deathbed. After his death, the political leaders of his land gave Constantine the status of a pagan god.

One historian explains how Constantine removed some paganism but left behind much:

> Shortly after Diocletian, the emperor Constantine converted to Christianity, and all the charming archaic features of paganism, naked athletes at the Olympics, priestesses of Apollo in trances, ithyphallic Hermae on street corners, priests of Astarte cutting off their genitals, orgiastic Dionysiacs, etc., began to disappear. … Constantine then built his New Rome, a Christian Rome, decorated with the spoils of the dying paganism (including great bronze horses from Delphi, later relocated to Venice, and the Wonder of the World Statue of Zeus from Olympia, whose face evidently inspired portraits of Christ[1]), but also with its own Senate, its own chariot races (in the hippodrome), its own factional riots, and its own grain subsidies, drawn from Egypt and North Africa like those of Rome itself. [2]

When Constantine made Christianity Rome's official religion, Christians were no longer persecuted by the pagans. However, Constantine ordered the persecution of all Jews, including the Jewish followers of Christ, by taking away their legal rights. Constantine issued laws forbidding Jewish believers to keep Saturday as the Sabbath, circumcise their children, celebrate Passover, etc. The punishments included imprisonment, and even death.

Underlined text refers to Internet link at http://Homeschool-Books.com

He made many changes to Christianity. Under his rule, many ideas and pagan practices of Mithras were incorporated into Christianity, and carry over to churches today. Constantine replaced the Biblical Holidays with alternative forms of celebrations adopted from other religions. The biblical festivals were replaced by the traditional holidays of Constantine's time. He made December 25th, the birthday of the pagan Unconquered Sun god, the official birthday of Jesus. He also instituted celebrating Easter and Lent based on pagan holidays. Constantine made these changes from 330-337 to separate all Jewish association from Christianity. He was trying to suggest that Jesus was a Christian, not a Jew, which meant that he could continue persecuting the Jews.

The church, largely Gentile in makeup, would now become "de-Judaized"—severed from its Jewish roots. This de-Judaizing developed into a history of anti-Judaism, a travesty that has extended from the second century to the present day.

Watch a video. (Look for the videos below at your local video store, or watch television schedules for local listings.)

Hail Caesar Volume V: Constantine ◆▯
Modern scholars explore Constantine's conversion to Christianity. Location footage from twenty-three countries shows the splendid ruins of Imperial Rome. Originally seen on A&E's "Biography." See full description of the six-volume series in the Resources Section.

Biography: Constantine: The Christian Emperor
Biography explores Constantine's life and legacy through ancient art and artifacts, expert commentary and historic re-enactments. Trace his 20-year struggle to take control of the splintered empire, and see how he restored it to its former glory through masterful diplomacy and the judicious use of force. Explore the dramatic story of his conversion, and the momentous changes in the Empire and the world that resulted. And walk the streets of the city he founded as the capital of his reborn empire. This is the definitive portrait of the ruler who saved his nation and transformed the world—Constantine the Great.

Step 2 Examine

Find several articles about Constantine from both Christian and secular resources. Use these primary resources to build original historical interpretations about Constantine. Analyze interpretations of events from the perspectives of various groups, and evaluate the credibility of differing accounts. Make a list of the conflicts you find. Use any resource (an encyclopedia, nonfiction book, historical novel, or the Internet). We recommend the following:

Resources recommended in ◆several lessons, ★ several units, ♥ other HOW Units. ●—Key Resource (see beginning of unit or page 32).

Heart of Wisdom Publishing   623

The Usborne Book of the Ancient World ●— ★
Read: "The Empire After Constantine" (257).

The Penguin Historical Atlas of Ancient Rome ●— ♦
Read: "Constantine the Great" (126-127).

Caesar and Christ (Story of Civilization III) ♦
Read: "The Rise of Constantine" (653-664).

Internet Sources

Constantine the Great
Description: *Encarta* article.

Anti-Judaism and the Council of Nicaea by Rick Aharon Chaimberlin
Description: Article from From *Petah Tikvah Magazine*.

Legitimization Under Constantine
Description: Article from the site "From Jesus to Christ."

The Emperor Constantine and Jerusalem
Description: Article from the Jerusalem Mosaic site.

Constantine the Great (A.D. ca. 285-A.D. 337)
Description: Article from the site RomanEmpire.net.

Step 3 Expand

Choose and complete one of the following activities:

Activity 1: Add to Your Time Line Book
Add Constantine to your Time Line Book. Include a summary.

Activity 2: Contrast and Compare
Write a summary explaining how the Roman Empire in the time of Constantine differed from the Roman Empire of the past.

Activity 3: Make a Map
Research and re-create maps of the Roman Empire during Constantine's reign and other reigns. Use these maps to illustrate the differences in the Roman Empire under different emperors.

Underlined text refers to Internet link at http://Homeschool-Books.com

Activity 4: Write a Summary

Write a summary explaining Constantine's conversion to Christianity. How did it occur? What were some of the reactions of the people of the Roman Empire to Constantine's conversion?

Activity 5: Answer Questions

The following questions are recommended by A&E in the Classroom to use before and after watching the video *Hail Caesar Volume II: Constantine: The Christian Emperor*:

1. Things began to go wrong in the Roman Empire in the third century. Why was the Roman Empire under siege? Who challenged Rome for supremacy? How did this affect the empire?
2. How was the Roman Empire in the time of Constantine different than the Roman Empire of the past?
3. Constantine came from a humble background—his mother was a barmaid. How did Constantine rise from such humble beginnings to be one of the most powerful men in the world?
4. Compare Constantine's Rome with Hadrian's Rome.
5. Constantine's father tried to arrange a politically advantageous marriage for his son, but Constantine refused. Why did Constantine refuse to marry the girl his father chose to be his wife?
6. Although it is impossible to know the exact population of Christians in the third century, historians estimate it to be between two and ten percent. If Christians were such a numeric minority, why were they so feared? Why did Christians have so much influence, good and bad, in the Roman Empire?
7. Why did pagans find Christians to be offensive?
8. Constantine changed the course of history when he converted to Christianity. How did Constantine's conversion occur?
9. What were some of the reactions of the people of the Roman Empire to Constantine's conversion?
10. How did Constantine's conversion help determine the course of European history and Western Civilization?

Activity 6: Write an Article

Write an article, as if for a magazine, about Constantine's life and significance. Use a wide variety of primary and secondary sources that present conflicting interpretations. Use at least five different sources for your research. Include this information:

• His parents
• His young years
• Where he started to rule as Caesar
• How he gained power over Rome

Resources recommended in ◆several lessons, ★ several units, ● other HOW Units. ●—Key Resource (see beginning of unit or page 32).

Heart of Wisdom Publishing   625

- How he ruled
- Who helped him
- The policy of tolerance of Christianity
- The drastic changes he made in the early church
- The Council of Nicaea
- The influence of Christian teachings upon his laws
- His cruelty toward members of his family
- His three sons

Activity 7: Expand Your Research

Constantine was a pagan who followed the religion of Mithras, the most powerful and influential religion in the first to the fourth centuries. In actuality, Christianity was a distant second to Mithras. Upon the conversion of his mother, Constantine became tolerant of Christianity and later forbade the persecution of Christians. Upon the formation of the church and its council of Nicaea in A.D. 325, he proclaimed himself the head of the church. He forced certain decisions and had a great deal of influence in church decisions, but at no time during this period was he a Christian. He was reported to have seen a cross in the sky, and in the vision a voice told him that under this sign he would conquer and rule. Some church history reports this as the cross of the crucifixion. Other historians report that what he actually saw was the cross of Mithras, which was the "tau" or known as the Egyptian "ankh" (a cross with a loop on top). Do further research on this topic. Was there fruit in Constantine's life?

Step 4 Excel

Share your work from Step 3 with someone. Explain what you have learned in this lesson. Correct written work to demonstrate correct punctuation and spelling, and effective use of grammar. Add corrected written work or any illustrations to your portfolio.

Footnotes

1. The video "The Seven Wonders of the Ancient World" reveals the amazing resemblance of art depicting the Messiah and the Statue of Zeus.
2. Jones, A. (1986). *The Later Roman Empire: 284-602*, Johns Hopkins Univ Pr; ISBN: 0801832853.

Underlined text refers to Internet link at http://Homeschool-Books.com

The Birth of Christianity A.D. 379

Step 1 Excite

Discuss what you know about the church's beginnings. Was Jesus the founder of Christianity? When did Christianity become separate from Judaism?

Imagine and discuss what it would be like if laws in your country were passed to put to death all those who professed to believe in Jesus. What if your family and friends who refused to renounce Christ were put to a gruesome death by fighting in arenas with wild animals or gladiators? Imagine that your friends and family were driven underground to survive.

Watch a video. (Look for the videos below at your local video store, or watch television schedules for local listings.)

Rome: Power and Glory, Volume V: The Cult of Order ◆
When the Roman people grow weary of the Empire's moral decay many turn to Christianity. As these beliefs spread, however, the emperor's influence wanes and Christians fall subject to cruel oppression. See description of this six-volume set in the Resources Section.

Ancient Rome: The Story of an Empire That Ruled the World ◆
Volume 4, "The Enduring Legacy," looks at Rome's early indifference to Christianity and how this religion came to dominate the world through Rome's dominance, even as the empire itself was about to crumble. See description of this four-volume set in the Resources Section.

Step 2 Examine

Christianity was conceived in an environment in which there was a general acceptance of Canaanite, Egyptian, Greek, and Roman gods. The Canaanite god Baal, the Egyptian god Amon, and the Persian god Ahura Mazda were identified with the Greek god Zeus. The Romans called him Jupiter. Only the Hebrews worshiped the one true God.

Jesus was born, lived, and died in a small corner of the Roman Empire. During His lifetime the Romans allowed the Jews to practice their faith and did not make them worship Roman gods.

Resources recommended in ◆several lessons, ★ several units, ● other HOW Units. ●━Key Resource (see beginning of unit or page 32).

Heart of Wisdom Publishing   627

Jesus was a faithful and observant Jew. He loved the Torah and observed it with the deepest faithfulness and spiritual dedication. He lived by it until his last breath. In the first century, there were literally hundreds of thousands of Jews that believed in Jesus (Acts 2:41,47, 4:4; 6:7; 9:31; 21:20). Very few Gentiles converted before Peter and Paul were sent out to spread the good news to the Gentiles. When God miraculously showed the believing Jews that Jesus was the Messiah for both Jew and Gentile alike, then Gentiles from every nation began to pour into this Jewish faith. The followers of Christ, whether Jewish or Gentile, were seen as one family. Both considered themselves part of Israel. The Gentiles saw themselves as grafted into Israel (Romans 11), not replacing Israel.

By the end of the 1st century A.D. three main movements remained:

1. Pauline Christians: A group of mainline congregations, largely of non-Jewish Christians.
2. Gnostic Christians: Later declared heretics by a series of church councils, and suppressed.
3. Jewish Christians: Remnants of the group originally headed by James, and including Jesus' disciples. Rejected by traditional Judaism because of their faith in Yeshua, and rejected by Christianity as well because they continued their Jewish way of life, Messianic Jews dwindled in numbers until, in the fourth century, they ceased to be a cohesive community.

The word "Christian" was not used until A.D. 42 in Antioch (Acts 11:26). Later, it was adopted to set apart Jews believing in Jesus from unbelieving Jews. Ultimately, it became an identity for the entire Church.

Christianity was first ignored, then persecuted, and finally supported by the Roman government. But it continued to grow, and it became a menace to the empire, threatening to exalt itself above the Caesar. Laws were passed to put to death those who professed belief in Jesus of Nazareth. The Church was driven underground, even into the Catacombs under Rome. When Christians were caught, they were told to renounce their faith in Jesus; if they would not, they were killed. Many times, the method of execution was a sporting event in front of the citizens of the Roman Empire. This was intended to send a clear message to all. Some were put into arenas with wild animals, some into arenas with gladiators. Some were simply put to a gruesome death. In spite of the extreme penalties, this sect called Christians continued to grow and multiply. (Jesus spoke of "persecutions" coming upon His followers in Matt. 5:10-12 and 10:23.)

By the time of the Council of Nicaea (A.D. 325), Constantine, Emperor of Rome, claimed conversion to Christianity and considered himself the leader in the Christian church. He even made it the official religion of the Empire, though he himself worshiped the sun. Life changed drastically for the Gentile believers; they were no longer persecuted. The Jews who accepted Jesus as the Messiah were forced to give up all ties with Judaism, Jewish practices, Jewish friends, and anything Jewish.

Research Christianity's beginnings in Rome. Use any resource (an encyclopedia, nonfiction book, historical novel, or the Internet). We recommend the following:

Books

Encyclopedia of the Bible (Nelson's Illustrated) ◉⇌ ♥
"The Birth of Christianity" (42-43), "The Earliest Christians" (172-173).

The Usborne Book of the Ancient World ◉⇌ ★
Read: "Alternatives to State Religion" (257).

The Greco-Roman World of the New Testament Era ◉⇌ ♥
Read: "Influences on Christian Organization" (71-88).▯

The Penguin Historical Atlas of Ancient Rome ◉⇌ ◆
Read: "The Spread of Christianity" (124-125).

Caesar and Christ (Story of Civilization III) ◆
Read: Book V "The Youth of Christianity" (552-664).

Our Father Abraham ◉⇌ ♥
Read: Chapter 6 "The Jewish Revolts and the Parting of the Way," and Chapter 7 "A History of Contempt, Anti-Semitism in the Church."

Sketches of Church History From A.D. 33 to the Reformation
Read: Chapter 1 "The Age of the Apostles (A.D. 33-100)" (Available online).

Restoring of the Early Church ◉⇌ ♥
Read: Chapter 7 "The Roman Conquest of the Church"(See description in the Ancient Israel Resources Section).

Jesus & the Rise of Early Christianity: A History of New Testament Times by Paul Barnett
Description: The pathway to understanding the New Testament leads through the vibrant landscape of the first-century Greco-Roman world. The New Testament is rooted in the concrete historical events of that world. We cannot understand the rise of Christianity apart from this. This is the story of Jesus, the Messiah of Israel, and the spiritual and intellectual impact which he had on his immediate followers and those who succeeded them. Barnett offers fresh insights. In its engagement with contemporary scholarship and its emphasis on the propelling

Resources recommended in ◆several lessons, ★ several units, ♥other HOW Units. ◉⇌Key Resource (see beginning of unit or page 32).

Heart of Wisdom Publishing   629

role of the historical and risen Jesus in the rise of Christianity, this book provides a timely rejoinder to current revisionism in the exploration of Christian origins. Hardcover - 500 pages (November 1999) Intervarsity Pr; ISBN: 0830815880.

Introduction to the History of Christianity by Tim Dowley (Editor) ♥ Description: The 2,000-year history of Christianity is a dramatic, intriguing, and often surprising story, told here by more than sixty specialists from ten countries in the most popular one-volume illustrated reference book on church history ever published. The book's strong points include readability, easy transition from one time period to another, a "bird's-eye-view" of church history, highlights concerning most important ideas and/or events, and a good presentation of the unity of Christian faith throughout the centuries, countries, and denominations. Hardcover - 688 pages (July 1995) Augsburg Fortress Publishing; ISBN: 0800629353.

Backgrounds of Early Christianity by Everett Ferguson Description: Widely used as a textbook since its publication in 1987, this work provides an analytical and systematic introduction to the Roman, Greek, and Jewish political, social, literary, and religious backgrounds necessary for a historical understanding of the New Testament and the early church. Now, Everett Ferguson has thoroughly revised *Backgrounds of Early Christianity*, completely updating the bibliographies, rewriting and adding sections, and incorporating many of the critical suggestions received from professors who have used his book. As a result, the book will inform today's students even better than before. Paperback - 611 pages 2nd edition (September 1993) Wm. B. Eerdmans Publishing Co.; ISBN: 0802806694.

Judaism and Christianity in First-Century Rome ♦ See description in the Resource section.

Internet Sources

The Birth of Christianity Description: Concise article about Christianity's beginnings.

The Transformation of Rome from a Pagan into a Christian City by Rodolfo Lanciani Description: Chapter One from *Pagan and Christian Rome*, originally published by Houghton, Mifflin and Company Boston and New York, 1892.

Christian Origins and the New Testament by James Tabor Description: An overview of Christian origins and the New Testament, by the author of The Jewish Roman World of Jesus.

The Birth and Rise of the Christian Church
Description: Links to several historical articles about Christianity's beginnings.

Christian Churches by Rodolfo Lanciani
Description: Chapter Three from *Pagan and Christian Rome*, originally published by Houghton, Mifflin and Company Boston and New York, 1892.

The Collision With Paganism by Wayne A. Meeks
Description: Article by Woolsey Professor of Biblical Studies, Yale University.

The Catacombs: A Place of Hiding and Worship For the Early Church
Description: An explanation of why Christians used these underground rooms and passageways.

Chronology and History of Early Christianity
Description: A time line of events in early Christianity.

Christian Catacombs
Description: This site is intended for people who wish to deepen their knowledge of the Christian Catacombs of Rome and of the Church history in its origins. It provides extensive material, in separate sections, dealing with this fascinating and largely unknown topic.

Step 3 Expand

Choose and complete one of the following activities:

Activity 1: Write a Story
Write a fictional story depicting the effect that seeing a Christian martyred for his faith might have on a pagan Roman. Choose either a pagan main character who witnessed an execution or a Christian main character who observes the reaction to his imprisonment of an unbelieving friend. The conflict of the story should be an inner conflict, a struggle between doubt and faith. Younger students can narrate (orally tell) their story.

Activity 2: Answer Questions
Little is known of Nero's alleged persecution of Christians after the fire in Rome in A.D. 64. Learn about the severest persecutions that came during the reigns of the emperors Domitian, Marcus Aurelius, Decius, and Valerian. Investigate the Roman persecution of Christians. Who made the attempt to extin-

Resources recommended in ◆several lessons, ★ several units, ● other HOW Units. ●—Key Resource (see beginning of unit or page 32).

Heart of Wisdom Publishing   631

guish Christianity altogether? Who was Julian the Apostate? Where did Christians have to hide? What were the stories of Vibia Perpetua, Polycarp, and Justin Martyr?

Activity 3: Write a Summary
Write a summary explaining why many Romans that were not spiritual converted to Christianity.

Activity 4: Write a Short Work
Write a short work of historical fiction based on the martyrdom of either Vibia Perpetua, Justin Martyr, or Polycarp.

Activity 5:Create a Monologue
Write a fictional story, turning it into a monologue. Portray your main character in a soliloquy, as if he is speaking aloud his inner struggles.

Step 4 Excel

Share what you have learned about the Gentile Christians and Jewish believers in Rome with a friend or family member. Correct written work to demonstrate correct punctuation and spelling, and effective use of grammar. Add corrected written work or any illustrations to your portfolio.

The Fall of the Roman Empire

Step 1 Excite

Watch a-video. (Look for the videos below at your local video store, or watch television schedules for local listings.)

The Fall of the Roman Empire
Description: Hollywood's story about a dying ruler's efforts to prevent his mad son from inheriting the throne. The Roman general Livius follows the precepts of Marcus Aurelius, in hopes of creating an empire at peace within and without its borders. The accession of the unstable Commodus puts this goal in jeopardy. Considered above-average by critics due to strong performances and an intelligent script. Enjoyable for fans of lavish epics. Starring: Sophia Loren, Alec Guinness. Director: Anthony Mann. (Caution: some romance and immodest dress.)

Rome: Power and Glory, Volume VI: The Fall ♦
Rome's grasp finally weakens due to invasions, an enormous bureaucracy, an overtaxed populace and arrogant rulers. The Emperor Constantine moves the Empire east, clearing the way for anarchy. See description of this six-volume set in the Resources Section.

Ancient Rome: The Story of an Empire That Ruled the World ♦
Volume 4, "The Enduring Legacy," looks at Rome's early indifference to Christianity and how this religion came to dominate the world through Rome's dominance, even as the empire itself was about to crumble. See description of this four-volume set in the Resources Section.

Step 2 Examine

Rome's Decline and Fall covers a vast period of time—beginning at Rome in the reign of the first emperor, Augustus (31 B.C.-A.D. 14), and ending with the fall and capture of Constantinople in 1453. There were many causes of the collapse of the Roman Empire. Look at some of the following and discuss why they could have led to Rome's fall:

* The empire became too large to control politically.
* The military became weak.
* The morale of the people declined.

Resources recommended in ♦several lessons, ★ several units, ♥other HOW Units. ☛Key Resource (see beginning of unit or page 32).

Heart of Wisdom Publishing   633

- Christianity spread and interfered with the methods of the ruling powers.
- Large irrigation projects required water to be stored in large reservoirs (malaria).
- Germanic neighbors of the Roman Empire assimilated themselves into the empire.

Investigate the Fall of Rome. The fundamental seriousness that had characterized the conduct of ancient Rome was gone. The passion for a life of luxury existed in all classes. The poor had their panem et circenses ('pan-em-et-kir-'kan-sas)—"bread and circuses." What did this phrase describe? The middle class had almost disappeared. Roman society became stagnant—politically, industrially, and mentally. The old Roman Empire fell into weakness and decline. Learn about Gaul's invasion of Italy and the sacking of Rome. How do you understand the meaning of the phrase "the geese saved Rome"? Who was the last ruler of the West? When and by whom was he deposed?

Use any resource for your research (an encyclopedia, nonfiction book, historical novel, or the Internet). We recommend the following:

Books

The Usborne Book of the Ancient World ●— ★
Read: "The End of the Roman Republic" (204-205), "The Early Republic" (216-217), "The Empire After Constantine" (270-271), and "The Byzantine Empire" (272-273).

Kingfisher History Encyclopedia ●— ♥
Read: "The Roman Empire 27 B.C.-A.D. 475" (64-65).

Kingfisher Illustrated History of the World ●— ♥
Read: "The Decline of Rome" (140-145).

The Penguin Historical Atlas of Ancient Rome ●— ♦
Read: Part V "Restoration and Fall" (114-135).

Caesar and Christ (Story of Civilization III) ♦
Read: "The Collapse of the Empire" (620-645).

Streams of Civilizations: Earliest Times to Discovery ★
Read: "Fall of the Roman Republic" (150-155).

The Decline and Fall of the Roman Empire: An Abridged Version (Penguin Classics) by Edward Gibbon
Description: British parliamentarian and soldier Edward Gibbon (1737-1794) conceived of his plan for Decline and Fall while "musing amid the ruins of the Capitol" on a visit to Rome. For the next ten years he worked away at his great history, which traces the decadence of the late empire from the time of the Antonines and

the rise of Western Christianity. "The confusion of the times, and the scarcity of authentic memorials, pose equal difficulties to the historian, who attempts to preserve a clear and unbroken thread of narration," he writes. Despite these obstacles, *Decline and Fall* remains a model of historical exposition, and required reading for students of European history. (Amazon review).

Internet Sources

The Fall of Rome
Description: Some of the most interesting and widely articulated theories about the fall of Rome.

Rome's Decline and Christianity's Ascent
Description: Chapter 24 from Antiquity Online, "Rome and Christianity from A.D. 200 to 306."

Fall of Roman Empire - Live!
Description: LookSmart Live! community member recommends a series of guides, essays, stories, and theories on why the Roman Empire fell.

Temple of Serapis - Destruction of Paganism
Description: An excerpt from *The Decline and Fall of the Roman Empire* by Edward Gibbon. A description of the destruction of the temple of Serapis.

The Fall of the Roman Empire
Description: A summary sheet in outline form.

The "Best of" Edward Gibbon's Decline and Fall of the Roman Empire
Description: A list of inspiring quotations, in context and cross-indexed, from the classic *The Decline and Fall of the Roman Empire* by Edward Gibbon.

Poem: The Fall of Rome
Description: A brief poem from the Academy of American Poets.

Fall of Rome, Christianity and the Barbarian Invasions
Description: Lecture supplement features resources for the study of the barbarian invasions of the crumbling Roman Empire and the rise of Christianity.

Resources recommended in ♦several lessons, ★ several units, ♥other HOW Units. ☜Key Resource (see beginning of unit or page 32).

Heart of Wisdom Publishing   635

Chronology of Ancient Rome
Description: Provides a chronological history of Rome, beginning with the Etruscans in the eighth century B.C.E. and ending with the fall of Rome in 568 C.E.

Step 3 Expand

Choose and complete one of the following activities:

Activity 1: Discuss the Fall of the Roman Empire
Discuss the different reasons given for the decline and fall of the Roman Empire. What lessons can be learned from this decline and fall?

Activity 2: Write a Summary
Write a summary of what you have earned about the fall of the Roman Empire. Younger students can narrate (orally tell) what they have learned.

Step 4 Excel

Share what you have learned about the fall of the Roman Empire with a friend or family member. Correct written work to demonstrate correct punctuation and spelling, and effective use of grammar. Add corrected written work or any illustrations to your portfolio.

Science in Ancient Rome

Step 1 Excite

Brainstorm and discuss roads, aqueducts, and bridges. How many of these do you think are still in use? Make a list of some of the places where Roman roads and bridges are still in use.

Step 2 Examine

Research Roman engineering accomplishments such as aqueducts, bridges, glass making, sewers, roads, pesticides, refrigeration, sewers, fish farming, eye operations, lighthouses, tunneling, and watermills. Use any resource (an encyclopedia, nonfiction book, historical novel, or the Internet). We recommend the following:

Books

Usborne Book of Discovery: Inventors/Scientists/Explorers ♥
Read: All references to Rome in the index.

Ancient Rome (Eyewitness) ⊙– ◆
Read: "Builders and Engineers" (26-27), "Writing it all Down" (40-41), "Craftsworkers and Technology" (42-43), "First Catch Your Dormouse" (44-46).

Caesar and Christ (Story of Civilization III) ◆
Read: "Roman Science" (307-310), "Roman Medicine" (311-314), "The Engineers" (326-327), "The Progress of Science" (502-506).

Internet Sources

Agricultural Machinery of Rome
Description: Essay examining the various types of agricultural machinery used in ancient Rome and Greece. Offers blueprints and technical drawings.

Roman Technology - Electronic Passport
Description: Studies the development of Roman engineering technology and its use in the empire's many great public building projects.

Resources recommended in ◆several lessons, ★ several units, ♥other HOW Units. ⊙–Key Resource (see beginning of unit or page 32).

Heart of Wisdom Publishing   637

Ancient Roman Technology
Description: Directory of articles on the development and use of technology in ancient Rome. Research the tools used in arts, warfare, and basic survival.

History of Plumbing
Description: Explore the origins of plumbing in the ancient Roman bath houses. Features photos.

Roman Roads
Description: Extensive project devoted to research of ancient Roman roads. See photos of original roadways, and view maps of the Roman roads.

Step 3 Expand

Choose and complete one of the following activities:

Activity 1: Add to Your Time Line Book
As you study the different scientific inventions and discoveries during this period, add each to your Time Line Book.

Activity 2: Make a Model
Make a model of a Roman bridge.

Activity 2: Make a Model
After researching how Roman roads were constructed, make a model using pebbles, stones, sand, and broken tiles. Don't forget the curbstones.

Activity 3: Draw a Picture
Draw pictures of glass vessels in the styles that the Romans produced.

Activity 4: Make an Educational Display
Use the models that you made to assemble an educational display titled "Technology in Ancient Rome."

Step 4 Excel

Explain orally to your parents what you've learned in this lesson. Correct all written work to demonstrate correct punctuation and spelling, and effective use of grammar. Add corrected written work or any illustrations to your portfolio.

Underlined text refers to Internet link at http://Homeschool-Books.com

Agriculture in Ancient Rome

Step 1 Excite

Think about the climate of the Mediterranean region. What crops can be easily grown there? What animals are raised in southern Europe and northern Africa, where Roman settlements were located? Where do you think that Romans obtained wool? (Britain) Cotton? (Egypt) Do you think that periods of warfare ever disrupted the food supply? Do you think that famine was a problem in ancient Rome?

Step 2 Examine

Agriculture was a main part of ancient Rome's economy. "Roman agriculture changed as the empire progressed. In the beginning, the main sources of agriculture were small estates cultivated and owned by small farmers. This was subsistence farming since they only grew enough to feed their own families. However, as the empire became increasingly military and it became involved in more wars, the taxes also increased. The small farmers couldn't afford to keep their land and had to sell to a big landowner for protection and help. This caused the main agriculture unit to become the latifundia, or a huge estate owned by a single landholder and operated by many slaves" (ThinkQuest Team 16325, 1998).

Many agricultural manuals were written in Rome; for instance, *About Agriculture* by Caton (160 B.C.), *De Re Rustica by* Marcus Porcius Cato, *De Re Rustica* by Columnella (c. A.D. 60), and the *Georgics* of Vergil (38 and 30 B.C.). In addition to using the technology that was recorded in farming handbooks, Romans had superstitions about farming. Like other pagans, Romans worshiped many gods and goddesses who, according to their belief, could provide a good crop. In April and May there were special celebrations devoted to Ceres and Flora, the goddesses of agriculture and of flowers, respectively. The Latin adjective Cerealis, "of Ceres," gave us our word cereal.

Research agriculture in ancient Rome. Use any resource (an encyclopedia, nonfiction book, historical novel, or the Internet). We recommend the following:

Book

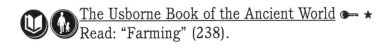 The Usborne Book of the Ancient World ●— ★
Read: "Farming" (238).

Resources recommended in ◆several lessons, ★ several units, ♥other HOW Units. ●—Key Resource (see beginning of unit or page 32).

Heart of Wisdom Publishing   639

Step 3 Expand

Choose and complete one of the following activities:

Activity 1: Answer Questions
Agriculture was a main part of ancient Rome's economy. Answer these questions: When did the Romans plow and sow? What animals did they use to pull their plows? What vegetables and fruits did they produce, and what domestic birds and animals did they raise?

Activity 2: Make a Chart
Compare agriculture in your state with that in ancient Rome. Compare the following: principal crops cultivated, principal animals raised, major products exported, and percentage of the population employed in agriculture. The local county extension office is a good source for up-to-date agricultural information.

Activity 3: Write a Report
Retell, in writing, what you have learned about Roman agriculture. Write at least two paragraphs. Younger students can copy one or two sentences or narrate (tell back) what has been learned.

Step 4 Excel

Share what you have learned about agriculture in Rome with a friend or family member. Correct written work to demonstrate correct punctuation and spelling, and effective use of grammar. Add corrected written work or any illustrations to your portfolio.

Underlined text refers to Internet link at http://Homeschool-Books.com

Architecture in Ancient Rome

Step 1 Excite

Ancient Roman societies were organized What is a praetorium? The Latin word praetorium first meant "a tent of a general" in a Roman army's camp. Later, the word was applied to a palace where a governor of a province lived and made judgment, as well as to the emperor's fortified palaces.

Read Matthew 27:27; Mark 15:16; John 18:28, 33; 19:9; Acts 23:35; and Philippians 1:13 to find out the usage of "praetorium."

Make a list of the types of buildings that you would see in an ancient Roman city.

Step 2 Examine

Explore images of ancient Roman architecture. Make a note of the building that you find to be the most beautiful. Use any resource (an encyclopedia, art books, or the Internet). We recommend the following:

Books

The Usborne Book of the Ancient World ●— ★
Read: "Architecture" (262).

Ancient Rome (Eyewitness) ●— ◆
Read: "Builders and Engineers" (26-27).

The Greco-Roman World of the New Testament Era ●— ♥
Read: "The City in the Greco-Roman World" (48-70). This chapter includes physical setting, the landmarks that dominated various types of cities, and the housing in Greco-Roman cities

Caesar and Christ (Story of Civilization III) ◆
Read: "The Engineers" (326-327), "Architecture" (355-362).

City: A Story of Roman Planning and Construction by David MacAulay
Fabulous text and black-and-white illustrations show how the Romans planned and constructed their cities for the people who lived within them. (October 24, 1983) Houghton Mifflin Co (Juv); ISBN: 0395349222. Reading level: Ages 9-12.

Resources recommended in ◆several lessons, ★several units, ♥other HOW Units. ●—Key Resource (see beginning of unit or page 32).

Heart of Wisdom Publishing   641

Video

Roman City by David Macaulay
Description: This PBS show is also available on video. An excellent resource, it includes an animated story line that ties together a very good look at the "how" and "why" of various important functions and considerations which were contemplated by planners of a Roman city. It also gives a strong overview of life, politics, and architecture in a Roman city.

Internet Sources

Inside Architecture - Roman and Romanesque
Description: Read an overview of ancient Roman architecture, as well as an introduction to Romanesque architecture, which began around A.D. 1000.

Roman Architecture - Digital Archive
Description: Find seven thumbnail images of various examples of Roman architecture found in France. Enlargements are very high quality.

Roman Architecture - Architecture on the Web
Description: Provides links to Roman construction techniques, the history of Roman architecture, and the architecture of Pompeii and Rome.

Roman Architecture
Description: Roman architecture through the ages, architecture links, and Fine Art.

Roman Architecture in Pompeii
Description: Explore ancient Pompeii through interactive maps, virtual reality panoramas, and hundreds of color photos.

Ancient Roman Architecture
Description: Explore ancient Roman architecture, from Great Buildings Online.

Step 3 Expand

Choose and complete one of the following activities:

Activity 1: Write a Description
Write a detailed description of your favorite picture of ancient Roman architecture. Younger students can narrate (orally tell) their description.

Activity 2: Make a Model
Build and display a model of the city of Rome. Include buildings with aqueducts, roads, temples, the Tiber River, Seven Hills, the Forum, Colosseum, etc. Use any materials available—paper, clay, etc.

Activity 3: Make a Roman Fort
Make a Roman fort using the Usborne cut-out book Make This Roman Fort.

Activity 4: Make a Roman Villa
Make a Roman villa with Usborne's book Make this Roman Villa.

Activity 5: Make an Edible Roman House
Make an edible Roman House out of gingerbread. Combine your culinary skills and your knowledge of Roman culture to create one of the following: a villa rustica, a villa urbana, a domus, or an insula.

Activity 6: Make a Roman Amphitheater
Make a Roman amphitheater using the Usborne cut-out book Make This Roman Amphitheater.

Activity 7: Write an Essay
Write an essay explaining the significance to the Roman community of these locations: the Forum, the baths, and the Colosseum. Write a paragraph for each, then add an introductory paragraph and a conclusion to complete your essay.

Activity 8: Write a Description
Jacopo Robusti, called Tintoretto (1518-1594), was a famous Venetian painter. It is said that he wrote on his workshop wall "The drawing of Michelangelo and the color of Titian." Look at his picture, Christ Before Pilate, in an art book or on the Internet. Describe a praetorium, using as many adjectives as possible. Refer to "Writing a Description" in Writers INC.

Step 4

Share what you have learned about architecture in ancient Rome with a friend or family member. Correct written work to demonstrate correct punctuation and spelling, and effective use of grammar. Add corrected written work or any illustrations to your portfolio.

Resources recommended in ♦several lessons, ★ several units, ♥other HOW Units. ☞—Key Resource (see beginning of unit or page 32).

Heart of Wisdom Publishing   643

Art In Ancient Rome

Step 1 Excite

Art was a very important part of Roman culture. The purpose of Roman art was to show beauty and record special events. The Romans created and enjoyed art in many different mediums and styles.

Sculpture

The Romans liked to sculpt in marble, and often copied Greek statues. When they designed their own sculptures of people, they chose to make them look realistic. Famous Romans depicted in marble will often be wrinkled, bald, and/or fat. These signs of age were thought to give them an air of wisdom.

Mosaics

During the time of Flavian, much of the mosaic art was impressionistic. However, during the time of Hadrian, mosaics became more realistic and detailed. Later, spiritual motifs and romanticism were used. Some of the mosaics depicted a scene of battle or other events. These designs were skillfully decorated with lustrous colors. Christian motifs were introduced in the beginning of the fourth century A.D. Mosaics in basilicas and tombs often portrayed birds, fish, and lambs. Others simply had an epitaph (Caputo & Driss, 1962, p.20).

Relief Sculptures

"Displaying of relief sculpture on the walls of public monuments became popular during imperial times. In this kind of sculpture, particular emperors and their family members were shown in imposing positions, commanding the army, or giving out food to the poor. Many subjects were often used in Roman art. One of the examples of a frequently used subject was the emperor addressing a crowd. In this image, the emperor was either rising above the others or standing in front of a large group. This motif is called adlocutio in Latin because it has a meaning of a formal speech, often given by the emperor to his troops. Therefore, these traditional stances are associated with such a speech. Romans tended to portray real events in sculpture, and often they overstate these events with their point of view. These sculptures were found in public buildings as temples, monuments, or decorative frieze. Not only were these historical reliefs depicting real events but they also described myths. In these combined sculptures, there was a line between real events and myths. Also, Romans liked to mix the figures from the divine world and ordinary people." (Sculpture).

Underlined text refers to Internet link at http://Homeschool-Books.com

Step 2 Examine

Look at examples of Roman murals, sculptures, and mosaics. Use any resource (an encyclopedia, art books, or the Internet). We recommend any of the following:

Books

The Usborne Book of the Ancient World ⊶ ★
Read: "Decorations" (229).

Ancient Rome (Eyewitness) ⊶ ♦
Read: "City-state to Super Power" (6-7), "The Theater" (36-37).

Caesar and Christ (Story of Civilization III) ♦
Read: Chapter XVI "Rome and Its Art" (338-362).

Internet Sources

The Detroit Institute of Arts site
Description: Detroit Institute of Arts: Permanent Collection of ancient art of Rome.

Looking at Art of Ancient Greece and Rome
Description: An Online Exhibition. ArtsEdNet's exclusive presentation of selected works from the J. Paul Getty Museum. This virtual exhibition draws from art objects that appear in Beyond Beauty: Antiquities as Evidence.

Museum of Art - Greek and Roman Art
Description: Site includes samples of the museum's collection of ancient Greek and Roman art. Examine a Roman wall painting, a tombstone, and a cameo of Augustus.

Roman Museums Guide to Ancient Art
Description: Includes descriptions of Capitoline, Conservators' Palace, Pius-Clementine, Nat'l Roman, Borghese, and Roman Civilization.

Gallery of Roman Art
Description: Features a variety of images taken largely from coins in the author's collection of ancient Roman artifacts.

Roman Art
Description: Images of Ancient Greece and Rome art from Niagara County Community College.

Resources recommended in ♦several lessons, ★ several units, ♥other HOW Units. ⊶Key Resource (see beginning of unit or page 32).

Heart of Wisdom Publishing   645

Step 3 Expand

Choose and complete one of the following activities:

Activity 1: Write an Essay
From ancient times, Romans made death masks. When the head of the household died, an image of him was made by pressing wax on his face. The image was then placed in a family shrine, to be venerated. Members of the patrician class eventually had busts made in marble, replacing the wax masks. Write an essay about household idols. What other ancient cultures practiced ancestor worship? Was ancestor worship reflected in the art of these other cultures? What are some other examples of household shrines? In your essay, discuss household idols that are mentioned in the Bible (1 Samuel 19:13; Genesis 31:19) and the commandment against making images for worship (Exodus 20:4,5).

Activity 2:Create a Paper Mosaic
Involve your family in creating mosaic pictures. For a simple project, design and draw a simple outline on stiff paper. Cut an assortment of colored paper into small pieces. Glue them inside the picture outlines. Do not allow the pieces of paper to overlap each other; there should be gaps between scraps of paper. For a more elaborate project, follow the instructions for a broken-tile mosaic table using real ceramic tiles (see below).

Activity 3: Make a Mosaic Tiled Table
Supplies: Ceramic tiles, small table, utility knife, putty knife, mastik, grout, sponge, white glue, latex primer, semigloss or high-gloss latex paint. Optional: tile nibbler, grout trowel.

Find tiles for your project. You can either buy some, or you can find free tiles by asking around for leftovers. Get a variety of brightly colored tiles. The color scheme for your project depends upon the colors of tiles that you have. Stick to one color scheme, such as primary colors only, pastel colors only, blue and white only, or perhaps the colors of a sunset. Put the tiles in an old towel and smash them with a hammer. Most of the fragments should be larger than one inch in diameter.

Find a small table for your project. A rectangular tabletop will be much easier to work on, so avoid circles and ovals. Good sources are a second-hand furniture store, an unfinished furniture store, or a thrift store. Perhaps someone you know has a table to give you. Select a paint color from your color scheme. Again, ask around; someone may have some leftover paint to give you.

Prime and paint the entire table. Now you're ready to design your mosaic. A bold design is best. You can choose either to make a simple picture or to place tiles randomly. Your design should be bordered by an outside band of smaller tiles. To decide on your design, first cut a piece of paper the same size as your tabletop, and arrange your tiles on it. Allow spaces between your tiles, no more than 1/8 to 1/4 of an inch wide. Select larger tiles to fill in the main design in the center. Arrange smaller tiles around the edge to make a border. If you have a tile nibbler, you can cut tiles to the size and shape you want.

Once you have worked out the design on paper, you are ready to stick the tiles onto the tabletop. To make sure that the tiles will adhere well, score the tabletop with a utility knife, and then lightly coat it with watered-down glue. Allow the glue to dry. Use a putty knife to put adhesive or mastik on the tabletop. To select the right product, ask for help at a hardware store. Place the tiles on the tabletop, starting in the center and working outward. Pay attention to the spaces you leave between tiles: the gaps should be only 1/8 to 1/4 of an inch wide. Let your project completely dry overnight.

Next, fill in the gaps between the tiles with grout. A grout trowel is the best tool for this step, but you can use a putty knife. Smear the grout across the tiles, pressing it into all of the gaps. Let the grout set up for a few minutes. Lightly and carefully wipe the surface of the tabletop, using a damp sponge. Make the grout lines even and smooth. After the grout has dried, you will need to wipe the tile to rinse off the excess grout. Once it is all dried, you are finished. You now have a beautiful mosaic-tiled table.

Step 4 Excel

Share your work from Step 3 with someone. Explain what you have learned in this lesson. Correct all written work to demonstrate correct punctuation and spelling, and effective use of grammar. Add corrected written work or any illustrations to your portfolio.

Resources recommended in ◆several lessons, ★ several units, ♥other HOW Units. ◉━Key Resource (see beginning of unit or page 32).

Calendars in Ancient Rome

Step 1 Excite

List the months of the year. Brainstorm and discuss: Which names refer to Romans or Roman gods? List the days of the week. Which day is named after a Roman god? Why do you think that people have tried new calendars throughout history? Do you think it would be difficult to change calendars? Is more than one type of calendar currently in use throughout the world?

Step 2 Examine

Research the calendar systems of ancient Rome. When was the Julian calendar introduced? Why was calendar reform needed at that time? What changes did Octavian make? How long was the Julian calendar in use, and why was it corrected in the time of Pope Gregory XIII?

Read online about future calendar reform. See Future calendars. Do you think modern people would want to reform the calendar? Is there any kind of crisis that would require calendar reform? If you had the privilege of choosing one calendar to be used worldwide, which would you choose? Would you invent a new one or use an old one?

Internet Sources

Early Roman Calendars
Chronicles the development of the Roman calendar from the writings of Ovid and Plutarch. Examines the origins of each month's name.

Roman Calendar
An example of an ancient Roman calendar, with an explanation of symbols and uses. Includes a historical background, including archaeological information, and a bibliography.

Step 3 Expand

Choose and complete one of the following activities:

Activity 1: Make a Chart
Make a chart comparing calendars. Begin by comparing the Julian and Jewish calendars. Compare how long each system was in use, how each calendar was developed, how the lengths of the months and the year were determined, how the months were named, and how many days there were per week, month, and

---

Underlined text refers to Internet link at http://Homeschool-Books.com

year. Then choose from this list two more types of calendars for your chart: Coptic, Ethiopic, Islamic civil, modern Persian, Mayan, French Revolutionary, Chinese, and Hindu.

Activity 2: Write an Article

Write an article explaining your opinion about whether one standard calendar should be used worldwide. If you think that the world should have one calendar, which calendar should be chosen? Your editorial article can be in any style that you choose; the only requirement is that you must somewhere cite Daniel 7:25. Refer to Argumentative Essays.

Activity 3: Memorize

Obtain a Jewish calendar and try to learn the names of the days and months. Try using the Jewish calendar in your daily life. Add new words to your Hebrew notebook.

Step 4 Excel

Explain to your family, using the narration method, what you have learned about how our calendar developed. You should narrate aloud, without looking at books or notes.

Resources recommended in ◆several lessons, ★ several units, ♥ other HOW Units. ☞ Key Resource (see beginning of unit or page 32).

Heart of Wisdom Publishing   649

Citizenship in Ancient Rome

Step 1 Excite

If you were born in the United States, or if you were born abroad but one or both of your parents were American citizens, you have American citizenship automatically. Do you know your rights and responsibilities as an American citizen? Make a list of at least ten rights and responsibilities.

Step 2 Examine

Romans were divided into two main groups: Roman citizens and noncitizens. Write down privileges of Roman citizens. To whom was citizenship given at birth? How else could citizenship be obtained? Who were kept from exercising the rights of citizens?

Read Acts 16:37 and 22:24-30. What citizenship privilege did the apostle Paul use? Read Acts 22:28. Why did Paul appeal to Caesar? Find out how former royal slave Felix received his citizenship and became a procurator of Judea in Acts 23:24.

In 90 B.C., the Italian allies, who had demanded full Roman citizenship for a long time, rose in a revolt that lasted two years and resulted in bestowal of citizenship. Find out when the rights of Roman citizens were given to all free men in the Empire. Who had a so-called "citizen's voice in government"?

Research citizenship in Rome. Use any resource (an encyclopedia, nonfiction book, historical novel, or the Internet). We recommend the following:

Book

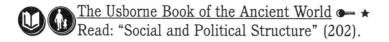
The Usborne Book of the Ancient World ●— ★
Read: "Social and Political Structure" (202).

The Greco-Roman World of the New Testament Era ●— ♥
Read: "Citizenship" (197-210).

Step 3 Excel

Choose and complete one of the following activities:

Activity 1: Write a Report
Write a report about Paul's Roman citizenship. Explain the rights that he had as a citizen, how he obtained his citizenship, and how his ancestors might have obtained citizenship.

Activity 2: Narrate What You Have Learned
Retell what you learned about Roman citizenship using the narration method. Show the Bible passages that mention Paul's citizenship, and tell what it meant when Paul appealed to Caesar. Narrate aloud from memory. You can use an outline to prompt you, but don't read from your notes.

Step 4 Excel

Share your work from Step 3 with someone. Explain what you have learned in this lesson. Correct written work to demonstrate correct punctuation and spelling, and effective use of grammar. Add corrected written work or any illustrations to your portfolio.

Resources recommended in ◆several lessons, ★ several units, ♥ other HOW Units. ◐—Key Resource (see beginning of unit or page 32).

Heart of Wisdom Publishing   651

Clothing in Ancient Rome

Step 1 Excite

Can you think of other cultures in which the people have worn clothes that resemble Roman tunics and togas? Why do you think that only citizens were allowed to wear togas? How do you think Romans ironed tunics? How much time do you think it would take to wash and dry a soft woolen toga? How was Lydia of the Bible involved in the textile industry? Were textiles and clothing a major industry in ancient Rome?

Step 2 Examine

The ancient Roman women loved ornate necklaces, pins, earrings, bracelets, and friendship rings. Pearls were favorites. Women often dyed their hair, usually golden-red. They used false hairpieces to make their hair thicker or longer. Sometimes, Roman women wore their hair up, in carefully arranged styles held with jeweled hairpins, and sometimes they wore it down, curled in ringlets. Women might carry parasols, or fans made of peacock feathers, wood, or stretched linen. Women enjoyed using mirrors of highly polished metal (not glass).

Hairstyles and beards varied with the time. In early Roman times, men wore long hair and full beards. For a while, they were clean-shaven with short hair. About 1AD, longer hair and beards were fashionable again. Different styles of haircuts and beards depended upon the fashion of the time. Rings were the only jewelry worn by Roman citizens, and good manners dictated only one ring. Some men did not wore many rings.

What were clothes made from? What were men's clothes? Could freedmen wear togas? What did a senator's toga look like? When did men put on purple togas? What were women's clothes like? How did they cover their heads? What cosmetics were used? What were children's clothes like? When did a boy receive the right to wear a toga?

Research how men and women dressed during the time of the Roman Empire. Find out about hair coverings, beards for men, footwear, and religious garments.

Books

The Usborne Book of the Ancient World ◉— ★
Read: "Clothes and Fashion" (234).

Ancient Rome (Eyewitness) ◉— ◆
Read: Browse through the whole book to see several different types of Roman clothing.

Caesar and Christ (Story of Civilization III) ◆
Read: "Dress" (372-373). Also see references to clothing in the index.

Internet Sources

Ancient Roman Clothing (women)
Description: Pictures of women in various dress.

Ancient Roman Clothing (men)
Description: Pictures of men in various dress.

Smith's Dictionary: Articles on Clothing & Adornment
Description: This index page collects the articles in *Smith's Dictionary* on clothing, shoes, cosmetics, hairstyles, etc.

Ancient Roman Accessories
Description: Pictures of shoes, helmets, wigs, jewelry, and more.

Ancient Roman Hair Styles, Clothing Styles, Shoes
Description: Pictures of women's hairstyles, clothing, and shoes.

How to Make a Tunic
Description: Instructions for making a tunic.

Resources recommended in ◆several lessons, ★ several units, ❤other HOW Units. ◉—Key Resource (see beginning of unit or page 32).

Heart of Wisdom Publishing   653

How to Make a Bedsheet Toga
Description: Here is a way to make a fairly effective—and easy-to-wear—Roman toga out of materials you probably have at home.

Step 3 Expand

Choose and complete one of the following activities:

Activity 1: Add to Your Time Line Book
Add illustrations of Roman clothing to the proper pages in your Time Line Book.

Activity 2: Copy Bible Passages
Look up and copy each of the following verses: 1 Timothy 2:9 and 1 Peter 3:3. Were Christians living in ancient Rome expected to dress differently than fashionable Romans? Write a paper about proper Christian attire using historical information from ancient Rome.

Activity 3: Look up Words
Find out what these words mean: tunica talaris, camisia, strophium, tunic, pallium, stola, palla, toga, toga praetexta, toga purpurea, toga candida, toga virilis.

Activity 4: Make a Tunic
Make a Roman tunic (see directions from Internet sites above).

Activity 5: Illustrate the Following
Illustrate Acts 10:24-48 and Acts 16:13,14: Peter preaching to the household of Cornelius, and Paul preaching to Roman women by the river. In your pictures, pay special attention to making the clothing authentic.

Step 4 Excel

Share what you have learned about clothing in ancient Rome with a friend or family member. Correct all written work to demonstrate correct punctuation and spelling, and effective use of grammar. Add corrected written work or any illustrations to your portfolio.

Underlined text refers to Internet link at http://Homeschool-Books.com

Customs in Ancient Rome

Step 1 Excite

Have you ever attended a ceremony? Marriages, graduations, baptisms, ordinations, funerals, baby dedications, awards ceremonies, and club-induction ceremonies are all common in American culture. Who invented the way that these ceremonies are conducted? Where did the traditions come from? Are they biblical? Do they vary from community to community, from family to family? Are ceremonies important?

Step 2 Examine

Research the customs and practices of marriages and funerals in ancient Rome. Use any resource (an encyclopedia, nonfiction book, historical novel, or the Internet). We recommend the following:

The Usborne Book of the Ancient World ●— ★
Read: "Marriage and Child Birth" (240), "Funerals and Burial" (241).

Ancient Rome (Eyewitness) ●— ◆
Read: "A Roman Wedding" (22), "Death and Burial" (56-58).

The Greco-Roman World of the New Testament Era ●— ♥
Read: "Life & Death in the First Century" (19-47), "The Family, Women & Education" (237-258). Includes several aspects of the everyday life in the world of the first century A.D., such as food production and eating habits, trade, banking and business, crafts and manufacturing, leisure and games, travel, attire and fashion and burial practices of the Romans and Jews.

Caesar and Christ (Story of Civilization III) ◆
Read: "The Family" (56-58), "Weddings" (223, 379), "Post Mortem" (83-84).

Step 3 Expand

Choose and complete one of the following activities:

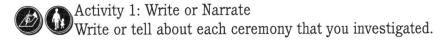
Activity 1: Write or Narrate
Write or tell about each ceremony that you investigated.

Resources recommended in ◆several lessons, ★ several units, ♥other HOW Units. ●—Key Resource (see beginning of unit or page 32).

Heart of Wisdom Publishing   655

Activity 2: Make a Silhouette

Choose one of the ceremonies to illustrate with a silhouette. To make a silhouette, simply draw an outline without filling in details. Place your drawing over a black piece of paper, and cut the outline and the paper underneath, so that you produce a black shape that looks like a shadow of a scene. Mount the silhouette on a sheet of contrasting paper as a background, such as white. Or, for a more dramatic result, choose red or yellow for your background.

Activity 3: Answer Questions

Answer the following about Roman marriages:

- Who chose the spouse?
- At what age were girls given in marriage?
- How did families celebrate the engagement?
- What present did the bride receive?
- Who was in charge of a wife's money and belongings?
- What day and month were considered unlucky for a wedding?
- What happened on the eve of the wedding?
- What happened in the beginning of a wedding?
- What object was present?
- How were the vows exchanged?

Activity 4: Answer Questions

Answer the following about Roman funerals:

- What happened to the spirit of a dead man, according to Roman belief?
- Why did the Romans put a coin under a dead man's tongue?
- How were funeral announcements made?
- How did women participate in a funeral ceremony?
- How long was the corpse displayed?
- What does The Law of the Twelve Tablets say about a place for burial?
- What types of funeral rites were present in the Roman Empire?
- Compare funeral ceremonies of a pagan Roman man and a Christian Roman man.

Activity 5: Contrast and Compare

Create a contrast-and-compare graphic (see page 26) to show how weddings or funerals differed in ancient Rome, Greece, Egypt, and Israel.

Step 4 Excel

Explain orally to your parents what you've learned in this lesson. Correct all written work to demonstrate correct punctuation and spelling, and effective use of grammar. Add corrected written work or any illustrations to your portfolio.

Underlined text refers to Internet link at http://Homeschool-Books.com

Daily Life in Ancient Rome

Step 1 Excite

Browse through the books or Internet sites on ancient Rome suggested in the Resources Section. Find illustrations of family life, types of housing, household furnishings, bathing, sports, musical instruments, and games.

Step 2 Examine

Research family life and entertainment in ancient Rome. Use any resource (an encyclopedia, nonfiction book, historical novel, or the Internet). We recommend the following:
Books

The Usborne Book of the Ancient World ⊙— ★
Read: "Entertainments" (248), "Festivals" (258), "Food and Dining" (230), "Townhouses" (226).

Kingfisher History Encyclopedia ⊙— ♥
Read: "Roman Life" (66-67).

Ancient Rome (Eyewitness) ⊙— ◆
Read: "Growing Up" (20-21), "Family Life" (22-23), "House and Home" (24-25), "A Trip to the Baths" (38-39), "Writing it all Down" (40-41), "Craftsworkers and Technology" (42-43), "First Catch Your Dormouse" (44-46), "Making Music" (48-49), "Country Life" (58-59).

The Greco-Roman World of the New Testament Era ⊙— ♥
Read: "Social Class & Status in the Empire" (180-196), "Citizenship (197-210).

Resources recommended in ◆several lessons, ★ several units, ♥other HOW Units. ⊙—Key Resource (see beginning of unit or page 32).

Internet Sources

ⓘ Ancient Rome: Daily Life
Description: Article from SPQR Online (a premier Web resource concerning ancient Rome). Includes several links to related topics such as: Fashions, ceremonies, society, entertainment, and diet.

ⓘ Roma: Culture
Description: This site includes several links to informative articles such as: "Family House," "Education," "Clothes," "Food," "Games," and "A day in Rome."

ⓘ BBC Roman History
Description: Educational resource outlines most areas of life and culture in ancient Rome. Read articles on "Leisure," "Families & Children," and "Religion."

ⓘ Daily Life in Rome
Description: This site from Odyssey Online explores both public and private life in ancient Rome.

ⓘ People in Rome
Description: This site from Odyssey Online explores a few of the people you might meet if you traveled back in time to ancient Rome: rulers, senators, soldiers, craftsmen and merchants' slaves.

ⓘ Roles of Men, Women and Children in Ancient Rome
Description: This site was designed to introduce elementary-school students to the ancient Roman civilization.

ⓘ Ancient Rome Daily Life
Description: Article describing family life in Rome, with links to explanations of Roman social classes and education.

Step 3 Expand

Choose and complete one of the following activities:

Activity 1: Write a Diary Entry
Write a diary entry that might have been written by a Roman adult. How did the day start? What were the activities of the day? What items were used? How did the day conclude?

Activity 2: Play a Roman Game
Find directions and play one of these Roman board games: Knucklebones (Tali & Tropa), Dice (Tesserae), Roman Chess (Latrunculi), Roman Checkers (Calculi), The Game of Twelve Lines (Duodecim Scripta), Tic-Tac-Toe (Terni Lapilli), Roman Backgammon (Tabula), Egyptian Backgammon (Senet).

Activity 3: Play a Musical Instrument
Find out about Roman musical instruments such as: lute, organ, cithara, flutes, tympani, trumpet, panpipes, harp, and drum. Visit a music store or borrow one of these instruments, and try to play it.

Activity 4: Copy Illustrations
Find and copy or trace some illustrations of Roman households for your portfolio or Time Line Book.

Activity 5: Make a Book
Put together your diary entry and your illustrations to make a book titled "A Day in Ancient Rome."

Step 4 Excel

Explain orally to your parents what you've learned in this lesson. Correct written work to demonstrate correct punctuation and spelling, and effective use of grammar. Add corrected written work or any illustrations to your portfolio.

Resources recommended in ◆several lessons, ★ several units, ● other HOW Units. ●–Key Resource (see beginning of unit or page 32).

Men in Ancient Rome

Step 1 Excite

In order to understand attitudes toward men in today's society, we must review the history of the Greco-Roman society on which Western civilization was founded. Once we have done so, we will be resolved to embrace fully the biblical Hebraic models for men's ministry. In order to understand proper roles for men in the church and in the family, we must return to the Scriptures for our patterns—then we will discover the biblical man. Brainstorm and discuss the lives of men in ancient Rome. Make a list of daily duties, problems, responsibilities, dress, etc. What character traits would differ between a Jewish man and a Roman man?

Step 2 Examine

Research men in Rome. Use any resource (an encyclopedia, nonfiction book, historical novel, or the Internet). We recommend the resources in the "Daily Life in Ancient Rome" lesson and the following:

Books

The Usborne Book of the Ancient World ●— ★
Read: "Jobs and Occupations" (244), "A Soldier's Life" (208).

Kingfisher History Encyclopedia ●— ♥
Read: "Roman Life" (66-67).

The Greco-Roman World of the New Testament Era ●— ♥
Read: "Social Class & Status in the Empire" (180-196), "Citizenship" (197-210), Slavery (220-236).

Step 3 Expand

Activity 1: Write an Autobiography
Write an autobiography as if you were a man in ancient Rome. Answer these questions:
- What is your name?
- Are you married or unmarried, free or slave?
- What kind of clothes do you wear?
- What do you look like?

Underlined text refers to Internet link at http://Homeschool-Books.com

- What country are you from?
- Describe your home.
- What do you do for fun?
- What kinds of foods do you eat?
- What hardships do you face?
- Which machines, conveniences, or technologies do you use every day?
- What are the major differences between your life and a modern life?
- Describe how world, national, or local events have affected you.
- What do you hope for?
- What or whom do you fear?
- Whom do you admire?
- What are your beliefs (religious, political, personal, and so on)?

Activity 2: Write and Perform a Monologue
Perform, in costume, a dramatic soliloquy portraying a Roman Christian man. He describes the type of life he leads, and his hopes for the future. He is looking for a wife to marry, and he describes the qualities he's looking for in a woman and the kind of life that she will lead in his household. Put a copy of the monologue in your portfolio.

Step 4 Excel

Share your work from Step 3 with someone. Explain what you have learned in this lesson. Correct all written work to demonstrate correct punctuation and spelling, and effective use of grammar. Add corrected written work or any illustrations to your portfolio.

Resources recommended in ◆several lessons, ★ several units, ♥ other HOW Units. ●━Key Resource (see beginning of unit or page 32).

Heart of Wisdom Publishing   661

Women in Ancient Rome

Step 1 Excite

A famous ancient-Roman myth is "The Rape of the Sabine Women," recounted by Livy in his *History of Rome*. This tale explains how the city of Rome was first populated, at the time that Romulus founded the city. The event was commemorated with a yearly celebration, The Feast of the Women. Read any version of the story that you can locate. What does this myth tell you about ancient-Roman attitudes toward women? What does it tell you about ancient-Roman men? This event was supposed to have happened in the 700s B.C., around the time that the Northern Kingdom of Israel went into exile. Does this example of Gentile behavior give you insight into why the Israelites' obedience to God's law was needed as a light to the nations?

Brainstorm and discuss the lives of women in ancient Rome. Make a list of daily duties, problems, responsibilities, dress, etc. What character traits would differ between a Jewish woman and a Roman woman?

Step 2 Examine

In order to understand attitudes toward women in today's society, we must review the history of the Greco-Roman society on which Western civilization was founded. Once we have done so, we will be resolved to embrace fully the biblical Hebraic models for women''s ministry. In order to understand proper roles for women in the church and in the family, we must return to the Scriptures for our patterns—then we will discover the biblical woman. The Roman wife was her husband's companion and helper: she was next to him at parties and banquets, shared his authority over the children and slaves, and participated in the dignity of his position in public life. Read Matthew 27:19, and Acts 25:13,23, and 30-31.

Research the role of women in ancient Rome. Use any resource (an encyclopedia, nonfiction book, historical novel, or the Internet). We recommend the following:

Books

The Usborne Book of the Ancient World ●━ ★
Read: "In the Kitchen" (232), "Marriage and Childbirth" (240).

Ancient Rome (Eyewitness) ●━ ◆
Read: "The Women of Rome" (18-19), "Family Life" (22-23), "House and Home" (24-25).

The Greco-Roman World of the New Testament Era

Read: "The Family, Women & Education" (237-258).

Caesar and Christ (Story of Civilization III) ◆
Read: "The Sexes" (369-371).

Jewish Women in Greco-Roman Palestine by Tal Ilan
This study explores the real—versus the ideal—
social, political, and religious status of women in
Palestinian Judaism during the Hellenistic and Roman
periods. This investigation concludes that extreme religious groups in Judaism of that period influenced other
groups, classes, and factions to tighten their control of
women. They also encouraged an understanding of the
ideal relationships between men and women as represented in the literature and the legal codes of the time, which
required increasing chastity. Despite this, the lives of real
women and their relationships to men continued to have
variation and nuance. 270 pages (April 1996) Hendrickson
Publishers, Inc.; ISBN: 1565632400.

Internet Sources

First Century Women Hellenic and Latin Influences on Western Views of
Women
Description: An article explaining that in order to understand attitudes toward
women in today's society, we must review the history of the Greco-Roman society
on which Western civilization was founded.

Ancient Roman Women
Description: This site examines the prejudices facing Roman women in the
ancient world.

Wives and Mothers
Description: Article explaining that the ancient-Roman family unit was
strong, and became Rome's first abiding strength. Includes excerpts from Caesar
and Christ: A History of Roman Civilization and of Christianity From Their
Beginnings to A.D. 325.

Deification of Roman Women
Description: An essay which examines the historical, social, and psychologi-
cal conditions that led to divine honors being bestowed on women.

Resources recommended in ◆several lessons, ★ several units, ● other HOW Units. ●━Key Resource (see beginning of unit or page 32).

Heart of Wisdom Publishing   663

Educated Women in Ancient Society
Description: This site explores the perception of education in ancient times, and researches the effect of education on women.

Roman Ladies
Description: On this site, you can read biographies of the famous women of ancient Rome, and view ancient coins bearing the likenesses of these women.

Women of Rome
Description: An article exploring the roles of women in ancient Rome. Includes research on marriage; and guardianship laws and customs.

Step 3 Expand

Choose and complete one of the following activities:

Activity 1: Write an Autobiography
Write an autobiography as if you were a woman in ancient Rome. Answer these questions:

- What is your name?
- Are you married or unmarried, free or slave?
- What kind of clothes do you wear?
- What do you look like?
- What country are you from?
- Describe your home.
- What do you do for fun?
- What kinds of foods do you eat?
- What hardships do you face?
- Which machines, conveniences, or technologies do you use every day?
- What are the major differences between your life and a modern life?
- Describe how world, national, or local events have affected you.
- What do you hope for?
- What or whom do you fear?
- Whom do you admire?
- What are your beliefs (religious, political, personal, and so on)?

Activity 2: Contrast and Compare
Create a contrast-and-compare graphic (see page 26) to compare traits of Jewish and Roman women. Which type of individual more closely resembles today's American woman?

Underlined text refers to Internet link at http://Homeschool-Books.com

Activity 3: Contrast and Compare
Create a <u>contrast-and-compare graphic</u> (see page 26) to compare the position of women in ancient Greece (or another ancient culture that you have studied) and ancient Rome.

Activity 4: Discuss Women in the Roman Empire
Discuss the role of women in the Roman Empire. How were women used as tools to gain political power through marriage alliances? What does this say about the way women were viewed?

Activity 5: Write and Perform a Monologue
Perform, in costume, a dramatic soliloquy portraying an ancient-Roman Christian woman. As she prepares the evening meal for her family, she describes what her day was like and discusses news that she has heard. Put a copy of the monologue in your portfolio.

Step 4 Excel

Share your work from Step 3 with someone. Explain what you have learned in this lesson. Correct all written work to demonstrate correct punctuation and spelling, and effective use of grammar. Add corrected written work or any illustrations to your portfolio.

Resources recommended in ◆several lessons, ★ several units, ♥ other HOW Units. ●–Key Resource (see beginning of unit or page 32).

Heart of Wisdom Publishing   665

Economy in Ancient Rome

Step 1 Excite

Think of New Testament stories that mention some kind of business enterprise (tent making, ship building, selling fabric, selling divination, selling idols, agriculture, sewing garments, transportation by ship, fishing, carpentry). Make a list of the industries and the verses where they are found.

Step 2 Examine

Investigate the economy of the Roman Empire. How could an ambitious Roman get rich? How were goods transported around the empire? What kinds of goods were in demand by small villages and peasants, by city dwellers, by soldiers, and by patricians? Use any resource (an encyclopedia, nonfiction book, historical novel, or the Internet). We recommend the following:

Books

Encyclopedia of the Bible (Nelson's Illustrated) ●— ♥
"Travel and Transport" (122-123), "Trade and Commerce" (124-125).

The Usborne Book of the Ancient World ●— ★
Read: "Ships and Shipping" (212-213), "Jobs and Occupations" (244-245).

Ancient Rome (Eyewitness) ●— ♦
Read: "Craftworkers and Technology" (42-43), "Transportation, Travel and Trade" (60-61).

The Penguin Historical Atlas of Ancient Rome ●— ♦
Read: "Trade and Transport" (80-81).

The Greco-Roman World of the New Testament Era ●— ♥
Read: "Tools of Governance: Finances, Law & the Military" (142-154).

Caesar and Christ (Story of Civilization III) ♦
Read: Chapter XV "Rome at Work" (319-337).

Step 3 Expand

Choose and complete one of the following activities:

Activity 1: Write an Essay
Choose one of the major industries of Rome: agriculture or trading in textiles. Write an essay describing how you would operate a business in that industry. With whom would you trade? Who would your employees be? How would you get your goods to market? Where would you market your products? What kinds of products are in demand? Younger students can copy one or two sentences from research or narrate (tell back) what has been learned.

Activity 2: Write a Journal Entry
Choose a New Testament character who was employed in a business, such as Lydia, Paul, Peter, or Joseph. Write a journal entry as if you were that character, describing a day at work.

Activity 3:Perform in Costume
Dramatize the journal entry that you wrote. Dress in costume as your character, and describe to an audience the work that you do in a normal business day.

Step 4 Excel

Explain orally to your parents what you've learned in this lesson. Correct all written work to demonstrate correct punctuation and spelling, and effective use of grammar. Add corrected written work or any illustrations to your portfolio.

Resources recommended in ◆several lessons, ★ several units, ● other HOW Units. ●—Key Resource (see beginning of unit or page 32).

Heart of Wisdom Publishing   667

Education in Ancient Rome

Step 1 Excite

Do you think that home education was common in ancient Rome? Brainstorm and discuss what school was like in ancient Rome. Where was it? Who taught? What types of materials were used?

Step 2 Examine

Rome absorbed the Greek culture in the second century, and attempted to establish pagan schools throughout the Empire by way of taxes. The public school during this time period was primarily literal in curriculum and rhetorical in content. During the first three centuries of the Christian church, there was little contact between the believers (later called "Christians") and the pagan educational system.

> The classical public schools, with their intention to produce perfect citizens through education, produced only an artificial and cruel society. Men still look back on the "golden Days" of Greece for personal and cultural inspiration, but they fail to realize that the true nobility that they aspired to was never obtainable on any humanistic premise. True nobility, which the Greek and Roman ideal correctly identified, to some extent, is only available through the obedience to the Gospel of Christ, with its insistence on our recognition and confession of sin and its promise of containing sanctification. This is never attainable though education, but only through the free mercies of Christ our Savior.[1]

Research education in ancient Rome. Use any resource (an encyclopedia, nonfiction book, historical novel, or the Internet). We recommend the following:

Books

The Usborne Book of the Ancient World ●━ ★
Read: "Education" (242).

Ancient Rome (Eyewitness) ●━ ◆
Read: "Growing Up" (20-21).

The Greco-Roman World of the New Testament Era ●━ ♥
Read: "Education in the Greco-Roman Culture and the New Testament" (253-258).

Underlined text refers to Internet link at http://Homeschool-Books.com

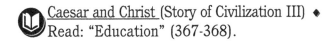
Caesar and Christ (Story of Civilization III) ◆
Read: "Education" (367-368).

Internet Sources

Ancient Roman Education
Description: Description of the goals and typical school in ancient Rome.

Daily Life, Ancient Rome
Overview of Roman culture for the young reader. Describes daily life in ancient Rome, covering topics such as school, families, and life in the country.

Step 3 Expand

Choose and complete one of the following activities:

Activity 1: Discuss
Discuss the ways in which ancient Roman schooling differs from modern education in the United States. Was it in any way similar?

Activity 2: Answer Questions
Answer the following:
- At what age did boys attended school?
- Who were their teachers?
- What was the role of a pedagogue?
- What did boys learn at elementary and at grammar schools?
- Which subject was considered the most important?
- What did boys learn after fourteen years of age?
- How they were prepared for careers as statesmen?
- What kind of school supplies did they use?

Step 4 Excel

Share what you have learned about education in ancient Rome with a friend or family member. Correct written work to demonstrate correct punctuation and spelling, and effective use of grammar. Add corrected written work or any illustrations to your portfolio.

Footnote

1. Mulligan, David. (1994). Far Above Rubies: Wisdom in the Christian Community. VT: Messenger Publishing.

Resources recommended in ◆several lessons, ★ several units, ♥other HOW Units. ☛─Key Resource (see beginning of unit or page 32).

Heart of Wisdom Publishing   669

Famous Romans

Step 1 Excite

Read scripture to learn how the life of Jesus was connected with the Roman people. He was born in Bethlehem as a result of a census required by the Roman Caesar Augustus (Luke 2:1-4), responded to the requests of Roman centurions about healing (Matthew 8:5-13; Luke 7:2-10), was arrested and beaten by Roman soldiers (John 19:1-3), and was sentenced to death by a Roman governor (John 19:15-16).

Step 2 Examine

Select a name from each column: Notable Romans, Politicians, and Authors.

Notable Romans	Politicians	Authors
Epictetus	Mark Antony	Aurelius
Livia Augustus	Marcus Aurelius	Cato
Lucius Z. Cincinnatus	Cassius	Catullus
Lucretia	Cleopatra	Cicero
Helena, wife of Constantius I and mother of Constantine	Commodus	Horace
	Diocletian	Julius Caesar
Felix	Domitian	Josephus
Aelia Flaccilla	Hadrian	Livy
Galen	Julian the Apostate	Lucan
Herod Antipas	Marius	Lucretius
Herod the Great	Nero	Martial
Hillel	Scipio "Africanus"	Ovid
Josephus	The Gracchus brothers	Petronius
Maecenas	Servius Tullius (578-535 B.C.)	Pliny the Elder
Musonius Rufus	Tiberius	Pliny the Younger
Pontius Pilate	Trajan	Plutarch
Plotinus	Octavian (Caesar Augustus)	Propertius
	Pompey	Seneca
	Romulus Augustulus	Suetonius
	Sulla	Tacitus
	Vespasian	Publius Terentius Afer or Terence
		Virgil

Underlined text refers to Internet link at http://Homeschool-Books.com

Investigate the life and significance of each person you chose. Use any resource (an encyclopedia, nonfiction book, historical novel, or the Internet). We recommend the following:

Books

The Usborne Book of the Ancient World ☞ ★
Read: "Who was Who in Ancient Rome" (276).

Famous Men of Rome   edited by Rob and Cyndy Shearer
The history of Rome is taught chronologically as students read short biographical sketches. Paperback (June 1989) Greenleaf Pr; ISBN: 1882514033. Reading level: Ages 9-12.

Internet Sources

New Testament Roman Emperors
Description: Brief biographical sketches of Emperors-during New Testament times.

Roman Byzantine People
Description: Biographies of: The Emperor Constantine, Helena, The Empress Eudocia, and The Emperor Justinian.

Emperors, Leaders, Famous Romans
Description: Includes details about: Justinian, Constantine, Hadrian, Trajan, Augustus, Valens, Commodus, Elagabalus, Nero, Caligula, Caesar, Scipio Africanus, Marius, Pompey, Hannibal, Pyrrhus, Geiseric, Surenas, Arminius.

Step 3 Expand

Choose and complete one of the following activities:

Activity 1: Add to Your Time Line Book
Add each of the people you selected from the chart in Step 2 to your Time Line Book. Include summaries.

Activity 2: Write Biographies
Write a brief biography of each of the people you selected from the chart in Step 2. Include the time period in which they lived and a minimum of three facts about each. Refer to "Writing About a Person" in *Writers INC* or to the Biography Maker on the Internet. Biography Maker walks students through the steps of choosing a topic, researching the answers to probing questions, pulling together resources, and creating an engaging story. Younger students can narrate (tell back) what they remember about each person.

Resources recommended in ◆several lessons, ★ several units, ♥other HOW Units. ☞Key Resource (see beginning of unit or page 32).

Activity 3: Make a Biography Box
Cover a cereal box with paper and decorate the box with an image and information about a character from ancient Rome (similar to the sports figure on a box of Wheaties). Include facts about the character's life, illustrations, and a motto that makes clear why the figure has been chosen.

Step 4 Excel

Explain orally to your parents what you've learned in this lesson. Correct all written work to demonstrate correct punctuation and spelling, and effective use of grammar. Add corrected written work or any illustrations to your portfolio.

Food in Ancient Rome

Step 1 Excite

Try a Roman dessert. Stuffed dates were very popular; to make them, chop apples and nuts finely and mix with bread or cookie crumbs. Add a little bit of cinnamon and moisten with fruit juice. Pit dates and stuff them with the mixture.

Step 2 Examine

Research food in Rome. Use any resource (an encyclopedia, nonfiction book, historical novel, or the Internet). We recommend the following:

Books

The Usborne Book of the Ancient World ●— ★
Read: "Food and Dining" (230-231), "In the Kitchen" (232-233), "Entertainments" (248-249), "Festivals" (258-259).

Ancient Rome (Eyewitness) ●— ◆
Read: "House and Home" (24-25), "A Dinner Party" (46-47).

Internet Sources

What Did the Romans Eat?
Description: A sensible site explaining that ancient Romans ate good food, and most of the time, it was simple. Includes recipes adapted from various sources.

Social Position and Food in the Roman Empire
Description: An overview of ancient Roman eating patterns as determined by social position.

Roman Meals: Come Starve with Me
Description: From a Classics professor's recipe pages.

Resources recommended in ◆several lessons, ★ several units, ●other HOW Units. ●—Key Resource (see beginning of unit or page 32).

Step 3 Excel

Choose and complete one of the following activities:

Activity 1: Answer Questions
Learn about dining ancient-Roman style.
- What did they eat for breakfast, lunch ("prandium"), and dinner ("cena")?
- What was the most popular food for cena during the Republic?
- When did Romans add meat to their diets?
- What did they eat at the beginning, and at the end?
- What is the meaning of the expression "ab ovo usque ad mala" (ab-'o-vo-'us-kwe-'ad-ma-la\ L.), "from egg to apples?"
- What furniture was in a Roman dining room?
- Did they use spoons, forks, knives, towels, or napkins?
- What kinds of entertainment did the host provide?
- Romans drank a great deal of wine. Whose tradition did they use in mixing wine with water?

Activity 2: Research
Learn about native Roman ingredients. Discuss why these were popular: Caroenum, Defritum, Liquamen, Passum, Poleiminze, Saturei: Silphium or Laser.

Activity 3: Find Ancient-Roman Recipes
Find old Roman recipes, then use them to plan a full dinner, including an appetizer, entree, side dish, and dessert. A Roman dinner may consist of dishes such as: pepones et melones (water and honey melons), patina de pisciculis (soufflé of small fishes), isicia omentata (a kind of Roman burgers), patina de piris (pear soufflé), and dulcia domestica (dessert of dates and nuts).

Activity 4: Create a Menu and Serve a Dinner
Use the meal plan that you created to design and print a menu which explains the dishes served. Set a dinner table to be as authentically Roman as possible. Serve a Roman dinner to your family.

Step 4 Excel

Share what you have learned about food in ancient Rome with a friend or family member. Correct all written work to demonstrate correct punctuation and spelling, and effective use of grammar. Add corrected written work or any illustrations to your portfolio.

The Gladiators and Colosseum

Step 1 Excite

Have you ever seen a Spanish bullfight? What do bullfighters and gladiators have in common? Watch a video. (Look for the videos below at your local video store, or watch television schedules for local listings.)

Nova's Secrets of Lost Empires: Colosseum (1997)
Description: The 2,000-year-old Colosseum covers six acres, and could seat over 45,000 spectators. How did the Romans succeed in putting a roof across this enormous amphitheater, some 600 feet in diameter? Two experts, engineer and long-time sailor Owain Roberts, and classicist Norma Goldman, responded to selected questions during a live event from NOVA.

Rome and Pompeii
Description: The grandeur of the empire that changed the world is recreated through extraordinary computer modeling. Stand before the Colosseum in the first century, as it is built before your eyes. Step inside and see 50,000 Romans wildly cheering gladiators locked in duels to the death. Take a first-hand look at the lavish lifestyles of Rome and Pompeii—theaters, baths, markets, parties, and home life. 60 Minutes. From The Discovery Channel. 1-800-889-9950.

Step 2 Examine

As the gladiators marched about the amphitheater before engaging in combat with one another or with wild beasts, they saluted the Roman emperor with the words "Morituri te salutamus!" (mor-i-tur-e-'ta-sa-lu-'tam-us), "We who are about to die salute you!" The successful fighter was rewarded with a palm branch. This explains the origin of our phrases "take the palm" and "yield the palm."

Resources recommended in ♦several lessons, ★ several units, ♥other HOW Units. ☜—Key Resource (see beginning of unit or page 32).

Research the Colosseum and gladiators in ancient Rome. Use any resource (an encyclopedia, nonfiction book, historical novel, or the Internet). We recommend the following:

Books

The Usborne Book of the Ancient World ●– ★
Read: "Entertainments" (248-249), "Races and Games" (250-251), "Gladiator Fights" (251-252).

Kingfisher History Encyclopedia ●– ♥
Read: Entries for "Colosseum" (62, 72).

Kingfisher Illustrated History of the World ●– ♥
Read: Entries for "Colosseum" (117, 127).

Ancient Rome (Eyewitness) ●– ♦
Read: "The Bloody Arena" (28-29), "Mortal Combat" (30-31), "Steel and Claws" (32-33), "A Day at the Races" (34-35).

The Penguin Historical Atlas of Ancient Rome ●– ♦
Read: "The Roman Amphitheatre" (82-83). ▯

Caesar and Christ (Story of Civilization III) ♦
Read: "The Games" (381-387).

Internet Sources

Gladiator
Description: Article explaining that a gladiator was a trained warrior who fought bloody battles to entertain the ancient Romans. *A-to-Z History* is brought to you by DiscoverySchool.com, and powered by World Book Online.

The Colosseum
Description: The Colosseum, or Flavian Amphitheatre, is one of the most imposing monuments achieved by the ancient Romans. This site includes photos, articles and more.

Step 3 Expand

Choose and complete one of the following activities:

Activity 1: Write a Summary
Write a summary about the historical facts that you have learned about gladiatorial combat.

Underlined text refers to Internet link at http://Homeschool-Books.com

Activity 2: Answer Questions:
Answer the following:

- How did gladiatorial fights begin?
- When did the first gladiatorial combat in Roman history take place?
- Who gave gladiatorial shows?
- Who were gladiators? What did they learn in gladiatorial schools?
- What could be the reaction of the spectators when a gladiator was disarmed or disabled?
- Who could receive a wooden sword, and what did it mean?
- How many gladiators participated in combats?
- What gladiatorial shows did Julius Caesar and Trajan give?
- Who issued an edict forbidding such exhibitions, and why?
- What do you think is revealed about the people who enjoyed such bloody spectacles?
- What godly character traits were lacking in people who enjoyed this entertainment?

Activity 3: Write an Essay
Write an essay about the significance and meaning of gladiatorial combat in ancient Rome. Compare and contrast it with modern contact sports such as boxing, bullfighting, and football. What can we learn from the spectacles of the Roman amphitheater that will help us avoid temptations in modern entertainment?

Activity 4: Create a Brochure
Create a brochure advertising a day of entertainment at the Roman Colosseum. Include naval battles, gladiatorial fights, and other forms of ancient-Roman entertainment in your advertisement.

Activity 5: Illustrate a Story
One of Aesop's fables, "Androcles and the Lion," tells of the unusual fate of a slave who was put in the arena with a lion. Find the story on the Web or in a children's book. Illustrate your own version of this story and share the story and illustrations with a child.

Step 4 Excel

Share your work from Step 3 with someone. Explain what you have learned in this lesson. Correct all written work to demonstrate correct punctuation and spelling, and effective use of grammar. Add corrected written work or any illustrations to your portfolio.

Resources recommended in ◆several lessons, ★ several units, ♥other HOW Units. ☞–Key Resource (see beginning of unit or page 32).

Language of Ancient Rome

Step 1 Excite

Latin, at first, was a dialect spoken by the tribe of the Latins. Later, as Roman power expanded, Latin became the language of commerce, of government, and of law. Pilate wrote on Jesus' cross: "Jesus of Nazareth, the King of the Jews" in Hebrew, Greek, and Latin (Luke 23:38; John 19:20). When the barbarians overcame Italy, much of Latin literature was temporarily lost; however, Latin did not disappear. It continued to be spoken by the masses, and gradually evolved into the Romance languages; nearly 90 percent of their vocabularies are of Latin derivation.

Latin was the root of such widely spoken Romance languages as French, Italian, Portuguese, Spanish, and Italian, and influenced West Germanic languages like Dutch, English, and German. Throughout the Middle Ages in Europe, Latin served as the language of the Christian Church, and both religious and secular scholarship. To this day, Latin survives as the official tongue of Vatican City, and as the official language of communication of the Roman Catholic Church.

Step 2 Examine

The Romans controlled Britain from A.D. 43 until the fifth century. The invasion of the Saxons and other Germanic tribes caused the native Celtic speech of Britain and the official Latin to be replaced by the Anglo-Saxon language. Hence, English became a Germanic language. The Christianization of England introduced many Latin words. In 1066, the Normans subdued England. Their language, Norman French, had Latin as its basis. It mixed with the Anglo-Saxon language to form Chaucerian English. Latin words as scientific terms, such as bacilli, laboratory, carbon, stimulant, and vacuum, and ordinary Latin words and expressions, like animal, arena, circus, camera, omen, motor, campus, and splendor, without any change of form, are still used in the English language. Upward of 50 percent of our modern English vocabulary is Latin in origin. Knowing the most important roots, prefixes, and suffixes from Latin is invaluable in vocabulary building. For instance: the Latin word "anima" means "breath," "soul," or "spirit," and is seen in the English word "animate."

Research language in ancient Rome. Use any resource (an encyclopedia, nonfiction book, historical novel, or the Internet). We recommend the following:

Underlined text refers to Internet link at http://Homeschool-Books.com

Books

The Usborne Book of the Ancient World ⚷— ★
Read: "Language" (283). Also, see the glossary on page 273 (many Latin words are explained).

Kingfisher History Encyclopedia ⚷— ♥
Read: References to "Latin" in the index.

Kingfisher Illustrated History of the World ⚷— ♥
Read: References to "Latin" in the index.

Internet Sources

Latin Language
Description: An *Encarta Encyclopedia* article.

Latin Word Lists from About.com
Description: Over a dozen word lists, including body parts, poisonous plants, geography, and many more.

Step 3 Expand

Choose and complete one of the following activities:

Activity 1: Vocabulary
Play Rummy Roots and More Rummy Roots card games every day during your study of the ancient Rome unit. (Available through Eternal Hearts 509-732-4147.) These are fun card games designed to help increase English vocabulary in an enjoyable and challenging way. Vocabulary is increased by learning the forty-two Greek and Latin roots through playing each game (forty-two roots per deck). Greek and Latin roots, when combined, form many of our English words. Knowing these roots adds a deeper level of comprehension to reading, aids understanding of how to spell words, and will help increase SAT scores. These games can be played by the entire family, or by just two people. Add new words to your Vocabulary Notebook.

Activity 2: Make a List
Make a list of Latin terms that are used in English, such as a "priori" and "ad hominem." Select at least thirty words from a reference book or Internet site. Be certain that you know the meaning of each word or phrase.

Resources recommended in ♦several lessons, ★ several units, ♥other HOW Units. ⚷—Key Resource (see beginning of unit or page 32).

Activity 3: Learn Roman Numerals
If you haven't already learned Roman numerals, memorize them now. M=1000, D=500, C=100, L=50, X=10, V=5, and I=1. You must learn the system of writing numbers to master Roman numerals. Consult a reference book or Web site to make sure you understand writing and reading numbers using Roman numerals.

Activity 4: Play a Game
Play a game with your friends. Have each person make a list of all the English words with Latin roots that they can think of. Compare your lists. The person who writes the most words will be the winner. Then do the same with specific Latin roots: "bene," meaning "well"; "unus," meaning "one"; "bi," meaning "two"; "tri," meaning "three"; "dic," from dicere, meaning "to say" or "to tell"; "fac," from facere, meaning "to do" or "to make"; and "vol" from volens, meaning "wishing."

Step 4 Excel

Share your work from Step 3 with someone. Explain what you have learned in this lesson. Correct all written work to demonstrate correct punctuation and spelling, and effective use of grammar. Add corrected written work or any illustrations to your portfolio.

Laws in Ancient Rome

Step 1 Excite

Roman law has influenced the laws of every country in Western Europe. How do you think that the ancient Romans created a code of law, since they didn't accept Mosaic Law? Is a sense of fairness part of human nature? Can people recognize an unjust law without the guidance of the Holy Spirit? Do you suppose that ancient-Roman laws were made through trial and error, or that they were the result of careful deliberation?

Step 2 Examine

Investigate ancient-Roman laws. What was the "Law of the Twelve Tables"? Who organized the laws as the "Roman Civil Law," and when? What are the "Corpus Iuris" and the "Institutes of Gaius"? Learn about changes the imperial system brought into the law system and judgment. Who unified all local edicts? When proconsuls judged people, they took local traditions into consideration; thus, laws were different in every province. Read Matthew 27:15-17; 27:62-66; and John 19:31. What did Roman citizens gain after the reforms of Hadrian? Read Acts 25:11-14, 24-27; 26:1, 30-32.

What document guaranteed the equal protection under the law to every citizen of the United States? When was it instituted?

Books

The Usborne Book of the Ancient World ⊶ ★
Read: "Rome's Social and Political Structure" (202), "The Legal System" (266).

The Greco-Roman World of the New Testament Era ⊶ ♥
Read: "Tools of Governance: Finances, Law & the Military" (154-171). ▯

Caesar and Christ (Story of Civilization III) ♦
Read: Chapter XVIII "Roman Law" (391-406). Also see "The Lawmakers" (25-27), "The Magistrates" (28-30), "The Beginnings of Roman Law" (31-32).

Internet Sources

Legal Status in the Roman World
Description: Article that explains the customs and laws associated with marriage in ancient Rome.

Resources recommended in ♦several lessons, ★ several units, ♥ other HOW Units. ⊶—Key Resource (see beginning of unit or page 32).

Roman Law Resources
Description: This site provides information on ancient-Roman law sources and literature, the teaching of ancient-Roman law, and the persons who engage in the study of ancient-Roman law, from the University of Aberdeen.

Roman Law
Description: These pages are dedicated to ancient-Roman Law: the legal system invented by the ancient Romans more than 2,000 years ago, which—having undergone the process of decay, revival, transformation, and reinterpretation innumerable times—continues to influence legal thinking and legal practice to our day.

Step 3 Expand

Choose and complete one of the following activities:

Activity 1: Copy Paragraphs
Copy (by hand or typing) two or more paragraphs from your research which explain law in ancient Rome. Younger students can copy one or two sentences or narrate (tell back) what has been learned.

Activity 2: Paraphrase
Write paraphrases of the constitutional amendments that guarantee equality to United States citizens. Younger students can copy one or two sentences or narrate (tell back) what has been learned.

Activity 3: Discuss Roman Law
Discuss ancient-Roman law. Do you think that ancient-Roman law was a good basis for European common law? What do you think would have happened if the laws of ancient Rome had not been preserved and reinstituted in Europe during the Middle Ages?

Activity 4: Write a Summary
Write a summary of what you have learned about ancient-Roman law. Include the differences between Republican and Imperial laws.

Step 4 Excel

Share what you have learned about ancient-Roman law with a friend or family member. Correct all written work to demonstrate correct punctuation and spelling, and effective use of grammar. Add corrected written work or any illustrations to your portfolio.

Literature in Ancient Rome

Step 1 Excite

Brainstorm and discuss what you know about literature in ancient Rome. If the ancient Romans had books, how were they made? What types of materials were used? Did they have newspapers? What would be in a newspaper? What did books look like? Did they have libraries?

Step 2 Examine

Most of our knowledge about ancient Rome comes from written records of the Romans themselves (the language of ancient Rome is primarily Latin). These records include such documents as law codes, treaties, and decrees of the emperors and the Roman Senate. Other written records are masterpieces of Latin literature. In many works, the authors wrote about events which they lived through. Such works include the letters and speeches of Cicero and the letters of Pliny the Younger. Julius Caesar wrote about his conquest of Gaul in *Commentaries on the Gallic War*. Roman historians supplied the narrations that connected many of the events that other writers described. Livy told of Rome's development from its legendary origins to his own time, the Augustan Age. Tacitus described the period of Roman history from Emperors Tiberius to Domitian. Suetonius wrote biographies of the rulers from Julius Caesar to Domitian.[1]

Latin literary works have had a great influence on Western literature and culture. Famous writings include speeches and letters by Cicero, history by Tacitus, humor by Horace and Juvenal, and poetry by Ovid and Virgil.

Writing materials consisted of papyrus or parchment scrolls, and small wax tablets. Books were written by hand and copied by Greek slaves. Both the state and individuals set up large libraries. By the Late Empire there were twenty-nine libraries in Rome. A newspaper was distributed through Rome titled the *Acta Diurna* ("Daily Events").

Research ancient-Roman literature. Use any resource (an encyclopedia, a nonfiction book, or the Internet). We recommend the following:

Books

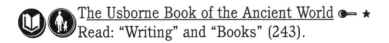 The Usborne Book of the Ancient World ●— ★
Read: "Writing" and "Books" (243).

Resources recommended in ◆several lessons, ★ several units, ● other HOW Units. ●—Key Resource (see beginning of unit or page 32).

Heart of Wisdom Publishing   683

The Penguin Historical Atlas of Ancient Rome ◉━ ◆
Read: "Writing and Literacy" (78-79). ▯

Caesar and Christ (Story of Civilization III) ◆
Read: "The Awakening of Literature" (97-101), "Literature Under the Revolution" (146-166).

Internet Sources

Latin Literature
Description: An *Encarta Encyclopedia* article.

Roman Literature
Description: An annotated list of links to samples of ancient-Roman literature and poetry.

Literary Resources
Description: Resources for Greek and Latin Classics from the Library of Congress.

Latin Literature
Description: MSN Encarta highlights the development of literature, dominant in the time of ancient Rome and much of the Middle Ages, that lasted into the Renaissance.

Works by Julius Caesar Internet Classics
Description: Archive provides Julius Caesar's *War Commentaries*, which chronicle many of ancient Rome's military conflicts.

Words Written Upon the Hide of a Cow
Description: Links to several articles pertaining to ancient-Roman literature.

Greek and Roman Comedy
Description: This site presents various literary and visual evidence of the performance of ancient Greek and Roman comedy, the development of the genre, and the cultural background of dramatic performance.

The Development of a Classical Style
Description: An encyclopedia article explaining that the last era of the Roman Republic produced some of the greatest figures in Latin literature.

Roman Mythology
Description: An encyclopedia article giving an overview of Roman mythology.

(i) Classical Greek and Roman Poets
Description: Links to information about: Catullus, Homer, Horace, Lucan, Ovid, Sappho, and Virgil.

Step 3 Expand

Choose and complete one of the following activities:

Activity 1: Make a Chart
Find a title written by each of the authors listed below. Make a chart displaying the authors' names, dates, book titles, and the type of literature the book represents: historical works, poetry, biography, etc.

Aurelius	Livy	Propertius
Cato	Lucretius	Seneca
Catullus	MartialOvid	Suetonius
Cicero	Petronius	Tacitus
Horace	Pliny the Elder	Publius Terentius Afer or
Julius Caesar	Pliny the Younger	Terence
Josephus	Plutarch	Virgil

Activity 2: Answer Questions
Answer the following:
- How were libraries established?
- How many libraries were in Rome during the time of the Late Empire?
- Who made books, and how?
- What materials were used to make books?
- What did books look like?
- When did the word "codex" appear?
- How did Christians use the word "codex"?
- Athens, Alexandria, and Rome were great centers of book production, and they exported books throughout the ancient world. Find out how the books were made.

Activity 3: Copy a Passage
Copy (by hand or typing) two or more paragraphs from literature in ancient Rome.

Resources recommended in ◆several lessons, ★ several units, ✿ other HOW Units. ☞ Key Resource (see beginning of unit or page 32).

Heart of Wisdom Publishing   685

Activity 4: Make a Book

Make a book of your own which tells an ancient-Roman legend or myth. Choose a creative title for your book and make a title page. Illustrate a cover, which should be made of cardstock or stiff cardboard. Your illustration could be a drawing, a photograph—photocopying a black-and-white photograph makes an effective illustration—or a collage of pictures cut out of magazines.

Activity 5: Make a Newspaper

Make a Roman newspaper titled *Acta Diurna* ("Daily Events"). Include headings, bylines, pictures, photographs, and anything else which you think will make your project better. You can create a newspaper online using <u>Create Your Own Newspaper</u>.

Step 4 Excel

Share what you have learned about literature in ancient Rome with a friend or family member. Correct all written work to demonstrate correct punctuation and spelling, and effective use of grammar. Add corrected written work or any illustrations to your portfolio.

Footnote
Gruen, Erich S. "Rome, Ancient," Discovery Channel School, original content provided by World Book Online, <http://www.discoveryschool.com/homeworkhelp/ worldbook/atozhistory/r/474350.html>, (Accessed 12/01/00).

Underlined text refers to Internet link at <u>http://Homeschool-Books.com</u>

Medicine in Ancient Rome

Step 1 Excite

The ancient Romans followed up the scientific methods which the ancient Greeks and Asians used in their development of medicine. The ancient Romans, like the ancient Greeks and medieval Europeans, believed that there were four "humors" in the body, and that an imbalance in these humors caused disease. Can you name the four humors? (Blood, phlegm, yellow bile (or choler), and black bile.) Does this belief have any scientific validity? [1]

Step 2 Examine

Research medicine in ancient Rome. Use any resource (an encyclopedia, nonfiction book, historical novel, or the Internet). We recommend the following:

Books

The Usborne Book of the Ancient World ●— ★
Read: "Medicine" (260-261).

Ancient Rome (Eyewitness) ●— ◆
Read: "Healing the Sick" (54-55).

Caesar and Christ (Story of Civilization III) ◆
Read: "Roman Medicine" (311-312).

Internet Sources

Ancient Medicine
Description: Read essays on the history of medicine in ancient Rome and Greece. Includes links to resources on the history of medicine.

Medicine of Ancient Rome
Description: Excellent overview of medicine and surgery in ancient Rome.

Discover Magazine - Lead Poisoning in the Roman Empire
Description: An article that relates recent archaeological discoveries which conclude that Rome's downfall was precipitated by the peoples' heavy use of lead in everyday life.

Resources recommended in ◆several lessons, ★ several units, ●other HOW Units. ●—Key Resource (see beginning of unit or page 32).

(i) <u>Etruscan and Roman Medicine</u>
Description: Explore the origins of medicine in ancient Roman civilization. Research the first doctor to arrive in Rome, and the role he played within society.

(i) <u>Greco-Roman Medicine</u>
Description: Resource for ancient Greco-Roman medicine, and medical thought from Mycenaean times until the fall of the Roman Empire.

(i) <u>Lancet Interactive - Cranial Surgery in Ancient Rome</u>
Description: Article by Renato Mariani-Costantini reports on new archaeological evidence related to the practice of cranial surgery in ancient Rome.

(i) <u>Roman Medicine</u>
Description: Provides essays, resources, and bibliographies on the study of ancient medicine as practiced in Greece and Rome.

Step 3 Expand

Choose and complete one of the following activities:

Activity 1: Research and Answer
Use your research to answer the following about the ancient Romans:
- What did they believe caused disease?
- What diseases were most troublesome?
- Did they practice good hygiene?
- Where did they receive most of their knowledge?
- When were the first medical schools opened?
- What subjects did students learn?
- What medical instruments did doctors use?
- What methods of curing diseases did they practice?
- Where was the first public hospital?
- What did women doctors do?
- How many different specialties did doctors have?
- Which of their methods of treatment do we still use?

Activity 2: Write a Textbook Entry
Write a "textbook entry" for an ancient-Roman medical school. Explain the four humors, tell about common diseases and their treatments, and explain the medical instruments that a doctor should be familiar with.

Activity 3: Give a Lecture
Wear a costume as you give a "lecture" (skit) for your "medical school class" (family), in which you explain to your students the basics of Roman medicine. Have a copy of your "textbook entry" available for your "students."

Step 4 Excel

Explain orally to your parents what you've learned in this lesson. Correct all written work to demonstrate correct punctuation and spelling, and effective use of grammar. Add corrected written work or any illustrations to your portfolio.

Resources recommended in ◆several lessons, ★ several units, ♥ other HOW Units. ◉━Key Resource (see beginning of unit or page 32).

Heart of Wisdom Publishing   689

Military in Ancient Rome

Step 1 Excite

Watch a video. (Look for the video below at your local video store or watch television schedules for local air times.)

The Legions of Rome
See description of this four-volume set in the Resources Section.

Step 2 Examine

Research the ancient-Roman army. Use any resource (an encyclopedia, a historical novel, or the Internet). We recommend the following:

Books

The Usborne Book of the Ancient World ☜ ★
Read: "The Army" (206-207), "A Soldiers Life" (208-209).

Kingfisher History Encyclopedia ☜ ♥
Read: "The Roman Army" (64-65).

Kingfisher Illustrated History of the World ☜ ♥
Read: "The Roman Army" (114-115).

Ancient Rome (Eyewitness) ☜ ♦
Read: "The Legionary" (10-11), "Battle and Defense" (12-13), "Soldiers in Society" (14-15).

The Greco-Roman World of the New Testament Era ☜ ♥
Read: "Tools of Governance: Finances, Law & the Military" (171-179). ▯

The Penguin Historical Atlas of Ancient Rome ☜ ♦
Read: "The Over-Mighty Generals" (28-19), "The Roman Army" (62-63), "Guarding the Frontiers" (86-87).

Underlined text refers to Internet link at http://Homeschool-Books.com

Caesar and Christ (Story of Civilization III) ◆
Read: "The Army of the Republic" (33-34). Also see references to "army" in the index.

The Eagle of the Ninth by Rosemary Sutcliff
In this fictional story set in A.D. 125, during the Roman Empire's occupation of Britain, a young Roman centurion must recover the infamous Ninth Legion's missing symbol of honor, the eagle standard. Sutcliff presents an unusual blend of stirring action and poetic symbolism in an authentic story from long ago. If you enjoy this book, you might want to read the next two books in the series: *The Silver Branch* and *The Lantern Bearers*. (September 1993) Sunburst; ISBN: 0374419302. Reading level: Young adult.

Roman Warfare by Adrian Goldsworthy, John Keegan (Editor)
Description: A well-constructed survey of how armies in ancient Rome prepared, equipped, manned, and made war, using selected illustrative examples from each stage of development over the thousand-year period.(April 2000) Cassell Academic; ISBN: 0304352659.

Internet Sources

The Roman Army
Description: Extensive resource on the origins of the military in ancient Rome, including the formation of the phalanx, and Roman army camps.

The Roman Army
Description: Primary School site with brief descriptions of military life in ancient Rome. Includes illustrations of weapons, uniforms, and forts.

Virtual Legion - Online History
Description: Animated graphics and sound files guide you to an understanding of the ancient-Roman military. (Move your cursor over the images, then click when something you wish to learn more about is highlighted.) This site might take awhile to load but it is well worth the wait.

Armamentarivm
Description: A dynamic illustrated source book about ancient-Roman military equipment. Includes weaponry, clothing, standards, etc.; combines archaeological and textual knowledge with practical experience drawn in part from modern reenactments and reconstructions.

The Roman Army Page
Description: An excellent general overview of the ancient-Roman army, in one lengthy page.

Resources recommended in ◆several lessons, ★ several units, ● other HOW Units. ●▬Key Resource (see beginning of unit or page 32).

Warfare in the Roman World
Description: A collection of resources relevant to the subject of Warfare in the ancient-Roman world. It covers material from the periods of the Republic and Empire. Originally prepared for a college course titled *Roman Warfare*.

The Roman Army
Description: An introduction to the organization and equipment of the ancient-Roman army, from the first century until the early fifth century.

Soldiers of the Roman Army
Description: Illustrations and a quiz to match names of soldiers: cavalarist, tribunus militum, hastatus, veles, legionarius, centurio, and praetorian.

Catapults of the Roman Empire
Description: Article explaining that ancient-Roman armies employed the largest, most sophisticated catapults of their time.

Step 3 Expand

Choose and complete one of the following activities:

Activity 1: Write Journal Entries
Based on information you have learned, imagine the life of an ancient-Roman soldier. Write several journal entries describing a day in the service of the ancient-Roman army.

Activity 2: Write an Essay
Write an essay on the Roman army either during the era of the Roman Republic or the Roman Empire.

Activity 3: Discuss Scriptures
The Roman army was one of the most disciplined in the ancient world. There were eighteen offenses for which a guard unit of Roman soldiers could be put to death; these included falling asleep, and leaving one's position unguarded. Read Matthew 28:2-4; and Luke 24:1-2. These scriptures prove that only a supernatural event—like the resurrection of Jesus—was an acceptable cause for a guard unit to flee. The penalty for this offense also explodes the theory that while the soldiers were sleeping, disciples of Jesus had stolen His body from the tomb. Read these scriptures to your family, and talk about the event from the Roman soldiers' point of view.

Activity 4: Answer Questions
Answer the following:

- Who joined the army during the times of the Early Republic and the Empire?
- How many soldiers were in a centuria, a cogorta, and a legion?
- Who reorganized the army, and when?
- How long did military service last?
- How much was a soldier's salary?
- How were soldiers trained, and what professions did they have to learn?
- How were they disciplined?
- Why were they called "Marius' mules"?
- Who provided their food?
- What armor and weapons did they have?
- How did the army influence political life?
- What were shields made from?

Step 4 Excel

Share what you have learned about the ancient-Roman military with a friend or family member. Correct all written work to demonstrate correct punctuation and spelling, and effective use of grammar. Add corrected written work or any illustrations to your portfolio.

Resources recommended in ◆several lessons, ★ several units, ♥other HOW Units. ◉—Key Resource (see beginning of unit or page 32).

Heart of Wisdom Publishing   693

Money in Ancient Rome

Step 1 Excite

Titian (1477-1576) was a celebrated Venetian painter. He developed coloristic style in the grand manner typical of the High Renaissance. His painting "The Tribute Money" illustrates Matthew 22:19-21. View this painting.

Step 2 Examine

The ancient Romans began making their own coins about the fourth century B.C., and laid the foundations of modern coinage. Explore the subject of ancient coins. Who minted the first coins? Why were coins invented? How do people carry on commerce without coins? (Bartering) What are the advantages of using coins?

Do research to find pictures of ancient-Roman money. Use any resource (an encyclopedia, nonfiction book, historical novel, or the Internet). Web sites that sell ancient-Roman coins have excellent images. Draw your own coin.

Books

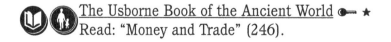
The Usborne Book of the Ancient World ●— ★
Read: "Money and Trade" (246).

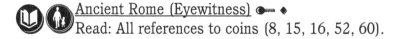
Ancient Rome (Eyewitness) ●— ◆
Read: All references to coins (8, 15, 16, 52, 60).

The Penguin Historical Atlas of Ancient Rome ☞ ♦
Read: All references to coins (30, 40, 72, 80, 111, 119).

Caesar and Christ (Story of Civilization III) ♦
Read: "The Bankers" (330-332), and all references to coinage in the index.

Step 3 Expand

Activity 1: Look up Bible Passages
Mentions of Roman coins in the Bible are found in Matthew 5:26, 10:29, 12:42, 22:19; Mark 12:15; and Luke 12:6 and 20:24. Write down all the kinds of coins mentioned there, and the circumstances under which they are mentioned. Which Roman coins were the most common in New Testament times? The first "denarii" bore a depiction of a Roman goddess in a helmet. Read Matthew 22:20, Mark 12:16, and Luke 20:24, and describe how a denarius looked in later times. Read Matthew 20:2,9, and 13. How long did a man have to work to earn one denarius? According to Roman historian Tacitus, one denarius was the daily salary of a soldier at the time of the Emperor Tiberius. Read Revelation 6:6 to learn the prices for food during hard times.

Activity 2: Add to Your Time Line Book
Add illustrations of coins to your Time Line Book.

Activity 3: Interview
Almost since the first known coins were minted, they have been collected. Coin-collecting as a hobby dates back more than two-thousand years to the ancient Greeks and Romans. The art of collecting and studying coins is known as "numismatics." A coin collector is called a "numismatist." These terms are derived from the Latin word "numisma," which means "coin." Perhaps you know someone who collects coins. If so, discuss ancient-Roman coins with him or her.

Step 4 Excel

If you would like to start a coin collection, the easiest and most inexpensive way is to begin with coins that are still in circulation. Books about coins can be found in public libraries or coin shops. If you live close to Philadelphia or Denver, you can visit U.S. Government mints with your family.

Resources recommended in ♦several lessons, ★ several units, ●other HOW Units. ☞Key Resource (see beginning of unit or page 32).

Heart of Wisdom Publishing   695

Philosophy in Ancient Rome

Step 1 Excite

What is your personal philosophy of life? What is the most important goal in your life? How did you adopt this philosophy? Do you find yourself fighting against the philosophies of the world? What is a common philosophy of life that you notice in other young adults? Do you know any hedonists? Any humanists? These are common non-Christian approaches to life. Into what kinds of behavior do these philosophies lead people in modern times? What kind of behavior does your philosophy of life call for?

Step 2 Examine

Research the most common philosophies of Rome: Stoicism, Neoplatonism, and Epicureanism. Who taught these philosophies? What were the basic teachings of each?

Books

The Greco-Roman World of the New Testament Era ◐— ♥
Read: "Influences on the Christian Organization" (71-88). The author explains that the synagogue and especially the household and the voluntary associations of the Greco-Roman world were the structures that the Christians borrowed from in order to organize their churches.

Caesar and Christ (Story of Civilization III) ◆
Read: "The Philosophers" (299-300) and all references to philosophy in the index.

Internet Sources

Roman Philosophy
Description: An annotated list of links to several sites on this topic.

Roman Philosophy
Description: Brief overview from the Internet Encyclopedia of Philosophy.

Step 3 Expand

Choose and complete one of the following activities:

Activity 1: Find Bible Verses
Which values in life seemed to be most important to the ancient Romans? Find Bible verses that teach us not to adopt these values.

Activity 2: Write Summary Paragraphs
Write three summary paragraphs defining these philosophies: Stoicism, Neoplatonism, and Epicureanism. Then write an introductory paragraph and a concluding paragraph, and choose an appropriate title for your essay on ancient-Roman philosophy.

Activity 3: Make a List
Read "Christian World View" in *The Heart of Wisdom Teaching Approach*. Make two columns on a piece of paper. List the Roman world view on one side and a biblical world view on the other.

Activity 4: Prepare an Inspirational Speech
Prepare an inspirational speech about how Christians should resist the philosophies of the world. Use clear words that will form a vivid image in the minds of your listeners. Use real-life examples that your audience can relate to. Write the speech out and show it to your parents or your pastor, in order to get suggestions for improvement. Once your speech is polished, record your voice reading the speech. Share the audio recording through a Web site, a local radio station, or by giving it to a library.

Step 4 Excel

Explain orally to your parents what you've learned in this lesson. Correct all written work to demonstrate correct punctuation and spelling, and effective use of grammar. Add corrected written work or any illustrations to your portfolio.

Resources recommended in ◆several lessons, ★ several units, ♥other HOW Units. ●—Key Resource (see beginning of unit or page 32).

Heart of Wisdom Publishing   697

Religion in Ancient Rome

Step 1 Excite

Some modern Americans are following various forms of pagan religions. "Paganism spans the globe with a vast family tree of traditions," one Web site touts. When you study accurate history about worship in ancient Rome, you will be horrified to see what pagan religion can be. Paul warns in 1 Corinthians 10:20 that pagan sacrifices are made to demons, and studying history shows us that Roman idol worship was demonic and evil. In the past, the word "pagan" has been used as a negative way of calling someone a non-Christian. In our day, the term "pagan" often refers to an actual religious belief. People generally define themselves as pagans if they practice a religion that does not accept the truth that there is one God: they worship deities, and they are more than merely followers of a philosophy. Romans worshiped many gods and were pagans in this sense.

The Word of God is our guidebook for life. Read Psalm 119:105 and 2 Peter 1:19. Where in the Bible are we taught to avoid pagan worship practices? Would you be ready to speak the truth of God's Word to a modern follower of a pagan religion?

Step 2 Examine

Ancient Romans, like virtually all peoples before "the Age of Reason," believed in supernatural powers. There was a general acceptance of Canaanite, Egyptian, and Greek gods. The Canaanite god Baal, the Egyptian god Amon, and the Persian god Ahura Mazda were identified with the Greek god Zeus. The Romans called him "Jupiter." The ancient Romans felt the state was inseparable from religion.

The people of ancient Rome had statues of their gods. Research the pagan religion of the ancient Romans. Use any resource (an encyclopedia, nonfiction book, historical novel, or the Internet). Be careful in doing Internet searches on this topic. People are actually trying to revive the worship of ancient pagan deities, and their presence on the Web is something you should strictly avoid. We recommend the following:

Books

> Encyclopedia of the Bible (Nelson's Illustrated) ●— ♥
> "Roman Religion and Beliefs" (74-75).

> The Usborne Book of the Ancient World ●— ★
> Read: "Religious Beliefs" (254-255), "Gods and Godesses" (256-257),
> "Festivals" (258-259).

Underlined text refers to Internet link at http://Homeschool-Books.com

Ancient Rome (Eyewitness) ◉— ◆
Read: "A World of So Many Gods" (50-51), "Worship and Sacrifice" (52-53).

The Greco-Roman World of the New Testament Era ◉— ♥
Read: "Religion in the Greco-Roman World" (89-110).:THis chapter explains the Empire was the home of various nations, which had different religions. The Roman attitude towards these religions was not uniform, and it ranged from toleration and acceptance to repression and persecution.

Caesar and Christ (Story of Civilization III) ◆
Read: "The Religion of Rome" (58-71), "The New Gods" (93-96), "The New Faiths" (388-390).

Internet Sources

Religion in Ancient Rome
Description: A good overview which includes: "Religious Practices," "Religious Festivals," and "Family Religious Practices."

Hellenistic/Roman Religion & Philosophy by James Tabor
Description: An overview of Hellenistic/Roman religion and philosophy by the author of The Jewish Roman World of Jesus.

Pagan Shrines and Temples
Description: Chapter 2 from Pagan and Christian Rome by Rodolfo Lanciani, originally published by Houghton, Mifflin and Company Boston and New York, 1892.

Step 3 Expand

Choose and complete at least two activities below:

Activity 1: Contrast and Compare
Create a contrast-and-compare graphic (see page 26) compare biblical celebrations with pagan Roman celebrations. Make a chart with the following columns: "Festival Name," "Date," "What was Celebrated," "Who was Honored," and "Type of Celebration." Include the biblical celebrations: Passover, Unleavened Bread, FirstFruits, Succoth, Feast of Trumpets, Day of Atonement, and Feast of Tabernacles. Include Roman celebrations: Floralia, Hallomas, Eastre, Ferrua, Cerealia, Saturnalia, Volcanalia, Lupercalia, and the Equiria. Follow the link for a chart that you can fill in.

Resources recommended in ◆several lessons, ★ several units, ♥other HOW Units. ◉—Key Resource (see beginning of unit or page 32).

Heart of Wisdom Publishing   699

Activity 2: Read and Summarize

Read and orally summarize the following verses: Exodus 19-24, especially 19:1-8, 20:3-5, and Chapter 23. Then read Leviticus 26:1; Deuteronomy 5:7-9; 29:17; 32:17; Joshua 24:14; Judges 2:2-3; Psalms 97:7; 106:19-22; Isaiah 40:18-25; 42:17; 44:9-19; 34-39; Romans 1:21-25; 1 Corinthians 10:14,20; and Colossians 3:5.

Activity 3: Write a Report

Write a report on ancient-Roman religion. Discuss the two main groups of gods; how Greek beliefs influenced ancient-Roman religion; the cult of Vesta; which cults came to Rome from the Etruscans, Indians, Gauls, Egyptians, Carthaginians, and peoples of Asia Minor; and how ancient Romans worshiped all their gods and goddesses. Younger students can narrate (orally tell) what they have learned.

Activity 4: Write a Paper

Write a paper explaining that the Bible condemns all kinds of occult practices and forbids any associations with people involved in them. Refer to Exodus 22:18; Leviticus 19:31; 20:6,27; Deuteronomy 18:10-12; 1 Samuel 15:23; 2 Kings 23:24; Isaiah 8:19; 44:25; 47:12-15; Jeremiah 27:9; Acts 9:24; 13:6-11; 19:13-20; Galatians 5:20; and Revelation 21:8 and 22:15.

Activity 5: Write an Open Letter

Think through how you could witness to someone who practices paganism. Write an open letter directed to anyone who is experimenting with pagan worship. Explain what the Bible teaches about idols and false gods. Show your letter to your parents and your pastor in order to get advice for improvement. Polish your words until they are godly, gracious, and persuasive.

Activity 6: Answer the Following

Why were the famous sibylline books so important for Romans, and who wrote them? What did astrologists do, and when did they become popular? Where did the sick sleep to see dreams about their healing? Who were augurs, and how did they predict the future?

Step 4 Excel

Share what you have learned about pagan religion with a friend or family member. Correct all written work to demonstrate correct punctuation and spelling, and effective use of grammar. Add corrected written work or any illustrations to your portfolio.

The Messiah Unit

Unit Overview

Messiah Overview 702

Messiah Objectives 704

Messiah Time Line 705

Messiah Resources 706

Messiah Lessons

Introduction: Mind of Christ 710

Messiah in the Old Testament

Messianic Prophecies 713

Christ, Our Passover Lamb 715

Type of Christ: Joseph 717

Type of Christ: Moses 721

Type of Christ: Boaz 723

Messiah in the Gospels

Geography at the Time of Christ .724

Culture at the Time of Christ 726

The Gospels 729

Genealogy of the Messiah 732

Birth of Christ 734

Christ's Disciples 737

The Bible Jesus Read 739

The Kingdom of God 742

Attitude Toward Lepers 744

Teachings on Law 746

Teachings Through Parables 750

Miracles Performed by Christ 754

Attitude Toward Adulteress 757

Christ, Our Shepherd 759

Attitude Toward Women 761

Attitude Toward Children 763

Christ, Our Bridegroom 765

Attitude Toward the Poor 767

Teachings on Love 769

Teachings on Forgiveness 772

Crucifixion and Resurrection 774

Names of the Messiah 780

Related Lessons in Other Units

Birth of Christianity (Rome) 627

Messiah Overview

Humankind was in peril. Adam and Eve had disobeyed God, choosing to think and act in a way that was contrary to what God had taught them. They had rebelled and behaved as they wished—not for God's glory, but for their own desires. And the consequences were dreadful: The two parents of all mankind were ashamed, accursed, and driven from their home (Genesis 2).

They must have felt profoundly sorrowful when they repented and were once again in fellowship with their Creator. But even though they repented and submitted to God, their offspring were also rebellious, as they had been. We are told that, from the earliest human history, *the wickedness of man was great in the earth* (Genesis 6:5). Likewise, in our own time, we see the ungodly deeds of people who are in rebellion against God.

Humankind needs a champion, a hero who can rescue us. But who is mighty enough to rescue us from our own rebellious folly? Who can save us from our sinful deeds? Who can prevent God from justly administering the punishment that each of us so richly deserves? People throughout history have rallied behind heroes, victorious conquerors, and "mighty men." The first such leader mentioned in Scripture was Nimrod, "a mighty one on the earth." But Nimrod was not the kind of hero who could lead people into righteousness or into the blessings that come with godly behavior. The foundations of government that Nimrod laid were built into the pagan civilizations of Babylon and Assyria (Genesis 10:8-12). Mankind has never produced a mighty hero who could rescue people from rebelliousness and ungodliness.

God, however, did provide someone to rescue mankind. His plan for providing a Savior is called a "mystery," a plan that God established before He created the world. Examine 1 Corinthians 2:6-8:

> Howbeit we speak wisdom among them that are perfect: yet not the wisdom of this world, nor of the princes of this world, that come to naught: But we speak the wisdom of God in a mystery, even the hidden wisdom, which God ordained before the world unto our glory: Which none of the princes of this world knew: for had they known it, they would not have crucified the Lord of glory.

The princes, the leaders, the conquerors in this world are powerless to meet the true needs of the souls of their earthly subjects. The Bible says that they come to nothing. But God ordained a plan, in His wisdom, to redeem mankind from sin. It is this plan, this "hidden mystery," and this Savior, whom you are preparing to study.

God's plan was to provide the Messiah to save mankind from sin. The word "Messiah" in Hebrew means the "anointed one," signifying a king. The chosen people of Israel believed in the Word of God as revealed through the prophets, which promised that God would send them a king and savior. Such was their messianic expectation. God sent this Messiah in the person of Jesus, also called "Christ," the Greek translation of Messiah.

> For by him [Jesus] were all things created, that are in heaven, and that are in earth, visible and invisible, whether they be thrones, or dominions, or principalities, or powers: all things were created by him, and for him: And he is before all things, and by him all things consist. And he is the head of the body, the church: who is the beginning, the firstborn from the dead; that in all things he might have the preeminence. For it pleased the Father that in him should all fulness dwell; And, having made peace through the blood of his cross, by him to reconcile all things unto himself; by him, I say, whether they be things in earth, or things in heaven. …In whom are hid all the treasures of wisdom and knowledge. And this I say, lest any man should beguile you with enticing words (Colossians 1:15-20; 2:3-4).

What could be more exciting! All the treasures of wisdom and knowledge are hidden in the person of the Messiah! You have the opportunity to investigate ancient prophecies, hidden wisdom, things that people longed to know for centuries before the Messiah came to dwell on earth. You are in the privileged position of looking backward through history to see the Messiah as He was described in prophesy, as He dwelt on earth, as He is now, and as He speaks to you through His Word.

Recommended Literature for this Unit

Begin reading the Gospels now, and continue to do so throughout this unit. Read the passages chronologically, using *The Narrated Bible* (pages 1349-1484). If you are blessed by finishing your reading before you finish the lessons, then begin reading the Gospels over again, this time in the usual order.

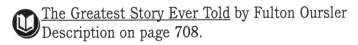
The Greatest Story Ever Told by Fulton Oursler
Description on page 708.

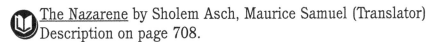
The Nazarene by Sholem Asch, Maurice Samuel (Translator)
Description on page 708.

Resources recommended in ◆several lessons, ★ several units, ♥ other HOW Units. ●━Key Resource (see beginning of unit or page 32).

Heart of Wisdom Publishing 703

Messiah Objectives

Upon completion of this unit your student should:

- Have an appreciation for the importance of the Old Testament and its relationship to the New Testament.
- Grasp the enormity of God's gift of forgiveness, and practice gratitude.
- Know the size of the geographic area in which Jesus ministered.
- Know what a "harmony of the Gospels" is.
- Know the ways in which each of the four Gospels is unique.
- Have practice in discussing favorite Bible passages with older people
- Be able to reflect on how Jesus participated in human history.
- Know how Jesus treated women.
- Be able to reflect on which words and actions express God's love.
- Know what the Messiah taught about forgiveness.
- Be able to reflect on the forgiveness that the Messiah makes available to us.
- Know how Jesus treated poor people.
- Minister to hungry people.
- Know-how Jesus ministered to lepers.
- Understand-the Messiah's attitude toward children.
- Know how the Messiah is described through metaphors and types.
- Understand the analogy of the union between husband and wife to the union between Christ and the Church.
- Be able to reflect on the sufferings of Jesus during the Crucifixion.
- Have practice in giving a defense of the historical Resurrection of Jesus.
- Understand-cultural practices that are mentioned in the Gospels.
- Know the characteristics of disciples of Jesus.
- Have an understanding of what is meant by the term "kingdom of God."
- Have-a concept of the Law as a tutor to lead us to Christ.
- Desire to allow God to transform him/her by "the renewing of his/her mind."
- Know the various names of the Messiah, and what they mean.
- Understand the nature and purpose of parables.
- Know what Jesus taught about love for God and for our neighbors.
- Know what Jesus taught about prayer.
- Be able to practice artistic expression.

Messiah Timeline

Childhood	Year of Opposition c. A.D. 29	The Last Week
Birth of Jesus c. 6/4 B.C. *	John the Baptist is killed by Herod	The Triumphal Entry
Visit by shepherds	Sends his 12 followers out to preach and heal	Curses the fig tree
Presentation in the temple	Feeds 5,000 people	Cleanses the temple
Visit by the Magi	Walks on water	His authority questioned
Escape to Egypt	Withdraws to Tyre and Sidon	Teaches in the temple
Return to Nazareth	Feeds 4,000 people	Anointed
Visit to temple as a boy 12 years old. Passover	Peter says that Jesus is the Son of God	The plot against Jesus
Adult Ministry c. A.D. 27	Tells his disciples he is going to die soon	Passover Supper
Baptized	Is transfigured	Comforts the disciples
Tempted by Satan	Pays his temple taxes	Gethsemane
First miracle	Attends the Feast of the Tabernacles	Arrest and trial
Cleansing of the temple	Heals a man who was born blind	Crucifixion and death on Passover. Jesus is our Passover Lamb (Jn 1:29)
Speaks with Nicodemus	Visits Mary and Martha	Burial on Feast of Unleavened Bread. Jesus is the Bread of Life (Jn 6:51).
Talks to the Samaritan woman	Raises Lazarus from the dead	Empty tomb
Heals a nobleman's son	Begins his last trip to Jerusalem	Resurrection on Firstfruits. Jesus is the original Firstfruits (1 Co. 15:23).
People of hometown try to kill him	Blesses the little children	Appears to the two going to Emmaus
The Year of Popularity c. A.D. 28	Talks to the rich and young man	Appears to 10 disciples
4 fishermen become His followers	Again tells about his death and resurrection	Appears to the 11 disciples
Heals Peter's mother-in-law	Heals blind Bartimaeus	Talks with some of his disciples
Begins his first preaching trip through Galilee	Talks to Zacchaeus	Ascends to his Father in heaven
Matthew decides to follow	Returns to Bethany to visit Mary and Martha	
Chooses the 12 disciples		
Preaches the "Sermon on the Mount"		
A sinful woman anoints Him		
Travels again through Galilee		
Teaches parables about the kingdom		
Calms the storm		
Brings Jairus's daughter back to life		

*Christ's birth was in the time of King Herod the Great (Matthew 2:1). Jesus' birth would not have taken place prior to 6 B.C. or later than Spring of 4 B.C., which was the time of King Herod's death.

Resources recommended in ◆ several lessons, ★ several units, ♥ other HOW Units. ◕━ Key Resource (see beginning of unit or page 32).

Heart of Wisdom Publishing   705

The Messiah Resources

Resources with a ◐ symbol are appropriate for grades 4-12 or family read aloud. All other books are appropriate for young adults or adults.

Key Resources

Daily Life at the Time of Jesus by Miriam Feinberg Vamosh ⊶ ♦
Description in the "Key Resources Recommended in Several Units" beginning on page 33.

The Holman Bible Atlas ⊶ ♥
See description in the "Key Resources" section beginning on page 32.

Yeshua: A Guide to the Real Jesus and Original Church by Ron Mosley ⊶ ♥
This is a well-researched and fascinating study of the Jewishness of the historical Jesus. The author explores the structure and mission of the original church in the Jewish culture of the first century. The book combines scholarship with an understandable writing style resulting in a book that can be easily read but challenging to the reader. This book is a must for every serious student of the Bible in enlightening us as to our Jewish heritage. With forwards by Brad Young, Ph.D., Dr. Marvin Wilson, and Dwight Prior. We recommend readings in the "Ancient Israel Unit," this Unit, and the "Early Church Unit" (not published at the time of this writing). Paperback - 213 pages (July 1998) Jewish New Testament Publishers; ISBN: 1880226685. Reading level: Grades 9 and up.

Alternative Resources

Discovering the Bible: Jesus in Galilee by Victoria Parker, Janet Dyson
The Bible is perhaps the most influential book in the history of the world, and every child should be familiar with its timeless stories. This new *Discovering the Bible* series of books brings them to children everywhere in an accessible, lively, informative fashion, and is an invaluable addition to every home library. (June 9, 2000) Lorenz Books; ISBN: 0754804771.

A Novel Idea The Greatest Story Ever Told: The Timeless Bestselling Life of Jesus Christ by Fulton Oursler
The compelling fictionalized narrative, which remains faithful to the scriptures throughout, can be heard now on cassette via the talents of Tony Award- winning actor Edward Herrmann. Listeners will experience a sense of "being there," as

---

Underlined text refers to Internet link at http://Homeschool-Books.com

author and narrator capture the essence of the compassionate yet forceful Son of God and his mission amidst the political, religious, and social turmoil of the early first century. Random House (1949). ISBN: 038508028X.

The Hem of His Garment by Dr. John Garr ★
As you read this volume, you'll be simply amazed at just how Jewish Jesus really was! You'll also be enriched by a comprehensive understanding of spiritual lessons found in biblically Hebraic dress. The story in Matthew 9 is not just an isolated, one-of-a-kind event in the life of Jesus, a time when one lone woman reached out and touched the hem of his garment to be healed. Hidden from the eye of the reader of these stories is an enriching key to understanding what actually happened in these days of deliverance. Most versions of the Bible tell us that she touched the "hem of his garment" or the "border of his garment" or the "edge of his cloak" or the "fringe of his cloak." None of these translations, however, adequately conveys one important detail of the event. Without this detail (which you will learn about in this book), we simply miss the richness of this event and of an entire tradition in biblical history. Golden Key Books (423-472-7321). ISBN: 0-9678279-0-6. Available online!

The Jesus I Never Knew by Philip Yancey ◆
Philip Yancey realized that despite a lifetime attending Sunday school topped off by a Bible College education, he really had no idea who Jesus was. In fact, he found himself further and further removed from the person of Jesus, distracted instead by flannel-graph figures and intellectual inspection. He determined to use his journalistic talents to approach Jesus, in the context of time, within the framework of history. In *The Jesus I Never Knew*, Yancey explores the life of Jesus, as he explains, "'from below,' to grasp as best I can what it must have been like to observe in person the extraordinary events unfolding in Galilee and Judea" as Jesus traveled and taught. Hardcover 288 pages (September 1995) Zondervan Publishing House; ISBN: 0310385709.

Jesus the Jewish Theologian by Brad Young, Marvin R. Wilson, David Wolpe
This book establishes Jesus firmly within the context of first-century Judaism and shows how understanding Jesus' Jewishness is crucial for interpreting the New Testament and for understanding the nature of Christian faith. Paperback - 308 pages (November 1995) Hendrickson Publishers, Inc.; ISBN: 1565630602. Reading level: Adult.

Knowing Jesus Through the Old Testament by Christopher J. H. Wright ★
Has the Christian Bible bound believers to a narrow and mistaken notion of Jesus? Christopher Wright is convinced that Jesus' own story is rooted in the story of Israel. Throughout his life Jesus lived by the script of Israel. Only as we come to understand Jesus as a man with a story—an Old Testament story—will we come to know who Jesus truly is. To change that narrative is to deface our only

Resources recommended in ◆several lessons, ★ several units, ● other HOW Units. ●–Key Resource (see beginning of unit or page 32).

Heart of Wisdom Publishing   707

reliable portrait of Jesus. Here is a book that traces out the face of Christ in the textual tapestry of the Old Testament. But it also outlines the pattern of God's design for Israel as it is lived out in the story of Jesus. (March 1995) Intervarsity Pr; ISBN: 0830816933.

The Life and Times of Jesus the Messiah by Alfred Edersheim ◆
Alfred Edersheim's heritage as a Messianic Jew gives the description of Jewish culture in *The Life and Times of Jesus the Messiah* an authenticity that a non-Jew would be hard-pressed to duplicate. The culture of Israel during the Roman occupation comes alive in Edersheim's writing in a way that goes beyond scholastic study, by blending his own Jewish heritage, archaeological fact, and keen spiritual insight. Jesus is steeped in the culture of Israel as it progressed from Abraham to Herod. Used as a reference, *The Life and Times* gives Bible studies the context for the illustrations of Jesus, and its index is arranged according to verses and events. Read as a book, Edersheim is ponderous; however, a contiguous reading gives one a consistent Hebrew framework within which the New Testament fit 2,000 years ago. Hardcover - 1109 pages New Updtd edition (April 1997) Hendrickson Publishers, Inc.; ISBN: 0943575834.

Messianic Christology by Arnold Fruchtenbaum ★
Dr. Fruchtenbaum works his way through the Old Testament following the first-century Jewish arrangement of the books, the arrangement that Jesus was familiar with. He shows how the revelation of the Messiah gradually progressed and built-up to reveal a magnificent picture of the Deliverer to come. *Messianic Christology* is an absorbing study that will strengthen your faith, bless your heart, and invigorate your worship. (1998) Ariel Ministries; ISBN: 091486307X.

 The Nazarene by Sholem Asch, Maurice Samuel (Translator)
The story of Jesus is told by three different witnesses: Cornelius, Pontius Pilate's governor of Jerusalem; the fragmentary gospel of Judas Iscariot; and the narrative of Joseph, a young student of Nicodemus, presenting a sweeping panorama of the Holy Land nearly two thousand years ago. This book will give you an appreciation for the Old Testament and the Jewish heritage of the Christian faith. Paperback 2nd edition (1996). Carroll & Graf; ISBN: 0786703792.

 No Wonder They Call Him the Savior: Chronicles of the Cross by Max Lucado
In this compelling quest for the Messiah, Max Lucado presents a poignant narrative that sheds new light on a story which readers thought they already knew by heart: the story of Christ's crucifixion. This book truly shows the power and "awesomeness" of our Lord and Savior. (September 1998) Multnomah Publishers Inc.; ISBN: 1576733882.

The Robe by Lloyd C. Douglas
A Roman soldier, Marcellus, wins Christ's robe as a gambling prize. He then sets forth on a quest to find the truth about the Nazarene's robe-a quest that reaches to the very roots and heart of Christianity and is set against the vividly limned background of ancient Rome. Here is a timeless story of adventure, faith, and romance, a tale of spiritual longing and ultimate redemption. Houghton Mifflin Co Paperback. (1986). ISBN: 0317387987.

A Shepherd Looks at Psalm 23 by W. Phillip Keller
A genuine classic about how a real-life shepherd views the love that Jesus the Shepherd has for his flock. The book draws on the firsthand experiences of one who has developed and managed sheep ranches. An inspirational and refreshing look at one of the best-loved portions of Scripture. Timeless. In Mass Market format. Mass Market Paperback (December 1996) Zondervan Books; ISBN: 031021435 1.

Twelve Words Jesus Knew by Irene Lipson
Imagine learning Hebrew and learning about the character of God at the same time! Irene Lipson accomplishes this feat through an in-depth study of twelve Hebrew words spoken by Yeshua. These words, including "Berith" (covenant), "Shabbat" (Sabbath), and "Torah" (direction), illustrate God's relationship with his people and introduce us to the world of Jewish religious thought and practice. Lipson then points us toward a life-style shaped by our relationship with the God whom these words reveal. 224 pages (1998) Monarch Books; ISBN: 1854244256.

Understanding the Difficult Words of Jesus by David Blivin, Roy Blizzard
The authors do an excellent job of placing Jesus in his proper historical context, as highly educated in both the study of the Torah and in the culture of his day. Many scholars believe Jesus' teachings were originally transmitted in Hebrew and can therefore be fully understood only from their Hebraic context. Many of Jesus' sayings contain Hebrew idioms that are meaningless in either Greek or English. When the Greek text is translated back into Hebrew, Hebrew idioms appear that illuminate the teaching. This light of understanding reveals the wonders of our Savior's life and teachings. (February 1995) Destiny Image; ISBN: 156043550X.

Videos

Jesus In His Jewish World by Dwight A. Pryor
Drawing upon the very latest biblical research, Pryor opens up the Gospels to wonderfully new and inspiring insights into the life of our Lord. A picture is drawn of the historical Jesus—living in the land of Israel and within the Jewish culture of the first century—that dramatically illuminates the method and meaning of his teachings. Seven 60-minute messages on four videos.

Resources recommended in ◆several lessons, ★ several units, ● other HOW Units. ●━Key Resource (see beginning of unit or page 32).

Heart of Wisdom Publishing   709

Introduction: Mind of Christ

Step 1 Excite

To have the mind of Christ is to think like He does, to have His attitudes toward life and people. To follow His example and to be His disciples, we must have the mind of Christ. As we learn to have the mind of Christ, the people around us will notice. In fact, people will be watching us to see how Christians handle responsibilities and trials.

Brainstorm and discuss these two verses: 1 Cor. 2:16 says, *For who hath known the mind of the Lord, that he may instruct him? But we have the mind of Christ.* Rom. 8:6 says *For to be carnally minded is death; but to be spiritually minded is life and peace.*

What is meant by "the mind of Christ"? Who is "we" in this verse? What is meant by being "carnally minded"? "spiritually minded"? Make a list of character traits in someone who has the mind of Christ. As you continue your study through this unit add to this list. Here are a few character traits to get you started: Compassion, humility, self sacrifice, obedience.

Step 2 Examine

We cannot possess the mind of Christ at all unless we first have asked Jesus Christ to come into our hearts and have become, as John 3:3 says, "born again." We must study the life of Christ and His teachings. In addition to reading and studying the Bible, how is the mind of Christ revealed? What did Jesus tell His disciples about how they would learn what Jesus thought and said? John 14:26 - *But the Comforter, which is the Holy Ghost, whom the Father will send in my name, he shall teach you all things, and bring all things to your remembrance, whatsoever I have said unto you.* John 15:26 - *But when the Comforter is come, whom I will send unto you from the Father, even the Spirit of truth, which proceedeth from the Father, he shall testify of me.*

Do more research about the mind of Christ. We recommend the following:

Books

What Would Jesus Do? by Mac K. Thomas
This book presents a variety of situations and discusses how Jesus would behave in them, covering such qualities as sharing, living in peace with others, and being truthful. Includes 140 full-color illustrations, plus discussion questions in the back of the book from each of the eighteen chapters. (March 1997) Zondervan Publishing House; ISBN: 1576730530. Reading level: Ages 4-8. Interest level: All ages.

Underlined text refers to Internet link at http://Homeschool-Books.com

In His Steps by Charles M. Sheldon
A ragged man tells a Midwestern church congregation "It seems to me there's an awful lot of trouble in the world that somehow wouldn't exist if all the people who sing such songs went and lived them out." The man later passes away. The Minister and Congregation are shocked and ashamed and proceed to pledge to live their everyday lives asking themselves, "What Would Jesus Do?" This is the book that started the WWJD fad. (December 1993) Barbour & Co; ISBN: 1557483469.

What Would Jesus Do? by Deborah Morris, Garrett Ward Sheldon
A contemporary retelling of In His Steps, the story that started a movement among today's youth. (1998) Broadman & Holman Publishers; ISBN: 080540189X.

The Mind of Christ: The Transforming Power of Thinking His Thoughts by W. Hunt, T. W. Hunt
Description: This book is an introduction to the lifelong process of becoming like Jesus. It will help you understand how God works within you and transforms you by continually renewing and reshaping your mind to reflect more closely the mind of Christ. (April 1997) Broadman & Holman Publishers; ISBN: 0805463496.

Internet Source

The Mind of Christ
Description: A study by Ray C. Stedman from Peninsula Bible Church, written to call men back to reality, away from the confusion and the illusion, and the delusions and fantasies by which the world lives, to the realities of life as it is in Christ.

Step 3 Expand

Choose and complete one of the following activities:

Activity 1: Write a Prayer
Write a prayer asking God to give you the mind of Christ. (Luke 11:11-13).

Activity 2: Write a Letter
Reflect upon ways that you can be *transformed by the renewing of your mind, that ye may prove what is that good, and acceptable, and perfect, will of God* (Romans 12:2). Write a letter to yourself that you can read after months, or perhaps years, have elapsed. Talk about the ways that your thinking needs to change. Talk about your hopes for your future and for how you will think in ways that are acceptable to God.

Resources recommended in ◆several lessons, ★ several units, ● other HOW Units. ◕—Key Resource (see beginning of unit or page 32).

Heart of Wisdom Publishing   711

Activity 3: Play a Game
You have probably seen the letters W W J D on a bracelet, a T-shirt, a cap, or some other article of clothing. It stands for "What would Jesus do?" and is inspired by Charles Sheldon's book *In His Steps*. Write individual descriptions of difficult situations people face daily on several index cards. Example: "A friend begins telling you a long boring story." Or "Someone asks to borrow an item from you. They have borrowed items in the past without returning them." Have each person in your family draw a card and explain how they would handle the situation.

Activity 4: Discuss Scripture
Read Philippians 2:1-4. Discuss with your parents what "double minded" means.

Step 4 Excel

Put away the letter that you wrote to yourself, in a safe, private location where you can retrieve it later. Make a note of the date on which you intend to open and read it. Next, surrender your mind to God, preferring God's ways to your own. Pray that God will transform your mind.

Messianic Prophecies

Step 1 Excite

Read Luke 2:25-38. How did Simeon and Anna learn about the Messiah? What Scriptures would they have had to read in order to know the prophecies about Jesus?

Step 2 Examine

Jesus is the prophesied Christ. Several Old Testament prophets foretold Jesus' birth, life, and death. Read each of the following prophecies and its fulfillment.

Prophesy	Old Testament	New Testament
Descendant of Abraham	Genesis 12:3	Matthew 1:1-17
Descendant of Isaac	Genesis 17:19	Luke 3:34
Descendant of Jacob	Numbers 24:17	Matthew 1:2
From tribe of Judah	Genesis 49:10	Luke 3:33
Heir to throne of David	Isaiah 9:7	Luke 1:32-33
Born in Bethlehem	Micah 5:2	Luke 2:4-7
Time for His birth	Daniel 9:25	Luke 2:1-2
Born of a virgin	Isaiah 7:14	Luke 1:26-31
Enters Jerusalem on a donkey	Zechariah 9:9	Matthew 21:1-11

Research Messianic Prophecies. Use any resource (a non-fiction book, or the Internet). We recommend the following:

Books

Messianic Christology ◆
Read: The "Introduction" (8-12) and browse the rest of the book. Assigned readings will appear throughout this unit. See description in the Resources Section.

Knowing Jesus Through the Old Testament ◆
Read: Chapter 1 "Jesus and the Old Testament Story"(1-54). Browse the rest of the book. See description in the Resources Section.

New Evidence That Demands A Verdict by Josh McDowell
Description: In this revised edition, Part I addresses the trustworthiness of the Bible; Part II offers historical evidence and supporting attestations for Jesus'

Resources recommended in ◆several lessons, ★ several units, ◆other HOW Units. ◕━Key Resource (see beginning of unit or page 32).

Heart of Wisdom Publishing   713

claim to God; Part III addresses "radical Christian criticism" of the Bible; Part IV is devoted to quelling the voice of numerous skeptics, including "a defense for the existence of miracles" and "answers to divergent worldview." (December 1999) Word Books; ISBN: 0785243631.

Internet Sources

Messiah Revealed: Fulfilled Messianic Prophecies
Description: a comprehensive single source of all prophecies related to the first coming of God's promised Messiah, Jesus of Nazareth.

324 Messianic Prophecies
Description: A list of prophecies and their fulfillment with references.

Step 3 Expand

Choose and complete one of the following activities:

Activity 1: Research
This activity will involve a good share of "Bible thumping." You will need to do a bit of research to find all of the scriptures that prophesy these events, as well as those demonstrating their fulfillment. Make a chart with the headings: Prophecies, Fulfillment, Reference. Use Bible study tools to fill in at least 30 prophecies and their fulfillment.

Activity 2: Make a Chart
Jesus' death, burial, resurrection, and Second Coming are all foretold in the biblical holidays listed in Leviticus 23. Make a chart showing the Messianic significance of each of the biblical holidays: Passover, Unleavened Bread, Firstfruits, Pentecost, Trumpets, Day of Atonement, and Tabernacles. Use a Bible dictionary or a book like A Family Guide to the Biblical Holidays.

Step 4 Excel

Share your work from Step 3 with someone. Explain what you have learned in this lesson. Correct all written work to demonstrate correct punctuation and spelling, and effective use of grammar. Add corrected written work or any illustrations to your portfolio.

Christ, Our Passover Lamb

Step 1 Excite

Jesus is continually referred to by the title "Lamb of God," or simply, "Lamb." Revelation refers to Him this way twenty-eight times. Read about Passover in Exodus 12:3-19; 23:15-18; Leviticus 23:4-8; Numbers 9:2-5,13-14; 28:16-25; and Psalms 81:3-5.

Step 2 Examine

In the first century, the High Priest chose a lamb outside of Jerusalem each year on the tenth of Nisan. Then, the priest would lead this lamb into the city while crowds of worshippers lined the streets waving palm branches and singing Psalm 118, "Blessed is He that comes in the name of the Lord."

Jesus our Messiah entered Jerusalem this same day, on a donkey (usually ridden by a king), probably right behind the High Priest's procession. The crowds that had just heralded the entrance of the sacrificial lamb heralded the entrance of the Lamb of God. Accordingly, Jesus identified himself with the Passover sacrifice (John 12:9-19). As Jesus entered Jerusalem, His entry fulfilled prophecy. Enthusiasm filled the air. All Israel knew that it would be in Jerusalem that the Messiah would be enthroned as their King. Edersheim writes:

> Everyone in Israel was thinking about the Feast. Everyone was going to Jerusalem, or had those near and dear to them there, or at least watched the festive processions to the Metropolis of Judaism. It was a gathering of universal Israel, that of the memorial of the birth-night of the nation, and of its Exodus, when friends from afar would meet, and new friends be made; when offerings long due would be brought, and purification long needed be obtained and all worship in that grand and glorious Temple, with its gorgeous ritual. National and religious feelings were alike stirred in what reached far back to the first, and pointed far forward to the final Deliverance.[1]

The High Priest would then take the lamb to the Temple, where it would be tied in public view so that it could be inspected for blemishes. In the same way, Yeshua sat and taught in the Temple courtyard for four days. He was inspected and questioned as the Sadducees, the Pharisees, and the teachers of the Law sought to trip him up in His words and entrap Him. They could not, because He was perfect and without blemish.[2]

Resources recommended in ◆several lessons, ★ several units, ● other HOW Units. ●━Key Resource (see beginning of unit or page 32).

Heart of Wisdom Publishing   715

Passover pronounces redemption. To believers in the Messiah, the Passover feast has a special meaning. Though we are not slaves, as God's people in Egypt, we were slaves to our sin, our own wants and desires. Sin was our master until Jesus, the Passover Lamb, delivered us from our Egypt. The lamb slain during Passover foreshadowed the redemption we find in Jesus; the Messiah, our Passover lamb. The principle of redemption is the concept of bondage to the slavery of sin and freedom from its domination (John 8:31-36). To be "redeemed" means to be purchased from slavery. Jesus Christ purchased our freedom with His blood as the payment for the redemption (Ps. 34:22; 1 Pet. 1:18, 19; Gal. 3:13; Eph. 1:7; 1 John 1:7).

Jesus ate the Passover meal with eleven of His disciples. Just as the priest was to teach, pray, and offer sacrifice, so Christ, the High Priest, taught, prayed, and then offered Himself as our sacrifice.

For more on this subject see the resources in "The Exodus and Passover" lesson in the Ancient Israel Unit or any of the resources below:

Encyclopedia of the Bible (Nelson's Illustrated) ❤
Part 2 "Jesus the Saviour" (190-191).

The Victor Journey through the Bible ⊶ ❤
Read: The Last Supper (316-317).

Step 3 Excel

Choose and complete one of the following activities:

Activity 1: Write a Comparison
Write a comparison of at least seven things that Jesus had in common with the Passover Lamb.

Activity 2: Write a Poem
Write a poem titled "Mary had a Little Lamb." Add it to your portfolio.

Step 4: Excel

Share your work from Step 3 with someone. Explain what you have learned in this lesson. Correct all written work to demonstrate correct punctuation and spelling, and effective use of grammar. Add corrected written work or any illustrations to your portfolio.

Footnotes
1. Edersheim, Alfred (1994), *The Temple: Its Ministries and Service*, Peabody, MA, Hendrickson Publishers,
2. Lancaster, Daniel (1996), "Pictures of the Messiah: The Spring Festivals," *First Fruits of Zion Magazine*.

Type of Christ: Joseph

Step 1 Excite

Do this activity before you read the text below. Read <u>Genesis 37-50</u>. Set a timer for twenty minutes. Brainstorm with your family and make a list of as many parallels as you can think of between Joseph and Christ, before the timer goes off.

Step 2 Examine

Here are some of the parallels between Joseph and Christ:

- Both were loved by their father above all their other children.
- Both were hated by their brothers.
- Both were hated because of their words.
- Both were sent by their fathers to their brothers and their flocks.
- Their brothers conspired against them to kill them.
- Both were stripped of their garments.
- Both were buried.
- Both went down to Egypt.
- Both were "dead."
- Both were found to be alive—Not in the Pit/Tomb.
- Both were sold.
- Their fathers tore their clothes (Jacob tore his clothes, and the veil of the Temple tore).
- Both sat at the right hand of the King.
- Both were given charge over all of the King's matters.
- Both were falsely accused.
- Both were not recognized by their brothers.
- Both provided bread (grain) in a time of famine.

Do research to find more parallels between Joseph and Christ. Use any resource (Bible, a nonfiction book, or the Internet). We recommend the following:

Book

> <u>Gleanings in Genesis</u> by Arthur W. Pink
> Description: Pink shows 100 points in which Joseph is a picture of our Savior. Genesis, the seed plot of the Bible, gives in germ form all the doctrines of the Bible—the Trinity, man's depravity, salvation by substitution, justification by faith. These are examined along with character studies and biblical types. (December 1922) Moody Press; ISBN: 0802430023.

Resources recommended in ◆several lessons, ★ several units, ❤other HOW Units. ◉━Key Resource (see beginning of unit or page 32).

Heart of Wisdom Publishing   717

Internet Sources

The Life and Times of Joseph
Description: An extensive nine-part Bible study on Joseph.

Joseph—A type of Christ Genesis Chapter 32
Description: A Bible commentary on Joseph as a type of Christ, from Grace Baptist Church of Danville.

Christ as Typified by Joseph
Description: A sermon on Joseph as a type of Christ, by the pastor of Redeemer Baptist Church.

Step 3 Expand

Choose and complete one of the following activities:

Activity 1: Make a Contrast-and-Compare Chart
Read Genesis 37–50. Make a contrast-and-compare chart similar to the table below to compare Joseph and Jesus. Include Bible references.

Joseph	Jesus

Activity 2: Make a Storyboard
A storyboard is a graphic, sequential depiction of a narrative. Gather the materials you would need to tell the story of Joseph on a storyboard. You can either draw this story or cut out pictures to tell this story to your family and friends. Refer to Storyboard directions (see page 26).

Activity 3: Make a Scrapbook Page
Read Genesis 37–50. Draw or print out pictures of the story of Joseph similar to those below. Label with Bible references. Discuss how each reminds you of Christ. Idea: Make a background with a shape of a coat of many colors.

Step 4 Excel

Share what you have learned about Joseph as a type of Christ with a friend or family member. Correct all written work to demonstrate correct punctuation and spelling, and effective use of grammar. Add corrected written work or any illustrations to your portfolio.

Resources recommended in ◆several lessons, ★ several units, ♥ other HOW Units. ◉━Key Resource (see beginning of unit or page 32).

Heart of Wisdom Publishing   719

Type of Christ: Moses

Step 1 Excite

At the time of Jesus, the Romans ruled the Jews, who were a people constantly waiting for a Messiah to deliver them to freedom as Moses had led them into deliverance. Many of the Jews at that time did not understand what kind of freedom Jesus was to bring them. Brainstorm and make a list of the ways in which Moses and Christ are similar.

Step 2 Examine

The Messiah delivers his people from slavery to sin. A story illustrates this:

There once was a man who owned several slaves. He was mean and wicked to his slaves; they were beaten and starved so badly that they could scarcely work. He decided to sell his slaves to buy new ones, so he took them to the slave market. A rich, generous man came into the crowd as the auction began. His heart leaped for joy as he recognized one of the boys as his own son, who had been kidnapped many years earlier. He bid the highest and was able to buy his son. The son now had a new owner—his true father. How different his life would be now; he was no longer a slave to evil but a slave to love.

Read Romans 6:15-23. We are no longer slaves to sin but slaves to righteousness. Compare what the boy's life was like under each master.

Discuss Matthew 6:24, *No one can serve two masters.* Exodus 6:6-7 explains God's promises: *Wherefore say unto the children of Israel, I am the Lord, and I will bring you out from under the burdens of the Egyptians* [the world], *and I will rid you out of their bondage* [sin], *and I will redeem you with a stretched out arm and with great judgments* [bought with a price]*: And I will take you to me for a people, and I will be to you a God* [our new loving Master].

Research how Moses is a type of Christ. Use any resource (an encyclopedia, non-fiction book, historical novel, or the Internet). We recommend the following:

Books

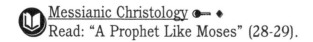

Messianic Christology ●▬ ◆
Read: "A Prophet Like Moses" (28-29).

Step 3 Expand

Choose and complete one of the following activities:

Activity 1: Make a Chart
Make a chart similar to the one below. Fill in the middle column with the events from scriptures that show the similarities between Jesus and Moses.

Moses		Jesus
Ex. 1:22		Mat. 2:16
Deut. 6:4-5		Mark 12:29
Num. 12:10-15		Luke 17:12-19
Ex. 17:6		John 4:10-14
Ex. 34:29		Luke 9:29
Deut. 18:18		John 12:49-50

Activity 2: Make a List
Make a list of adjectives describing your life both before and after receiving Christ. Explain your life when you were a slave to sin and your life now as a slave to Christ.

Activity 3: Write a Journal Entry
The Jewish people were awaiting a Messiah who was a mighty military conqueror (a lion), not one who was a suffering servant (a lamb). Write about the times in your life when your prayers have been answered, but not in the way you had expected. Be sure to describe your reaction, and explain how much better God's answer was than yours. Younger students can narrate (orally tell) what they have learned.

Step 4 Excel

Share your work from Step 3 with someone. Explain what you have learned in this lesson. Correct all written work to demonstrate correct punctuation and spelling, and effective use of grammar. Add corrected written work or any illustrations to your portfolio.

Resources recommended in ♦several lessons, ★ several units, ♥other HOW Units. ☛Key Resource (see beginning of unit or page 32).

Heart of Wisdom Publishing   721

Type of Christ: Boaz

Step 1 Excite

Boaz was a Kinsman-Redeemer. Read the book of Ruth. Make a list of ways that the Messiah is symbolized in the love story of Ruth and Boaz.

Step 2 Examine

Provision was made in the Law of Moses for the poor person who was forced to sell part of his property or to sell himself into slavery. His nearest of kin could step in and "buy back" what his relative was forced to sell (Leviticus 25:48). The kinsman-redeemer was a rich benefactor, or person who frees the debtor by paying the ransom price. *If a fellow countryman of yours becomes so poor he has to sell part of his property, then his nearest kinsman is to come and buy back what his relative has sold* (Leviticus 25:25; Ruth 4:4,6). [1]

Research how Boaz is a type of Christ. Use any resource (an encyclopedia, non-fiction book, historical novel, or the Internet). We recommend the following:

Internet Sources

Our Kinsman-Redeemer by Wil Pounds
Description: Bible study on the meaning of "nearest kinsman" or "kinsman-redeemer."

Christ Our Kinsman-Redeemer by Robert A. Peterson
Description: Article revealing that Boaz, in his role as kinsman-redeemer, is a type of Christ.

Christ Our Kinsman Redeemer by Don Fortner
Description: Bible study explaining that the Book of Ruth is a beautiful picture of the work of our Lord Jesus Christ as our kinsman-redeemer.

Underlined text refers to Internet link at http://Homeschool-Books.com

Step 3 Expand

Activity 1: Make Charts
Make charts similar to the ones below. Fill in the middle column showing the similarities between Boaz and Christ and Ruth and the church.

Boaz		Jesus
Ruth 2:14		Mark 14:22
Ruth 2:15, 18		Mat. 7:7
Ruth 4:1		1 Tim. 2:5
Ruth 4:10		1 Cor. 6:20
Ruth		Church
Ruth 1:16		Acts 10:35
Ruth 2:9		John 7:38,39
Ruth 2:11		Mat. 10:37
Ruth 2:14		Mark 14:22

Activity 2: Write an Essay
Explain the idea of "kinsman-redeemer" to other students, or write an expository essay on the topic and publish it on the Internet.

Step 4 Excel

Explain orally to your parents what you've learned in this lesson. Correct all written work to demonstrate correct punctuation and spelling, and effective use of grammar. Add corrected written work or any illustrations to your portfolio.

Footnote
1. Pounds, WII, (1999), Our Kinsman Redeemer, <http://www.abideinchrist.com/messages/lev25v25.html> (Accessed Jan 2001).

Resources recommended in ◆several lessons, ★several units, ♥other HOW Units. ☞Key Resource (see beginning of unit or page 32).

Heart of Wisdom Publishing   723

Geography at the Time of Christ

Step 1 Excite

In the Bible, the actions of God are closely associated with nations and geographical areas. Getting a grasp of where Jesus lived and traveled will give you a deeper understanding of Scripture, particularly the Gospels. Before you start this lesson, find Israel on a globe or map. Brainstorm and list cities or provinces relating to Jesus.

Step 2 Examine

Research the geography during the time of Christ. Use any resource (an encyclopedia, non-fiction book, historical novel, or the Internet). We recommend the following:

Books

Encyclopedia of the Bible (Nelson's Illustrated) ❤
"In the Steps of Jesus (40-41).

The Holman Bible Atlas ☞ ❤
Read: "The Life and Ministry of Jesus" (216-235).

Reproducible Maps, Charts, Timelines & Illustrations ☞ ❤
Read: "Journey to Bethlehem" (183), "Jesus in Judea and Samaria" (205), "Jesus in Galilee" (207), "Palestine Under Herod the Great" (197).

Daily Life at the Time of Jesus ☞ ♦
Read: Maps on pages 4 and 7.

The Greco-Roman World of The New Testament Era: Exploring the Background of Early Christianity ☞ ❤
Read: "Provinces and Cities of The New Testament Era" (259-292). Also see maps beginning on page 324. See description in the Ancient Israel Resources Section.

Go to Galilee: The Spiritual Geography of the Gospels by Virginia Marie Butler
Description: From the birth of Jesus in a cave in Bethlehem to his burial in a cave outside of Jerusalem, from his hidden life in the hills of Nazareth to his public life along the Sea of Galilee, from his Transfiguration on the Mount called Tabor to his Sermon on the Mount in Galilee and his Ascension on the Mount of Olives, from

his forty-day sojourn in the desert to his baptism in the waters of the Jordan—this book follows in the footsteps of Jesus. (January 2001) Alba House; ISBN: 0818908874.

Internet Sources

Bible Map of the Holy Land (Israel) in Time of Jesus
Description: Map from JesusAnswers.com.

Palestine in the Time of Jesus
Description: This site includes links to several Ancient Near East maps.

Videos

Land & Word: A Biblical Journey
Three videos. See description in the Ancient Israel Resources Section.

Step 3 Expand

Choose and complete one of the following activities:

Activity 1: Map Work
Locate the following modern territories on a map of Palestine in the time of Jesus: Bethany, Bethlehem, Galilee, Samaria, Judea, Perea.

Activity 2: Write a Travelogue
Select one of Jesus' journeys and assume that you were a member of the traveling group. Then, create a travelogue describing your experience on that journey. Using the first person (I, me, we, us), write a narrative (essay) of the events and describe the geographical areas that your group visited.

Activity 3: Play a Game
You'll need a Bible, *The Holman Bible Atlas* (or a similar resource), and a timer. To play: A parent looks up a Bible story and calls out the title (Examples: Birth of Christ, John Baptizes Jesus). The student uses the index to find a map or illustration of the Bible story as the parent times the student. Do this for several different events.

Step 4 Excel

Share your work from Step 3 with someone. Explain what you have learned in this lesson. Putmaps in your portfolio.

Resources recommended in ◆several lessons, ★ several units, ♥ other HOW Units. ●—Key Resource (see beginning of unit or page 32).

Culture at the Time of Christ

Step 1 Excite

Jesus lived in Israel. He came from the Jewish people. He lived as a Jew and followed Jewish religious practices. He refused to abolish biblical Judaism (Matthew 5:17). Read Ephesians 2:11-13; 3:4-6; Romans 11:11-18; 15:27; Galatians 3:29. Discuss the importance of Christians understanding their Hebraic heritage.

Step 2 Examine

Its important for us to understand Jewish culture to understand Jesus. It is also important for us to understand the Greek and Roman cultures to understand the world during the time of Christ and the early church. Learning about the Jewish customs and idioms can help us understand Jesus and His teachings. Studying Christ from our Western/American/Greek view is like looking for gold in a dark mine with a dim pen light—you can see enough to stumble around, but you need more light to see clearly. A good grasp of the ancient Hebraic customs and terminology is a powerful floodlight that will allow you to reexamine Christ's life, exposing intricate details and treasures.

> Think of such common English idioms as "hit the ceiling," "kill time," "eat one's heart out," "lose one's head," "be in hot water," "throw in the towel," or "kick the bucket." A non-English-speaker who heard these idioms translated literally into his own language would probably find them amusing. However, if he did not suspect that they were literal translations of English idioms and took them at face value, the information he received would be very misleading. The Hebrew language has hundreds of idioms. For example: be'arba enayim, literally "with four eyes," means face to face without the presence of a third person, as in, "The two men met with four eyes." lo dubim ve lo ya'ar is literally "[There are] neither bears nor forest," but means that something is completely false. And taman et yado batsalahat, "buried his hand in the dish," means that someone idles away his time. A translator faced with putting these idioms into another language such as English must be careful to find an equivalent idiom for each Hebrew expression. If he merely translates them word for word, he will not end up with English but Hebrew in English dress.[1]

Investigate the culture of Judea during the time Jesus lived there. Use any resource (an encyclopedia, non-fiction book, or the Internet). Many of the books in the Resources Section have this information. We recommend the following:

Books

Daily Life at the Time of Jesus ⊙— ◆
Read: "Introduction" (3), "When Worlds Collide" (6-19).

The Holman Bible Atlas ⊙— ♥
Read: "The World of Jesus" (207-215), "The Life and Ministry of Jesus" (216-235).

Yeshua: A Guide to the Real Jesus and the Original Church ⊙— ♥
Read: "Jewish Idioms in the Teachings of Jesus" (13-28).

The Jesus I Never Knew ◆
Read: "Background: Jewish Roots and Soil" (47-66).

The Life and Times of Jesus the Messiah ◆
Read: Book I. Introductory. The Preparation for the Gospel; the Jewish world in the days of Christ. Available online.

Revealing Jesus as Messiah: A Portrait of the Messiah and His People by Stuart Sacks Thirteen short, readable chapters—taken from the Book of Isaiah—that provide insight into the nature and work of Jesus as Messiah. The author offers encouragement for those who want to know Jesus and be like Him. This book is both enlightening and practical! (March 2000) ISBN: 1857923111.

Christianity Is Jewishby Edith Schaffer
Edith Schaeffer, wife of the late Francis Schaeffer, wrote that Christianity, no matter how un-Jewish some of its current forms of expression may be, has its roots in Judaism and in the Jewish people. The very concept of a Messiah is nothing but Jewish. Finally, Yeshua (Jesus) himself was Jewish - was then and apparently is still, since nowhere does Scripture say or suggest that he has ceased to be a Jew. (1977) Tyndale House Pub; ISBN: 0842302425

Internet Sources

ⓘ Customs by Peter M. Lechner
Description: Tutorial from *Jerusalem Perspective* explaining the importance of understanding the customs that were common knowledge to the writers and early readers of the Gospels.

ⓘ Jesus' Jewishness by Dr. R. Steven Notley
Description: Article from Bridges for Peace.

ⓘ Knowing Him and Following Him by Rev. Terril D. Littrell, Ph.D.
Description: Article explaining the lessons that we can learn from the shepherd/sheep paradigm in Scripture, which will help us to know and follow our Lord.

Resources recommended in ◆several lessons, ★ several units, ♥other HOW Units. ⊙—Key Resource (see beginning of unit or page 32).

Heart of Wisdom Publishing   727

Significance of Idioms by Peter M. Lechner
Description: Tutorial from *Jerusalem Perspective* explaining that the problem with translating one language into another is dealing with idioms.

The Contours of Hebrew Thought by Marvin R. Wilson, Ph.D.
Description: Article explaining that Christianity does not derive from pagan, Hellenistic sources or from speculative worldviews but is securely anchored in the Hebrew Bible—the Law, Prophets, and Writings.

Step 3 Expand

Choose and complete one of the following activities:

Activity 1: Brainstorm and List
Brainstorm and make a list of Jewish idioms that most people would not understand unless they studied the culture of ancient Israel (examples "Moses' seat," "finger of God," "binding and losing," "the golden vine," "the good eye"). Add to this list as you study the other lessons in this unit.

Activity 2: Make a List
What Jewish customs can you find mentioned in the Gospels? (Phylacteries, ceremonial hand washing, circumcision, and the celebration of Passover, for example.)

Activity 3: Prepare a Lesson
Prepare a lesson, under the guidance of your parents or a spiritual leader, detailing what you have learned about Jewish customs that are found in the Gospels. Explain tzitzit, ceremonial hand washing, and the rules about observing the Sabbath. Read verses from the Gospels in which these are mentioned. Share the lesson that you have prepared by teaching other students or by giving the lesson to a teacher.

Step 4 Excel

Explain orally to your parents what you've learned in this lesson. Correct all written work to demonstrate correct punctuation and spelling, and effective use of grammar. Add corrected written work or any illustrations to your portfolio.

Footnotes
1. Bevin, David. "Hebrew Idioms in the Gospels" *Jerusalem Perspective*, No. 22 (Sept./Oct. 1989).

The Gospels

1350-1352

The Narrated Bible

Step 1 Excite

Interview five adult Christians of various ages. Which is their favorite Gospel book to study: Matthew, Mark, Luke, or John? Why? Ask for their insights into the overall theme of each book. Take careful notes to use later. Refer to "Conducting Interviews" in *Writers INC.*

Step 2 Examine

Read the gospels' events in chronological order in *The Narrated Bible* or another resource. When the Bible stories are assembled in this fashion, it is called a "harmony of the Gospels." Harmonies of the Gospels are typically an attempt to organize the Four Gospels into some chronological sequence. Each harmonizer has made some decisions regarding various passages. Not all harmonizers have every event in the same order.

Matthew, Mark, and Luke are called the synoptic gospels, in contrast with John, because they can readily be arranged in a three-column harmony called a "synopsis." Unlike John, the synoptic gospels share a great number of parallel accounts and parables, arranged in mostly the same order, and told with many of the same words. [1]

Research the Gospels. Use any resource (an encyclopedia, non-fiction book, historical novel, or the Internet). We recommend the following:

Book

Jesus Rabbi and Lord by Robert Lindsey
In 1945, Robert Lindsey from Norman, Oklahoma, found himself pastor of a small Baptist congregation in Jerusalem, Israel. With his Hebrew-speaking congregants in mind, he began a translation of the Greek texts of Matthew, Mark, and Luke into modern Hebrew. He soon concluded there must lie behind these Gospels, even if distantly, an early Hebrew story of Jesus. To his surprise he also found that Luke almost always showed Greek texts which could easily be translated literally to Hebrew. The same was true of Matthew, where he was not copying Mark's Gospel. In 1962, Lindsey met Professor David Flusser of Hebrew University and the two pursued the question of whether we can get back to the earliest semitic story and words of Jesus. "It is clear," say Lindsey and Flusser, "that our synoptic texts originated mainly in one Greek translation of a Hebrew biography of Jesus, probably written by the Matthew of tradition. The materials are too Hebraic to have originated in Greek, as many scholars mistakenly think today. Happily, if we use the right tools we can still hear Jesus speak as His fellow

Resources recommended in ♦several lessons, ★ several units, ♥other HOW Units. ●—Key Resource (see beginning of unit or page 32).

Heart of Wisdom Publishing   729

Jews of the first-century heard Him." Lindsey tells here the warm, personal account of how he and Flusser struggled over many years to discover the earliest form of Jesus' words and narratives of His life. They believe that the records, when properly analyzed and studied, show us an authentic picture of Jesus interacting with the people of Jerusalem and Galilee. (August 1989). Cornerstone Pub; ISBN: 0962395005.

Internet Sources

An Overview of the Four Gospels of the New Testament
Description: From the Web site Jesus to Christ, explaining that the four Gospels, though they tell the same story, reflect very different ideas and concerns.

The Book of Jesus
Description: A chronological listing of events based upon where they appear in the four Gospels. (You can download the entire *The Book of Jesus: A Chronological Harmonization of the Gospels of Matthew, Mark, Luke, and John* by Dennis F. McCorkle from this site.)

Step 3 Expand

Choose and complete one of the following activities:

Activity 1: Outline
Choose one of the Gospels to outline. Refer to Creating an Outline.

Activity 2: Write a Speech
Write a speech in which you explain the similarities and differences between the Gospel accounts. Refer to "Planning Your Speech," "Writing Your Speech," and "Preparing Your Speech Script," in *Writers INC*.

Activity 3: Research Different Styles
Each of the four Gospels is written from a different perspective. Research the different styles of writing and themes in the Gospels. What is unique in each book with regard to the following:
- The style of writing
- The kinds of anecdotes told
- The number of quotations
- The number of parables recounted
- The number of cultural references
- The length
- The degree of emphasis on miracles
- The degree of emphasis on Jesus' teachings

- The amount of attention given to Passion Week
- The amount of attention given to the birth of Jesus
- The information given about what Jesus did after the resurrection
- The amount of emphasis on action
- Stories that are uniquely found in one Gospel

Step 4 Excel

Share what you have learned about the Gospels with a friend or family member. Correct written work to demonstrate correct punctuation and spelling, and effective use of grammar. Add corrected written work or any illustrations to your portfolio.

Footnotes
1. Throckmorton, Burton H., Jr. *Gospel Parallels: A Comparison of the Synoptic Gospels.*

Resources recommended in ◆several lessons, ★ several units, ♥ other HOW Units. ●━ Key Resource (see beginning of unit or page 32).

Heart of Wisdom Publishing   731

The Genealogy of the Messiah

Step 1 Excite

Prophets had foretold that a son (descendant) of David would restore Israel's kingdom to its former zenith (see Isa. 11:1-9; Jer. 23:5-6). According to Matthew 1:1-16, Jesus was descended from David. David, like Jesus, was born in Bethlehem; of the tribe of Judah; root of Jesse (see Isa. 11:1); of lowly origin, but exalted; after God's own heart. Read and discuss the following: Matthew 12:23; 15:22; 20:30-31; and 21:9. Why did people call Jesus "Son of David"?

Step 2 Examine

Read Matthew 22:41-46. What did the Pharisees say about the relationship between the Messiah and King David? What promise was given to King David about one of his descendants? Read 1 Chronicles 17:11-14. What prophecies and promises are contained in these verses?

Matthew 1 opens with the genealogy of Christ. Luke 3 offers a different lineage. Matthew's genealogy begins with Abraham and moves forward to Jesus. Luke's genealogy begins with Christ and traces the line backward to Adam. Both genealogies skip generations. It was a common practice to skip a generation and go from grandfather to grandson. Sometimes that generation was skipped due to a spiritual failure in the person in question; more often, there is no reason given.[1] Some believe the differences between the genealogies of Matthew and Luke may be attributed to the fact that Matthew traced the ancestry of Joseph, while Luke traced the that of Mary. Other scholars provide different theories.

Matthew's genealogy record included five women: Tamar, Rahab, Ruth, Bathsheba, and Mary. Four of the women are not Jews. The four Gentile women show that the descendants of Abraham are not limited by racial purity. These women testify to God's initiative in incorporating outsiders into Israel by placing these women in the royal lineage.

Research the lineage from David to Jesus. Use any resource (a Bible commentary, Bible dictionary, or the Internet). The book Messianic Christology explains the two genologies in the Gospels in the chapter "Christ's Right to David's Throne" (135-139). We also recommend the following:

Books

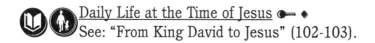 Daily Life at the Time of Jesus ●— ◆
See: "From King David to Jesus" (102-103).

Underlined text refers to Internet link at http://Homeschool-Books.com

Messiah Christology ⚷— ◆
Read: "The Seed of Abraham" (19-20), "The Seed of Judah" (21-23), "The Davidic Covenant" (78-79), "Christ's Right to David's Throne (135-139)."

Our Father Abraham ⚷— ♥
Read: "Discovering the Jewish Jesus" (115-118).

The Bible Comes Alive: Volume Two, Moses to David ⚷— ◆
Read: "A Greater-Than-David Is Here" (143).

Internet Source

Life of Christ: Genealogy of Jesus Christ
Description: The genealogy of Jesus Christ explained, from www.LifeofChrist.com.

Step 3 Expand

Activity 1: Make a Contrast-and-Compare Chart
Make a contrast-and-compare graphic (see page 26) to compare King David and King Jesus. Use your chart to discuss how David was a type of Christ.

Activity 2: Make a Family Tree
Make a family tree tracing Jesus' lineage back to David. See *Daily Life at the Time of Jesus,* page 102.

Step 4 Excel

Share what you have learned about the genealogy of the Messiah with a friend or family member. Correct written work to demonstrate correct punctuation and spelling, and effective use of grammar. Add corrected written work or any illustrations to your portfolio.

Footnotes
1. Doud, Warren. Grace Notes, Village Missions International, Austin, Texas 78757.

Resources recommended in ◆several lessons, ★ several units, ♥ other HOW Units. ⚷—Key Resource (see beginning of unit or page 32).

Heart of Wisdom Publishing 733

Birth of Christ

1353-1355

The Narrated Bible

Step 1 Excite

Read the account of the birth of the Messiah in Luke 2, paying special attention to the shepherds' point of view. When the shepherds visited Jesus, did they realize that they were meeting the Messiah? Who were "all they" in verse 18? Do you think that these shepherds were still living in the area when Herod ordered the murder of the babies in the region of Bethlehem (Matthew 2:16)? How do you think the shepherds thought and felt about this disaster, having recently seen the angels, with the glory of God shining around them?

Step 2 Examine

The Bible verse 1 John "In the beginning was the Word . . ." tells us of the eternity of the Lord Jesus Christ. When other things began, He was. He was from all eternity and He is from all eternity. Jesus Christ is eternal. His human life began when He was born to the virgin Mary.

The birth of Christ fulfills many Bible prophecies, all made at least 500 years before Jesus was born: Isaiah 7:14, of the virgin birth; Genesis 3:15, that he was born of the seed of woman; Isaiah 11:1, that he would descend from the line of Jesse (King David); Micah 5:2, that he would be born in Bethlehem; Matthew 2:18 and Jeremiah 31:15, that Herod would slaughter all the children in an attempt for the Devil to kill the Christ child.

The Bible does not specifically state the date of Jesus' birth (it is a controversial subject in some circles). We do know it was in the time of King Herod the Great (Matthew 2:1). Jesus' birth could not have taken place prior to 6 B.C., or later than Spring of 4 B.C., which was the time of King Herod's death. We know that it was not during the winter months because the sheep were in the pasture (Luke 2:8).

Many scholars believe that Jesus was born during the Feast of Tabernacles. Matthew Henry states:

> It is supposed by many that our blessed Saviour was born much about the time of this holiday; then He left his mansions of light above to tabernacle among us (John 1:14), and he dwelt in booths. And the worship of God under the New Testament is prophesied of under the notion of keeping the feast of tabernacles, Zec. 14:16. For,

---

Underlined text refers to Internet link at http://Homeschool-Books.com

[1.] The gospel of Christ teaches us to dwell in tabernacles, to sit loose to this world, as those that have here no continuing city, but by faith, and hope and holy contempt of present things, to go out to Christ without the camp, Heb. 13:13,14.

[2.] It teaches us to rejoice before the Lord our God. Those are the circumcision, Israelites indeed, that always rejoice in Christ Jesus, Phil. 3:3. And the more we are taken off from this world the less liable we are to the interruption of our joys.[1]

Research Christ's birth. Use any resource (an encyclopedia, non-fiction book, or the Internet). We recommend the following:

Books

Encyclopedia of the Bible (Nelson's Illustrated) ♥
"Jesus is Born" (200-201).

The Victor Journey through the Bible ☞ ♥
Read: "Matthew" (246-247

A Family Guide to the Biblical Holidays ★
Read: "Was the Birth of Christ During the Feast of Tabernacles?" (352-356). (See links to the online pages below.)

The Holman Bible Atlas ☞ ♥
Read: "The Birth of Jesus and His Childhood" (217).

The Jesus I Never Knew ♦
Read: "Birth: The Visited Planet" (47-66).

Messianic Christology ☞ ♦
Read: "The Seed of a Woman" (14-17), "Born of a Virgin" (37), "Unto Us a Son is Given" (39-41).

The Life and Times of Jesus the Messiah ♦
Read: Book II. From the Manger in Bethlehem to the Baptism in Jordan. Available online.

Internet Sources

Was the Birth of Christ During the Feast of Tabernacles?
Description: An excerpt from the book A Family Guide to the Biblical Holidays.

Resources recommended in ♦several lessons, ★ several units, ♥other HOW Units. ☞—Key Resource (see beginning of unit or page 32).

Life of Christ: Birth of Jesus Christ
Description: Part 1 of 5 in a brief summary of the life of Christ, from the Life of Christ Web site.

The Word Became Flesh
Description: Bible study on John 1:1-18.

Biblical Dates for Messiah's Conception and Birth
Description: Article exploring possible dates for the conception of John the Baptist and Jesus, based on Bible passages.

Step 3 Expand

Choose and complete one of the following activities:

Activity 1: Write a Journal Entry
Based on the information you have learned, imagine the experience of a common shepherd of Bethlehem who saw the angels, the Messiah, and the slaughter of babies by Roman soldiers. Write a journal entry for each event.

Activity 2: Listen to a Recording
Listen to a recording of the Christmas portion of Handel's *Messiah*.

Activity 3: Add to Your Time Line Book
Add the birth of Christ to your Time Line Book. Refer to Reproducible Maps, Charts, Timelines & Illustrations (#170-184).

Share what you have learned about the birth of Christ with a friend or family member. Correct all written work to demonstrate correct punctuation and spelling, and effective use of grammar. Add corrected written work to your portfolio.

Footnote
1. Henry, Matthew.(1706), *Matthew Henry Complete Commentary on the Whole Bible*.

Christ's Disciples

Step 1 Excite

1367-1375

The Narrated Bible

Answering the call to be a sage's disciple in first-century Israel often meant leaving relatives and friends and traveling the country under austere conditions. It also meant total commitment. A prospective disciple first had to be sure his priorities were in order. [1]

Write a classified ad looking for an employee to "work" as a disciple. Include a list of the qualifications for the "job," describe the responsibilities of being a disciple, and mention the pay, benefits, and job security.

Step 2 Examine

The word "disciple" is a derivative of the word "discipline." The word "Christian" occurs only three times in the New Testament. The word "disciple" occurs over 270 times. Read what Jesus said about Discipleship:

- Follow Me, I will make you fishers of men (Matthew 4:19).
- As you wish that men would do to you, do so to them (Luke 6:31).
- Whoever of you does not renounce all that he has cannot be My disciple (Luke 14:33).
- If anyone serves Me, he must follow Me; and where I am, there shall My servant be also (John 12:26).
- Behold, I send you out as sheep in the midst of wolves; so be wise as serpents and innocent as doves (Matthew 10:16).
- Preach as you go, saying, 'The kingdom of heaven is at hand.' Heal the sick, raise the dead, cleanse lepers, cast out demons (Matthew 10:7-8).
- Do not labor for the food which perishes, but for the food which endures to eternal life, which the Son of Man will give to you, for on Him has God the Father set His seal (John 6:27).
- Blessed are you when men revile you and persecute you and utter all kinds of evil against you falsely on My account. Rejoice and be glad, for your reward is great in heaven, for so men persecuted the prophets who were before you (Matthew 5:11-12).

Research Jesus Disciples.

Encyclopedia of the Bible (Nelson's Illustrated) ♥
"Jesus Disciples" (181), In the Steps of Jesus (40-41).

The Victor Journey through the Bible ●— ♥
Read: "Jesus Calls Four Disciples"(230-231), "Jesus Calls Matthew" (238-239), "Choosing the Tellve" (248-249).

Resources recommended in ♦several lessons, ★ several units, ♥ other HOW Units. ●—Key Resource (see beginning of unit or page 32).

Heart of Wisdom Publishing   737

Step 3 Expand

Choose and complete one of the following activities:

Activity 1: Do a Word Study
Use the Bible study tools (available in the Research Area) to do a word study on "disciple." Use your word study and the list above to make a list of traits that it takes to be a disciple (a follower) of Jesus.

Activity 2: Write a Letter
Imagine that you are living in the Holy Land at the time of our Lord and you've just been invited by Jesus to become a disciple. Write a letter home to your family, telling them about this wonderful man and why you have decided to follow Him.

Activity 3: Memorize the Disciples' Names
"The Twelve" is one of the special names for the group of men Jesus selected as His original apostles (Mark 4:10; Luke 6:13). The number twelve is significant to the twelve tribes of Israel (Matt. 19:28). Memorize the 12 names by singing them in the order below to the tune of *Jesus Loves Me.*

Peter, James, John, Andrew
Phillip and Bartholomew
Matthew, Thomas, another James,
Thaddaeus, Simon, Judas too.

Activity 4: Learn Hebrew Words
The Hebrew word for Disciple is *talmidim.*
Look up *talmidim* in a Hebrew lexicon. Add the word, phonetic spelling, and meaning to your Hebrew Notebook. See The Old Testament Hebrew Lexicon. Disciple, which in Greek is *mathetes*, comes "from the verb *manthano*, 'to learn,' whose root math suggests thought with effort put forth. A disciple is a learner, one who follows both the teaching and the teacher. The word is used first of the Twelve and later of Christians generally".[2] It basically describes any convert to Christianity, as well as those truly devoted to pressing in to His life.

Step 4 Excel

Explain discipleship to younger students. Define the word "disciple," and explain the relationship between a disciple and the one he/she follows. Tell a Bible story to show an example of Jesus' disciples. Then give examples of what it means for us to be disciples of Jesus.

Footnotes

1. Bivin, David. "First-century Discipleship," Jersulam Perspective.

2. *Spirit-Filled Life Bible* (1991), 1421, Nashville: Thomas Nelson, "Word Wealth: Matt. 10:1 disciples."

Underlined text refers to Internet link at http://Homeschool-Books.com

The Bible Jesus Read

Step 1 Excite

Brainstorm and discuss: what Bible did Jesus have? Where did He learn the Scriptures He quoted?

Step 2 Examine

Except for a few familiar passages—Genesis 1, Psalm 23, Isaiah 53—The Old Testament is a mystery to most Christians. Yet it is three-quarters of the Bible and the only form of Scripture which was used by Jesus Christ, the Apostles, and the first Christian community. Jesus referred to the OT consistently. When the words were written, *All scripture is inspired by God and is useful for teaching, for reproof, for correction, and for training in righteousness* (1 Timothy 3:16), they referred to what we call the Old Testament and what was then known as "Scripture."

The written Torah was accepted by all sects of Judaism, and Jesus himself said about the Torah, *For verily I say unto you, Till heaven and earth pass, one jot or one tittle shall in no wise pass from the law, till all be fulfilled.* (Mat. 5:18). Without a grasp of the Old Testament, the New Testament cannot be fully understood or appreciated.

> The Old Testament contains the prayers Jesus prayed, the poems he memorized, the songs he sang, the bedtime stories he heard as a child, [and] the prophecies he pondered. He revered every "jot and tittle" of the Hebrew Scriptures. The more we comprehend the Old Testament, the more we comprehend Jesus. Said Martin Luther, "the Old Testament is a testamonial letter of Christ, which he caused to be opened after his death and read and proclaimed everywhere through the Gospel. [1]

Once, a government tried to amputate the Old Testament from Christian Scriptures. The Nazis in Germany forbade study of this "Jewish book," and Old Testament scholarship disappeared from German seminaries and journals. In 1940, at the height of Nazi power, Dietrich Bonhoeffer defiantly published a book on the Psalms, and was fined. In letters of appeal, he argued convincingly that he was explicating the prayer book of Jesus Christ himself. Jesus quoted often from the Old Testament, Bonhoeffer noted, and never from any other book. Besides, much of the Old Testament explicitly or implicitly points to Jesus.

Resources recommended in ◆several lessons, ★ several units, ♥other HOW Units. ●—Key Resource (see beginning of unit or page 32).

Do research about the Torah and Tanakh, the Scripture that was read in the synagogue during the time Jesus was on earth. Use any resource (an encyclopedia, non-fiction book, historical novel, or the Internet). We recommend the following:
Books

Encyclopedia of the Bible (Nelson's Illustrated)
"Understanding the Bible" (194-195), "The Torah" (196-203).

Our Father Abraham: Jewish Roots of the Christian Faith
Read: "The Old Testament: Hebraic Foundation of the Church" (107-134).
Also see "Allegory: An Attempt to Rescue the Jewish Scriptures" (96-98).

The Bible Jesus Read by Philip Yancey
Yancey challenges the perceptions that the New Testament is more important than the Old, and that the Hebrew Scriptures aren't worth the time they take to read and understand. Writing, as always, with keen insight into the human condition and God's provision for it, Yancey refutes these opinions once and for all. As he personally discovered, the Old Testament is full of rewards for one who embraces its riches. Yancey unfolds his interactions with the Old Testament from the perspective of his own deeply personal journey. From Moses, the amazing prince of Egypt, to the psalmists' turbulent emotions and the prophets' oddball rantings, Yancey paints a picture of Israel's God—and ours—that fills in the blanks of a solely New Testament vision of the Almighty. Yancey says that, reading the Scriptures that Jesus so revered gives believers a profound new understanding of Christ, the Cornerstone of the New Covenant. The better we comprehend the Old Testament, Yancey writes, the better we comprehend Jesus. (July 1999) Zondervan Publishing House; ISBN: 0310228344.

From Mesopotamia to Modernity: Ten Introductions to Jewish Literature
Read: "The Hebrew Bible" (9-36). See description on page 37.

Internet Sources

Is the Old Testament for Christians?
Description: Article explaining the importance of proper study of the Old Testament.

Why Biblical Literacy Matters
Description: Crossways International president Harry Wendt discusses why we need to understand the Bible's 'big story.'

The Tanakh
Description: A brief definition of the Tanakh and its divisions from the perspective of Judaism.

Step 3 Expand

Choose and complete one of the following activities:

Activity 1: Write a Summary
Read Luke 4:16-20. What does this passage show about the importance of the Old Testament? Write what you learn in the form of a summary. Refer to "Writing a Summary," in *Writers INC*. Younger students can narrate (orally tell) what they have learned.

Activity 2: Write a Letter
Write a convincing letter to someone who thinks the Old Testament isn't important to a Christian's life. Refer to "Writing to Persuade" in *Writers INC* and to the article on this site, The Importance of Both Testaments. Younger students can narrate (orally tell) why both Testaments are important.

Activity 3: Answer Questions:
Answer the following about the Tanakh:

- Where did the name "Tanakh" come from?
- What were the names of the three sections of the Old Testament?
- Which books belonged in each division?
- How were Scripture portions recorded on scrolls?
- Were Bible books all written on the same scroll, or was there a different scroll for each book?

Activity 3: Write a Report
Write a report on Marcion explain the Marcionite position and its effects on the church today.

Step 4 Excel

Share what you have learned about the Bible Jesus read with a friend or family member. Correct all written work to demonstrate correct punctuation and spelling, and effective use of grammar. Add corrected written work or any illustrations to your portfolio.

Footnote

1. Yancey, Philip. (1999) *The Bible Jesus Read*, Zondervan Publishing House, Grand Rapids, Mich.

Resources recommended in ◆several lessons, ★ several units, ♥other HOW Units. ☯—Key Resource (see beginning of unit or page 32).

Heart of Wisdom Publishing   741

The Kingdom of God

Step 1 Excite

The popular Israelite tradition of kingship [had] three principal characteristics: kingship was constituted by popular election or anointing; it was conditional on the king's maintenance of a certain social policy, and the anointing of a new king was generally a revolutionary action.[1]

Read: Mark 4:30-32; Matthew 13:33; 18:3; Luke 13:20-21; Matthew 12:28; and Luke 11:20 and 17:20-21. Brainstorm and discuss what the Kingdom of God is.

Step 2 Examine

The "Kingdom of Heaven" or "Kingdom of God" (occurring over 100 times in the Bible) is the central theme of Jesus' preaching. The Hebrews did not use the sacred name of God. Many times they used the expressions "Kingdom of Heaven" or "Kingdom of God"—just as today we say, "Heaven help me." We are not asking for heaven's help. We are asking for God's help.

Look at the phrase *The Kingdom of God has come near you* (Luke 10:9-11). The Kingdom of Heaven or God is described by most commentaries as God's kingdom to come sometime in the future. Some teach that it means the second coming of Christ (Jesus called the second coming "the coming of the Son of Man").

Examining the gospel passages in their Hebraic context will clarify what Jesus meant when he spoke of the "kingdom of God" or the "kingdom of Heaven." The Greek word *"engiken"* means "about to appear" or "is almost here"; however, if it is translated back to Hebrew, the verb *"karav"* means "to come up to," "to be where something or someone is." In the Greek, the Kingdom is at a distance. In the Hebrew—it is here! Jesus' Messiahship is present, here and now. The "Kingdom of Heaven" is not futuristic, but rather a present reality wherever God is ruling...when one is able to put [Greek] passages back into Hebrew, it is immediately obvious that the Kingdom has already arrived, is in fact already here—almost the exact opposite of the Greek meaning.[2]

Jesus Himself proclaimed that the Kingdom was at hand. This proclamation involved an awakening cry of sensational and universal significance. He was referring to Himself as the King being at hand—being present. He was already present in His person, and He is the King. For one to follow Him, he had to make Him his King and follow His rules. *Not every one that saith unto me, Lord, Lord, shall enter into the kingdom of heaven; but he that doeth the will of my Father which is in heaven* (Matthew 7:21) takes on a whole new meaning. It is not heaven

---

that they won't be entering. It is His Kingdom now, of peace, following His ways.[3] *Blessed are the poor in spirit: for theirs is the Kingdom of Heaven* (Matthew 5:3) also takes on a new meaning.

Step 3 Expand

Activity 1: Read and Discuss
Jesus did not come right out and say, "I am the Messiah." In Hebrew there are far more powerful ways of making that claim. Read the following verses in this new light. It may change your opinion of these teachings: Mark 4:30-32; Matthew 13:33; 18:3; Luke 13:20-21; Matthew 12:28; Luke 11:20; 17:20-21.

Activity 2: Write a Parable
Begin your parable, "Once upon a time there was a wonderful King that mercifully ruled His kingdom. The King was always doing fine and wonderful things for His people..." Finish the story. For help refer to the online story, The Holiday Parable. Younger students can narrate (orally tell) their story.

Activity 3: Write a Paper
Seeking first the Kingdom of God is making Jesus Lord of your life today. Write a paper titled "The Kingdom of God" using the verses in this lesson.

Step 4 Excel

Share your work from Step 3 with someone. Explain what you have learned in this lesson. Correct all written work to demonstrate correct punctuation and spelling, and effective use of grammar. Add corrected written work or any illustrations to your portfolio.

Footnotes
1. Horsley, Richard A. and Hanson, John S. (1985). *Bandits, Prophets, and Messiahs: Popular Movements in the Time of Jesus.*
2. Bivin, Blizzard (1995). *Understanding the Difficult Words of Jesus: New Insights from a Hebraic Perspective.* Destiny Image. ISBN: 156043550X.
3. Wilson, Marvin R. (1989). *Our Father Abraham: Jewish Roots of the Christian Faith.* Grand Rapids, MI: William B. Eerdmans Publishing Company, and Dayton, OH: Center For Judaic-Christian Studies; ISBN: 0802804233.

Resources recommended in ◆several lessons, ★ several units, ◆other HOW Units. ◉━Key Resource (see beginning of unit or page 32).

Heart of Wisdom Publishing   743

Christ's Attitude Toward Lepers

Step 1 Excite

Jesus drew much criticism from his contemporaries because he allowed lepers to be near him. Who are the "lepers" in our society today? Make a list of all the different types of people who are treated like lepers by our society. Are you acquainted with anyone who is shunned by other people?

Step 2 Examine

Read these passages: Matthew 8:2-4; 10:7,8; 11:2-6; 26:6; Mark 1:40-45; 14:3; Luke 4:27; 7:22; 17:12-19. Next, look up these verses in the Bible study tools that are available in the Research Area. Find out how unusual the way that Jesus treated lepers actually was in that place and time.

Research lepers in the Bible. Use any resource (a non-fiction book, or the Internet). We recommend the following:

Book

Manners and Customs of the Bible
Read: "Leprosy" (125-126). See description in the Ancient Israel Resources Section.

Step 3 Expand

Use the Scripture passages Matthew 8:3; Mark 1:40-42; Luke 5:13; 17:12-14 to complete one of the activities below:

Activity 1: Copy Passages
Copy the Bible passages telling how Jesus dealt with the lepers, or have someone dictate the passage to you. Younger students can copy one or two sentences or narrate (tell back) the stories.

Activity 2: Think and Discuss
Discuss the proper attitude Jesus calls us to have toward those who are today's "unclean" in our society.

Underlined text refers to Internet link at http://Homeschool-Books.com

Activity 3: Illustrate a Story
Draw a comic-book page, complete with conversations in "bubbles," showing Jesus' conversation with lepers.

Activity 4: Write an Essay
Using the Bible passages you read, write an essay titled "Jesus Cleansed the Lepers." Explain what the Bible passages show about lepers, how the Messiah treated them, and how they responded to Jesus. Refer to "Structure of the Traditional Essay" and "Sample of a Traditional Essay" in *Writers INC*, or "How to Write an Essay".

Step 4 Excel

Share what you have learned about Jesus' attitude toward lepers with a friend or family member. Correct written work to demonstrate correct punctuation and spelling, and effective use of grammar. Add corrected written work or any illustrations to your portfolio.

Resources recommended in ◆several lessons, ★ several units, ❤ other HOW Units. ●—Key Resource (see beginning of unit or page 32).

Heart of Wisdom Publishing   745

Christ's Teachings on Law

1446-1448

The Narrated Bible

Step 1 Excite

Read Matthew 22:36-40 and Hebrews 13:8. Read Romans 10:4 and Galatians 3:24, and the context of each of these verses. Discuss what these verses tell us about the Messiah teaching about God's Law.

Brainstorm and discuss the following:

- What did Jesus say is the most important commandment?
- Is Jesus the same in the twenty-first century as he was in the first century?
- Are His teachings the same?
- Are His expectations the same?
- Are His activities the same?
- What do these truths mean in your life?
- Read Romans 13:8-10, Galatians 5:13-14, and the context which surrounds these verses. What do they teach you about the law?

Step 2 Examine

Jesus is the living Torah, the Word and Law of God made flesh. We cannot love Him without loving His law. Jesus says in John 14:15, *If you love Me, keep My commandments.* This is speaking about the commands of the New Testament; however, the implications go deeper, and even include the Old Testament, or Tenach.[1]

When asked "which is the great commandment?," Jesus summed up the law, saying, *Thou shalt love the Lord thy God with all thy heart, and with all thy soul, and with all thy mind. This is the first and great commandment. And the second is like unto it, Thou shalt love thy neighbour as thyself. On these two commandments hang all the law and the prophets* (Matthew 22:36-40).

Jesus was often accused by the Pharisees of violating ceremonial law, but he was the fulfillment of what these laws represented and were pointing to at that very moment in time. Jesus said, *Do not think that I have come to abolish the Law or the Prophets; I have not come to abolish them but to fulfill them* (Matthew 5:17). Is it breaking the law of gravity if a man jumps off a twenty-story building? No; it is an illustration of the law of gravity. In the same way, Jesus is an illustration of the Law of God. Jesus fulfilled the Law in such a way as to perfect a foundation. Jesus is the Law—the perfect life—our instruction, our example. The only negative thing about the Law is the consequences of breaking it—receiving our deserved punishment—death! Christ came and died as our replacement, receiving our punishment Himself. If

---

we accept His free gift, then we are set free from the Law of sin and death! Jesus did not come to kill, steal, or destroy. He came that we might have life more abundantly—an extraordinary life surrounded by His love.

Jesus kept the law, but by Jesus' time, religious leaders had added on to God's law and changed the meaning into a confusing mass of rules. Jesus taught to bring people back to its original purpose. Jesus never spoke against the law itself but against the abuses and excesses to which it had been subjected. The Pharisees of Jesus' times were fiercely proud of the righteousness they felt they had earned because of their meticulous obedience to all the regulations (a lot of added-on Rabbinical rules). Jesus showed the Pharisees that their narrow interpretation of the Law blurred God's intention in creating the Law. He publicly rebuked them for putting their laws and regulations above the people. Jesus pointed out that what is in a man's heart is more important. Jesus affirmed the necessity of putting God's laws paramount above any tradition or requirement of any man or group of men.

The attitude of the heart is the important thing is the message found throughout Jesus' teachings. In the story of the Good Samaritan, Jesus gives a lesson on the law. Robert Lindsey explains in *Jesus, Rabbi, Lord*:

> In the story the priest and the Levite are really prisoners of their own liturgical regulations: they are not allowed to touch a body and this half dead body of a man thrown by the wayside may defile them. Jesus contrasts them with the good Samaritan, who simply takes pity on a fellow human being....How easy these [legalistic] acts can imprison us and make us no longer sensitive to a hurting world![2]

Often Jesus went beyond the letter of the Law and instructed His disciples in the spirit of the Law. In Matthew 5:21-22 Jesus taught about the law against murder. He said that not only was it wrong to murder but also wrong to have hatred in your heart.

> *Ye have heard that it was said by them of old time, Thou shalt not kill; and whosoever shall kill shall be in danger of the judgment: But I say unto you, That whosoever is angry with his brother without a cause shall be in danger of the judgment: and whosoever shall say to his brother, Raca, shall be in danger of the council: but whosoever shall say, Thou fool, shall be in danger of hell fire.*

By His life, His death, and His glorious resurrection, He [Jesus] gave believers the dynamic power to keep His law. Paul says in Galatians 2:20: *I have been crucified with Christ; it is no longer I who live, but Christ lives in me...* In Philippians 2:13 he says, *for it is God who works in you both to will and to do for His good pleasure.* God will keep the law in us if we will let Him. Also, it

Resources recommended in ◆several lessons, ★ several units, ● other HOW Units. ●━ Key Resource (see beginning of unit or page 32).

Heart of Wisdom Publishing   747

should be pointed out that we are no longer trying to keep the law to gain God's approval. Those who believe in Jesus have His approval already, and are now "justified" so far as the law is concerned (Rom. 8:30).[3]

Research what Jesus taught about the law. Refer to "The Law" lesson in the Ancient Israel Unit (page 335). We also recommend the following:

Books

> Yeshua: A Guide to the Real Jesus and the Original Church ○── ♥
> Read: "Misconceptions Concerning the Law" (29-48).

> Our Father Abraham: Jewish Roots of the Christian Faith ○── ♥
> Read: "The Problem with Judaizing" (24-26), "Salvation: By Grace or Works" (20-21), and "Paul and the Law" (27-28).

> Ancient Israel: Its Life and Institutions ○── ★
> Read: "Law and Justice" (143-160). See description in the Ancient Israel Resources Section.

Internet Source

> The Spirit of the Law by Ron Mosley
> Book online. See description in the Ancient Israel Resources Section.

> Law Written on the Heart
> Description: Article from *Bridges for Peace* by Jim Gerrish, explaining that divine intention is that the Law would be perfectly fulfilled in each individual's life.

Step 3 Expand

> Activity 1: Art Project
> Design an art project to reflect the two commandments that Jesus emphasized. Use whatever medium you have access to: paint, charcoal, water colors, magic markers, calligraphy pen, etc.

> Activity 2: Read and Discuss Scripture
> Read and discuss Psalms 19:7-9, 119:1-8; Proverbs 28:4,5; Luke 13:10-16; and Mark 2:25-26, 7:1-23 with your parents. What do you learn about the Law from these verses?

Activity 3: Learn Hebrew Words

Roy Blizzard, concerning the origination of the word Law, says, "The English word law is used to translate the Hebrew word *Torah*. Torah is the feminine noun from the root *yarah*. The root *yarah* means to throw, or to shoot, or to cast, as in the casting of lots, or the shooting of arrows. It means to point out, to show. It means to direct, to teach, to instruct. A *moreh*, in Hebrew, is a teacher, or one who throws out, or points out; one who directs or instructs. Torah is direction, or instruction. It sets forth the way man is to live. It instructs man as to how he is to live in an ethical and moral way among his fellow man and before God."[4]

Activity 4: Write a Summary

Once the Jewish leaders tried to show that Jesus was a lawbreaker. Pharisaic traditions specified thirty-nine unlawful Sabbath activities, including shelling and eating grain.[5] Jesus used two Old Testament examples to illustrate that the Pharisees used the Law wrongly. He spoke of what David did (Matt. 12:3, 4) and what the priests did (Matt. 12:5-7). Write a summary explaining what each example implies about Jesus and the Law.

Activity 5: Write a Précis

Write a précis explaining your view of Jesus and God's Law. Reveal how the law shows us our sins and the need for a savior, Jesus, to justify us. Discuss the précis that you wrote with a spiritual leader such as a parent, pastor, or teacher.

Step 4 Excel

Explain what Jesus taught about the law to a younger student. Define the word "law" and give examples of what it means for us to love Jesus.

Footnotes
1. Gerrish, Jim (1999). <u>Law Written on the Heart</u>, The Dispatch from Jerusalem, Bridges for Peace, Jerusalem, Israel.
2. Lindsey, Robert (1990). *Jesus, Rabbi, Lord: The Hebrew Story Behind Our Gospels*, Cornerstone Publishing, Oakcreek, WI.
3. Gerrish, Jim (1999). IBID.
4. Bivin, Blizzard (1995). *Understanding the Difficult Words of Jesus: New insights from a Hebraic Perspective.* Destiny Image. ISBN: 156043550X.
5. Keener, Craig S. *The IVP Bible Background Commentary: New Testament.* (Downers Grove, IL: InterVarsity Press, 1993), 78.

Resources recommended in ♦several lessons, ★ several units, ♥other HOW Units. ●━Key Resource (see beginning of unit or page 32).

Heart of Wisdom Publishing 749

Christ's Teachings Through Parables

1394-1397

The Narrated Bible

Step 1 Excite

A Parable is a sort of 'extended metaphor' illustrating spiritual things by using ordinary things. Roughly speaking, parables are stories to illustrate certain truths. ...In interpreting the parables, the problem is to know which details are significant, and which are incidents necessary to the story. Ordinarily a parable was meant to show *one* point, and should not be pressed for lessons in every detail. The number of parables is variously given from 27 to 50. What some call parables others call metaphors. Ordinarily the number of parables is reckoned as about 30. Some of them are quite similar. Jesus used different stories to illustrate the same point, and sometimes the same story to illustrate different points.[1]

Try to make up a parable to illustrate an idea. Think of a simple bit of truth or common-sense advice that you would like to communicate.

Step 2 Examine

Jesus chose to deliver His teachings by using stories that biblical scholars agree are as powerful—and as relevant—today as they were 2,000 years ago. Research the parables. Use any resource (Bible commentary, Bible dictionary, Bible handbook, or the Internet). We recommend the following:

Books

Encyclopedia of the Bible (Nelson's Illustrated) ❤
"Jesus the Teacher" (182-183).

The Victor Journey through the Bible ⊶ ❤
Read: "The Sower and Other Parables"(252-253

The Parables of Jesus: The Teachings of Jesus
Description: A short narrative of the action, along with the biblical text and an application section encourage children to focus not only on "who" and "what," but "why" and "how" the lessons learned by men and women of the Bible can be applied to our lives today. Paperback - 40 pages (February 2001) Master Books; ISBN: 089051331. Reading level: Ages 9-12

The Parables of Jesus: A Commentary
Description: Arland Hultgren's outstanding work features fresh translations of the parables in the Synoptic Gospels and the Gospel of Thomas, followed by interpretive notes and commentary on the theological meaning and significance of

---

Underlined text refers to Internet link at http://Homeschool-Books.com

each parable for readers today. After an introductory chapter on the nature of parables and their interpretation, Hultgren studies the thirty-eight parables of Jesus thematically, exploring in turn "parables of the revelation of God," "parables of exemplary behavior," "parables of wisdom," "parables of life before God," "parables of final judgment," "allegorical parables," and "parables of the kingdom." Eerdmans; ISBN: 0802844758. Reading level: Adult.

The Parables: Jewish Tradition and Christian Interpretation by Dr. Brad H. Young
Description: Fully one-third of Jesus' words in the Synoptic Gospels occur in parables. It could be said that knowing the parables is essential for understanding the person of Christ. In his newest work on the parables, Brad displays his unique perspective as a scholar steeped in both Jewish and Christian studies. While parables have timeless messages, reinterpretations in new contexts throughout the centuries have distorted the original meanings and undermined the essence of what Jesus intended for his initial listeners. Young examines the parables that best illustrate the parallels between Rabbinic and Gospel parables. Hendrickson Publishers, Inc.; ISBN: 1565632443. Reading level: Adult.

Step 3 Expand

Choose and complete one of the following activities:

Activity 1: Write Summaries
Use the chart on the following page. Look up and read each parable. Write a summary of one or two sentences for each parable.

Activity 2: Write a Paraphrase
Write a paraphrase of one of the parables. Refer to "Writing a Paraphrase" in *Writers INC*.

Activity 3: Answer Questions
Answer the following:
- What does the Old Testament tell you about parables? (Psalms 78:2; Ezekiel 17:2; Hosea 12:10).
- What reason is given here for Jesus speaking in parables? (Matthew 13:34-35).
- What reason did Jesus give for speaking in parables? (Matthew 13:10-17; Mark 4:10-13).
- How did the audiences respond to the parables when they heard them spoken by Jesus? (Mark 12:12; Luke 8:9-10).
- What insight does Luke give into the purpose of some of the parables? (Luke 18:1,9; 19:11)

Resources recommended in ♦several lessons, ★ several units, ♥other HOW Units. ☞Key Resource (see beginning of unit or page 32).

Heart of Wisdom Publishing   751

The two debtors	Lu 7:40-43
The strong man armed	Mt 12:29; Mr 3:27; Lu 11:21,22
The unclean spirit	Mt 12:43-45; Lu 11:24-26
The sower of Galilee	Mt 13:3-9,18-23; Mr 4:3-9,14-20; Lu 8:5-8,11-15
The tares and wheat	Mt 13:24-30,36-43
The mustard seed	Mt 13:31,32; Mr 4:30-32; Lu 13:18,19
The seed growing secretly	Mr 4:26-29
The leaven	Mt 13:33; Lu 13:20,21
The hid treasure	Mt 13:44
The pearl of great price	Mt 13:45,46
The draw net	Mt 13:47-50
The unmerciful servant	Mt 18:21-35
The good Samaritan	Lu 10:29-37
The friend at midnight	Lu 11:5-8
The rich fool	Lu 12:16-21
The barren fig tree	Lu 13:6-9
The great supper	Lu 14:15-24
The lost sheep	Mt 18:12-14; Lu 15:3-7
The lost piece of money	Lu 15:8-10
The prodigal son	Lu 15:11-32
The good shepherd	Jh 10:1-18
The unjust steward	Lu 16:1-8
The rich man and Lazarus	Lu 16:19-31
The profitable servants	Lu 17:7-10
The importunate widow	Lu 18:1-8
The Pharisees and publicans	Lu 18:9-14
The laborers in the vineyard	Mt 20:1-16
The pounds	Lu 19:11-27
The two sons	Mt 21:28-32
The wicked husbandmen	Mt 21:33-44; Mr 12:1-12; Lu 20:9-18
The marriage of the king's son	Mt 22:1-14
The ten virgins	Mt 25:1-13
The talents	Mt 25:14-30

• What were the reasons that Jesus told each parable, according to Luke's report? What does each of the above show about the character of the Messiah?

Activity 4: Make a Chart
Make a chart like the one on the next page listing each of Jesus' parables. Write a brief description of each parable.

Activity 5: Write a Summary
Jesus said to *learn a parable of the fig tree* (Matthew 24:32; Mark 13:28). Fig trees are mentioned thirty-three times in the Bible. Memorize these two passages. Write a personal summary of the Parable of the Fig Tree. Refer to "Writing to Learn Activities," and "Personal Summary" in *Writers INC*.

Activity 6: Write an Essay
Carefully read Jesus' parable about the vine and the branches. Write a short (250-word) essay that describes how Jesus (the vine) provides you (the branches) with life-sustaining energy, and how you would wither if you were cut off. Refer to "Writing an Essay" in *Writers INC*.

Step 4 Excel

Share what you have learned about the parables with a friend or family member. Correct all written work to demonstrate correct punctuation and spelling, and effective use of grammar. Add corrected written work or any illustrations to your portfolio.

Footnotes
1. Halley, Henry H. (1965). *Halley's Bible handbook*. Grand Rapids, Michigan: Zondervan Publishing House.

Resources recommended in ◆several lessons, ★ several units, ♥ other HOW Units. ●—Key Resource (see beginning of unit or page 32).

Heart of Wisdom Publishing   753

Miracles Performed by Christ

1397-1415

The Narrated Bible

Step 1 Excite

Have you ever witnessed a miracle? If not, interview someone who has. If you are not acquainted with someone who has witnessed a miracle, then read a non-fiction account of a modern-day miracle. Take careful notes on your memory, interview, or reading. How many books do you think the miracles of Jesus could fill?

The Gospel of John concludes by saying, *And there are also many other things which Jesus did, the which, if they should be written every one, I suppose that even the world itself could not contain the books that should be written. Amen* (John 21:25).

Step 2 Examine

Jesus' miracles recorded in the New Testament were more than wonders. They were signs. He did them to encourage men and women to believe in Him for everlasting life. He healed a crippled man to affirm His right to forgive sins. He fed thousands of people with a little boy's lunch, setting the stage for His claim to be the "bread of life." He walked on water, stilled angry seas, healed the sick, restored paralyzed limbs, gave sight to the blind and hearing to the deaf, and even raised from the dead an embalmed man by the name of Lazarus. Another reason Jesus performed miracles was to support His claim to be God. The apostle John wrote, "Truly Jesus did many other signs in the presence of His disciples, which are not written in this book; but these are written that you may believe that Jesus is the Christ, the Son of God, and that believing you may have life in His name" (John 20:30-31).[1]

Research the miracles performed by Jesus. Use any resource (Bible commentary, Bible dictionary, Bible handbook, or the Internet). We recommend the following:

Books

Encyclopedia of the Bible (Nelson's Illustrated) ♥
"Jesus is Born" (200-201).

The Victor Journey through the Bible ●– ♥
Read: The Wedding at Cana" (216-217), "The Miracle of Fish" (228-229), "The Withered Hand"(246-247), The Fringe of His Garment" (256), Jarrus' Daughter" (257), Jesus' Miracles"(258).

The Holman Bible Atlas ●– ♥
See: Maps between pages 218-228 that show where the miracles occurred.

Underlined text refers to Internet link at http://Homeschool-Books.com

Water made wine	Jh 2:1-11
Traders cast out out of the temple	Jh 2:13-17
Nobleman's son healed	Jh 4:46-54
First miraculous draught of fishes	Lu 5:1-11
Leper healed	Mt 8:2-4; Mk 1:40-45; Lu 5:12-15
Centurion's servant healed	Mt 8:5-13; Lu 7:1-10
Widow's son raised to life	Lu 7:11-17
Demoniac healed	Mk 1:21-28; Lu 4:31-37
Peter's mother-in-law healed	Mt 8:14,15; Mk 1:29-31; Lu 4:38,39
Paralytic healed	Mt 9:2-8; Mk 2:1-12; Lu 5:17-26
Impotent man healed	Jh 5:1-16
Man with withered hand healed	Mt 12:10-14; Mk 3:1-6; Lu 6:6-11
Blind and dumb demoniac healed	Mt 12:22-24; Lu 11:14
Tempest stilled	Mt 8:23-27; Mk 4:35-41; Lu 8:22-25
Demoniacs dispossessed	Mt 8:28-34; Mk 5:1-20
Jairus' daughter raised to life	Mt 9:18-26; Mk 5:22-24; Lu 8:41-56
Issue of blood healed	Mt 9:18-26; Mk 5:22-24; Lu 8:41-56
Two blind men restored to sight	Mt 9:27-31
Dumb demoniac healed	Mt 9:32-34
Five thousand men miraculously fed	Mt 14:13-21; Mk 6:31-44; Lu 9:10-17; Jh 6:5-14
Jesus walks on the sea	Mt 14:22-33; Mk 6:45-52; Jh 6:15-21
Syrophoenician daughter healed; Sidon	Mt 15:21-28; Mk 7:24-30
Deaf and dumb man healed	Mk 7:31-37
Four thousand men fed	Mt 15:32-39; Mk 8:1-9
Blind man restored to sight	Mk 8:22-26
Demoniac and lunatic boy healed	Mt 17:14-21; Mk 9:14-29; Lu 9:37-43
Miraculous provision of tribute	Mt 17:24-27
The eyes of one born blind opened	Jh 9:1-41
Woman, of 18 years' infirmity, cured	Lu 13:10-17
Dropsical man healed	Lu 14:1-6
Ten lepers cleansed	Lu 17:11-19
Lazarus raised to life	Jh 11:1-46
Two blind beggars restored to sight	Mt 20:29-34; Mk 10:46-52; Lu 18:35-43
Barren fig tree blighted	Mt 21:12,13,18,19; Mk 11:12-24
Buyers and sellers again cast out	Lu 19:45,46
Malchus' ear healed	Mt 26:51-54; Mk 14:47-49; Lu 22:50,51; Jh 18:10,11
Second draught of fishes	Jh 21:1-14

Resources recommended in ◆several lessons, ★ several units, ♥other HOW Units. ●—Key Resource (see beginning of unit or page 32).

Yeshua: A Guide to the Real Jesus and the Original Church ●▬ ◆
Read: "The Verification of Miracles" (125-126).

The Jesus I Never Knew ◆
Read: "Miracles: Snapshot of the Supernatural" (163-184).

Step 3 Expand

Choose and complete one of the following activities:

Activity 1: Write Summaries
Use the chart on the previous page to look up and read each miracle. Study each miracle, determine what truths it teaches, and then determine how the truths apply to you (application). Write a summary of one or two sentences for each.

Activity 2: Write a Skit
Imagine that Jesus was on the earth today and performed His loaves-and-fishes miracle at a public gathering. How would the news media cover such an event? Whom would they interview? What would they say about the miracle, and what would they say about Jesus? Write a skit to depict how the modern news media would cover this miracle.

Activity 3: Answer Questions
Answer the following: What disease does Jesus call by name? What was required in those who received the miracles? (Matthew 17:20; 21:21; John 14:12; Acts 3:16; 6:8).What happened after witnesses saw that Jesus raised Lazarus from the dead? (John 11:1-45).

Activity 4: Write a Story
Write a true account of a modern-day miracle. Make your writing as vivid and concise as possible. Next, read a Bible account of the miracle that Jesus performed in feeding the five thousand. Is the description very detailed? Are the essential facts given? Revise your modern-day miracle account to make it as brief as the Bible story.

Step 4 Excel

Share what you have learned with a friend or family member. Correct written work to demonstrate correct punctuation, spelling, and effective use of grammar. Add corrected written work or any illustrations to your portfolio.

Footnotes
1. *10 Reasons To Believe God Became Man.* (2000). Radio Bible Class, Ministries-Grand Rapids MI.

Christ's Attitude Toward the Adulteress

1418

The Narrated Bible

Step 1 Excite

One of the most powerful lessons from Jesus occurred when he saved the life of an adulteress who was about to be stoned to death by an accusing crowd. When Jesus had lifted up himself, and saw none but the woman, he said unto her, *Woman, where are those thine accusers? hath no man condemned thee? She said, No man, Lord. And Jesus said unto her, Neither do I condemn thee: go, and sin no more.* (John 8:10-11).

Read John 7:53-8:11. What do you think Jesus wrote on the ground? Why did the people go away? Reflect on how this incident applies to your life today as it pertains to the way we judge other people.

If you haven't already, memorize 1 John 1:9—do it today: *If we confess our sins, He is faithful and righteous to forgive us our sins and to cleanse us from all unrighteousness.*

Step 2 Examine

A hallmark of the teachings of Jesus is His emphasis on forgiveness. Use Bible study tools in the Research Area to look up "forgiveness." Read any or all of the following Bible messages about sinners:

Internet Sources

ⓘ Save the Adulteress! by Brad Young, Ph.D.
Description: Article explaining the ancient Jewish response to the Gospels through the story of Jesus and the adulteress.

ⓘ I Am All That I Need to Be for God to Use Me Right Now by David Hodge
Description: A devotional on John 8:10-11.

ⓘ The Life and Times of Jesus the Messiah ◆
Read: The Woman Which Was A Sinner. Available online.

Step 3 Expand

Choose and complete one of the following activities:

Resources recommended in ◆several lessons, ★ several units, ♥other HOW Units. ●━Key Resource (see beginning of unit or page 32).

Heart of Wisdom Publishing 757

Activity 1: Write a Summary

Forgiveness as "the act of setting someone free." Sin is "the state of being in bondage—in need of being set free." Write a short summary that describes an episode in your life in which you have been forgiven, and an instance when you have forgiven someone else. Pay particular attention to describing how each act of forgiveness made you feel.

Activity 2: Write a Paraphrase

Write the story of Jesus and the adulteress in your own words. Refer to "Writing a Paraphrase" in *Writers INC*.

Activity 3: Write a Thank-You Card

To be pardoned is an act by which an individual is freed from the consequences of having committed a breach of the law. Pardons can be conditional or unconditional. Christ's blood bought us an unconditional pardon for our sins. Read Ephesians 4:1-3 and write a thank-you card to show gratitude to God for the sacrifice of His Son. What can we do in our lives to show gratitude?

Step 4 Excel

Explain forgiveness to a younger child. Tell a Bible story to show an example of forgiveness. Then give examples of how we can forgive others.

Christ, Our Shepherd

Step 1 Excite

Discuss the figurative uses of the words "sheep" and "shepherd": Jesus is our Passover Lamb. "Sheep" is also figurative of believers who follow the shepherd. One without a leader is like a sheep without a shepherd. Jesus is our Shepherd. Discuss the responsibilities of a shepherd: to protect, feed, shelter, etc.

Step 2 Examine

Research the Bible's use of the words "sheep" and "shepherd." Use any resource (a book, Bible study tools, or the Internet). We recommend the following:

Books
Books

Encyclopedia of the Bible (Nelson's Illustrated) ♥
"Jesus the Leader" (180-181).

The Victor Journey through the Bible ●─ ♥
Read: "Jesus the Good Shepherd" (280).

Daily Life at the Time of Jesus ●─ ◆
Read: "The Shepherd" (48).

Our Father Abraham: Jewish Roots of the Christian Faith ●─ ♥
Read: About Jesus' parables on pages 120-121.

A Shepherd Looks at Psalm 23 by W. Phillip Keller
See description in the Resources Section.

Lessons from a Sheepdog by Phillip Keller
Keller draws spiritual truth from his experience in training and using a sheep dog named Lass on his sheep ranch in the American West. With love, compassion, and patience, the dog became not only a friend, but also a valuable co-worker on the ranch. From his experiences, Keller draws parallel lessons to what God wants each of us to do and be as His co-worker. The story of Lass is a modern day parable that's heart warming and powerful. (May 1988) Word Books; ISBN: 0849931304.

Internet Sources

Resources recommended in ◆several lessons, ★ several units, ♥other HOW Units. ●─Key Resource (see beginning of unit or page 32).

Heart of Wisdom Publishing   759

(i) <u>Knowing Him and Following Him</u> by Rev. Terril D. Littrell, Ph.D.
Description: Article explaining the lessons that we can learn from the shepherd/sheep paradigm in Scripture.

(i) <u>Sheep and Shepherd</u>
Description: Entries from *Easton's Bible Dictionary.*

Step 3 Expand

Choose and complete one of the following writing activities:

Activity 1: Write a Summary
Write a summary about a shepherd and his relationship with his sheep. Younger students can narrate (orally tell) what they have learned.

Activity 2: Write a Story
Write an allegory, a folktale, or a story for children about the relationship between sheep and their shepherd. Younger students can narrate (orally tell) their story.

Activity 3: Write a Poem
Learn about different types of poetry (figurative, narrative [epics, ballads], dramatic, or lyric). Choose one of these forms in which to write a poem about a lamb.

Step 4 Excel

Share your creative writing with others. Read it aloud to your family or friends. Say a prayer to good thanking Hime for Jesus our shepherd.

Christ's Attitude Toward Women

Step 1 Excite

How can you tell when someone truly cares about you and values you? Do they patronize you? Treat you like a baby? Ignore you? Humiliate you? Or do they listen to you? Encourage you? Accept help from you? Correct you, lovingly? Give you gifts? Accept gifts from you? Give you responsibility? Do you believe Jesus had respect for women? Which of these things do you think Jesus did for the women He knew as He lived on earth?

Step 2 Examine

> In Jesus' time, women participated fully in the religious life of the community. This included participation in synagogue services and in the regular study sessions that were conducted in the synagogue's bet midrash (house of study). There was no separation of the sexes in synagogues and women could be counted as part of the required congregational quorum of ten adults. There was, however, one inequality. For social reasons, women were not allowed to read the Scriptures publicly[1]

Women were important to Jesus. Jesus interacted with many women in His ministry. He taught women(Luke 10-38:42). He ignored ritual impurity laws (Mark 5:25-34) when a woman needed healing. He talked to foreign women (the woman of Samaria: John 4:7 to 5:30, and a Canaanite woman: Matthew15:21). He used terminology which treated women as equal to men (Luke 13:16). He forgave a woman's sins (Luke 7:35 to 8:50). He accepted women in his inner circle (Luke 8:1-3). He appeared first to a woman after his resurrection (Mat 28:9-10). Women were present at Jesus' death (Matthew 27:55-56 and Mark 15:40-41). He expressed concern for widows (Luke 2:36, 4:26, 7:11, 18:1, 20:47 and 21:1)

Research Jesus' treatment of women. Use any resource (a Bible concordance, commentary, Bible dictionary, or the Internet). We recommend the following:

Books

Our Father Abraham: Jewish Roots of the Christian Faith
Read: "Marriage and Family Through Hebrew Eyes"(195-236).

Sketches of Jewish Social Life
Read: Chapter 8 Mothers, Daughters, and Wives in Israel. See description in the Ancient Israel Resources Section.

Resources recommended in ◆several lessons, ★ several units, ♥other HOW Units. ●—Key Resource (see beginning of unit or page 32).

Heart of Wisdom Publishing   761

<u>Women, Class, and Society in Early Christianity, Models from Luke-Acts</u>
See description in the "<u>Women in Ancient Israel</u>" lesson in the Ancient Israel Unit.

Internet Sources

<u>Jesus and women: What Did Jesus do?</u> by Joe E. Trull
Description: Article by a Professor, New Orleans Baptist Theological Seminary.

Step 3 Expand

Choose and complete one of the following activities:

Activity 1: Write a Journal Entry
Choose one of the following women as a subject of creative writing. Imagine how she felt the day after a miracle was performed in her life. (Refer to Scripture to discover what the miracle was.) What did she think, hope, and do? What difference did the miracle make in her life? Write a journal entry, as if you were she.
- Widow of Nain (Luke 7:11-12)
- Gentile woman (Mark 7:26)
- Elizabeth (Luke 1)
- Mary Magdalene (Luke 8:2)

Activity 2: Make a Chart
Make a chart with the following headings: Encouragement, Accepting Help, Loving Correction, Giving and Accepting Gifts, Giving Responsibility, Listening, Understanding the Other's Point of View, Discussing, Graciously Hearing Complaints, Teaching. Look up the following verses: Luke 10:38-42; John 11:1-15; 12:2-3; Luke 7:12-15; Matthew 9:20-22; 15:22-28; 26:7; 27:55-56; Mark 5:25-34; 7:25-30; 15:40; Luke 7:37-38; 7:44-50; 8:1-3; 11:27-28; 13:11-13; 23:27-28; John 2:4; 4:7-26; 8:9-11; 16:21; 19:26-27; 20:15-17. List each passage under all appropriate headings. Younger students can choose three passages to read and narrate (tell back) what they learned.

Step 4 Excel

Share your work from Step 3 at the Heart of Wisdom Internet site.

Footnotes
1. Safrai, Shmuel. (1999). "The Place Of Women In First-century Synagogues," *Jerusalem Perspective* Sep-Oct 1993 p3-6, 14.

Underlined text refers to Internet link at <u>http://Homeschool-Books.com</u>

Christ's Attitude Toward Children

Step 1 Excite

1436

The Narrated Bible

Jesus loved children. In fact, one of the instances in which He openly rebuked His disciples took place when they were trying to keep little children away from Him. *Let the children come unto me,* He said. (Matthew 19:14)

Discuss our society's attitude toward children today, particularly regarding abortion. Are we placing the same value on children as Jesus did?

Step 2 Examine

Research Jesus' attitudes toward children. Use any resource (a Bible commentary, Bible dictionary, or the Internet). We recommend the following:

Book

The Victor Journey through the Bible ●— ♥
Read: "Jesusand the Children" (296).

Our View of Children by Rebecca Prewett
Description: Article by a homeschool mother, from a Family Issues site.

Jesus' Compassion For Children
Description: Excerpt from the booklet *The Compassion of Jesus* by Vernon Grounds, a directors of RBC Ministries.

Step 3 Expand

Choose and complete one of the following activities:

Activity 1: Write an Article
Write a feature article (with a headline) that tells the story of Jesus blessing the children (Matthew 19:13-15; Mark 10:13-16; Luke 18:15,16) as it might be found on the front page of a newspaper in the town where the story takes place.

Resources recommended in ♦several lessons, ★ several units, ♥ other HOW Units. ●—Key Resource (see beginning of unit or page 32).

Heart of Wisdom Publishing   763

Activity 2: Answer Questions
Answer the following about your community: Where are Christians showing Jesus' love to the children? Where are hungry children being fed? Where are neglected children being cared for? Where are they being taught God's Word? Where are they encouraged and loved?

Activity 3: Make a Directory
Make a directory of people and places in your community that are serving children in the name of Jesus. Share the directory with others and ask them if they can help in ministering to children.

Activity 4: Think and Discuss
Discuss how to show love to a young child. What helps a child know the love of Jesus? What types of activities could you share with a child to show them your undivided attention? What could you say to encourage a child? What are some ways you could point a child toward Jesus?

Step 4 Excel

Share the plan of salvation with a child. If you don't know someone to share with now put your own salvation expierence in writing as if you were sharing it with a child. THen you will be prepared!

Correct all written work to demonstrate correct punctuation and spelling, and effective use of grammar. Add corrected written work or any illustrations to your portfolio.

Christ, Our Bridegroom

Step 1 Excite

A beautiful picture of God's love is found in the ancient Jewish wedding. In the Jewish wedding the bridegroom is the important figure. In the Bible Jesus is the Bridegroom and the elect will be the bride of Christ (Revelation 19). The "Church's Bridegroom" is found in many places in Scripture. In Matthew 22:1-14, Christ gives the parable of the King who gave a wedding feast for his son, an obvious reference to the union between Christ and His believing people. In Matthew 25:1-13, Christ gives another parable of the ten virgins who went to meet the bridegroom, typifying the church going out to meet Christ when He returns. In John 3:29, John the Baptist said of Christ, *He who has the bride is the bridegroom; but the friend of the bridegroom, who stands and hears him, rejoices greatly because of the bridegroom's voice.*

Examine 2 Corinthians 11:2 and Revelation 19:7-9. How do these verses relate to the bridegroom?

Step 2 Examine

Investigate the symbolism found in Jewish wedding ceremonies, such as those that Jesus uses in His parables. We recommend the following:

Books

Encyclopedia of the Bible (Nelson's Illustrated) ♥
"Marriage and Weddings" (96-97).

The Victor Journey through the Bible ◉— ♥
Read: "Jesus the Good Shepherd" (280).

Daily Life at the Time of Jesus ◉— ♦
Read: "A Wedding Feast" (58-59).

Our Father Abraham: Jewish Roots of the Christian Faith ◉— ♥
Read: "Marriage and Family Through Hebrew Eyes" (195-236).

Here Comes the Bride by Richard Booker
Description: One of the most beautiful pictures of God's love is the ancient Jewish wedding. In this publication, Booker explains the biblical concept of marriage as a covenant between God and his people; ancient Jewish wedding customs and how they point to the Messiah; and how God is calling both Jews and Gentiles to be His bride. This Book will warm your heart and give you hope for the future.

Resources recommended in ♦several lessons, ★ several units, ♥other HOW Units. ◉—Key Resource (see beginning of unit or page 32).

Internet Source

> The Marriage of Jesus and the Elect
> Description: Dr. Zola Levitt's description of Jewish marriage customs in first-century Jerusalem.

Step 3 Expand

Choose and complete one of the following activities:

Activity 1: Think and Discuss
God's never-ending love for us is far beyond our understanding. To help us know Him better, God made us male and female, in part so that we could experience the pleasures of an intimate personal relationship. The marital relationship between husband and wife is ordained by God to be a picture of the spiritual relationship of Christ, our husband, and us, his bride. Discuss with your parents some of the ways that a human marriage can be compared and contrasted with the union of Christ and the Church.

Activity 2: Write a Summary
Write a summary of what you know about the religious symbolism of marriage.

Activity 3: Research
Read and study the parable of the Ten Virgins in Matthew 25:1-12.

Step 4 Excel

Discuss with your parents how being in a marriage could help someone grow spiritually. How do your parents think that being in a marital relationship could help someone better understand, and develop a deeper relationship with, Jesus?

Christ's Attitude Toward the Poor

Step 1 Excite

The Bible tells us, *For everyone to whom much is given, from him much will be required* (Luke 12:48). (Note: The Bible does NOT say "God helps those who help themselves." That is a Ben Franklin quote.) Reflect on how much we Christians have been given in the person of Jesus and what we are expected to give in return.

Step 2 Examine

Poverty in Scripture can be both social and spiritual. The words "poor" and "poverty" cover a wide range of meaning, overlapping with terms like "widow" or "orphan," which underscores the expansive nature of the topic. In addition, because not all poor people are destitute the meaning of these terms is heavily dependent upon context.... Jesus understood the reality of poverty in society (Matt 26:9-11) and the difficulties of the poor (Mark 12:42-44). He stressed the need to give to the poor (Matt 19:21; Luke 12:33) and to provide for them (Luke 14:13,21). Jesus himself identified with poor people and, like many poor persons, did not have a home (Luke 9:58). He taught how difficult it was to be rich (Matt 19:23-24) and the necessity of spiritual poverty for a relationship with God (Matt 5:3).[1]

Recall Jesus' wonderful reminder that *Assuredly, I say to you, inasmuch as you did it to one of the least of these My brethren, you did it to Me.* Read Matthew 25:34-40. Jesus indicates that it is the poor and destitute who are indeed the most fortunate of individuals, for it is they who have the honor of being participants in the age of the Messiah.

Step 3 Expand

Activity 1: Copy Passages
Read all of the following passages: Mark 12:42-44; Matthew 5:3;19:21-24; Luke 9:58; 12:33; 14:13. Choose one passage that speaks to you. Copy it.

Activity 2: Volunteer
Find a way to use the gifts God has given you to minister to others by volunteering for one of the following: the Crisis Pregnancy Center, Meals on Wheels, helping at retirement centers or homeless shelters, writing letters to female prison inmates, helping with housework for a shut-in or handicapped person, baby-sitting for a working mother, or anything else that would serve others.

Resources recommended in ◆several lessons, ★ several units, ●other HOW Units. ●—Key Resource (see beginning of unit or page 32).

Heart of Wisdom Publishing   767

Step 4 Excel

Read Jesus' words in Matthew 25:40-46. Find out how you can help the hungry. Here are a few organizations:

- Compassion International, P.O. Box 7000, 3955 Cragwood Dr., Colorado Springs, CO 80933, offers opportunities for Child sponsorship.
- Feed My People, 3805 Walker Rd., Colorado Springs, CO 80908 (719) 481-2083, offers starter kits for helping the hungry in your community.
- Food for the Hungry, 7729 E. Greenway Rd., Scottsdale, AZ 85260
- World Vision, Box O, Monrovia, CA 91016, famine and disaster relief. Offers a "Planned Famine" program.

Footnote
1. Elwell, Walter A. "Entry for 'Poor and Poverty, Theology of'". *Evangelical Dictionary of Theology*.

Christ's Teachings on Love

Step 1 Excite

Jesus is an example of perfect, unconditional love. God's love is the unselfish giving of Himself to us in order to bring goodness and blessing into our lives. It is far more than simply an emotion.

> Love for the Master is not some sweet sentimental emotion that sweeps over the soul in moments of special piety. Love for Christ is a deliberate setting of the will to carry out His commands at any cost. It is the fixed attitude of heart that decides to do His will at all times. It is the desire and delight of accomplishing our Father's highest purposes, no matter how challenging.
> The end result of such conduct for a Christian is to bring sweet satisfaction to the great Good Shepherd of his soul. Because of such bold and single-minded service we sense His approval of our behavior. We sense and know of a surety that we are loved and appreciated. We are His friends. And the ultimate end is that others benefit; others are blessed; others are cared for....
> In our highly permissive society, where the so-called "me" generation is encouraged to be so self-centered and so self-preoccupied, the call to obey Christ and comply with His commands cuts across our culture and our cynical conduct.
>
> It simply is not normal nor natural for most of us to "love" God or "love" others in the drastic discipline of a laid-down life. We are a selfish, self-serving people. And when called upon to serve others we feel insulted. We have the strange, worldly idea that to be of lowly service is to be "used" or "abused." Yet God, very God, in Christ came among us in lowly service. He came to minister to us. He came to give Himself to us. And so, because He first "loved" us, we in turn are to be willing and ready to "love" Him and others.[1]

Brainstorm and make a list of what Jesus taught about love.

Step 2 Examine

Because God loves us, our sin-debt was paid in full. Because we accept Christ, we can face tomorrow with confidence, assurance, and perfect peace. Read these words of Jesus about love:

- Simon, son of John, do you love Me? (John 21:17).
- If you love Me, you will keep my commandments (John 14:15).

Resources recommended in ♦several lessons, ★ several units, ♥other HOW Units. ●━Key Resource (see beginning of unit or page 32).

Heart of Wisdom Publishing   769

- Greater love hath no man than this, that a man lay down his life for his friends (John 15:13).
- The Father himself loves you, because you have loved Me and have believed that I came from the Father (John 16:27).
- If a man loves Me, he will keep My word, and My Father will love him, and We will come to him and make Our home with him (John 14:23).
- For the Father loves the Son, and shows him all that he himself is doing; and greater works than these will he show him, that you may marvel (John 5:20).
- As the Father has loved Me, so have I loved you; abide in My love. If you keep My commandments, you will abide in My love, just as I have kept My Father's commandments and abide in His love (John 15:9-11).
- If the world hates you, know that it has hated Me before it hated you. If you were of the world, the world would love its own; but because you are not of the world, but I chose you out of the world, therefore the world hates you (John 15:18-19).
- You did not chose Me, but I chose you and appointed you that you should go and bear fruit and that your fruit should abide; so that whatever you ask the Father in My name, He may give it to you. This I command to you, to love one another (John 15:16-17).
- You have heard that it was said, 'You shall love your neighbor and hate your enemy.' But I say to you, love your enemies and pray for those who persecute you, so that you may be sons of your Father who is in heaven (Matthew 5:43-45).
- A new commandment I give to you, that you love one another; even as I have loved you, that you also love one another. By this all men will know that you are My disciples, if you have love for one another (John 13:33-35).
- If you love those who love you, what credit is that to you? For even sinners love those who love them. And if you do good to those who do good to you, what credit is that to you? For even sinners do the same (Luke 6:32-33).

Charles Stanley explains the reasons that we have difficulty believing in unconditional love[2]:

- We think about God's love in the same way we think about how we love other people (Matthew 6:25-26).
- It's our natural response to love some people conditionally and some unconditionally (Hebrews 13:5).
- We experience guilt in our life.
- We don't feel worthy.
- We've heard legalistic teaching.
- We misunderstand the whole idea of unconditional love.
- There seems to be conflict in the Scripture concerning God's unconditional love and such things as divine discipline, His anger and wrath, hell and judgment (Hebrews 12:5-6; Ezekiel 7:8-12; John 3:36; Revelation 6:12-17).

Research Jesus' teachings on love. Use any resource (a concordance, Bible commentary, Bible dictionary, or the Internet). We recommend the following:

Book

A Touch of His Love by Dr. Charles Stanley
Description: God's love is unconditional and unending. It is the only source of true security and fulfillment. *A Touch of His Love* helps you grasp the magnitude of that love. Containing supporting Scriptures, prayers, and touchstones, this book is a wellspring of encouragement and growth for the believer. Each meditation is accompanied by black-and-white photography taken by Dr. Stanley.

Internet Sources

Jesus' Jewish Command To Love
Description: Article from Bridges for Peace by Dr. R. Steven Notley.

Listen to Love in Action
Description: Dr. James Boice's broadcast about Romans 12:11-13.

Step 3 Excel

Choose and complete one of the following activities:

Activity 1: Make a List
Brainstorm and list what you do now to show love to God and to other people. Now, think of several people your age, either from books or from among your acquaintances, whom you admire. List the things that they do or say to show Christian love. Which things are difficult for you? What steps could you take to improve your ability to express love to God and to other people?

Activity 2: Write an Essay
Use the list from the activity above. Write an essay explaining how you can best exemplify Christlike love toward God and toward others in your life. Younger students can narrate (orally tell) what they have learned.

Activity 3: Write and Share
Write and share John 21:16 and 17 in your own words.

Step 4 Excel

Explain orally to your parents what you've learned in this lesson. Correct all written work to demonstrate correct punctuation and spelling, and effective use of grammar. Add corrected written work or any illustrations to your portfolio.

Resources recommended in ◆several lessons, ★ several units, ♥ other HOW Units. ●—Key Resource (see beginning of unit or page 32).

Heart of Wisdom Publishing   771

Christ's Teachings on Forgiveness
Step 1 Excite

To be pardoned is an act by which an individual is freed from the consequences of having committed a breach of the law. Pardons can be conditional or unconditional. Christ's blood bought us an unconditional pardon for our sins. Read Ephesians 4:1-3.

Step 2 Examine

"Redemption" is a word taken from the slave market. The basic idea is that of obtaining release by payment of a ransom. Jesus paid for (ransomed) us. God loved us enough to pay the ultimate price for us. On the cross, Jesus said, "It is finished!" (John 19:30). Then he bowed his head and died. According to the Bible Knowledge Commentary, "Tetelestai" is the word in Greek translated here "it is finished." Papyri receipts for taxes have been recovered with the Greek word Tetelestai written across them, meaning "paid in full." God proved His love and concern for us by giving us His greatest gift. He did not spare His son, but gave Him up for us—you and me. Since He did that, He will graciously give us all things. The word "graciously" means that God does what He does for us out of a heart of grace.

Read Jesus' Words on forgiveness:

*   Father, forgive them, for they don't know what they do (Luke 23:34).
*   I have not come to call the righteous, but sinners to repentance (Luke 5:32).
*   I tell you, there is joy before the angels of God over one sinner who repents (Luke 15:10).
*   Receive the Holy Spirit (If you forgive the sins of any, they are forgiven; if you retain the sins of any, they are retained (John 20:23).
*   Therefore I tell you, every sin and blasphemy will be forgiven men, but the blasphemy against the Spirit will not be forgiven (Matthew 12:31).
*   I tell you, there will be more joy in heaven over one sinner who repents than over ninety-nine righteous persons who need no repentance (Luke 15:7).
*   Why do you question thus in your hearts? Which is easier, to say to the paralytic, 'Your sins are forgiven', or to say 'Rise, take up your pallet and walk'? Mark 2:8-9).
*   Truly, I say to you, all sins will be forgiven the sons of men, and whatever blasphemies they utter: but whoever blasphemes against the Holy Spirit never has forgiveness, but is guilty of an eternal sin (Mark 3:28-29).
*   Thus it is written, that the Christ should suffer and on the third day rise from the dead, and that repentance and forgiveness of sins should be preached in His name to all nations, beginning from Jerusalem (Luke 24:46-47).

- For if you forgive men their trespasses, your heavenly Father also will forgive you; but if you do not forgive men their trespasses neither will your father forgive your trespasses (Matthew 6:14-15).
- My son, your sins are forgiven (Mark 2:5).
- Let him who is without sin among you be the first to throw a stone at her (John 8:7).
- Do you see this woman? You gave Me no water for My feet, but she has wet My feet with her tears, and wiped them with her hair. You gave Me no kiss, but she, since the time I came in, has not ceased to kiss My feet. You did not anoint My head with oil, but she anointed My feet with perfume (For this reason I say to you, her sins, which are many, have been forgiven, for she loved much; but he who is forgiven little, loved little. (Luke 7:44-47)).
- Therefore I say to you, all things for which you pray and ask, believe that you have received it, and they shall be granted to you. And whenever you stand praying, forgive, if you have anything against anyone; so that your Father also who is in heaven may forgive you your transgressions (Mark 11:24-26).
- For if you forgive men their transgressions, your heavenly Father will also forgive you; but if you do not forgive men, then your Father will not forgive your transgressions (Matthew 6:14-15).
- It is not those who are healthy who need a physician, but those who are sick. But go and learn what this means, I desire compassion and not sacrifice, for I did not come to call the righteous but sinners (Matthew 9:12-13).
- If your brother sins, rebuke him, and if he repents, forgive him; and if he sins against you seven times a day, and returns to you seven times saying 'I repent,' forgive him (Luke 17:3-4).
- So also my heavenly Father will do to you if you do not forgive your brother from your heart (Matthew 18:3).

Step 3 Expand

Choose and complete one of the following activities:

Activity 1: Illustrate and Memorize
Illustrate that Jesus paid for (ransomed) us by designing a T-shirt or sweatshirt with a giant "SOLD" sign. Be prepared to answer when someone asks you what this means by memorizing one of the following verses: 1 Corinthians 7:23; 6:19-20; Romans 6:20-22; 3:24-25; Colossians 1:14; Acts 20:28; Ephesians 1:7.

Resources recommended in ◆several lessons, ★ several units, ◆other HOW Units. ◉—Key Resource (see beginning of unit or page 32).

Heart of Wisdom Publishing   773

Activity 2: Copy Words Jesus Spoke on Forgiveness
Copy (by hand or typing) the words that Jesus spoke on forgiveness. (Copying is a good exercise for teaching yourself accuracy and attention to detail, and you will probably discover things about the text you are copying that you would be unlikely to notice otherwise).

Activity 3: Write or Narrate a Parable
Show your understanding of grace by writing or narrating a parable about a mother and/or father showing grace to her or his child who has broken a rule. Include repentance and the giving of a gift (because God gave us a gift), and why parents make rules (laws). Include a dialog about obeying parents' rules even though one can be forgiven easily and get gifts anyway (easy grace).

Activity 4: Write a Thank-you Card
Write a thank-you card to show gratitude to God for the sacrifice of His Son. What can we do in our lives to show gratitude?

Activity 5: Write an Essay
A hallmark of the teachings of Jesus is His emphasis on forgiveness. Write a short essay that describes an episode in your life in which you have been forgiven, and an instance when you have forgiven someone else. Pay particular attention to describing how each act of forgiveness made you feel.

Step 4 Excel

Share what you have learned about forgiveness with a friend or family member whom you have had to ask forgiveness from. Correct all written work to demonstrate correct punctuation and spelling, and effective use of grammar. Add corrected written work or any illustrations to your portfolio.

Christ's Crucifixion and Resurrection

Step 1 Excite

Brainstorm and discuss what it would be like to slowly die of crucifixion. Think about what it would be like to receive a death penalty if you were innocent.

Step 2 Examine

Many of us have a difficult time grasping the pain and suffering that Christ went through on the crucifixion day. Television today has de-sensitized our feelings pertaining to the horrifying violence of the torture and slow death of Jesus.

The following is just a portion of an article by Dr. C. Truman Davis, M.D., M.S., titled: *The Crucifixion Of Jesus: The Passion Of Christ From A Medical Point Of View*, which explains some of the agony Christ experienced:

> In the early morning, Jesus, battered and bruised, dehydrated, and exhausted from a sleepless night, is taken across Jerusalem to Pontius Pilate. The prisoner is stripped of His clothing and His hands tied to a post above His head. A short whip consisting of several heavy, leather thongs with two small balls of lead attached near the ends of each is brought down with full force again and again across Jesus' shoulders, back, and legs.
>
> The condemned man was forced to carry the patibulum [cross bar], apparently weighing about 110 pounds, from the prison to the place of execution. Without any historical or Biblical proof, medieval and Renaissance painters have given us our picture of Christ carrying the entire cross. Many of these painters and most of the sculptures of crucifixes today show the nails through the palm. Roman historical accounts and experimental work have shown that the nails were driven between the small bones of the wrists and not through the palms. Nails driven through the palms will strip out between the fingers when they support the weight of the human body. The misconception may have come about through a misunderstanding of Jesus' words to Thomas, "Observe my hands." Anatomists, both modern and ancient, have always considered the wrists as a part of the hand.

Resources recommended in ◆several lessons, ★ several units, ♥other HOW Units. ●—Key Resource (see beginning of unit or page 32).

Heart of Wisdom Publishing   775

A titulus, or small sign, stating the victim's crime was usually carried at the front of the procession and later nailed to the cross above the head. A small bundle of flexible branches covered with long thorns (commonly used for fire-wood) are plaited into the shape of a crown and this is pressed into His scalp. The heavy patibulum [crossbar] of the cross is tied across His shoulders, and the procession, headed by a centurion, begins its slow journey along the Via Dolorosa. In spite of His efforts to walk erect, the weight of the heavy wooden beam, together with the shock produced by copious blood loss, is too much. He stumbles and falls. The centurion, anxious to get on with the crucifixion, selects a stalwart North African onlooker, Simon of Cyrene, to carry the cross.

The crucifixion begins. The legionnaire drives a heavy, square, wrought iron nail through the wrist and deep into the wood. The patibulum is then lifted in place at the top of the stripes and the titulus, reading "Jesus of Nazareth, King of the Jews," is nailed in place.

Hours of this limitless pain, cycles of twisting, joint-rending cramps, intermit-tent partial asphyxiation, searing pain as tissue is torn from His lacerated back as He moves up and down against the rough timber; then another agony begins: a crushing pain deep in the chest as the pericardium slowly fills with serum and begins to compress the heart.

The body of Jesus is now in extremis, and He can feel the chill of death creep-ing through His tissues. This realization brings out possibly little more than a tortured whisper, "It is finished."

His mission of atonement has been completed. Finally He can allow His body to die.

With one last surge of strength, He once again presses His torn feet against the nail, straightens His legs, takes a deeper breath, and utters His seventh and last cry, "Father, into thy hands I commit my spirit." [1] (Truman 1965).

Jesus died as the lambs for the Passover meal were being slain. Not a bone was to be broken in these sacrificial lambs (Ex. 12:46; Num. 9:12). Jesus, the Lamb of God, was the perfect sacrifice for the sins of the world (1 Cor. 5:7).

During the Passover time, a sign hung from each lamb's neck, bearing the name of the owner of the lamb. Jesus was crucified with a sign hung over His head with the name of His Father. Studies have shown the Tetragrammaton probably appeared over Jesus when He hung on the cross. During Bible times, messages were commonly written with the first letter of each word. An example in English: "UPS" stands for "United Parcel Service." The phrase "Jesus of

Nazareth and King of the Jews" was written in three languages on a sign above Jesus as He hung on the cross (John 19:19). The Hebrew initials for "Jesus of Nazareth and King of the Jews" were YHWH. That is why the priest asked Pilate to change the writing.[2] *Then said the chief priests of the Jews to Pilate, "Write not, The King of the Jews; but that he said, I am King of the Jews." Pilate answered, "What I have written I have written"* (John 19: 21-22).

The story does not end with the death of Jesus. His body was placed in a new tomb that belonged to a man named Joseph of Arimathea (Luke 23:50-56; John 19:38-42). The greatest event that separates Jesus from all others is the fact that He overcame death. In three days He rose again and lives today. He arose from the grave on the Feast of Firstfruits! On Nisan 17, when Israel emerged from the Red Sea, this emergence was a shadow of the fulfillment of the day of Firstfruits (Lev. 23:9-14). These were the first of God's people to emerge from sin (Egypt). The day of Firstfruits was truly fulfilled 1,478 years later on Nisan 17, A.D. 30, when Jesus was resurrected and ascended to heaven as our high priest, the Firstfruit of the resurrected (John 20:17).

Christ's resurrection was foretold by the Old Testament prophets. It was recorded as a matter of history by the writers of the Gospels. It is maintained as fact by the Apostles in their epistles. We know that it was uniformly believed by the early Christians, even to the point of death.

Research the crucifixion and resurrection of Jesus. Use any resource (an encyclopedia, nonfiction book, historical novel, or the Internet). We recommend the following:

Books

Daily Life at the Time of Jesus ●— ◆
Read: "Crucifixion" (35-37).

The Holman Bible Atlas ●— ♥
Read: "The Last Week of Jesus" (233-235). Note: There is controversy concerning the days of the week in this text.

Our Father Abraham: Jewish Roots of the Christian Faith ●— ♥
Read: "Belief in the Resurrection of Jesus" (58).

The Jesus I Never Knew ◆
Read: "Death: The Final Week" (185-206), "Resurrection: A Morning Beyond Belief" (207-222).

Messianic Christology ●— ◆
Read: "The Death of Messiah" (82), "The Suffering & Exaltation of Messiah" (83-86), "Why Did Messiah Have to Die" (129-134).

Resources recommended in ◆several lessons, ★ several units, ♥other HOW Units. ●—Key Resource (see beginning of unit or page 32).

Heart of Wisdom Publishing   777

The Life and Times of Jesus the Messiah ◆
Read: Book V. The Cross and the Crown. Available online.

Internet Sources

The Chronology of Christ's Crucifixion & Resurrection
Description: This site explains that the key to understanding the chronology of the events leading up to and including Jesus' crucifixion and resurrection is this: there were two Sabbaths in that week, with a day of preparation between them. This makes all of the Gospels' accounts fall into place.

The Resurrection of Jesus: Hoax or History
Description: Dr. Howard Morgan uses a courtroom analogy to show facts of the resurrection as a historical matter.

Step 3 Expand

Choose and complete at least one of the following activities:

Activity 1: Write a Letter
The Resurrection of Jesus is the ultimate victory over sin and death. Imagine that you are one of the apostles to whom Jesus appears after His Resurrection. Write a letter to a friend, telling him or her how excited you are about Jesus' Resurrection.

Activity 2: Answer Questions
Answer the following:
1. What was the result for you when Jesus died on the cross? (2 Corinthians 5:21)
2. What did Christ teach concerning His death (Mark 8:31,32)?
3. How did Christ feel about such a death (Hebrews 12:2)?
4. Was Jesus in complete control of the circumstances? (Matthew 26:53; John 10:17-18).
4. Why did Jesus die for us (1 Peter 3:18)?
5. How did Christ's death affect your relationship with God (Colossians 1:21,22; Romans 5:10,11)?

Activity 3: Write a Journal Entry
Write in a personal journal answering the following questions: Why is Christ's resurrection important for believers? (1 Corinthians 15:12-19.) What does Christ's resurrection mean to you? How can the victory of Christ's resurrection bring victory to your life?

Activity 4: Make a Chart
Make a chart showing how each of the following reacted and contributed to the suffering of Jesus as He hung on the cross:

- The Roman execution squad (Matt. 27:33-37)
- The chief priests, scribes, and elders (Matt. 27:41-43)
- The two thieves (Matt. 27:38, 44)
- Spectators (Matt. 27:47-49)

Activity 5: Add to Your Time Line Book
Add the story of Christ's crucifixion and resurrection to your Time Line Book. Refer to <u>Reproducible Maps, Charts, Timelines & Illustrations</u> (175, 193).

Activity 6: Write a Summary
John 18: 1-12 records Judas Iscariot carrying out what Scripture had said he would do. Retell this event in your own words.

Activity 7: Write a Summary
Before Jesus was crucified, He went to pray in Gethsemane, which means "an oil press." Oil presses were used to extract oil from the fruit. Find and read about this event in one of the Gospels. Write a summary of it in your own words. Include what spiritual application it has in your life.

Activity 8: Write a Summary
Read Isaiah 50:5-10; Matthew 16:21-24; 26:53-56; John 3:16,17; and Romans 3:22, and write a summary explaining who killed Jesus.

Activity 9: Write a Letter
The Resurrection is central to the faith and hope of every believer. As the apostle Paul stated in 1 Corinthians 15:16-19, *For if the dead rise not, then is not Christ raised: And if Christ be not raised, your faith is vain; ye are yet in your sins. Then they also which are fallen asleep in Christ are perished. If in this life only we have hope in Christ, we are of all men most miserable.* Write a letter, as to an unbelieving acquaintance, explaining why you believe in the Resurrection of Jesus.

Step 4: Excel

Share what you have learned about Jesus' Crucifixion and Resurrection with a friend or family member. Correct all written work to demonstrate correct punctuation and spelling, and effective use of grammar. Add corrected written work or any illustrations to your portfolio.

Footnotes
1. Davis, Dr. C. Truman. A Physician Analyzes the Crucifixion, *Arizona Medicine*, March 1965, Arizona Medical Association.
2. Michas, Peter A. & Christie D., and Vander Maten, Robert, *God's Master Plan From Aleph to Tav*, Troy, IL, Messengers of Messiah International Ministries, 1994.

Resources recommended in ◆several lessons, ★ several units, ♥other HOW Units. ◉—Key Resource (see beginning of unit or page 32).

Heart of Wisdom Publishing   779

Names of the Messiah

The name "Jesus" is a combination of the Greek "Iesous" and the Latin version employing the letter J. This name commonly used in Christianity did not exist until about 500 years ago. The Messiah's name is Yeshua. It's His Hebrew name, the name His mother and others called him. His name has been translated into other names, with "Jesus" probably being the most recognized. For more on this subject visit the Internet site http://BiblicalHolidays.com

In Genesis he is the Seed of the Woman

In Exodus he is the Paschal Lamb.

In Leviticus he is the Atonement for Sin.

In Numbers he is the Brazen Serpent.

In Deuteronomy he is the City of Refuge.

In Joshua he is Rahab's Scarlet Cord.

In Judges he is the Angel of the Lord.

In Ruth he is our Kinsman Redeemer.

In I Samuel he is the Slayer of our Enemies.

In II Samuel he is the Gracious King.

In I Kings he is the Builder of His Temple.

In II Kings he is the Great Prophet.

In I Chronicles he is the Ark of Blessing.

In II Chronicles he is the Defender Of His People.

In Ezra he is the Restorer of His People.

In Nehemiah he is the Rememberer of His People.

In Esther he is the Preserver of His People.

In Job he is the Daysman.

In Psalm he is the Good Shepherd.

In Proverbs he is the Wisdom of God.

In Ecclesiastes he is the Teacher of Wisdom.

In Solomon's Song he is the Beloved of His Church.

In Isaiah he is the Substitute for Sinners.

In Jeremiah he is the Lord our Righteousness.

In Lamentations he is the Lord our Portion.

In Ezekiel he is the Glory of the Lord.

In Daniel he is the Messiah the Prince.

In Hosea he is God my Husband.

In Joel he is the Hope of His People.

In Amos he is the Sifter of His People.

In Obadiah he is the Searcher of Hearts.

In Jonah he is the Sovereign Delieverer.

In Micah he is Bethlehem's Infant.

In Nahum he is the Great One.

In Habbakkuk he is the Faithful One.

In Zephaniah he is the Mighty One.

In Haggai he is the Desire of All Nations.

In Zechariah he is the Fountain Opened for Sinners.

In Malachi he is the Sun of Righteousness.

In Matthew he is the Son of David.

In Mark he is the Son of Man.

In Luke he is the Son of God.

In John he is the Lamb of God.

In Acts he is the Ascended Lord.

In Romans he is the Just God our Savior.

In I Corinthians he is the Power of God.

In II Corinthians he is the Reconciler.

In Galatians he is the End of the Law.

In Ephesians he is the Effectual Savior.

In Philippians he is the Joy of Saints.

In Colossians he is the Pre-eminent One.

In I Thessalonians he is the Hope of Salvation.

In II Thessalonians he is the Coming Lord.

In I Timothy he is the Preacher's Doctrine.

In II Timothy he is the Eternal Surety.

In Titus he is the Grace of God.

In Philemon he is the Intercessor.

In Hebrews he is the Fulfillment of the Law.

In James he is the Giver of Grace.

In I Peter he is the Effectual Redeemer.

In II Peter he is the Longsuffering Lord.

In I John he is the Propitiation for Our Sins.

In II John he is the Doctrine of God.

In III John he is the Truth of God.

In Jude he is Our Security

In Revelation he is the Fulness of God.

Underlined text refers to Internet link at http://Homeschool-Books.com

Heart of Wisdom
Paper People

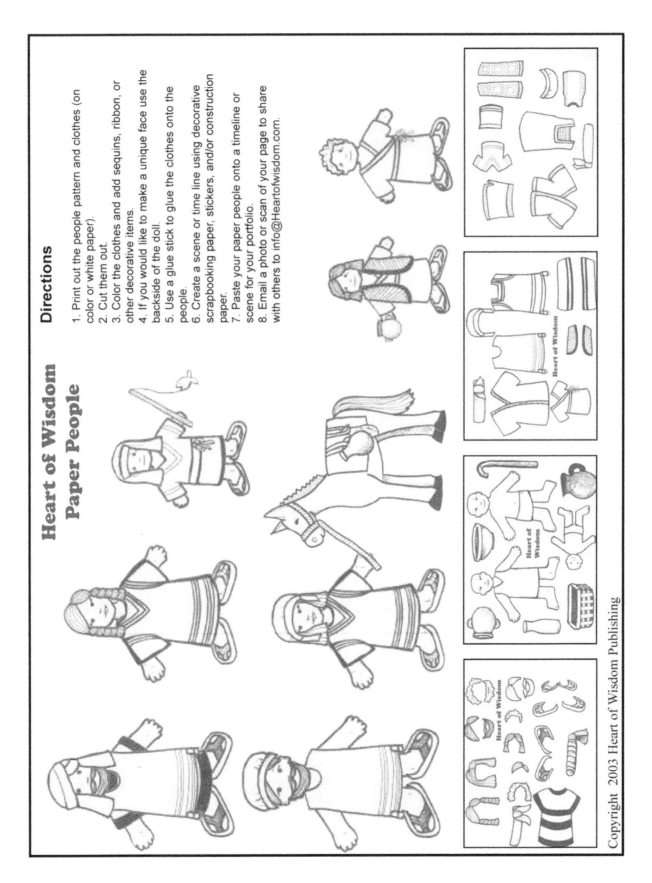

Directions

1. Print out the people pattern and clothes (on color or white paper).
2. Cut them out.
3. Color the clothes and add sequins, ribbon, or other decorative items.
4. If you would like to make a unique face use the backside of the doll.
5. Use a glue stick to glue the clothes onto the people.
6. Create a scene or time line using decorative scrapbooking paper, stickers, and/or construction paper.
7. Paste your paper people onto a timeline or scene for your portfolio.
8. Email a photo or scan of your page to share with others to info@Heartofwisdom.com.

Copyright 2003 Heart of Wisdom Publishing

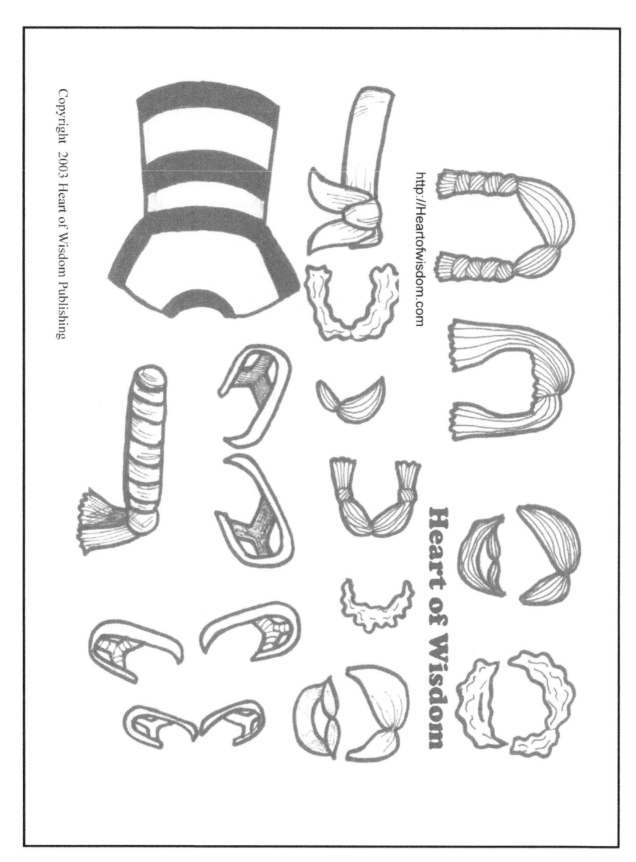

http://Heartofwisdom.com

Heart of Wisdom

Heart of Wisdom

http://Heartofwisdom.com

Copyright 2003 Heart of Wisdom Publishing

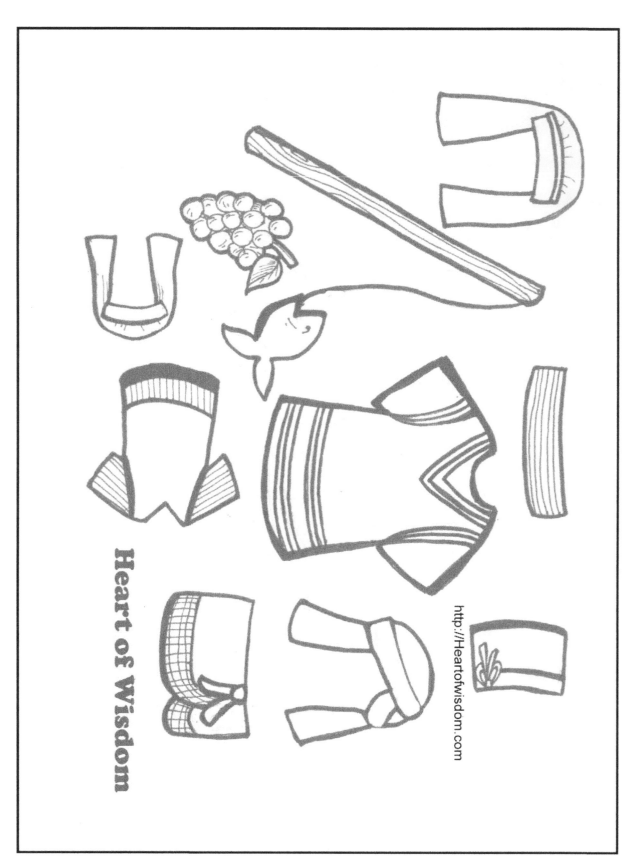

Heart of Wisdom

http://Heartofwisdom.com

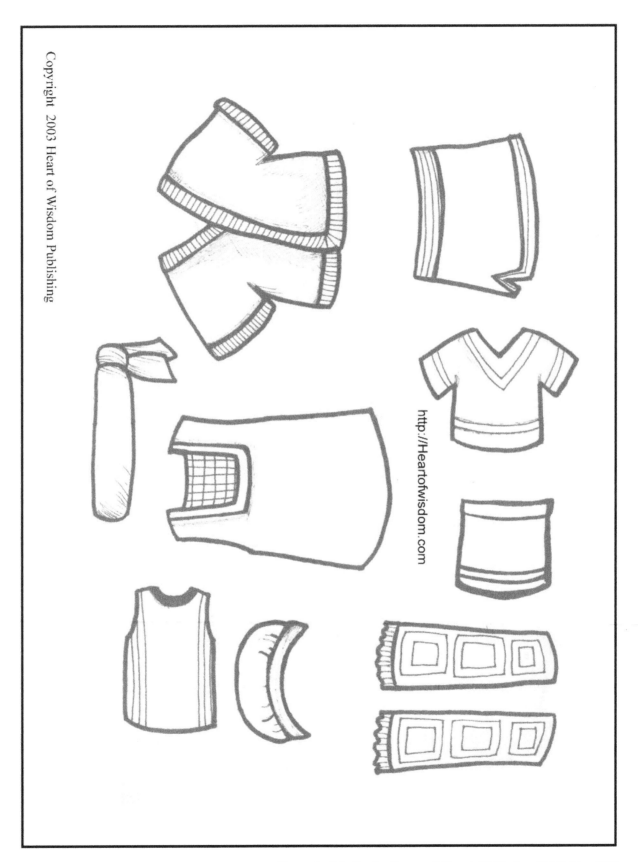

http://Heartofwisdom.com

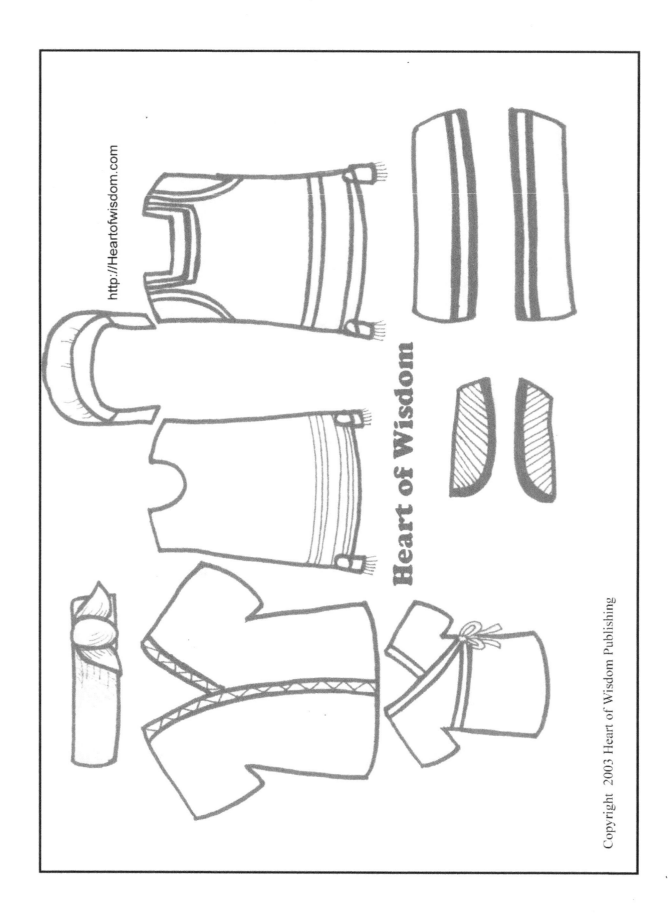

http://Heartofwisdom.com

Heart of Wisdom

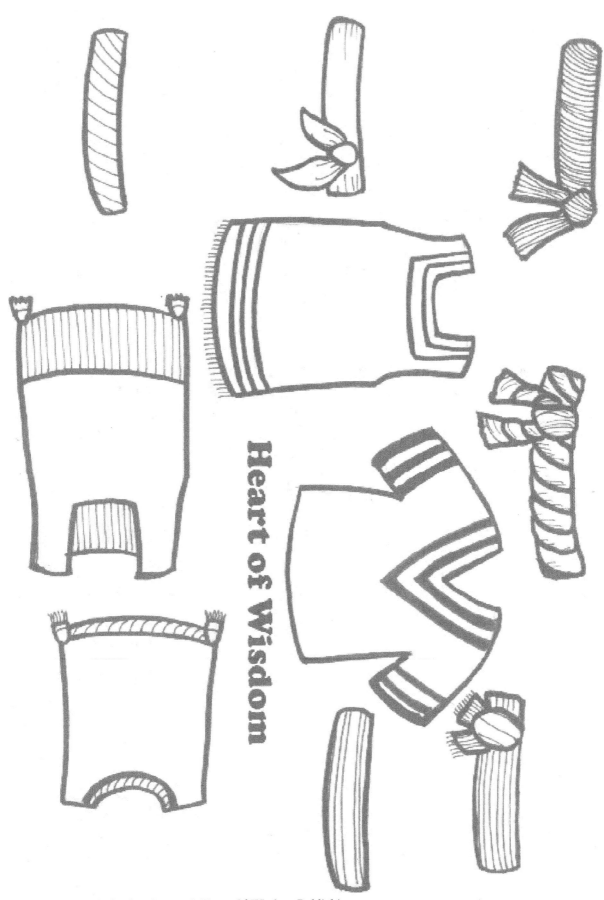

Heart of Wisdom